STATE ARCHIVES OF ASSYRIA

VOLUME II

I0354801

FRONTISPIECE. *Shalmaneser III clasping hands with Marduk-zakir-šumi of Babylon (c. 850 BC).* IM 65574.

STATE ARCHIVES OF ASSYRIA

Originally published by the Neo-Assyrian Text Corpus Project
of the Academy of Finland
in co-operation with
Deutsche Orient-Gesellschaft

Reprinted by Eisenbrauns

Editor in Chief
Simo Parpola

Managing Editor
Robert M. Whiting

Editorial Committee
Karlheinz Deller, Frederick Mario Fales, Simo Parpola,
Nicholas Postgate

VOLUME II

Simo Parpola and Kazuko Watanabe

NEO-ASSYRIAN TREATIES AND LOYALTY OATHS

© 1988 by the Neo-Assyrian Text Corpus Project
and the Helsinki University Press

Original publication of this volume was made possible in part by a grant
from the Research Council for the Humanities of
the Academy of Finland

Reprinted 2014 by permission of the Neo-Assyrian Text Corpus Project
With a new printed score in the back of the volume
Printed in the United States of America

www.eisenbrauns.com

ISBN 978-1-57506-332-4

Set in Times
Typography and layout by Teemu Lipasti
The Assyrian Royal Seal emblem drawn by Dominique Collon from original
Seventh Century B.C. impressions (BM 84672 and 84677) in the British Museum
Typographical encoding by Laura Kataja and Raija Mattila
Photocomposition by Tuula Hauhia
Pasteup by Jouni Laakso

The paper used in this publication meets the minimum requirements of the American National Standard for Information Sciences—Permanence of Paper for Printed Library Materials, ANSI Z39.48–1984. ∞™

NEO-ASSYRIAN TREATIES AND LOYALTY OATHS

Edited by
SIMO PARPOLA
and
KAZUKO WATANABE

Illustrations
edited by
JULIAN READE

Winona Lake, Indiana
EISENBRAUNS
2014

FOREWORD

The manuscript of the present volume was originally scheduled to be prepared by Dr. Watanabe alone. However, as she was unable to complete the manuscript by the required deadline, Professor Parpola undertook the completion of the manuscript so that the projected publication schedule could be more or less kept. The roles of the two editors in the preparation of the manuscript and their respective responsibilities for the final product are described in more detail in the Preface to the volume.

Robert M. Whiting

PREFACE

The texts included in the present volume were computerized by the Neo-Assyrian Text Corpus Project staff in Spring, 1986, from transliterations previously prepared by myself (Texts 1-5 and 7 13), Prof. A. K. Grayson (Text 14) and my co-editor, Dr. Watanabe (the score of Text 6, kindly made available by Prof. K. Deller before its publication in book form in *Baghdader Mitteilungen,* Beiheft 3). Complete word and reverse word indices, as well as a Key-Word-In-Context concordance and a printout of the texts, were subsequently generated from this material and handed over, in September, 1986, to Watanabe, who had undertaken to complete the basic manuscript of the volume by the end of 1987.

Unfortunately various circumstances prevented Watanabe from embarking on the work until she was invited to visit Helsinki as recipient of a scholarship from the Academy of Finland in December 1987/January 1988. During this visit she prepared, in close collaboration with me, a draft translation of the texts and proofread the transliterations made available to her earlier, as well as the composite transliteration of Text 6 compiled for the volume by Raija Mattila of the project staff. She also discussed with me in depth two central issues relating to the translation of the texts where we disagreed, viz. the meaning of the term *adê* by which the texts are designated, and the rendering of the subjunctive *šumma* clauses occurring prominently in the texts.

Upon departure from Helsinki, Watanabe spent a week in London collating the texts, and was expected to submit the rest of the manuscript (the critical apparatus and the introduction) by the end of April. By the end of June it became evident, however, that she would not be able to provide these sections within foreseeable time. Accordingly, in order not to delay the publication of the volume indefinitely, the manuscript was completed by myself with the assistance of the project staff.

Watanabe's responsibility for the volume is thus limited to the preliminary transliterations and translations completed in January, 1988. Since then, both have been substantially revised on the basis of further collations and research by myself, as well as suggestions by the other members of the Editorial Committee. The introduction, all the indices, and the final version of the critical apparatus are entirely my own work. The variant list included in the critical apparatus was compiled according to my instructions by Hannes Hägglund and Laura Kataja of the project staff. The list of manuscript sigla and the basic manuscript of the score transliteration of Text 6 were prepared by Raija Mattila using as a point of departure the data found in BaM Bh 3. The line boundaries of individual manuscripts indicated in the score were supplied by Hannes Hägglund.

Thus, once again, we have a volume of the SAA series which would not have appeared without the cooperation of many people. In addition to Dr. Watanabe and the members of the project already mentioned, the volume owes particularly much to Dr. Julian Reade, who edited the illustrations and provided many valuable remarks on the translations and name indices. Prof. Benjamin Foster and Dr. Gary Beckman of Yale University thoroughly and competently collated Text 11 at my request. My colleagues Karlheinz Deller, F. M. Fales and Nicholas Postgate read the galley proofs suggesting several improvements. Dr. Robert Whiting, Managing Editor of the project, checked the page proofs and edited the English of the introduction as well as the final (microfiche) version of the score of Text 6. To all these friends and colleagues who were directly involved in the preparation of the volume I wish to express my deep gratitude and appreciation for the work they did.

I also wish to extend my thanks to the following museum authorities and colleagues who granted publication permissions for the texts and photographs included in this volume, or were helpful in obtaining fresh photographs and prints for the volume: Drs. C. B. F. Walker and I. L. Finkel of the Department of Western Asiatic Antiquities of the British Museum; Dr. Annie Caubet of the Département des Antiquités Orientales du Musée du Louvre; Dr. Evelyn Klengel of the Vorderasiatisches Museum, Berlin; and Prof. Paul Garelli of the Sorbonne. I am indebted to the entire staff of the Department of Western Asiatic Antiquities of the British Museum for the help rendered to me and my co-editor during the collation of the originals, and to the Photographic Service of the British Museum for the excellent prints prepared for this volume.

This book would not have appeared without the computer hardware and software donated by the Olivetti (Finland) Corporation, and this valuable support is here gratefully acknowledged. In this context I also wish to record my gratitude to Mr. Pasi Tapanainen, who rewrote the programs used in the preparation of the volume in C and thus enabled their use on the new VAX mainframe of the University of Helsinki.

Our publisher, the Helsinki University Press, has helped in the production of this volume in every possible way. I greatly appreciate the smooth collaboration we have been able to establish, and the dedication and care by which every part of the manuscript has been handled by the staff.

The publication of this volume has been supported by a grant from the Ministry of Education of the Government of Finland, and I take this opportunity to thank Marita Savola of the Ministry personally for the interest she has taken in our project.

My principal thanks of course go to our funding institution, the Academy of Finland, without which the research behind this volume would not have been possible.

November 1988 Simo Parpola

CONTENTS

FOREWORD VII

PREFACE IX

INTRODUCTION XIII

Treaties as Instruments of Neo-Assyrian Imperialism XV
The Treaty Corpus XXVI
Contexts and Dates XXVI
Structural and Formal Analysis XXXV
Manuscripts XLIII
On the Present Edition LI
Notes LIV
Abbreviations and Symbols LVI
Manuscript Sigla LIX

TRANSLITERATIONS AND TRANSLATIONS 1

Treaties of the Ninth and Eighth Centuries B.C. 1
1. Treaty of Šamši-Adad V with Marduk-zakir-šumi, King of Babylon 4
2. Treaty of Aššur-nerari V with Mati'-ilu, King of Arpad 8
Treaties of the Seventh Century B.C. 15
3. Sennacherib's Succession Treaty 18
4. Accession Treaty of Esarhaddon 22
5. Esarhaddon's Treaty with Baal, King of Tyre 24
6. Esarhaddon's Succession Treaty 28
7. Oath of Loyalty to Esarhaddon 59
8. Zakutu Treaty 62
9. Assurbanipal's Treaty with Babylonian Allies 64
10. Assurbanipal's Treaty with the Qedar Tribe 68
11. Sin-šarru-iškun's Treaty with Babylonian Allies 72
12. Extract from a Treaty of Sin-šarru-iškun 73
13. A Vassal Treaty 76
14. Esarhaddon's Treaty Inscription 77

GLOSSARY AND INDICES 81

Logograms and Their Readings 81

Glossary 83
Index of Names 108
Personal Names 108
Place Names 109
God, Star, and Temple Names 110
Subject Index 112
Index of Texts 120
By Publication Number 120
By Museum Number 120
List of Illustrations 121

COLLATIONS AND COPIES 122

PLATES I-X 124

SCORE OF TEXT 6 (Microfiche) ..... Inside Back Cover

INTRODUCTION

The corpus of treaties edited in the present volume represents only a small fraction of all the treaties once concluded by the Neo-Assyrian emperors. Many treaties recorded on papyrus and leather were burnt to ashes during the destruction of Nineveh in 612 B.C.,[1] and innumerable treaties on clay and stone have either been destroyed or remain buried in the ruins of Assyrian palaces in Nineveh and elsewhere. Even the few extant texts edited here are only fragmentarily preserved. A mere glance at the diagrams on pp. XLIVf will reveal that large chunks of text have broken away from almost all of them, and every one of them has suffered at least some sort of textual damage.

Of course, the state of preservation of these documents has nothing to do with their intrinsic value as authentic treaties of an ancient superpower which once held in its iron grip half of the civilized world. To bring out their significance fully, one may add that the might of that superpower was to a very significant extent based on this very type of document, and that some of the treaties that helped it rule the world are actually included in the present volume.

Having access to such documents in the form of originals is a rare privilege indeed, considering that we do not possess a single copy of a treaty concluded by imperial Rome. In fact, precious few original treaties are available from ancient times altogether,[2] and none of the ancient states from which treaties are available can match the Assyrian empire at the apex of its power in significance. The treaties edited in the present volume span a period of 200 years from about 825 to 625 B.C., the time of Assyria's greatest territorial expansion, and they give first-hand testimony of how that expansion was achieved and how it was maintained.

Almost all the treaties included in the present edition have been previously available in English translation. However, most of the texts have been scattered in many specialized scholarly publications, which has made them in practice inaccessible for the general reader, and many of the available editions suffer from various inaccuracies and flaws, which has rendered a serious study of the genre difficult even for the specialist. It is hoped that the present volume, which is the first comprehensive edition of the whole Neo-Assyrian treaty corpus, will ameliorate this situation by making this important body of texts accessible in its entirety both for the specialist and the non-specialist in a reliable and easy-to-use edition.

It is clear that future excavations both in museums and in the field will add to the corpus and render the present edition obsolete in due course. However, we believe that for the moment and the immediate future, this edition will serve an important function. Many things which seemed to be obscure in the past become understandable once the texts are put together in a coherent fashion. One of the myths that the present volume is sure to bury is the popular notion of Assyria as a primitive and crude military power. We believe this notion should be replaced by one of a superpower relying on power politics rather than arms, but prefer to leave that for the reader himself or herself to judge. The purpose of the following introduction is to put together the basic facts needed for making the texts speak for themselves to an attentive reader.

Treaties as Instruments of Neo-Assyrian Imperialism

As the title of the present volume indicates, texts definable as 'loyalty oaths' make up a considerable portion of the Neo-Assyrian treaty corpus. In fact, such texts dominate the corpus so overwhelmingly that it has been questioned whether any of these texts, called *adê* in Neo-Assyrian, should be regarded as 'treaties' in the proper sense of the word. Following I.J. Gelb, many scholars have since the early sixties taken all *adê* texts as sworn pacts of loyalty imposed by the Assyrian king on his vassals or subjects. Some have even gone as far as to claim that in the final analysis all these texts are simply oaths, not treaties, pacts, or indeed any sort of formal agreements between two parties at all.[3]

A closer look at the texts will make it clear, however, that taking all of them for loyalty oaths just does not work. While all of them apparently did involve an oath, a few of them (cf. nos. 1, 5 and 13) are unquestionably bilateral agreements between rulers and hence treaties by the modern definition. One of these texts (no. 5) is explicitly designated as an *adê*, and all of them agree in structure and formulation with *adê* texts taken to be loyalty oaths. This indicates that despite differences in content, all the texts in the corpus belong to the same genre, and accordingly the 'loyalty oaths' too were basically conceived as agreements between the parties specified at the beginning of these texts.

Further study bears out that a schematic division of the corpus into treaties and loyalty oaths (here adopted for practical reasons) is artificial rather than real. The seemingly homogenous group of 'loyalty oaths' actually consists of many different types of pacts concluded under different circumstances and for a variety of different purposes. The small group of 'treaties' likewise consists of texts of different type and background. Significantly, some texts in the corpus (e.g., nos. 2 and 9-10) combine features of both groups so that the decision whether to classify them as 'treaties' or 'loyalty oaths' becomes rather arbitrary.

Bilateral and Unilateral Treaties

These facts suffice to show that it is a mistake to approach the *adê* texts from the narrow viewpoint of 'loyalty oaths'. Basically, they are all binding polical agreements, pacts or treaties, whose exact nature was determined by the mutual status of the contracting parties. The particular nature of the present corpus derives from the gross imbalance of power between the contracting parties, the other party being the king of Assyria.

As ruler of a superpower, the Assyrian king was in a position to dictate the terms of most agreements he concluded and to obtain unilateral concessions from the other contracting party. However, it is important to realise that this was not always the case. Situations arose in which the Assyrian ruler too was forced (or saw it as advantageous) to make concessions in order to obtain an agreement he desired. The extent of the concessions he was ready to make was of course directly related to the bargaining power of the other contracting party. Seen in this light, the texts in this book can be conveniently divided into two basic types: agreements involving, and ones not involving, concessions from the Assyrian king. In other words, we are simply dealing with various types of 'bilateral' and 'unilateral' agreements. We shall refer to them as treaties, since the other contracting party in each text was either a ruler or a nation, usually both.

In order to fully understand the nature and function of these treaties, it is necessary to carefully consider the typical situations in which Neo-Assyrian treaties were concluded. We can study the matter from royal inscriptions and other contemporary documents, which refer to numerous treaties in addition to those actually preserved. Sifting this evidence, one is struck by an interesting and rather unexpected observation:

Relatively few of the treaties were actually 'imposed' on the other contracting party. On the contrary, most of them, even ones clearly belonging to the category of unilateral treaties, were concluded at the initiative of the other, 'subordinate', party. How is this possible, if the terms of the treaties were as unequal as they seem to us?

The answer should be obvious. In each case, the other party had temporarily something very important to gain from Assyria (mostly military aid, but also political backing, alliance, or simply peace) in exchange for the concessions it made. In other words, even seemingly unequal treaties may once have been viewed as 'pretty good deals' by the party whom we now classify as the losing one.

This, in any case, was the official Assyrian position in the matter. Every treaty concluded by the Assyrian king was portrayed as a royal favour toward the other party, who came to beg for it on his knees – the idiom was "to grasp the king's feet" – so that "favour", "benefit" (*ṭābtu*) in effect became a synonym of "treaty" (*adê*). These 'favours' had a price tag attached to them though, the treaty terms, which may not have seemed of great consequence at the time when they were imposed but in practice often meant the loss of the 'beneficiary's' political independence.

Nonaggression Pacts

Before proceeding further, let us pause for a moment to have a look at the sources themselves. Rather than skimming through all the available references, we shall concentrate on a few paradigmatic examples only, selected to illustrate different types of treaties in their historical contexts. The function of treaties in Neo-Assyrian imperial policies will, we believe, emerge clearly from even these few examples. We shall begin with a treaty with Elam, Assyria's perennial foe on the southeastern frontier.

The background of this treaty, concluded between Esarhaddon (of Assyria) and Urtaku (of Elam) in 674 B.C., is described in Assyrian royal inscriptions as follows:

"The Elamite and the Gutian, obstinate kings whose relations with my royal forefathers had been inimical, heard of the might of Aššur that I had displayed to all enemies; fear overcame them, and in order to keep the border of their countries unviolated they dispatched their messengers of friendship and peace (*ša ṭūbi u sulummê*) to me to Nineveh and swore an oath by the great gods." (Borger Esarh. p. 58f.)

The passage refers to two kings, but nothing is known of a treaty with a "Gutian" king. On the other hand, the Elamite peace initiative is confirmed by a contemporary oracle query (AGS 76). A later letter (CT 54 580) shows that the treaty was preceded by intensive negotiations:

"A message from the Crown Prince to Šulmu-ahu: The king of Elam and the king of Assyria, having repeatedly consulted with each other, have by the command of Marduk made peace with one another (*isselmū*) and become treaty partners (*bēl adê ša ahāmiš*)."[4]

Note that the treaty is here explicitly identified as an *adê*, and compare the phrasing of the royal inscription, which simply shows that a sworn agreement was in question. Both the letter and the inscription speak of a peace treaty. One could also call it a nonaggression pact, as the motive behind the Elamite peace drive clearly was fear of an Assyrian invasion. That such a pact was of interest to Assyria too is made patently clear by the following letter passage, referring to the very treaty in question:

"Last year when the Palace Superintendent and the Magnates went down to Chaldea, the brothers of the king of Elam tried to incite their brother the king, saying: 'Let us gather an army, cross over to Chaldea and take it away from Assyria.' The king of Elam, however, did not sin, but refused to listen to them, saying: 'I shall not violate the treaty (*adê*).'" (ABL 328:9-15.)

Even though the treaty itself has not been preserved, there is every reason to believe that it was fully bilateral. A piece of correspondence between the contracting kings (ABL 918) implies that they went so far as to exchange children to make sure that the treaty terms would be kept. Note the care taken in the letter to convey a tone of absolute equality:

"A letter from Esarhaddon, king of Assyria, to Urtaku, king of Elam, my brother: I am well, your sons and daughters are well, my country and magnates are well. May Urtaku, king of Elam, my brother, be well, may my sons and daughters be well, may your magnates and your country be well.

"Now that the gods Aššur, Sin, Šamaš, Bel, Nabû, Ištar of Nineveh, Ištar of Arbela and Manziniri have completed and stabilized what they promised ..."

To summarize briefly, we have here an indisputable case of a fully bilateral treaty between Assyria and another major power, referred to as *adê* in contemporary letters and as a "peace and friendship" treaty in the royal inscriptions. The treaty was sworn, confirmed by an exchange of children between the contracting parties, and evidently meant to last. In fact, it did last for ten years, and when it was finally broken, this came as a total surprise to the Assyrian party:

"On my 6th campaign I marched against Urtaku, king of Elam, who had forgotten the favours (*ṭābtu*) of my father and did not guard my friendship... The Elamite, whose attack I had never seriously considered and whose hostility I did not suspect..." (Streck Asb p. 105.)

Peace and Friendship Treaties

A whole series of 'peace and friendship' treaties between Assyria and Babylonia is recorded in the Synchronistic History, a chronicle totally devoted to the theme of Assyro-Babylonian interrelations. The following examples are just a few out of many:

"Karaindaš, king of Karduniaš, and Aššur-bel-nišešu, king of Assyria (1419-1411), made an agreement (*riksāni urakkisū*) with each other and gave sworn assurances (*māmītu*) to each other concerning this very boundary."

"Adad-nerari II (911-891) and Nabû-šuma-iškun ... gave their daughters to each other in marriage and established perfect friendship and peace (*ṭūbta u sulummâ gamra*) with each other. The peoples of Assyria and Babylonia were joined together. They established a boundary from Til-Bit-Bari to Til-ša-Batani."

"At the time of Shalmaneser III, king of Assyria (858-824), Nabû-apla-iddina was the king of Karduniaš. They established perfect friendship and peace with each other. At the time of Shalmaneser, king of Assyria, Marduk-zakir-šumi I ascended his father's throne. Marduk-bel-usate, his brother, rebelled against him... Shalmaneser, king of Assyria, went to the aid of Marduk-zakir-šumi, king of Karduniaš..." (Grayson Chronicles pp. 158 and 166ff.)

That these passages refer to written treaties and not just "verbal agreements between monarchs", as recently alleged,[5] can be taken as certain. Compare the discussion of Text 1 below, p. XXVII. It seems clear that these treaties not only served as peace and border settlements but also as means of guaranteeing the stability and continuity of the ruling dynasties in both Assyria and Babylonia. As such, they also offered a convenient excuse to interfere in the affairs of the other country at times of political turmoil.

Mutual Assistance Pacts

A totally different kind of treaty with a major foreign power is hidden behind this episode from the inscriptions of Assurbanipal, dating from the time Assyria was at the zenith of its power:

"Gyges, the king of Lydia, an overseas territory, a distant place whose name my royal ancestors had not even heard of, was shown my royal name in a dream by Aššur, the god who created me, who spoke thus: 'Grasp the feet of Assurbanipal, king of Assyria, and defeat your enemies by the mere mention of his name.' The day he saw this dream he sent his mounted messenger to greet me and had the dream he had seen narrated to me by his messenger.

From the moment he grasped my royal feet, he, with the support of Aššur and Ištar, defeated the Cimmerians who had harassed the people of his country... He threw into iron fetters and handcuffs two of the Cimmerian chieftains he had defeated and sent them into my presence together with his weighty audience gift.

"(Later) he cut off the mounted messenger whom he had regularly been sending to my audience. Not guarding the word of Aššur, the god who created me, he trusted in his own power, grew haughty, and sent his troops to help Psammetikos, king of Egypt, who had thrown off my yoke. When I heard this, I prayed to Aššur and Ištar, saying: 'May his corpse be cast before his enemy and may they bring me his bones.' And see: what I had prayed for to Aššur happened; his body was thrown before his enemy and his bones were brought to me. The Cimmerians who at the mention of my name had submitted to him invaded and devastated his entire land.

"Afterwards his son ascended his throne. He reported to me by his messenger the evil fate which my gods at my request had prepared for his father, and grasped my feet saying: 'You are a king whom God cares for: you cursed my father, and evil befell him. Now bless me, your servant who fears you, and I will pull your yoke.'" (Streck Asb p. 20ff.)

Even though the word 'treaty' is not explicitly mentioned here, two subsequent treaties concluded at Lydian initiative are clearly implied. Both provided the country with Assyrian military aid at the time of a dire emergency; in return, we see Lydia joining the ranks of Assyria's allies and vassals at the royal audience in Nineveh. One can be sure that such an arrangement, meaning a heavy economic burden to Lydia, was not set up without a written agreement – a 'mutual assistance pact' – attached as a precondition to the aid provided by Assyria.[6]

Alliance Treaties

The classic method of forming alliances by political marriage is well attested in Assyria. And as the following oracle query (PRT 16) shows, these marriages were routinely adorned with a suitable treaty:

"O Šamaš, great lord, give a firm answer to the question I am asking you: Will Protothyes, king of Scythia, who has now sent his messengers to Esarhaddon, king of Assyria, on account of the king's daughter – if Esarhaddon gives him a princess, will Protothyes speak true and honest words of peace with Esarhaddon, will he keep the treaty (*adê*) of Esarhaddon, king of Assyria, and do whatever is good to Esarhaddon?"

This marriage certainly looks like a good deal to both parties. To the Scythian king it meant a powerful ally on top of a sizable dowry; to the prospective father-in-law, a cheap and easy way of acquiring control over a dangerous nomad nation looming up within the borders of the empire. Note the end of this quotation and compare it with Text 13 ii 3ff.

To add to the loyalty of his treaty partners, the Assyrian king did not shun assuming the role of a happy bridegroom himself every now and then:

"Mugallu, king of Tabal, who had defied my royal fathers, sent his own daughter with ample dowry to me to Nineveh and kissed my feet. I imposed upon him a yearly tribute of stately horses." (Streck Asb p. 18.)

Treaties with Exiled Foreign Royalty

We now turn to an interesting category of treaties: those concluded with expatriated princes and nobility seeking shelter at the court of Nineveh. The Assyrian king had a 'soft spot' for these people and gladly provided them with the asylum they needed. He was even willing to help them return to their home country and, with the help of the Assyrian army, correct the injustice that had been done to them. All this naturally on the condition that the favour would be paid back.

The role of treaties in this game is illustrated by an episode from the reign of Assurbanipal. Following the death of Urtaku in 664, an usurper named Teumman seized the throne of Elam and started eliminating his adversaries. Subsequently, "Ummanigaš, Ummanappa, and Tammaritu, sons of Urtaku, king of Elam, fled before Teumman's murderous rage and grasped my royal feet... Even though he repeatedly sent his officials to demand the extradition of Ummanigaš, Ummanappa and Tammaritu, I did not grant their extradition." (Piepkorn Asb p. 61.)

Ten years later, using an alleged provocation by Teumman as an excuse, Assurbanipal launched a destructive attack against Elam. "I cut off the head of Teumman before his assembled troops ... and seated Ummanigaš, who had fled and grasped my feet, upon his throne; Tammaritu, his third brother, I established as king in Hidalu." (ibid. p. 71.)

There are three significant points in the process of bringing the two princes to power in Elam which do not clearly emerge from the above condensed account but are well attested in other sources. First, the Assyrian troops invaded Elam under Elamite leadership:

"When Ummanigaš came and grasped my feet, and I sent my troops with him, and they fought with Teumman, did we set out feet in the temples, cities or anywhere? Did we take plunder? Did we not pour oil upon blood and become your benefactors?" (Letter of Assurbanipal to Elamite elders, BM 132980:8ff.)

Secondly, despite all the official propaganda, the real objective of the operation certainly was to turn Elam into an Assyrian dependency. This appears clearly from a contemporary letter (ABL 839 r.14ff), where it is suggested that the king "should place one of the princes among his servants to the governorship (*pāhatūtu*) of Elam."[7] An overlooked royal inscription (Bauer Asb pl. 45) explicitly states that tax and tribute were imposed upon Elam, and also mentions other administrative measures normally carried out when turning a country into a province.

Thirdly, as could be expected, the Elamite puppets were bound to their 'benefactor' by means of sworn treaties. The existence of these treaties is not revealed in passages describing the installation of the princes, but is made more than explicit in passages describing their later perfidious behaviour:

"Ummanigaš, for whom I had done many favours, whom I had established as king of Elam, but who was not mindful of my kindness and did not keep the treaty sworn by the great gods (*adê māmīt ilāni rabûti*) but accepted bribes from the hands of the messengers of Šamaš-šumu-ukin, my faithless brother and enemy, and sent troops with them to fight my forces..." (Piepkorn Asb p. 77.)

In a letter to one of the princes, Tammaritu, Assurbanipal plainly tells what he expected from his puppet:

"What (even) a father does not do for a son, I have [done] and given to you! As for you, remember [this], strive to return to me in full these favours [that I have done to you], and keep the [treaty] that I have made you swear before the gods of heaven and earth!" (ABL 1022 r. 19ff.)

Treaties with Assyrianized Foreign Royalty

Another way of gaining control over a country through a native puppet was to import children of foreign kings to Nineveh, educate them at the royal court until they had been completely Assyrianized, and then, at a suitable moment, install them on their fathers' thrones. The status and obligations of the puppets in this case too were defined in a treaty:

"As for Ṣidqâ, king of Ashkelon, who had not submitted to my yoke – the gods of his dynasty, himself, his wife, his sons, his daughters, his brothers, the offspring of his dynasty I tore away and brought to Assyria. Šarru-lu-dari, the son of Rukibti their former king, I set over the people of Ashkelon, imposed upon him the payment of taxes and presents to my majesty, and he accepted my yoke." (Luckenbill Senn. p. 30.)

The Assyrian name of this new king, which means "may the king live forever", suffices to make clear what sort of a man he must have been.

Other examples: Sennacherib installed "a native of Babylon who had grown up in my palace like a puppy" on the throne of Babylon (Luckenbill p. 54). Esarhaddon placed an Arab princess, "Tabu'a, raised in my father's palace, to kingship over them and returned her with her gods to her country." (Borger p. 53.) Note also Streck Asb p. 21, referring to nine sons of the king of Arwad sent to Nineveh, robed in purple, given golden bracelets and incorporated in Assurbanipal's entourage.

Treaties with Submissive Adversaries

Many treaties were concluded with enemies surrendering before an approaching Assyrian army or after a display of force:

"Natnu, king of distant Nabatea, heard of the power of Aššur and Marduk, and he who had never sent his messenger to my royal fathers to ask about the well-being of their majesties, now sent his 'messenger of health' to me to kiss my feet and to implore my lordship in order to conclude a treaty of peace and vassalage (*adê sulummê u epēš ardūti*) with me. I looked at him kindly, turned my gracious face upon him, and imposed a yearly tax and tribute upon him." (Piepkorn Asb p. 85.)

"Layalê, king of Yadi', who had fled before my weapons, became scared for his life, came to my presence to Nineveh and kissed my feet. I had mercy on him and pardoned him; I inscribed the might of Aššur my lord on his gods that I had plundered, returned them to him, entrusted him that region of Bazu and imposed the tax and tribute of my lordship upon him." (Borger Esarh. p.56f.)

By contrast, one looks in vain for treaties imposed on defeated enemies. Such people were of no use to Assyria; they were eliminated and replaced with people ready and willing to cooperate:

"The governors, nobles and people of Ekron, who had thrown Padî their king, bound by treaty and oath (*bēl adê u māmīt*) to Assyria, into iron fetters and given him over to Hezekiah the Jew, became afraid ... I drew near to Ekron and slew the governors and nobles who had committed sin, and hung their corpses on stakes around the city. The citizens who had sinned I counted as spoil, the rest who were not guilty of sin I pardoned. I brought Padî their king out of Jerusalem, set him on the royal throne over them and imposed upon him the tribute of my lordship." (Luckenbill Senn. p. 31.)

Broken Treaties

All Neo-Assyrian treaties were sworn treaties, and those which were not kept turned into a curse against the treacherous party – a curse, or rather curses, literally written in the treaty itself. Compare the following episode from the inscriptions of Assurbanipal with the curses in Text 2 v 1ff:

"Yauta' the son of Hazael, king of Qedar, who had submitted to me, appealed to me about his gods and entreated my lordship. I had him swear an oath by the great gods and gave the god Atar-samain back to him. Later he sinned against my treaty (*adê*), did not respect my favours, threw off the yoke of my dominion, stopped asking about my health and withheld my audience gift. He incited the people of Arabia to revolt with him, and they repeatedly plundered Syria.

"I dispatched against him my troops which were stationed at the border of his land and they defeated him. They struck down with weapons all the Arab people who had risen in rebellion, set on fire and burnt down the tents where they dwelt, and took as spoils countless numbers of cattle, sheep, asses, camels and slaves... As for Yauta' and the rest of the Arabs, his troops who had not kept my treaty, who had fled before my weapons, the warrior Erra struck them down; famine broke out among them, and to still their hunger they ate the flesh of their own children.

"Aššur, Sin, Šamaš, Bel, Nabû, Ištar of Nineveh and Ištar of Arbela, the great gods, my lords, brought upon them word for word all the curses that were prescribed in their treaty. Young camels, young asses, calves and spring lambs sucked their nursing mothers seven times and still could not satisfy their stomachs with milk. People in the Arab land, one after the other, kept asking one another: 'Why has this misfortune befallen the Arab land? Because we did not keep the great treaty of Aššur, and sinned against the favour of

Assurbanipal, the king whom the god Illil loves.'" (Piepkorn Asb p. 80ff; cf. Streck Asb p. 74ff.)

A letter (ABL 350) from the Assyrian governor who carried out this punitive operation is extant, and it is important to note how he reports on the result of his mission:

"As to the Qedarites concerning whom the king my lord gave me orders, I went to the country and by the king my lord's destiny afflicted a crushing defeat on them.

"They have become terrified; and as the king my lord's treaty (*adê*) has overcome them, those who escaped the iron sword will die of hunger."

The inevitability of the treaty curses stressed here is a constantly recurring theme in the royal inscriptions:

"At that time Nabû-zer-kitti-lišir, son of Merodach-Baladan, governor of the Sealand, who did not keep the treaty (*adê*) and was not mindful of the favours of Assyria, forgot the favours of my father, and during the confusion in Assyria mustered his troops... This seditious rebel heard of the approach of my troops and fled to Elam like a fox. Because he had transgressed the oath by the great gods, Aššur, Sin, Šamaš, Bel and Nabû imposed upon him a heavy punishment and killed him with a weapon in Elam..." (Borger Esarh. p. 46f.)

"Urtaku, king of Elam, who had not kept friendship with me, met a premature death, perished and oozed away in weariness, setting no more his feet on the ground of the living: his life ended the very same year, and he passed away. Bel-iqiša the Gambulean who had cast off the yoke of my dominion lost his life through the bite of a rat. Dropsy, accumulation of fluid, carried off Nabû-šum-eriš, the governor of Nippur who did not keep the treaty (*adê*). Marduk, king of the gods, imposed his heavy punisment on Marduk-šum-ibni, his eunuch, the instigator who had induced Urtaku to plan evil. In a single year they all laid down their lives, one after another." (Piepkorn Asb p. 58f.)

Expansion through Treaties

The Assyrian empire has gone into history as a ruthless military power. Consequently, one is easily led to think that it expanded primarily by means of arms and unrestrained aggression. As we have seen, however, the truth is somewhat different. In reality, the expansion of Assyria took place less dramatically, almost imperceptibly, through political deals with foreign rulers (or would-be rulers) seeking military aid, peace or other favours from the Assyrian king. By signing a treaty with the Assyrian emperor, these rulers traded off their national independence for Assyrian vassalage. And once Assyria's overlordship had been formally established, there was no escaping from it. Broken treaties were severely punished; sooner or later Assyrian armies poured into the rebel country, which was utterly destroyed and annexed to Assyria.

No doubt the Assyrian kings preferred 'expansion by treaties' to expansion by aggression. Waging war was costly and time-consuming, and wasted the resources of both Assyria and the target country. By contrast, the advantages of acquiring vassals and allies by diplomacy were self-evident. Shrewdly drawn-up treaties added the vassal's troops to the imperial army, channeled a significant portion of his wealth to the imperial treasury, and subjected his country to a process of gradual Assyrianization, sure to make total annexation so much easier at a later stage — all this for little or no extra cost. What more could even a greedy emperor have hoped for?

On the other hand, broken treaties also worked to Assyria's advantage. The brutal military measures needed to annex a country were now conveniently sanctioned by the curses written in the treaties. On the ideological level, every broken treaty was a sin against the god Aššur, and thus the invading Assyrian army could be portrayed as the 'sword of Aššur' which the perfidious vassal himself had called upon his land.[8]

Loyalty Pacts

The more the power of Assyria grew, the greater became the role treaties played in its territorial expansion, as more and more nations exposed to its threat sought peace or alliance with it. Using a parable, one could say that from the early 7th century on, the empire grew by its own weight like a downhill-rolling snowball. The only major problem the expansionists in Nineveh faced was the internal stability of the empire. While external threats and local uprisings could under normal conditions be easily contained even by provincial governors, the capability to meet these challenges was seriously weakened at times of power struggles in the core, which paralyzed the normal functions of the state.

The Assyrian solution to the problem was to set up a mechanism geared to detect and nip all treacherous activities in the bud: pacts of loyalty obliging every Assyrian subject to accept and protect the sovereignty of the ruling king (or his heir apparent) and to immediately report any activities undermining this sovereignty to the king.

Such pacts seem to have been typically imposed after civil wars and at the official appointment of the heir apparent. All extant specimens are from the 7th century and they are therefore generally believed to represent a comparatively late development. However, a loyalty oath imposed on Assyrian citizens is already attested in an inscription of Šamši-Adad V dating from the 9th century B.C. (see below, p. XXVI), and it should be noted that stipulations typical of the 7th century 'loyalty pacts' also occur in the mid-8th century treaties from Sefire and other treaties not belonging to the category of 'loyalty pacts'. It would thus seem that the Assyrian royal house had already quite early recognized the gravity of the problem it was facing, and thus treaties comparable to the 7th century 'loyalty pacts' may well have existed considerably earlier.

Power Politics

We thus see that treaties performed several centrally important functions in Assyrian imperialistic policy:

They were the very means of enlarging the empire, binding new acquisitions to it permanently, regulating international trade, channeling a flow of goods and raw materials to the centre of the empire, adding to the imperial army, tying the hands of enemy powers, and securing the safety of the king and the transfer of power to a successor of the emperor's own choice. In short, they were the very thing that made the Assyrian empire an empire. From the systematic and routine way in which they were used in daily politics it is clear that they were part of a sophisticated and well-tested strategy designed to bring ever new nations under the sway of the Assyrian emperor. Naturally, they could not have had their desired impact without the backing of a strong army, and a willingness to use it ruthlessly and unhesitatingly, but their central role in the imperial policies shows that Assyria was something more than just the crude military power which it is pictured as in the schoolbooks.

It was above all a true superpower making use of all the classic means of political manipulation in its dealings with other nations. It concluded mutual friendship and assistance pacts, only to later invade a country by invitation; it sold arms and military assistance to shaky governments, only to add them to its sphere of influence; it acquired zones of satellites by methodically installing its puppets in exposed countries. These methods sound so familiar that the Assyrians might well have written the modern textbook for territorial expansion by diplomatic means.

The Treaty Corpus

Contexts and Dates

Text 1

No. 1 is a treaty between Šamši-Adad V, king of Assyria (823-811), and Marduk-zakir-šumi I, king of Babylon (c. 850-820, exact regnal years unknown). In addition, an otherwise unknown individual named Marduk-rimanni seems to figure as a third contracting party. Judging from the context where he appears, he may have been a Babylonian, but this is uncertain. He may be identical with the governor mentioned in obv. 3', in which case he would be an Assyrian.[9]

The extant clauses of the treaty are almost entirely military. Of the principal contracting parties, Marduk-zakir-šumi is called king, while Šamši-Adad is not. This indicates that the treaty was concluded before Šamši-Adad's accession and can accordingly only date from the stormy last years (827-824) of Shalmaneser III, the time of the great rebellion of Aššur-da''in-aplu. The present treaty was thus probably occasioned by an internal power struggle in Assyria, described in Šamši-Adad's inscriptions as follows (1 R 29 i 39ff):

"When Aššur-da''in-aplu, in the time of Shalmaneser, his father, acted wickedly, bringing about sedition, rebellion and evil plotting, caused the land to rise in revolt, prepared for war, brought the people of Assyria, north and south, to his side, strengthened (his position by) oath, made all the cities obey him and set his mind to begin strife and battle – the cities of Nineveh, Adia, Šibaniba, Imgur-Illil, Iššabri, Bet-šašširi, Šimu, Šibhiniš, Tamnuna, Kipšuna, Kurbail, Tidu, Nabulu, Kahat, Assur, Urakka, Sallat, Huzirina, Dur-balaṭi, Dariga, Zabban, Lubdu, Arrapha, Arbail, Amidi, Til-abnâ, and Hindanu, a total of 27 cities, along with their fortresses, which had revolted against Shalmaneser, my father, and gone to the side of Aššur-da''in-aplu, at the command of the great gods, my lords, I brought into submission at my feet."

Šamši-Adad's father, Shalmaneser III, had years earlier concluded a bilateral friendship and peace treaty with the father of Marduk-zakir-šumi I, the other treaty party, and actually gone to the aid of the latter at the time of a revolt (Grayson Chronicles p. 167, and cf. above p. XVIII). By providing military assistance to Shalmaneser's (legitimate) heir, to which he was evidently obligated by oath, Marduk-zakir-šumi was thus simply returning a favour rendered to him earlier. There is no reason to take the treaty to indicate Babylonian supremacy over Assyria, as has been hitherto done. On the contrary, the treaty terms (cf. especially obv. 8-13) imply perfect equality between the contracting parties.

It is possible that the present treaty is referred to in a fragmentary entry in the Synchronistic History (col. iii 1'-5'):

"They [Šamši-Adad and Marduk-zakir-šumi] established [perfect friendship and peace (*ṭūbta sulummâ gamra*) with each other; the peoples of Assyria and Babylonia] were joined [together. ......] They fixed [a boundary line by mutual consent]."

If so, the text can be defined as a 'mutual frienship and peace treaty' comparable with the other similar treaties in the Synchronistic History. For the restorations, which are certain, see Grayson Chronicles pp. 167f and 286; the break preceding the passage is at least 10 lines wide and actually requires a reference to the Aššur-da"in-aplu rebellion (compare, e.g., col. ii 29'-37' of the same text).

Text 2

No. 2 is a treaty between Aššur-nerari V, king of Assyria (754-745), and Mati'-il, king of Arpad, an Aramaic city-state north of Aleppo. It was probably concluded in Aššur-nerari's very first year and it seems to have been duly observed by Mati'-il, since, while Arpad was the target of an Assyrian campaign in 754, the city does not figure in Assyrian sources later in Aššur-nerari's reign.

The situation changed in the reign of Tiglath-Pileser III, who succeeded Aššur-nerari after a coup d'état. Possibly feeling no longer bound by the treaty, Mati'-il soon joined an anti-Assyrian revolt in coalition with other Syrian city-states and Urarṭu – an alliance expressly forbidden in the present treaty (cf. the fragmentary lines in col. iii 5'-10'). The revolt was a failure; Urarṭu was defeated in 743, while Arpad fell after a three-year siege and was reduced to a province in 740.

No account of the circumstances which led to the conclusion of the present treaty is extant, but it is very unlikely that Mati'-il was actually defeated in the 754 campaign. After all, it took Tiglath-Pileser III three years to take Arpad by siege. By analogy to other comparable cases, it can be assumed that the treaty was the result of a political surrender in the face of the advancing Assyrian troops; that is, it too represents a 'favour' of the Assyrian king, 'granted' at the request of Mati'-il himself.

The text has remarkable affinities with three Aramaic treaties found at Sefire near Aleppo (KAI 222-224), all of them likewise concluded between Mati'-il of Arpad and a mysterious Bar-ga'yah of KTK, who figures in the texts as Mati'-il's overlord. Since, despite extensive debate, the identity of Bar-ga'yah and KTK has not yet been established, it is necessary to point out that all the essential features in these treaties (the treaty gods, the structure and formulation of the texts, and the actual treaty terms) imply that the other contracting party was the king of Assyria.

Since there is no evidence that Mati'-il was forced to conclude a treaty with any Assyrian king other than Aššur-nerari – no Assyrian campaigns to Arpad are recorded between 805 and 754 – the conclusion seems inevitable that Bar-ga'yah ("son of majesty") in fact is a pseudonym for this king. We accordingly hold that KTK too stands for Assyria,[10] and that the Sefire treaties are the Aramaic counterpart – though not an exact translation – of our Text

2. It does not require much imagination to find a reason for the use of a pseudonym (or euphemism) for a hated overlord in a text like this. It may well have been 'part of the deal', the only feasible way by which Mati'-il could accept the treaty without being ousted from his throne by the anti-Assyrian elements of his population. One only needs to recall what happened within the walls of Jerusalem at the time Sennacherib's troops were besieging the city (2 Kings 18:13ff) to understand the delicacy of the situation.

A detailed comparison of these two treaties falls outside the scope of the present edition, but it may be pointed out that all of the few extant treaty clauses in Text 2 find a parallel in the Sefire treaties (cf. iii 9-10 = KAI 224:2-3 and 19-20; iii 21-22 = KAI 224:4-6; iii 23-27 = KAI 222 B 23-25; iv 1-3 = KAI 222 B 28-33; v 1-4 = KAI 224:11-13), and all the clauses extant only in Sefire would comfortably fit in the breaks of our text. Note also the affinities between the ceremonial acts and curses in both treaties (e.g., no. 2 i 10ff // KAI 222 A 36-40; 2 i 4 // KAI 222 A 32; 2 v 14 // KAI 222 A 29), not to speak of individual details of formulation and the general structure of the texts. Parallels with other texts of the present volume are easy to find, as in KAI 222 C compared with no. 6:283ff, 385ff and 494ff.

Text 3

No. 3 is a fragment of an intriguing treaty of Sennacherib, king of Assyria (704-681). It seems to concern the royal succession, the extant clauses closely paralleling those found in nos. 6 and 8. The peculiar list of gods appearing in the curse sections makes it likely that the text dates from either 683 or 682 B.C.[11]

Even though the name of the heir apparent is broken away, there is thus every reason to believe that the treaty concerned the controversial promotion of Esarhaddon, which was soon to plunge Assyria into a bloody civil war. The background of this treaty is described as follows in Esarhaddon's inscriptions:

"Although I was younger than my big brothers, my father and begetter, by command of the gods, justly preferred me to my other brothers, saying: 'This is my heir.' Respecting the weighty decree of Šamaš and Adad, he assembled the people of Assyria, great and small, my brothers and the seed of my father's house, and before Aššur, Sin, Šamaš, Nabû and Marduk, the gods of Assyria and the gods inhabiting heaven and earth, made them pronounce their weighty names in order to protect my succession." (Borger Esarh. p. 40, Nin. A i 8-19; cf. ibid. i 50f and 80f.)

Text 4

No. 4 is a fragment of a treaty of Esarhaddon, king of Assyria (681-669), likewise belonging to the category of loyalty oaths. Since the extant treaty clauses exclusively consist of assurances of loyalty to Esarhaddon, who is not referred to as king but 'my lord' only, it seems likely that the treaty was imposed shortly before Esarhaddon's accession in late Adar (March), 681 B.C. No references to it are found in contemporary sources.

Text 5

No. 5 is a treaty between Esarhaddon and Baal, king of Tyre, probably concluded after the conquest and destruction of Sidon in 676 B.C. The inscriptions of Esarhaddon imply that a treaty with Baal was concluded on that occasion:

"From these cities of his (i.e. Abdi-Milkutti, king of Sidon) I entrusted Ma'rubbu and Ṣariptu in the hands of Baal, king of Tyre, and imposed upon him, in addition to the previous yearly tax, a tribute to my lordship." (Borger Esarh. p. 49.)

This statement is broadly in agreement with the spirit of the present treaty, which can be regarded as relatively favourable to Baal, giving him free access to all ports of trade on the Mediterranean coast and limiting Assyrian control of Tyre to the presence of a royal agent and collection of toll, "as in the past". The references to the "destroyed cities" and "the Sidonites" in col. iii 4' and 30' further support the dating of the text to 676 B.C.

Sidon's ruthless destruction and reduction into an Assyrian province were doubtless intended as warning signals to all Phoenician cities harbouring dreams of total independence from Assyria. Accordingly, it seems certain that the present treaty, with its relatively lenient terms, must have been preceded by gestures of submission from Baal.

Five years later, having refused cooperation with the Assyrian troops invading Egypt, Baal had to suffer a totally different kind of treatment from Esarhaddon. The Assyrian monarch tersely notes:

"I conquered Tyre, which lies in the middle of the sea, and took away from its king Baal, who relied on Taharka, king of Egypt, all his cities and possessions." (Borger Esarh. p. 86.)[12]

Text 6

No. 6 is the composite text of a treaty of Esarhaddon concerning the succession of his son Assurbanipal, concluded in Iyyar, 672 B.C. The purpose and date of the treaty are clearly stated in the text itself and confirmed by other contemporary sources, e.g., the later inscriptions of Assurbanipal (Streck Asb p. 2f):

"Esarhaddon, king of Assyria, my father and begetter, heeded the command of Aššur and Mullissu, the gods in whom he trusted, who told him that I was to exercise the kingship. On the 12th of Iyyar, at the noble command of Aššur, Mullissu, Sin, Šamaš, Adad, Bel, Nabû, Ištar of Nineveh, Ištar of Arbela, Ninurta, Nergal and Nusku, he convened the people of Assyria, great and small, from coast to coast, made them swear a treaty oath by the gods (*adê nīš ilāni*) and established a binding agreement to protect my crown-princeship and future kingship over Assyria."

The composite text of the treaty has been reconstructed from hundreds of fragments reduceable to eight separate manuscripts, all found in the Nabû temple of the city of Calah. The manuscripts contain orthographic and linguistic variants, as well as occasional errors and omissions, but are otherwise for all practical purposes identical. The only significant differences lie in the treaty preamble, where each manuscript has a different 'city-ruler' as the other contracting party:

Manuscript	H:	Humbareš	of Nahšimarti
	G:	Bur-Dadi	of Karzitali
	T:	Hatarna	of Sikris
	a:	Larkutla	of Mazamua
	A:	Ramataja	of Urakazabanu
	F:	Tunî	of Ellipi
	d:	NN	of Izaja
	I:	(destroyed)	

Primarily for this reason, the texts were dubbed 'the Vassal-Treaties of Esarhaddon' in Wiseman's editio princeps. This designation has recently been critisized by Watanabe, who regards it as misleading insofar as the texts were evidently imposed in identical form on the whole population of Assyria, not just on vassals. "It is only due to an accident that the VTE tablets drawn up for the Median chieftains have come down to us."[13]

This may be so, but there is another side to the matter that should not be overlooked. The texts are, as a matter of fact, formulated as bilateral agreements between rulers, and in addition they share many features with the Mati'-il and Sefire treaties (see under no. 2), which incontestably represent the classic type of a vassal treaty. Thus, while primarily drawn up for a different purpose, they could also secondarily be put to use as treaties concluded with vassals. In this context, note particularly lines 393f of the treaty, where the other party is pledged to accept the supremacy of Assyria and its chief god. This is a stipulation suiting a treaty with a newly acquired vassal, not a loyalty oath imposed on the whole empire, and its significance increases when it is considered together with the background of the 'city-rulers' with whom the treaties were concluded.

All of them ruled areas in the eastern periphery of Assyria. Excepting Mazamua (modern Sulaimaniya), these places were all situated in Media (today's Iran), and none of them appear to have been firmly under Assyrian control. In fact, at the time the treaties were drawn up, most of them must have been only recently reduced into vassal status. Ellipi, a vassal state under Sargon II and Sennacherib, was certainly independent at the accession of Esarhaddon. Ramataja of Urakazabanu joined the ranks of vassals in 675 B.C. — three years before the present treaty — as a result of a military operation described as follows in Esarhaddon's inscriptions:

"Fear of the nimbus of Aššur my lord overcame Uppis, city-ruler of Partakka, Zanasana, city-ruler of Partukka, and Ramateia, city-ruler of Urakazabarna, distant Medes who under my royal forefathers had not crossed the border of Assyria nor trodden her ground, and they brought big stallions and blocks of genuine lapis lazuli to Nineveh, my capital, and kissed my feet. They implored my lordship on account of city-rulers who had attacked them and asked for my help (*kitru*). I sent with them eunuchs of mine, governors of the districts next to their countries; they defeated the people living in those cities and made them bow at their feet. I imposed upon them tax and tribute to my lordship.

"(From) Patušarri, a region on the border of the Salt Desert in the land of the distant Medes, near Mt. Bikni (= Mt. Demavend near Teheran), the lapis-lazuli mountain, the ground of whose land none of my royal ancestors had trodden, I took as spoils of war to Assyria Šidirparna and Eparna, two mighty city-rulers who had not submitted to yoke, along with their people, riding horses, oxen, sheep, camels, and a heavy tribute." (Borger Esarh. p. 54 iv 32ff.)

A fragmentary oracle query from the time before the Salt Desert venture suggests that Bur-Dadi of Karzitali became a vassal at this juncture:

"Should Esarhaddon, king of Assyria, send troops to the city of Andarpati[anu ......] to collect a tribute of horses [......]? Should they advance as far as the Salt Desert [......] and from there [......] to the city of Karzi[tali? ......] the house of Tatt[î [......] Karzita[li ......] Eparna ... ... Will they return [aliv]e and safely?" (AGS 33+)

The reference to tax and tribute imposed on Ramataja shows that he had to pay dearly for the aid (*kitru*) he had received. It can accordingly be no coincidence that at least two further rulers figuring in the present treaties (Humbareš of Nahšimarti and Tunî of Ellipi) also received military aid from Esarhaddon. See AGS 52 and CT 53 638, both texts explicitly using the same word for the help given (*kitru*) as in the case of Ramataja. Neither of these texts can be exactly dated, but 673 should not be far off the mark.

An oracle query from about the same time (PRT 22) concerns a tribute-collecting expedition to Sikris, whose ruler Hatarna appears as a treaty party in manuscript T. The vassal status of Sikris is clear from the text, but there is no evidence when it had been established. Under Sargon II, the city had been part of the province of Harhar. The city and ruler of Izaia (manuscript d) are not otherwise known.

In sum, it can be stated that at least four, and possibly as many as seven, of the eight 'city-rulers' figuring in these treaties had become Assyrian vassals within a period of three years before the treaties were concluded. This being so, it seems quite possible that these texts really were meant to function as 'vassal-treaties', instruments relegating the oath-taking rulers to a status of permanent vassalage. This interpretation is not in conflict with the texts' obvious character as loyalty oaths; the two concepts are not mutually exclusive.

Text 7

No. 7 is a fragment of a treaty of Esarhaddon, possibly imposed upon the king's subjects after an abortive coup d'état attempted in early 670 B.C.[14] The tiny size of the fragment naturally makes this interpretation very tentative.

Text 8

No. 8 is a pact of loyalty to Assurbanipal (king of Assyria, 669-627 B.C.) imposed on the Assyrian royal family, aristocracy and nation at large by the queen dowager Zakutu after Esarhaddon's death in November 669 B.C. This treaty maintained the internal stability of the empire for 17 years but was ultimately to be broken by Assurbanipal's brother Šamaš-šumu-ukin, the most prominent 'contracting party' in the document. Assurbanipal's inscriptions dealing with the outbreak of Šamaš-šumu-ukin's rebellion refer to it as follows:

"That faithless brother of mine, Šamaš-šumu-ukin, who did not guard my treaty (*adê*), made the people of Babylonia, Chaldea, Aram and the Sealand, my servants and subjects, defect from me..." (Streck Asb, p. 30:96ff.)

Text 9

No. 9 is a treaty of Assurbanipal dating from the time of the Šamaš-šumu-ukin rebellion (652-648 B.C.), and phrased in the form of a vow made in the first person plural. The identity of the group(s) of people involved remains uncertain, but judging from obv. 26ff, it seems certain that they had initially taken part in the rebellion and later changed sides. This strongly points to Sealanders, the Chaldean tribes inhabiting the shore of the Persian Gulf, who under the leadership of Nabû-bel-šumati had sided with Šamaš-šumu-ukin but by 650, when the tide turned, had started going over to the Assyrian side. Compare ABL 289, a letter of Assurbanipal assuring that the king was favorably disposed to the Sealanders and did not associate them with the crimes of Nabû-bel-šumati, as well as the following letter from Assurbanipal's general Bel-ibni, sent to make use of the situation:

"On the 16th I entered the city of Kissik with the Palace Superintendent; many troops of the Sealanders, the king my lord's servants, came to see me in Kissik. On the 17th we imposed the treaty (*adê*) upon them, and on the 18th we went down to the Sealand. The whole Sealand is firmly set to become the king's servants again." (ABL 521 r.7-15.)

Alternatively, one may compare the following royal letter, probably addressed to Assurbanipal's staunch supporter Nabû-ušabši, the governor of Uruk:

"[The king's] w[ord to NN. From the beginning you have ......] guarded my [treaty], and not sinned against my favour and oath. You have fallen and died on account of all the messages and orders I have been sending to you. And truly by these recent things that you have done you have surpassed everything.

"The fact that for the sake of my name you have isolated yourself, [keeping on the side of] the representative of Aššur and Marduk; that you have kept [my watch] and not made common cause with my enemy; the fact that ever since you returned [from] my presence and saw that the Babylonians, Chaldeans and Arameans were not loyal, you sent [...] your countrymen [...] and made them conclude (this) treaty with me: 'We will not change nor [violate] the treaty of Assurbanipal; we will not side with his enemy; as long as we [live], we will keep the treaty [we have concluded with him]; [...] his ally shall be our ally, and we will walk with him [...]' – from these facts I have experienced your [genuine love] and loyalty [to me].

"[*Now* ...] this campaign [...] set for your life. This very day, those who have sinned against my treaty – your eyes will notice how the god will once again swiftly call to account those who tampered with the treaty. As for you, remain under the protection of Aššur and Marduk, and you will thrive within their castle.

"Now then I am sending to you my eunuch Nabû-eriba, my 'third man' Nergal-šarru-uṣur, and Akkullanu of the clergy of Aššur with my treaty tablet. *Join* the treaty, let the *confidence* of my servants settle upon your countrymen and let them become confident. For my part, let me see your love and affection even more clearly, multiply the numerous favours I have already granted to you, pay back fully my debt with you, and make your name great in the assembly of Babylonia." (ABL 539)

Text 10

No. 10 is a treaty of Assurbanipal with the Arab tribe of Qedar, probably concluded just before the outbreak of the rebellion of Šamaš-šumu-ukin in 652 B.C. (see Weippert, WO 7 [1976] 69ff). The background to the treaty is described in the passage from Assurbanipal's inscriptions cited above, p. XXII; the actual conclusion of the treaty is described later in the same inscriptions as follows:

"Abiyate', the son of Te'ri, came to Nineveh and kissed my feet. I concluded with him a treaty of vassalage to me, put him as king in place of Yauta', and imposed upon him a yearly tribute of gold, beads, pappardillu stones, antimony, camels and stud-asses." (Piepkorn Asb p. 85.)

If the readings in line 1' of the treaty are correct, a son of the defeated Yauta', who had fled to Nabatea, was also included in the treaty. Considering the situation, it seems likely that he was detained in Nineveh in order to be brainwashed and kept in store as a possible later candidate for the kingship of Qedar.

Text 11

No. 11 is a treaty of Sin-šarru-iškun, king of Assyria (ca. 627-612 B.C.) with three unidentifiable individuals, who judging from their names seem to have been Babylonians. The name of the Assyrian king was tentatatively given (following Clay, Goetze, and Borger) as Sin-šumu-lešir in Grayson's recent edition of the text, but collation by Foster indicates that Scheil's original reading Sin-šarru-iškun (ZA 11 47) is preferable. This reading is also the only acceptable one from the viewpoint of space considerations; there just is not enough room for restoring S[I.SÁ LÚ.GAL—SAG *ša* mAN.ŠÁR—NIR.GÁL—DINGIR.MEŠ] in Obv. 1.

In the absence of the body of the document containing the treaty stipulations, it is fruitless to spend many words on its date or purpose. It seems likely, though, that the persons figuring as the other treaty party were Sin-šarru-iškun's allies in his struggle with Nabopolassar for the control of Babylonia. Note that five letters from Babylonia addressed to Sin-šarru-iškun (ABL 412, 469, 1089, 1365 and 1366) indicate that the king had supporters in the country until late in his reign.

Text 12

No. 12 is only an extract from the curse section of a treaty of Sin-šarru-iškun; judging from its place of discovery (a house of exorcists in Assur, see p. L), it may have belonged to a loyalty pact imposed on the Assyrian population after the king's accession following a civil war in 627(?) B.C. Compare above, under no. 4.

Text 13

No. 13 is an interesting vassal treaty resembling in its formulation no. 5 (Baal treaty). Unfortunately, the preamble has not been preserved and no names are found in the extant portion of the text, so that the identity of the contracting parties as well as the date and historical context of the treaty remain obscure. If the restoration of col. ii 8' is correct, which seems quite possible (cf. Text 10:6 and Borger Esarh. p. 54 ii 24), then the text is a treaty with an Arab king. In view of its affinities with no. 5 (cf. also ii 6'f with PRT 16:9f, cited above, p. XIX), it may date from the reign of Esarhaddon, in which case it would be Esarhaddon's treaty with Hazael of Qedar or his son Yauta' (Borger Esarh. p. 53f), but all this is very conjectural.

Text 14

No. 14 is not a treaty but part of an inscription of Esarhaddon relating to the succession treaty which he imposed on his subjects in Iyyar 672 B.C. (see no. 6). The text is not only unique as a royal inscription but is also badly damaged and difficult. Especially at the beginning of col. i it is hard to grasp the nature of the narrative. It does seem, however, that its purpose was to justify the unorthodox way in which the king settled his succession, and if the beginning and the end of the text were better preserved, they might well shed interesting new light on the motives underlying the king's decision.

It seems that the king had repeatedly approached the mother goddess Belet-ili with a query ("[When] ([*i-nu-ma*]) I *ten times over* (*ešrāti*) had asked Belet-ili: 'Why?'", col. i 1), presumably through extispicy, and obtained an answer, cited in i 2-5, which probably led to the decision about the succession and the imposition of the treaty. While the nature of both the query and the answer to it remain obscure, the fact that the king turned to the goddess of birth implies that he was concerned about his sons. Whether this concern was based on his own tragic experiences during his time as crown prince (see under no. 3) or on the behaviour of the princes themselves, as suggested by LAS 170, remains obscure.

Col. ii of the reverse, which contains a prayer section customarily concluding royal inscriptions in the Babylonian formulary, seems to link the succession settlement with the planned return of Marduk's statue to Babylon. The first part of the prayer is addressed to several gods (perhaps all the Babylonian gods 'deported' by Sennacherib to Assyria), the latter part to Belet-ili alone. A more detailed analysis of this intriguing text fallsside the scope of the present edition.

Structural and Formal Analysis

While all the treaties edited in the present volume differ somewhat in form and structure from one another, they also display considerable structural and formal similarities. It is easy to see that they consist of a limited number of structural elements, which may not all be obligatory or appear in the same order in every document, but have a well-defined function and are formulated according to well-established conventions. Chart 1 presents a survey of the attested elements in the order in which they appear in no. 6, the longest and best preserved text in the corpus.

Chart 1. Attested Structural Elements

Element	1	2	3	4	5	6	7	8	9	10	11	12	13
Preamble					+	+		+		+	+		
Seal Impressions	-		-			+		-		-	-	-	
Divine Witnesses						+		-	+	+			
Oath/Adjuration		+				+		-	+	+			
Historical Introduction						+		-	-	+			
Treaty Stipulations	+	+	+	+	+	+	+	+	+	+			+
Violation Clause	+	+	*	*		+		+	+	*	+		
Traditional Curses	+	+	+	+	+	+		+	+	+	+	+	
Vow	-			+	-	+		-	+				
Ceremonial Curses		+			-	+		-					
Colophon and Date					+	+		-					

Explanation:
\+ indicates attested elements - indicates omitted elements
* indicates omitted but structurally implicit elements
Lack of +/-/* indicates textual damage

A detailed analysis of these elements is not within the scope of the present edition, and the following discussion will hence limit itself to the barest essentials.

Preamble

The Preamble, which can be taken as obligatory in all texts, opens the document by identifying the contracting parties. Its standard form is *adê ša* A *issi* B "Treaty of A with B", where A stands for the Assyrian king with his title and parentage and B for the other contracting party, usually another king (with his title) and a nation. This formula is attested in nos. 5, 6, 8, 10 and 11, and corresponds to the phrase *adê ša* A "treaty of A" by which the texts are referred to in the treaties themselves (no. 1 i 13, ii 17, v 8; 6:390, 555A, 612A, 666; 12:1f) and elsewhere.[15]

adê ša "treaty of" can also mean "treaty which", depending on the context.

This latter meaning occurs in the second paragraph of no. 6 (divine witnesses), where the words *adê ša* have been omitted as unnecessary but are implied by the subjunctive predicates concluding the paragraph, as well as further down in the same text (lines 41 and 283). It would, however, be a mistake to apply the meaning "treaty which" to the preamble also, as was done in earlier editions of the text.[16] Both the preamble and the witness section are independent, though interconnected, structural elements, as shown by the rulings and seal impressions separating them in all manuscripts, and they have to be rendered accordingly. Note the unambiguous formulation of these sections in the Sefire treaties: "Treaty of A with B; this treaty which A concluded [before Aššur] and Mullissu..." (KAI 222 A).

Seal Impressions

Inserted between the preamble and the witness section in no. 6 are three cylinder-seal impressions; a caption describing the seals is inscribed at the head of the four columns of the obverse (i-iv) and separated from the text by a dividing line; see the copy on p. 28.

The middle seal, with the short legend "Of the God Aššur and the City Hall", dates from the time of the Old Assyrian city-state.

The impression on the left, from a Neo-Assyrian seal, shows the king of Assyria standing between the gods Aššur and Mullissu, and has the following legend:

"The Seal of Destinies, with which Aššur, king of the gods, seals the destinies of the Igigi and Anunnaki of heaven and earth, and of mankind. What he seals with it, he does not alter. He who should alter (it), may Aššur, king of the gods, and Mullissu, together with their children kill him with their mighty weapons. I am Sennacherib, king of Assyria, a prince who fears you. Whoever erases my name and discards this Seal of Destinies of yours, erase his name and seed from the land!"

The impression on the right, showing the king kneeling between the gods Aššur and Ninurta, is from a Middle-Assyrian seal; both gods are mentioned in the largely illegible legend (lines 4f).

As recently pointed out by A. George, there can be little doubt that the document ratified by these sealings became, on the mythological plane, a 'Tablet of Destinies'.[17] In impressing them, the king of Assyria was 'sealing destinies' as Aššur's earthly representive. These sealings thus had a dual function: to add to the eternal validity of the treaty terms, and to sanctify and protect the treaty tablet by portraying the god Aššur himself as its ratifier and guardian. Compare lines 400ff of Text 6.

How many treaty tablets were actually sealed remains unclear. In the present corpus, the only text with a sealing is no. 6. It is definitely missing in nos. 1, 3, 8, and 10-12, all of which are one-column tablets. On the other hand, it could have been impressed on nos. 2, 5 and 13, all of which, like no. 6, are multi-column tablets.

Divine Witnesses

All Neo-Assyrian treaties appear to have been sworn agreements, witnessed and sworn by the gods of both contracting parties. A list of divine witnesses (or an adjuration formula mentioning the same gods) is found in five texts of the corpus, and is certainly missing only in one (no. 8). The reasons for its omission in this treaty, which certainly was a sworn document, are unclear but possibly related to the small size of the text. As the gods by which the treaty was sworn were listed in the curse section, it may be that it was omitted as unnecessary in order to save space. Note that other stereotyped structural elements of the treaties, such as the adjuration or the treaty violation clause, could also be given in abbreviated form or even omitted altogether (see below).

Where given, the witness list immediately follows the preamble. In accordance with the order of the contracting parties, which reflects their mutual status, the gods of Assyria precede those of the other contracting party. This order is also followed in the Sefire Treaties (KAI 222 A), in the curse sections of the treaties, and in references to treaty gods outside the treaty corpus itself (compare, e.g., ABL 918 cited above, p. XVII).

From the reign of Esarhaddon on, astral gods start heading the witness list prominently (cf. nos. 6, 8 and 11, but also references to sworn agreements such as Iraq 34 p. 23). This surely reflects increased interest in astrology, and it may be that having the treaties concluded "under the stars" was thought to add to their durability.

As it appears from no. 6 (lines 153ff and 494), and passages such as ABL 213:7ff ("let the gods come for the treaty"), the treaty gods were, at least in theory, physically present at the oath-taking ceremony in the form of their statues or otherwise. Whether this was always the case cannot of course be determined. But it should be noted that all the astral gods mentioned in the witness list of no. 6, with the exception of Mars, were indeed visible at the time this treaty was concluded.[18]

Adjuration

An adjuration clause is attested in four texts (nos. 2, 6, 9 and 10); it is missing in no. 8, but may have been included in all the remaining texts. In nos. 6ff, it immediately follows the list of treaty gods; in no. 2, it is inserted at the end of the document.

The clause is slightly differently formulated in all the texts where it occurs. In no. 6, it is phrased in the imperative, "Swear by the god (...)!" In no. 10, the verb "swear" is for reasons of space omitted altogether, and only the gods sworn by are given. The relevant passage in no. 9 is broken, but it is likely that the adjuration there was expressed in the form of a 1st person plural vow, as the rest of the text. The formulation in no. 2 resembles that of no. 6, but the verbal form is different: "You are sworn by the god (...)!"[19]

This last formula is psychologically interesting, because it reveals something of the Assyrian attitude towards the other contracting party. The same formula is quite well known from Mesopotamian exorcistic literature, where it is used for conjuring evil demons (e.g., *nīš ilāni rabûti ša šamê u erṣeti tummâtunu* "you are sworn by the great gods of heaven and earth", KAR 227 ii 45). What is more, these conjuration formulae are followed by exorcisms formulated exactly like the stipulations of the present treaties! (In addition to KAR 227 ii 50, *šumma tumaššarūšunūtimma*, see also the Lamaštu passages cited by W. Farber, ZA 64 177f.) One gets the impression that the Assyrian kings were approaching their treaty partners – mostly strangers and actual or potential enemies – basically as evil demons, to be treated with the methods tested and found effective by domestic science.

Historical Introduction

A formal introduction to the contents of a treaty is attested in two texts of the corpus only (nos. 6 and 10), and in both cases it is very short. On the other hand, it is certainly missing only in two texts (nos. 8 and 9), and may have been included in the others. In any case, judging from the brevity of the attested examples, it seems that, possibly due to Assyrian superiority, the introduction was losing ground as a structurally significant element in Neo-Assyrian treaties, even though it was not omitted altogether.[20]

Formulation of Treaty Stipulations

The various kinds of stipulations attested in the texts are surveyed in Chart 2. In most texts, individual stipulations are divided by rulings into separate sections corresponding to modern treaty articles. The order of the sections in no. 6 reveals a well thought-out logical scheme systematically covering all possible forms of threat against the ruling house, starting from the definition of loyal conduct, and gradually proceeding to open rebellion and murder of the king.

Typologically, the attested stipulations fall into declarations, demands, injunctions, obligations, commands and prohibitions, and they are usually phrased in the form of sentences beginning with the particle *šumma* and ending in a subjunctive predicate. 'Normal' main clauses with indicative predicates are

Chart 2. Attested Types of Stipulations

	1	2	3	4	5	6	7	8	9	10	11	12	13
loyalty to Assyrian king		+	+	+		+	+	+	+			+	
obligation to inform/report			+	+		+		+	+				+
relations toward enemies		+				+			+	+			+
military cooperation	+	+				+			+				
extradition of rebels etc.	+	+				+	+		+				
commercial regulations					+								
recognition of royal deputy					+				+				
accepting Aššur as god						+							
mutual nonviolation clause	+												
Assyrian concessions	+								+				+

interspersed among the subjunctive ones, but they form a clear minority. The meaning of the subjunctive clauses has been the subject of much controversy and confusion and must hence be briefly discussed here.

The predominance of these clauses in the treaties is due to their character as sworn documents. Most of the stipulations are things that the other contracting party was pledged under oath to accept, do, or avoid doing; they thus carry the implication of a solemn, oath-bound pledge. This implication was expressed in Akkadian by a special linguistic formula used in all kinds of solemn, oath-bound statements. In 1st person verbal forms, it marks solemn promises or assertions, in 2nd and 3rd person forms, solemn pledges or assertions, depending on the tense of the verb.

A survey of the relevant formulae, which differed from dialect to dialect, is given in Chart 3. They all involve a predicate in the subjunctive and are mostly preceded by an oath formula (e.g., "I swear by god so-and-so"), which could occasionally be omitted. The subjunctive verbal forms in the treaty stipulations are correspondingly connected with the preceding adjuration formula ("Swear/You are sworn by ...!").

Chart 3. Vow, Pledge and Assertion Formulae

		FUTURE POSITIVE	
	1st person vow	2nd and 3rd person pledge	
	"I will speak"	"you shall speak"	"he shall speak"
OAkk/OA	*aqabbiu*	*lu taqabbiu*	*lu iqabbiu*
OB	*lu aqabbû*	*lu taqabbû*	*lu iqabbû*
MA/NA	*šumma la aqabbûni*	*šumma la taqabbûni*	*šumma la iqabbûni*
MB/SB	*šumma la aqabbû*	*šumma la taqabbû*	*šumma la iqabbû/iqtabû*
NB/LB	*kî aqabbû*	*kî taqabbû*	*kî iqabbû*
	(= *aqabbi)*	(= *taqabbi)*	(= *iqabbi)*
		FUTURE NEGATIVE	
	1st person vow	2nd and 3rd person pledge	
	"I will not speak"	"you shall not speak"	"he shall not speak"
OAkk/OA	*la aqabbiu*	*la taqabbiu*	*la iqabbiu*
OB	*la aqabbû*	*la taqabbû*	*la iqabbû*
MA/NA	*šumma aqabbûni*	*šumma taqabbûni*	*šumma iqabbûni*
MB/SB	*šumma aqtabû(ma)*	*šumma taqabbû(ma)*	*šumma iqabbû/iqtabû(ma)*
NB/LB	*kî aqtabû*	*kî taqtabû*	*kî iqtabû*
	(= *la aqabbi)*	(= *la taqabbi)*	(= *la iqabbi*)
		PAST NEGATIVE	
	1st person assertion	2nd and 3rd person assertion	
	"verily I did not speak"	"verily you did not speak"	"verily he did not speak"
OAkk/OA	*la aqbiu*	*la taqbiu*	*la iqbiu*
OB	*la aqbû*	*la taqbû*	*la iqbû*
MA/NA	*šumma aqbûni*	*šumma taqbûni*	*šumma iqbûni*
MB/SB	*šumma aqbû*	*šumma taqbû*	*šumma iqbû*
NB/LB	*kî aqbû*	*kî taqbû*	*kî iqbû*

Since the Neo-Assyrian formulae begin with the conjunction *šumma*, which usually means "if", they have in some editions been rendered as conditional sentences,[21] but this is a mistake. These formulae have no more to do with conditional sentences than the corresponding formulae in other dialects of Akkadian; their origin may lie in oath-bound conditional clauses ("I'll be damned if...") , but in their actual usage they simply are the linguistic form of solemn statements in this dialect. As far as the treaties are concerned, note that the word *šumma* is missing in several subjunctive clauses in Text 6 where it is expected (e.g., in lines 49, 167, 283, 306, and 407) and hence must have been semantically redundant. The specific meaning of the formulae resided in their subjunctive predicates, which when negated indicated a positive vow or pledge, and when positive, a negative one.

Thus a subjunctive expression like (*šumma*) *la taqabbûni* "you shall say" was functionally more or less equivalent to indicative *taqabbi* "you will say", the only difference being – as in English – that the former was more solemn and binding than the latter. The equivalence of the two expressions is put beyond doubt by the fact that they occur as textual variants in different manuscripts of Text 6:

la tu-šá-aṣ-bat-a-ni "you shall install" (line 85, ms. G)
= *tu-šá-aṣ-ba(t)-ta* "you will install" (ibid. AId);
ta-šá-kan-a-ni "you shall not place" (line 301, B)
= *la ta-šá-ka-na* "do not place" (ibid. H).

Similar variation between other functionally equivalent expressions also occurs elsewhere in the same text:

li-ra-ah-ṣa "may they (the chariots) get drenched" (line 615, GH)
= *lu-šar-hi-ṣu* "may they drench (the chariots)" (ibid. AK);
lib-('i)-iš "may it stink" (605, HLTh)
= *lu-ba-i-šu* "may they make it stink" (ibid. frg.);
lu-ú-pal-li-šu "may they pierce (your women)" (line 598, h)
= *lu pal-lu-šá* "may (your women) be pierced" (ibid. T);
li-tah-li-qa-ku-nu "may it get lost for you" (line 445, A)
= *lu tah-[li-qa-ku-nu]* "may it disappear from you" (ibid. g).

That the difference between indicative verbs and subjunctive *šumma* clauses was relatively slight is further indicated by the fact that in Text 13 a single subjunctive *šumma* clause (iii 4) appears inserted between several indicative sentences, and contrariwise indicative clauses are found among strings of subjunctive *šumma* clauses in Texts 4 and 6 (lines 83-91, 198-211, 380-384). The same phenomenon is attested in the Aramaic Sefire treaties, where paronomastic constructions with infinitive absolutus alternate with simple verbal forms (e.g., *hskr thskrhm* "you must surrender them" followed by simple *yhskr* in KAI 224:2f, *rqh trqhm* "you must conciliate them" followed by *'rqhm* ibid. 6f; see also ibid. 12f and 18).

No subjunctive *šumma* clauses are found in Text 5, where all stipulations are phrased as indicative main clauses.

Of the contracting parties, the king of Assyria is basically identified by his name and title, occasionally by 1st person verbal forms and suffixes ("you shall send to me" 2 iii 10', "our life" ibid. v 1; "these cities which I destroyed" 5 iii 4', "I have appointed" ibid. 6; "if you do what is good to me" 13 ii 7' etc.).

The other party is basically addressed in the 2nd person, but may also be referred to by name (nos. 1, 2 and 5).

Violation Clauses

The stipulations are followed by a clause for the case of treaty violation, leading to the subsequent curse section. This clause is phrased slightly differently in every text of the corpus where it is extant, but it basically resembles similar clauses found in other types of texts involving curses or penalties (royal inscriptions, decrees, grants, legal documents, epitaphs, etc.). The best preserved versions of the clause in Texts 6 and 11 read:

"Whoever changes, disregards, transgresses or erases the oath of this treaty tablet, or disregards this treaty and transgresses its oath" (6:397ff, followed by curse);

"Whoever alters the wording of this tablet, or sins against the treaty of the great gods" (11 r.5f, followed by curses).

In the former case, the clause cited is followed by injunctions against destroying the treaty documents, after which the curse section proper begins. The injunctions, formulated as subjunctive *šumma* clauses, have (by analogy to the violation clauses leading to the ceremonial curse section) been rendered as conditional sentences, but it is possible that they in fact represent treaty stipulations and have to be rendered accordingly ("You shall not remove it, consign it to fire, etc."). In that case, the curse section would lack an immediately preceding violation clause, like nos. 3, 4 and 10 (see below).

In no. 9, a treaty in the form of a 1st person vow, the clause is formulated "If we should transgress, break, erase or [...] this treaty". In no. 1, the relevant passage is broken but seems to have read "Whoever sins against this treaty and does not carry out his duty" (line 15'). In no. 8, the clause is abbreviated into the form "Whoever (sins) against this treaty", and it is omitted altogether in nos. 3, 4, and 10, obviously as redundant. No data are available from nos. 5, 7 and 13.

In no. 12, the clause takes the form of a conditional sentence identical with the repetitive clause preceding the ceremonial curses (see below) in Texts 2 and 6: "If you should sin against this treaty". The predicate of this conditional sentence is abnormally in the subjunctive in all three texts, but appears at least once in the normal indicative mood in no. 2 (*iḫtiṭi*, v 9). It seems likely that the abnormal subjunctives in this clause are due to a contamination with the clauses preceding traditional curses, which involve a relative pronoun (*mannu ša*) and hence a predicate in the subjunctive. Note that one of these clauses in text 2 actually reads "If PN, his sons, or his magnates who(!) sin against this treaty".

Curses

As already pointed out, curses formed the very backbone of Assyrian treaties in that they defined and sanctioned the punitive measures resorted to after a possible treaty violation. Accordingly, they were certainly included in every treaty. A curse section is actually attested in every text of the present corpus, except for two texts, both of which are very fragmentary, and it always follows right after the stipulations (and the violation clause).

Structurally, the curse section forms an independent unit within the treaty which has nothing to do with the preceding stipulation section. It is comparable to the penalty section of legal documents, which is likewise preceded by a violation clause and forms a self-contained unit within the document. Taking the curses as 'apodoses' to the stipulations, as done in some earlier editions, is out of the question even in cases where the violation clause has been omitted as unnecessary. Simply note the 3rd person object suffixes in the curse section of Text 4, and compare the 2nd person prefixes in the preceding *šumma* clauses.

An analysis of the curses occurring in the texts falls out of the scope of the present edition. It will suffice to call attention to the fact that they fall into two classes, 1) curses involving individual witness gods as agents of punishment and destruction, and 2) curses effected collectively by all the treaty gods. The former are referred to in this book as 'traditional curses', because they largely consist of curses taken over from the Mesopotamian literary tradition and attested in an identical or nearly identical form in several other texts and text genres. The latter are referred to as 'ceremonial curses', because they involve parables or references to symbolic acts actually carried out during the conclusion of the treaties.

Ceremonial curses are attested only in two texts (nos. 2 and 6). In the latter, they make up a long section concluding the treaty; in the former, they occupy a position right at the beginning, between the divine witnesses and the treaty articles. In either case, they occupy a very prominent position and are of such a nature as to have a clearly calculated effect: the other party was to witness and to have vividly and undeletably impressed on his mind the consequences a violation of the treaty would entail.

Vow

Inserted between the two long curse sections in Text 6 (lines 414-493 and 518-663) is a short section containing a solemn vow in the first person plural to abide by the terms of the treaty. It is phrased according to the classic Assyrian formula for a promissory oath, being headed by an invocation of gods already attested in the Old Assyrian period, and was certainly to be pronounced by the other contracting party. The individual clauses of the vow are couched as the subjunctive *šumma* sentences (see above, p. XL) recapitulating the central points of the treaty. An affirmatory sentence resembling ones found in contemporary legal documents closes the vow.

A similar section is attested in two other texts of the present corpus only (nos. 4 and 9), and in both of these it seems to have constituted the entire text of the treaty proper. On the other hand, it seems to have been missing in at least nos. 1, 5 and 8. It would thus seem that the vow was an alternative way of phrasing treaties unilaterally accepted by the other party, and that the presence of a vow and treaty stipulations in the same text was an exception rather than a rule.

Colophon and Date

Only two texts of the corpus end in a colophon specifying their purpose and date. However, it is quite possible that many more texts originally contained this entry, since it is certainly missing in only one text (the Zakutu treaty), which also contains many other atypical features.

Manuscripts

Text 1

No. 1 (Rm 2,427) is a fragment of the lower left half of a polished black stone tablet measuring 4.4 x 12.5 x 8.6 cm. It was found in Nineveh by H. Rassam and is now in the collections of the British Museum. Judging from the curvature, which swells towards the centre, at least half of the slab's original height and about 1/6 of its original width has been lost. In its original shape, it probably measured about 14 cm (width) x 18 cm (height). See Diagram 1.1 on p. XLIV.

The extant portion is inscribed with 14 lines of text on the obverse, 5 lines on the lower edge, and 16 lines on the reverse. The script density is 1.7 lines to 1 cm on the obverse and 2 lines to 1 cm on the reverse. Assuming the estimate of the original height as 18 cm to be correct, this means that the obverse originally contained 30 lines and the reverse, if fully inscribed, 36 lines. The original line total would thus have been 30 + 5 + 36 = 71 lines, of which 35 lines, or a little less than 50%, are preserved.

Each line of the text is separated from the next by a horizontal dividing line. The script is clearly executed early NB cursive, not lapidary script.

Text 2

No. 2 is a fragmentarily preserved three-column clay tablet from Nineveh consisting in its present condition of three separate fragments, all in the collections of the British Museum. The largest one, K 15272 + Rm 120 + Rm 274, measuring 15 cm (width) by 10 cm (height), is the lower half of the tablet containing remains of two columns (I and III) on the obverse and the upper portions of three columns (IV-VI) on the reverse. Two small fragments, 79-7-8,195 and BM 134596, measuring 4.1 x 3.8 cm and 3.5 x 3.7 cm, contain portions of columns V and III-IV respectively.

Assuming that the ratio between the short and long axis of the tablet was 2:3, as normal in three-column tablets, the original tablet height would have been about 22.5 cm (see Diagr. 1.2). The script density is 3.75 lines to 1 cm in cols. I-IV, and 3.5 lines to 1 cm in cols. V-VI. This means that cols. I-IV were originally inscribed with c. 82 lines and cols. V-VI with c. 78 lines each. The original line total of the tablet would thus have been 82 + 82 + 82 + 82 + 78 + 78 = 484 lines, of which 35 + 0 + 28 + 33 + 27 + 26 = 149, i.e. less than 31%, are actually extant.

1. Rm 2, 427 (Šamši-Adad)

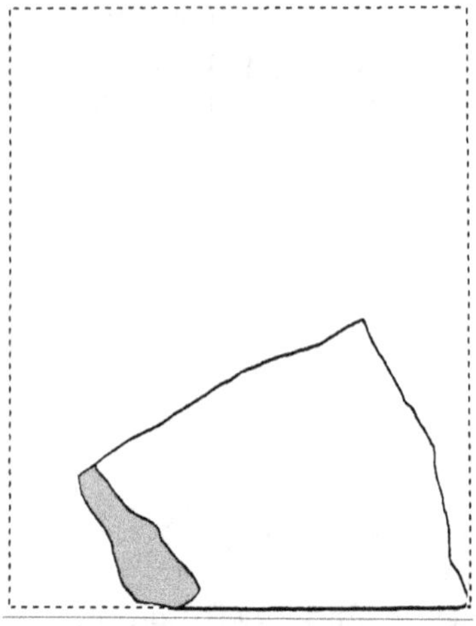

2. K 15272+ (Mati'-il), rev.

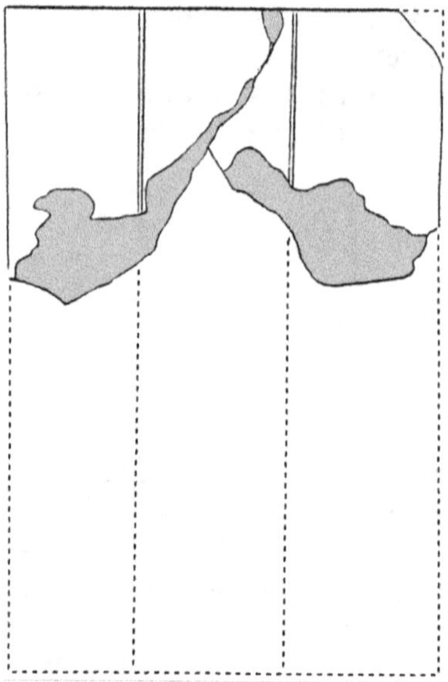

3. VAT 11449

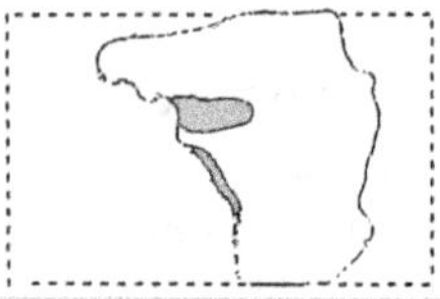

7. Bu 91-5-9,22

4. 83-1-18,420+ (Esarhaddon)

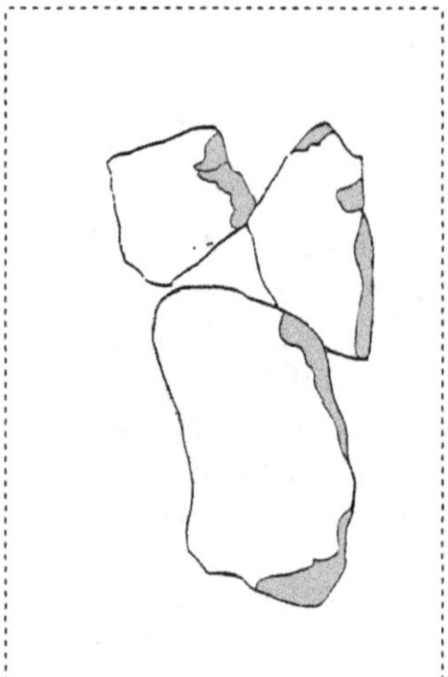

5. K 3500+ (Baal), rev.

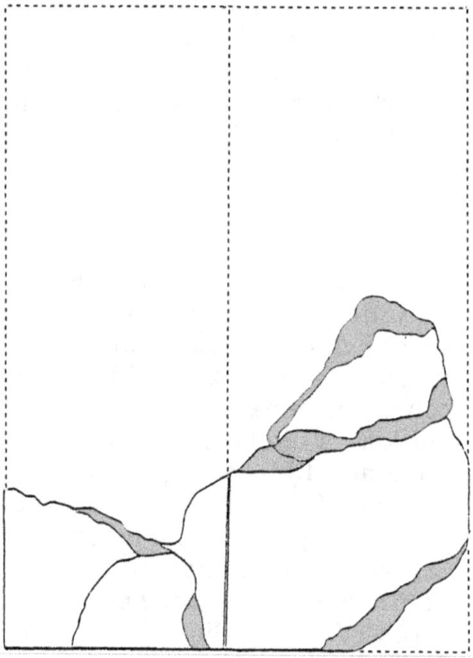

DIAGR. 1. *Outlines of nos. 1-5 and 7.*
Note: Broken lines indicate reconstructions, solid lines actual outlines and rulings drawn by scribes, shaded areas broken or obliterated portions of text.

Scale 1:3 10 cm

6. ND 4327 (Esarhaddon's succession treaty)

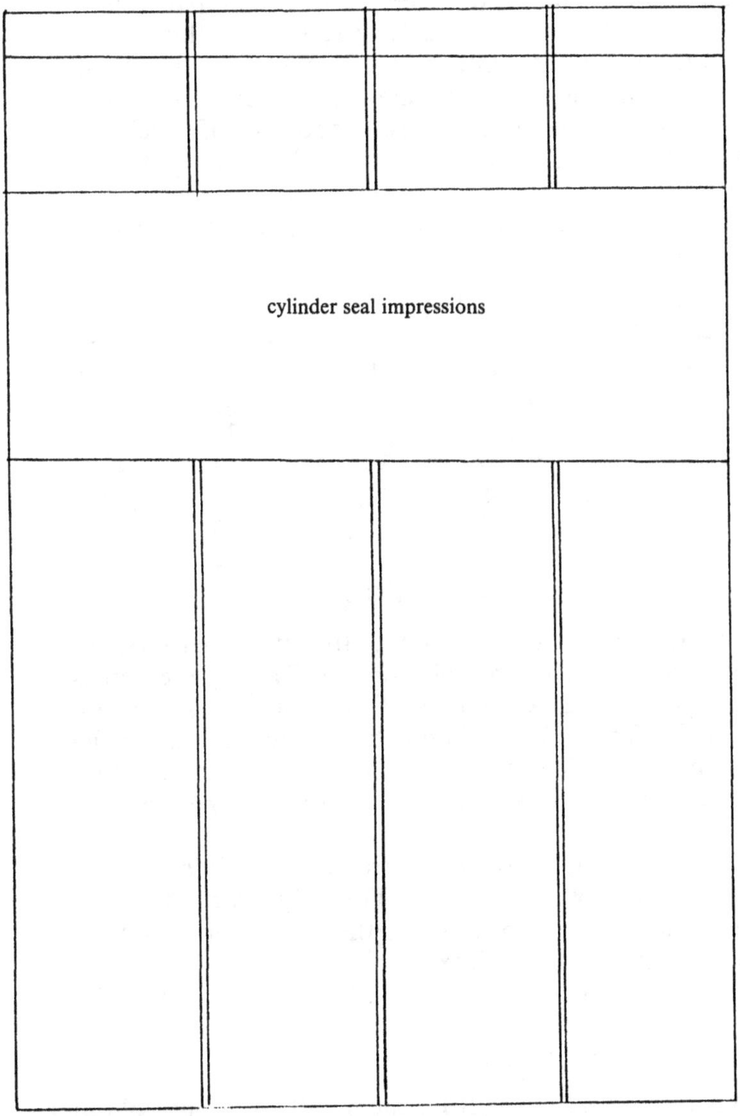

11. MLC 1302, rev.

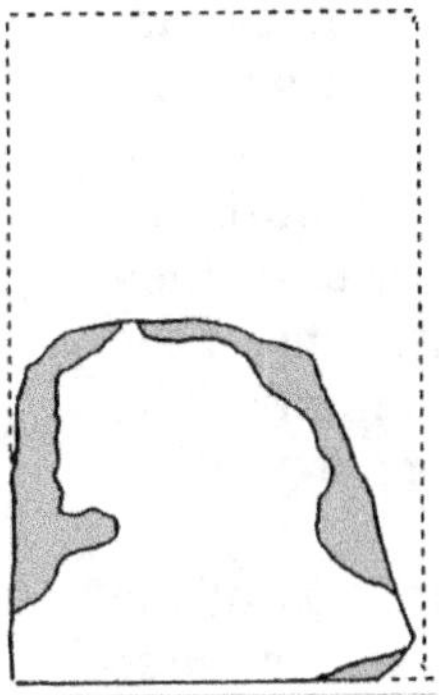

13. K 4439, rev.

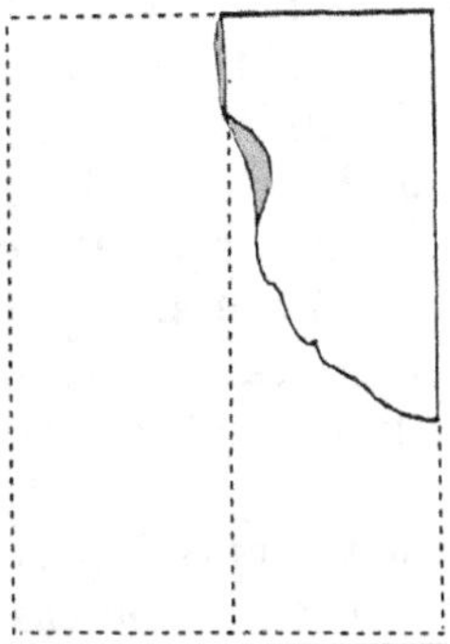

8. 83-1-18,45+ (Zakutu)

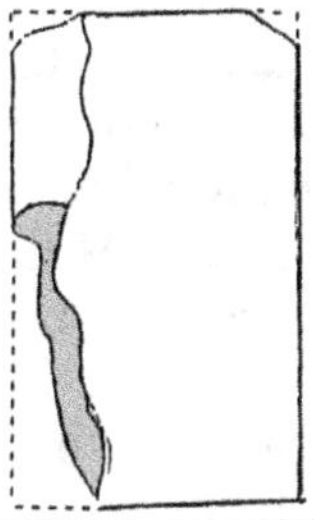

9. 82-5-22,130

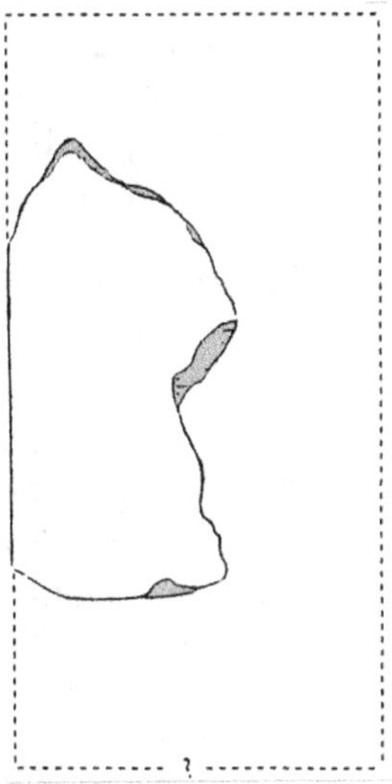

10. Bu 91-5-9,178 (Qedar)

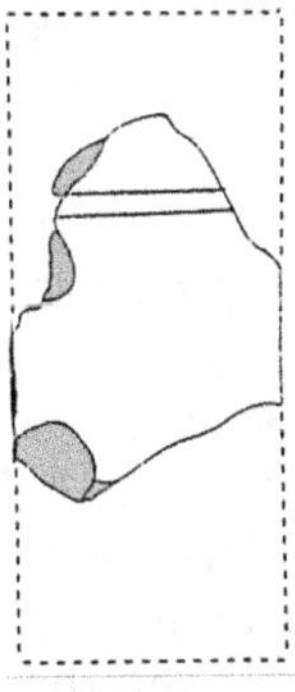

12. Ass 13955z

DIAGR. 2. *Outlines of nos. 6 and 8-12.*

The beginning of col. I, now lost, contained the treaty preamble and divine witnesses; the rest of the column is devoted to ceremonies accompanying the conclusion of the treaty. Col. II through IV 3, all together 167 lines (= ll. 83-249 according to the above reconstruction), contained the treaty stipulations, of which only 31 fragmentary lines are extant. Col. IV 4 through VI 5, in all 161 lines (= ll. 250-411), contained the curse section, of which 38% (62 lines) is extant. The rest of the text (VI 6-end, about 73 lines) was devoted to the adjuration and the colophon. The original structure of the text, compared with what is actually left, would accordingly appear as follows in table form:

	original lines	%	extant lines	%
Preamble, divine witnesses	c. 40	8.3	0	0.0
Treaty ceremonies	c. 42	8.6	35	23.5
Treaty stipulations	167	34.5	31	20.8
Curse section	162	33.5	62	41.6
Adjuration	c. 68	14.0	21	14.1
Colophon	c. 5	1.1	0	0.0
Total	484	100.0	149	100.0

It can thus be seen that the state of preservation of the text rather seriously distorts our view of its original structure and content. Treaty ceremonies, curses, and adjuration, which now make up 80% of the extant text, originally constituted only 56% of it. On the other hand, treaty stipulations, which originally constituted more than 1/3 of the whole text, now make up only 1/5 of it, and only ten of the extant 31 lines (6.7% of the original line total) are complete.

In sum, the text may have resembled the other treaties, particularly no. 6, more closely that the extant text would suggest. The only major structural difference seems to lie in the relative positions of the adjuration and ritual sections, which appear in inverted order in Text 6.

Text 3

No. 3 (VAT 11449) is a small fragment from the middle of a one-column clay tablet, measuring 4.2 x 5.4 cm. It was found in the excavations at Assur and is now in the collections of the Vorderasiatisches Museum, Berlin. According to collation by D. Frayne, "the curvature suggests that the original tablet was very small, but it is difficult to say how much is missing."[22] According to Ebeling's copy in PKTA pl. 31, the lower parts of both the obverse and the reverse extend all the way to the edges. If this is the case, then the first extant line of the obverse(?) would have to be the very first line of the text. Restoring it [*a-de-e ša* etc.], "[treaty of Senna]cherib" seems impossible, however, because it would leave no room for the other contracting party either in line 1 or 2.

It is therefore possible that the tablet did not contain the entire text of the treaty but merely excerpts from it, as in the case of no. 12. Since the curse section of the obverse is repeated in an almost identical form on the reverse, it is also possible that the tablet contained excerpts from two different treaties. However, as long as the original format of the tablet cannot be reliably determined, the question of the nature of the text is best left open.

The excavation number of the tablet is not known, and so nothing certain can be said about its exact provenance.

Text 4

No. 4 consists of three separate fragments, 83-1-18,420, 83-1-18,493 and Bu 91-5-9,131, which definitely belong to the same tablet and lightly touch each other at three points, but do not constitute a good physical join. Pieced together, the whole thing measures 7.8 cm (width) x 14 cm (height). Judging from the number of signs missing on each line, the original width must have been about 13 cm. The original height is more difficult to determine; using as a point of departure the ratio between the short and long axis of no. 8 (the Zakutu treaty), it would have been about 22 cm, but it may have been more. The length of the lines makes it evident that the tablet did not have more than one column of text on each side (see Diagr. 1.4). All three fragments were found in the excavations of Nineveh and are now in the British Museum.

The script density is 2.3 lines to 1 cm. Thus the original line total must have been at least 51 + 51 = 102 lines, of which 28 are extant. The extant lines, from the middle of the reverse, cover part of the loyalty vow (in first person singular), treaty violation clauses (in second person singular), and the beginning of the curse section (in third person singular). The obverse, which probably contained the preamble, divine witnesses, adjuration formula, and the beginning of the vow, is entirely destroyed.

Text 5

No. 5 consists of two separate pieces of a two-column tablet: a large fragment (K 3500 + K 4444 + K 10235) from the top of the tablet containing a few lines of cols. I and II and the ends of cols. III and IV, and a small chip (Sm 964) from the left half of col. I. The larger piece measures 19.4 cm (full width) x 14.2 cm (height), the smaller one 4.4 x 3.8 cm. Assuming cautiously that the ratio between the tablet's short and long axis was 3:4, the original height of the tablet can be estimated as about 26 cm (see Diagr. 1.5). If the ratio was 2:3, as in Texts 2 and 6, the height would have been about 29 cm.

The vertical script density is 2.75 lines to 1 cm. This means that each column contained about 71 to 80 lines of text, depending whether the original height was 26 or 29 cm. Accordingly, the original line total can be estimated as about 284 or 320, of which 12 + 5 + 30 + 21 = 68 lines are extant. In other words, as much as 3/4 or 4/5 of the text has been lost.

The extant fragments were found in the excavations of Nineveh and are now in the collections of the British Museum.

Text 6

No. 6 has been pieced together out of more than 350 fragments of baked clay tablets found in the British excavations of Nimrud (ancient Calah) in 1955.[23] Subsequent joins have reduced the total number of separate fragments to 92, and many joins are still likely to be discovered. The different manuscripts and scribal hands hidden behind the fragments have so far not been subject to serious study, even though three of the manuscripts (ND 4327 = A, ND 4331 = F and ND 4336 = H) have been assembled so efficiently that their original shapes and dimensions are either known or can be accurately reconstructed (cf. Diagr. 2.6 = A).

A, F and H are all large four-column tablets showing the ratio 2:3 between their short and long axes; A measures 30 x 45 cm, F 28.4 x *42.5 cm, and H 28 x *42 cm. The script density in all three tablets is 2.5 signs to 1 cm, so that theoretically they could have accommodated 8 x 110 = 880 lines of text each, but because of an 11 cm (H: 10 cm) high seal space running across the obverse the average number of lines per column is only 80 on the obverse of A and 85 on that of B. The many dividing lines reduce the average number of lines per column to about 90 on the reverse of A; data for B and C are not available. The total number of lines in A was thus about 680.

While corresponding data on the other manuscripts are as yet not available, it is clear that they were all basically identical, though different in detail. Thus they all had the same (2:3) format, were all divided into four columns, had seal impressions across the obverse after the preamble, and (in contrast to normal practice) turned around their long axis like the pages of a book. On the other hand, their individual line totals differed depending on tablet height, column width, vertical script density, and other factors. The line count of the composite text (670 lines + 11 'ABC' lines not attested in all manuscripts) is an abstraction probably not having an exact counterpart in any of the manuscripts.

A further manuscript of no. 6, apparently basically identical with the Nimrud texts, is known from Assur (VAT 11534, excavation number and exact provenance unknown). This is just a small fragment (5.2 x 4.1 cm), but clearly part of a multi-column tablet and (save for orthographic variants and a superfluous dividing line) an exact duplicate of lines 229-236 of the composite text.

Text 7

No. 7 (Bu 91-5-9,22) is a tiny fragment of the left half of a clay tablet, measuring 2 cm (width) x 4.4 cm (height). Neither the shape nor the size of the original tablet can be determined; the script density is 3 lines to 1 cm. The tablet was found in Nineveh and is now in the British Museum.

Text 8

No. 8 (83-1-18,45 + 266) is an almost complete one-column tablet from Nineveh in the collections of the British Museum. It measures 6.3 cm (complete width) x 10.2 cm (complete height); only a small fragment from the lower left corner is missing. The script density is 2.7 lines to 1 cm on the obverse and 3 lines to 1 cm on the reverse.

Text 9

No. 9 (82-5-22,130) is a portion of the left half of a one-column tablet, measuring 6.1 x 12 cm. The original width of the tablet can be estimated as about 10 cm on the basis of textual analysis. The script density is 3.25 lines to 1 cm. Since both the preamble and the divine witnesses are missing, it is clear that at least 3 cm (= 10 lines) are broken away from the top of the tablet. How much of the bottom is missing cannot be established with certainty. The reconstruction shown in Diagr. 2.9 is based on the ratio 1:2 holding between the short and long axis of most (but not all) one-column tablets. This reconstruction would imply that the tablet was originally inscribed with about 65 + 65 = 130 lines of text, of which 39 + 27 = 66 are actually extant.

The text was found in Nineveh and is now in the collections of the British Museum.

Text 10

No. 10 (Bu 91-5-9,178), from Nineveh and now in the British Museum, is a portion out of the middle of a one-column tablet, measuring 5.9 cm (complete width) x 7.9 cm. Judging from the curvature, at least 5 lines are broken away from the top and at least 8 lines from the bottom of the tablet. The script density is 2.5 lines to 1 cm. Accordingly, the tablet probably originally measured 5.9 x 12.6 cm and was inscribed with about 31 + 31 = 62 lines of text, of which 16 + 11 = 27 (about 43%) are extant at present.

Text 11

No. 11 (MLC 1302) is the upper portion of a one-column clay tablet measuring c. 7.5 cm (width) x 8 cm (height). Very little of the original width is missing (cf. rev. 11'-14'). Assuming cautiously that the original proportions of the tablet were the same as in no. 8, the original height would have been at least 13.3 cm (see Diagr. 2.11). If the ratio between the short and long axis of the tablet was 1:2, as normal in one-column tablets, the original height was 15 cm. The script density is 3.5 lines to 1 cm. Accordingly, the original line total can be estimated as 46 to 52 lines, of which 20 lines (= 43.5 to 38.5%) are actually extant.

The tablet, now in the Yale Babylonian Collection, very probably originated in Nineveh since its first possessor, V. Scheil, says in his edition of the text (ZA 11 [1896] 47ff) that the tablet "provient de Mossoul". Tablets later acquired by Scheil in Mosul did include a number of legal documents from Assur (see K. Deller, BaM 15 [1984] 225ff), but Assur is for all practical purposes excluded as a provenance for the present text since systematic excavations in the city did not begin until 1903.

Text 12

No. 12 (Ass 13955z = A 2409) is a complete clay tablet measuring 7.2 cm (width) x 3.8 cm (height). It was found in the excavations of Assur and comes from the archives of a family of exorcists attached to the Aššur temple; see Pedersén Archives II, p. 60. The original is now in Istanbul.

Pace Grayson, JCS 39 154, the text is not a school tablet. These are typically clumsily shaped and round or ovoid, whereas the present tablet has the standard format of excerpt tablets, showing the ratio 2:1 between its horizontal and vertical axis.

Text 13

No. 13 (K 4439) is a fragment out of the lower right-hand corner of a multi-column tablet, measuring 5 cm (width) x 8.2 cm (height). It was found in the excavations of Nineveh and is now in the Kuyunjik Collection of the British Museum. Only one column of text has been preserved on each side, but traces of two vertical inter-column rulings to the left of the column are visible on the other side. Judging from the curvature, no more than about half of the original tablet width seems to have been lost, which points to a two-column tablet originally measuring c. 9 x 13.5 cm; however, it is not totally excluded that the tablet originally had three columns, in which case the dimensions would have been something like 13.5 x 20 cm. The mutual order of the sides can be determined by textual analysis, which indicates that the extant columns are the last column of the obverse and the first column of the reverse, the text on the former being continued immediately on the latter.

The script density is 3 lines to 1 cm. This means that that the original line total was either about 4 x 40 = 160 lines (two-column alternative) or 6 x 60 = 360 lines (three-column alternative), of which only 20 + 23 = 43 lines survive.

Text 14

No. 14 consists of two fragments of a two-column clay tablet. The smaller one, BM 51098, is a fragment from the upper left corner measuring 5.5 cm (width) x 5.25 cm (height), and contains the beginning of col. I (14 lines) and the end of col. IV (15 lines). The larger one, BM 50666 + 50857 + 53678 + 53728, measuring 7.5 x 9 cm, is from the lower portion of the tablet and contains parts of cols. I (18 lines) and II (27 lines). The original column width seems to have been about 6 cm. Both fragments are in the collections of the British Museum and were probably found in the city of Sippar.

The break separating the two fragments in col. I seems to have been very short, only a few lines at most; at least 7 lines, but not necessarily many more, are missing at the end of the column in BM 50666+. Consequently, the original column length seems to have been about 17 cm (= 5.25 + 1 + 9.5 + 1 cm). This would mean that the tablet originally measured about 12 x 17 cm, which seems realistic. Script density is 2.7 lines to 1 cm, and the original number of lines per column may accordingly have been about 45 (= 14 + 3? + 18 + 10?) lines. The original line total can be estimated as about 180 (= 4 x 45), of which 41% (74 lines) is extant.

On the Present Edition

Purpose and Scope

The present volume has a limited but challenging objective: to provide an edition of the Neo-Assyrian treaty corpus that meets the needs of both the specialist and the general reader. To this end, no effort has been spared to make it as accurate, reliable and easy to use as possible, and to provide the reader with the basic information necessary for understanding the texts edited in their original setting. On the other hand, we have purposely refrained from analysing the texts in detail and from comparing the Assyrian treaty practices with other similar systems, ancient or modern. These are matters better left to the users of the book, and fall out of the scope of the present edition.

General Structure

Structurally, the edition follows the norm established for the SAA series in the Editorial Manual of the Neo-Assyrian Text Corpus project. It consists of three principal parts: an introduction, a critical edition of the texts in transliteration and translation, based on fresh collation of the originals, and exhaustive computer-generated indices. In addition, a limited number of illustrations, copies and photographs of the originals are included. The principles followed in the preparation of each of these sections are defined in the Editorial Manual, and only some main points specific to the present volume will be discussed below.

Texts Included and Excluded

In line with the goals of the SAA series, the edition contains all extant treaties and loyalty oaths of the Neo-Assyrian empire identified to date, regardless of the language in which they were drawn up. We have taken care to include even the smallest fragments that can certainly be shown to belong to the genre. The only exception is constituted by the Old Aramaic treaties from Sefire, which were imposed by an Assyrian overlord but drawn up in Aramaic, and hence are not compatible with the scope of the SAA series.

In the interest of comprehensiveness, we have also included a text not strictly belonging to the category of treaties (no. 14). On the other hand, two small fragments (ABL 1186 and CT 35 33) previously tentatively assigned to the genre have been excluded as not pertinent.

Transliterations

The transliterations, addressed to the specialist, render the text of the originals in roman characters according to standard Assyriological conventions and the principles outlined in the Editorial Manual. Every effort has been taken to make them as accurate as humanly possible. All the texts edited have been recently collated either by the editors or a competent colleague.

Results of collation are indicated with exclamation marks. Single exclamation marks indicate corrections to published copies, double exclamation marks, scribal errors. Question marks indicate uncertain or questionable readings. Broken portions of text and all restorations are enclosed within square brackets. Parentheses enclose items omitted by ancient scribes.

No. 6 is presented in composite transliteration (combining the evidence of all available manuscripts to produce a single continuous text) rather than in score transliteration (presenting all manuscripts separately line by line), because the latter way of presentation, ideal as it is for purposes of research, is not compatible with the format of the SAA series.

Since all the fragments of Text 6 cannot yet be assigned to definite manuscripts, the composite text presented here is not oriented after any particular manuscript. Rather, it is a conglomeration reflecting the idiosyncracies of several different scribes. Syllabic and 'full' spellings have generally been preferred to logographic and defective ones at the sacrifice of orthographic consistency. Restorations (i.e. items not preserved in any manuscript) are enclosed in square brackets, while items found in some manuscripts but omitted as unnecessary in others are enclosed within parentheses. All variants, even insignificant ones, are listed in the critical apparatus.

In the interest of economy, the manuscript fragments of Text 6 have been assigned new sigla replacing the (abbreviated) excavation numbers (46A = ND 4346A, etc.) by which the texts are identified in earlier editions. A concordance of the sigla and the excavation numbers is found on p. LIXff. Capital letters indicate large fragments, lower case letters, smaller ones; fragments containing less than 10 lines of text are simply identified as "frg." For practical reasons, the order and numbering of lines follows BaM Bh 3.

A score transliteration of Text 6 in microfiche format is provided in the pocket inside the back cover.

Translations

The translations seek to render the tenor and meaning of the texts as accurately as possible in readable, contemporary English. In the interest of clarity, the line structure of the originals has not been retained in the translation but the text has been rearranged into logically coherent paragraphs. Badly broken passages are generally translated only if the isolated words occurring in them yield some meaningful information. Uncertain and conjectural restorations and translations are indicated by italics. Interpretative additions to the translation are enclosed within parentheses. (In Text 6, parentheses also enclose words or phrases omitted as redundant in certain manuscripts.) All major restorations are enclosed within square brackets matching the corresponding items in the transliteration. Untranslatable passages are indicated by dots, unrestorable breaks by dots within parentheses.

Personal, divine and geographical names are rendered conventionally if a well-established and functional English or Biblical equivalent exists (e.g., Melqarth, Nineveh); otherwise, the name is given in transcription with length marks deleted. Month names are rendered by their Hebrew equivalents. The rendering of names of professions is a compromise between the use of accurate but impractical Assyrian terms and inaccurate but practical modern or classical equivalents.

Critical apparatus

The primary purpose of the critical apparatus is to support the readings and translations established in the edition, and it consists chiefly of references to collations of questionable passages either by the editor himself or by others. Other essential matters covered in the apparatus are textual variants, scribal mistakes corrected in the transliteration, and alternative readings or translations of problematic or ambiguous passages. Restorations based on easily verifiable evidence (parallels or duplicates) are basically not explained in the apparatus, conjectural restorations only if their conjectural nature is not made explicit by italics in the translation.

Copies and collations published at the end of the volume are referred to as "see copy" and "see coll." The abbreviations KW and SP identify collations and interpretations by the two editors whenever necessary.

The critical apparatus does contain some additional information relevant to the interpretation of the texts, but it is not a commentary. While references to related or associated texts are meant to facilitate the study of the texts until a true commentary is available, they are by no means exhaustive. Comments on individual names and lexical items are kept to a minimum and generally limited to new words and/or forms not to be found in the standard dictionaries or even specialized literature.

Glossary and Indices

The glossary and indices have been generated with the help of the computer and are for all practical purposes complete. The glossary, which is really a word index, contains all the occurrences of even the most common words, listed in alphabetic order under the relevant lemmas. The forms listed are not grouped semantically, and only the basic meanings of the words are given for the lemmas. Verbal adjectives are listed under verbs. References to the different manuscripts of Text 6 are indentified by ms. sigla following the line number. For the sake of clarity, half brackets, exclamation and question marks, as well as primes have been deleted from all references. The lemmas are given in their Assyrian form (e.g., *uṣû* not *aṣû*), with cross references under corresponding Babylonian forms. A complete list of the logograms occurring in the volume with their Assyrian readings precedes the glossary.

The name indices are styled like the glossary. To enhance their utility, identifications are consistently given (in parentheses) for every name whenever possible. The lemmas are again given in their normalized Assyrian form (Issar, Inurta, Ninua), which is not necessarily identical with the name form used in the translations (Ištar, Ninurta, Nineveh). Cross-references are given whenever necessary.

The subject index has been automatically generated from the translations and includes all the words occurring in them, with the exception of particles, common verbs and adjectives and the Assyrian names included in the name indices. Singular and plural forms have often been listed separately to obviate unnecessary checking.

Copies and Photographs of Tablets

In line with the general format of the SAA series, only previously unpublished texts are given in copy in the present volume. References to published copies or photographs are to be found under each text at the beginning of the translation column.

NOTES

[1] See A. H. Layard, *Discoveries in the Ruins of Nineveh and Babylon* (London 1853), 153-159, for clay sealings of destroyed papyrus and leather documents discovered in Nineveh, including a bulla bearing the impressions of royal Egyptian (Shabako II) and Assyrian signet rings and thus almost certainly once attached to a treaty between the two countries.

[2] Apart from the Neo-Assyrian treaties edited in this volume, about 35 cuneiform treaty fragments (twenty Hittite fragments, six fragments from Alalakh, several fragments from Ugarit, and possibly one Middle Assyrian fragment) are extant from the 2nd millennium B.C., see R. Borger, *Handbuch der Keilschriftliteratur* III (1975), p. 41. The only treaty extant from Egypt is the Hattusili-Ramses treaty edited by K. A. Kitchen, *Ramesside Inscriptions* II (Oxford 1977), p. 225ff. The oldest surviving treaties are the Treaty of Naram-Sin of Akkad with Elam (W. Hinz, ZA 58 [1967] 66ff) from c. 2250 B.C. and the Treaty of Ebla (E. Sollberger, Studi Eblaiti 3 [1980] 129ff, see W. G. Lambert in L. Cagni (ed.), *Ebla 1975-1985. Atti del convegno internationale* [Napoli 1987], 353ff) about 2400 B.C.

[3] The previous discussion is conveniently surveyed by K. Watanabe in BaM Bh 3 (1987), p. 6ff; see further ibid. 24 and S. Parpola, JCS 39 (1987) 180-183, excursus on the term *adê*.

[4] The crown prince figuring in this letter may be either Assurbanipal or Šamaš-šumu-ukin. In either case, the letter dates from 672-669 B.C.

[5] A.K. Grayson, JCS 39 (1987) 129.

[6] Compare with this passage the more explicitly worded Natnu episode cited p. XXI, and note that explicit references to treaties are often omitted in royal inscriptions even in cases where we certainly know that a treaty existed (cf., e.g., p. XXf).

[7] See R. Mattila, "The political status of Elam after 853 B.C. according to ABL 839," SAAB 1 (1987) 27ff.

[8] Compare ABL 292:5ff, a letter of Assurbanipal to his general Bel-ibni dating from the final phase of the Šamaš-šumu-ukin rebellion: "You know that through the iron sword of Aššur and my gods you destroyed that country by fire, (so) that the country backed down and could be subjugated, and you returned it to my control."

[9] One Marduk-rimanni, chief cupbearer, is known as the eponym of year 779, and another one was the governor of Calah in 728. Since sons of prestigious families often were named after their grandfathers, it is possible that these officials represent different generations in the same family, and accordingly an Assyrian official with the same name may also have been active in the mid-820's.

[10] We prefer to leave the interpretation of KTK open for the time being, but we believe that it is not the name of a country but rather an epithet or pseudonym that refers to Assyria in a manner that masked the participation of Assyria in the treaty from the Aramaic speaking population of Arpad.

[11] See JCS 39 (1987) 164 and 180.

[12] This later incident is described in more detail in another inscription of Esarhaddon: "[On my return (from Egypt) I marched against Baal, king of] Tyre, who lives [in the middle of the sea, and trusting in his friend Taharka, king of Kush], had thrown off the yoke [of Aššur my lord. The terrible sheen of] Aššur, king of the gods, and the splendour of my lordship [overwhelmed him; he submitted to my yoke, and crouching before] me on his knees supplicated my majesty. [... In an effort to appease] my angry mind, [he brought] his daughters along with an [ample] dowry and all the [taxes and tribute] which he had ceased paying [to Nineveh into my presence] and kissed my feet [......]. I took away from him his cities on the continent, [reorganized that district], placed [it in the hands of my eunuch] and turned it into Assyrian territory." (Borger Esarh. p. 110, Frt. A, rev.)

[13] BaM Bh 3 (1987), p. 4.

[14] See JCS 39 (1987) 175.

[15] E.g., *adê ša šarri bēlīja* "the treaty of the king, my lord", ABL 350 r.4; *adê ša abīka u ... adêka* "the treaty of your father and your own treaty", ABL 1217:4f // CT 53 17:4 // CT 53 938:5; *adê ša šarri* "the king's treaty" LAS 247:22 and often in contemporary legal documents.

[16] E. Reiner, ANET[3] (1969) p. 544a, correctly translates "(the treaty) which he has made..."

[17] See A. George, "Sennacherib and the Tablet of Destinies," Iraq 48 (1986) 133ff, especially p. 141.

[18] See LAS II (1983), p. 5.

[19] Instead of the D-stem stative *tummātunu* occurring in Text 2, line 384 of Text 6 has the corresponding Neo-Assyrian G-stem form *ta''ākunu* (from **tam'ākunu*) "you are sworn". The forms are semantically free variants, and corresponding variation is also attested in exorcistic adjuration formulae, e.g. *nīš* DN *lū tāmāta* // [*nīš*] DN *tāmāta*, W. Farber, *Beschwörungsrituale an Ištar und Dumuzi* (Wiesbaden 1977), pp. 231 and 232.

[20] A historical introduction appears to have been an integral element of most 2nd millennium treaties, even though it was occasionally omissible in these too, see e.g. J. Nougayrol, *Le palais royal d'Ugarit* IV (1956), p. 153f (no. 61).

[21] E. Reiner, ANET[3] (1969) 535ff; R. Borger, TUAT 1/2 (1983), 161ff; K. Watanabe, BaM Bh 3 (1987), 147ff; correctly D.J. Wiseman, VTE (1958), 34ff and Grayson, JCS 39 (1987) 134ff.

[22] D. Frayne apud Grayson, JCS 39 (1939) 133.

[23] See in more detail M. E. L. Mallowan in the foreword to VTE (1958), and D.J. Wiseman, ibid. 1ff.

Abbreviations and Symbols

Bibliographical Abbreviations

A	tablets in the collections of Istanbul Arkeoloji Müzeleri
ABL	R. F. Harper, *Assyrian and Babylonian Letters* (London and Chicago 1892-1914)
AfO	Archiv für Orientforschung
AGS	J. A. Knudtzon, *Assyrische Gebete an den Sonnengott* (Leipzig 1893)
AlT	D. J. Wiseman, *The Alalakh Tablets* (London 1953)
ANET	J. B. Pritchard (ed.), *Ancient Near Eastern Texts Relating to the Old Testament* (3rd edition, Princeton 1969)
AO	tablets in the collections of the Musée du Louvre
Ass	field numbers of tablets excavated at Assur
BaM Bh	Baghdader Mitteilungen, Beihefte
Bauer Asb	Th. Bauer, *Das Inschriftenwerk Assurbanipals* (Leipzig 1933)
Biggs Šaziga	R. D. Biggs, ŠÀ.ZI.GA*: Ancient Mesopotamian Potency Incantations* (Texts from Cuneiform Sources 2, Glückstadt 1967)
BM	tablets in the collections of the British Museum
Borger Esarh.	R. Borger, *Die Inschriften Asarhaddons, Königs von Assyrien* (AfO Beiheft 9, Graz 1956)
Böhl Chrestomathy	F. M. T. Böhl, *Akkadian Chrestomathy* (Leiden 1947)
Börker-Klähn, Bildstelen	J. Börker-Klähn, *Altorientalische Bildstelen und vergleichbare Felsreliefs* I-II (Baghdader Forschungen 4, Mainz 1982)
BRM	Babylonian Records in the Library of J. Pierpont Morgan
BSOAS	Bulletin of the School of Oriental and African Studies
Bu	tablets in the collections of the British Museum
BWL	W. G. Lambert, *Babylonian Wisdom Literature* (Oxford 1960)
CAD	Chicago Assyrian Dictionary
CH	Codex Hammurapi
CRRAI	Rencontre assyriologique internationale, comptes rendus
CT	Cuneiform Texts from Babylonian Tablets in the British Museum
Grayson Chronicles	A. K. Grayson, *Assyrian and Babylonian Chronicles* (Texts from Cuneiform Sources 5, Glückstadt 1975)
JCS	Journal of Cuneiform Studies
K	tablets in the Kuyunjik collection of the British Museum
KAI	H. Donner and W. Röllig, *Kanaanäische und Aramäische Inschriften* (2nd edition, Wiesbaden 1966-1968)
KAJ	E. Ebeling, *Keilschrifttexte aus Assur juridischen Inhalts* (Leipzig 1927)
KAR	E. Ebeling, *Keilschrifttexte aus Assur religiösen Inhalts* (Leipzig 1919)

LAS	S. Parpola, *Letters from Assyrian Scholars to the Kings Esarhaddon and Assurbanipal* I-II (Alter Orient und Altes Testament 5/1-2, Neukirchen-Vluyn 1970, 1983)
Luckenbill Senn.	D. D. Luckenbill, *The Annals of Sennacherib* (Oriental Institute Publications 2, Chicago 1924)
MLC	tablets in the collections of the J. Pierpont Morgan Library
ND	field numbers of tablets excavated at Nimrud
NL	H. W. F. Saggs, "The Nimrud Letters", *Iraq 17* (1955), 21ff, etc.
Or.	Orientalia, Nova Series
Pedersén Archives	O. Pedersén, *Archives and Libraries in the City of Assur* I-II (Uppsala 1985-1986)
Piepkorn Asb	A. C. Piepkorn, *Historical Prism Inscriptions of Ashurbanipal* (Assyriological Studies 5, Chicago 1933)
PKTA	E. Ebeling, *Parfümrezepte und kultische Texte aus Assur* (Roma 1952)
PRT	E. Klauber, *Politisch-Religiöse Texte aus der Sargonidenzeit* (Leipzig 1913)
R	H. C. Rawlinson, *The Cuneiform Inscriptions of Western Asia* (London 1861-1884)
Rm	tablets in the collections of the British Museum
SAA	State Archives of Assyria
SAAB	State Archives of Assyria Bulletin
Sm	tablets in the collections of the British Museum
Streck Asb	M. Streck, *Assurbanipal* I-III (Vorderasiatisches Bibliothek 7, Leipzig 1916)
TUAT	Texte aus der Umwelt des Alten Testaments
Uruanna	pharmaceutical series uruanna : *maštakal*
VAT	tablets in the collections of the Staatliche Museen, Berlin
VS	Vorderasiatische Schriftdenkmäler der Königlichen Museen zu Berlin
VTE	D. J. Wiseman, *The Vassal Treaties of Esarhaddon* (London 1958)
WO	Die Welt des Orients
ZA	Zeitschrift für Assyriologie

Other Abbreviations and Symbols

Aram.	Aramaic
Babyl.	Babylonian
LB	Late Babylonian
MA	Middle Assyrian
NA	Neo-Assyrian
MB	Middle Babylonian

NB	Neo-Babylonian
OA	Old Assyrian
OAkk	Old Akkadian
OB	Old Babylonian
SB	Standard Babylonian
e.	edge
obv.	obverse
r., rev.	reverse
s.	(left) side
coll.	collated, collation
frg.	fragment
MS	manuscript
unpub.	unpublished
var.	variant
!	collation
!!	emendation
?	uncertain reading
: ∴ ::	cuneiform division marks
*	graphic variants (see LAS I p. XX)
0	uninscribed space or nonexistent sign
x	broken or undeciphered sign
( )	supplied word or sign
[[ ]]	erasure
[...]	minor break (one or two missing words)
[......]	major break
...	untranslatable word
......	untranslatable passage
→	see also
/	(in score transliteration) line boundary
+	joined to, (in score transliteration) continuing line

Manuscript Sigla

Pl(s). refers to VTE, Tf. to BaM Bh 3.

SIGLUM	FIELD NUMBER	LINES	COPY	PHOTO
A	ND 4327	480	Pls.1-9	Pl.I and III; Tf.1 and 16 (Obv.) Pl.IX; Tf.2 (Rev.)
B	35+	189	Pl.35,26-27	Tf.5d
C	29	120	Pls.30-31	Tf.3c
D	37	119	Pls.38-39	Pl.XI; Tf.6b
E	46E	100	Pls.18-20	Tf.9a
F	31(+)51E	97+10	Pls.13-15,42	Pl.X 2
G	28A(+)48D	95+19	Pls.12-13,20	Tf.3a,3b (Obv.) Tf.4 (Rev.)
H	36	89	Pls.9-11	Pl.X 1
I	39	84	Pl.21	Tf.7d
J	45G	75	Pls.28-29	Pl.XII 2; Tf.8b
K	28C(+)50P	45+10	Pl.16,46	
L	BM 1959-4-14,90	46	Tf.15b	Tf.14b
M	ND 4338A	45	Pls.24,48	Tf.3e
N	28B	36	Pl.32	Tf.7e
O	55F	36	Pl.23	Tf.11c
P	45D	35	Pl.23	Tf.7b
Q	36C	34	Pl.43	Pl.XII 3; Tf.6a
R	X 15+	33	Pl.36	Tf.11f
S	4347A	32	Pl.20	Tf.9c
T	32	28	Pl.11	Pl.XII 1 left; Tf.5c
U	30B	27	Pl.16	Tf.5a
V	46C	27	Pl.41	Tf.8f
W	30A	25	Pl.19	Tf.3d
X	46A	25	Pl.32	Tf.8d
Y	X 7	24	Pl.27	Tf.11e
Z	4354A	22	Pl.44	Tf.10k
a	43+	19	Pl.11	Pl.XII 1 right; Tf.7a
b	47D	19	Pl.44	Tf.10a
c	56	19	Pl.36	
d	45I	18	Pl.13	Tf.7f
e	47C	17	Pl.33	
f	48A	17	Pl.32	Tf.10b
g	50A	17	Pl.40	Tf.10h
h	30C	16	Pl.45	
i	36B	16	Pl.33	Pl.XII 4; Tf.5b
j	51C	16	Pl.45	

SIGLUM	FIELD NUMBER	LINES	COPY	PHOTO
k	X 12	16	Pl.40	
l	4346EE	15	Pl.40	
m	50B	15	Pl.46	Tf.10i
n	55G	15	Pl.20	Tf.11d
o	55I	15	Pl.24	
p	46N+49Q	14	Pls.33,36	Tf.9e
q	49B(+)49S	14+	Pl.41	Tf.10c(+)
r	46B	13	Pl.18	Tf.8e
s	48B	13	Pl.37	
t	49E	13	Pl.24	
u	49L	13	Pl.28	Tf.10f
v	51G	13	Pl.45	Tf.10j
w	48K	12	Pl.36	
x	49I	12	Pl.21	Tf.10e
y	46I	11	Pl.22	Tf.9b
z	46J	11	Pl.37	
frg.	45M	1 (i)	Pl.13	
	47H	1 (ii)	Pl.48	
	46P	3 (iii, 177-179)	Pl.25	
	45F	8 (iv, 244-251)	Pl.33	Tf.8c
	51T	7 (iv, 266-271)	Pl.34	
	45A	54 (13-40b, 109-134	Pl.17	Tf.8a
	45H	5 (24-28)	Pl.17	
	45L	8 (40-47)	Pl.17	
	46W	6 (45-50)	Pl.17	
	BM 1959-4-14,71	8 (54-61)	Tf.13u	Tf.12u
	ND 4348S	5 (59-63)	Pl.20	
	BM 1959-4-14,72	4 (62-65)	Tf.13b	Tf.12b
	73	6 (65-70)	Tf.13c	Tf.12c
	ND 4355P	11 (86-96)	Pl.22	
	BM 1959-4-14,74	5 (87-91)	Tf.13h	Tf.12h
	ND 4355CC	9 (88-96)	Pl.22	
	49K	8 (88-95)	Pl.22	
	46Q	7 (88-94)	Pl.22	
	46Z	7 (92-98)	Pl.22	
	45E	19 (94-112)	Pl.22	
	55W	5 (94-98)	Pl.22	
	49M	7 (101-107)	Pl.22	
	46X	5 (103-107)	Pl.22	
	49R	15 (108-122)	Pl.23	
	BM 1959-4-14,75	7 (108-114)	Tf.13d	Tf.12d
	76	3 (119-121)	Tf.13i	Tf.12i
	ND 4346S	6 (131-136)	Pl.24	
	46T	5 (142-146)	Pl.24	
	47E	8 (147-154)	Pl.24	
	55L	7 (170-176)	Pl.25	
	55KK	7 (170-176)	Pl.25	
	55AA	5 (170-174)	Pl.25	
	BM 1959-4-14,78	3 (173-175)	Tf.13n	Tf.12n
	ND 4347G	6 (174-179)	Pl.25	
	55EE	5 (177-181)	Pl.25	
	55C	10 (181-190)	Pl.25	Tf.11a

SIGLUM	FIELD NUMBER	LINES	COPY	PHOTO
frg.	BM 1959-4-14,79	3 (183-185)	Tf.13e	Tf.12e
	ND 4345P	7 (185-191)	Pl.25	
	49G	10 (188-197)	Pl.25	
	55LL	7 (192-198)	Pl.25	
	49D	11 (194-204)	Pl.25	Tf.10d
	55HH	7 (198-204)	Pl.28	
	48O	9 (205-213)	Pl.28	
	48V	5 (210-214)	Pl.29	
	46CC	7 (217-223)	Pl.29	
	BM 1959-4-14,80	6 (228-233)	Tf.13f	Tf.12f
	VAT 11534	8 (229-236)	AfO 13, Tf.XIV	
	ND 4348Q	9 (240-248)	Pl.31	
	BM 1959-4-14,81	4 (240-243)	Tf.13j	Tf.12j
	ND 4348C	10 (242-251)	Pl.29	
	48R	9 (245a-253)	Pl.33	
	46FF	8 (260-267)	Pl.33	
	55D	20 (267-287)	Pl.34	Tf.11b
	55U	8 (268-275)	Pl.33	
	46O	9 (278-286)	Pl.34	
	48F	8 (283-290)	Pl.34	
	49H	10 (300-309)	Pl.34	
	38B	10 (327-336)	Pl.34	
	X 16	8 (328-335)	Pl.35	
	BM 1959-4-14,82	3 (336-338)	Tf.13o	Tf.12o
	ND 4352G	6 (339-344)	Pl.35	
	49F	2 (336-337)	Pl.35	
	49V	6 (341-346)	Pl.36	
	46V	5 (346-350)	Pl.37	
	45C	9 (356-364)	Pl.37	
	48T	10 (360-369)	Pl.37	
	50Z	10 (360-369)	Pl.37	
	X 14	11 (370-380)	Pl.37	
	ND 4345J	4 (373-376)	Pl.37	
	X 13	8 (211-218)	Pl.29	
	ND 4350S	2 (418-419)	Pl.41	
	51F	9 (425-433)	Pl.39	
	BM 1959-4-14,83	2 (425-426)	Tf.13k	Tf.12k
	ND 4346M	5 (451-455)	Pl.40	Tf.9d
	50N	4 (451-454)	Pl.40	
	X 20	4 (455-458)	Pl.41	
	ND 4348U	6 (457-462)	Pl.40	
	BM 1959-4-14,84	1 (459)	Tf.13p	Tf.12p
	X 17	7 (460-466)	Pl.40	
	BM 1959-4-14,85	4 (466-469)	Tf.13g	Tf.12g
	ND 4348Y	7 (482-488)	Pl.42	
	50C	9 (484-492)	Pl.42	
	52F	4 (490-493)	Pl.41	
	46JJ	4 (494-497)	Pl.48	
	BM 1959-4-14,87	4 (494-497)	Tf.13a	Tf.12a
	86	3 (494-496)	Tf.13l	Tf.12l
	88	8 (505-512)	Tf.13q	Tf.12q
	ND 4347I	5 (508-512)	Pl.41	
	49O	7 (516-522)	Pl.48	
	51N	3 (529-531)	Pl.42	
	50G	6 (534-539)	Pl.42	

SIGLUM	FIELD NUMBER	LINES	COPY	PHOTO
frg.	X 19	4 (537-540)	Pl.42	
	ND 4346II	4 (541-544)	Pl.42	
	46BB	7 (545-551)	Pl.42	
	50M	5 (545-549)	Pl.42	
	49U	9 (549-557)	Pl.42	Tf.10g
	51I	9 (551-559)	Pl.42	
	50F	7 (564-570)	Pl.44	
	BM 1959-4-14,89	3 (567-569)	Tf.13r	Tf.12r
	ND 4354B	10 (570-575, 662-665)	Pl.44	
	50T	4 (570-573)	Pl.43	
	48I	9 (579-587)	Pl.45	
	51S	4 (579-582)	Pl.43	
	X 21	11 (601-611)	Pl.46	
	ND 4350U	6 (610-615)	Pl.46	
	X 9	6 (613-618)	Pl.46	
	ND 4345N	2 (617-618)	Pl.46	
	X 22	4 (618-621)	Pl.46	
	ND 4351A	10 (620-629)	Pl.46	
	46G	10 (621-630)	Pl.47	
	50I	8 (629-636)	Pl.47	
	52E	5 (632-636c)	Pl.47	
	55R	11 (633-643)	Pl.47	
	50Y	6 (636a-641)	Pl.47	
	51J	11 (637-647)	Pl.47	
	51L	6 (637-642)	Pl.47	
	X 18	6 (643-648)	Pl.47	
	ND 4352C	7 (645-651)	Pl.48	
	48L	5 (647-651)	Pl.48	
	51H+	8 (656-663)	Pl.48 Tf.15a	Tf.14a
	54F	2 (664-665)	Pl.49	
	54D	1 (664)	Pl.49	
	54G	2 (665-666)	Pl.49	Tf.10l
	BM 1959-4-14,91	1 (665)	Tf.13s	Tf.12s
	ND 4344B	5 (666-670)	Pl.49	Tf.7c
	54C	2 (666-667)	Pl.49	
	54E	4 (667-670)	Pl.49	
	BM 1959-4-14,92	2 (668-669)	Tf.13	Tf.12t

TRANSLITERATIONS AND TRANSLATIONS

Treaties of the Ninth and Eighth Centuries B.C.

Šamši-Adad V (823-811)

COURTESY TRUSTEES OF THE BRITISH MUSEUM

FIG. 1. *Stela of Šamši-Adad V dedicated to the war-god Ninurta.*
BM 118892.

1. Treaty of Šamši-Adad V with Marduk-zakir-šumi, King of Babylon

Rm 2,427

beginning broken away

1′ [*x x x x x x x x x x x x x x x x*] *hi* [*x x x x*]

2′ [*x x x x x x x x x x x x x x* ANŠ]E.KUR.RA.ME[Š *x x x*]

3′ [*x x x x x x x x x x x*]*x ki-i* LÚ*.EN.NAM *x*[*x x*]

4′ [*x x x x x x x x x*] *e-mu-qí il-tap-ru* LUGAL *mim-m*[*a*$^{?}$ *x x x*]

5′ [*x x x x x x ina ku-u*]*n* ŠÀ-*bi-šú-nu la it-ták-lu na-a-*[*x x x*]

6′ [*x x x x x x x*]*x* KUR—URI.KI *u* KUR—*aš-šur*.KI *ul-te-eg-lu-ma šu*[*m-ma*]

7′ [*x x x x x i*]*ṣ*$^{?}$*-ṣab-tu-ma šum-ma a-na* URU.*bi-ra-a-ti a-na šu-*[*lu*$^{?}$*-ti*]

8′ [*x x x x x x*]*x šum-ma* ^{m}*šam-ši*—^{d}IM *a-mat* MÍ.HUL *šá* ^{md}AMAR.UTU—*ri-man-ni* [*x* (*x*)]

9′ [(*x*) *x x x*] LUGAL *iq-ta-bu-ú um-ma du-*⸢*ú-ku*⸣ *nu-up-pil ṣu-ub-*[*bit(-su)*]

10′ [*šum-ma* ^{md}AMA]R.UTU—MU—⸢MU⸣ LUGAL *il-te-mu-šu-ma šum-*[*ma*]

11′ [*x x x x x x*]*x-šu-ma* IGI.2 *še-pi-tu* ŠU.SI *ta-r*[*a-ṣu*$^{?}$]

12′ [*x x x x x x*]*x u* KUR-*šu ul-*⸢*x*⸣*-šu-ma hu-ub-ta-a-ni* [0]

13′ [*x x x x x x x u*]*t-tir-ru-ma it-tan-nu-ma mun-nab-t*[*u*]$^{!}$

14′ [*x x x x x x in-n*]*a-bi-tu-ni* LUGAL [*l*]*a i-qab-ba-áš-šú* [0]

e.15′ [*šá ina* ŠÀ *a-de-e an-nu-ti*] ⸢*i*⸣*-haṭ-ṭu-ú la il-ka-šu* [0]

16′ [*il-la-ku*$^{?}$ *x x x x x x*]*-nu* ^{d}AMAR.UTU EN GAL-*ú šá a-mat-su ina mah-ri* DU$^{!}$-*ku* [0]

17′ [*x x x x x x x*]*x la šá-lam-šu u sa-pa-ah* UN.MEŠ-*šú* 0$^{!}$

18′ [*x x x x x li*]*q-bi* ZI-*šú* GIM A.MEŠ *lit-bu-*

AfO 8 28

(Beginning destroyed)

2 [......] horses [......].

3 If the governor [......] sends troops [to ......], the king [shall ... *no*]thing [......].

5 [......] *he shall trust* [in] their [*stead*]*fast* heart ...[...].

6 [......] he shall not deport [......] Babylonia and Assyria nor seize [......].

7 He shall [......] to the forts and *gar*[*risons* ......].

8 Šamši-Adad shall not say (any) evil words about Marduk-rimanni [... to] the king, (viz.): "Kill, blind, or se[ize him", nor] shall King Marduk-zakir-šumi listen to him (should he say such things).

11 [He shall not ......] him, [nor ...] *to poi*[*nt*] an eye, toe or finger [......, nor] ... [...... of his ...] and his country.

12 He shall not give back the captives [......].

13 The king shall indicate to him the fugitives [who] fled [*from Assyria to Babylonia*].

15 [Whoever] sins [against this treaty *and does*] not [*carry out*] *his duty*,

16 May Marduk, the great lord whose commands take precedence, [*by his unalterable word*] order his decay and the dispersion of his people [...]; may he pour out his life like water, [may he destroy] his

1 Previous edition (with no translation): E. Weidner, AfO 8 (1932/3) 27ff. — The number of signs missing on the left side of the document has been determined on the basis of the curses on the reverse, particularly r.8ff and 12ff, which, excepting occasionally omitted divine epithets, are largely identical with those found in Codex Hammurapi (cf. Borger, Or 34 [1965] 168f). Thus, while the present text omits CH's *nābû palēja* in r.3, *mušarbû šarrūtīja* in r.4, and *rubû rabiu ša šīmātūšu ina mahra illakā* as well as *mušāriku ūm balāṭīja* in r.7, the wording of the relevant curses otherwise agrees with CH. Further differences vis-à-vis CH are noted below insofar as they affect the restorations. 5 *it-ták-lu*: or *id-dag-lu* "(he shall) look, wait". 6 *du-*⸢*ú-ku*⸣: the second sign is headed by three horizontals and followed by tablet damage affecting part of ⸢*ku*⸣ (coll. KW; cf. photo on pl. I). Watanabe accordingly suggests reading *du-*⸢*luh-ma*⸣ "hasten to", which seems epigraphically possible; however, Weidner's reading *du-*⸢*ú-ku*⸣ fits the traces as well and makes better sense. Note that the sequence "kill — blind — seize" is also encountered in a contemporary literary text, the well-known Dialogue of Pessimism (*šum-ma di-i-ku šum-ma ki-ṣi šum-ma nu-up-pu-lu šum-ma ṣa-bit*, BWL 146:44f). 9 Restore possibly [*ina ma-har*] "before". r.3 There may be room for restoring *uk* KUR-*s*[*u*]

19′ [*li-hal-liq ina bu-bu-t*]*i*! *u hu-šah-hi* UN.MEŠ-*šú li-šam-qit* 0!

r.1 [(*x*) *x x x x x x*]-*li li-ir-di-šu* ^{d}AG DUMU.UŠ *ṣi-ru* [0]

2 [*x x x x x x*]*x gal-le-e lem-nu-ti la i-gam-mi-la nap-šat-su*

3 [^{d}*a-num a-b*]*i* DINGIR.MEŠ GIŠ.PA-*šú liš-bir* $^{d+}$EN.LÍL *be-lum mu-šim* NAM.M[EŠ]

4 [*šá qí-bi-sa la ut-tak-k*]*a-ru pa-le-e ta-né-hi* UD.MEŠ *i-ṣu-ti* MU.MEŠ *hu-*[*šah-hi*]

5 [*a-na šim-ti li*]-*šim-šú* ^{d}NIN.LÍL *um-mu* GAL-*tu šá qí-bit-sa i-n*[*a* É.KUR]

6 [*kab-ta-at*] *a-šar šip-ṭi u* EŠ.BAR *i-na ma-har* $^{d+}$EN.LÍL *a-bu-us-*[*su*]

7 [*a-a iṣ-bat*] ^{d}É.A NUN.ME DINGIR.MEŠ *mu-de-e mim-ma šum-šu* ÍD!.[MEŠ-*šú*]

8 [*ina nag-bi lis*]-*kir* ^{d}UTU *da-a-a-nu* GAL-*ú šá* AN-*e u* KI.TIM *m*[*uš-te-šir*]

9 [*šik-nat* ZI-*tim* EN *tuk*]*ul-ti šar-ru-su li-is-kip di-in-šu a-a* ⸢*i*⸣-[*di-in*]

10 [^{d}30 EN AN-*e šá*] *še-ret*!-*su ina* DINGIR.MEŠ *šu-pa-a*[*t* 0]

11 [*x x x x šir-t*]*a ra-bi-ta šá ina* SU-*šú la* KÚR-*ru* [*li-mid-su-ma*]

12 [UD.MEŠ ITI.MEŠ MU.MEŠ *pa*]-*le-e-šú i-na ta-né-hi* ⸢*ù*⸣ [*dim-ma-ti li-šaq-ti*]

13 [^{d}IM GÚ.GAL AN-*e u* KI.TIM A.A]N *ina* AN-*e* A.KAL *ina nag-bi* [*li-ṭir-šu*]

14 [KUR-*su ina hu-šah-hi*] *li-hal-*[*liq* 0]

15 [UGU URU-*šú ez-zi-iš li-is-si-ma* KUR]-*su*! *a*!-*n*[*a* DU$_{6}$ *a-bu-bi*]

16 [*li-tir* ^{d}*za-ba*$_{4}$-*ba*$_{4}$ *qar-ra-du* GAL-*u a-l*]*i*-[*ku x x x*]

rest broken away

country, strike down his people [through hunge]r and famine, and lead him [to *captivity* ...].

r.1 May Nabû, the august heir [*who* ......] evil demons, not spare his life.

3 [May Anu, fat]her of the gods, break his sceptre; may lord Illil, decreer of fates [whose command is un]alterable, decree him a reign of exhaustion, scarce days and years of f[amine].

5 May Mulliltu, the great mother whose utterance [carries weight] in [Ekur], not intercede for him before Illil at the site of judgment and decision.

7 May Ea, the sage of the gods who knows everything, dam his rivers [in their sources].

8 May Šamaš, the great judge of heaven and earth w[ho provides justice for all living beings, the source of con]fidence, reject his kingship and not [judge] his case.

10 [May Sin, the *lord* of heaven, whose] punishment is renowned among the gods, [inflict upon him] a severe puni[shment] which is not to be removed from his body; may he [make the days, months and years] of his reign [end] in sighing and [moaning].

13 [May Adad, the canal inspector of heaven and earth, deprive him of rain] from the heaven, and of seasonal flooding from the underground water; may he destroy [his land through famine, roar fiercely at his city], and turn his [land into ruins by means of a flood].

16 [May valiant Zababa, *the great warrior*, who w]alk[s ......]

(Rest destroyed)

[GAL-*ú*] "great" after ^{d}*a-num* in accordance with CH. 5 Before *a-na šim-ti* CH has *mūt niṭil īnim*, but there is no room to restore this in the break. 6f CH has *awassu lilemmin* for *a-bu-us-*[*su a-a iṣ-bat*. 11 CH's *agâm kussiam ša šarrūtim līṭeršu* does not fit in the break. 13 The string of epithets in CH (*Adad bēl nuhšim gugal šamê u erṣetim rēṣūʾa*) is too long to fit completely in the break.

Aššur-nerari V (754-745)

COURTESY VORDERASIATISCHES MUSEUM

FIG. 2. *King Bar-rakib of Sam'al, a younger contemporary of Mati'-ilu of Arpad, depicted with his secretary (late 8th century BC).*
VA 2817.

2. Treaty of Aššur-nerari V with Mati'-ilu, King of Arpad

K 15272 + Rm 120 + Rm 274 (+) BM 134596 (+) 79-7-8,195

AfO 8 17 (+) Iraq 32 pl.36 (+) unpub.

I beginning (at least 30 lines) broken away

1′ [*x x*] *pa*! [*x x x x x x x x x*]

2′ ⸢DUMU.MEŠ-*šú*⸣ DUMU.MÍ.MEŠ-*šú* G[AL.MEŠ-*šú* UN.MEŠ KUR-*šú*]

3′ *am—mar x*[*x x x x x x x*]

4′ KUR-*su am—mar har*-⸢*ba*⸣-*t*[*i x x x*]

5′ *kaq-qa-ru am—mar* SIG_4 *ina ú*-[*zu-zi-šú*]

6′ *a-na ú-zu-zi šá* DUMU.MEŠ-*šú* DUMU.MÍ.ME[Š-*šú* GAL.MEŠ-*šú*]

7′ [U]N.MEŠ KUR-*šú li-ih-liq* ^{m}*ma-ti-i*ʾ—DINGIR [DUMU.MEŠ-*šú*]

8′ [DUMU].MÍ.MEŠ-*šú* GAL.MEŠ-*šú* UN.MEŠ KUR-*šú* GIM *pu-l*[*i x x x*]

9′ *šu-tú a-di* UN.MEŠ KUR-*šú* GIM *gaṣ-ṣi lip-p*[*ar-ri-ir*]

10′ UDU.NIM *an-ni-ú* TA* ŠÀ *pit-qí-šú la a-na* UDU.SISKUR *še-lu*-[*a*]

11′ *la a-na qa-ri-ti še-lu-a la a-na qí-ni-ti še*-[*lu-a*]

12′ *la a-na mar-ṣi še-lu-a la a-na ṭa-ba-hi a-n*[*a x x še-lu-a*]

13′ *a-na a-de-e šá* ^{m}*aš-šur*—ERIM.GABA MAN KUR—[*aš-šur*]

14′ [T]A* ^{m}*ma-ti-i*ʾ—DINGIR *šá-ka-ni še*-[*lu-a*]

15′ *šúm-mu* ^{m}*ma-ti-i*ʾ—DINGIR *ina a-de-e ta-mi-ti an*-[*nu-ti i-ha-ṭi*]

16′ *ki-i šá* UDU.NIM *an-ni-u* TA* *pit-qí-šú še-lu*-[*u-ni*]

17′ *a-na pit-qí-šú la* GUR-*ni pa-ni šá pit-qí-šú* [*la e-mar-u-ni*]

18′ *a-hu-la* ^{m}*ma-ti-i*ʾ—DINGIR *a-di* DUMU.MEŠ-*šú* [GAL.MEŠ-*šú*]

19′ UN.MEŠ KUR-*šú* TA* ŠÀ KUR-*šú li*-[*ih-liq*]

20′ *a-na* KUR-*šú la* GUR-*ra pa-ni šá* KUR-*šú la* [*em-mar*]

21′ ⸢SAG⸣.DU *an-ni-u la* SAG.DU *ša* UDU.NIM [*šu-tú*]

(Beginning destroyed)

i 1 [... may Mati'-ilu], his sons and daughters, his mag[nates and the people of his land become] altogether like [...], may his land [be reduced] to wasteland, may only an area of the size of a brick (be left) for [him to stand upon], may nothing be left for his sons, [his daughters, his magnates and the peo]ple of his land to stand upon. May Mati'-ilu [together with his sons], daughters, magnates and the people of his land [...] like limestone, and may he, together with the people of his land, be cru[shed] like gypsum.

---

10 This spring lamb has not been brought out of its fold for sacrifice, nor for a banquet, nor for a purchase, nor for (divination concerning) a sick man, nor to be slaughtered for [...]: it has been brought to conclude the treaty of Aššur-nerari, king of Assyria with Mati'-ilu. If Mati'-ilu [sins] against th[is] sworn treaty, then, just as this spring lamb has been brought from its fold and will not return to its fold and [not behold] its fold again, (in like manner) may, alas, Mati'-ilu, together with his sons, daughters, [magnates] and the people of his land [be ousted] from his country, not return to his country, and not [behold] his country again.

2 Previous edition: E. Weidner, AfO 8 (1932/3) 17ff. → E. Reiner, ANET^3 (1969), p. 532f; R. Borger, TUAT 1/2 (1983), p. 155ff. – In accordance with earlier editions, the name of the ruler of Arpad is here normalized as Mati'-ilu. A more appropriate normalization would, however, be Matiʾ-il, judging from the personal name ^{m}*mat—il*—DINGIR-*a-a* "Mat(i)-il is my god" attested in ND 3429 r.24, where the final element of the name is exceptionally spelled syllabically.

I 1, 3 See coll. 15 There is not enough room to restore [*i-ha-ṭu-ni*] (i 32, iv 18) or [*ih-ti-ṭi*] (v 9) at the end of the line (coll. SP).

22′ SAG.DU *šá* ^{m}*ma-ti-i*ʾ—DINGIR [*šu-u-tú*]
23′ SAG.DU *šá* DUMU.MEŠ-*šú* GAL.MEŠ-*šú* UN.MEŠ K[UR-*šú šu-tú*]
24′ *š*[*úm-m*]*u* ^{m}KI.MIN *ina a-de-e an-nu-t*[*i i-ha-ṭu-ni*]
25′ *ki-i šá* SAG.DU *šá* UDU.NIM *an-ni-u qa-*[*ti-pu-u-ni*]
26′ [*ku*]*r-sin-nu-šu ina* KA-*šú šak-na-tu-n*[*i x x x*]
27′ S[AG.D]U *ša* ^{m}KI.MIN *lu qa-ti-ip* DUMU.[MEŠ-*šú* GAL.MEŠ-*šu*]
28′ *ina* ⸢É⸣ *lu ka-*[*ar-ru*]
29′ UZU.ZAG ⸢*an-ni*⸣-*tú la* UZU.ZAG *šá* UDU.[NIM *ši-i-ti*]
30′ UZU.ZAG *šá* ^{m}KI.MIN *ši-i-ti* UZU.ZAG *šá* DU[MU.MEŠ-*šú* GAL.MEŠ-*šú*]
31′ UN.MEŠ KUR-*šú ši-i-ti šúm-mu* ^{m}*ma-ti-i*[ʾ—DINGIR *ina* ŠÀ *a-de-e*]
32′ *an-nu-ti i-ha-ṭu-*[*ni k*]*i-i šá* UZU.Z[AG *ša* UDU.NIM *an-ni-u*]
33′ *na-as-ha-tu-ni ina* [*x x x x x x x šak-na-tu-ni*]
34′ UZ[U.ZAG *ša* ^{m}K]I.MIN DUMU.⸢MEŠ⸣-[*šú* GAL.MEŠ-*šú*] UN.[MEŠ KUR-*šú*]
35′ [*l*]*u na-as-ha-at ina x*[*x x x x*] *lu* [*šak-na-at*]

21 This head is not the head of a spring lamb, it is the head of Mati'-ilu, it is the head of his sons, his magnates and the people of [his la]nd. If Mati'-ilu [should sin] against this treaty, so may, just as the head of this spring lamb is c[ut] off, and its knuckle placed in its mouth, [...] the head of Mati'-ilu be cut off, and his sons [and magnates] be th[rown] into [...].

29 This shoulder is not the shoulder of a spring lamb, it is the shoulder of Mati'-ilu, it is the shoulder of his so[ns, his magnates, and the people of his land. If Mati'-ilu] should sin against this [treaty], so may, just as the shou[lder of this spring lamb] is torn out and [placed in ...], the shoulder of Mati'-ilu, of his sons, [his magnates] and the people of his land be torn out and [placed] in [...].

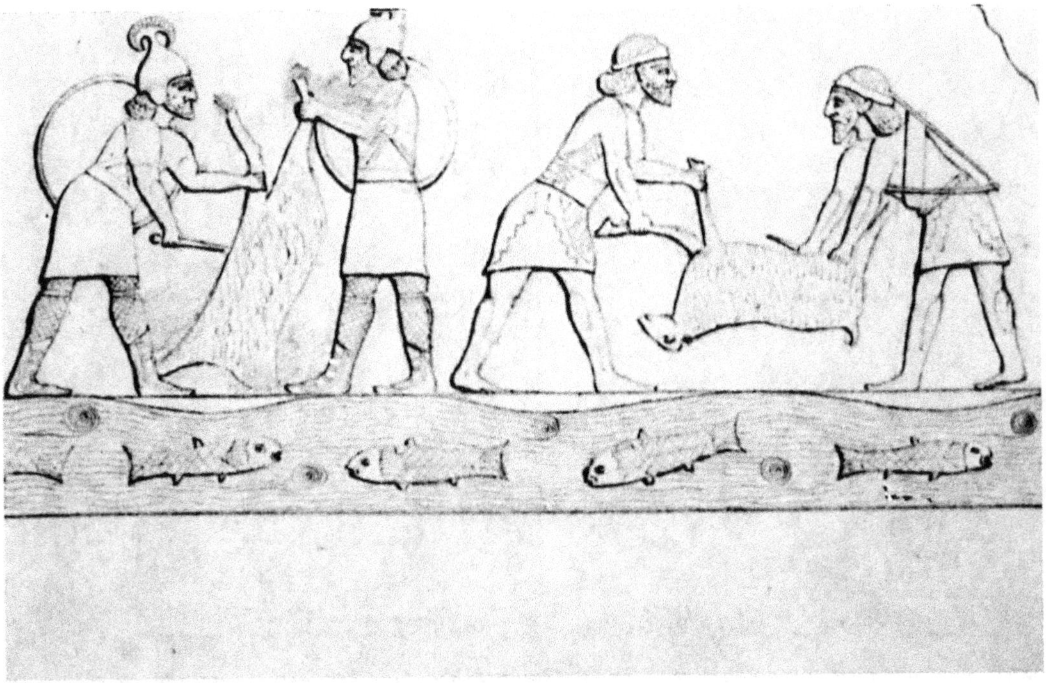

COURTESY TRUSTEES OF THE BRITISH MUSEUM

FIG. 3. *Assyrian soldiers slaughtering sheep (reign of Sennacherib).*
ORIGINAL DRAWING IV, 25.

II	broken away	(Break)
III	beginning broken away	
1′	[*x x x x x x x x x x x x*] *x*[*x x x*]	
2′	[*x x x x x x x x x x x x x x x*]*x*	
3′	[*x x x x x x x x x x x x x x x-b*]*a-ku*	
4′	[*x x x x x x x x x x x x x x a*]*n-nu-ti*	iii 4 [......] this [......]
5′	[*x x x x x x x x x x x x x*.ME]*Š-ni ša* KUR.*hat-ti*	5 [......]... of Hatti
6′	[*x x x x x x x x x x x x x*]*x-du-ni*	6 [......]...
7′	[*x x x x x x x x x x x in-n*]*é-piš*	7 [......]
8′	[*x x x x x x x x x x x* K]UR.*ú-ra-ar-ṭa-a-a*	8 [......] Urarṭian
9′	[*x x x x x x x x x x x x*] *la* (*ta*)-*ṣab-ba-tú-ni*	9 [... You] shall seize [...]
10′	[*x x x x x x x x x la t*]*u-še-bal-an-n*[*i-n*]*i*	10 [... and shall] send [......]
	break	(Break)
11′	[*x x x x x x x x x x x x*]*x x*[*x x*]	
12′	[*x x x x x x x x x x x x x*]*x-hu-u*[*m x*]	
13′	[*x x x x x x x x x x x x*]*x man ša x*[*x* (*x*)]	
14′	[*x x x x x x x x x x x t*]*a*!*-ha-ṭu-ni*	14 [... *If*] you *should* sin [against ......]
15′	[*x x x x x x x x x x x x*]*x ina* ŠÀ-*šú ta-ha-ṭu-*[*ni*]	15 [... *If*] you *should* sin against it [......]
16′	[*x x x x x x x x x x x*]*x* GAZ-*šú*	16 [......] you *shall* kill him
17′	[*x x x x x x x x x x x*]*x ta-lak-ni*	17 [......] you shall come to me
18′	[*x x x x x x x x x x a*]*n-nu-te*	18 [...] this [......]
19′	[*x x x x x x x x x x x x x x x-n*]*i*	
20′	[*x x x x x x x x x x x x x x x-z*]*i*	

III 4 and 18 Restore possibly, in accordance with the Sefire Treaty: "[(then) you will have sinned against] this [treaty]" (cf., e.g., KAI 224:9 and 19). 5 Restore possibly [LUGAL].MEŠ-*ni* "[king]s". 12ff See coll. At the end of l.13

COURTESY TRUSTEES OF THE BRITISH MUSEUM

FIG. 4. a, b. *Chariot and foot-soldiers of the city of Carchemish, not far from Arpad (late 10th and early 9th centuries BC).*
HITTITE MUSEUM, ANKARA 94 AND 116.

21′ [*lu*] ⸢LÚ*!.EN⸣—GIŠ.GIGIR ⸢*lu*!⸣ *šá*!—*pet*!-*hal*!-*li ina*? U[GU?*x x x*]
22′ *šúm-mu tu-pa-za-ru-ni ta-ha-ṣi-nu-*[*u*]-*ni*
23′ [*š*]*úm-mu a-na* KUR 2-*te tu-še-bal-ni šúm-m*[*u* ^{m}KI.M]IN
24′ [T]A* ^{m}*aš-šur*—ERIM.GABA *la ke-nu-ni šúm-mu* ŠÀ-[*ba-k*]*a*
25′ [TA*] ^{m}*aš-šur*—ERIM.GABA MAN KUR—*aš-šur la šá-ki-nu-*⸢*ni*⸣
26′ [*šúm-mu a*]*t-ta* DUMU-*ka* UN.MEŠ KUR-*ka* [*x*]-*nu*!
27′ [*tu-b*]*a*!-ʾ*u-*⸢*ú*!⸣-[*n*]*i*!
28′ [*x x x x x x x x x x x x x x x x*]*x*
rest (about 12 lines) broken away

Reverse

IV 1 *ina qí-bit* ^{m}*aš-šur*—ERIM.GABA MAN KUR—*aš-šur a-na* KÚR-*šú* DU-*k*[*u-ni*]
2 ^{m}*ma-ti-i*ʾ—DINGIR *a-di* GAL.MEŠ-*šú* Á.KAL.MEŠ-*šú* GIŠ.GI[GIR.MEŠ-*šú*]
3 *a-na ga-mur-ti* ŠÀ-*bi-šú la* È-*ni la* DU-*k*[*u-ni*]
4 ^{d}30 EN GAL-*u a-šib* URU.KASKAL *a-na* ^{m}*ma-ti-i*ʾ—DINGIR DUM[U.MEŠ-*šú*]
5 GAL.MEŠ-*šú* UN.MEŠ KUR-*šú* SAHAR.ŠUB.BA-*a* GIM *na-ha-lap-ti l*[*i-hal-lip*]
6 EDIN *li-ir-pu-du a-a* TUK-*šú-nu re-e-mu*
7 *ka*!-*bu*!-*ut*! GUD ANŠE UDU.MEŠ ANŠE.KUR.RA.MEŠ *ina* KUR-*šú a-a ib-ši*
8 ^{d}IM GÚ.GAL AN-*e* KI.TIM *ina su-un-qi*
9 SU.KÚ *hu-šah-hi šá* ^{m}*ma-ti-i*ʾ—DINGIR KUR-*su* UN.MEŠ KUR-*šú*
10 *liq-qat-ti-ma* UZU DUMU.MEŠ-*šú-nu* DUMU.MÍ.MEŠ-*šú-nu le-ku-lu-ma*
11 GIM UZU UDU.NIM MÍ.NIM UGU-*šú-nu li-ṭib*
12 *ik-kil* ^{d}IM *li-za-me-ú-ma*
13 A.AN.MEŠ *a-na ik-ki-bi-šú-nu liš-šá-kín*
14 SAHAR.MEŠ *a-na* KÚ-*šú-nu qi-ru a-na* ŠÉŠ-*šú-nu*
15 KÀŠ ANŠE *a-na* NAG-*šú-nu ni-a-ru ana lu-bu-uš-ti-šú-nu*
16 *liš-šá-kín ina tub-ki-ni lu ma-a-a-al-šú-nu*
17 BE-*ma* ^{m}*ma-ti-i*ʾ—DINGIR DUMU.MEŠ-*šú* GAL.MEŠ-*šú šá ina a-de-e*
18 *šá* ^{m}*aš-šur*—ERIM.GABA MAN KUR—*aš-šur i-ha-ṭu-u-ni*
19 LÚ.ENGAR-*šú ina* EDIN *a-a il-sa-a a-la-la*
20 *ur-qit* EDIN *lu la* È-*a* ^{d}UTU *lu la*! IGI
21 [M]Í!.*ha-*⸢*bi*!⸣-*t*[*i* A].⸢ME⸣ *a-a ih-ba-a* A.MEŠ *nag-bi*
22 [*x x x x lu ma*]-*ka-al-šu-nu*
23 [*x x x x x lu m*]*aš-ti-su-nu*
24 [*x x x x x*] *li-ir-x*[*x x*]*x*
25 [*x x x x x x*]*x x*[*x x x*]
26 [*x x x x x x*]*x*[*x x x*]*x*

19 [......]. You shall not conceal (or) protect (any) chariot-[figh]ter or cavalryman [...], nor send him to another country. If you should prove disloyal to Aššur-nerari, and if your heart should not be devoted to Aššur-nerari, king of Assyria, [if] you, your sons, and the people of your land [should s]eek [...

(Break)

iv 1 [If the Assyrian army] goes to war at the orders of Aššur-nerari, king of Assyria, and Mati'-ilu, together with his magnates, his forces and his char[iotry] does not go forth (on the campaign) in full loyalty,

4 May Sin, the great lord who dwells in Harran, clothe Mati'-ilu, [his so]ns, his magnates, and the people of his land in leprosy as in a cloak; may they have to roam the open country, and may there be no mercy for them. May there be no more dung of oxen, asses, sheep, and horses in his land.

8 May Adad, the canal inspector of heaven and earth, put an end to Mati'-ilu's land, and the people of his land through hunger, want, and famine, may they eat the flesh of their sons and daughters, and may it taste as good to them as the flesh of spring lambs. May they be deprived of Adad's thunder so that rain become forbidden to them. May dust be their food, pitch their ointment, donkey's urine their drink, papyrus their clothing, and may their sleeping place be in the dung heap. the dung heap.

17 If Mati'-ilu, his sons, or his magnates who (sic!) sin against this treaty of Aššur-nerari, king of Assyria, may his farmers not sing the harvest song in the fields, may no vegetation spring forth in the open country and see the sunlight, may women fetching water not draw water from the springs, [may ...] be their food, [...] their drink, [...

read possibly *ša ina* U[GU]. 21 See coll.; reading *šú*]*m-*⸢*mu*⸣ GIŠ.GIGIR excluded. 26f See coll. At the end of the line restore possibly [*lum*]-*nu* "[ev]il".
IV 21, 31 See coll.

break
27′ [*x x x x x x x x x x m*]*a-a ina ta*$^{!}$*-mit*
28′ [*šá* ^{m}*aš-šur*—ERIM.GABA MAN KUR—*aš-šur ni-i*]*h-ti-ṭi*

(Break)
27 [...... "Woe, we have sin]ned against the oath [of Aššur-nerari, king of Assyria]."

29′ [*šúm-mu* ^{m}KI.MIN *ina a-de-e an-nu-ti šá* ^{m}]*aš-šur*—ERIM.GABA MAN KUR—*aš-šur*
30′ [*i-ha-ṭu-ni x x x x x l*]*a*$^{!}$ *i-da-gal-u-ni*
31′ [*x x x x x x x x x x*] *u* URU.NINA KI.MIN
32′ [*x x x x x x x x x x*] UN.MEŠ KUR-*šú*
33′ [*x x x x x x x x x l*]*a ta-ga-lu-ni*
V 1 *šúm-mu mu-a-tin-ni la mu-at-ka šúm-mu ba-*[*la-ṭi*]*n-ni*
2 *la ba-laṭ-ka-ni ki-i šá* TI.LA *šá* Z[I.MEŠ]-*ka*
3 DUMU.MEŠ-*ka* GAL.MEŠ-*ka ku-*[*nu*]*-ni*
4 TI.LA *šá* ^{m}*aš-šur*—ERIM.GABA DUMU.MEŠ-*šú* GAL.MEŠ-*šú la tú*$^{!}$-[*b*]*a-ʾu-u-ni*
5 *aš-šur* AD DINGIR.MEŠ *na-din* LUGAL-*ti* KUR-*ka ana tú-šá-ri*
6 UN.MEŠ-*ka ana* GÌR.BAL URU.MEŠ-*ka ana* DUL.ME É-*ka*
7 *ana har-ba-ti lu-tir*

29 [If Mati'-ilu sins against this treaty of] Aššur-nerari, king of Assyria, and *looks* [......],

31[......] and Nineveh, ditto,

32 the people of his land [......] (and) you *shall be deported* [......];

v 1 If our death is not your death, if our life is not your life, if you do not seek (to protect) the life of Aššur-nerari, his sons and his magnates as your own life and the life of your sons and officials, then may Aššur, father of the gods, who grants kingship, turn your land into a battlefield, your people to devastation, your cities into mounds, and your house into ruins.

---

8 *šúm-mu* ^{m}KI.MIN *ina a-de-e an-nu-ti šá* ^{m}*aš-šur*—ERIM.[GABA] MAN KUR—*aš-šur*
9 *ih-ti-ṭi* ^{m}KI.MIN *lu* MÍ.*ha-rim-tú* LÚ*.ERIM.[MEŠ-*šú*] *lu* MÍ.MEŠ
10 GIM MÍ.*ha-rim-tú ina re-bit* URU-*šú-n*[*u nid*$^{?}$*-n*]*u lim-hu-ru*
11 KUR *ana* KUR *lid-hu-šú-nu* TI$^{!}$ *ša* ^{m}KI.[MIN *lu šá*$^{?}$] ANŠE.GÌR.NUN
12 *áš-šá-tu-šú li-tu-tu* [^{d}15 *be-l*]*it* NITA.MEŠ GAŠAN MÍ.MEŠ
13 GIŠ.BAN-*su-nu li-kim* [*x*]*x bal-tu-šú-nu liš-kun*
14 *lim-ru-ur bi-k*[*it*$^{!}$*-su-nu m*]*a-a a-hu-la ma-a ina a-de-e*
15 *šá* ^{m}*aš-šur*—ERIM.GABA MAN [KUR—*aš-šur*] *ni-ih-ti-ṭi*

8 If Mati'-ilu sins against this treaty with Aššur-nerari, king of Assyria, may Mati'-ilu become a prostitute, his soldiers women, may they receive [*a gift*] in the square of their cities like any prostitute, may one country *push* them to the next; may Mati'-ilu's (sex) life be that of a mule, his wives extremely old; may Ištar, the goddess of men, the lady of women, take away their bow, bring them to shame, and make them bitterly weep: "Woe, we have sinned against the treaty of Aššur-nerari, king of Assyria."

---

16 *šúm-mu* ^{m}K[I.MIN *ina a-de-e an-nu-t*]*i* ⌜*šá*⌝ [^{m}*aš-šur*—ER]IM.GABA MAN KUR—*aš-šur*
17 [*ih-ti-ṭi x x x x x x x x x x x x x*]*x*
18 [*x x x x x x x x x x x x x x x x*]*x*
19 [*x x x x x x x x x x x x x x x x*]*x*
break
20′ ⌜*x a x x*⌝ [*x x x x x x x x x x*]
21′ *ina* IGI MAN.MEŠ-*ni mi-*[*x x x x x x x x x*]
22′ *sar-ti* DINGIR.MEŠ *x*[*x x x x x x x x x x x*]
23′ *a-ha-iš x*[*x x x x x x x x x x x x*]

16 If Ma[ti'-ilu sins against thi]s [treaty] of [Aššur-n]erari, king of Assyria [......
(Break)

21 ...] before the kings [......]

22 a divine punishment [......]

23 each other [......]

24′ *šúm-mu* ^{m}KI.MIN *ina a-de-e* [*x x x x x x x x*]
25′ KÁ-*šú li-pi-hi-ma ku-x*[*x x x x x x x x x x*]

24 If Mati'-ilu [sins against this] treaty [of Aššur-nerari, king of Assyria], may his door

V 1 *mu-at-ka* sic (not *-ni* despite *ba-laṭ-ka-ni* in l. 2). 11 *lid-hu-šú-nu* TI sic (coll. SP; signs clear). 20-27 Placement of the fragment 79-7-8,195 here by K. Watanabe. 22 "divine punishment": instead of *sar-ti*, read possibly *šèr-ti* DINGIR.MEŠ (K. Deller).

26′ *hab-ba-ti* KÁ *ša* UN.MEŠ-[*šú x x x x x x*]
27′ *li-ni-la mu-x*[*x x x x x x x x x x*]

VI 1 [BURU$_5$.MUŠEN *lit-ba*]-*am-ma* KUR-*su* KÚ
2 [*x x x x*]*x-ma* IGI.2-*šú-nu lu-na-pi-il*
3 [URU *šá*] 1-*lim* É.MEŠ *a-na* 1 É *li-tur*
4 [0] 1-*lim* TÚG.*maš-ku-nu a-na* 1 TÚG.*maš-ki-ni li-tur*
5 *ina* ŠÀ URU 1 LÚ *a-na di-li-li li-ni-zib*

---

6 ^{d}*aš-šur* MAN AN KI *tùm-ma-tú-nu*
7 ^{d}*a-nu-um an-tum* KI.MIN ^{d}BE ^{d}NIN.LÍL KI.MIN
8 ^{d}1 ^{d}*dam-ki-na* KI.MIN ^{d}30 ^{d}NIN.GAL KI.MIN
9 ^{d}UTU ^{d}A.A KI.MIN ^{d}IM ^{d}*ša-la* KI.MIN
10 ^{d}AMAR.UTU ^{d}*zar-pa-ni-tum* KI.MIN ^{d}AG ^{d}LÁL KI.MIN
11 ^{d}MAŠ ^{d}ME KI.MIN ^{d}IB ^{d}NIN.É.GAL KI.MIN
12 ^{d}*za-ba$_4$-ba$_4$* ^{d}BA.Ú KI.MIN ^{d}U.GUR ^{d}*la-aṣ* KI.MIN
13 ^{d}DI.KUD ^{d}NIN.GÍR.SU KI.MIN
14 ^{d}*hum-hum-mu* ^{d}*i-šum* KI.MIN
15 ^{d}GIŠ.BAR ^{d}PA.TÚG KI.MIN ^{d}15 NIN URU.*ni-na-a* KI.MIN
16 ^{d}INNIN NIN URU.*arba-ìl* KI.MIN
17 ^{d}IM *šá* URU.*kur-ba-ìl* KI.MIN
18 ^{d}IM *šá* URU.*hal-la-ba* KI.MIN
19 ^{d}IGI.DU *a-lik mah-ri* KI.MIN
20 ^{d}7.BI *qar-du-ti* KI.MIN
21 ^{d}[*d*]*a-*⸢*gan*⸣ 0! ⸢^{d}⸣[*m*]*u*?*-ṣur-u-na* KI.MIN
22 ^{d}*m*[*i-il-qar-tu* ^{d}*ia-s*]*u*!*-mu-na* KI.MIN
23 ^{d}*k*⸢*ù*⸣!*-b*[*a-ba* ^{d}*kar*]*-hu-ha* KI.MIN
24 ^{d}IM ^{d}[*x*] ⸢*x* ^{d}!*ra*!*-ma*!*-nu*!⸣
25 *ša* UR[U.*di-maš-qa* KI.MIN]
26 ^{d}*za-*[*x x x x x x x x*]
rest broken away

be closed and [......; may] robbers [...] the door of [his] people [......], may he sleep [......];

vi 1 may [*locusts*] appear and devour his land, may [...] blind their eyes; may [*a city of*] one thousand houses decrease to one house, may one thousand tents decrease to one tent, may (just) one man be spared in the city to (proclaim my) glory.

---

6 You are sworn by Aššur, king of heaven and earth!

7 Ditto by Anu and Antu! Ditto by Illil and Mullissu!

8 Ditto by Ea and Damkina! Ditto by Sin and Nikkal!

9 Ditto by Šamaš and *Nur*! Ditto by Adad and Šala!

10 Ditto by Marduk and Zarpanitu! Ditto by Nabû and Tašmetu!

11 Ditto by Ninurta and Gula! Ditto by Uraš and Ninegal!

12 Ditto by Zababa and Babu! Ditto by Nergal and Laṣ!

13 Ditto by Madanu and Ningirsu!

14 Ditto by Humhummu and Išum!

15 Ditto by Girra and Nusku! Ditto by Ištar, Lady of Nineveh!

16 Ditto by Ištar, Lady of Arbela!

17 Ditto by Adad of Kurbail!

18 Ditto by Hadad of Aleppo!

19 Ditto by Palil, who marches in front!

20 Ditto by the heroic Pleiades!

21 Ditto by Dagan and [*M*]*uṣ*uruna!

22 Ditto by M[elqarth and Esh]mun!

23 Ditto by Kub[aba and Kar]huha!

24 Ditto by Hadad, [...] and Ramman of [Damascus]!

26 [Ditto by] ...[......]!

(Break)

VI 21 ⸢d⸣[*m*]*u-ṣur-u-na*: The determinative actually does look more like UR[U], as copied by Weidner, but the reading ⸢d⸣ also seems within possibilities and has been adopted in view of the continuation. The next sign is either [*m*]*u* or [*š*]*e*. Watanabe suggests that the name be connected with KUR.*mu-ṣu-ru-na*, Iraq 21 154:19. 22f Readings ^{d}*ia-s*]*u-mu-na* and ^{d}*kù-b*[*a-ba* by KW, ^{d}*m*[*i-il-qar-tu*, ^{d}*kar*]*-hu-ha* and ^{d}*ra-ma-nu* by SP. See coll.

Treaties of the Seventh Century B.C.

Bavian Bavian - Rock Sculp

Sennacherib (704-681)

FIG. 5. *Sennacherib facing Aššur and Mullissu, from the Bavian rock reliefs.*
ORIGINAL DRAWING II, 25.

COURTESY TRUSTEES OF THE BRITISH MUSEUM

3. Sennacherib's Succession Treaty

VAT 11449

beginning broken away

1′ [*x x x x ša* ^{md}30—PAB.M]EŠ$^!$—⸢SU⸣ MAN$^!$ KUR—*aš-šu*[*r*.KI EN-*ku-nu*]

2′ [*x x x x iš*]-⸢*ku*$^!$⸣-*na-k*[*a-nu-ni*] *a-bu-tú* ⸢*la*$^!$ *de*$^!$⸣-*iq*-⸢*tú*⸣ [*ta-šam-ma-a-ni*]

3′ [*la ta-qab-ba*]-⸢*a*$^!$-*ni*$^!$⸣ *a-na* ^{md}30—PAB.MEŠ—SU MAN KUR—*aš-šur*.[KI EN-*ku-nu*]

4′ [*la ta-lak-a-ni-ni* Š]À$^!$-⸢*ba*$^!$⸣-*ku-nu a-na* LUGAL EN-*ku-nu* ⸢*la*$^!$ *ga*$^!$⸣-*mur*-[*u-ni* 0]

5′ [*šum-ma* ^{m}*aš-šur*—PAB—AŠ DUMU—MAN GAL *ša* É—UŠ-*ti ù*] ⸢*re-eh*⸣-*ti* DUMU.MEŠ LUGAL [*ša* ^{md}30—PAB.MEŠ—SU]

6′ [MAN KUR—*aš-šur*.KI *ú-kal-lim*]-⸢*ú*$^!$⸣-*ka-nu-ni la ta-na-ṣar-šá-n*[*u*$^!$-*ni* 0]

7′ [*aš-šur* ^{d}NIN.LÍL ^{d}*še-ru-u-a*] ⸢^{d}⸣30 ^{d}NIN.GAL ^{d}UTU ^{d}⸢A⸣.[A 0]

8′ [^{d}*a-num an-tum* ^{d}EN.LÍL ^{d}IM ^{d}*š*]*a-la* ^{d}*kip-pat*—KUR [0]

9′ [^{d}15 *ša* AN-*e* ^{d}15 *ša* URU.NINA.KI] ^{d}15 *ša* URU.[*arba-ìl*.KI]

10′ [^{d}15 *aš-šur-i-tú* ^{d}*za-ba*$_4$-*ba*$_4$ ^{d}BA].Ú ^{d}MAŠ ^{d}PA.⸢TÚG$^?$ *x*⸣ [*x x*]

11′ [DINGIR.MEŠ *šá* É.*á-ki-it x x x ar*]-*rat la nap-šur ma-r*[*u-uš-tu*]

12′ [*li-ru-ru-ku-nu x x x x x x i*]*na* URU—^{d}⸢*aš-šur lik*$^?$⸣-*x*[*x x x x*]

rest broken away

Rev. beginning broken away

1′ [*x x x x x x x x x x*] *ṣab ina* ŠÀ-*bi-šú x*[*x x x x x x x x x*]

2′ [*aš-šur* ^{d}NIN.LÍL ^{d}*še-ru-u-a*] ⸢^{d}⸣30 ^{d}NIN.GAL ^{d}UTU [^{d}A.A 0]

3′ [^{d}*a-num an-tum* ^{d}E]N.LÍL ^{d}IM ^{d}*ša-la* [^{d}GAM—KUR ^{d}15 *šá* AN-*e*]

4′ [^{d}15 *ša* NINA.KI ^{d}15 *šá arba*]-*ìl*.[K]I ^{d}15 *aš-šur*-[*i-tú* ^{d}*za-ba*$_4$-*ba*$_4$ ^{d}BA.Ú]

5′ ^{d}É.A DINGIR.MAH ^{d}*dam-ki-na* ^{d}GA.G]A ^{d}U.GUR DINGIR.MEŠ [*ša* É.*á-ki-it*$^?$]

6′ [*x x x ar-rat la nap-šur ma-ru-u*]*š*$^!$-*tu li*-[*ru-ru-ku-nu*]

7′ [*x x x x x x x x x x x x*]-⸢*ku*⸣-*nu ina nap-har* K[UR$^?$.KUR *x x x x x x*]

8′ [*x x x x x x x x x x x x in*]*a* É.*á-ki*-⸢*it*$^!$⸣ [*x x x x x x x x*]

rest broken away

PKTA 31

(Beginning destroyed)

1 [...... which Sennach]erib, king of Assyr[ia, your lord], has *set to* you;

2 [If you should hear] improper things, you shall speak out [going] to Sennacherib, king of Assyria, [your lord], and totally devote yourselves to the king, your lord;

5 you shall protect [*Esarhaddon*, the crown prince designate, and] the other princes [whom Sennacherib, king of Assyria, has presen]ted to you;(otherwise):

7 [May Aššur, Mullissu, Šerua], Sin, Nikkal, Šamaš, *Nu*[*r*, Anu, Antu, Illil, Adad, Š]ala, Kippat-mati, [Ištar of Heaven, Ištar of Nineveh], Ištar of [Arbela, the Assyrian Ištar, Zababa, Ba]bu, Ninurta, Nusku, and [..., the gods of the Akitu Chapel ... curse you with] an indissoluble, grievous curse [...] in the city of Aššur [...]

(Break)

r.1 [...] in his heart [...],

2 May [Aššur, Mullissu, Šerua], Sin, Nikkal, Šamaš, [*Nur*, Anu, Antu, I]llil, Adad, Šala, [Kippat-mati, Ištar of Heaven, Ištar of Nineveh, Ištar of Arb]ela, the Assyrian Ištar, [Zababa, Babu, Ea, Belet-ili, Kakk]a, and Nergal, the gods [of the Akitu Chapel ... curse you with an indissoluble, griev]ous [curse, may they ...] your [...] in all *l*[*ands*...] the Akitu Chapel [...]

(Rest destroyed)

3 Previous edition with full discussion: S. Parpola, JCS 39 (1987) 178ff and 163f. The order of obverse and reverse has been tentatively inverted in the present edition following a suggestion of Watanabe.

COURTESY TRUSTEES OF THE BRITISH MUSEUM

FIG. 6. *The Assyrian crown prince (reign of Sennacherib).*
ORIGINAL DRAWING VI, 46.

Esarhaddon (680-669)

FIG. 7. *Esarhaddon holding on a leash Baal of Tyre and Ušanahuru, crown prince of Egypt. Flanking the stela, the Assyrian crown princes Assurbanipal and Šamaš-šumu-ukin.*
VA 2708. *Drawing by J. Börker-Klähn, Altorientalische Bildstelen und vergleichbare Felsreliefs II (1982), no.* 219.

4. Accession Treaty of Esarhaddon

83-1-18,420 (+) 83-1-18,493 (CT 53 937) (+) Bu 91-5-9,131 — JCS 39 187

Obv. destroyed

Rev. beginning broken away

1′ [x x x x x x x x x x x]-⌜lu⌝-n[i x x x x]

2′ [x x x x x x x x x] ⌜i⌝-si-t⌜a⌝-[te x x x]x a-na L[Ú.x x x]

3′ [x x x a-na a-l]ik hu-li a-qab-bi [x x x x a]-na ZAG ⌜ù⌝ [KAB a-šap-par]

4′ [ù šúm-ma a-na-k]u a-bat-su la ⌜de⌝-i[q-t]ú [TA* pi]-i NUMUN-šú a-šam-mu-[u-ni]

5′ [ú-la-a šúm-ma] TA* pi-i ša 1-en T[A* ŠÀ L]Ú.GAL.MEŠ [LÚ.NAM.MEŠ]

6′ [TA* pi-i 1-en T]A* ŠÀ LÚ.šá—ziq-ni ú-la-a TA* pi-⌜i⌝ [1-en LÚ.SAG.MEŠ]

7′ [a-šam-mu-u-ni] ù a-na ^{m}aš-šur—PAB$^{!!}$—[SUM]-na EN-iá la a-qab-b[u-u-ni]

8′ [šúm-ma la ARAD-šú] a-na-ku-u-ni ù [de-i]q-tú-šú la a-zak-k[ar-u-ni]

9′ [šúm-ma e-ni-šú la] ⌜a⌝-dag-gal-⌜u-ni⌝ [pa-n]i šá ^{m}aš-šur—PAB—SUM-na E[N-iá]

10′ [x x x x x x x x x x x x x x šú]m-ma a-na-ku ma-mit [x x]

11′ [x x x x x x x x x]x ⌜ur hu⌝ [ma-mit p]a-šá-a-ru e-pa-šu-[u-ni]

12′ [x x x x x x e-pa]-šu-u-ni ù šúm-ma at-ta [x x x]

13′ [x x x x x x te]-pa-šu-u-ni ù šúm-[ma] at-ta [x x x]

14′ [x x x x x x x] te-pa-šu-u-ni ù šúm-m[a a]t-t[a x x x]

15′ [x x x x x x x]-ʾi-i šá pa-šá-a-ri šá [x x]x[x x x x]

16′ [AN.ŠÁR AD DINGIR.MEŠ LUGAL k]iš-šat AN-e u KI.TIM še-ret-s[u kab-tú li-mid-su]

17′ [x x x x x x x]x-ma ina ma-har DINGIR u LUGAL e-[reb-šú a-a iq-bi]

18′ [^{d}NIN.LÍL AMA GAL-tú hi]-ir-tu na-ram-ta-[šu x x x]

19′ [x x x x x x ṭè]-e-šú li-šá-ni x[x x x x]

20′ [^{d}15 be-let MURUB$_4$ u MÈ ina t]a-ha-a-zi dan-ni [GIŠ.BAN-šú liš-bir]

(Beginning destroyed)

r.1 [...... t]ower[s ...] I shall tell [...] to [... and] trav[ellers, *I shall send messengers*] to the south and [the north ...].

4 Should I he[ar an ug]ly word about him [from the mou]th of his progeny, [should I hear it] from the mouth of one of the magnates or [governors], [from the mouth of one o]f the bearded or from the mouth of [the eunuchs], I will go and tell it to Esarhaddon, my lord;

8 I [will] be [his servant] and speak good of him, I [will be] loyal to him and [... the *fa*]*ce* of Esarhaddon my lord, [...];

10 I will [keep] the oath [*of this treaty tablet*] and not perform the (rite of) undoing the [oath ...] or make [...].

12 Also, you shall not make [...], and you shall not make [...], and you shall not [......] of undoing ...[...]. (Whoever sins against this treaty tablet:)

16 [May Aššur, father of the gods, and king] of the totality of heaven and earth, [impose a heavy] punishment [upon him ... and forbid his ent]ering into the presence of god and king.

18 May [Mullissu, the great mother, his] beloved wife [...] alter his [mind].

20 [May Ištar, lady of warfare, break his

4 Editio princeps with discussion and commentary: S. Parpola, JCS 39 (1987) 170ff and 163. r.3 "to the south and [the north]": or "to right and [left]." The implication is in both cases "everywhere." Cf. crit. note on 6:634f. 7 PAB written AŠ (scribal slip).

21′ [*ina šá-pal* LÚ.KÚR-*šú l*]*i-še-ši-ib-šú ka-mì-iš* [0?]
22′ [^{d}UTU *x x x x x* GI]Š.*zi-ba-ni-tum la kit-ti* [*x x x*]
23′ [*x x x x x x* L]AK *ina re-bit* URU-*šú* [*x x x*]
24′ [^{d}NIN.GAL? *x x x x x x*]-*bi ina ma-har* ^{d}30 [*ha-*ʾ*i-ri-šá*]
25′ [*ab-bu-su a-a iṣ-bat a-mat*]-*su li-lam-mìn* [*x x x*]
26′ [^{d}U.GUR *dan-dan-nu* DINGIR.MEŠ *ina*] *šib-ṭi ù* NAM.ÚŠ.MEŠ [*x x x*]
27′ [*x x x x x x li-qa*]*t-ta-a* UN.MEŠ-[*šú* 0?]
28′ [*x x x x x x x i*]*š-*⌈*di-šu*⌉ *li-*⌈*x*⌉[*x x x x*]
rest broken away

bow in] the thick of battle, and have him crouch as a captive [under his enemy].

22 [May Šamaš ......] untruthful scales [......] in the plaza of his city.

24 [May Nikkal ...] worsen his case [and not intercede for him] in the presence of Sin [her husband].

26 [May Nergal, *the strongest among the gods*,] destroy [his] people through plague and pestilence [...

(Rest destroyed)

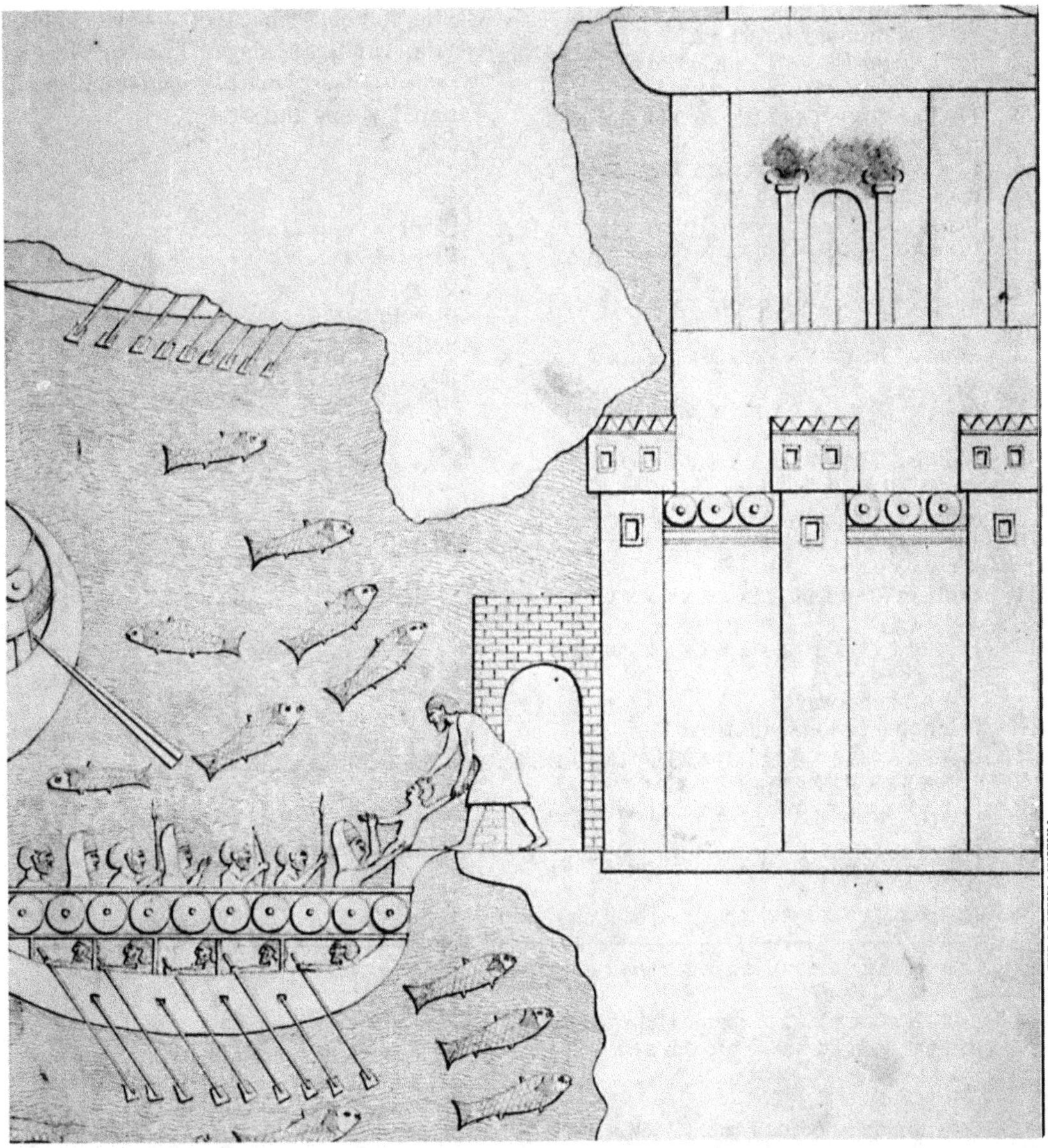

COURTESY TRUSTEES OF THE BRITISH MUSEUM

FIG. 8. *Phoenician ships and a city, probably Tyre; scene continues to left in Fig. 9 (reign of Sennacherib).* ORIGINAL DRAWING IV, 8.

5. Esarhaddon's Treaty with Baal, King of Tyre

K 3500 + K 4444 + K 10235 (+) Sm 964 (unpub.)

Borger Esarh. pl.3 (+) unpub.

I 1 [*a-de*]-*e šá* ^{m}⸢*aš-šur*⸣—PAB$^{!}$—⸢AŠ$^{!}$⸣ M[AN$^{!}$] KUR—*aš-šur*.KI DUMU $^{m!}$⸢$^{d!}$⸣[30—PAB.MEŠ—SU MAN KUR—*aš-šur*.KI-*ma*]
2 [TA* ^{m}*ba-a-l*]*u* MAN KUR.*ṣur-ri* TA* ^{m}*x*[*x x x x x x x x x x x x x x x*]
3 [TA* KUR.*ṣur-ri gab-b*]*i*$^{!}$-*šú*$^{!}$ TUR GAL [*x x x x x x x x x x x x x*]
4 [*x x x x x*] ⸢*x x x*⸣ [*x x x x x x x x x x x x x*]
break
5′ ⸢*lu-u x x*⸣ [*x x x x x x x x x x x x x x x x x x x x*]
6′ *lu-u e*-[*x x x x x x x x x x x x x x x x x x x x*]
7′ *lu-u* TA* [*x x x x x x x x x x x x x x x x x x x x*]
8′ *la* ⸢*x x*⸣ [*x x x x x x x x x x x x x x x x x x x*]
9′ *šúm-ma la x*[*x x x x x x x x x x x x x x x x x*]

10′ *šúm-ma* KUR—*aš-š*[*ur x x x x x x x x x x x x x x x x x*]
11′ [*na*$^{?}$]-*ṣa-ku-nu ma-a* [*x x x x x x x x x x x x x x x x*]
12′ [*x*] ⸢*ha x x*⸣ [*x x x x x x x x x x x x x x x x x x x*]
rest broken away
II beginning (7 lines) destroyed
8 [*x x x x x x x x x x x x x x x x x*] ⸢*x*⸣ [*x x x*]
9 [*x x x x x x x x x x x x x x x x x*] ⸢*x x*⸣ [*x x*]
10 [*x x x x x x x x x x x x x x x x x a*]-*na*$^{!}$ *pi*-⸢*i*⸣ [*x*]
11 [*x x x x x x x x x x x x x x x x*]*x lid*$^{!}$-*x*[*x x*]
12 [*x x x x x x x x x x x x x x x x x*] *áš*$^{!}$ [*x x*]

---

13 [*x x x x x x x x x x x x x x x x ina* UG]U$^{!}$ LÚ*$^{!}$.*zak*$^{!}$-[*ke-e*]
14 [*x x x x x x x x x x x x x x x x x x x*] *x*[*x x x*]
rest (at least 20 lines) broken away

i 1 [The treat]y of Esarhad[don, king] of Assyria, son of [Sennacherib, likewise king of Assyria, with Baa]l, king of Tyre, with [..., *his son, and his other sons and grandsons*, with a]ll [Tyrians], young and old [...

(Break)
5 or ...[......]
6 or [......]
7 or with [......]
8 not[......]
9 if [......] not ...[......]

---

10 If Assyr[ia ......]
11 ... you [......]...[......]
(Break)

ii 10 [......] according to [...]
11 [......] let [...]
12 [......] ...[...]

---

13 [...... *t*]*o the ex*[*empt*]
(Break)

5 Previous edition: Borger Esarh. (1956), p. 107ff. → E. Reiner, ANET[3] (1969), p. 533ff; Borger, TUAT 1/2 (1983), p. 158f.
I [1, 3] See coll. [5-12] Placement of the fragment Sm 964 here and copy p. 123 by KW.
II [8ff] All readings by SP; see copy.

Reverse

III beginning broken away

1′ [*x x x x x x x x x x x x x x* T]A! UGU! UD?-*m*[*e*? *x*] *a*!-*d*[*i*? *x x x x x*]

2′ [*x x x x x x x x x x x x x*].MEŠ-*šú-nu* m*aš-šur*—PAB—AŠ MAN KUR—*aš*-[*šur*.KI *x x x x*]

3′ [*x x x x x x x x x* URU.*ṣu*]*r*-[*r*]*i ina* UGU-*hi la* ⸢*x x*⸣ [*x x x x x*]

4′ [*x x x x x x x x an-n*]*u-te* URU.MEŠ *an-nu-te šá ah-pu-n*[*i x x x x*]

5′ [*x x x x x x x x x x*]*x il-la-ku-u-ni-ni* ⸢*la*! *ta*!-*šap*!-*par*! *la tu*⸣-*š*[*e*!-*ba-la-šú-nu*]

iii 1 [......] from ... until [......]

2 [......] their [...]s; Esarhaddon, king of As[syria ......]

3 [......] will not [...] upon it [...]

4 [......] these [...]s and these cities which I destroyed [......]

5 you must not send nor desp[atch] the [... which] (may) come [...].

6′ [*x x* LÚ*.*qe-e-pu šá ina*] UGU-*hi-ka áš-kun-u-ni* ⸢*me*!-*me*!-*ni ina*! *na*!⸣-*x*[*x x x x x x*]

7′ [*x x x x x x*]-*ka* LÚ.*par-šá-mu-te šá* KUR-*ka ina mil*-⸢*ki*⸣ [*x x x x x x*]

8′ [*x x x x x*]-*u-ni* LÚ*.*qe-e-pu is-si-šú-nu i*-[*x x x x x x x*]

9′ [*x x x x x x*]*x* ⸢*x šá* GIŠ⸣.MÁ.MEŠ *x*[*x x x x x x x x x x*]

10′ [*x x x x x x x x x x x x x*] *šá* [*x x x x*] *aš x*[*x x x x x*]

11′ [*x x x x x x x x x x x x x*] *šá ina* IGI-⸢*ka*!⸣ *ta*!-*lak-an*-[*ni la x x x*]

12′ [*x x x x x x šá*] *pi-i-šú la ta-šá-me* ⸢*šúm*⸣-*ma ba-la-at* LÚ*.[*qe*]-*e-bi*! [*x x x x*]

13′ *ù e-gír-tú* ⸢*šá*⸣ *a-šap-par-kan-ni ba-la-at* LÚ*.*qe-e*-⸢*bi*!⸣ *la ta-pat-t*[*i* 0]

14′ *šúm-ma* LÚ*.*qe-e-pu la qur-bu ina* IGI-*šú ta-da-gal ta-pat-ti ú-la-a* LÚ*!.A!—⸢KIN! *x*⸣

6 [*If* the royal deputy whom] I have appointed over you [...] *anything in* [...]

7 [...] the elders of your country [*convene to take*] counsel

8 the royal deputy [will ...] with them [......]

9 [......] of the ships [......]

(Break)

11 [You may not ... any ship ...] which comes to you; [if ......], do not listen to him, [do not ...] without the royal deputy; nor must you open a letter which I send you without the royal deputy. If the royal deputy is absent, wait for him and then open it, or [...] the messenger.

15′ *šúm-ma* GIŠ.MÁ *šá* m*ba-a-lu lu šá* UN.MEŠ KUR.*ṣur-ri šá ina* KUR.*pi-lis-ti lu ta-hu-me*

16′ *ša* KUR—*aš-šur*.KI *gab-bu ta-mah-ha-ṣu-u-ni am—mar šá ina* ŠÀ GIŠ.MÁ-*ni šá* m*aš-šur*—PAB—AŠ MAN KUR—*aš-šur*.K[I]

17′ *ù* UN.MEŠ *am—mar šá ina* ŠÀ GIŠ.MÁ *ina* ŠÀ-*šú-nu* ⸢*la*⸣ *i-ha-ṭi-u* ⸢*ina* KUR⸣-*šú-nu ú-sa-hu*!-⸢*ru*!⸣

15 If there is a ship of Baal or the people of Tyre that is shipwrecked off the land of the Philistines or within Assyrian territory, everything that is on the ship belongs to Esarhaddon, king of Assyria; however, one must not do any harm to any person on board the ship but one must return them all to their country.

18′ *an-nu-te* KAR.MEŠ KASKAL.MEŠ *šá* m*aš-šur*—PAB—AŠ MAN KUR—*aš-šur a-na* m*ba-a-lu* ARAD-*šú* ⸢*ip-qi*⸣-[*du-ni*]

19′ *a-na* URU.*a-ku-u* URU.*du-u*ʾ-*ri ina na-gi-e* KUR.*pi-lis-te gab*-[*bu* 0!]

20′ *ù ina* URU.MEŠ *ta-hu-me šá* KUR—*aš-šur*.KI *šá ši-di tam-tim gab*-[*bu* 0]

21′ *ù ina* URU.*gu-ub-lu* KUR.*lab-na*-[*na*] URU.MEŠ *šá ina* KUR-*i gab-b*[*u* 0]

22′ *am—mar* URU.MEŠ [*šá* m*aš-š*]*ur*—PAB—AŠ MAN KUR—*aš-šur* m*ba-a-lu* URU.MEŠ [*x x*]

23′ KUR.*ṣur-ra-a-a* ⸢*pit*!-*ti*! *šá*⸣ m*aš-šur*—PAB—AŠ MAN KUR—*aš-šur*.[KI] *i-din*!-[*áš-šú-ni*]

18 These are the ports of trade and the trade routes which Esarhaddon, king of Assyria, [entrusted] to his servant Baal: to Akko, Dor, to the entire district of the Philistines, and to all the cities within Assyrian territory on the seacoast, and to Byblos, the Lebanon, all the cities in the mountains, all (these) being cities of Esarhaddon, king of Assyria.

22 Baal [*may enter these*] cities. The people of Tyre [will], in accordance with what Esarhaddon, king of Assyria, has *per*[*mitted,*

III 1 See coll. 6 At the beginning of the line restore probably [*šúm-ma*; at end of line, *me-me-ni* etc. written over an erasure. 14, 17, 24 See coll.

COURTESY TRUSTEES OF THE BRITISH MUSEUM

FIG. 9. *Phoenician ships; scene continues to right in Fig. 8.*
ORIGINAL DRAWING IV, 7.

24′ *ina* ŠÀ GIŠ.MÁ.MEŠ-*šú-nu ù am—mar e*$^{!}$-⸢*rab*$^{!}$⸣-*u-ni ina* ŠÀ URU.MEŠ *šá* ^{m}[*x x x*]
25′ URU.MEŠ-*šú* URU.ŠE.MEŠ-*šú* KAR.MEŠ-*šú ša a-na na-še-e* [*x x x x xx x*]
26′ *am—mar a-hi-ta-te-šú-nu-u-ni ki-i šá ina la-bi-*[*ri x x x x x x x*]
27′ *in-na-*⸢*ga*⸣-*ru-u-ni me-me-ni pi-ir-k*[*u x x x x x x x x*]
28′ *ina* ŠÀ GIŠ.MÁ.MEŠ-*šú-nu la i-ha-ṭi ina* ŠÀ K[UR.*x x x x x x x xx x*]
29′ *ina na-gi-šú* URU.ŠE.MEŠ-*šú e-rim-tú* [*x x x x x x x x x x*]
30′ *ki-i šá la-bi-ri* KUR.*ṣi-du-*[*na-a-a x x x x x x x x x x*]
IV beginning broken away
1′ ^{d}[NIN.LÍL *a-ši-bat* URU.NINA.KI GÍR.AN.BAR *ha-an-ṭu it-ti-ku-nu li-ir-ku-su*]
2′ ^{d}IŠ.TAR ⸢*a*⸣-[*ši-bat* URU.*arba-ìl re-e-mu gim-lu lu la i-šá-kan* U]GU-*ku-un*
3′ ^{d}*gu-la a-zu-gal-la-t*[*ú* GAL-*tú* GIG *ta-né-hu ina* ŠÀ-*bi-k*]*u-nu*
4′ *si-im-mu la-zu ina zu-mur-ku-n*[*u liš-kun da-a-mu u šar-ku ki-ma* A.MEŠ] *ru*$^{!}$-*un-ka*
5′ ^{d}*si-bit-te* DINGIR.MEŠ *qar-du-te ina* GIŠ.TUKUL.MEŠ-*šú-nu* [*ez-zu-ti na-áš-pan-ta-k*]*u-nu liš-kun*
6′ ^{d}*ba-a-a-ti—*DINGIR.MEŠ ^{d}*a-na-ti—ba-*⸢*a*⸣-[*a-ti—*DINGI]R.MEŠ
7′ *ina* ŠU.2 UR.MAH *a-ki-*⸢*li*⸣ [*lim-nu-u-k*]*u-nu*
8′ DINGIR.MEŠ GAL.MEŠ *šá* AN-*e ù* KI.TIM DINGIR.MEŠ KUR—*aš-šur*.KI DINGIR.MEŠ KUR.URI.KI
9′ DINGIR.MEŠ *e-bir—*ÍD *ar-rat la nap-šú-ri li-ru-ru-*⸢*ku*⸣-*nu*
10′ ^{d}*ba-al—sa-me-me* ^{d}*ba-al—ma-la-ge-e* ^{d}*ba-al—ṣa-pu-nu*
11′ TU$_{15}$ *lem-nu ina* GIŠ.MÁ.MEŠ-*ku-nu lu-šat-ba* GIŠ.*mar-kas-ši-na lip-ṭu-ur*
12′ GIŠ.*ṭar-kul-la-ši-na li-is-su-hu e-du-u dan-nu ina* [*tam-t*]*im*
13′ *li-ṭa-bi-ši-na šam-ru a-gu-u e-li-ku-nu li-l*[*i-a*]
14′ ^{d}*mi-il-qar-tu* ^{d}*ia-su-mu-nu* KUR-*ku-nu a-na ha-p*[*e*$^{!}$]-⸢*e*$^{!}$⸣
15′ UN.MEŠ-*ku-nu a-na šá-la-li li-di-nu* TA* KUR-*ku-nu* [*lis-su-h*]*u*$^{!}$-⸢*ku*$^{!}$-*nu*$^{!}$⸣
16′ ŠUKU.MEŠ *ina pi-i-ku-nu ku-zip-pi*$^{!}$ *ina la-ni-ku-nu* [0$^{?}$]
e.17′ Ì.MEŠ *ina pa-šá-ši-ku-nu lu-hal-li-qu* [0]
18′ ^{d}*as-tar-tú ina ta-ha-zi dan-ni* GIŠ.BAN-⸢*ku-nu li-*(*iš*)*-bir ina šap*⸣-*l*[*a* LÚ*.KÚR-*ku-nu*]
19′ *li-še-ši-ib-ku-nu* LÚ*.KÚR *a-hu-u li-za-i-za mim-*[*mu-ku-nu*]
20′ *ṭup-pi a-d*[*e*]-*e kun-nu šá* ^{m}*ba-a-lu* KUR.*ṣu*[*r-ra-a-a*]
21′ (uninscribed space) *ina*$^{!}$ [*x x x*]

stay] in their ships, and all those who enter into the towns of [...], his towns, his villages, his ports of trade which [...] for collecting [*toll* ...], and all (the places) in their outskirts, will [*pay toll*], as in the past.

27 Nobody will [do] injustice [*to those*] who are hired [...] and nobody will harm their ships. In the coun[try of ...], in his district, in his villages ...[...] the people of Sidon [...] as in the past [...

(Break)

iv 1 [May Mullissu, who resides in Nineveh, tie to you a flaming sword].

2 [May] Ištar, [who resides in Arbela, not grant] you [mercy and forgiveness].

3 May Gula, the great physician, [put illness and weariness in] your [hearts] and an unhealing sore in your body; bathe [in blood and pus as if in water]!

5 May the Pleiades, the heroic gods, [smi]te you [down] with their [fierce] weapons.

6 May Bethel and Anath-Bethel [deliver] you to the paws of a man-eating lion.

8 May the great gods of heaven and earth, the gods of Assyria, the gods of Akkad and the gods of Eber-nari curse you with an indissoluble curse.

10 May Baal Shamaim, Baal Malagê and Baal Saphon raise an evil wind against your ships to undo their moorings and tear out their mooring pole, may a strong wave sink them in the sea and a violent tide [rise] against you.

14 May Melqarth and Eshmun deliver your land to destruction and your people to deportation; may they [uproot] you from your land and take away the food from your mouth, the clothes from your body, and the oil for your anointing.

18 May Astarte break your bow in the thick of battle and have you crouch at the feet of your enemy, may a foreign enemy divide your belongings.

20 Tablet of the treaty established with Baal of Tyre in [......].

IV 16 ŠUKU.MEŠ "food": possibly rather NINDA.MEŠ "bread", see Borger, ZA 54 183[3].

6. Esarhaddon's Succession Treaty

ND 4336 and duplicates

i NA$_4$.KIŠIB ^{d}*a-šur*$_4$ LUGAL DINGIR.MEŠ
ii EN KUR.KUR *ša la šu-un-né-e*
iii NA$_4$.KIŠIB NUN-*e* GAL-*e* AD DINGIR.MEŠ
iv *ša la pa-qa-a-ri*

Seal of the god Aššur, king of the gods, lord of the lands - not to be altered; seal of the great ruler, father of the gods - not to be disputed.

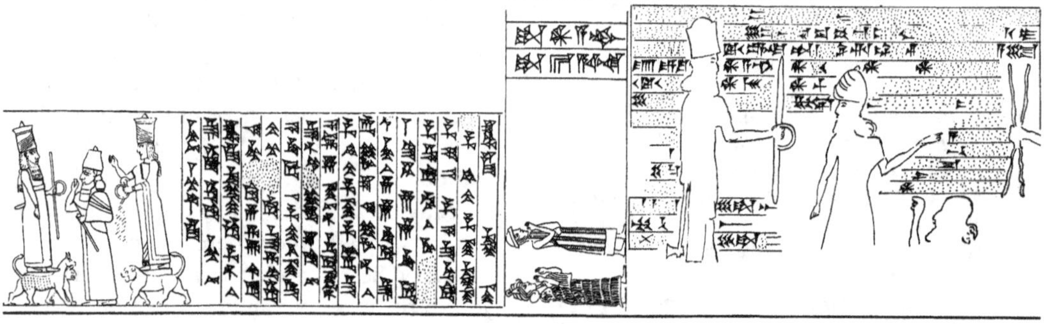

1 *a-de-e ša* ^{m}*aš-šur*—PAB—AŠ (MAN ŠÚ) MAN KUR—*aš-šur*.(KI)
2 DUMU ^{md}30—PAB.MEŠ—SU (MAN ŠÚ) MAN KUR—*aš-šur-*(*ma*)
3 TA* ^{m}*hum-ba-re-eš* LÚ.EN—URU URU.*na-ah-ši-mar-ti*
4 (TA*) DUMU.MEŠ-*šú* DUMU—DUMU.MEŠ-*šú* TA* URU.*na-ah-ši-mar-ta-a-a*
5 LÚ.ERIM.MEŠ ŠU.2-*šú gab-bu* TUR (*u*) GAL *ma-la ba-šu-u*
6 TA* *na-pa-ah* ^{d}UTU-*ši a-di ra-ba* ^{d}*šam-ši*
7 *am—mar* ^{m}*aš-šur*—PAB—AŠ MAN KUR—*aš-šur* LUGAL-*tu be-lu-tu*
8 *ina* UGU-*hi-šú-nu up-pa-áš-u-ni*
9 *is-si-ku-nu* (TA*) DUMU.MEŠ-*ku-nu* DUMU—DUMU.MEŠ-*ku-nu*
10 *ša* EGIR *a-de-e a-na* UD-*me ṣa-a-ti ib-ba-áš-šú-u-ni*

§ 1 Preamble

1 The treaty of Esarhaddon, (king of the world), king of Assyria, son of Sennacherib, (likewise king of the world), king of Assyria, with Humbareš, city-ruler of Nahšimarti (etc.), his sons, his grandsons, with all the Nahšimartians (etc.), the men in his hands young and old, as many as there are from sunrise to sunset, all those over whom Esarhaddon, king of Assyria, exercises kingship and lordship, (with) you, your sons and your grandsons who will be born in days to come after this treaty,

6 Previous editions: D.J. Wiseman, VTE (1958), K. Watanabe, BaM Bh 3 (1987); → E. Reiner, ANET^3 (1969), p. 534ff; R. Borger, TUAT 1/2 (1983), p. 160ff.

i ^{d}*a-šur*$_4$ AFHTa: ^{d}*aš-šur* G. iii NUN-*e* AFH: LÚ.⌈NUN⌉-[*e* I. 1 —PAB—AŠ AGFHTd: —ŠEŠ—SUM-*na* a; MAN ŠÚ AFTHa: caret Gd; KUR—*aš-šur*.KI Fd: .KI omitted in AGHTa. For the rendering "treaty of" (not: "treaty which") see Introduction. 2 MAN ŠÚ AFHa: caret GTd; KUR—*aš-šur-ma* AF: KUR—*aš-šur* GHa, KUR—*aš-šur*.KI Td. 3 Thus H, var. ^{m}*ra-ma-ta-a-a* EN—URU *ú-ra-ka-za-ba-nu* A, ^{m}*bur—da-di* LÚ.EN—URU *kar-zi-ta-li* G, ^{m}*tu-ni-i* EN—URU KUR.*el-pa-a-a* F, ^{m}*ha-tar-na* EN—URU URU.*sik-ri-si* T, ^{m}*la-ar-ku-ut-la* LÚ.EN—URU KUR—*za-mu-u-a* a, [PN] EN—URU URU.*i-za-a-a* d. 4 TA* AGa: caret FHT; DUMU—DUMU.MEŠ- AFGHTd: ŠEŠ.MEŠ-*šú qin-ni-šú* NUMUN É—AD-*šú* a; URU.*na-ah-ši-mar-ta-a-a* H: URU.⌈*ú-ra-ka*⌉-*za-ba-nu-a-a* A, URU.*kar-zi-ta-li-a-a* G, KUR.*el-pa-a-a* F, URU.*sik-ri-sa-a-a* T. 5 LÚ.ERIM.MEŠ ŠU.2-*šú* GFHTad: caret A; TUR u GAL F: TUR GAL AGHTa; *ma-la* GFH: *mal* AT; *ba-šu-u* F: -*ú* G, *ba-šú-u* AH, -*ú* T. 6 *na-pa-ah* GFHTa: *na-pah* A; ^{d}UTU-*ši* AFHTa: ^{d}*šam-ši* G; *ra-ba* FT: *ra-bé-e* H, *e-reb* AG; ^{d}*šam-ši* GF: ^{d}UTU-*ši* ATH. 7 LUGAL-*tu* AGF: -*tú* T, -*u-tu* H; *be-lu-tu* A: EN-*tu* GF, -*tú* T, -*u-tu* H. 8 UGU-*hi-šú-nu* GFHTa: UGU-*šú-nu* A; *up-pa-áš-u-ni* GF: *up-pa-áš-ú-ni* T: *up-pa-šú-u-ni* H: *ú-ba-šu-u-ni* A. 9 TA* T: caret AFGHa. Lines 9f follow line 5 in A. 10 *ša* AFGHa: *šá* T; a-na FHTa: *ina* AG; *ib-ba-áš-šú-u-ni* FH: *i*[*b-ba*]-*šu-u-ni* G, *ib-ba-šu-ú-*[*ni*] T, *ib-ba-šú-u-ni* A.

11 (*šá ina* UGU ^{m}*aš-šur*—DÙ—A DUMU—MAN GAL *ša* É—UŠ-*ti* DUMU ^{m}*aš-šur*—PAB—AŠ
12 MAN KUR—*aš-šur ša ina* UGU-*hi-šú a-de-e is-si-ku-nu iš-ku-nu-ni*)

---

13 *ina* IGI MUL.SAG.ME.GAR MUL.*dil-bat*
14 MUL.UDU.IDIM.SAG.UŠ MUL.UDU.IDIM.GUD.UD
15 MUL.*ṣal-bat-a-nu* MUL.GAG.SI.SÁ
16 *ina* IGI ^{d}*aš-šur* ^{d}*a-num* ^{d}EN.L[ÍL] ^{d}É.A
17 ^{d}30 ^{d}*šá-maš* ^{d}IM ^{d}AMAR.UTU
18 ^{d}PA ^{d}PA.TÚG ^{d}IB ^{d}U.GUR
19 ^{d}NIN.LÍL ^{d}*še-ru-u-a* ^{d}*be-lit*—DINGIR.MEŠ
20 ^{d}15 *ša* URU.NINA.KI ^{d}15 *ša* URU.*arba-ìl*
21 DINGIR.MEŠ *a-ši-bu-ti* AN-*e* KI.TIM
22 DINGIR.MEŠ KUR—*aš-šur* DINGIR.MEŠ KUR—*šu-me-ri u* [UR]I.[K]I
23 DINGIR.MEŠ KUR.KUR DÙ-*šú-nu ú-dan-nin-*[*u-ni*]
24 *iṣ-ba-tu iš-ku-nu-n*[*i*]

11 (concerning Assurbanipal, the great crown prince designate, son of Esarhaddon, king of Assyria, on behalf of whom he has concluded this treaty with you,)

§ 2 Divine Witnesses

13 (which he) confirmed, made and concluded in the presence of Jupiter, Venus, Saturn, Mercury, Mars and Sirius;

16 in the presence of Aššur, Anu, Ill[il], Ea, Sin, Šamaš, Adad, Marduk, Nabû, Nusku, Uraš, Nergal, Mullissu, Šerua, Belet-ili, Ištar of Nineveh, Ištar of Arbela, the gods dwelling in heaven and earth, the gods of Assyria, the gods of Sumer and [Akka]d, all the gods of the lands.

11f These lines in A only. 12 The referent of *ša* is Assurbanipal, not Esarhaddon (thus BaM Bh 3). 13 MUL.SAG.ME.GAR MUL.*dil-bat* GK: ^{d}SAG.ME.GAR ^{d}*dil-bat* A, MUL.SAG.ME.GAR ^{d}*d*[*il-bat*] frg. 16 ^{d}*aš-šur* GK frg: *aš-šur* A; ^{d}EN.L[ÍL] G: ^{d}BE A. 17 ^{d}*šá-maš* G: ^{d}UTU AKU. 18 ^{d}PA AU: ^{d}AG G frg. 19 ^{d}*be-lit*—DINGIR.MEŠ G: DINGIR.MAH AU; G: ^{d}*še-ru-u-a* not *-šá* (coll. from photo). 20 URU.NINA.KI AG: U frg omit .KI. 21 Thus all MSS (G: AN-⸢*e*⸣ KI.TIM, coll. from photo); cancel the alleged var. AN *ù* KI.TIM. 22 KUR—*aš-šur* G frg: U omits .[K]I; KUR—*šu-me-ri* U: KUR.EME.KU A frg. 23 *ú-dan-nin-*[*u-ni*] A: *ú-dan-ni-*[*nu-ni*] frg. 24 *iṣ-*⸢*ba-tu*⸣ *iš-ku-nu-n*[*i*] A: *iṣ-ṣi-bat-tu iš-ku-nu-*[*ni*] ND 4345A (see coll.; correct BaM Bh 3). The Babylonian subjunctive form *iṣ-ba-tu* (corresponding to NA *iškunūni*)

COURTESY TRUSTEES OF THE BRITISH MUSEUM

FIG. 10. ***Families from Iran, the men still bearing arms, received by Assyrian soldiers (reign of Sennacherib).*** ORIGINAL DRAWING IV, 54.

§ 3 Adjuration

25 ^{d}*aš-šur* AD DINGIR.MEŠ EN KUR.KUR *ti-t[am-ma-a]*
26 ^{d}*a-num* ^{d}EN.LÍL ^{d}É.A MIN
27 ^{d}30 ^{d}*šá-maš* ^{d}IM ^{d}AMAR.UTU MIN
28 ^{d}AG ^{d}PA.TÚG ^{d}IB ^{d}U.GUR MIN
29 ^{d}NIN.LÍL ^{d}*še-ru-u-a* ^{d}*be-lit*—DINGIR.M[EŠ] MIN
30 ^{d}15 *ša* URU.NINA.KI ^{d}15 *ša* URU.*arba-ìl* MIN
31 DINGIR.MEŠ DÙ-*šú-nu ša* URU.ŠÀ—URU MIN
32 DINGIR.MEŠ DÙ-*šú-nu ša* URU.NINA.KI MIN
33 DINGIR.MEŠ DÙ-*šú-nu ša* URU.*kal-ha* MIN
34 DINGIR.MEŠ DÙ-*šú-nu ša* URU.*arba-ìl* MIN
35 DINGIR.MEŠ DÙ-*šú-nu ša* URU.*kàl-zi* MIN
36 DINGIR.MEŠ DÙ-*šú-nu ša* URU.KASKAL MIN
37 DINGIR.MEŠ KÁ.DINGIR.RA.KI BÁR.SIPÁ.KI EN.LÍL.KI (DÙ-*šú-nu*) MIN
38 DINGIR.MEŠ KUR—*aš-šur* (DÙ-*šú-nu* MIN)
39 DINGIR.MEŠ KUR—*šu-me-ri u* URI.KI DÙ-*šú-nu* MIN
40 DINGIR.MEŠ KUR.KUR DÙ-*šú-nu* MIN
40A DINGIR.MEŠ *šá* AN-*e u* KI.TIM DÙ-*šú-nu* MIN
40B [DINGIR].MEŠ KUR-*šu*! *na-gi-šu* DÙ-*šú-nu* MIN

25 Sw[ear ea]ch individually by Aššur, father of the gods, lord of the lands!

26 Ditto by Anu, Illil and Ea!

27 Ditto by Sin, Šamaš, Adad and Marduk!

28 Ditto by Nabû, Nusku, Uraš and Nergal!

29 Ditto by Mullissu, Šerua and Belet-ili!

30 Ditto by Ištar of Nineveh and Ištar of Arbela!

31 Ditto by all the gods of the Inner City!

32 Ditto by all the gods of Nineveh!

33 Ditto by all the gods of Calah!

34 Ditto by all the gods of Arbela!

35 Ditto by all the gods of Kilizi!

36 Ditto by all the gods of Harran!

37 Ditto by all the gods of Babylon, Borsippa and Nippur!

38 Ditto by all the gods of Assyria!

39 Ditto by all the gods of Sumer and Akkad!

40 Ditto by all the gods of the lands; ditto by all the gods of heaven and earth! Ditto by all the gods of one's land and one's district!

§ 4 Assurbanipal Designated Heir to Throne

41 *a-de-e ša* ^{m}*aš-šur*—PAB—AŠ MAN KUR—*aš-šur ina* IGI DINGIR.MEŠ GAL.MEŠ
42 *šá* AN-*e u* KI.TIM *is-si-ku-nu iš-ku-nu-u-ni*
43 *ina* UGU ^{m}*aš-šur*—DÙ—A DUMU—MAN GAL *šá* É—UŠ-*ti*
44 DUMU ^{m}*aš-šur*—PAB—AŠ MAN KUR—*aš-šur* EN-*ku-nu šá a-na* DUMU—MAN-*u-te*
45 *šá* É—UŠ-*ti* MU-*šú iz-kur-u-ni ip-qi-du-šú-u-ni*
46 *ki-ma* ^{m}*aš-šur*—PAB—AŠ MAN KUR—*aš-šur a-na šim-ti it-ta-lak*
47 ^{m}*aš-šur*—DÙ—A DUMU—MAN GAL *šá* É—UŠ-*ti ina* GIŠ.GU.ZA-*e*
48 LUGAL-*ti tu-še-šab-ba* LUGAL-*u-tú* EN-*u-tú*
49 *(šá* KUR—*aš-šur) ina* UGU-*hi-ku-nu up-pa-áš ina* A.ŠÀ *ina bir-ti* URU
50 *la ta-na-ṣar-šú-u-ni ina* UGU-*hi-šú la ta-ma-qut-a-ni*

41 (This is) the treaty which Esarhaddon, king of Assyria, has concluded with you, in the presence of the great gods of heaven and earth, on behalf of Assurbanipal, the great crown prince designate, son of Esarhaddon, king of Assyria, your lord, whom he has named and appointed to the crown-princeship:

46 When Esarhaddon, king of Assyria, passes away, you will seat Assurbanipal, the great crown prince designate, upon the royal throne, and he will exercise the kingship and lordship of Assyria over you. You shall protect him in country and in town, fall and

can be explained as a stylistic device meant to reinforce the meaning of the sentence (cf., e.g., NB *lā banītu* beside NA *lā de'iqtu* in l.73 and passim, and note that the idiom *adê ṣabātu*, otherwise not attested in NA, clearly was the NB equivalent of NA *adê šakānu*). The variant *iṣ-ṣi-bat-tu* features NA phonetic changes pointing to a forward shift of stress before the subjunctive marker *-u* (*iṣbátu* → *iṣṣibáttu*). 27 ^{d}⌜*šá-maš*⌝ G: ^{d}UTU A frgg. 29 ^{d}*be-lit*—DINGIR.M[EŠ] G: DINGIR.MAH A frg. 30 URU.NINA.KI AEG: URU.NINA frg; URU.*arba-ìl* E: ^{d}⌜*arba*⌝-*ìl* A, *arba-ìl* frg. 31-36 *ša* AGE: *šá* frg. 32 URU.NINA.KI AE: NINA frg. 34 URU.*arba-ìl* AE; frg. omits URU. 37 DÙ-*šú-nu* frg: caret E. The order of lines 37f is inverted in A. 38 KUR—*aš-šur* AE: .KI frg; DÙ-*šú-nu* MIN A: caret E frg. 39 KUR.*šu-me-ri* AE: KUR.EME.KU frg; DÙ-*šú-nu* A frg: caret E. 40 DINGIR.MEŠ A frgg: DINGIR frg. 40A KI.TIM A frg: TIM.KI E; DÙ-*šú-nu* E frg: caret A. 40B Omitted in A. 41 *ša* frg: caret A. 42 AN-*e* KI.TIM A: AN-*e u* TIM.[KI E. 44 DUMU A: [*š*]*á* E, 0 *šá* frg; *šá a-*⌜*na* DUMU—MAN-*ti*⌝ A: *a-na* DUMU—MAN-*u-te* E. 45 UŠ-*ti* A: *-te* E frg; [*ip*]*-qi-du-* A: *ip-qid-du-* E. 46 *šim-ti* A: *-te* E. 47 UŠ-*ti* A: *-te* E; GIŠ.GU.ZA-*e* E: GIŠ.GU.ZA A. 48 LUGAL-*ti* A: *-u-te* frg; LUGAL-*u-tú* A: LUGAL-*tú* E, *-tu* frg; EN-*u-tú* A: EN-*tú* E. 49 *šá* KUR—*aš-šur* A: caret Er; UGU-*hi* A: UGU E; *ina bir-ti* An: *bir-ti* frg; *-te* E. The words *šum-ma at-tu-nu* supplied at the beginning of this line in BaM Bh 3 are definitely missing in A, E and ND 4346W, and probably in r and

51 *la ta-mut-ta-a-ni ina ket-ti šá* ŠÀ-*bi-ku-nu*
52 *is-si-šú la ta-da-bu-ba-a-ni mil-ku* SIG$_5$
53 *šá gam-mur-ti* ŠÀ-*bi-ku-nu la ta-mal-lik-a-šú-u-ni*
54 KASKAL SIG$_5$ *ina* GÌR.2.(MEŠ)-*šú la ta-šá-kan-a-ni*
55 *šum-ma at-tu-nu tu-nak-kar-a-šu-ni* TA* ŠÀ ŠEŠ.MEŠ-*šú*
56 GAL.MEŠ TUR.MEŠ *ina ku-mu-šú ina* GIŠ.GU.ZA KUR—*aš-šur*.KI
57 *tu-še-šab-a-ni šum-ma a-bu-tú šá* ^{m}*aš-šur*—PAB—AŠ MAN KUR—*aš-šur*.KI
58 *te-na-a-ni tu-šá-an-na-a-ni šum-ma* ^{m}*aš-šur*—DÙ—A DUMU—MAN GAL-*u*
59 *šá* É—UŠ-*ti šá* ^{m}*aš-šur*—PAB—AŠ MAN KUR—*aš-šur*.KI EN-*ku-nu*
60 ([*ú*]-*kal-lim-ka-nu-ni*) *ha-an-nu-um-ma la ta-da-gal-a-ni*
61 LUGAL-*u-tú* EN-*u-tú šá* KUR—*aš-šur ina* UGU-*hi-ku-nu la ú*-[*pa*]-*áš-u-ni*

die for him. You shall speak with him in the truth of your heart, give him sound advice loyally, and smooth his way in every respect.

[55] You shall not depose him nor seat (any)one of his brothers, elder or younger, on the throne of Assyria instead of him.

[57] You shall neither change nor alter the word of Esarhaddon, king of Assyria, but serve this very Assurbanipal, the great crown prince designate, whom Esarhaddon, king of Assyria, your lord, has presented to you, and he shall exercise the kingship and dominion over you.

---

§ 5 Obligation to Protect Heir

62 *šum-ma at-tu-nu a-na* ^{m}*aš-šur*—DÙ—A DUMU—MAN GAL *šá* É—UŠ-*ti*
63 *šá* ^{m}*aš-šur*—PAB—AŠ MAN KUR—*aš-šur*.KI *ú-kal-lim-u-ka-nu-ni*
64 *iq-ba-ka-nu-ni a-de-e ina* UGU-*hi-šú is-si-ku-nu*
65 *ú-dan-nin-u-ni iš-ku-nu-ni la ta-na-ṣar-a-ni*
66 *ina* ŠÀ-*bi-šú ta-ha-ṭa-a-ni* ŠU.2-*ku-nu a-na* HUL-*tim*
67 *ina* ŠÀ-*bi-šú tu-bal-a-ni ep-šú bar-tu a-bu-tú la* DÙG.GA-*tú*
68 *la* SIG$_5$-*tú te-ep-pa-šá-ni-šú-u-ni ina* LUGAL-*ti* KUR—*aš-šur*
69 *tu-nak-ka-ra-šú-u-ni* TA* ŠÀ-*bi* ŠEŠ.MEŠ-*šú* GAL.MEŠ TUR.MEŠ
70 *ina ku-mu-šú* GIŠ.GU.ZA KUR—*aš-šur tu-šá-aṣ-bat-a-ni*
71 LUGAL [*šá-nu-u*]*m-ma* EN *šá-nu-um-ma ina* UGU-*hi-ku-nu ta-šá-kan-a-ni*
72 *a-na* LUGAL *šá-ni-ma* DUMU—MAN *šá-ni-ma ma-mit ta-tam-ma-a-ni*

[62] You shall protect Assurbanipal, the great crown prince designate, whom Esarhaddon, king of Assyria, has presented and ordered for you, and on behalf of whom he has confirmed and concluded (this) treaty with you; you shall not sin against him, nor bring your hand against him with evil intent, nor revolt or do anything to him which is not good and proper;

[68] you shall not oust him from the kingship of Assyria by helping one of his brothers, elder or younger, to seize the throne of Assyria in his stead, nor set any other king or any other lord over yourselves, nor swear an oath to any other king or any other lord.

---

§ 6 Obligation to Report Opposition to Succession

73 *šum-ma at-tu-nu a-bu-tú la* DÙG.GA-*tú la ba-ni-tú*
74 *la ta-ri-su ša e-peš* LUGAL-*te šá ina* UGU

[73] If you hear any improper, unsuitable or unseemly word concerning the exercise of kingship which is unseemly and evil against

n as well, and hence cannot be regarded as an inadvertent scribal omission. 50 The reading *ta-ma-qut-a-ni* (not *ta-ma-haṣ-a-ni*) is made certain by the parallel *ki-i tan-qu-tu me-ta-ta* in ABL 539:9. 52f The signs *-a-ni* and *-u-ni* indicated in BaM Bh 3 as scribal omissions are actually broken away in n. 53 *šá* Ar: *ša* n; *gam-mur-ti* Arn: *-te* E; *ta-mal-l*[*ik-* W: *ta-ma-lik-a-* n, *ta-*[*mal*]*-li-ka-* A. 54 GÌR.2-*šú* A: MEŠ-*šu* r, -*šú*⌉ frg; *ta-šá-kan-a-ni* An: *-ša-* E, *-šak-* W. ⌈*la*⌉ in A is partially obliterated, not omitted by the scribe as alleged in BaM Bh 3 (coll. from photo). 55 *tu-nak-kar-a-šu-ni* r: *tu-nak-kar-šú-u-ni* A. 56 *ku-mu-šú* Ar: *-šu* frg. 57 *a-bu-tú* A:*-tu* r frg; KUR—*aš-šur*.KI Wn: .KI caret Ar. 58 GAL-*u* Wr: GAL A. 59 KUR—*aš-šur*.KI frg: KUR—*aš-šur* Wrn, KUR—*(aš-šur)* A; EN-*ku-nu* AW frg: caret r. 60 [*ú*]-⌈*kal-lim*⌉-*k*[*a*]-*nu-*[*ni* W: [*ú-kal*]-*lim-u-ka-nu-ni* n, caret Ar frg; *ha-an-nu-um-ma* Wrn frg: *-nu-ma* A. 61 LUGAL-*u-tú* An: LUGAL-*tu* r; EN-*u-tú* An: EN-*tu* r, *-tú* W; KUR—*aš-šur*.KI n frg: caret A, Wr omit .KI; *ú-*[*pa*]-⌈*áš*⌉-[*u-ni*] frg: A omits *-pa-* 63 KUR—*aš-šur*.KI W: A omits .KI; *ú-kal-lim-u-ka-nu-ni* A: *-ú-* W. 64 *iq-ba-ka-nu-ni* AW: *-kan-u-n*[*i* frg. 65 *iš-ku-nu-ni* A: *-kun-u-ni* W; *ta-na-ṣar-a-ni* A: -⌈*ṣar-ra*⌉-*ni* W. 66 *a-na* HUL-⌈*ti*⌉ A (coll. from photo): *ina* HUL-*tim* W. 67 *tu-bal-a-ni* A; *tú-* W; *bar-tu* A, *-tú* W; DÙG.GA-*tú* ESW: DÙG.GA A. 68 *te-ep-pa-šá-ni-šú-u-ni* A: *te-pa-šá-niš-šú-ni* W; LUGAL-*ti* AW: *-u-t*[*i*] frg. 69 *tu-nak-ka-ra-š*[*ú-ni*] W: *-kar-šú-u-ni* A; ŠÀ-*bi* A: ŠÀ W. 70 *ina ku-mu-šú* AS: caret W; GU.ZA KUR AW: GU.ZA *šá* KUR frg. 71 *šá-nu-um-ma* S: MAN-*ma* AW. 72 *šá-ni-ma* W: MAN-*ma* A; EN A: ⌈DUMU⌉—MAN W; *ma-mit* AS: *ta-me-tú* W; *ta-tam-ma-a-ni* Ax: *-ma-ni* WS. 73 *la* DÙG.GA-⌈*tu*⌉ *la ba-ni-tu* x: *la* DÙG.GA-*tú la*

^{m}*aš-šur*—DÙ—A
75 DUMU—MAN GAL-*u šá* É—UŠ-*te la tar-ṣa-tú-u-ni la ṭa-bat-u-ni*
76 *lu-u ina pi-i* ŠEŠ.MEŠ-*šú* ŠEŠ.MEŠ—AD.MEŠ-*šú* DUMU—ŠEŠ.MEŠ—AD.MEŠ-*šú*
77 *qin-ni-šú* NUMUN É—AD-*šú lu ina pi-i* LÚ.GAL.MEŠ LÚ.NAM.MEŠ
78 *lu ina pi-i* LÚ.*šá—ziq-ni* LÚ.SAG.MEŠ
79 *lu-u ina pi-i* LÚ.*um-ma-ni lu-u ina pi-i nap-har ṣal-mat*—SAG.DU
80 *ma-la ba-šu-u ta-šam-ma-a-ni tu-pa-za-ra-a-ni*
81 *la ta-lak-a-ni-ni a-na* ^{m}*aš-šur*—DÙ—A DUMU—MAN GAL-*u*
82 *šá* É—UŠ-*ti la ta-qab-ba-a-ni*

Assurbanipal, the great crown prince designate, either from the mouth of his brothers, his uncles, his cousins, his family (var. his people), members of his father's line; or from the mouth of magnates and governors, or from the mouth of the bearded and the eunuchs, or from the mouth of the scholars or from the mouth of any human being at all, you shall not conceal it but come and report it to Assurbanipal, the great crown prince designate.

83 *šum-ma* ^{m}*aš-šur*—PAB—AŠ MAN KUR—*aš-šur ina ṣa-ha-ri šá* DUMU.MEŠ-*šú*
84 *a-na šim-ti it-ta-lak* ^{m}*aš-šur*—DÙ—A DUMU—MAN GAL-*u*
85 *šá* É—UŠ-*ti* GIŠ.GU.ZA *šá* KUR—*aš-šur tu-šá-aṣ-ba-ta*
86 ^{md}GIŠ.ŠIR—MU—GI.NA ŠEŠ *ta-li-me-šú* DUMU—MAN *šá* É—UŠ-*ti*
87 *šá* KÁ.DINGIR.RA.KI *ina* GIŠ.GU.ZA LUGAL-*ti šá* KÁ.DINGIR.RA.KI
88 *tu-še-šá-ba* LUGAL-*tu* KUR—*šu-me-ri u* URI.KI KUR—*kar*—^{d}*dun-iá-àš*
89 DÙ.A.BI *ina pa-ni-šú tu-šad-ga-la ti-din-tú*
90 *am—mar* ^{m}*aš-šur*—PAB—AŠ MAN KUR—*aš-šur* AD-*šú id-din-na-šú-ni*
91 *is-si-šú ub-bal* 1-*en la ta-kal-la-a*

§ 7 Succession at Esarhaddon's Untimely Death

83 If Esarhaddon, king of Assyria, passes away while his sons are minors, you will help Assurbanipal, the great crown prince designate, to take the throne of Assyria, and you will help Šamaš-šumu-ukin, his equal brother, the crown prince designate of Babylon, to ascend the throne of Babylon. You will reserve for him the kingship over the whole of Sumer, Akkad and Karduniaš. He will take with him all the gifts that Esarhaddon, king of Assyria, his father, gave him; do not hold back even one.

92 *šum-ma* ^{m}*aš-šur*—DÙ—A DUMU—MAN GAL *šá* É—UŠ-*ti*
93 *šá* ^{m}*aš-šur*—PAB—AŠ MAN KUR—*aš-šur ú-kal-lim-u-ka-nu-ni*
94 *ù* ŠEŠ.MEŠ-*šú* DUMU AMA-*šú šá* ^{m}*aš-šur*—DÙ—A DUMU—MAN GAL-*u*
95 *šá* É—UŠ-*ti šá* ^{m}*aš-šur*—PAB—AŠ MAN KUR—*aš-šur ina* UGU-*hi-šú-nu*
96 *a-de-e is-si-ku-nu iš-ku-nu-ni ket-tu šá-lim-tu*
97 *la tu-kal-la-a-ni ina ke-na-a-te tar-ṣa-a-ti*

§ 8 Definition of Loyalty

92 You shall keep absolute honesty with respect to Assurbanipal, the great crown prince designate whom Esarhaddon, king of Assyria, has presented to you, and (with respect to) his brothers, sons by the same mother as Assurbanipal, the great crown prince designate, on behalf of whom Esarhaddon, king of Assyria has concluded (this) treaty with you; you shall always serve

SIG$_5$-*t*[*ú*] H, *la* SIG$_5$-*tú la ba-ni-tú* A. 74 LUGAL-*te* x: -*ti* A, MAN-*u-te* H; UGU Ax: UGU-*hi* H. 75 GAL-*u* H: GAL AS; É—UŠ-*te* Hx: -*ti* A; *tar-ṣa-tú-u-ni* H: -*tu-u-ni* Ax. 76 *lu-u* x: *lu* AH; *pi-i* Hx: *pi* A; ŠEŠ.MEŠ—AD.MEŠ-*šú* Hx: ŠEŠ.MEŠ—AD-*šú* A; DUMU—ŠEŠ.MEŠ—AD.MEŠ-*šú* Ax: caret H. 77 *qin-ni-šú* Ax: *lu-u* UN.MEŠ-*šu* H; *lu* Aa: *lu-u* H. 78 *lu ina pi-i* Aa: *lu-u* H, caret x; LÚ.*šá—ziq-ni* AHI: *šá*—LÚ.*ziq-ni* x; LÚ.SAG.MEŠ a: -ME A, LÚ.SAG I, [*ina*] *pi-i* LÚ.SAG.MEŠ x. 79 *lu ina pi-i* AGa: *lu-u (ina pi-i)* HI, caret x. 80 *ma-la* GHI: *mal* Aax; *ba-šu-u* Ax: -*ú* GI, -*šú-u* H; *ta-šam-ma-a-ni* GAx: -*ma-ni* AH; *tu-pa-za-ra-a-ni* AI: *tu-ba-za-ra-ni* H, *tu-pa-za*[*r*$_4$-*a-ni*] G, -*zar-a-ni* a. 81 GAL-*u* H: GAL AIa, caret G. 82 É—UŠ-*ti* AIG: -*te* Hx; *ta-qab-ba-a-ni* Ax: -*ba-niš-šú-un-ni* H, *ta-qa-ba-a-ni* I. 83 *šum-ma* AGa: [*k*]*i-ma* H; 84 GAL-*u* Gd: GAL A. 85 É—UŠ-*ti* AGI: -*te* d; *tú-šá-aṣ-ba-ta* I: -*bat-ta* A, ⸢*la tu*⸣-*šá-aṣ-bat-a-ni* G. 86 *ta-li-me-šú* AGI: -*mu* d; É—UŠ-*ti* AGI: -*te* d. 87 *šá* KÁ.DINGIR.RA.KI AGd frg: KÁ.DINGIR.KI I; *ina* Ad: caret GI; LUGAL-*ti* AGI: -*te* d frg; *šá* KÁ.DINGIR.RA.KI A: *šá* KÁ.DINGIR.KI G frg; I omits *ša*. 88 *tu-še-šá-ba* GI: -*šab* A, -*šab-šu* d; LUGAL-*ti* A: -*tu* GI, -*u-tu* d, -*tú* frg; KUR—*šu-me-ri* GI frg: KUR.EME.KU Ad; [KUR.*ka*]*r*—^{d}*dun-iá-àš* I: KUR.*kar*—^{d}*dun-iá* Ad, KUR.*kar*—^{d}*dun-iá*-[G. 89 *pa-ni-šú* frg: IGI-*šú* Id frg, IGI-*ni-šú* A; *tu-šad-ga-la* AGId: *tú*- frg; *ti-din-tú* A: -*tu* d. 90 *id-din-na-šú-ni* A: *i-di*-[*na-šu-u*]*n-ni* d, SUM-*šú-un-ni* I frg. 91 *ub-bal* GD frgg: *ú-bal* A frg; *ta-kal-la-a* Ad frg: *tak-la-a* I. 92 É—UŠ-*ti* AI: -*te* frg. 93 *ú-kal-lim-u-ka-nu-ni* A: -⸢*u*⸣-*ni* I frg. 94 GAL-*u* I frg: GAL AI frgg. 94f *šá* AF frgg: *ša* frg. 95 É—UŠ-*ti* AI: -*te* F frg. 96 *iš-ku-nu-ni* A frgg: -*u-ni* I, -*kun-u-ni* F. 97 *tu-kal-la-a-ni* AFI: -*la-ni* frg; *ke-na-a-te* AF: *ke-na-te* frgg;

98 *la ta-ta-nab-bal-a-šá-nu-u-ni ina ket-ti šá* ŠÀ-*bi-ku-nu*
99 *is-si-šú-nu la ta-da-bu-ba-ni ina* A.ŠÀ *bir-ti* URU
100 *la ta-na-ṣar-a-šú-nu-u-ni*

them in a true and fitting manner, speak with them with heartfelt truth, and protect them in country and in town.

§ 9 Prohibition of Disloyal Conduct

101 *šum-ma* ᵐ*aš-šur*—DÙ—A DUMU—MAN GAL-*u šá* É—UŠ-*ti*
102 *šá* ᵐ*aš-šur*—PAB—AŠ MAN KUR—*aš-šur iq-ba-ka-nu-u-ni*
103 *u* ŠEŠ.MEŠ-*šú* DUMU AMA-*šú šá* ᵐ*aš-šur*—DÙ—A DUMU—MAN GAL-*u*
104 *ša* É—UŠ-*te ina* UGU-*hi-šú-nu a-de-e is-si-ku-nu*
105 *iš-ku-nu-u-ni ta-ha-ṭa-a-ni qa-at-ku-nu ina* HUL-*tim*
106 *ina* ŠÀ-*bi-šú-nu tu-bal-a-ni*
107 *ep-šú bar-tú a-bu-tú la* DÙG.GA-*tú te-pa-šá-ni-šú-nu-u-ni*

101 You shall not sin against Assurbanipal, the great crown prince designate, whom Esarhaddon, king of Assyria, has ordered for you, nor against his brothers, sons by the same mother as Assurbanipal, the great crown prince designate, concerning whom he has concluded (this) treaty with you; you shall not bring your hands to (do) evil against them nor make insurrection or do anything which is not good to them.

§ 10 Obligation to Report Treason

108 *š[u]m-ma a-bu-tú la* DÙG.GA-*tú la de-iq-tú*
109 *la ba-ni-tú ina* UGU ᵐ*aš-šur*—DÙ—A DUMU—MAN GAL *ša* É—UŠ-*ti*
110 DUMU ᵐ*aš-šur*—PAB—AŠ MAN KUR—*aš-šur* EN-*ku-nu la tar-ṣa-at-u-ni*
111 *la ṭa-bat-u-ni lu-u ina pi-i* LÚ.KÚR-*šú*
112 *lu-u ina pi-i sal-me-šú*
113 *lu ina pi-i* ŠEŠ.MEŠ-*šú*
114 ŠEŠ.MEŠ—AD.MEŠ-*šú* DUMU—ŠEŠ.MEŠ—AD.MEŠ-*šú*
115 *qin-ni-šu* NUMUN É—AD-*šu lu-u ina pi-i* ŠEŠ.MEŠ-*ku-nu*
116 DUMU.MEŠ-*ku-nu* DUMU.MÍ.MEŠ-*ku-nu lu ina pi-i* LÚ.*ra-gi-me*
117 LÚ.*mah-he-e* DUMU *šá-ʾi-li a-mat* DINGIR
118 *lu-u ina pi-i nap-har ṣal-mat*—SAG.DU *mal ba-šú-u*
119 *ta-šam-ma-a-ni tu-pa-za-ra-a-ni*
120 *la ta-lak-a-ni-ni a-na* ᵐ*aš-šur*—DÙ—A DUMU—MAN GAL-*u*
121 *šá* É—UŠ-*te* DUMU ᵐ*aš-šur*—PAB—AŠ MAN KUR—*aš-šur*
122 *la ta-qab-ba-a-ni*

108 If you hear any evil, improper, ugly word which is not seemly nor good to Assurbanipal, the great crown prince designate, son of Esarhaddon, king of Assyria, your lord, either from the mouth of his enemy or from the mouth of his ally, or from the mouth of his brothers or from the mouth of his uncles, his cousins, his family, members of his father's line, or from the mouth of your brothers, your sons, your daughters, or from the mouth of a prophet, an ecstatic, an inquirer of oracles, or from the mouth of any human being at all, you shall not conceal it but come and report it to Assurbanipal, the great crown prince designate, son of Esarhaddon, king of Assyria.

§ 11 Injunction against Treason

123 *šum-ma at-tu-nu* ᵐ*aš-šur*—DÙ—A DUMU—MAN GAL-*u*
124 *šá* É—UŠ-*te ša* ᵐ*aš-šur*—PAB—AŠ MAN KUR—*aš-šur*

123 You shall not do (anything) that is evil and improper to Assurbanipal the great

tar-ṣa-a-ti A: *-te* E. 98 *ta-ta-nab-bal-a-šá-nu-u-ni* frg: *-bal-šú-u-ni* A, *ta-tan-nab-bal-a-šú-u-ni* F, *ta-ta-na-bal-a-šú-nu-u-ni* I; *ket-ti* AF frg: *-te* F. 99 *ta-da-bu-ba-ni* A: *ta-da-bu-ub-a-ni* I; *bir-ti* A: *-te* F. 100 *ta-na-ṣar-a-šú-nu-u-ni* AIE: *-ṣar-šú-nu-u-ni* frg. 101 GAL-*u* frg: GAL FE; ⌜É⌝—UŠ-*ti* A: É—UŠ-*t*[*e*] frg. 102 MAN KUR—*aš-šur* FE: caret frg; *iq-ba-ka-nu-u-ni* Ey frg: [*iq-ba*]*-ka-nu-ni* A. 103 *u* F: *ù* frg, caret E; GAL-*u* E frg: GAL y. 104 É—UŠ-*te* E: *-ti* frgg. 105 *iš-ku-nu-u-ni* E: *iš-kun-u-ni* frgg; *ta-ha-ṭa-a-ni* E: *-ṭa-ni* frg; *qa-at-ku-nu* E: ŠU.2-*ku-nu* frg. 106 ŠÀ-*bi-šú-nu* E frgg: ŠÀ-*šú-*[*nu*] y. 107 DÙG.GA-*tú* Ey frg: *ṭa-a*[*b-tu*] frg; *te-pa-šá-*[*ni-šú*]*-nu-u-ni* frg: *te-pa-šá-ni-šú-nu-ni* E. 108 *a-bu-tú* y frg: [*a-b*]*u-tu* frg; DÙG.GA-*tú* Ey frg: ⌜DÙG.GA-*tu*⌝ frg; *de-iq-tú* E: [S]IG$_5$-*tú* frg. 109 É—UŠ-*ti* E: *-te* frg. 110 KUR—*aš-šur* y frg: E adds .KI. 111 *lu-u* ND 4345A: *lu* AEy frg. 112 *ina* frg: caret E; *sal-me-šú* frg: *sa-*⌜*li*⌝*-me-*[*šú*] E (coll. from photo), [*sa-l*]*i-me-šú* frg. 114 ŠEŠ.MEŠ—AD.MEŠ-*šú* frg: ŠEŠ—AD.MEŠ-*šú* E frg; DUMU—ŠEŠ.MEŠ—[AD.MEŠ-*šú*] frg: DUMU—ŠEŠ—AD.MEŠ-*šú* E. 115 *pi-i* frg: *pi* E. 116 LÚ.*ra-gi-me* frgg: *ra-gi-me* E. 117 DINGIR frgg; DINGIR.MEŠ E. 118 *pi-i* A: caret o frg; *ṣal-mat*—SAG.DU frgg: —*qaq-q*]*a-di* E; *ba-šú-u* frg: *ba-šu-u* E frg. 119 *ta-šam-ma-a-ni* frg: *-ma-ni* Ao. 122 [*ta-qab-b*]*a-a-ni* EO frg: *ta-qab-ba-ni* frg. 123 *šum-ma* A frg: *šúm-mu* E; *at-tu-nu* A frg: *-tú-* Eo; GAL-*u* frg: GA]L E.

125 *iq-ba-ka-nu-u-ni la ṭa-ab-tú la de-iq-tú*
126 *te-ep-pa-šá-ni-šu-un-ni ta-ṣa-ba-ta-šu-u-ni*
127 *ta-du-ka-šú-u-ni a-na* LÚ.KÚR-*šú ta-da-na-šu-u-ni*
128 *a-na* LUGAL-*u-te* KUR—*aš-šur tu-nak-[ka]r-a-šú-u-ni*
129 *a-na* LUGAL *šá-nim-ma* EN *šá-nim-ma ma-m[it ta-tam]-ma-ni*

crown prince designate, whom Esarhaddon, king of Assyria, your lord, has ordered for you; you shall not seize him and put him to death, nor hand him over to his enemy, nor oust him from the kingship of Assyria, nor sw[ear an oa]th to any other king or any other lord.

---

130 *šum-ma me-me-ni a-na* ᵐ*aš-šur*—DÙ—A DUMU—[MAN GAL *š*]*á* É—UŠ-*te*
131 DUMU ᵐ*aš-šur*—PAB—AŠ MAN KUR—*aš-šur* EN-*ku-nu šá ina* [U]GU-*hi-šú*
132 *a-de-e is-si-ku-nu iš-ku-nu-u-ni*
133 *si-hu bar-tú šá d*[*u-a-ki*]-*šu ša-mut-ti-šu*
134 *hul-lu-qi-šú a-na ka-šu-nu* [*i*]*q-ba-ka-nu-u-ni*
135 *ù at-tu-nu ina pi-i me-me-ni ta-šam-ma-a-ni*
136 *e-piš-a-nu-te šá bar-te la ta-ṣab-bat-a-ni-ni*
137 *ina* UGU ᵐ*aš-šur*—DÙ—A DUMU—MAN GAL *ša* É—UŠ-*ti*
138 *la tu-bal-a-ni-ni šum-ma am—mar ṣa-ba-ti-šú-nu*
139 *du-a-ki-šú-nu ma-ṣa-ku-nu la ta-ṣab-bat-a-šá-nu-ni*
140 *la ta-du-ka-a-šá-nu-ni* MU-*šú-nu* NUMUN-*šú-nu*
141 *ina* KUR *la tu-hal-laq-qa-a-ni*
142 *šum-ma am—mar ṣa-ba-te-šú-nu du-a-ki-šú-nu*
143 *la ma-ṣa-ku-nu* PI.2 *šá* ᵐ*aš-šur*—DÙ—A DUMU—MAN GAL-*u*
144 *ša* É—UŠ-*ti la tú-pat-ta-a-ni is-si-šú*
145 *la* [*t*]*a-za-za-a-ni e-piš-a-nu-ti šá bar-te*
146 *la ta-*[*ṣ*]*ab-bat-a-ni la ta-du-ka-a-*[*ni*]

§ 12 Action against Those Suborning Treason

[130] If anyone should speak to you of rebellion and insurrection (with the purpose) of ki[lling], assassinating, and eliminating Assurbanipal, the [great crown] prince designate, son of Esarhaddon, king of Assyria, your lord, concerning whom he has concluded (this) treaty with you, or if you should hear it from the mouth of anyone, you shall seize the perpetrators of insurrection, and bring them before Assurbanipal, the great crown prince designate.

[138] If you are able to seize them and put them to death, then you shall destroy their name and their seed from the land. If, however, you are unable to seize them and put them to death, you shall inform Assurbanipal, the great crown prince designate, and assist him in seizing and putting to death the perpetrators of rebellion.

---

147 *šum-ma e-pi-šá-nu-te šá bar-te lu-u e-ṣu-te lu-u ma-a'-du-te*
148 *is-si-šú-nu ta-šá-kan-a-ni du-un-qu la du-un-qu*
149 *ta-šam-ma-a-ni*
150 *a-na* ᵐ*aš-šur*—DÙ—A DUMU—MAN GAL-*u šá* É—UŠ-*ti*
151 DUMU ᵐ*aš-šur*—PAB—AŠ MAN KUR—*aš-šur la ta-lak-a-ni-ni*

§ 13 Action against Traitors

[147] If you should come into contact with perpetrators of insurrection, be they few or many, and hear (anything, be it) favourable or unfavourable, you shall come and report it to Assurbanipal, the great crown prince designate, son of Esarhaddon, king of Assyria, being totally loyal to him.

[124] É—UŠ-*te* E frg: -*ti* AO. [125] *ṭa-ab-tú* E: DÙG.GA-*tu* frg; *de-iq-*[*tú*] E: SIG$_5$-*tú* O. [126] [*te-e*]*p-pa-šá-ni-šu-un-ni* frg: -*šú-un-ni* E, *te-ep-pa-šá-ni-šú-n*[*i* A (coll. from photo). [127] -*šú-* AEo: -*šu-* frg. [128] LUGAL-*u-te* frg: -*u-ti* A, -*ú-te* O, LUGAL-*te* E. [129] *šá-nim-ma* AE: MAN-*ma* frg; *šá-nim-m*[*a*] E: MAN-*ma* frg. [130] *šum-ma* A frg: *šúm-mu* E; É—UŠ-*te* E: [É—U]Š-*ti* O. [133] *bar-tu* A: -*tú* E; *šá* E: *ša* A; *ša-mut-ti-*⌜*šu*⌝ frgg: -*te-šu* E, -*ti-šú-nu* O. [134] *hul-lu-qi-šú* At: -*šú-nu* O; [*iq-ba-k*]*a-nu-u-ni* frg: [*i*]*q-ba-ka-nu-ni* E, *i*]-*qab-ba-ka-nu-u-ni* O. [135] *ta-šam-ma-a-ni* O: -*ma-ni* E. [136] *e-piš-a-nu-te* Et: *e-pi-šá-nu-ti* A; *ta-ṣab-bat-a-ni-ni* AO: *ta-ṣa-bat-* E. [137] GAL EO: GAL-*u* t; É—UŠ-*ti* AE: -*te* O. [138] *tu-bal-a-ni-ni* AO: *tú-* E; *šum-ma* At: *šúm-mu* E. [139] *du-a-ki-šú-nu* E: *du-u-a-ki-šú-nu* A. [140] *ta-du-ka-a-šá-nu-ni* E: *ta-du-ka-šá-nu-u-ni* At. [141] *tu-hal-laq-qa-a-ni* E: -*qa-ni* t. [142] *šum-ma* t frg: [*š*]*úm-mu* E. [143] Contra BaM Bh 3, *ma-ṣa-ku-nu* has not been omitted by the scribe but is broken away in E.

[144] *l*]*a tú-pat-ta-a-ni* E (coll. from photo): *tu-* t frg. [145] [*t*]*a-za-za-a-ni* P: -*za-ni* t; [*e-p*]*iš-a-nu-te* E: *e-pi-šá-nu-te* t, -*ti* frg. [147] *e-pi-šá-nu-te* H: -*ti* A -*pi*]*š-a-nu-ti* P, -*te* E; *bar-te* H: -*ti* P; *lu-u e-*[*ṣ*]*u-te* H: *lu e-ṣu-ti* P frg; [148] *du-un-qu* HE: SIG$_5$-*tú* AP, -*tu* frg. [149] thus HP; A inserts here *l*[*a ta-lak-a*]-*ni-*[*ni*] from l. 151 (coll. from photo). [150] GAL-*u* H: GAL PE, caret frg. [151] *ta-lak-a-ni-ni* E: [*ta*]-*lak-a-ni* A, *tal-lak-a-ni-ni* P frg. [152] *la ta-qab-ba-a-ni* P: *t*]*a-*⌜*qab*⌝*-ba-*

152 *la ta-qab-ba-a-ni lib-ba-ku-nu is-si-šu la gam-mur-u-ni*
153 *ša* DINGIR.MEŠ-*ni ú-še-šá-bu-u-ni a-de-e ina* IGI DINGIR.MEŠ-*ni*
154 *i-šá-kan-u-ni ina ri-k*[*is*] GIŠ.BANŠUR *šá-te-e ka-si*
155 *ni-pi-ih* ᵈGIŠ.BAR A.MEŠ Ì.MEŠ *ṣi-bit tu-le-e*
156 (*a-na*) *a-he-iš tu-tam-ma-a-ni a-na* ᵐ*aš-šur*—DÙ—A DUMU—MAN GAL-*u*
157 *šá* É—UŠ-*ti* DUMU ᵐ*aš-šur*—PAB—AŠ MAN KUR—*aš-šur* EN-*ku-nu*
158 *lá tal-lak-a-ni-ni la ta-qab-ba-a-ni*
159 *e-piš-a-nu-ti šá bar-ti ù* LÚ.ERIM.MEŠ EN—*hi-ṭi*
160 *la ta-ṣab-bat-a-ni-ni la ta-du-ka-a-ni*
161 MU-*šú-nu* NUMUN-*šú-nu ina* KUR *la tu-hal-laq-qa-a-ni*

[153] You shall not take a mutually binding oath with (any)one who installs (statues of) gods in order to conclude a treaty before gods, (be it) by sett[ing] a table, by drinking from a cup, by kindling a fire, by water, by oil, or by holding breasts, but you shall come and report to Assurbanipal, the great crown prince designate, son of Esarhaddon, king of Assyria, your lord, and shall seize and put to death the perpetrators of insurrection and the traitorous troops, and destroy their name and seed from the land.

§ 14 **Action against Open Rebellion**

162 *šum-ma lu* LÚ.*aš-šur-a-a lu da-gíl—pa-ni šá* KUR—*aš-šur*
163 *lu-u* LÚ.*šá—ziq-ni lu-u* LÚ.SAG *lu* DUMU KUR—*aš-šur*.KI
164 *lu* DUMU KUR *šá-ni-tim-ma lu ina šik-nat*—ZI-*tim ma-la ba-šú-u*
165 *a-na* ᵐ*aš-šur*—DÙ—A DUMU—MAN GAL *šá* É—UŠ-*te* (*lu*) *ina* A.ŠÀ
166 (*lu*) *ina* ŠÀ URU *e-ta-as-ru-šú si-hu bar-tú ina* UGU-*hi-šú e-tap-šu*
167 *at-tu-nu* TA* ᵐ*aš-šur*—DÙ—A DUMU—MAN GAL *šá* É—UŠ-*ti*
168 *la ta-za-za-a-ni la ta-na-ṣar-a-šú-u-ni*
169 LÚ.ERIM.MEŠ *šá bar-ti e-pa-šú-ni-šú-u-ni ina gam-mur-ti* ŠÀ-*bi-ku-nu*
170 *la ta-du-ka-a-ni a-na* ᵐ*aš-šur*—DÙ—A DUMU—MAN GAL
171 *šá* É—UŠ-*ti u* ŠEŠ.MEŠ-*šú* DUMU AMA-*šú is-si-šú*
172 *la tu-še-za-ba-a-ni-ni*

[162] If an Assyrian or a vassal of Assyria, or a bearded (courtier) or a eunuch, or a citizen of Assyria or a citizen of any other country, or any living being at all besieges Assurbanipal, the great crown prince designate, in country or in town, and carries out rebellion and insurrection,

[167] you shall take your stand with and protect Assurbanipal, the great crown prince designate, wholeheartedly defeat the men who revolted against him, and rescue Assurbanipal, the great crown prince designate, and his brothers, sons by the same mother.

§ 15 **Obligation to Escape from Rebels**

173 *šum-ma ša* TA* ᵐ*aš-šur*—DÙ—A DUMU—MAN GAL *šá* É—*re-du-ti*
174 DUMU ᵐ*aš-šur*—PAB—AŠ MAN KUR—*aš-šur* EN-*ku-nu šá ina* UGU-*hi-šú*

[173] You shall not make common cause with (any)one who may revolt against Assurbanipal, the great crown prince designate,

a-ni A (coll. from photo; correct BaM Bh 3); *lib-ba-ku-nu* A: ŠÀ-*ku-nu* E; *is-si-šu* E: -*šú* A frg; *gam-mur-u-ni* P frg: *ga-*⌜*ma-ru*⌝-[*ni*] A, *ga-mur-u-ni* E. [153] DINGIR.MEŠ-*ni* P: DINGIR.MEŠ E; *ú-š*]*e-šá-bu-u-*[*ni*] A: [*ú*]-*ši-šá-bu-u-n*[*i*] H, *ú-še-šab-u-ni* EP. [154] *i-šá-kan-u-ni* P: *ta-šá-kan-a-ni* E; *ri-k*[*is*] H: KÉŠ APE; GIŠ.BANŠUR HP: GIŠ.ABXAD.TIM AE; *šá-te-e* E: *šá-ti-e* frg; *ka-si* E: GÚ.ZI P. [155] Ì.MEŠ PE: caret A. [156] *a-na* P: caret AEH; *a-he-iš* AP: *a-ha-meš* EH; GAL-*u* H: GAL AEP. [157] É—UŠ-*ti* A: -*te* BEP; DUMU ABEP: A H. [158] *tal-lak-a-ni-ni* APS: *ta-lak-a-ni-ni* E. [159] *e-piš-a-nu-ti* EP: *e-pi-šá-nu-ti* A, *e-piš-šá-nu-te* S; *bar-ti* AP: -*te* ES; *ù* P: *u* AES; LÚ.ERIM.MEŠ AP: ERIM.MEŠ ES. [160] *ta-ṣab-bat-a-ni-ni* S: *ta-ṣab-bat-a-ni* P, *ta-ṣa-bat-a-ni-ni* E, *ta-ṣa-ba-(ta)-a-ni-ni* A; *ta-du-ka-a-ni* AES: *ta-du-(ka)-a-ni* P. [161] *tu-hal-laq-qa-a-ni* A: [*tu*]-*hal-la̤-qa-a-ni* B, *tu-hal-laq-a-ni* P, [*t*]*ú-hal-laq-qa-a-ni* E, *tu-hal-la-ka-a-*[*ni*] S. [162] LÚ.*aš-šur-a-a* PES: *aš-šur-a-a* A; *lu* PS: caret AE; KUR—*aš-šur* PS: KUR—*aš-šur*.KI ABE. [163] *lu-u* AM: *lu* BEIPS; LÚ.*šá—ziq-ni* AIP: *šá—ziq-ni* S; KUR—*aš-šur*.KI AB: KUR—*aš-šur* EPS. [164] DUMU IPS: DUMU.MEŠ A; *šá-ni-tim-ma* PS: -*ti-ma* I, *šá-(ni)-tim-(ma)* A; S inserts here *lu ina nap-har ṣal-mat*—SAG.DU *mal ba-šú-u* S (caret ABP); —ZI-*tim* BEPS: ZI AM; *ma-la* BEP: *mal* AMS; *ba-šú-u* BPS: *ba-šu-u* A, GÁL E. [165] É—UŠ-*te* P: -*ti* AES, -*ú-ti* B; *lu* P: caret AES; A.ŠÀ EPS: A adds -*šú*. [166] *lu* P: caret AES; *ina* ŠÀ EP: *bir-ti* AS; *e-ta-as-ru-šú* ABPS: -*šu* EM, -*uš* I; *bar-tú* EP: -*tu* AI, -*te* S; *e-tap-šu* ES: -*šú* P, *e-tap-pa-šu* M. [167] *at-tu-nu* AEIS: *at-tú-nu* P; *šá* AMPS: *ša* E; É—UŠ-*ti* AMS: -*te* E. [168] *ta-za-za-a-ni* AEIP: *ta-za-(za)-a-ni* S; *ta-na-ṣar-a-šú-u-ni* EMPS: *ta-na-ṣar-šú-u-ni* A. [169] *bar-ti* AP: -*tu* I, -*tú* E; *e-pa-šú-ni-šú-u-ni* A: -*šú-un-ni* E, *e-pa-šu-niš-šu-*⌜*un-ni*⌝ M, *e-pu-šu-niš-*[I, *e-pu-šú-niš-šú-*[P, *e-pa-áš-šu-ni-šu-u-ni* S; *gam-mur-ti* AS: -*te* P; ŠÀ-*bi* AIM: ŠÀ S. [171] É—UŠ-*ti* AIMS frg: -*te* P; *u* S: *ù* A frg, caret P; ŠEŠ.MEŠ-*šú* AIPS: -*šu* M, ŠEŠ.MEŠ frg; DUMU AIMS frg: DUMU.MEŠ frg; *is-si-šú* S: caret AIM frgg. [172] *tu-še-za-ba-a-ni-ni* S frg: -*ba-ni-ni* A. [173] *ša* A: *šá* GIPS frgg; É—*re-du-ti* frg: É—UŠ-*ti* AIMS. [174] UGU-*hi-šú* AIMS frg: -*šu* G. [175] *iš-ku-nu-u-ni* A frg: -*nu-ni* frg, *iš-kun-u-ni* M. [176]

175 *a-de-e is-si-ku-nu iš-ku-nu-u-ni ib-bal-kàt-u-ni*
176 *at-tu-nu is-si-šú ta-šá-kan-a-ni*
177 *šum-ma ki-i da-ʾa-a-ni iṣ-ṣab-tu-ku-nu*
178 *at-tu-nu la ta-hal-liq-a-ni ina* UGU ^{m}*aš-šur*—DÙ—A
179 DUMU—MAN GAL-*u šá* É—UŠ-*ti la tal-lak-a-ni-ni*

son of Esarhaddon, king of Assyria, your lord, concerning whom he has concluded (this) treaty with you, but, should they seize you by force, you shall flee and come to Assurbanipal, the great crown prince designate.

180 *šum-ma at-tú-nu lu in*[*a x*]-*e*$^{!}$ *hu-ra-di* [*x x x x x*]
181 *lu in*[*a* UD-*m*]*e*$^{?}$ *ra-qi ki-i qa-bal* KUR
182 *áš-ba-ka-*[*nu-ni*] *lu ki-i ina pi-ir-ri*
183 *te-rab-a-ni-ni a-bu-tú la* DÙG.GA-*tú*
184 *šá* ^{m}*aš-šur*—DÙ—A DUMU—MAN GAL-*u šá* É—UŠ-*ti*
185 *ina* ŠÀ-*b*[*i*]-*ku-nu ta-šá-kan-a-ni ina* UGU-*hi-šú*
186 *ta-bal-kàt-a-ni ep-šu bar-tu a-bu-tu*
187 *la* DÙG.GA-*tú te-pa-šá-niš-*[*u-ni*]

§ 16 Rejection of Rebellion

[180] You shall not, whether while *on a guard duty* [......] or on a [day] of rest, while resid[ing] within the land or while entering a *tax-collection point*, set in your mind an unfavourable thought against Assurbanipal, the great crown prince designate; you shall not revolt against him, nor make rebellion, nor do anything to him which is not good.

188 *šum-ma* ^{m}*aš-šur*—DÙ—A DUMU—MAN GAL-*u šá* É—[UŠ-*ti*]
189 DUMU ^{m}*aš-šur*—PAB—AŠ MAN KUR—*aš-šur* EN-*ku-nu ina* UD-*me šá* ^{m}*aš-šur*—PAB—AŠ
190 MAN KUR—*aš-šur* EN-*ku-nu a-na šim-ti il-lak-ú-ni*
191 *šu-u la* LUGAL-*ka-nu-ni la* EN-*ka-nu-u-ni*
192 *dan-nu la ú-šap-pal-u-ni šap-lu la i-ma-táh-u-ni*
193 *šá du-a-ki la i-du-ku-u-ni š*[*a*] *bal-lu-ṭí*
194 *la ú-bal-laṭ-u-ni am—mar i-qab-bu-u-ni*
195 *la ta-šam-ma-a-ni ki-i pi-i-šú*
196 *la te-pa-šá-a-ni* LUGAL MAN-*ma* EN MAN-*ma*
197 *ina* UGU-*hi-šú tu-ba-ʾa-a-ni*

§ 17 Succession of Assurbanipal

[188] On the day that Esarhaddon, king of Assyria, your lord passes away, (on that day) Assurbanipal, the great crown prince desi[gnate], son of Esarhaddon, your lord, shall be your king and your lord; he shall abase the mighty, raise up the lowly, put to death him who is worthy of death, and pardon him who deserves to be pardoned.

[195] You shall hearken to whatever he says and do whatever he commands, and you shall not seek any other king or any other lord against him.

198 *šum-ma me-me-ni ina* É.GAL *bar-tu lu ina kal* UD-*me*
199 *lu-u ina kal* MI [*l*]*u-u ina* KASKAL *lu ina qab-si* KUR *a-na*
200 ^{m}*aš-šur*—PAB—AŠ MAN KUR—*aš-šur e-ta-pa-áš a*[*t-tu*]-*nu*

§ 18 Rejection of Palace Revolt against Esarhaddon

[198] If anyone in the Palace makes an insurrection, whether by day or by night, whether on a campaign or within the land against Esarhaddon, king of Assyria, you must not obey him.

is-si-šú ABI: *-šu* M, *-šú-nu* S. [177] *da-ʾa-a-ni* MS: *da-ʾa-ni* A, *da-a-ni* BI. [178] *ta-hal-liq-a-ni* AS: *-li-qa-a-ni-ni* M, *-laq-a-*[*ni* frg. [179] GAL-*u* I: GAL frg; É—UŠ-*ti* AIM: *-te* frg; *tal-lak-a-ni-ni* A: *tal-lak-ni-ni* S, *ta-lak-a-ni-ni* BM. [180] *hu-ra-di* A: *hu-ra-a-*[*di* I (see coll.). The word *hurādu* is otherwise attested in Neo-Assyrian only in NL 41:26, where it occurs side by side with *ilku* "service" (*la* [*i*]*l-*[*k*]*u la hu-ra-du*). Beside "guard duty", the meanings "military duty, expedition, army" are well attested in Middle Assyrian (see Postgate, BSOAS 34 496ff and Freydank, AoF 4 111ff). [181] *ra-qi* AI (see coll.; correct BaM Bh 3); *lu* frg: caret AI; *qa-bal* frgg: $MURUB_4$ AI. [182] *pirru* is rendered "tax-collection (centre)" following Postgate, TCAE p.163ff, but note the MA evidence discussed by Freydank, AoF 4 115ff. [184] É—UŠ-*ti* I: *-te* frg. [185] ŠÀ-*b*[*i-ku-nu*] I: ŠÀ-*ku-nu* frg. [186] *ep-šu* I: *-šú* frg; *bar-tu* I: *-tú* frg; *a-bu-tu* FI: *-tú* frg. [187] DÙG.GA-*tú* frg: *-tu* I; *te-pa-šá-niš-*[*x x*] frg: *te*]*-pa-šá-ni-šu-*[*ni*] frg. [188] *šum-ma* FI: [*šúm*]*-mu* frg; GAL-*u* I: GAL frgg. [192] *ú-šap-pal-u-ni* J frg:]*-pa-lu-u-ni* frg. [194] *ú-bal-laṭ-u-ni* FJ frg: *ú-ba-la-*[*ṭa x x*] frg. [196] *te-pa-šá-a-ni* Y: *te-p*]*a-a-ša-a-ni* frg, *te-ep-pa-*[*šá-a-ni* frg. [197] *tu-ba-ʾa-a-ni* F frg: *t*]*u-ba-a-ni* Y. [198] *bar-tu* J: *-tú* frg. [200] *e-ta-pa-áš*

201 *la taš-me-a-šú [l]u-u ina kal* UD-*me lu-u ina kal mu-ši*
202 [*ina l*]*a si-me-ni-šú* LÚ.A—*šip-ri* TA* ŠÀ É.GAL
203 *ina* UGU DUMU—MAN *it-tal-ka ma-a* AD-*ka*
204 *re-eš-ka i-ti-ši ma-a* EN *lil-li-ka*
205 *at-tu-nu la ta-*[*šam-m*]*e-a-šú la tu-ra-ma-šú*
206 *la il-lak* [*ma-ṣar-t*]*u-šú tu-da-a-na*
207 *a-di* 1-*en ina* ŠÀ-*bi-ku-nu ša* EN-*šu i-ra-ʾa-mu-u-ni*
208 *ina* UGU É—EN.MEŠ-*šu mar-ṣa-šu-u-ni*
209 *il-lak-u-ni* (*ina* É.GAL) DI-*mu šá* LUGAL EN-*šu*
210 *e-mar-u-ni ha-ra-me-ma* TA* DUMU—MAN
211 EN-*ku-nu ina* É.GAL *tal-la-ka*

---

212 *šum-ma at-tu-nu pu-uh-ru ta-šá-kan-a-ni a-he-iš*
213 *tu-tam-ma-a-ni a-na* 1-*en ina* ŠÀ-*bi-ku-nu* LUGAL-*u-tu ta-dan-a-ni*

---

214 *šum-ma at-tu-nu* TA* ŠÀ-*bi* ŠEŠ.MEŠ-*šú* ŠEŠ.(MEŠ)—AD.MEŠ-*šú*
215 DUMU—ŠEŠ.MEŠ—AD.MEŠ-*šú qin-ni-šu* NUMUN É—AD-*šú*
216 *lu-u šá ina* KUR—*aš-šur šu-nu-u-ni lu šá ina* KUR *šá-ni-tim-ma*
217 *in-nab-tu-u-ni lu-u ina kal-zi* É.GAL *qur-bu-ti*
218 *lu-u ina kal-zi* É.GAL *pa-ti-ú-ti lu-u ina kal-za-a-ni*
219 GAL.MEŠ TUR.MEŠ *lu-u ina* GAL.MEŠ TUR.MEŠ-*te*
220 *lu-u ina* DUMU—SIG_5.MEŠ *lu-u ina* DUMU—*muš-ke-nu-ti*
221 *lu šá* LÚ.*ziq-ni lu* LÚ.SAG *lu-u ina* LÚ.ARAD.MEŠ
222 *lu-u ina* LÚ.ŠÁM.MEŠ *lu ina* DUMU KUR—*aš-šur lu ina* DUMU KUR
223 *šá-ni-tim-ma lu-u ina nap-har ṣal-mat*—SAG.DU *mal ba-šu-u*
224 1-*en ina* ŠÀ-*bi-ku-nu* GIŠ.GU.ZA KUR—*aš-šur tu-šá-aṣ-bat-a-ni*
225 LUGAL-*ú-tú* EN-*ú-*[*tú*] *šá* KUR—*aš-šur ta-da-na-niš-šú-ni*

201 If a messenger from within the Palace at an unexpected time, whether by day or by night, comes to the prince saying: "Your father has summoned you; let my lord come," you must not listen to him nor let him go away but you must guard him strongly until one of you, who loves his lord and feels concern over the house of his lords, goes to the Palace and ascertains the well-being of the king, his lord. (Only) afterwards you may go to the Palace with the prince, your lord.

§ 19 Prohibition against Seditious Meetings

212 You shall not hold an assembly to adjure one another and give the kingship to one of you.

§ 20 Action against Pretenders to Throne

214 You shall not help (anyone) from among his brothers, his uncles, his cousins, his family, or members of his father's line, whether those who are in Assyria or those who have fled to another country, or (anyone) in the closer palace groups or in the more remote palace groups or (any) groups great or small, or (any) of the old or young, of the rich or the poor, whether a bearded (courtier) or a eunuch, or (one) of the servants, or (one) of the bought (slaves) or any citizen of Assyria or any foreigner or any human being at all, any one of you, to seize the throne, nor shall you hand over to him the kingship and lordship of Assyria.

J: *e-tap-pa-*[*áš* frg. 201 ⌜*mu-ši*⌝ C: M[I] frg. 202 [*si*]-*me-ni-šú* J: *si-la-ma-n*[*i-šú*] frg. 204 *i-ti-ši* O: [*i*]*t-ti-ši* J, [*it*]-*te-ši* frg. 205 *at-tu-nu* C: *at-tú-nu* frg; *tu-ra-ma-šu* J: *tu-ra-ma-šú-nu* O. 207 EN-*šu* JO: -*šú* u frg; *i-ra-ʾa-mu-u-ni* Oe frg: *i-ra-a-mu-u-ni* Ju. 208 *mar-ṣa-šu-u-ni* u: -*šu-un-ni* J, -*šú-u-ni* O, -*áš-šú-un-ni* frg. 209 *il-lak-u-ni* eu: *i-lak-u-ni* J; *ina* É.GAL CJe: caret frg; EN-*šu* JO: -*šú* u frg. 210 *e-mar-u-ni* Ju frg: *e-rab-u-*[*ni*] O; *ha-ra-me-ma* J frg: *ha-ra-ma-a-ma* e. 212 *šum-ma* JOu: [*šú*]*m-mu* frg; *at-tu-nu* JO: *at-tú-nu* frg; ⌜*pu*⌝-*uh-ru* frg: UKKIN JOu; *a-he-iš* CJ: [*a-h*]*a-meš* frg, *a-na a-he-iš* frg. 213 ŠÀ-*bi-ku-nu* Ju: ŠÀ-*ku-nu* O frg; LUGAL-*u-tu* J: LUGAL-*tú* u; *ta-dan-a-ni* Je frg: *ta-da-na-a-ni* C frg, *ta-*⌜*dan*⌝-*na-a-ni* frg. 214 ŠEŠ.MEŠ—AD.MEŠ-*šú* Je; ŠEŠ—AD.MEŠ-*šú* C frg. 215 DUMU—ŠEŠ.MEŠ—AD.MEŠ-*šú* J: DUMU—ŠEŠ—AD.MEŠ-*šú* CO; *qin-ni-šu* J: [*q*]*in-ni-šú* u. 216 *šu-nu-u-ni* J: *šu-nu-ni* C; *šá-ni-tim-ma* Je frg: *šá-nim-tim-ma* C: MAN-*tim-ma* frg. 217 *kal-zi* "groups": taken to refer to the various groups of palace personnel listed as potential threats to the king's life in AGS 108ff and PRT 44. The adjectives "close" and "remote" are understood to indicate the distance of the threat from the king's person. 218 *pa-ti-ú-ti* H: -*u-te* J; *kal-za-a-ni* CHe: *kal-za-ni* J. 219 TUR.MEŠ-*te* J: TU]R.MEŠ H. 220 *muš-ke-nu-ti* CJ: -*te* e frg. 221 LÚ.ARAD.MEŠ CJ frg: ARAD.MEŠ H. 222 *ina* HJ: caret f; DUMU—KUR HJ: DUMU—KUR.KUR f. 223 *ba-šu-u* H: -*ú* C. 224 KUR—*aš-šur* f: caret J. 225 LUGAL-*ú-tú* H: -*u-tu* J; [*ta-d*]*a-na-niš-šu-un-ni* C:

226 *šum-ma* ^{m}*aš-šur*—DÙ—A DUMU—MAN GAL-*u šá* É—UŠ-*te*
227 GIŠ.GU.ZA *šá* KUR—*aš-šur*.KI *la tú-šá-aṣ-bat-a-ni*
228 LUGAL-*tú* EN-*tú šá* KUR—*aš-šur ina* UGU-*hi-ku-nu la ú-pa-áš-ú-ni*

[226] You shall help Assurbanipal, the great crown prince designate to seize the throne of Assyria, and he will exercise the kingship and lordship over you.

---

§ 21 **Allegiance to Assurbanipal**

229 *šum-ma at-tu-nu ina* UGU ^{m}*aš-šur*—DÙ—A DUMU—MAN GAL *šá* É—UŠ-*te*
230 DUMU ^{m}*aš-šur*—PAB—AŠ MAN KUR—*aš-šur* EN-*ku-nu la ta-ma-qut-a-ni*
231 *la ta-mut-ta-a-ni šá ina* UGU-*hi-šú ṭa-bu-u-ni*
232 *la tu-ba-ʾa-a-ni la te-ep-pa-šá-a-ni*
233 *šum-ma la* DÙG.GA-*tú te-ep-pa-šá-niš-šú-un-ni*
234 *mil-ku la dam-qu ta-mal-lik-a-šú-u-ni*
235 KASKAL *la šal-mu ina* GÌR.2-*šú ta-šá-kan-a-ni*
236 *ina ke-na-a-te tar-ṣa-a-te la ta-ta-nab-bal-a-šú-u-ni*

[229] You shall fall and die for Assurbanipal, the great crown prince designate, son of Esarhaddon, your lord, and seek to do for him what is good.

[233] You shall not do for him what is not good, nor give him an improper counsel or direct him in an unwholesome course, but continually serve him in a true and fitting manner.

---

§ 22 **Action against Murderer of Assurbanipal**

237 *šum-ma* ^{m}*aš-šur*—PAB—AŠ MAN KUR—*aš-šur* EN-*ku-nu ina ṣa-ha-ri šá* DUMU.MEŠ-*šú*
238 *a-na šim-te it-ta-lak lu* LÚ.SAG *lu* LÚ.*šá—ziq-ni*
239 *a-na* ^{m}*aš-šur*—DÙ—A DUMU—MAN GAL-*u*
240 *šá* É—UŠ-*te i-du-ak*
241 LUGAL-*u-tu šá* KUR—*aš-šur it-ti-ši*
242 *šum-ma at-tu-nu is-si-šú ta-šá-kan-a-ni*
243 *a-na* LÚ.ARAD-*nu-ti-šú ta-tu-ra-a-ni*
244 *la ta-bal-kàt-a-ni la ta-na-kir-a-ni*
245 KUR.KUR *gab-bu is-si-šú la tu-šam-kar-a-ni si-hu ina* UGU-*hi-šú la ta-šá-kan-a-ni*
246 *la ta-ṣab-bat-a-ni-šú-u-ni la ta-du-ka-šú-u-ni*
247 *ù* DUMU ^{m}*aš-šur*—DÙ—A DUMU—MAN GAL *šá* É—UŠ-*ti*
248 GIŠ.GU.ZA *šá* KUR—*aš-šur*.KI *la tu-šá-aṣ-bat-*[*a*]-*ni*

[237] If Esarhaddon, king of Assyria, passes away during the minority of his sons, and if either a bearded (courtier) or a eunuch puts Assurbanipal, the great crown prince designate, to death, and takes over the kingship of Assyria, you shall not make common cause with him and become his servant but shall break away and be hostile (to him), alienate all lands from him, instigate a rebellion against him, seize him and put him to death, and then help a son of Assurbanipal, the great crown prince designate to take the throne of Assyria.

---

249 *šum-ma at-tu-nu ina* IGI MÍ.*a-ri-ti*
250 *šá* ^{m}*aš-šur*—PAB—AŠ MAN KUR—*aš-šur*.KI *ù* DAM ^{m}*aš-šur*—DÙ—A DUMU—MAN GAL-*u*
251 *šá* É—UŠ-*ti la ta-da-gal-a-ni*

[249] You shall wait for a woman pregnant by Esarhaddon, king of Assyria, (or) for the wife of Assurbanipal, the great crown prince

t]*a-da-na-niš-šú-ni* H, *ta-da-ni-šú-nu* f. 226 É—UŠ-*te* HX: -*ti* Cf. 227 KUR—*aš-šur*.⌈KI⌉ f: KUR—*aš-šur* H. 228 LUGAL-*tú* Xf: -*u-tu* J; EN-*tú* Xf: -*u-t*[*u*] J; *ú-pa-áš-ú-ni* f: *up-pa-áš-u-n*[*i*] C. 229 *šum-ma* JX frg: *šúm-mu* f; *ina* Xf: caret frg. 230 EN-*ku-nu* JXf frg: -*ku* A. 231 *ta-mut-ta-a-ni* ANXf: *ta*-⌈*mu*⌉-*ta-a-n*[*i*] J frg; *ṭa-bu-u-ni* ACJX frg: DÙG.GA-*u-ni* f. 232 *la* JNX frg: caret A; *tu-ba-ʾa-a-ni* AX frg: *tu-ba-a-ni* J, [*t*]*ú-ba-ʾa-a-ni* f; *la* JNXf frg: caret A; *te-ep-pa-šá-a-ni* X: -*áš-a-ni* A, *te-pa-šá*-⌈*ni*⌉ J, -*šá-a-ni* f, -*áš-a-ni* N. 233 DÙG.GA-*tú* AXf: -*tu* CJ frg; *te-ep-pa-šá-niš-šú-un-ni* X: -*šá-ni-šú-u-ni* A, *te-pa-šá-niš-šu-un-ni* N, -*šá-a-ni-niš-šu-un-ni* f. 234 *dam-qu* frg: SIG_5 AJNX; *la* A: caret CJNXf; *ta-mal-lik-a-šú-u-ni* JX: *ta-ma-lik-a-šú-u-ni* ACN, *ta-mal-li-ka-šú-u-n*[*i*] f. 235 *ina* ANX: *ana* frg. 236 *ke-na-a-te* AJNX: -*ti* C; *tar-ṣa-a-te* X: -*ti* A, caret N; *ta-ta-nab-bal-a-šú-u-ni* N: (*ta*)-*ta-nab-bal-šú-u-ni* A, *ta-ta-na-bal-a-šú-u-ni* J. 237 EN-*ku-nu* NX: caret AJ. 238 LÚ.SAG NX: *šá—ziq-ni* A, *šá*—LÚ.*ziq-ni* J. 239 GAL-*u* J: GAL AX frg. 240 É—UŠ-*te* JX: -*ti* N. 241 [LUG]AL-*u-tu* J: LUGAL-*tú* X frg; KUR—*aš-šur* JX: KUR—*aš-šur*.KI A. 243 LÚ.ARAD-*nu-ti-šú* A: LÚ.ARAD.MEŠ-*šú* X; *ta-tu-ra-a-ni* A: [*t*]*a-tú-ra-a-ni* frg. 244 *ta-na-kir*-[*a-ni*] frg: *ta-na-ki-ir-ra-ni* A, *ta-na-ki-ra-ni* frg, *ta-na-kír-a-ni* frg. 245 KUR.KUR A frg: [KU]R.KUR.MEŠ frg; *gab*-⌈*bu*⌉ frg: *šá-ni-a-ti* A; *si-hu ina* [U]GU-*hi-šú la ta-šá-kan-a-ni* X frgg: caret A. 246 *ta-ṣab-bat-a-ni-šú-u-ni* A: *ta-ṣab-bat-a-šú-u-ni* frg. 247 GAL A frg: GAL-*u* frg; 249 MÍ.*a-ri-ti* A frg: MÍ.$PEŠ_4$ I frg. 250 KUR—*aš-šur*.KI I: KUR—*aš-šur* A; *ù* BI frg: caret A; DAM ABI: MÍ.DAM frg; GAL-*u* I: GAL AB frg. 251 É—UŠ-*ti* AB: É—[UŠ]-*ti* I (UŠ obliterated, not omitted by the scribe, as indicated in BaM Bh 3). 252 *tu-rab-ba-a-ni* AB: *tu-ra-ba-a-ni*

252 *ki-ma it-tab-ši la tu-rab-ba-a-ni*
253 GIŠ.GU.ZA *šá* KUR—*aš-šur*.KI *la tu-šá-aṣ-bat-a-ni*
254 *e-pi-šá-nu-ti šá bar-ti la ta-ṣab-bat-a-ni-ni*
255 *la ta-du-ka-a-ni* MU-*šú-nu* NUMUN-*šú-nu*
256 *ina* KUR *la tu-hal-laq-qa-a-ni da-me ku-um da-me*
257 *la ta-ta-ba-ka-a-ni gi-im-lu*
258 *šá* ^{m}*aš-šur*—DÙ—A DUMU—MAN GAL-*u šá* É—UŠ-*te*
259 *la tu-tar-ra-a-ni-ni šum-ma at-tu-nu*
260 *a-na* ^{m}*aš-šur*—DÙ—A DUMU—MAN GAL-*u šá* É—UŠ-*te*
261 DUMU ^{m}*aš-šur*—PAB—AŠ MAN KUR—*aš-šur* EN-*ku-nu*
262 *šam-mu šá mu-a-ti-šú tu-šá-kal-a-šú-u-ni*
263 *ta-šá-qi-a-šú-u-ni ta-pa-šá-šá-šú-u-ni*
264 *kiš-pi te-ep-pa-šá-niš-šú-u-ni* DINGIR.(MEŠ) *u* ^{d}IŠ.TAR
265 *is-si-šú tu-šá-az-na-a-ni*

---

266 *šum-ma at-tu-nu a-na* ^{m}*aš-šur*—DÙ—A DUMU—MAN GAL-*u šá* É—UŠ-*te*
267 DUMU ^{m}*aš-šur*—PAB—AŠ MAN KUR—*aš-šur* EN-*ku-nu*
268 *ki-i nap-šá-te-ku-nu la tar-ʾa-ma-a-ni*
269 *šum-ma at-tu-nu ina* IGI ^{m}*aš-šur*—DÙ—A DUMU—MAN GAL *šá* É—UŠ-*ti*
270 *šá* ŠEŠ.MEŠ-*šú* DUMU AMA-*šú kar-ṣi-šú-nu ta-kal-a-ni*
271 *la* MUN-*šú-nu ta-qab-ba-a-ni* Á.2-*ku-nu*
272 *ina* É.MEŠ-*šú-nu tu-bal-a-ni ina* ŠÀ-*bi-šú-nu ta-ha-ṭa-a-ni*
273 TA* ŠÀ-*bi ti-din-tú šá* ^{m}*aš-šur*—PAB—AŠ MAN KUR—*aš-šur* AD-*šú-nu i-din-na-šá-nu-ni*
274 *qi-ni-tu šá šú-nu iq-nu-u-ni ta-na-áš-šá-a-ni*
275 *šum-ma ti-din-tú* A.ŠÀ.MEŠ É.MEŠ GIŠ.SAR.MEŠ
276 UN.MEŠ *ú-nu-tú* ANŠE.KUR.RA.MEŠ ANŠE.GÌR.NUN.NA
277 ANŠE.MEŠ GUD.MEŠ UDU.MEŠ *šá* ^{m}*aš-šur*—PAB—AŠ MAN KUR—*aš-šur*.KI
278 *a-na* DUMU.MEŠ-*šú id-din-u-ni la ina pa-ni-šú-nu la šu-tú-u-ni*

designate (to give birth), and after (a son) is born, bring him up and set him on the throne of Assyria, seize and slay the perpetrators of rebellion, destroy their name and their seed from the land, and by shedding blood for blood, avenge Assurbanipal, the great crown prince designate.

§ 23 **Prohibition against Killing Assurbanipal**

[259] You shall not give Assurbanipal, the great crown prince designate, son of Esarhaddon, king of Assyria, your lord, a deadly drug to eat or to drink, nor anoint him with it, nor practice witchcraft against him, nor make gods and goddesses angry with him.

§ 24 **Action in Favour of Assurbanipal's Brothers**

[266] You shall love Assurbanipal, the great crown prince designate, son of Esarhaddon, king of Assyria, your lord, like yourselves.

[269] You shall not slander his brothers, his mother's sons, before Assurbanipal, the great crown prince designate, nor speak anything evil about them, nor lift your hands against their houses or commit a crime against them, nor take anything away from the gift which their father has given them, or the acquisitions which they themselves have made.

[275] The gift of lands, houses, orchards, peoples, implements, horses, mules, donkeys, cattle and flocks which Esarhaddon, king of Assyria, has given to his sons, shall be theirs.

I. [254] *e-pi-šá-nu-ti* AI: *e-piš-a-nu-ti* B; *ta-ṣab-bat-a-ni-ni* I: *-a-ni* A, *ta-ṣa-bat-a-ni-ni* B. [256] *tu-hal-laq-qa-a-ni* AB: [*t*]*u*-[*ha*]*l*-⌜*la-qa*⌝-*a*-[*ni*] M; *da-me* AIi: *da-a-me* B. [257] *ta-ta-ba-ka-a-ni* ABi: *ta-ta-bak-a-ni* I; *gi-im-lu* AIi: *-li* B. [258] GAL-*u* i: GAL ABI; É—UŠ-*te* i: *-ti* ABI. [260] GAL-*u* i: GAL Bp; É—UŠ-*te* i: *-ti* ABp. [263] *ta-pa-šá-šá*-⌜*a*⌝-*šu-u-ni* B: *ta-pa-šá-šá-šú-u-ni* i. [264] [*t*]*e-ep-pa-šá-niš-šú-u-ni* B: *t*[*e-e*]*p-pa-šá-ni-šú-u-ni* A, *te-ep-pa-šá-niš-un-ni* F, *te-pa-šá-ni-šu-un-ni* i, *-niš-šú-ni* frg; DINGIR.MEŠ BFi: DINGIR frg; ^{d}IŠ.TAR Bi: ^{d}15 F. [265] *is-si-šú* ABFi: *-šu* M; *tu-ša-az-na-a-ni* I: *tu-šá-za-na-a-ni* Fi, *tu-šá-za-a-na-a-ni* B. [266] *a-na* AFi frg: *a-(na)* B; GAL-*u* i frg: GAL ABF; É—UŠ-*te* i frg: *-ti* AB. [268] *nap-šá-te-ku-nu* i: *nap-šat-ku-nu* A, ZI.MEŠ-*ku-nu* B; *tar-ʾa-ma-a-ni* A: *tar-a-ma-a-ni* B frg, *ta-ram-ma-ni* i: *tar-a-ma-ni* M. [269] GAL ABM frg: GAL-*u* frg; É—UŠ-*ti* AB frg: *-te* Fi frg. [270] ŠEŠ.MEŠ-*šú* A frg: *-šu* i; *ta-kal-a-ni* AF frgg: [*t*]*a-kal-ni* frg. [271] MUN-*šú-nu* AB: DÙG.GA-*ta-šú-nu* F; *ta-qab-ba-a-ni* A: *ta-qa-ba-a-ni* frg. [272] É.MEŠ-*šú-nu* AB: *-šu-nu* frg; ŠÀ-*bi-šú-nu* F frgg: *-šú* A, ŠÀ-*šú-nu* B; *ta-ha-ṭa-a-ni* B frg: *-ṭa-ni* AF. [273] ŠÀ-*bi* A: ŠÀ frg; *ti-din-tú* AF: *-tu* frg, *-te* frg; ^{m}*aš-šur*—PAB—AŠ MAN KUR—*aš-šur* FB frg: caret A; *i-din-na-šá-nu-ni* frg: *id-din-áš-šá-nu-u-ni* A, *id-di-na-áš-šú*-[*u-ni*] frg. [274] *qi-ni-tu* A frg: *-tú* BF; *šú-nu* AB: *šu-nu* frg; *iq-nu-u-ni* A frgg: *iq-qi-nu-u-n*[*i*] B; *ta-na-áš-šá-a-ni* AB: *ta-na-šá-a-ni* frg. [275] *ti-din-tú* A: *-tu* B frg. [276] *ú-nu-tú* AB: *-tu* frg. [277] KUR—*aš-šur*.KI B: KUR—*aš-šur* A. [278] *a-na* BY: *a-(na)* A; *id-din-u-ni* A: *i-din-u-ni* B; *pa-ni-šú-nu* AY: IGI-*šú-nu* B; *šu-tú-u-ni* A: *šu-tu-u-ni* B. [280] *ta-qab-ba-a-ni* A:

279 *šum-ma de-iq-ta-šú-nu ina* IGI ᵐ*aš-šur*—DÙ—A DUMU—MAN GAL
280 *šá* É—UŠ-*ti la ta-qab-ba-a-ni*
281 *šum-ma ina* IGI-*ni-šú la i-za-zu-u-ni is-si-ku-nu*
282 *la ú-sa-ta-mah-u-ni*

---

283 *a-de-e an-nu-ti šá* ᵐ*aš-šur*—PAB—AŠ MAN KUR—*aš-šur*.KI
284 *ina* UGU ᵐ*aš-šur*—DÙ—A DUMU—MAN GAL *šá* É—UŠ-*ti*
285 (*ù*) ŠEŠ.MEŠ-*šú* DUMU AMA-*šú šá* ᵐ*aš-šur*—DÙ—A DUMU—MAN GAL
286 *šá* É—UŠ-*ti ú-dan-nin-u-ni is-si-ku-nu*
287 *iš-kun-u-ni ta-me-tú ú-tam-mu-ka-nu-ni*
288 *a-na* DUMU.M[EŠ-*k*]*u-nu* DUMU—DUMU.MEŠ-*ku-nu a-na* NUMUN-*ku-nu*
289 *a-na* NUMUN—NUMUN-[*ku-n*]*u šá* EGIR *a-de-e a-na* UD-*me ṣa-a-ti*
290 *ib-ba-šú-u-ni la ta-qab-ba-a-ni ṭè-mu*
291 *la ta-šá-ka*[*n*]-*šú-u-ni ma-a a-de-e an-nu-te*
292 *uṣ-ra ma-a ina* ŠÀ-*bi a-de-e-ku-nu la ta-ha-ṭi-a*
293 ZI.MEŠ-*ku-nu la tu-hal-la-qa*
294 *ma-a* KUR-*ku-nu a-na ha-pe-e* UN.MEŠ-*ku-nu*
295 *a-na šal-la-li la ta-da-na ma-a a-bu-tú*
296 *an-ni-tu šá ina* IGI DINGIR.MEŠ *a-me-lu-te mah-rat-u-ni*
297 *ši-i ina pa-ni-ku-nu lu mah-rat ina* UGU-*hi-ku-nu lu ṭa-bat*
298 ᵐ*aš-šur*—DÙ—A DUMU—MAN GAL *šá* É—UŠ-*ti a-na be-lu-ti*

279 You shall speak good of them before Assurbanipal, the great crown prince designate. They shall stand before him and be united with you.

§ 25 Perpetuating Allegiance to Assurbanipal

283 This treaty which Esarhaddon, king of Assyria, has confirmed and concluded with you on behalf of Assurbanipal, the great crown prince designate and his brothers, sons by the same mother as Assurbanipal, the great crown prince designate, by making you take an oath, you shall speak to your sons and grandsons, your seed and your seed's seed which shall be born in the future, and give them orders as follows:

292 "Guard this treaty. Do not sin against your treaty and annihilate yourselves, do not turn your land over to destruction and your people to deportation. May this matter which is acceptable to god and mankind, be acceptable to you too, may it be good to you. May Assurbanipal, the great crown prince designate, be protected for (his) lordship

⌜*ta*⌝-*qa-ba-a-ni* frg, [*t*]*a-qab-ba-ni* Y. 282 ⌜*ú*⌝-*sa-ta-mah*-⌜*u-ni*⌝ A (coll. from photo): -*ta-a-mah-u-ni* B. 283 KUR—*aš-šur*.KI B: KUR—*aš-šur* A frg. 284 É—UŠ-*ti* BY: -*te* frg, É—*re-(du)-u-ti* A. 285 *ù* frg: caret ABJ; GAL ABY frg: GAL-*u* frg. 286 É—UŠ-*ti* AB: -*te* J. 287 *iš-kun-*[*u*]-*ni* B: *iš-ku-nu-u-ni* J; *ta-me-tú* AB: -*tu* C; *ú-tam-mu-ka-nu-ni* B: -*ka-nu-u-ni* frg, *ú-ta-mu-ka-nu-u-ni* A. 290 *ib-ba-šú-u-ni* B: -*áš-š*[*u-u-n*]*i* A; *ta-qab-ba-a-ni* A: -*ba-niš-*[C, -*ba-a-ni-šú-ni* A. 291 *an-nu-te* A: -*ti* BH. 292 *uṣ-ra* AH: *la u*[*ṣ*]-*ra-a* C; ŠÀ-*bi* AH: [Š]À B. 294 *ha-pe-e* ABH: *ha-bé-e* C. 295 *ta-da-na ma-a* C: *ta-da*-⌜*na*⌝ [*ma-a*] A (coll. from photo). 296 *an-ni-tu* H:-*tú* B; DINGIR.MEŠ CH: DINGIR A; *u* A: caret CH; *a-me-lu-te* H: LÚ-*ti* AC. 297 *pa-ni-ku-nu* C: IGI.MEŠ-*ku-n*[*u*] B. 298 GAL CB: GAL-*u* H; *be-lu-ti* C: -*te* H, *be-lut* A, EN-*ut* B. 300

COURTESY TRUSTEES OF THE BRITISH MUSEUM

FIG. 11. *Deportation and execution of rebels (reign of Sennacherib).*
ORIGINAL DRAWING IV, 53.

299 KUR *u* UN.MEŠ *lu na-ṣir*
300 EGIR *a-na* LUGAL-*ú-ti lu na-bi* MU-*šú*
301 LUGAL MAN-*ma* EN MAN-*ma ina* UGU-*hi-ku-nu la ta-šá-ka-na*

---

302 *šum-ma me-me-ni ina* UGU ᵐ*aš-šur*—PAB—AŠ MAN KUR—*aš-šur*
303 *si-hu bar-tu e-tap-áš ina* GIŠ.GU.ZA LUGAL-*ti-šú*
304 *it-tu-šib šum-ma a-na* LUGAL-*ti-šú*
305 *ta-ha-du-a-ni la ta-ṣab-bat-a-niš-šú-u-ni*
306 *la ta-du-ka-a-šú-u-ni šum-ma am—mar ṣa-ba-ti-šú*
307 *du-a-ki-šú la ma-ṣa-ku-nu a-na* LUGAL-*u-ti-šú*
308 *ta-ma-gúr-a-ni ta-me-tú ša* LÚ.ARAD-*nu-ti*
309 *ta-tam-ma-a-ni-šú-u-ni ina* UGU-*hi-šu*
310 *la ta-bal-kàt-a-ni ina gam-mur-ti* ŠÀ-*bi-ku-nu*
311 *qa-ra-a-bu is-si-šú la tu-pa-áš-a-ni*
312 KUR.KUR *šá-ni-a-te is-si-šú la tu-šam-kar-a-ni*
313 *hu-ub-tu-šú la ta-hab-bat-a-ni-ni*
314 *de-ek-tu-šú la ta-du-ka-a-ni*
315 MU-*šú* NUMUN-*šú ina* KUR *la tu-hal-laq-a-ni*
316 ᵐ*aš-šur*—DÙ—A DUMU—MAN GAL-*u ša* É—UŠ-*u-te*
317 GIŠ.GU.ZA AD-*šú la tu-šá-aṣ-bat-a-ni*

---

318 *šum-ma at-tu-nu* TA* ŠÀ-*bi* ŠEŠ.MEŠ-*šú*

over the land and the people, (and) may his name later be proclaimed for the kingship. Do not place any other king or any other lord over you."

§ 26 **Action against Usurper of Esarhaddon's Throne**

302 If anyone makes rebellion or insurrection against Esarhaddon, king of Assyria and seats himself on the royal throne, you shall not rejoice over his kingship but shall seize him and put him to death. If you are unable to seize him and put him to death, you shall not submit to his kingship nor swear an oath of servitude to him, but shall revolt against him and unreservedly do battle with him, make other lands inimical to him, take plunder from him, defeat him, destroy his name and his seed from the land, and help Assurbanipal, the great crown prince designate, to take his father's throne.

§ 27 **Injunction against Fomenting Strife between King and Crown Prince**

318 If (any) one of his brothers, his uncles,

LUGAL-⸢*ú*⸣-[*ti*] B: -*u-te* H; MU-*šú* B: -*šu* C. 301 UGU-*hi*-⸢*ku*⸣-*nu* B: -*hi-šú* frg; *ta-šá-ka-na* H: -*kan-a-ni* B, ⸢*taš-(ka)-na*⸣ C. 302 *me-me-ni* AC: *me-me-(ni)* frg; MAN KUR—*aš-šur* AB: caret C frg. 303 *e-tap-áš* BC: *e-ta*-⸢*pa*⸣-*áš* A; LUGAL-*ti-šú* B: LUGAL-*ti* C, -*u-te* frg, MAN-*ti* A. 304 LUGAL-*ti-šú* BC: -*u-te-šú* frg. 305 *ta-ha-du-a-ni* B: *tah-du-a-ni* C; *ta-ṣab-bat-a-ni-šú-u-ni* A: -*a-šú-u-ni* C, *ta-ṣa-bat-a-šú-u-ni* frg. 306 *ṣa-ba-ti-šú* A: -*šu* C, *ṣa-ba-te*-⸢*šú*⸣ frg, *ṣa-bat-ti-šú* B. 307 *du-a-ki-šú* A: -*šu* C; LUGAL-*u-ti-šú* A: -*u-te-šú* frg. 308 *ta-me-tú* A: -*tu* C; LÚ.ARAD-*nu-ti* A: LÚ.ARAD.MEŠ-*ti* C, LÚ].ARAD.MEŠ-*a-nu*-[*ti*] B. 310 *gam-mur-t*[*i* A: *gu-mur-ti* C. 311 *qa-ra-a-bu* C: *qa-ra-bu* A; *tu-pa-áš-a-ni* C: *tu-pa-šá-ni* J. 312 *šá-ni-a-te* A: -*ti* C. 314 *ta-du-ka-a-ni* C: -*ka-ni* J. 315 MU-*šú* AJ: MU C; *tu-hal-laq-a-ni* J: -*la-qa-a-ni* C. 316 GAL-*u* J: GAL AC; É—UŠ-*u-te* J: É—UŠ-*ti* BC. 317 caret CJ: *ina* A; AD-*šú* AC: -*šu* J; *tu-šá-aṣ-bat-a-ni* CJ: [*tu-ša-a*]*ṣ-bat-t*[*a-a-ni*] A. 318 ŠÀ-*bi* JN: ŠÀ BC. 319 ŠEŠ.MEŠ—AD.MEŠ-*šú* N: —AD-*šú* J, ŠEŠ—AD.MEŠ-*šú* ABC; DUMU—ŠEŠ.MEŠ—

COURTESY TRUSTEES OF THE BRITISH MUSEUM

FIG. 12. *Spoils of war: cattle, sheep and goats (reign of Sennacherib).*
ORIGINAL DRAWING IV, 15.

319 ŠEŠ.MEŠ—AD.MEŠ-*šú* DUMU—ŠEŠ.MEŠ—AD.MEŠ-*šú*
320 TA* ŠÀ-*bi* NUMUN É—AD-*šú* TA* ŠÀ-*bi* NUMUN MAN *pa-ni-ú-ti*
321 TA* ŠÀ-*bi* LÚ.GAL LÚ.NAM LÚ.SAG TA* ŠÀ-*bi* DUMU KUR—*aš-šur*
322 TA ŠÀ-*bi* DUMU KUR *šá-ni-tim-ma ú-šak-pa-du-ka-nu-u-ni*
323 *i-qab-ba-ak-ka-nu-u-ni ma-a kar-ṣi šá* ^{m}*aš-šur*—DÙ—A
324 DUMU—MAN GAL-*u šá* É—UŠ-*ti ina* IGI AD-*šú ak-la*
325 *ma-a a-bat-su la* DÙG.GA-*tu la* SIG$_5$-*tu qi-bi-a*
326 *ina bir-tu-šú ina bir-ti* AD-*šú tu-šam-ha-ṣa-a-ni*
327 *a-na zi-a-ri ina* IGI *a-he-iš ta-šá-kan-a-šá-nu-ni*

his cousins, his family, (any) one of his own dynastic line, or any descendant of former royalty or (any) one of the magnates, governors or eunuchs, (or any) one of the citizens of Assyria, (or) any foreigner, involves you in a plot, saying to you: "Malign Assurbanipal, the great crown prince designate, in the presence of his father. Speak evil and improper things about him," you shall not make it come to a fight between him and his father by stirring up mutual hatred between them.

§ 28 **Response to Fomentors of Strife**

328 EN—*qi-ʾi šá ṭè-e-mu i-šá-kan-u-ka-nu-u-ni*
329 *ú-šá-an-za-ru-ka-nu-ni* [*q*]*i*?-*b*[*a*?-*n*]*i*?-*šú*
330 *ma-a lu* ŠEŠ.MEŠ-*šú ma-a lu* LÚ.ARAD.MEŠ-*ni*
331 *ša ina* UGU AD-*šú ú-*[*šá-an-z*]*i-ru-u-ni*
332 *ša kar-ṣi-šú ina* IGI AD-*šú* [*e-k*]*al-u-ni a-le-eʾ*
333 *ma-a la šá* ^{d}*aš-šur* ^{d}UTU *ù* [^{d}IM? *ina* UG]U-*šú iq-bu-u-ni ta-kun*
334 *ma-a ina ba-lat aš-šur* ⸢*ù*?⸣ ^{d}UTU AD-*ku-nu* LU TI *ú* ŠID
335 *ma-a šá* ŠEŠ-*ku-nu kab-bi-da* ZI.MEŠ-*ku-nu uṣ-*[*r*]*a*

[328] (Instead) say to the envious person who commands you and would make you *become accursed*: "Where are his brothers or the servants who *made themselves accursed* to his father by slandering him in the presence of his father? Has not what Aššur, Šamaš and [Adad] said about him proved to be true? Did your father ...... without (the consent of) Aššur and Šamaš? Let your brother be honoured, and stay alive."

§ 29 **Injunction against Fomenting Strife between Prince and His Brothers**

336 *šum-ma me-me-ni ú-šak-pa-du-ka-nu-u-ni i-qab-ba-kan-u-ni*
337 TA ŠÀ-*bi* ŠEŠ.MEŠ-*šú* ŠEŠ—AD.MEŠ-*šú* [DUMU—ŠEŠ].MEŠ—AD.MEŠ-*šú qin-ni-šú*
338 NUMUN É—AD-*šú lu* L[Ú.SAG] *lu* LÚ.*šá—ziq-ni lu* DUMU KUR—*aš-šur*
339 *lu* DUMU KUR *šá-ni-nim-ma lu ina nap-har ṣal-mat*—SAG.DU
340 *ma-la ba-šu-u i-qab-ba-ka-nu-u-ni*
341 *ma-a kar-ṣi šá* ŠEŠ.MEŠ-*šú* DUMU AMA-*šú ina pa-ni-šú*
342 *ak-la ma-a šam-hi-ṣa ina bir-tu-šú-nu*

[336] If someone involves you in a plot, be it one of his brothers, his [unc]les, his relations, a member of his father's line, a bearded (courtier) or a e[unuch], an Assyrian or a foreigner, or any human being at all, saying: "Slander his brothers, sons by his own mother, before him, make it come to a fight between them, and divide his brothers, sons of his own mother, from him," you shall not

AD.MEŠ-*šú* JN: -ŠEŠ—⸢AD-*šú*⸣ C; caret BJN: *q*]*in-ni-šú* c. 320 TA* ŠÀ-*bi* AN: TA* ŠÀ BCJ, caret c; É—AD-*šú* BN: -*šu* Jc, AD-*šú* A; MAN CN: LUGAL B; *pa-ni-ú-ti* B: -*ú-ut-ti* C, -*u-ti* N, -*u-tú* c. 321 ⸢ŠÀ⸣-*bi* N: ŠÀ Cc, caret B; LÚ.GAL AC, LÚ.⸢NUN⸣ N, NUN-*e* Bc; ŠÀ-[*b*]*i* N: ŠÀ BCc; KUR—*aš-šur* BC: .KI Nc. 322 ŠÀ-*bi* N: ŠÀ BCc; *šá-ni-tim-ma* N: *šá-nim-tim-ma* C, *ša-ni-tim-ma* c, MAN-*tim-ma* B; *ú-šak-pa-du-ka-nu-u-ni* N: *ú-šak-pa-du-u-ka-(nu)-u-ni* C, *ú-šak-pa-ad-u-ka-nu-ni* c, [*ú*]-*šá-ak-pa-du-ka-nu-ni* B. 323 *i-qab-ba-ak-ka-nu-u-ni* c: *i-qab-ba-ka-nu-ni* BC, *iq-qa-ba-kan-u-ni* N (coll. from photo). 324 GAL-*u* N: GAL BCc; É—UŠ-*ti* BCN: -*te* c. 325 DÙG.GA-*tu* BCN: -*tú* c; SIG$_5$-*tu* CN: -*tú* Bc. 326 *ina bir-ti* Bc: *bir-ti* CN; *tu-šam-ha-ṣa-a-ni* C: -*ṣa-ni* B. 327 *ta-šá-kan-a-šá-nu-ni* BC: -*šú*-⸢*nu-ni*⸣ frg,]-*a-šu-n*[*u-ni*] c. 329 *ú-šá-an-za-ru-ka-nu-ni* B: -*za-ar-u-ka-nu*-⸢*ni*⸣ frg. For the rendering of *šanzuru* "to make hateful (*nazru*)" see CAD N/2 139ff, and cf. NA *šanmuru* "to light" (lit. "to make bright", *namru*)" corresponding to Babyl. *nummuru* (CAD N/1 217). The causative translation "zu schimpfen veranlassen" given in BaM Bh 3 is out of the question. 332 Context requires restoring [*e-k*]*al-u-ni* (pret. with a dissimilated root vowel) rather than [*ek-k*]*al-u-ni* (BaM Bh 3, etc.). 333 ^{d}*aš-šur* B: *aš-šur* frg. The word *abutu* supplied in BaM Bh 3 is unnecessary. 334 End of the line obscure (B only); the interpretation offered in BaM Bh 3 p.159 and 187 ("Did your father recite the *udutilû* (formula) without Aššur and Šamaš") involves several difficulties and is not convincing. 336 [*i-qab*]-*ba-kan-u-ni* frg: *i-qab-ba-ka-*[*nu-ni*] F. 337 *qin-ni-šú* F: -⸢*šu*⸣ frg. 338 LÚ.*šá—ziq-ni* R: *šá*—L]Ú*.*ziq-ni* B. 340 *ba-šu-u* F: *ba-š*]*ú-u* B, GÁL frg. 341

343 *ma-a* ŠEŠ.MEŠ-*šú* DUMU AMA-*šú* TA* *pa-ni-šú pur-sa*
344 *at-tu-nu ta-šam-ma-a-ni la* DÙG.GA-*tú*
345 *ša* ŠEŠ.MEŠ-*šú ina* IGI-*šú ta-qab-ba-a-ni*
346 TA* IGI ŠEŠ.MEŠ-*šú ta-par-ra-sa-a-šú-u-ni*
347 *šum-ma qa-bi-a-nu šá a-bu-tú an-ni-tú*
348 *iq-ba-ka-nu-u-ni tu-ra-ma-šú-u-ni*
349 *šum-ma la tal-lak-a-ni-ni a-na* ^{m}*aš-šur*—DÙ—A DUMU—MAN GAL
350 *šá* É—UŠ-*te la ta-qab-ba-a-ni*
351 *ma-a* AD-*u-ka a-de-e ina* UGU *is-si-ni*
352 *is-sa-kan ú-tam-ma-na-a-*[*ši*]

obey nor speak evil about his brothers in his presence, nor divide him from his brothers; you shall not let those who speak such things go free but shall come and report to Assurbanipal, the great crown prince designate as follows: "Your father imposed a treaty on us and made us swear an oath concerning it."

---

353 *šum-ma ta-da-ga-la-n*[*i*? *ina*? IGI? ^{m}*aš-šur*—DÙ—A DUMU—MAN] GAL *šá* É—UŠ-*ti*
354 ŠEŠ.MEŠ-*šú* [*x*] *kan šu x*[*x x*]*x-ku-uš*
355 *ma*!-*ṣar-t*[*u x x x x x x x*] *at-tu-nu*
356 *ki-i ra-ma-*[*ni-ku-nu*] *la ta-ga-ri-šú-nu-ni*
357 *pu-x*[*x x x x x*] *ina* ŠÀ-*bi-šú-nu*
358 *la tu-še-*[*x x x*] *ma-a* AD-*ku-nu ina* ŠÀ-*bi a-de-e*
359 *is-sa-kan ú-ta*[*m-ma-na-a-ši*]

§ 30 **Response to Attempts to Foment Strife**

353 You shall not *look on* [...... Assurbanipal], the great crown [prince], his brothers [......]. You shall contest them as you would on [your] own [behalf], and rouse [*fear*] in their heart, saying: "Your father set (this) in a treaty and made [us] swear it."

---

360 *šum-ma at-tu-nu ki-ma* ^{m}*aš-*[*šu*]*r*—PAB—AŠ MAN KUR—*aš-šur* EN-*kunu*
361 *a-na šim-ti it-ta-lak* ^{m}*aš-šur*—DÙ—A
362 DUMU—MAN GAL-*u šá* É—UŠ-*ti ina* GIŠ.GU.ZA LUGAL-*u-te it-t*[*u-šib*]
363 *a-bu-tú la* DÙG.GA-*tu šá* ŠEŠ.MEŠ-*šú* DUM[U AM]A-*šú*
364 *ina* IGI ŠEŠ-*šú-nu ta-qab-ba-a-ni tu-šá-an-za-ra-ni*
365 *ma-a* ŠU.2-*ka ina* HUL-*tim ina* ŠÀ-*bi-šú-nu ub-bíl*
366 *šum-ma* TA* IGI ^{m}*aš-šur*—DÙ—A DUMU—MAN GAL-*u*
367 *šá* É—UŠ-*te tu-na-kar-a-šá-n*[*u-u-ni*]
368 *di-ib-bi-šú-nu la* SIG$_5$.MEŠ *ina* IG[I Š]EŠ-*šú-nu*
369 *ta-*[*qa*]*b-ba-a-ni ma-za-a-su šá* ^{m}[*aš-šur*—PAB—AŠ]
370 MAN KUR—*aš-šur* AD-*šú-nu ú-kal-lim-u-šú-nu-*[*ni*] *ina* IGI ^{m}*aš-šur*—DÙ—A
371 DUMU—M[AN GAL *ša*] É—UŠ-*t*[*i*] *ta-qab-ba-a-ni*
372 *x*[*x x x x x x*] *ú-na-kar-šú-*[*nu-u-ni*]

§ 31 **Injunction against Fomenting Strife after Assurbanipal's Accession**

360 When Esarhaddon, king of Assyria, your lord, passes away and Assurbanipal, the great crown prince designate, ascends the royal throne, you shall not say any evil word about his bro[thers, sons of] his own mo[ther], before their brother nor try to make them *accursed* (saying): "Bring your hand against them for an evil deed." You shall not alienate them from Assurbanipal, the great crown prince designate, nor shall you say any evil word about them in the presence of their brother. (As for) the positions which Esarhaddon, king of Assyria, their father, assigned them, you shall not speak in the presence of Assurbanipal, the great crown prince designate, (trying to make him) remove them [from these *positions*].

---

373 *šum-ma sar-bu šá ina* UGU DINGIR.MEŠ *ša pu-uh-ri*

§ 32 **Prohibition against Invalidation of Oath**

373 You shall not smear your face, your hands, and your throat with ... *against* the

pa-ni-šú p: IGI-*šú* FR frg. 342 *šam-hi-ṣa* frg: *šá-an-hi-ṣa* F. 343 *pa-ni-šú* F: IGI-*šú* w. 344 DÙG.GA-*tú* F: -*tu* Aw. 345 IGI-*šú* FR: IGI.MEŠ-*šú* frg, *pa-*[*ni-šú* p. 346 [*ta-par-r*]*a-sa-a-šú-u-ni* A: -*sa-šú-u-ni* w, *ta-par-ra-sa-*⸢*šú-ni*⸣ R, -*sa-šú-nu-u-ni* F. 347 *a-bu-tú* F frg: -*tu* R; *an-ni-tú* Fw: -*tu* AR. 348 *tu-ra-ma-šú-u-ni* F: -*šá-nu-u-ni* R. 349 *tal-lak-a-ni-ni* Fw: *ta-lak-a-ni-ni* BR. 350 É—UŠ-*te* w: -⸢*ti*⸣ BR. 351 AD-*u-ka* B: AD-*ka* F. 352 *is-sa-kan* R: *i-sa-kan* AB. 353 É—UŠ-*ti* R: -*te* A. 356 *ta-ga-ri-šú-nu-ni*⸣ frg: *tu-ga-ri-a-šá-nu-u-*[*ni*] R. 357 ŠÀ-*bi-šú-nu* R frg: ŠÀ-*šú-nu* B. 358 ŠÀ-*bi* frg: ŠÀ R. 362 LUGAL-*u-te* frg: LUGAL-*tu* z, -*ti* R. 363 DÙG.GA-*tu* Rz frg: -*tú* frg. 364 ŠEŠ-*šú-nu* Rz frg: ŠE]Š.MEŠ-*šú-nu* frg. 365 ŠÀ-*bi-šú-nu* R: ŠÀ-*šú-nu* frg. 367 É—UŠ-*te* frgg: -*ti* z. 373ff For a discussion of this difficult passage see BaM Bh 3 p.187f. The interpretation of *sar-bu* as "tallow" favoured there is difficult to reconcile with the fact that the word occurs as the object of *rakāsu* "to bind" in l. 376; it is also unlikely on the grounds that *sarbu* "tallow" is otherwise not attested in NA and only known lexically from one occurrence in the rare-word column of the synonym list Malku. Similar objections apply to other proposed or thinkable readings like *sar-bu* "moisture", *šar-še-rum* "red paste", or

374 *lu pa-ni-ku-nu lu* ŠU.2-*ku-nu lu na-pul-ta-ku-nu*
375 *ta-pa-šá-áš-a-ni lu-u ina si-qi-ku-nu*
376 *ta-rak-kas-a-ni šá ma-mit pa-šá-ri te-ep-pa-šá-a-ni*

gods of the assembly, nor tie it in your *lap*, nor do anything to undo the oath.

---

§ 33 Probition against Undoing the Oath

377 *šum-ma at-tu-nu tur-tu tu-tar-ra-[a-ni]*
378 *ma-mit ta-pa-šar-a-ni ši-in-ga-te [x x x]*
379 *[ina* I]GI-*ni šá [tu]r-tu tur-ri ma-mit pa-šá-a-ri ta-ha-sa-sa-[a-ni]*
380 *[t]e-pa-šá-a-ni ta-me-tu an-[ni-tu ina* UGU$^{?}$] ^{m}*aš-šur*—DÙ—A DUMU—MAN GAL
381 *šá* É—UŠ-*ti* DUMU ^{m}*aš-šur*—PAB—AŠ MAN KUR—*aš-šur* EN-*ku-nu*
382 *šá ul-tú* UD-*me an-ni-e a-[d]i ša* EGIR *a-de-e*
383 *ib-ba-áš-ši-u-[ni at]-tu-nu* DUMU.MEŠ-*ku-nu šá a-na*
384 UD-*me ṣ[a-a-t]i ib-ba-áš-šú-u-ni ta-ʾa-ku-nu*

377 You shall not revoke or undo (this) oath ... [...]; you shall neither think of nor perform a ritual to revoke or undo the oath. You and your sons to be born in the future will be bound by this oath concerning Assurbanipal, the great crown prince designate, son of Esarhaddon, your lord, from this day on until what(ever) comes after this treaty.

---

§ 34 Attitude toward Swearing the Oath

385 *[šu]m-ma at-tu-nu ki-i (ina) kaq-qar ta-me-ti an-ni-tu*
386 *[t]a-za-za-a-ni ta-me-tu ša da-bab-ti šap-ti*
387 *ta-tam-ma-a-ni ina gu-mur-[t]i* ŠÀ-*ku-nu la ta-ta-ma-a-ni a-na* DUMU.MEŠ-*ku-nu ša* EGIR *a-de-e*
388 *ib-ba-áš-šú-u-ni la tu-šal-mad-a-ni*
389 *šu[m-m]a at-tu-nu* [G]IG *la pa$^{!}$-aṭ$^{!}$-ru$^{!!}$ ina* UGU
390 *r[a-ma-ni-k]u-nu ta-šá-kan-a-ni [in]a* ŠÀ-*b[i] a-de-e*
391 *šá* ^{m}*aš-šur*—PAB—AŠ MAN KUR—*aš-šur šá ina* UGU ^{m}*aš-šur*—DÙ—A DUMU—MAN GAL-*u*
392 *šá* É—UŠ-*te la te-rab-a-ni*
393 *a-na* EGIR UD-*me a-na* UD-*me ṣa-a-ti aš-šur* DINGIR-*ku-nu*
394 ^{m}*aš-šur*—DÙ—A DUMU—MAN GAL *šá* É—UŠ-*ti* EN-*ku-nu*
395 DUMU.MEŠ-*ku-nu* DUMU—DUMU.MEŠ-*ku-nu*
396 *a-⸢na šá⸣-[a]-šú lip-lu-hu*

385 While you stand on the place of this oath, you shall not swear the oath with your lips only but shall swear it wholeheartedly; you shall teach it to your sons to be born after this treaty; you shall not feign incurable illness but take part in this treaty of Esarhaddon, king of Assyria, concerning Assurbanipal, the great crown prince designate. In the future and forever Aššur will be your god, and Assurbanipal, the great crown prince designate, will be your lord. May your sons and your grandsons fear him.

---

§ 35 Obligation to Guard the Treaty Document

397 *šá ma-mit ṭup-pi an-ni-i e-nu-u e-gu-u*
398 *i-ha-ṭu-u i-pa-sa-su* x *šú a-de-e* ⸢x x⸣
399 *[e$^{?}$]-gu-ma i-par-ra-ṣu ma-mit-su-un*
400 [EN$^{?}$ *ṭup*]-*pi a-de-e an-ni-i*
401 [^{d}*aš-šur*] MAN DINGIR.MEŠ *u* DINGIR.MEŠ

397 Whoever changes, disregards, transgresses or erases the oaths of this tablet or [dis]regards ... *this* treaty and transgresses its oath, [*may the guardian(s) of*] this treaty tablet, [Aššur], king of the gods, and the

šar/šir-pu "combustible". The ambiguity of the preposition *(ina) muhhi* also leaves it unclear whether a substance found *upon* or to be used *against* the "gods of the assembly" (i.e. the divine statues witnessing the oath-taking ceremony) is in question. 373 DINGIR.⸢MEŠ⸣ frg: DINGIR-ME frg. 374 *na-pul-ta-ku-nu* frg: *lu-bul-[ta-ku-nu]* frg, TÚG.*lu-bul-ta-ku-n[u]* B. 376 *ta-rak-kas-a-[ni]* B: *-kas-ni* frg, *-kás-a-ni* frg. 379 *ši]-in-ga-te* A: *ši-in-ga-a-[te* s; cf. *ši-in-⸢ga⸣-am-ma id-du-nu* KAJ 47:21 and (wool) *a-na ši-in-gi* VS 19 54:2 (both MA). 383f *šá a-na* UD-*m[e* s: *[š]a ina* UD-*me* D (coll. from photo; correct BaM Bh 3). 384 *ib-ba-áš-šú-u-ni* D: *-šu-u-ni* s. 385 *ina* D: caret As; *kaq-qar* Ds: GAG *kaq-qar* A; *ta-me-ti* A: *-tu* D. 386 *ta-me-tu* Ds: *-tú* A. 387 *ta-ta-ma-a-ni* s: *ta-tam-ma-a-ni* D. 388 *tu-šal-mad-a-ni* As: *-ma-da-⸢ni⸣* D. 389 *la pa-aṭ-ru$^{!!}$*: *la pa$^{?}$-la$^{?}$-⸢lu$^{?}$⸣* D, *[l]a [pa-a]ṭ-lu* A (coll. from photo). 391 GAL-*u* H: ⸢GAL⸣ D. 392 É—UŠ-*te* H: *-ti* D. 393 *a-na* UD-*me* H: *ina* UD-⸢*me*⸣ D (coll. from photo, correct BaM Bh 3). 393f These lines are independent nominal sentences and cannot be taken as objects of *lipluhū* in l. 396 as done in BaM Bh 3. 396 *a-⸢na šá⸣-[a]-šú* coll. from photo; reading *a-⸢de-e⸣-šú* (BaM Bh 3) excluded. 401 Nothing missing in the break before

GAL.MEŠ EN.MEŠ-*ia*
402 [*x x x-š*]*ú*? *lu-u ṣa-lam* ^{m}*aš-šur*—PAB—AŠ MAN KUR—*aš-šur*
403 *lu ṣa-lam* ^{m}[*aš-šur*—DÙ—A DU]MU—MAN GAL *šá* É—UŠ-*ti*
404 *lu ṣa-lam* Š[EŠ?.MEŠ?-*šú x x x x x*]
405 NA$_4$.KIŠIB NUN-⌜*e*!⌝ [GAL-*e* AD] DINGIR.MEŠ [*x x x x*]
406 *šá* É ⌜*x*⌝ [*x x x x x x x x* (*x*)]
407 *ina* (ŠÀ-*bi*) NA$_4$.KIŠIB *šá* ^{d}*aš-šur* MAN DINGIR.MEŠ-*ni*
408 *ka*-⌜*ni*⌝*k*!-*u-ni ina* IGI-*ku-nu šá-kín-u-ni*
409 *ki-i* DINGIR-*ku-n*[*u*] *la ta-na-ṣar-a-ni*

---

410 *šum-ma at-tu-nu tu-na-kar-*[*a*]*-ni a-na* ^{d}GIŠ.BAR
411 *ta-pa-qid-a-*[*ni*] *ina* A.MEŠ *ta-na-da-a-ni*
412 *ina ep-ri ta-*[*kar-ra-ra-a-ni*] *ina mim-ma ši-pir ni-kil-ti*
413 *ta-bat-a-ni tu-hal-la-q*[*a-a-ni*] *ta-sa-pan-a-ni*

---

414 AN.ŠÁR LUGAL DINGIR.MEŠ *mu-šim* [NAM.MEŠ] *ši-mat* MÍ.HUL
415 *la* DÙG.GA-*ti li-š*[*im-k*]*u-nu a*-⌜*rak*!⌝ UD *še-bu-ti*
416 [*k*]*i-šid lit-tu-*[*ti a*]*-a i-qiš-ku-nu*

---

417 ^{d}NIN.LÍL *hi-ir-tu na-ram-ta-šú a-mat* KA-*šú*
418 *li-lam-mìn-ma a-a iṣ-bat ab-bu-ut-ku-un*

418A ^{d}*a-num* MAN DINGIR.MEŠ GIG *ta-né-hu di-*ʾ*u di-lip-tu*
418B *ni-is-sa-tu la* DÙG.GA NUMUN UGU *nap-har*
418C É.MEŠ-*ku-nu li-šá-az-nin*

---

419 ^{d}30 *na-an-nar* AN-*e u* KI.TIM *ina* SAHAR.ŠUB-*pu*
420 *li-hal-lip-ku-nu ina* IGI DINGIR.MEŠ *u* LUGAL *e-rab-ku-nu a-a iq-bi*
421 *ki-i sír-ri-me* MAŠ.DÀ (*ina*) EDIN *ru-up-da*

---

422 ^{d}UTU *nu-úr šá-ma-mi u kaq-qar di-in ket-ti* (*me-šá-ri*)
423 *a-a i-di-in-ku-nu ni-ṭil* IGI.2.MEŠ-*ku-nu liš-ši-ma*
424 *ina ek-le-ti i-tal-la-ka*

---

great gods, my lords, [......] the statue of Esarhaddon, king of Assyria, or the statue of Assurbanipal, the great crown prince designate, or the statue of [his] *b*[*rother* ......] the seal of the [great] ru[ler, father] of the gods, [......]. You shall guard [*this treaty tablet* which] is sealed with the seal of Aššur, king of the gods, and set up in your presence, like your own god.

§ 36 **Injunction against Destroying the Document**

410 If you should remove it, consign it to the fire, throw it into the water, [bury] it in the earth or destroy it by any cunning device, annihilate or deface it,

§ 37-56 **Standard Curse Section**

414 May Aššur, king of the gods, who decrees [the fates], decree an evil and unpleasant fate for you. May he not gra[nt yo]u long-lasting old age and the attainment of extreme old age.

§ 38 ———

417 May Mullissu, his beloved wife, make the utterance of his mouth evil, may she not intercede for you.

§ 38A ———

418A May Anu, king of the gods, let disease, exhaustion, malaria, sleeplessness, worries and ill health rain upon all your houses.

§ 39 ———

419 May Sin, the brightness of heaven and earth, clothe you with leprosy and forbid your entering into the presence of the gods or king. Roam the desert like the wild ass and the gazelle!

§ 40 ———

422 May Šamaš, the light of heaven and earth, not judge you justly. May he remove your eyesight. Walk about in darkness!

[^{d}*aš-šur*]. 404 Instead of Š[EŠ read (according to photo) rather DU[MU—MAN KÁ.DINGIR.RA.KI]. 405 NUN-⌜*e*⌝ clear in A (coll. from photo). 406 The sign after É is not N[A$_4$ (BaM Bh 3; coll. from photo). There is room for 8-9 signs only in the break, and accordingly the restoration [KIŠIB NAM.MEŠ *šumma attunu ṭuppi adê anniu*] (requiring a minimum of 16 signs) suggested in BaM Bh 3 is out of the question. 407 *ina* ŠÀ-*bi* NA$_4$.KI[ŠIB A: [*in*]*a* NA$_4$.KIŠIB C (coll. from photo; correct BaM Bh 3); nothing missing before *ina*. 408 *ka*-⌜*ni*⌝*k-u-ni* A sic (coll. from photo): not *-nik$_5$-* (BaM Bh 3). See coll. 410 *a-na* C: *ina* A. 412 Restoring *ta-*[*qab-bi-ra-a-ni*] in line with BaM Bh 3 is also possible. 414 MÍ.HUL C: H]UL-*ti* A. 415 DÙG.GA-*ti* A: *-tu* C; *a-rak*! UD *še-bu-ti* A (coll. from photo): caret C. 416 [*k*]*i-šid lit-tu-*[*ti a*]*-a i-qiš-ku-nu* A: caret C. 418 *iṣ-bat* C: *iṣ-ba-ta* A; *ab-bu-tu-ku-un* A: *-tú-k*[*u-un*] C; 418A-C caret A; *di-lip-tu* C: *-tú* frg; *ni-is-sa-tu* C: *-tú* B; *la* C: NU B; NUMUN C: UZU B. 419 *na-an-nar* ACc: *na-nar* B; AN-*e* Bc: AN.MEŠ C. 420 *e-rab-ku-nu* Cc: *e-(re)-eb-ku-nu* B. 421 *ki-i* c: *ki-ma* AB, GIM Cx; *ina* c: caret ABC. 422 *šá-ma-mi* C: *-me* Bc; *kaq-qar* C: *-qa-ri* Ac, caret B; *ket-ti* C: *-te* c; *me-šá-ri* A: caret BCc. 423 IGI.2.MEŠ-*ku-nu* C: IGI.2-*ku-nu* Bc; *li-ši-ma* B: *-mu* c, *liš-ši-ma* A. 424 *ek-le-ti* C: *ek-let-te* c: *i-tal-la-ka* AC: ⌜*it*⌝-*la-ka* c. 425 *šil-ta-hi-šu* B: *-šú* A: *li-šam-qit-ku-nu* A: ⌜*lu*⌝- c.

425 ^{d}MAŠ *a-šá-rid* DINGIR.MEŠ *ina šil-ta-hi-šu šam-ri li-šam-qit-ku-nu*
426 MÚD.MEŠ-*ku-nu li-mal-[li]* EDIN UZU-*[k]u-nu* Á.MUŠEN *zi-i-bu*
427 *li-šá-kil*

428 ^{d}*dil-bat na-bat* MUL.MEŠ *ina ni-ṭil* IGI.2-*ku-nu hi-ra-a-te-ku-nu*
429 *ina* ÚR LÚ.KÚR-*ku-nu li-šá-ni-il* DUMU.MEŠ-*ku-nu*
430 *a-a i-bé-lu* É-*ku-un* LÚ.KÚR *a-hu-u li-za-i-za mim-mu-ku-un*

431 ^{d}SAG.ME.GAR EN DINGIR.MEŠ *ṣi-i-ru e-rab* EN *ina* É.*sag-gíl*
432 *a-a ú-kal-lim-ku-nu li-hal-li-qa nap-šat-ku-un*

433 ^{d}AMAR.UTU DUMU.UŠ *reš-tu-u hi-i-ṭu kab-tu ma-mit la pa-šá-ri*
434 *a-na ši-im-[t]i-ku-nu li-šim*

435 ^{d}NUMUN-DÙ-*tú na-di-na-at* MU *u* NUMUN MU-*ku-nu* NUMUN-*ku-nu*
436 *ina* KUR *lu-hal-liq*

437 ^{d}*be-lit*—DINGIR.MEŠ ^{d}*be-lit nab-ni-ti ta-lit-tu ina* KUR-*ku-nu*
438 *lip-ru-us ik-kil* [TU]R.DIŠ *u la-ke-e*
439 *ina* SILA *re-bit li-za-a[m-mi ta]-rit-ku-un*

440 ^{d}IM GÚ.GAL AN-*e* KI.TIM ⸢A⸣.[KAL?] *ina* KUR-*k[u-nu] lip-ru-[us]*
441 *ta-me-ra-a-ti-ku-nu li-za-a[m-mi]*
442 *ina ri-ih-ṣi dan-ni* KUR-*ku-nu [x x x]* BURU$_{5}$
443 *mu-ṣa-hi-ir* KUR BURU$_{14}$-*ku-nu* ⸢*le*⸣-[*kul*] *ik-kil* NA$_{4}$.UR$_{5}$ *u* NINDU
444 *ina* É.MEŠ-*ku-nu a-a* GÁL-*ši* ŠE.PAD.MEŠ *a-na ṭi-ia-ni*
445 *lu tah-li-qa-ku-nu ku-um* ŠE.PAD.MEŠ *eṣ-ma-ti-ku-nu*
446 DUMU.MEŠ-*ku-nu* DUMU.MÍ.MEŠ-*ku-nu li-ṭi-nu ki-ṣir šá* ŠU.SI-*ku-nu*
447 *ina le-e-še lu la i-ṭa-ab-bu [x x x] a-ṣu-da-ti-ku-nu le-e-šu*
448 *le-kul* AMA UGU DUMU.MÍ-*šá* [KÁ-*šá le-di-il*]
449 *ina bu-ri-ku-nu* UZU.MEŠ DUMU.MEŠ-*ku-nu ak-la ina bu-b[u-ti]*
450 *hu-šah-hu* LÚ UZU LÚ *le-e-kul* LÚ KUŠ LÚ
451 *li-la-biš* UZU.MEŠ-*ku-nu* UR.KU.MEŠ ŠAH

§ 41 ———
[425] May Ninurta, the foremost among the gods, fell you with his fierce arrow; may he fill the plain with your blood and feed your flesh to the eagle and the vulture.

§ 42 ———
[428] May Venus, the brightest of the stars, before your eyes make your wives lie in the lap of your enemy; may your sons not take possession of your house, but a strange enemy divide your goods.

§ 43 ———
[431] May Jupiter, exalted lord of the gods, not show you the entrance of Bel in Esangil; may he destroy your life.

§ 44 ———
[433] May Marduk, the eldest son, decree a heavy punishment and an indissoluble curse for your fate.

§ 45 ———
[435] May Zarpanitu, who grants name and seed, destroy your name and your seed from the land.

§ 46 ———
[437] May Belet-ili, the lady of creation, cut off birth from your land; may she deprive your nurses of the cries of little children in the streets and squares.

§ 47 ———
[440] May Adad, the canal inspector of heaven and earth, cut off sea[sonal flooding] from your land and deprive your fields of [grain], may he [submerge] your land with a great flood; may the locust who diminishes the land devour your harvest; may the sound of mill or oven be lacking from your houses, may the grain for grinding disappear from you; instead of grain may your sons and your daughters grind your bones; may not (even) your (first) finger-joint dip in the dough, may the [...] of your bowls eat up the dough. May a mother [bar the door] to her daughter. In your hunger eat the flesh of your sons! In want and famine may one man eat the flesh of another; may one man clothe himself in another's skin; may dogs and swine eat your

[427] *li-šá-kil* B: *lu-šá-kil* N. [428] IGI.2-*ku-nu* B: IGI.2.ME[Š]-*ku-nu* A; *hi-ra-a-te-ku-nu* B: *hi-ra-*⸢*ti*⸣-*ku-nu* A. [431] ^{d}SAG.ME.GAR B frg: MUL.SAG.ME.GAR C; *ṣi-i-ru* B: MAH AI; É.*sag-gíl* ACI: É.SAG.ÍL B. [433] *hi-i-*⸢*ṭu*⸣ B: *hi-ṭu* AI. [437] *nab-ni-ti* I: *nab-n[i-t]ú* F. [445] ŠE.PAD.MEŠ Ag: ŠE.PAD l. [447] *le-e-še* g: ⸢*le-ši*⸣ A; *i-ṭa-ab-b[u]* g: ⸢*i-ṭa-bu*⸣ A. [449] *ina bu-ri-ku-nu* A: caret g; UZU.MEŠ Ag: UZU l. [450] *le-e-kul* g: *le-kul* A. [451] ŠAH g: ŠAH.MEŠ A; *le-e-ku-lu* g: *le-kul* A,

FIG. 13. *Rape of Arab woman (reign of Assurbanipal). Cf. curse formula, l. 428.*
BM 124927.

FIG. 14. *Rebels compelled to grind up their own father's bones (reign of Assurbanipal). Cf. curse, l. 445f.*
BM 124801.

le-e-ku-lu
452 *e-ṭím-ma-ku-nu pa-qi-du na-aq* A.MEŠ *a-a ir-ši*

flesh; may your ghost have nobody to take care of the pouring of libations to him.

§ 48

453 ᵈIŠ.TAR *be-lit* MURUB$_4$ *u* MÈ *ina* M[È] *dan-ni* GIŠ.BAN-*ku-nu liš-bir*
454 *i-di-ku-nu lik-si ina* KI.TA LÚ.KÚR-*ku-nu li-še-šib-ku-nu*

453 May Ištar, lady of battle and war, smash your bow in the thick of ba[ttle], may she bind your arms, and have you crouch under your enemy.

§ 49

455 ᵈU.GUR *qar-rad* DINGIR *ina* GÍR-*šú la ga-me-li nap-šat-ku-nu*
456 *li-bal-li šá-ga-áš-tú mu-t[a-a]-nu ina* ŠÀ-*bi-ku-nu liš-kun*

455 May Nergal, hero of the gods, extinguish your life with his merciless sword, and send slaughter and pes[til]ence among you.

§ 50

457 ᵈNIN.LÍL *a-ši-bat* URU.NINA.KI
458 *pat-ru ha-am-ṭu it-ti-ku-nu li-ir-ku-su*

457 May Mullissu, who dwells in Nineveh, tie a flaming sword at your side.

§ 51

459 ᵈIŠ.TAR *a-ši-bat* URU.*arba-ìl re-e-mu gim-lu*
460 [*lu l*]*a*! *i-šá-kan* UGU-*ku-un*

459 [May] Ištar, who dwells in Arbela, [no]t show you mercy and compassion.

§ 52

461 ᵈ*gu-la a-zu-gal-la-tú* GAL-*tú* GIG *ta-né-hu* [*ina* ŠÀ-*bi-ku-nu*]
462 *si-mu la-zu ina zu-um-ri-ku-nu liš-k*[*un da-mu u šar-ku*]
463 *ki-ma* A.MEŠ *ru-*[*un-ka*]

461 May Gula, the great physician, put sickness and weariness [in your hearts] and an unhealing wound in your body. Bathe in [blood and pus] as if in water!

§ 53

464 ᵈ*si-bit-ti* DINGIR.ME[Š *qa*]*r-d*[*u-te ina* GIŠ.TUKUL.MEŠ-*šú-nu*]

464 [May] the Pleiades, the [heroic] gods,

le-ku-lu l. 452 *e-ṭím-*⌜*ma-ku*⌝*-nu* frg: GIDIM-*ku-nu* l; *ir-ši* frg: *-še* frg. 453 *be-lit* lg: EN A. 454 *lik-si* Al frg: *li-ik-si* g. 455 *qar-rad* Ag: UR.SAG l. 456 *šá-ga-áš-tu* k: *-t*[*ú*] A, *šag-gaš-tú* g, *šag-ga-aš-tu* frg; *mu-t*[*a-a*]*-nu* A: NAM.ÚŠ k; ŠÀ-*bi-ku-nu* A: Š]À-*ku-nu* B; *liš-kun* AB frg: [*li*]*-iš-ku-nu* k. 457 URU.NINA.KI A: NINA.KI frgg, [NI]NA k. 458 *pat-ru* frg: *-ri* k, [GÍ]R.AN.BAR A. 459 *re-e-mu* Ak: ARHUŠ frg. 462 *zu-um-ri-*[*ku-nu* k: *zu-um-(ri)-ku-nu* frg, ⌜SU⌝*-ku-*⌜*nu*⌝ frg. 470

COURTESY TRUSTEES OF THE BRITISH MUSEUM

FIG. 15. *An Elamite surrenders by cutting his own bow (reign of Assurbanipal). Cf. curse, ll. 453 and 573f.*
BM 124941.

465 *ez-zu-ti na-aš-pan-*[*ta-ku-nu liš-ku-nu*]

---

466 [^{d}]*a-ra-miš* EN *im*? *x*[*x x x x x x x x x*]*-ku-n*[*u x x x x x x x x x x x*]*-tu*

---

467 [^{d}*ba-a-a-ti*—DINGIR.MEŠ ^{d}*a-na-t*]*i—ba-a-a-ti*—DINGIR.[MEŠ]
468 *ina* ŠU.2 UR.M[AH *a-ki-li*] *lim-nu-ku-nu*

---

469 ^{d}*kù*-KÁ ^{d}I[5 *ša* URU].*gar-ga-mis*
470 *ri-im-ṭu dan-nu ina* ŠÀ-*ku-nu liš-kun* [KÀŠ].MEŠ-*ku-nu*
471 *ki-ma ti*!*-ki ana kaq-qar lit-ta-tuk*!

---

472 DIN[GIR.MEŠ G]AL.MEŠ *šá* AN-*e* KI.TIM *a-ši-bu-tu kib-ra-*⸢*a-ti*⸣
473 *ma-la ina ṭup-pi an-ni-e* MU-*šú-nu zak-r*[*u*]
474 *lim-ha-ṣu-ku-nu li-kil-mu-ku-nu*
475 *ár-ra-tu ma-ru-uš-tu ag-giš li-ru-ru-ku-nu*
476 *e-liš* TI.LA.MEŠ *li-sa-hu-ku-nu šap-liš ina* KI.TIM
477 *e-ṭím-ma-ku-nu* A.MEŠ *li-za-mu-u* GIŠ.MI *u* UD.DA
478 *li-ik-ta-ši-du-ku-nu ina pu-uz-ri šá-h*[*a-ti*]
479 *la ta-nim-me-da* ⸢NINDA⸣.MEŠ *u* A.MEŠ *li-z*[*i-b*]*u-ku-nu*
480 *su-un-qu hu-šah-hu bu-bu-tu* NAM.[Ú]Š.MEŠ
481 TA IGI-*ku-nu a-a ip-pi-ṭir*! *si-si šá ar-da-te-ku-nu*
482 *mat-nat šá* LÚ.GURUŠ.MEŠ-*ku-nu ina ni-ṭil* IGI.2-*ku-nu* UR.KU ŠAH.MEŠ
483 *ina re-bit* URU.*aš-šur li-in-da-šá-ru* LÚ.ÚŠ.MEŠ-*ku-nu* KI.TIM
484 *a-a im-hur ina kar-ši* UR.KU ŠAH.MEŠ *lu na-aq-bar-ku-nu*
485 UD.MEŠ-*ku-nu* [*lu*] *e-ṭu-u* MU.MEŠ-*ku-nu lu ek-la ek-le-tú*
486 *la na-ma-a-r*[*i*] *a-na šim-ti-ku-nu li-ši-i-mu*
487 *ina ta-n*[*é-hu d*]*i-lip-tu na-piš-ta-ku-nu liq-ti*
488 *bu-bu-lu a-bu-bu la mah-ru ul-tú* (ŠÀ) KI.TIM
489 *li-la-a-ma na-aš-pan-ta-ku-nu liš-kun mim-ma* DÙG.GA *lu ik-kib-ku-nu*
490 *mim-ma* GIG *lu ši-mat-ku-nu qi-i-ru ku-up-ru lu ma-ka-la-ku-nu*
491 KÀŠ ANŠE.NITÁ *lu maš-qit-ku-nu nap-ṭu lu pi-šat-ku-nu*
492 *e-la-pu-u-a šá* ÍD *lu tak-tim-ku-nu*
493 *še-e-du ú-tuk-ku ra-bi-ṣu lem*!*-nu* É.MEŠ-

mas[sacre you with their] fierce [weapons].

§ 54

466 [May] Aramiš, lord of [..., ...] you, [...]...

§ 54A

467 May [Bethel and Ana]th-Bethel hand you over to the paws of [a man-eating] lion.

§ 55

469 May Kubaba, the god[dess of] Carchemish, put a serious *venereal* disease within you; may your [*urine*] drip to the ground like raindrops.

§ 56

472 May all the grea[t go]ds of heaven and earth who inhabit the universe and are mentioned by name in this tablet, strike you, look at you in anger, uproot you from among the living and curse you grimly with a painful curse.

476 Above, may they take possession of your life; below, in the netherworld, may they make your ghost thirst for water. May shade and daylight always chase you away, and may you not find refuge in a hidden cor[ner]. May food and water abandon you; may want and famine, hunger and plague never be removed from you.

481 Before your very eyes may dogs and swine drag the *teats* of your young women and the *penises* of your young men to and fro in the squares of Assur; may the earth not receive your corpses but may your burial place be in the belly of a dog or a pig.

485 May your days be dark and your years dim, may darkness which is not to be brightened be declared as your fate. May your life end in exha[ustion and slee]plessness.

488 May an irresistible flood come up from the earth and devastate you; may anything good be forbidden to you, anything ill be your share; may tar and pitch be your food; may urine of an ass be your drink, may naphtha be your ointment, may duckweed be your covering. May demon, devil and evil spirit select your houses.

Watanabe (BaM Bh 3) restores [MÚD.MEŠ] "blood". 481f Watanabe (BaM Bh 3 p.167), following Deller, Or 53 83f, renders *si-si* and *mat-nat* "curls" and "locks" (CAD: "wart" and "sinew, bowstring" respectively). The present rendering takes *si-si* as a variant of *zi-zi* "teats" (cf. English tit vs. teat) and *matnu* as a euphemism for "penis" (cf. Biggs Šaziga p.17 and passim). 483 URU.*aš-š*[*ur*] frg: *aš-šur* D. 484 [*n*]*a-*⸢*aq-bar*⸣*-ku-*[*nu*] frg: *naq-bar-qa-ku-nu* D. 485 ⸢*e*⸣*-ṭu-u* D: *-ú* frg; MU.MEŠ-*ku-nu* D: MU.AN.NA.MEŠ-*ku-*[*nu* frg; *ek-le-tú* D: *-tu* frg. 486 [*šim-t*]*i-ku-nu* frg: *šim-*⸢*ti*⸣ D; *li-ši-i-*[*mu*] frg: *li-ši-mu* D frg. 487 [*d*]*i-lip-tu* D: *-ti* frg. 488 *bu-bu-lu* D: [UD.N]Á.À[M] frg; *la mah-ru* D: caret frg *ul-tu*

ku-nu li-hi-ru

494 DINGIR.MEŠ an-nu-te lid-gu-lu šum-ma a-ni-nu ina UGU ᵐaš-šur—PAB—AŠ
495 MAN KUR—aš-šur (EN!-ni) ina UGU ᵐaš-šur—DÙ—A DUMU—MAN GAL šá É—UŠ-ti
496 ŠEŠ.MEŠ-šú DUMU AMA-šú šá ᵐaš-šur—DÙ—A DUMU—MAN GAL šá É—UŠ-ti
497 ù re-eh-ti DUMU.MEŠ ṣi-it—ŠÀ-bi šá ᵐaš-šur—PAB—AŠ MAN KUR—aš-šur EN-i-ni
498 si-hu bar-tu né-ep-pa-áš-u-ni pi-i-ni TA*
499 LÚ.KÚR-šú ni-šá-kan-u-ni šum-ma
500 mu-šam-hi-ṣu-u-tú mu-šad-bi-bu-tu li-ih-šu
501 šá a-mat MÍ.HUL la DÙG.GA-tu la ba-ni-tu
502 da-bab sur-ra-a-ti u la ke-na-a-te
503 šá ina UGU ᵐaš-šur—DÙ—A DUMU—MAN GAL-u šá É—UŠ-te
504 ù ŠEŠ.MEŠ-šú DUMU AMA-šú šá ᵐaš-šur—DÙ—A DUMU—MAN GAL
505 šá É—UŠ-ti ni-šam-mu-u-ni nu-pa-za-ru-u-ni
506 a-na ᵐaš-šur—DÙ—A DUMU—MAN GAL šá É—UŠ-ti be-lí-ni
507 la ni-qa-bu-u-ni UD-mu am—mar a-ni-nu DUMU.MEŠ-ni
508 DUMU—DUMU.MEŠ-ni bal-ṭa-a-ni-ni ᵐaš-šur—DÙ—A DUMU—MAN GAL šá É—UŠ-ti
509 la LUGAL-ni-ni la EN-ni-ni šum-ma LUGAL MAN-ma DUMU—LUGAL MAN-ma
510 ina UGU-hi-ni DUMU.MEŠ-ni DUMU—DUMU.MEŠ-ni ni-šá-kan-u-ni
511 DINGIR.MEŠ ma-la MU-šú-nu zak-ru ina ŠU.2-i-ni
512 NUMUN-[i]-ni NUMUN—NUMUN-i-ni lu-ba-ʾi-ú

§ 57 Vow of Allegiance to Assurbanipal

494 May these gods be our witnesses: We will not make rebellion or insurrection against Esarhaddon, king of Assyria, against Assurbanipal, the great crown prince designate, against his brothers, sons by the same mother as Assurbanipal, the great crown prince designate, and the rest of the sons of Esarhaddon, king of Assyria, our lord, or make common cause with his enemy.

500 Should we hear of instigation to armed rebellion, agitation or malicious whispers, evil, unseemly things, or treacherous, disloyal talk against Assurbanipal, the great crown prince designate, and against his brothers by the same mother as Assurbanipal, the great crown prince designate, we will not conceal it but will report it to Assurbanipal, the great crown prince designate, our lord.

507 As long as we, our sons (and) our grandsons are alive, Assurbanipal, the great crown prince designate, shall be our king and our lord, and we will not set any other king or prince over us, our sons or our grandsons. May all the gods mentioned by name (in this treaty) hold us, our seed and our seed's seed accountable (for this vow).

513 šum-ma at-tú-nu ina ŠÀ a-de-e an-nu-te šá ᵐaš-šur—PAB—AŠ MAN KUR—aš-šur EN-[ku-nu]
514 [ina] UGU ᵐaš-šur—DÙ—A DUMU—MAN GAL-u šá É—UŠ-t[e]
515 [ŠEŠ].MEŠ-šú DUMU [AMA-šú ša ᵐaš-š]ur—D[Ù—A] DUMU—MAN GAL-u šá É—UŠ-te
516 u re-e[h-ti DUMU.MEŠ] ṣi-it—ŠÀ-bi šá ᵐaš-šur—[PAB—AŠ MAN] KUR—aš-šur
517 EN-ku-nu is-si-ku-nu [iš-kun-u]-ni ta-ha-ṭa-[a-n]i
518 ᵈaš-šur AD DINGIR.MEŠ ina GIŠ.TUKUL.ME[Š-šú] ez-zu-u-ti li-[šam]-qit-[ku-nu]

§ 58-106 Ceremonial Curse Section

513 If you should sin against this treaty which Esarhaddon, king of Assyria, [your] lord, [has concluded] with you concerning Assurbanipal, the great crown prince designate, (and concerning) his [brother]s, sons by [the same mother as Ass]urba[nipal], the great crown prince designate, and the re[st of the off]spring of Esar[haddon, king] of Assyria, your lord,

518 May Aššur, father of the gods, st[ri]ke [you] down with [his] fierce weapons.

ŠÀ frg: ul-tú D. 489 liš-kun D: liš-ku-[nu] frg. 492 e-la-pu-u-a D: -pu-u frg. 494 an-nu-te D: -ti frg. 495 EN-ni frg: caret D frg; GAL Dq: GAL-ú frg. 496 GAL Dq: GAL-u frg. 497 DUMU.MEŠ q: DUMU D frg; line missing in V. 498 bar-tu Dq: -tú V. 500 mu-šam-hi-ṣu-u-tú D: -ṣu-tu Vq; mu-šad-bi-bu-tu Dq: -tú V; li-ih-šu D: -šú V. 501 MÍ.HUL DV: HUL-tim q; DÙG.GA-tu Dq: -tú V; ba-ni-tu Dq: -tú V. 502 sur-ra-a-ti D: [s]u-ra-a-te A, su-ra-a-ti V; ke-na-a-te V: -ti Dq. 503 GAL-u V: GAL ADq; É—UŠ-te V: -ti ADq. 504 DUMU DVq: DUMU.MEŠ A; GAL ADq: GAL-u V. 505 É—UŠ-ti AD: -te V; ni-šam-mu-u-ni AD: ni-šá-mu-u-ni V; nu-pa-za-ru-u-ni D: -zar-u-ni A, -za-ar-u-ni V; re-eh-t]i DUMU.MEŠ ... EN-i-ni q only, caret ADV. 506 É—UŠ-ti AD: -te V; be-lí-ni D: EN-ni AV. 507 UD-mu D: -me V, UD.MEŠ A. 508 É—UŠ-ti AD: -te V. 510 UGU-hi-ni D: UGU-ni V; ni-šá-kan-u-ni D: GAR-nu-n[i] frg. 511 ŠU.2-i-ni D: [Š]U-ni frg. 513 at-tú-nu V: caret D. 517 EN-ku-nu V: šá ina UGU-h[i-šú-nu a-de-e frg, -š]u-nu a-de-e frg. 521 MAN I: LUGAL A. 522 a-ga-nu-ti-l[a-

519 ^{d}IGI.DU EN *a-šá-[ri-du]* UZ[U-*ku-nu*]
520 Á.MUŠEN *zi-i-bu [li-šá-kil]*

---

521 ^{d}É.A MAN ZU.AB EN IDIM A.MEŠ *la* TI.LA
522 *liš-qi-ku-nu a-ga-nu-ti-la-a li-mal-li-ku-nu*

---

523 DINGIR.MEŠ GAL.MEŠ *šá* AN-*e* KI.TIM A.MEŠ Ì.MEŠ [*a-na* NÍG.GIG]-*ku-nu liš-ku-nu*

---

524 ^{d}GIŠ.BAR *na-din ma-ka-le-e a-na* TUR.MEŠ GAL.MEŠ
525 MU-*ku-nu* NUMUN-*ku-nu liq-mu*

---

526 KI.MIN KI.MIN DINGIR.MEŠ *ma-la ina ṭup-pi a-d[e]-e an-[ni-e* MU-*šú-nu zak-ru]*
527 *am—mar* SIG$_4$ *kaq-qu-ru lu-si-qu-ni-ku-nu*
528 *kaq-qar-ku-nu ki-i* AN.BAR *le-pu-šú me-me-ni*
529 *ina* ŠÀ-*bi lu la i-par-ru-ʾa*

---

530 *ki-i šá* TA* ŠÀ AN-*e šá* UD.KA.BAR A.AN *la i-za-nun-a-ni*
531 *ki-i ha-an-ni-e zu-un-nu na-al-šú ina* ŠÀ A.ŠÀ.MEŠ-*ku-nu*
532 *ta-me-ra-ti-ku-nu lu la [i]l-lak ku-um zu-un-nu*
533 *pe-eʾ-na-a-ti ina* KUR-*ku-nu li-iz-nu-na*

---

534 *ki-i šá* AN.NA *ina* IGI IZI *la i-za-zu-u-ni*
535 *at-tu-nu ina* IGI LÚ.KÚR-*ku-[nu la t]a-za-za* DUMU.MEŠ-*ku-nu*
536 DUMU.MÍ.MEŠ-*ku-nu ina* ŠU.2-*ku-nu [la t]a-ṣa-ba-ta*

---

537 KI.MIN *ki-i šá* NUMUN *šá* ANŠE.*k[u-di-ni la-á]š?-šu-u-ni*
538 MU-*ku-nu* NUMUN-*ku-nu* NUMUN *šá* DUMU.MEŠ-*ku-nu*
539 DUMU.MÍ.MEŠ-*ku-nu* TA* KUR *li-ih-liq*

---

540 *ki-i šá qar-nu šá* M[UNU$_4$ *ki-i ti*]-*ta-bi*
541 *ina* ŠÀ-*bi šak-nu-ni* K[I *x x x x*] *la i-par-ru-ʾu-u-ni*
542 [*x x*] *šú? ra x[x x]x-ni-šá la ta-sa-h[ar-u-ni]*
543 [NUMU]N-*ku-nu* NUMUN.MEŠ *šá* D[UMU?.MEŠ-*ku-n*]*u*
544 [TA?] UGU *pa-ni ša kaq-qa-ri li-ih-liq*

---

545 ^{d}UTU *ina* GIŠ.APIN *šá* AN.BAR URU-*ku-[nu] na-gi-ku-nu*

§ 59

519 May Palil, the fore[most] lord, let eagles and vultures [eat your f]lesh.

§ 60

521 May Ea, king of the Abyss, lord of the springs, give you deadly water to drink, and fill you with dropsy.

§ 61

523 May the great gods of heaven and earth *turn* water (and) oil [into a *curse* for] you.

§ 62

524 May Girra, who gives food to small and great, burn up your name and your seed.

§ 63

526 Ditto, ditto, may all the gods that are [mentioned by name] in th[is] treaty tablet make the ground as narrow as a brick for you. May they make your ground like iron (so that) nothing can sprout from it.

§ 64

530 Just as rain does not fall from a brazen heaven so may rain and dew not come upon your fields and your meadows; instead of dew may burning coals rain on your land.

§ 65

534 Just as lead does not stand up before a fire, so may you [not s]tand before yo[ur] enemy (or) take your sons and your daughters in your hands.

§ 66

537 Just as a m[ule has n]o offspring, may your name, your seed, and the seed of your sons and your daughters disappear from the land.

§ 67

540 Just as a germinal shoot of ma[lt, if it] is soaked with ma[sh ...], does not sprout (and) a [...] does not *return* [...], may your [see]d and the seed of y[our] s[ons] and your daughters disappear [from] the face of the ground.

§ 68

545 May Šamaš with an iron plough [overtu]rn yo[ur] city and your district.

a] A: *-til-la-a* I. 524 *ma-ka-le-e* G: *-li* AB. 525 ⌜MU⌝-*ku-nu* A: NUMUN.MEŠ-*ku-nu* B; NUMUN-*ku-nu* AG: NUMUN—NUMUN-*ku-n[u* B. 526 *ina* A: caret B; line omitted in G. 527 KI.MIN KI.MIN F: caret AB; *kaq-qu-ru* AGB: [*kaq*]-*qar* FM. 528 *le-pu-šú* F: *-šu* G: *le-e-pu-šú* B. 529 *i-par-ru-ʾa* F: *-ru-a* GM. 530 ŠÀ AGFB: ŠÀ-*bi* frg; *i-za-nun-a-ni* AG: *-u-ni* F. 531 *zu-un-nu* B frg: A.A[N A; *na-al-šú* AB: *-šu* M; *ina* ŠÀ A: *ina* GM. 532 *ta-me-ra-ti-ku-nu* G: *-rat-k[u]-nu* A, *-ra-a-ti-ku-nu* B; *la* AFM: caret(?) B; *i*]*l-lak* G: *i-lak* M, DU-*ak* AF; *ku-u*]*m zu-un-*⌜*nu*⌝ K: *ku-um* [*na-a*]*l-šú* A, *ku-um* A.AN G, caret F. 533 *pe-eʾ-na-a-ti* GB: *pe-eh-n[a-a-ti]* A; [*li-iz*]*-nu-na* K: *li-iz-nun* GM. 537 KI.MIN k: caret F frg. 538 NUMUN *šá* A frg: caret F; DUMU.MEŠ-*ku-nu* Fk: ŠEŠ.MEŠ-[*ku-nu*] frg. 540 *qar-nu* k: SI F frg. 541 *šak-nu-ni* k: *-u-n[i]* F; *i-par-ru-ʾu-u-ni* k: *-ru-u-[ni]* F. The break in k between K[I and *la* is much wider (4 signs) than indicated in BaM Bh 3. 543 NUMUN.MEŠ A: NUMUN F. 544 [TA] UGU *pa-ni ša kaq-qa-ri* A: *ina* KUR k. 547 KI.MIN KI.MIN M: caret A. 549

546 *lu-[šá-b]al⸣-kit*

§ 69

547 (KI.MIN KI.MIN) *ki-i šá* U$_8$ *[an-ni]-tú šal-qa-[t]u-u-ni* UZU *šá* DUMU-*[šá]*
548 *ina pi-i-šá šá-kín-u-ni ki-i ha-an-ni-e*
549 UZU *šá* ŠEŠ.MEŠ-*ku-nu* DUMU.MEŠ-*ku-nu* DUMU.MÍ.MEŠ-*ku-nu*
550 *a-na bu-ri-ku-nu lu-šá-kil-u-ku-nu*

547 (Ditto, ditto;) just as [thi]s ewe has been cut open and the flesh of [her] young has been placed in her mouth, may they make you eat in your hunger the flesh of your brothers, your sons and your daughters.

§ 70

551 *ki-i šá kab-su kab-su-tú* UDU.NIM MÍ.UDU.NIM-*tú šal-qu-u-ni*
552 *ir-ri-šú-nu* TA* GÌR.2.(MEŠ)-*šú-nu kar-ku-u-ni*
553 *ir-ri-ku-nu ir-ri šá* DUMU.MEŠ-*ku-nu* DUMU.MÍ.MEŠ-*ku-nu* TA* GÌR.2.(MEŠ)-*ku-nu*
554 *li-kar-ku*

551 Just as young sheep and ewes and male and female spring lambs are slit open and their entrails rolled down over their feet, so may (your entrails and) the entrails of your sons and your daughters roll down over your feet.

§ 71

555A *[šum-ma at-tu-nu ina* ŠÀ *a-de]-⸢e⸣ an-nu-ti šá* ^{m}*aš-šur*—PAB—AŠ MAN KUR—*⸢aš-šur⸣*
555B *[šá ina* UGU ^{m}*aš-šur*—DÙ—A DUMU—MAN GAL *šá* É—U]Š-*ti ta-ha-ṭa-a-ni*
555 [KI.M]IN *ki-i šá* MU[Š] *ù* ^{d}NIN.KILIM *ina* ŠÀ-*bi* 1-*et hu-ri-ti*
556 *la er-rab-u-ni la i-rab-bi-ṣu-u-ni*
557 *ina* UGU *na-kas* ZI.MEŠ *šá a-he-iš i-da-ba-bu-u-ni*
558 *at-tu-nu* MÍ.MEŠ-*ku-nu ina* ŠÀ-*bi* 1-*en* É *la te-ra-ba*
559 *ina* UGU 1-*et* GIŠ.NÁ *la ta-ta-la ina* UGU *na-kas* ZI.MEŠ *šá a-he-iš du-ub-ba*

555A [If you] should sin [against] this [trea]ty of Esarhaddon, king of Assyria, [concerning Assurbanipal, the great crown prince design]ate, (ditto;) just as a sna[ke] and a mongoose do not enter the same hole to lie there together but think only of cutting each other's throats, so may you and your women not enter the same room to lie down in the same bed; think only of cutting each other's throats!

§ 72

560 KI.MIN KI.MIN *ki-i šá* NINDA.MEŠ *u* GEŠTIN.MEŠ *ina* ŠÀ-*bi ir-ri-[ku-nu] er-rab-u-ni*
561 *[ki-i ha-an-ni]-i ta-me-tú an-ni-tú ina* ŠÀ-*bi ir-ri-[ku-nu]*
562 *ir-ri šá* DU[MU.MEŠ-*ku-nu* DUMU.M]Í.MEŠ-*ku-nu lu-še-ri-bu*

560 Ditto, ditto; just as bread and wine enter into the intestines, [so] may they (= the gods) make this oath enter into [your] intestines and into those of [your] so[ns] and your [daught]ers.

§ 73

563 KI.[MIN KI.MIN *k*]*i-i šá* A.MEŠ *ina* ŠÀ *ta[k-k]u-si ta-nap-pa-ha-a-ni*
564 *a-n[a k]a-šú-nu* MÍ.MEŠ-*ku-nu* DUMU.MEŠ-*ku-nu* DUMU.MÍ.MEŠ-*ku-nu*
565 *li-p[u-h]u-ku-nu* ÍD.MEŠ-*ku-nu* IGI.2.MEŠ-*ku-nu* A!.MEŠ-*ši-na*
566 *a-na qí-in-niš lu-sa-hi-ru*

563 Dit[to, ditto; j]ust as you blow water out of a t[ub]e, may they blow out you, your women, your sons and your daughters; may your streams and your springs make their waters flow backwards.

§ 74

567 KI.MIN KI.MIN NINDA.MEŠ *ina pi-it-ti* KUG.GI *ina* KUR-*ku-nu lu-šá-li-ku*

567 Ditto, ditto; may they make bread to be worth gold in your land.

ŠEŠ.MEŠ-*ku-nu* A: caret frg. 550 *lu-šá-kil-u-ku-nu* frg: *lu-šá-kil-ku-n[u]* A, *lu-šá-ki-li-ku-n[u]* frg. 551 UDU.NIM D frg: NIM A frg; MÍ.UDU.NIM-*tú* frg: MÍ.NIM-*tú* A, ⸢MÍ.NIM⸣ D; *šal-[q]u-u-ni* A: ⸢*šal*⸣-*qu-u-ni* D (coll. from photo; correct BaM Bh 3). 552 GÌR.2.MEŠ-*šú-nu* A frg: GÌR.2-*šú-nu* frg, -*šú* D. 553 *ir-ri-ku-nu* D: caret A frg; GÌR.2.MEŠ-*ku-nu* A: GÌR.2-*ku-nu* D. 555 [KI.MI]N D: caret A frg; ŠÀ-*bi* AD: ŠÀ frg; *hu-ri-ti* D frg: -*te* A. 556 *er-rab-u-ni* D frg: *e-* A. 557 *na-kas* A: caret frg. 558 *at-tu-nu* AD: *at-tú-nu* frg; ŠÀ-*bi* A: ŠÀ D frg; *te-ra-ba* D: *te-rab-ba* A. 559 *ina* UGU 1-*et* GIŠ.NÁ *la ta-ta-la* D frg: caret A; *na-kas* AD: -*kás* frg. 560 GEŠTIN.MEŠ D: GEŠTIN A; ŠÀ-*bi* A: ŠÀ D; *ir-ri-[ku-nu]* D: *ir-ri* A; *er-rab-u-ni* D: *e-rab-u-ni* A. 561 *ta-me-tú* A: -⸢*tu*⸣ D; ŠÀ-*bi* A: ⸢ŠÀ⸣ D. 565 A.MEŠ-*ši-na* D (coll. from photo): PÚ.M[EŠ frg (not collatable). 567 NINDA.MEŠ D (coll. from photo); [*p*]*i*-⸢*it*⸣-*ti* Q: *pi-it* frg, *p*]*u-ut* KUG.GI D (correct BaM Bh

§ 75

568 (KI.MIN KI.MIN) *ki-i šá* LÀL *ma-ti-qu-u-ni* MÚD.MEŠ *šá* MÍ.MEŠ-*ku-nu*
569 DUMU.MEŠ-*ku-nu* DUMU.MÍ.MEŠ-*ku-nu ina pi-i-ku-nu li-im-ti-iq*

568 (Ditto, ditto;) just as honey is sweet, so may the blood of your women, your sons and your daughters be sweet in your mouth.

§ 76

570 (KI.MIN) *ki-i šá šá-aṣ-*⌜*bu*?*-tu*⌝? *tul-tu ta-kul-u-ni*
571 *ina bal-ṭu-te-ku-nu* UZU.MEŠ-*ku-nu* UZU *šá* MÍ.MEŠ-*ku-nu*
572 DUMU.MEŠ-*ku-nu* DUMU.MÍ.MEŠ-*ku-nu tu-is-su lu ta-kul*

570 (Ditto;) just as a worm eats ..., so may the worm eat, while you are (still) alive, your own flesh and the flesh of your wives, your sons and your daughters.

§ 77

573 (KI.MIN) DINGIR.MEŠ *ma-la ina ṭup-pi a-de-e an-ni-i* MU-*šú-nu zak-ru* GIŠ.BAN-*ku-nu liš-bi-ru ina* KI.TA LÚ.KÚR-*ku-nu*
574 *lu-še-šib-u-ku-nu* GIŠ.BAN *ina* ŠU.2-*ku-nu lu-šá-bal-ki-*[*tu*]
575 GIŠ.GIGIR.MEŠ-*ku-nu a-na qí-niš lu-šá-di-lu*

573 (Ditto;) may all the gods who are called by name in this treaty tablet break your bow and subject you to your enemy; may they turn over the bow in your hands and make your chariots run backwards.

§ 78

576 (KI.MIN) *ki-i šá a-a-lu ka-šu-du-u-ni de-ku-u-ni*
577 *a-na ka-šú-nu* ŠEŠ.MEŠ-*ku-nu* DUMU.MEŠ-*ku-nu* EN—[MÚD.M]EŠ-*ku-nu*
578 *lu-ka-ši-du li-du-ku-ku-nu*

576 (Ditto;) as a stag is pursued and killed, so may your [mortal] enemy pursue and kill you, your brothers and your sons.

§ 79

579 (KI.MIN) *ki-i šá bur-di-šá-hi la ta-da-gal-u-ni*
580 *a-na bi-iš-ka-ni-šá la ta-sa-har-u-ni ki-i ha-an-ni-e at-tu-nu*

579 (Ditto;) as a caterpillar does not see and does not return to its cocoon, so may you not

3). 568 KI.MIN D: [K]I.MIN KI.MIN frg: caret frg. 569 DUMU.MÍ.MEŠ-*ku-nu* frg: caret Q; ⌜*li*⌝-*in-ti-iq* Q: ⌜*li*⌝-AH-*ti-iq* D, *li-im-ti-iq* frg. 570 KI.MIN D: caret Q; *šá-*⌜*aṣ-bu*⌝-[*t*]*ú tul-tú* Q: ⌜*šá*⌝-[*aṣ-b*]*u-*⌜*tu tul*⌝-*t*[*u* frg (coll. from photo), *šá-aṣ-b*[*u-tú tul*]-*tu* D; the readings *šá-as-s*[*u-ru* (for Q) and *šá-as-r*[*u* (for D) assumed in BaM Bh 3 are excluded. *šaṣbutu* (also attested in LAS 248:9) possibly "preparations, provisions", from *ṣabātu* Š "to prepare, provide for" (cf. ABL 317:17, 556 r.6, 1039 r.3, 1065:4, CT 53 110+ s.6, LAS 174:7, 211:18, ND 2803 r. i 5, NL 25:9, 28:12, SAA 1 128:12 and passim). 571 *bal-ṭu-te-ku-nu* DQ: *-ti-* frg. 572 *tu-is-su* DQ: *-si* frg. 573 thus Q; b adds KI.MIN, d has KI.MIN KI.MIN only. 574 *lu-še-šib-u-ku-nu* frg: *-ši-bu-ku-nu* D, *lu-še-šib-šib-bu* Q. 575 GIŠ.GIGIR.MEŠ-*ku-nu* DQb: GIŠ.GIGIR-*ku-nu* Z; *lu-šá-di-lu* D: *-di-il-lu* Q. 576 KI.MIN DQb: caret v; *ka-šu-du-u-ni* D: *-du-ni* Q; *de-ku-u-ni* DZ: -⌜*ú*⌝-[*ni*] Q. 577 *ka-šú-nu* Dv: *-šu-*[*n*]*u* b. 579 KI.MIN D: caret bv; *ta-da-gal-u-ni* Z frg: *ta-da*]-*gal-ni* Q. Despite BaM Bh 3 and earlier editions, the meaning of *burtišahhe* is not "butterfly" (*k/gurṣiptu*) but with CAD B 333, "caterpillar". Note especially the frequent equation of the word with *harsapnu* "date-worm, larva" (CAD H 115) and the sequence *munu* "larva" –

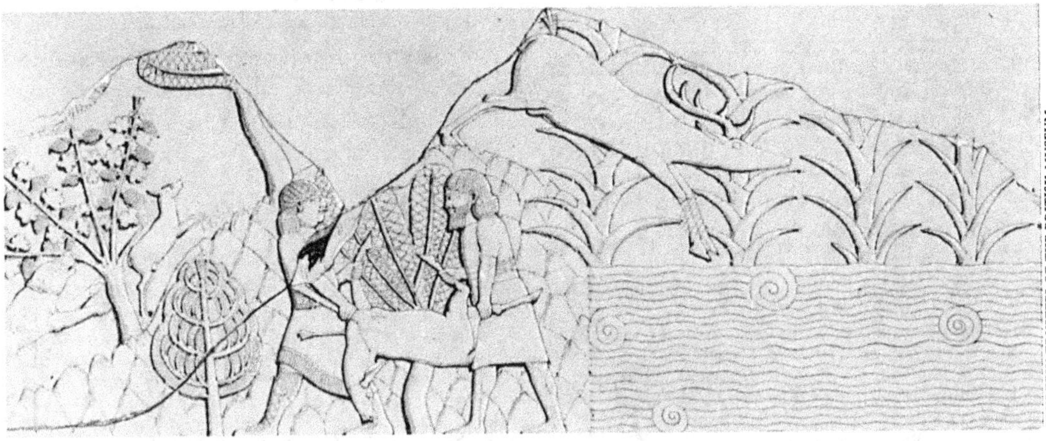

COURTESY TRUSTEES OF THE BRITISH MUSEUM

FIG. 16. *Stag pursued and killed (reign of Assurbanipal). Cf. curse, l. 576.*
ORIGINAL DRAWING VI, 19.

COURTESY TRUSTEES OF THE BRITISH MUSEUM

FIG. 17. *Birds in hand (reign of Sennacherib). Cf. curse, l. 582.*
ORIGINAL DRAWING IV, 70.

581 *ina* UGU MÍ.MEŠ-*ku-nu* DUMU.MEŠ-*ku-nu* DUMU.MÍ.MEŠ-*ku-nu a-*[*na*] É.MEŠ-*ku-nu la ta-sa-ah-hu-ra*

return to your women, your sons, your daughters, and to your houses.

---

§ 80

582 (KI.MIN KI.MIN) *ki-i šá* MUŠEN *ina tu-ba-qi iṣ-ṣab-bat-u-ni*
583 *a-na ka-šú-nu* ŠEŠ.MEŠ-*ku-nu* DUMU.MEŠ-*ku-nu ina* ŠU.2 EN—MÚD.MEŠ-*ku-nu*
584 *liš-ka-nu-ku-nu*

582 (Ditto, ditto;) just as one seizes a bird by a trap, so may they deliver you, your brothers and your sons into the hands of your mortal enemy.

---

§ 81

585 (KI.MIN KI.MIN) UZU.MEŠ-*ku-nu* UZU *šá* MÍ.MEŠ-*ku-nu* ŠEŠ.MEŠ-*ku-nu*
586 DUMU.MEŠ-*ku-nu* DUMU.MÍ.MEŠ-*ku-nu* ⸢*ki*!-*i*! *qí*!⸣-*ru*
587 *ku-up-ri nap-ṭi lu-ṣal-li-mu*

585 (Ditto, ditto;) may they make your flesh and the flesh of your women, your brothers, your sons and your daughters as black as [*bitu*]*men*, pitch and naphtha.

---

§ 82

588 KI.MIN *ki-i šá ha-e-ru-uš-hi ú-ma-mu ina kip-pi*
589 *is-sa-pa-ku-u-ni a*[*t-t*]*u-nu* [MÍ.MEŠ]-*ku-nu* ŠEŠ.MEŠ-*ku-nu* DUMU.MEŠ-*ku-nu*
590 DUMU.MÍ.MEŠ-*ku-nu ina* ŠU.2 LÚ.KÚR-*ku-nu na-aṣ-bi-ta*

588 Ditto; just as a ... beast is caught in a snare, may you, your [women], your brothers, your sons and your daughters be seized by the hand of your enemy.

---

§ 83

591 (KI.MIN K[I.M]IN) UZU.MEŠ-*ku-nu* UZU.MEŠ *šá* MÍ.MEŠ-*ku-nu* ŠEŠ.MEŠ-*ku-nu*
592 DUMU.MEŠ-*ku-nu* DUMU.MÍ.MEŠ-*ku-nu*
593 *ki-i* UZU.MEŠ *šá hur-ba-bíl-li li-ga-am-ru*

591 (Ditto, ditto;) may your flesh and the flesh of your women, your brothers, your sons and your daughters be wasted like the flesh of a chameleon.

---

§ 84

594 (KI.MIN KI.M[IN]) *ki-i šá ina* ŠÀ-*bi ka-ma-a-ni ša* LÀL
595 HABRUD.MEŠ *pal-lu-šá-a-ni*

594 (Ditto, ditto;) just as the honeycomb is pierced with holes, so may they pierce your

burtišamhat — hallulija "centipede" in Uruanna III 250ff. 580 *bi-iš-ka-ni-šá* DQv: *bé-eš-ka-n*[*i-šá* frg, *biš-ka-ni-šá* Zb; *ha-an-ni-e* b: *-ni-i* Zv; *at-tu-nu* Qb: caret Zv. 581 DUMU.MEŠ-*ku-nu* bv frg: caret D; DUMU.MÍ.MEŠ-*ku-nu* b frg: caret D;
burtišamhat — hallulija "centipede" in Uruanna III 250ff. 580 *bi-iš-ka-ni-šá* DQv: *bé-eš-ka-n*[*i-šá* frg, *biš-ka-ni-šá* Zb; *ha-an-ni-e* b: *-ni-i* Zv; *at-tu-nu* Qb: caret Zv. 581 DUMU.MEŠ-*ku-nu* bv frg: caret D; DUMU-MÍ.MEŠ-*ku-nu* b frg: caret D;
a-[*na*] b: *ina* Zv. 582 KI.MIN KI.MIN D: caret v frg; *tu-ba-qi* b: *du-ba-qi* Dv; *iṣ-ṣab-bat-u-ni* Zbv: *iṣ*]-*ṣab-bat-ni* Q, *i*]*ṣ-ṣa-bat-u-ni* frg. 583 *ka-šú-nu* DQZv frg: *-šu-nu* b. 584 *liš-ka-nu-ku-nu* QZbv frg: *li-iš-ku-nu-ku-*[*nu*] D. 585 KI.MIN KI.MIN D: caret v; UZU b: UZU.MEŠ v. 586 sic (collated from photo). 587 *nap-ṭi* DQbv frg: *na*]*p-ṭu* Z; *lu-ṣal-li-mu* Qb: *lu-ṣa-li-m*[*u*] frg, *li-ṣal-li-mu* Z. 590 *na-aṣ-b*[*i-ta*] hj: *na-ṣa-bi-ta* Q. 591 KI.MIN K[I.M]IN D: caret Lhj. 592 DUMU.MÍ.MEŠ-*ku-nu* K: DUMU.MÍ-*ku-nu* Dh. 593 UZU.MEŠ h: UZU j; *hur-ba-bíl-li* Qh: *hur-ba-bi-li* Lj; *li-ga-am-ru* "be wasted": the emendation *li-*^{ga}*gàr*$^{!?}$*-ru* proposed in BaM Bh 3 is unwarranted and unnecessary. 594 KI.MIN KI.M[IN D:

596 *ina* ŠÀ-*bi* UZU.MEŠ-*ku-nu* UZU.MEŠ *šá* MÍ.MEŠ-*ku-nu*
597 ŠEŠ.MEŠ-*ku-nu* DUMU.MEŠ-*ku-nu* DUMU.MÍ.MEŠ-*ku-nu*
598 *ina bal-ṭu-te-ku-nu* HABRUD.MEŠ *lu-ú*!-*pal-li-šu*

---

599 (KI.MIN KI.MIN) BURU$_5$ NUMUN! *bar*!-*mu kal-mu-tú mu-nu a-ki-lu*
600 URU.MEŠ-*ku-nu* KUR-*ku-nu na-gi-ku-nu lu-šá-ki-lu*

---

601 KI.MIN (KI.MIN) *ki-i zu-um-bi ina* ŠU.2 LÚ.KÚR-*ku-nu le-pa-šu-ku-nu*
602 LÚ.KÚR-*ku-nu li-im-ri-is-ku-nu*

---

603 *ki-i šá pi-is-pi-su (an-ni-u) bi-ʾi-šu-u-ni*
604 *ki-i ha-an-ni-i ina* IGI DINGIR *u* LUGAL *a-me-lu-te*
605 *ni-piš-ku-nu lib-ʾi-iš*

---

606 ([KI].MIN KI.MIN) *a-na ka-na-šú-nu* MÍ.MEŠ-*ku-nu* ŠEŠ.MEŠ-*ku-nu* DUMU.MEŠ-*ku-nu*
607 DUMU.MÍ.MEŠ-*ku-nu ina pi-til-ti li-ih-na-qu-ku-nu*

---

608 *ki-i šá ṣal-mu šá* DUH.LÀL *ina* IZI *iš-šar-rap-u-ni*
609 *šá ṭi-ṭi ina* A.MEŠ *i-mah-ha-hu-u-ni*
610 ([*k*]*i-i ha-an-ni-e*) *la-an-ku-nu ina* ^{d}GIŠ.BAR *liq-mu-u*
611 *ina* A.MEŠ *lu-ṭa-bu-u*

612A [*šum-ma at-tu-nu ina* ŠÀ *a-d*]*e-e an-nu-ti šá* ^{m}*aš-šur*—PAB—AŠ MAN KUR—*aš-šur*
612B [*u* DUMU].MEŠ-*šú* DUMU—DUMU.MEŠ-*šú* [*ṭa-ha*]-*ṭa-a-ni*
612 KI.MIN *ki-i šá* GIŠ.GIGIR *an-ni-tu a-di sa-si-šá*
613 *ina* MÚD.MEŠ *ra-ah-ṣa-tu-u-ni ki-i ha-an-ni-e*
614 *ina* MURUB$_4$ LÚ.KÚR-*ku-nu* GIŠ.GIGIR.MEŠ-*ku-nu*
615 *ina* (ŠÀ) MÚD.MEŠ *šá ra-me-ni-ku-nu li-ra-ah-ṣa*

---

flesh, the flesh of your women, your brothers, your sons and your daughters with holes while you are alive.

§ 85

599 (Ditto, ditto;) may they cause locusts, ..., lice, caterpillars and other field pests devour your towns, your land and your district.

§ 86

601 Ditto, ditto; may they make you like a fly in the hand of your enemy, and may your enemy squash you.

§ 87

603 Just as (this) bug stinks, just so may your breath stink before god and king (and) mankind.

§ 88

606 (Ditto, ditto;) may they strangle you, your women, your sons and your daughters with a cord.

§ 89

608 Just as an image of wax is burnt in the fire and one of clay dissolved in water, (so) may your figure be burnt in the fire and sunk in water.

§ 90

612A ([If you should sin against] this [treaty] of Esarhaddon, king of Assyria, [and of] his sons and grandsons,) ditto; just as this chariot is drenched with blood up to its baseboard, so may your chariots be drenched with your own blood in the midst of your enemy.

---

caret KLj; ŠÀ-*b*[*i* K: ŠÀ LThj. 596 ŠÀ-*bi* K: ŠÀ LThj. 597 DUMU.MÍ.MEŠ-*ku-nu* Khj: caret T. 598 *bal-ṭu-te-ku-nu* Th: -*ti-ku-nu* j; HABRUD.MEŠ h: HABRUD Tj; *lu*-⸢*ú*⸣-*pal-li-šu* h: *lu pal-lu-šá* T. The reading *lu*-⸢pa⸣*pal-li-šu* proposed in BaM Bh 3 is unlikely considering the spacing of the signs in h and the fact that *pal* was not a polyphonic sign needing a phonetic complement. 599 KI.MIN KI.MIN BURU$_5$ *x*[*x* j: [0 BUR]U$_5$! NUMUN! *bar*! A (coll. from photo); see coll. 601 KI.MIN KI.MIN KTj: KI.MIN h, caret A frg; *zu-um-bi* hj frg: NUM AT; LÚ.KÚR-*ku-nu* h frg: KÚR-*ku-nu* T, (KÚR)-*ku-nu* A; *le-pa-šu-ku-nu* KTj frg: -*šú-ku-nu* Ah. 603 *an-ni-u* H frg: caret ALTh; *bi-ʾi-šu-u-ni* HKLh frg: -*šu-ú-ni* Tj, -*šú-u-ni* A. 604 *ki-i ha-an-ni-i* H: -*ni-e* A, *ha-ni-i* L, caret frg; DINGIR AH frg: DINGIR.MEŠ h; *a-me-lu-te* Th frg: -*ti* K, LÚ-*ti* Aj, LÚ-*u-te* H. 605 *lib-ʾi-iš* H: -*ʾi-ši* h, *lib-iš* L, *li-ib-ʾi-iš* T, -*ši* A, [*l*]*u-ba-i-šu* frg. 606 [KI].MIN KI.MIN frg: caret A; ŠEŠ.MEŠ-*ku-nu* HT frg: caret A; DUMU.MEŠ-*ku-nu* AKh frg: -*(nu)* H, *at-tu-nu* T. 607 DUMU.MÍ.MEŠ-*ku-nu* AHL: caret frg; *pi-til-ti* A: -*te* frg; *li-ih-na-qu-ku-nu* AK frg: *li-ih-nu-qu-ku-nu* HLM. 608 *ṣal-mu šá* DUH.LÀL A: *ṣa-lam* DUH.LÀL frg, *ṣa-lam šá* DUH.LÀL M; *iš-šar-rap-u-ni* HM: *i-šar-rap-u-ni* L frg, *i-šá-rap-u-ni* AK, *i-ša-r*]*a-pu-u-ni* T. 609 *ṭi-ṭi* M: IM G; *i-mah-ha-hu-u-ni* A frg: *i-ma-ha-hu-u-ni* M. 610 [*k*]*i-i ha-an-ni-e* AH: caret GM frg; *liq-mu-u* AKL frg: -*ú* M. 611 *lu-ṭa-bu-u* H: -*ú* A, *li-ṭa-bu-u* G, -*ab-bu-ú* M. 612A-B only in K: caret AGMm frg. 612 KI.MIN Mm: caret GK; GIŠ.GIGIR AKMm: -MEŠ G; *an-ni-tu* K: -*tú* A, caret GM; *sa-si-šá* GM frg: *sa-s*]*i-i-šá* K, *sa-se-e*-[*šá*] A. 613 *ra-ah-ṣa-tu-u-ni* GL frg: -*tú*- A. 614 Thus AK; GIŠ.GIGIR.MEŠ-*ku-nu ina* MURUB$_4$ LÚ.KÚR-*ku-nu* Gm frg. 615 *ina* ŠÀ K: *ina* G frgg; *ra-me-ni-kù-nu* AK: *ra-ma-ni-ku-nu* GLm frgg; *li-ra-ah-ṣa* G: *lu ra*]-*ah-ṣa-at* L, *lu-šar-hi-ṣu* A. 616A Thus m frg; caret AGKL. 616

COURTESY TRUSTEES OF THE BRITISH MUSEUM

FIG. 18. *An enemy chariot crashing (reign of Assurbanipal). Cf. curses ll. 579 and 612A.*
BM 124801.

616A (DINGIR.MEŠ *ma-la ina ṭup-pi a-de-[e] an-ni-e* MU-*šu-nu zak-[ru]*)
616 *ki-i* GIŠ.*pi-laq-qi lu-šá-aṣ-bi-ru-ku-nu*
617 *ki-i* MÍ *ina* IGI LÚ.KÚR-*ku-nu le-pa-šu-ku-nu*

618A (DINGIR.MEŠ *ma-la ina ṭup-pi an-ni-i* MU-*šú-nu zak-ru*)
618 *a-na ka-šú-nu* ŠEŠ.MEŠ-*ku-nu* DUMU.MEŠ-*ku-nu*
619 DUMU.MÍ.MEŠ-*ku-nu ki-i al-lu-ti a-na qi-in-niš*
620 *lu-šá-di-lu-ku-nu*

---

621 *ki-i* IZI *la* DÙG.GA-*tú la* SIG_5-*tú lu-šal-bu-ku-nu*

---

622 *ki-i šá* Ì.MEŠ *ina* ŠÀ-*bi* UZU.MEŠ-*ku-nu er-rab-u-ni*
623 (*ki-i ha-an-ni-e*) *ta-me-tú an-ni-tu ina* ŠÀ-*bi* UZU.MEŠ-*ku-nu*
624 UZU.MEŠ *šá* MÍ.MEŠ-*ku-nu* DUMU.MEŠ-*ku-*

§ 91 ———

616A May all the gods who are called by name in this treaty tablet spin you around like a spindle-whorl, may they make you like a woman before your enemy.

§ 92 ———

618A May all the gods who are mentioned by name in this treaty tablet make you, your brothers, your sons, and your daughters go backward like a crab.

§ 93 ———

621 May they make evil and wicked things surround you like fire.

§ 94 ———

622 Just as oil enters your flesh, so may they cause this oath to enter into your flesh, the flesh of your brothers, your sons and your

GIŠ.*pi-laq-qi* Lm frg: *pi-laq-qi* K, GIŠ.BAL G; *lu-šá-aṣ-bi-ru-ku-nu* AL: *-bir-ku-nu* G, *lu-šá-ṣa-bir-ku-nu* K. 617 *le-pa-šu-ku-nu* GL: *-šú-ku-nu* A, *l[e-p]a-šú-(ku)-nu* K. 618A only in G: caret AKLm frgg. 618 *ka-šú-nu* GK frgg: *ka-šu-nu* L; ŠEŠ.MEŠ-*ku-nu* A: *-ku-(nu)* K, caret G. 619 DUMU.MÍ.MEŠ-*ku-nu* GL: DUMU.MÍ-*ku-nu* K; *al-lu-ti* AG: *al-lut-te* frg; *qi-in-niš* GL: *qí-in-niš* A, *qí-niš-ši* K. 621 Thus A; *la* DÙG.GA]-*tu* K, *la* DÙG.GA *la* SIG_5 G, *la* DÙG.GA]-*tu la* SIG_5-*tu* L, *la de-i]q-tú la* ⌜DÙG.GA-*tú* frg. 622 Š]À-*bi* G: ŠÀ frgg, caret K; UZU.MEŠ-*ku-nu* AK: UZU.MEŠ G frg, UZU frg; *er-rab-u-ni* L frg: *e-* (AGK frg. 623 *ki-i ha-an-ni-e* K: caret GL; *ta-me-tu* GL: *-tú* Km; *an-ni-tu* KL: *-tú* A frg; ŠÀ-*bi* AG: ŠÀ K frgg; 624

nu DUMU.MÍ.MEŠ-*ku-nu*
625 *lu-še-ri-bu*

daughters.

626 *ki-i šá a-ra-ri a-na* ᵈEN *ih-ṭu-u-ni*
627 *kap-pi šá* Á.2.MEŠ-*šú-nu* GÌR.2.MEŠ-*šú-nu* *ú-bat-ti-qu-u-ni*
628 IGI.2.MEŠ-*šú-nu ú-ga-lil-u-ni*
629 *ki-i ha-an-ni-e lig-ma-ru-ku-nu*
630 *ki-i* GI.AMBAR *ina* A.MEŠ *lu-ni-šú-ku-nu*
631 *ki-i qa-né-[e] ina rik-si* LÚ.KÚR-*ku-nu* *lu-šal-lip-ku-nu*

§ 95

626 Just as the *Cursers* sinned against Bel and he cut off their hands and feet and blinded their eyes, so may they annihilate you, and make you sway like reeds in water; may your enemy pull you out like reeds from a bundle.

632 *šum-ma at-tu-nu* ᵐ*aš-šur*—PAB—AŠ MAN KUR—*aš-šur*
633 *ù* ᵐ*aš-šur*—DÙ—A DUMU—MAN GAL-*u šá* É—UŠ-*te*
633A *u* ŠEŠ.MEŠ-*šu* [DUMU AMA]-*šú šá* ᵐ*aš-šur*—DÙ—A
633B DUMU—MAN GAL *šá* É—UŠ-*ti re-eh-ti* DUMU.MEŠ
633C *ṣi-it*—ŠÀ-*bi šá* ᵐ*aš-šur*—PAB—AŠ MAN KUR—*aš-šur*
634 *tu-ram-ma-a-ni a-na* ZAG *u* KAB *tal-lak-a-ni*
635 *šá a-na* ZAG *il-lak-u-ni* GÍR.MEŠ *le-kul-a-šú*
636 *šá a-na* KAB *il-lak-u-ni* GÍR.MEŠ-*ma le-kul-a-šú*

§ 96

632 If you should forsake Esarhaddon, king of Assyria, Assurbanipal, the great crown prince designate, (his brothers, [sons by the same mother] as Assurbanipal, the great crown prince designate, and the other sons, the offspring of [Esa]rhaddon, king of Assyria), going to the south or to the north, may iron swords consume him who goes to the south and may iron swords likewise consume him who goes to the north;

636A *a-na ka-a-šú-nu* MÍ.MEŠ-*ku-nu* ŠEŠ.MEŠ-*ku-nu*
636B DUMU.MEŠ-*ku-nu* DUMU.MÍ.MEŠ-*ku-nu*
636C *ki-i* UDU.NIM *ga-de-e lu*-⌜*x x x*⌝-[*ku-nu*]

§ 96A

636A may they [*slaughter*] you, your women, your brothers, your sons, and your daughters like a spring lamb and a kid.

637 (KI.MIN) *ki-i šá kil-lu šá su-ʾi (an-nu-te) i-ha-lul-u-ni*
638 *ki-i ha-an-ni-e at-tu-nu* MÍ.MEŠ-*ku-nu* DUMU.MEŠ-*ku-nu*
639 DUMU.MÍ.MEŠ-*ku-nu la ta-nu-ha la ta-ṣa-la-la*
640 *eṣ-ma-te-ku-nu a-na a-he-iš lu la i-qar-ri-ba*

§ 97

637 (Ditto;) just as the noise of (these) doves is persistent, so may you, your women, your sons and your daughters have no rest or sleep and may your bones never come together.

641 *ki-i šá lib-bu šá hu-up-pi ra-qu-u-ni*
642 [*li*]*b-bi-ku-nu li-ri-qu*

§ 98

641 Just as the inside of a hole is empty, may your inside be empty.

643 *ki-i* LÚ.KÚR-*ku-nu ú-pa-ta-hu-ka-nu-ni*
644 LÀL Ì.MEŠ *zi-in-za-ru-ʾu* MÚD—GIŠ.ERIN
645 *a-na šá-kan pi-it-hi-ku-nu li-ih-liq*

§ 99

643 When your enemy pierces you, may there be no honey, oil, ginger or cedar-resin available to place on your wound.

UZU.MEŠ GK: UZU L; MÍ.MEŠ-*ku-nu* G: ŠEŠ-ME-*ku-nu* L, ŠEŠ.MEŠ K. 626 *a-ra-ri* frg: -*ru* KL frg. 627 GÌR.2.MEŠ-*šú-nu* FGK frg: GÌR.2-*šú-nu* L; *ú-bat-ti-qu-u-ni* frg: -*ti-qu-ni* L, -*tú-qu-u-ni* F, *ú-pa-ti-qu-u-ni* GK. 628 *ú-gal-lil-u-ni* FL: *ú-ga-li-lu-u-ni* K, -*lil-u-*[*ni*] frg. 629 *ha-an-ni-e* GKL frg: -*i* F; *lig-ma-ru-ku-*⌜*nu*⌝ G: *li-ig-mur-u-ku-nu* K, *li-gi-(ma)-ru-ku-nu* frg. 630 GI.AMBAR F: AMBAR L, x] ⌜*a*⌝-*pa-r*[*i* frg; *lu-ni-šú-ku-nu* L frg: -*šú-u-ku-nu* K, -*šu-ku-nu* G. 631 *qa-né-*[*e* A: GI.MEŠ frg; [*lu*]-*šal-lip-ku-nu* frg: *lu-šá-lip-ku-nu* KL. 632 EN-*ku-nu* L: caret FGK frgg. 633 GAL-*u* frg: GAL FK; É—UŠ-*te* F frg: -*ti* L frg. 633A-C only in L frg. 634 *tu-ram-ma-a-ni* AFL: *tu-ra-ma-a-ni* frg; *u* F frg: caret KL frg. 634f "Going to the south (*imitti*) or to the north (*šumēli*)": or "to right or left," cf. Isaiah 30:21 etc. The implication is in either case "anywhere". 635 GÍR.MEŠ F frgg: GÍR.AN].BAR.MEŠ frg; *le-kul-a-šú* L frg, *le-ku-la-šú* F frgg, *l*]*e-ku-lu-šú* K. 636 GÍR.MEŠ-*ma* AF frgg: GÍR.AN.B]AR-*ma* frg; *le-kul-a-šú* frg: -*a-*⌜*šu*⌝ L, *le-kul-š*[*ú*] A, *le-ku-la-šú* F frg, -*lu-šú*⌝ K; 636A-C thus F frgg; caret AKL. 637 KI.MIN frg: caret A frg; *an-nu-te* frg: caret A. 638 *ha-an-ni-e* frg: *ha-ni-e* A. 640 *eṣ-ma-te-ku-nu* A frg: -*a-te-ku-nu* frg; *a-na a-he-iš* frgg, *a-na-he-iš* A; *i-qar-ri-ba* frg: *i-qa-ri-ba* A. 641 *lib-bu* frg: ŠÀ-*bu* A frg; *hu-up-pi* frg: -*pu* A. 642 [*li*]*b-bi-ku-nu* A: ŠÀ-*ba-*[*ku-nu* U. 644 LÀL A frg: LÀL.MEŠ U frg; Ì.MEŠ AU frg: caret

§ 100

646 *ki-i šá mar-tu mar-rat-u-ni*
647 *at-tu-nu* MÍ.MEŠ-*ku-nu* DUMU.MEŠ-*ku-nu* DUMU.MÍ.MEŠ-*ku-nu*
648 *ina* UGU *a-he-iš lu mar-ra-ku-nu*

646 Just as gall is bitter, so may you, your women, your sons and your daughters be bitter towards each other.

§ 101

649 KI.MIN ^{d}UTU *hu-ha-ru šá* UD.KA.BAR *ina* UGU-*hi-ku-nu* DUMU.MEŠ!-*ku-*[*nu*]
650 [DUMU.M]Í.MEŠ-*ku-nu li-is-hu-pu ina giš-par-ri šá la na-par-šu-di*
651 *li-di-ku-nu a-a ú-še-ṣi nap-šat-kun*

649 Ditto; may Šamaš clamp a bronze bird trap over you, (your sons and your [daught]ers); may he cast you into a trap from which there is no escape, and never let you out alive.

§ 102

652 *ki-i šá* KUŠ.*na-a-du šal-qa-tu-u-ni* A.MEŠ-*šá*
653 *ṣa-ap-pa-hu-u-ni*! *ina kaq-qar ṣu-ma-mit lap-lap-tu*
654 KUŠ.*na-da-ku-nu lu ta-hi-bi*
655 [*ina ṣ*]*u-um* A.MEŠ *mu-u-ta*

652 Just as (this) waterskin is split and its water runs out, so may your waterskin break in a place of severe thirst; die [of th]irst!

§ 103

656 [*k*]*i-i šá* KUŠ.E.SÍR *šal-qa-tu-u-ni*
657 *ina kaq-qar pa-qut-ti* [KUŠ.E.SÍR.ME]Š-*ku-nu*
658 *li-par-ma ina* UG[U *x x-k*]*u-nu x*[*x x x*]

656 Just as (these) shoes are split, so may your [shoes] be torn in a region of brier. [*Go around barefooted!*]

§ 104

659 ^{d}EN.LÍL EN GIŠ.GU.ZA [GIŠ.G]U.ZA-*ku-n*[*u lu-šá-bal-kit*]

659 May Illil, lord of the throne, [*overthrow*] your throne.

§ 105

660 ^{d}PA *na-ši ṭup-pi* NAM.MEŠ DINGIR.MEŠ
661 MU-*ku-nu lip-ši-ṭi* NUMUN-*ku-nu ina* KUR *lu-hal-liq*

660 May Nabû, bearer of the tablet of fates of the gods, erase your name, and destroy your seed from the land.

§ 106

662 GIŠ.IG *ina* IGI.MEŠ-*ku-nu lu x*[*x x x x x*]
663 GIŠ.IG.MEŠ-*ku-n*[*u x x x*]*x*[*x x x x x*]

662 May the door [...] before your eyes, may your doors [......].

§ 107 **Date and Colophon**

664 ITI.GUD.SI.SÁ UD-18-KÁM
665 *lim-mu* ^{md}PA—EN—PAB LÚ.GAR.KUR URU.BÀD—LUGAL-*uk-ku*
666 *a-de-e šá* ^{m}*aš-šur*—PAB—AŠ MAN KUR—*aš-šur*.KI [*šá*]! *ina* UGU ^{m}*aš-šur*—DÙ—A
667 DUMU—MAN GAL *šá* É—UŠ-*ti šá* KUR—*aš-šur*.KI
668 *ù ina* UGU ^{md}GIŠ.ŠIR—MU—GI.NA
669 DUMU—MAN *šá* É—UŠ-*ti* [*šá*] KÁ.DINGIR.RA.KI
670 *šak-n*[*u-u-ni*]

664 18th (var. 16th) day of Iyyar, eponymy of Nabû-belu-uṣur, governor of Dur-Šarrukku. The treaty of Esarhaddon, king of Assyria, conclu[ded] on behalf of Assurbanipal, the great crown prince designate of Assyria, and Šamaš-šumu-ukin, the crown prince designate of Babylon.

frg. 646 *mar-tu* AU frg: *-tú* frg, ZÉ-*tú* frg; *mar-rat-*⸢*u-ni*⸣ U frg: *mar-ra-tú-u-ni* A. 648 UGU U: UGU-*hi* frg; *mar-ra-ku-nu* A frg: *ma-ra-ku-*[*nu*] U. 650 [DUMU.M]Í.MEŠ-*ku-nu* frg: caret U; *li-is-hu-pu* frg: *-up* U. 651 *nap-šat-kun* U: *-ku-nu* frg. 661 MU-*ku-nu lip-ši-ṭi* frg: ⸢*lip-ši*⸣-[*ṭi* MU-*ku-nu* Q; *lu-hal-liq* Q: *li-hal-*[*liq*] frg. 664 UD-18-KÁM frgg: UD-16-KÁM Q. 665 ^{md}PA—EN—PAB Q frg: ^{md}AG—E[N—PAB frg; URU.BÀD—LUGAL-*uk-*⸢*ku*⸣ Q: *-u*]*k-k*[*a*] frg. 666 *šá* ^{m}*aš-šur*—PAB—AŠ MAN KUR—*aš-šur*.KI frg: caret Q; ⸢*šá*⸣ *ina* UGU Q: [*šá ina* UG]U frgg (coll. from photo). 667 GAL Q frg: caret frg; É—UŠ-*ti* Q frgg: *-te* frg; KUR—*aš-šur*.KI frg: KUR—*aš-šur* Q. 668 *ina* UGU frg: caret QZ frg; ^{md}GIŠ.ŠIR—MU—GI.NA Q frg: ^{m}GIŠ.ŠIR—MU—GI.NA frg. 669 É—UŠ-*ti* Q: [É—*re-du*]-*ú-*[*ti* frg.

7. Oath of Loyalty to Esarhaddon

Bu 91-5-9,22

beginning broken away

1′ ⸢*lu*⸣ [*x x x x x x x*

2′ *a-na* UR[U.*x x x x x x*

3′ *a-na* ^{m}*aš-šur*—P[AB—AŠ LUGAL KUR—*aš-šur x x*

4′ *šum-ma* LÚ.[*x x x x x x*

5′ *iz-za-zu-u-n*[*i x x x x x*

6′ NUMUN-*šú ù* U[N.MEŠ-*šú x x x*

7′ *la tu-raq-q*[*a-x x x x*

8′ *iq-qu-u-ku*[*n*$^{?}$*-u-ni x x x*

9′ *qu-ta-a-r*[*i x x x x*

10′ *la tu-raq-q*[*a-x x x x*

11′ LUGAL KUR—*aš-šur* [*x x x x x*

12′ ⸢*x x*⸣ [*x x x x x*

rest broken away

Rev. beginning broken away

1′ *i-*[*x x x x x x*

2′ *la* [*x x x x x x*

3′ *šum-m*[*a x x x x x*

4′ *šá at-t*[*u-nu x x x x*

5′ *ina gu-m*[*ur-ti x x x x*

6′ *an* [*x x x x x*

rest broken away

JCS 39 188

(Beginning destroyed)

1 ..[......]

2 to the ci[ty ......]

3 to Esarh[addon ......]

4 you shall [......]

5 standing [......]

6 his seed and his fa[mily ......]

7 you shall ...[......]

8 has *sacrificed* yo[u ......]

9 fumigant[s ......]

10 you shall ...[......]

11 king of Assyria [......]

(Break)

r.2 not [......]

3 you s[hall ......]

4 what you [......]

5 whol[eheartedly ......]

(Rest destroyed)

7 Previous edition: S. Parpola, JCS 39 (1987) 174f. 3 The reading of the second element of the royal name as P[AB not D[Ù is certain. 7, 10 Possibly *la tu-raq-q*[*a-qa-ni* "you shall *flat*[*ten out*" or "*ref*[*ine*". r.5 See coll.

Assurbanipal (668-627)

COURTESY TRUSTEES OF THE BRITISH MUSEUM

FIG. 19. *Stela of Assurbanipal carrying basket, from Babylon.*
BM 90864.

8. Zakutu Treaty

83-1-18,45 + 83-1-18,266

1 [*a-d*]*e-e* ⌜*šá*⌝ MÍ.*za-ku-u-te* MÍ.KUR *šá* ^{m}30—P[AB$^{!}$.MEŠ—SU]
2 [MA]N KUR—*aš* AMA ^{m}*aš-šur*—PAB—AŠ MAN KUR—*aš-šur*
3 TA* ^{md}GIŠ.ŠIR—MU—G[I].NA PAB *ta-li-me-šú*
4 TA* ^{md}GIŠ.ŠIR—UG$_{5}$.GA—TI.LA *ù*
5 *re-eh-te* PAB.MEŠ-*šú* TA* NUMUN LUGAL TA*
6 LÚ.GAL.MEŠ LÚ.NAM.MEŠ LÚ.*šá—ziq*$^{!}$*-ni*
7 [L]Ú.SAG.MEŠ LÚ.GUB—IGI TA* LÚ.⌜*zak*⌝-*ke-e*
8 *ù* LÚ.TU—KUR *gab-bu* 0$^{!}$ TA* DUMU.MEŠ KUR—*aš-šur*
9 ⌜LÚ⌝.[*qà*]*l-lu* LÚ.*dan-*⌜*nu*$^{!}$⌝ *man-nu šá ina* ŠÀ *a-de-e*
10 ⌜*an-nu*⌝-*te šá* MÍ.*za-ku-u-te* MÍ.KUR *ina* UGU
11 [^{m}*aš-šur*—D]Ù—A DUMU ŠÀ—ŠÀ-*bi-šá* HÚL TA* UN.MEŠ KUR *gab-bu*
12 [*taš-k*]*un-u-ni man-nu šá a-bu-tú la de-iq-tú*
13 [*la ṭ*]*a-ab-tú ù na-bal-kàt-tu*
14 [*ina* UG]U ^{m}*aš-šur*—DÙ—⌜A MAN⌝ KUR—*aš-šur* EN-*ku-nu*
15 [*x x t*]*a-sa-*⌜*li*⌝*-a-ni te-ep-pa-šá-a-ni*
16 [*nik-l*]*u*$^{!}$ *la da-an-qu da-ba-a-bu*
17 [*la ṭa*]-⌜*a*⌝-*bu ina* UGU ^{m}*aš-šur*—DÙ—A MAN KUR—*aš*
18 [EN-*ku-nu ina* Š]À ŠÀ-*bi-ku-nu ta-nak-kil-a-nin-ni*
19 [*ta-dáb-bu-b*]*a-a-ni us-su-uk-tú*
20 [*la de-i*]*q*$^{!}$*-tú mil-ku*$^{!!}$ *la ṭa-a-bu šá si-hi bar-te*
21 [*ina* ŠÀ-*bi-ku*]-*nu*$^{!}$ *ina* UGU ^{m}*aš-šur*—DÙ—A MAN KUR—*aš* EN-*ku-nu*
22 [*ta-mal-l*]*ik*$^{!}$*-a-ni ta-dáb-bu-ba-a-ni*
23 [TA* *x x x*]*x* 2-*e ina* UGU *du-a-ki*
24 [*šá* ^{m}*aš-šur*—DÙ—A MAN] KUR—*aš* EN-*ku-nu ta-dáb-bu-ba-a-*[*ni*]
25 [*aš-šur* ^{d}30 ^{d}UTU] ^{d}SAG.ME.GAR ^{d}*dil-bat*
e.26 [^{d}UDU.IDIM.SAG].⌜UŠ⌝$^{!}$ $^{d!}$⌜UDU⌝$^{!}$.[IDI]M$^{!}$.GUD.[UD]

ABL 1239 + JCS 39 189

The treaty of Zakutu, the queen of Senna[cherib, ki]ng of Assyria, mother of Esarhaddon, king of Assyria,

3 with Šamaš-šumu-ukin, his equal brother, with Šamaš-metu-uballiṭ and the rest of his brothers, with the royal seed, with the magnates and the governors, the bearded and the eunuchs, the royal entourage, with the exempts and all who enter the Palace, with Assyrians high and low:

9 Anyone who (is included) in this treaty which Queen Zakutu has concluded with the whole nation concerning her favourite grandson [Assurba]nipal,

12 anyone (of you) who should [...] fabricate and carry out an ugly and evil thing or a revolt against your lord Assurbanipal, king of Assyria,

16 in your hearts conceive and put into words an ugly [sch]eme or an evil plot against [your lord] Assurbanipal, king of Assyria,

19 [in yo]ur [hearts] deliberate and formulate an ugly suggestion and evil advice for rebellion and insurrection against your lord Assurbanipal, king of Assyria,

23 (or) plot [with] another [...] for the murder of your lord [Assurbanipal, king] of Assyria:

25 [May Aššur, Sin, Šamaš], Jupiter, Venus, Saturn, Mercury, [Mars, and Sirius ......

8 Previous edition: S. Parpola, JCS 39 (1987) 165ff. 2 The scribe has either omitted AMA ^{m}*aš-šur*—DÙ—A-*ma* "likewise mother of Assurbanipal" at the end of the line, or mistakenly written Esarhaddon instead of Assurbanipal. See discussion in JCS 39 168f. 20 Text *mil*-LU (scribal slip). r.1f See coll. 2 Text TA* TA* (scribal error).

COURTESY MUSÉE DU LOUVRE

FIG. 20. *Queen mother Naqia (Zakutu) with her son Esarhaddon (or grandson Assurbanipal).* AO 20185.

27 [^{d}*ṣal-bat*]-⸢*a*$^{!}$⸣-[*nu* ^{d}GAG.SI.SÁ *x x x*]
two lines destroyed
r.1 [*x x x x* Z]AG$^{?}$ ⸢*ù*⸣ [KAB *x x*]

---

2 [*ù šum-ma*] *at-tu-nu* TA* ŠÀ$^{!!}$ UD-*me an-ni*-⸢*e*⸣
3 [*a-bu-tú la*] *de-iq-tú šá si-hi bar-te*
4 [*šá ina* UGU ^{m}]*aš-šur*—DÙ—A MAN KUR—*aš be-lí-ku-nu*
5 [*i-dáb-bu*]-*bu-u-ni* (*ta-šam-ma-a-ni*) *la tal-la-ka-nin-ni*
6 [*uz-ni*] *šá* MÍ.*za-ku-u-te* AMA-*šú ù šá* ^{m}*aš-šur*—DÙ—A
7 [MAN KUR—*aš* E]N-*ku-nu la tu-pat-ta-a-ni* ⸢*ù*⸣ [*š*]*um-ma*

(Break)

sou]*th and* [*north*].

---

r.2 [And if] you from this day on (hear) an ugly [word] of rebellion and insurrection being spo[ken against] your lord Assurbanipal, king of Assyria, you shall come and inform Zakutu his mother and Assurbanipal, [king of Assyria], your lord;

8 *[at-tu]-nu šá da-a-ki ù hul-lu-qí*
9 *[šá* ^{m}*aš-šur]*—DÙ—A MAN KUR—*aš* EN-*ku-nu ta-šam-ma-a-ni*
10 *[la ta]l-la-ka-nin-ni uz-ni šá* MÍ.*za-ku-te* 0!
11 [AMA-*šú*] ⸢*ù*⸣ *šá* ^{m}*aš-šur*—DÙ—A MAN KUR—*aš be-lí-ku-nu*
12 *[la tu-pa]t-ta-a-ni ù šum-ma at-tu-nu*
13 *[ki-i nik-l]u la da-an-qu ina* UGU ^{m}*aš-šur*—DÙ—A
14 ⸢MAN KUR—*aš be-lí*⸣-*ku-nu i-nak-kil-an-ni*
15 *ta-šam-ma-a-ni la tal-la-ka-nin-ni*
16 *ina* IGI MÍ.*za-ku-te* AMA-*šú ù ina* IGI ^{m}*aš-šur*—DÙ—A
17 ⸢MAN KUR—*aš be-lí*⸣-*ku-nu la ta-qab-ba-a-ni*
18 *ù šum-ma at-tu-nu ta-šam-ma-a-ni*
19 *tu-da-a-ni ma*!-*a* ERIM.MEŠ *mu-šam-hi-iṣ-ṣu-u-te*
20 *mu-šad-bi-bu-u-te [[šá]] ina bir-tuk-ku-nu lu-u*
21 *ina* LÚ.*šá—ziq-ni lu-u ina* LÚ.SAG.MEŠ *lu-u ina* PAB.MEŠ-*šú*
22 *lu-u ina* NUMUN MAN *lu-u* PAB.MEŠ-*ku-nu lu-u* EN *ṭa-ba*!-*te-ku-nu*
23 *[lu-u] ina* UN.M[EŠ K]UR *gab-bu ta-šam-ma-a-ni*
24 *[tu-da-a-ni l]a ta-ṣab-ba-ta-nin-ni*
25 *[la ta-du-ka-ni ina]* ⸢UGU MÍ⸣.*za-ku-t[e]*!
26e [AMA-*šú ù ina* UGU ^{m}*aš-šur*—DÙ]—⸢A⸣ [MAN KUR—*aš*]
27e *[be-lí-ku-nu la tu-bal]*-⸢*a*!⸣-*n[in-ni]*
blank space of two lines

[7] and if you hear of (a plan) to kill or eliminate your lord [Assur]banipal, king of Assyria, you shall come and inform Zakutu [his mother] and your lord Assurbanipal, king of Assyria;

[12] and if you hear of an ugly [scheme] being elaborated against your lord Assurbanipal, king of Assyria, you shall speak out in the presence of Zakutu his mother and your lord, Assurbanipal, king of Assyria;

[18] and if you hear and know that there are men instigating armed rebellion or fomenting conspiracy in your midst, be they bearded or eunuchs or his brothers or of royal line or your brothers or friends or any one in the entire nation — should you hear and [know] (this), you shall seize and [kill] them and bring them to Zakutu [his mother and to Assurbani]pal, [king of Assyria, your lord.]

9. Assurbanipal's Treaty with Babylonian Allies

82-5-22,130

beginning broken away
1′ *[x x x]* ^{d}*be-lit*—*[x x x x x x x x x x x x x x x]*
2′ [DÙ]-*šú*!-*nu* DINGIR.MEŠ GAL.M[EŠ *ša* AN-*e u* KI.TIM *x x x x x x x x x x x]*
3′ *[ki-i] ul-tu* UD-*mu an-ni*-⸢*i*⸣ *[a-di* UD-*mu ma-la bal-ṭa-a-ni x x x x x x x]*
4′ *[šu]-u* ^{m}AN.ŠÁR—DÙ—DUMU.UŠ LUGAL KUR—*aš-šur*.[KI LUGAL-*a-ni* EN-*a-ni* ŠÀ-*bi-ni*]
5′ *it-ti* ^{m}AN.ŠÁR—DÙ—DUMU.UŠ LUGAL KUR—*aš-šur*.KI EN-*[i-ni gu-um-mu-ru lu-ú ši-pir-ti]*

ABL 1105

(Beginning destroyed)

[1] *[We swear by Aššur, Šerua,] Bel[et-ili,* ......, a]ll [the gods of Assyria and Babylonia], and [all] the great gods [of heaven and earth, ...],

[3] (that) from this day on [for as long as we live we will be subjects of Assurbanipal, king of Assyria], (that) Assurbanipal, king of Assyria [shall be our king and lord, and (that) we will be totally devoted] to Assurbanipal, king of Assyria, [our] lord.

26f See coll. (SP 18/3/88). There is absolutely no doubt that e. 26f (followed by two blank lines) are the last inscribed lines of this document.

9 Previous edition: A.K. Grayson, JCS 39 (1987) 139ff. — The number of signs missing at the ends of the lines has been determined on the basis of restorations made in Obv. 11', 16', 23', 25' and Rev. 3, all of which can be considered reasonably certain. 1 Restore probably [^{d}*še-ru-a*] ^{d}*be-lit*—[DINGIR.MEŠ DINGIR.MEŠ *šá* KUR—*aš-šur*.KI *u* KUR—URI.KI] in accordance with r.2 and Text 6:19ff. 2 See coll. 3 For restorations cf. Obv. 17' and 32'f.

6′ *lu-ú* LÚ*.A—KIN *šá* ^{md}GIŠ.ŠIR—MU—GI.NA LU[GAL TIN.TIR.KI *x x x x x x*]
7′ *i-pu-šu lu-ú ul-tu pa-an* DUMU.MEŠ *šá* ^{md}[GIŠ.ŠIR—MU—GI.NA *x x x x lu-ú*]
8′ *ul-tu pa-ni* LÚ*.EN—KÚR *šá* ^{m}AN.ŠÁR—DÙ—DUMU.UŠ LUGAL KUR—[*aš-šur*.KI EN-*i-ni il-li-ka*]
9′ *ni-ip-te-eṣ-nu u a-na pa-ši-ri ni-il-ta-kan-*⌜*ú*⌝ [*x x x a-na* ^{m}AN.ŠÁR—DÙ—DUMU.UŠ]
10′ LUGAL KUR—*aš-šur*.KI EN-*i-ni ni-šap-par-uš tab-bi*$^{!}$*-x*[*x ma-aṣ-ṣar-tú šá* ^{m}AN.ŠÁR—DÙ—DUMU.UŠ]
11′ LUGAL KUR—*aš-šur*.KI EN-*i-ni ni-na-aṣ-ṣa-ru u ma-aṣ-*[*ṣar-tú šá* LÚ*.EN—*pi-qit-ti šá ina* UGU-*hi-ni*]
12′ *ip-qí-du ni-na-aṣ-ṣa-ru lu-ú mam-ma na-az-ru x*[*x x x x x x* LÚ*.*mu-šam-hi-ṣu*]
13′ LÚ*.*mu-šad-bi-bu šá a-mat la ṭa-ab-ti a-na* UGU-*hi* ^{m}A[N.ŠÁR—DÙ—DUMU.UŠ LUGAL KUR—*aš-šur*.KI EN-*i-ni*]
14′ *i-qab-bu-ú lu-ú a-na* UGU-*hi* LÚ*.EN—*pi-qit-ti šá* ^{m}[AN.ŠÁR—DÙ—DUMU.UŠ LUGAL KUR—*aš-šur*.KI EN-*i-ni*]
15′ *i-qab-bu-ú u a-ni-ni ni-il-te-mu-ú u ni-qit-*[*x x x x x x ina iṣ—qa-ti*]
16′ *se-me-re-e ni-nam-du-ši-na a-na* ^{m}AN.ŠÁR—DÙ—DUMU.UŠ [LUGAL KUR—*aš-šur*.KI EN-*i-ni ni-šap-par-uš*]
17′ *ul-tu* UD-*mu an-ni-i a-di* UD-*mu ma-la ba*[*l-ṭa-a-ni a-na* UGU-*hi* ^{m}AN.ŠÁR—DÙ—DUMU.UŠ]

6 We will not conceal nor hide [*any message*] or messenger whom Šamaš-šumu-ukin, ki[ng of Babylonia] has [sent or] made [... or who has come to us] from the sons of Š[amaš-šumu-ukin] or from the enemy of Assurbanipal, king of [Assyria], but will send him [to Assurbanipal], king of Assyria, our lord.

10 We will protect [Assurbanipal], king of Assyria, our lord, and [the official whom] he has appointed [over us].

12 We will not listen to nor [...] any detestable person [..., agitator] or conspirator who speaks evil words against [Assurbanipal, king of Assyria, our lord], or against an official of [*Assurbanipal, king of Assyria, our lord*], but will throw him in [handcuffs] and [send him] to Assurbanipal, [king of Assyria, our lord].

17 From this day on for as long as we live

10 *tab-bi-x*[sic, see coll. 12-16 → 6:500-507 and 8 r.18-27. 15 *ni-qit-*[sic. 16 For restoration cf. Obv. 10’ and 32’f.

COURTESY TRUSTEES OF THE BRITISH MUSEUM

FIG. 21. *The royal tiara and other regalia of Šamaš-šumu-ukin displayed to Assurbanipal after the fall of Babylon in 648.*
BM 124945–6.

18′ LUGAL KUR—*aš-šur*.KI LÚ*.*ra-ʾi-ma-ni-šú u* KUR-*šú la ṭ[a-ab-ti x x x x x x]*

19′ *ni-te-ep-šu nu-ul-te-pi-šu ni-iq-ta-[bi x x x x x x x x x x x x x]*

20′ LÚ*.EN—*na-kar šá* ^{m}AN.ŠÁR—DÙ—DUMU.UŠ LUGAL KUR—*aš-š[ur*.KI EN-*i-ni x x x x x x x]*

21′ *la* LÚ*.EN—*sa-lam-i-ni mim-ma ma-la* [^{m}AN.ŠÁR—DÙ—DUMU.UŠ LUGAL KUR—*aš-šur*.KI EN-*a-ni*]

22′ *i-qab-ba-an-na-a-šú a-ki-i pi-[i-šú ni-ip-pu-šu x x x x x x x x x]*

23′ GIŠ.BAN.MEŠ-*ni ni-de-ek-ku-ú-ma it-t[i* ^{m}*aš-šur*—DÙ—DUMU.UŠ LUGAL KUR—*aš-šur*.KI EN-*i-ni*]

24′ *ni-iz-zi-iz-zu-ú-ma ṣal-ti a-na* ŠÀ-[*bi* LÚ*.KÚR-*šú ni-ip-pu-šu x x x x x x*]

25′ LÚ*.KÚR-*šú ina bi-bil* ŠÀ-*bi-ni ni-sek-ki-pu x[x* MU-*ni ina pa-an* ^{m}AN.ŠÁR—DÙ—DUMU.UŠ LUGAL KUR—*aš-šur*.KI]

26′ EN-*i-ni nu-ban-nu-ú hi-ṭu-ú-ni šá x[x x x x x x x x x x x x x x x]*

27′ *a-na* ^{m}AN.ŠÁR—DÙ—DUMU.UŠ LUGAL KUR—*aš-šur*.KI EN-*i-[ni ina* UGU ^{md}GIŠ.ŠIR—MU—GI.NA *ni-ih-ṭu-ú*]

28′ *ina pa-an* ^{m}AN.ŠÁR—DÙ—DUMU.UŠ LUGAL KUR—*aš-šur*.KI EN-*i-[ni ia-aʾ-nu x x x x x lu-ú*]

29′ *šá* ^{md}GIŠ.ŠIR—MU—GI.NA *lu-ú* KUR *šá-ni-tú m[a-la* ^{m}AN.ŠÁR—DÙ—DUMU.UŠ LUGAL KUR—*aš-šur*.KI]

30′ EN-*i-ni la i-šad-da-du a-na pa-ni-ni it-[tal-ka x x x x x x x x x x x x]*

31′ *ab-lu ni-ṣab-bat-ú-ma a-na* LUGAL EN-*i-ni ni-[šap-pa-ru x x x* ^{m}AN.ŠÁR—DÙ—DUMU.UŠ]

32′ LUGAL KUR—*aš-šur*.KI EN-*i-ni ni-ra-ʾa-a-mu u* LÚ*.[KÚR-*šú ni-ze-ʾi-i-ru ul-tu* UD-*mu*]

33′ *an-ni-i a-di* UD-*mu ma-la bal-ṭa-a-ni* ^{m}AN.ŠÁR—DÙ—[DUMU.UŠ LUGAL KUR—*aš-šur*.KI LUGAL-*a-ni* EN-*a-ni*]

34′ *šu-tu-ú-ma* LUGAL *šá-nam-ma* EN *šá-nam-ma a-na* U[GU-*hi-ni ni-il-ta-kan-ú*]

35′ *nu-ub-te-ʾu-ú ši-pir-ti a-na* LÚ*.KÚR *šá* ^{m}AN.ŠÁR—DÙ—[DUMU.UŠ LUGAL KUR—*aš-šur*.KI EN-*i-ni x x x*]

36′ [*lu*]-*ú ši-pir-ti lu-ú* LÚ*.A—KIN *šá ul-tu* KUR *šá-ni-tú-ma a-n[a pa-ni-ni*]

37′ [*i*]*t*-⌜*tal*!⌝-*ka* KASKAL.2 *a-na* GÌR.2-*šú ni-šak-kan-ú-ma a-na pa-[ni* ^{m}AN.ŠÁR—DÙ—DUMU.UŠ LUGAL KUR—*aš-šur*.KI]

38′ [*ni-šap-par*] ⌜*x x*⌝ *mam*!-*ma*! *šá a-na pa-ni* ^{m}AN.ŠÁR—DÙ—DUMU.UŠ LUGAL [KUR—*aš-šur*.KI *x x x x x x x x*]

we will neither do nor cause anyone to do, nor speak [evil things ...... against Assurbanipal], king of Assyria, those who love him, and his land.

20 The enemy of Assurbanipal, king of Assyria, [......] shall not be our ally.

21 [We will do] everything that Assurbanipal, king of Assyria, our lord, tells us (to do) according to his command; [when Assurbanipal, king of Assyria, our lord, goes against his enemy], we will muster our bow[men] and stand with [*Assurbanipal, king of Assyria, our lord*, make] battle against [his foes], overwhelm, as is our fervent desire, his enemy, and make [our name] good [in the eyes of Assurbanipal, king of Assyria], our lord.

26 Our crimes which [we committed because of Šamaš-šumu-ukin] against Assurbanipal, king of Assyria, [our] lord, [have been forgiven] by Assurbanipal, king of Assyria, [our] lord, [......].

29 [If any *subject*] of Šamaš-šumu-ukin, or of another land, w[hom Assurbanipal, king of Assyria], our lord, does not *tolerate*, c[omes] to us [or ...] is brought to us, we will seize (him) and [send him] to the king, our lord.

32 We will love [Assurbanipal], king of Assyria, and [hate his enemy]. [From] this [day] on for as long as we live, Assurbanipal, [king of Assyria], shall be [our king and lord. We will not install] nor seek another king or another lord for [ourselves]. [We will not send] a(ny) report to the enemy of Assurbanipal, [king of Assyria, our lord]; (if) a report or a messenger from another land reaches [us], we will put him on the road and [*send him*] into the presence [of Assurbanipal, king of Assyria, our lord].

38 [We will ......] anyone who [is ...] to Assurbanipal, king [of Assyria, our lord ...

26-28 The restorations in these lines are based on ABL 968 r.6, *hi-ṭu ša be-li-i-ni i-na pa-an* LUGAL *ia-a-nu.* 30 *i-šad-da-du*: the suggested translation is uncertain since the text has EN-*i-ni* instead of expected EN-*a-ni*. Grayson's reading *i-mad-da-du* seems excluded by the context. 33f → 6:507-510 and 191-197. 34 Note the Assyrianism *šu-tu-ú-ma* indicating that the text was composed in Nineveh. 38, r.1 See coll.

39′ [*x x x x x x x x*]*x*[*x*]*x*[*x x x x x x x x x x x x x x x x x x x x x x*] rest broken away	
Rev. beginning broken away	(Break)
1′ [*x x x x x x x*]-⸢*a*⸣!-*mu*! *šá* [*x x x x x x x x x x x x x x x*] 2′ [DINGIR.MEŠ *š*]*á* KUR—*aš-šur*.KI *u* KUR—UR[I.KI *x x x x x x x x x x x x x x x*]	r.2 ..., by the gods o]f Assyria and Babylonia [......]:
3′ *ki-i a-ni-ni a-na a-de-e a*[*n-nu-ti šá* ^{m}AN.ŠÁR—DÙ—DUMU.UŠ LUGAL KUR—*aš-šur*.KI EN-*i-ni*] 4′ *ni-mi-is-su ni-pa-as-s*[*a-su x x x x x x x x x x x x x x x*]	3 If we should [transgress], break, erase, [or ...] t[his] treaty [with Assurbanipal, king of Assyria, our lord],
5′ AN.ŠÁR AD DINGIR.MEŠ *mu-šim ši-ma-*[*a-ti ši-mat* MÍ.HUL-*ti la* DÙG.GA-*ti li-šim-an-na-a-ši*]	5 May Aššur, father of the gods, ordainer of fates, [ordain for us an evil and untoward fate].
6′ ^{d}AMAR.UTU LUGAL DINGIR.MEŠ EN KUR.KUR *a-x*[*x x x x x x x x x x x x x x x x x*]	6 May Marduk, king of the gods, lord of the lands, [......].
7′ ^{d}AG *pa-qid kiš-šat* AN-*e u* KI.TIM *is-*[*x x x x x x x x x x x x x xx*]	7 May Nabû, trustee of the entire heaven and underworld, [......].
8′ ^{d}UTU! DI.KUD.GAL AN-*e u* KI.TIM *be* [*x x x x x x x x x x x x x x*] 9′ *di-i-ni pa-rik-ti li-di-n*[*a-na-ši x x x x x x x x x x x x*] 10′ *ni-iṭ-lu* IGI.2-*ni liš-ši i-n*[*a ek-le-ti ni-tal-la-ka*]	8 May Šamaš, the great judge of heaven and earth, [......] render an unjust judgment [against us ......]. May he remove our eyesight, [may we wander about in darkness].
11′ ^{d}30 *na-an-na-ru* AN-*e u* KI.TIM [*x x x x x x x x x x x x x x x*] 12′ É.KUR *u* É.GAL ⸢*e*⸣*-re-ba-nu ú-*[*x x x x x x x x x x x x x x x x*]	11 May Sin, light of heaven and earth, [...... *prohibit*] our entry into temple and palace [...].
13′ ^{d}É.A LUGAL ZU.AB A.MEŠ *nag-bi* [*x x x x x x x e-liš ina* TI.LA.MEŠ] 14′ *li-is-suh-an-na-a-šú šap-l*[*iš ina* KI.TIM *e-ṭím-ma-a-nu* A.MEŠ *li-za-me*]	13 May Ea, king of the Abyss, [......] water from the springs; [above, may he] uproot us [from among the living, and bel]ow, [make our ghosts thirst for water].
15′ ^{d}IM GÚ.GAL-*la* AN-*e u* KI.TIM [*x x x x x x x x x x x x x x x x*] 16′ *mim-ma ina* ŠÀ-*bi la il-la-a la x*[*x x x x x x x x x x x x x x x x*]	15 May Adad, canal inspector of heaven and earth, [...... *so that*] whatever is therein cannot rise [......].
17′ ^{d}NIN.URTA DUMU.UŠ SAG-*tu-ú* [*x x x x x x x x x x x x x x x x*]	17 May Ninurta, the foremost heir, [......].
18′ ^{d}U.GUR *dan-nu-dan-nu* DINGIR.MEŠ *ina* [*x x x x x x x x x x x x x x x x x x*]	18 May Nergal, the strongest among the gods, with [*his (merciless) sword extinguish our lives*].
19′ ^{d}*za-ba*$_{4}$*-ba*$_{4}$ EN *šá-qu-ú šá* [*x x x x x x x x x x x x x x x x x x*]	19 May Zababa, exalted lord, who [......].
20′ ^{d}IGI.DU LUGAL EDIN *i-na x*[*x x x x x x x x x x x x x x x x*]	20 May Palil, king of the desert, with [......].

21′ ^{d}*zar-pa-ni-tum na-di-na-at* M[U *u* NUMUN x x x x x x x x x x]

21 May Zarpanitu, provider of [name and progeny, *drive our name and progeny from the land*].

22′ ^{d}*na-na-a be-lit re-e-mu u* [x x x x x x x x x x x x x x x x x]

23′ IDIM *u* NUN *tu-šam-ri-iṣ-an-na-ši* [x x x x x x x x x x x x x x x x x]

22 May Nanai, mistress of love and [peace, ...] make us an abomination to (both) nobleman and prince [......].

24′ $^{d+}$INNIN *a-ši-bat arba-ìl*.KI *i-lat ta-ha-za-a-ti* [x x x x x xx x x x x x x x]

25′ [*ina šá-pal* GÌR.2 *šá* LÚ*].KÚR-*ni li-šak-mì-is-an-n*[*a-ši* x x x x x x x x x x]

24 May Ištar, who resides in Arbela, goddess of battle, [*break our bow in the thick of battle* and] make us crouch [under the feet of] our enemy [......].

26′ [*x x x x x x x x*]*x x*[*x x*]*x* [*x x*]*x x x*[*x*] *x*[*x x x x x x x x x x x x*]

27′ [x x x x x x x x x x x x x x x] *sik* [x x x x x x x x x x]

---

rest broken away

(Rest destroyed)

10. Assurbanipal's Treaty with the Qedar Tribe

Bu 91-5-9,178

beginning (at least 5 lines) broken away

1′ [TA* ^{m}*x x x*] A ^{m}⸢*ia-ú*⸣-[*ta-a*ʾ *x x x*]

2′ [(IGI) DINGIR.MEŠ KUR]—*aš-šur* DINGIR.MEŠ KUR.*qi-id*-[*ri* DÙ-*šú-nu*]

3′ [*aš-šur*] ^{d}NI[N].LÍL $^{d!}$*š*[*e*$^{!}$-*ru-u-a*]

4′ [*pit*$^{?}$-*ti*$^{?}$ *š*]*á* ^{m}*ia-ú-ta-a*ʾ *la* MU[N-*a-nu*$^{?}$]

5′ [*pi-i* G]ÍR.AN.BAR *a-na ha-lu-*[*qi* 0$^{!}$]

6′ [KUR.*a-ru-b*]*u*$^{?}$ *gab-bu id-din*-⸢*u*⸣-[*ni* 0$^{!}$]

7′ [*ina pi*]-⸢*i*⸣ GÍR.AN.BAR *iš-kun-u-ka-nu-n*[*i*]

8′ [^{m}*aš-šur*]—⸢DÙ⸣—A ⸢MAN⸣ KUR—*aš-šur* EN-*ku-nu*

9′ ⸢Ì⸣.GIŠ *iš-kun-ak-ka-nu-u-ni*

10′ *pa-ni-šú* SIG$_{5}$.MEŠ *ina* UGU-*hi-ku-nu*

11′ *iš-kun-u-ni*

12′ *šum-ma at-tu-nu* TA* ^{m}*ia-ú-ta-a*ʾ

13′ *a-na* MUN *ta-qar-rib-a-ni*

14′ *šum-*[*ma* TA*] ŠEŠ.MEŠ-*ku-nu* ŠEŠ.ME A[D.MEŠ-*ku-nu*]

15′ [*x x x x*]*x tu* KUR [*x x x x*]

16′ [*x x x x x*]*x is* [*x x x x*]

rest (at least 8 lines) broken away

JCS 39 159

[The treaty of Assurbanipal, king of the world, king of Assyria, son of Esarhaddon, likewise king of the world, king of Assyria, with *Abiyate' son of Te'ri,* his sons, grandsons, brothers and nephews, with all Qedarites, young and old, and with ...] son of Yau[ta', in the presence of all the gods of] Assyria and Qedar:

---

3 [(*Swear* by) Aššur], Mullissu and *Š*[*erua*]:

---

4 [*Considering* th]at Yauta' (your) malef[actor] handed all [Arab]s over to destruction [through] the iron sword, and put you to the sword,

8 [and that Assur]banipal, king of Assyria, your lord, put oil on you and turned his friendly face towards you,

12 you shall not strive for peace with Yauta',

14 you shall not [... with] your brothers, [your] unc[les ...

10 Previous edition: A.K. Grayson, JCS 39 (1987) 147ff. 1f Restoring [TA* ^{m}*a-bi—ia-te-e*ʾ] at the beginning of the line is difficult, since there is room for 5 signs at most in the break. After ^{m}⸢*ia-ú*⸣-[*ta-a*ʾ], restore possibly [*ina pa-an*], in which case (IGI) at the beginning of the next line should be deleted. 3 See coll. There is no room for [*ti-ma-a*] "swear" or the like at the end of the line. 4 There is room for two small or one long sign only at the beginning of the line. The restoration at the end of the line is conjectural but fits the available space. 6 See coll. r.1 Despite Grayson, JCS 39 150, the reading *at*]-*tu*-⸢*nu*⸣ is possible. 3 See coll.

Rev. beginning (at least 6 lines) broken away
1′ [*x at*]-*tu*-⸢*nu*⸣ [*x x x x x x x*]
2′ [*šum-m*]*a* GÌR.2-*šú* [*x x x x x x x x*]
3′ [*i—d*]*a-tu-uš*-[*šu x x x x x x x*]
4′ *ina* ŠU.2 *me-me-ni ta-šap-pa*[*r*]-⸢*a*⸣-[*ni*-(*šú-ni*)]
5′ *ina pu-ut sa-an-ka-a-te šá e-p*[*u-šu-u-ni*]
6′ *ina* [U]GU *du-a-ki-šú la ta-kap-pu-d*[*a-a-ni*]
7′ *la ta-ṣa*[*r*]-*rim-a-ni*

8′ [^{d}*aš-šur* ^{d}NI]N.LÍL ^{d}30 ^{d}UTU
9′ [^{d}EN ^{d}P]A ^{d}⸢15⸣ [*šá*] NINA.[KI ^{d}1]5
10′ [*ša arba-ìl* ^{d}]U.GUR *x*[*x x x*]
11′ [*x x x x x x*]*x*[*x x x x*]
rest broken away

(Break)

r.1 You shall [......];

2 [you] sh[all keep] his feet [off ...], and shall not send [...] after him by the hand of anyone,

5 (but), considering the *terrible* things which he did, you shall make every effort to kill him.

---

8 [May Aššur, Mu]llissu, Sin, Šamaš, [Bel, Na]bû, Ištar [of Nineveh, Iš]tar [of Arbela], Nergal [...

(Rest destroyed)

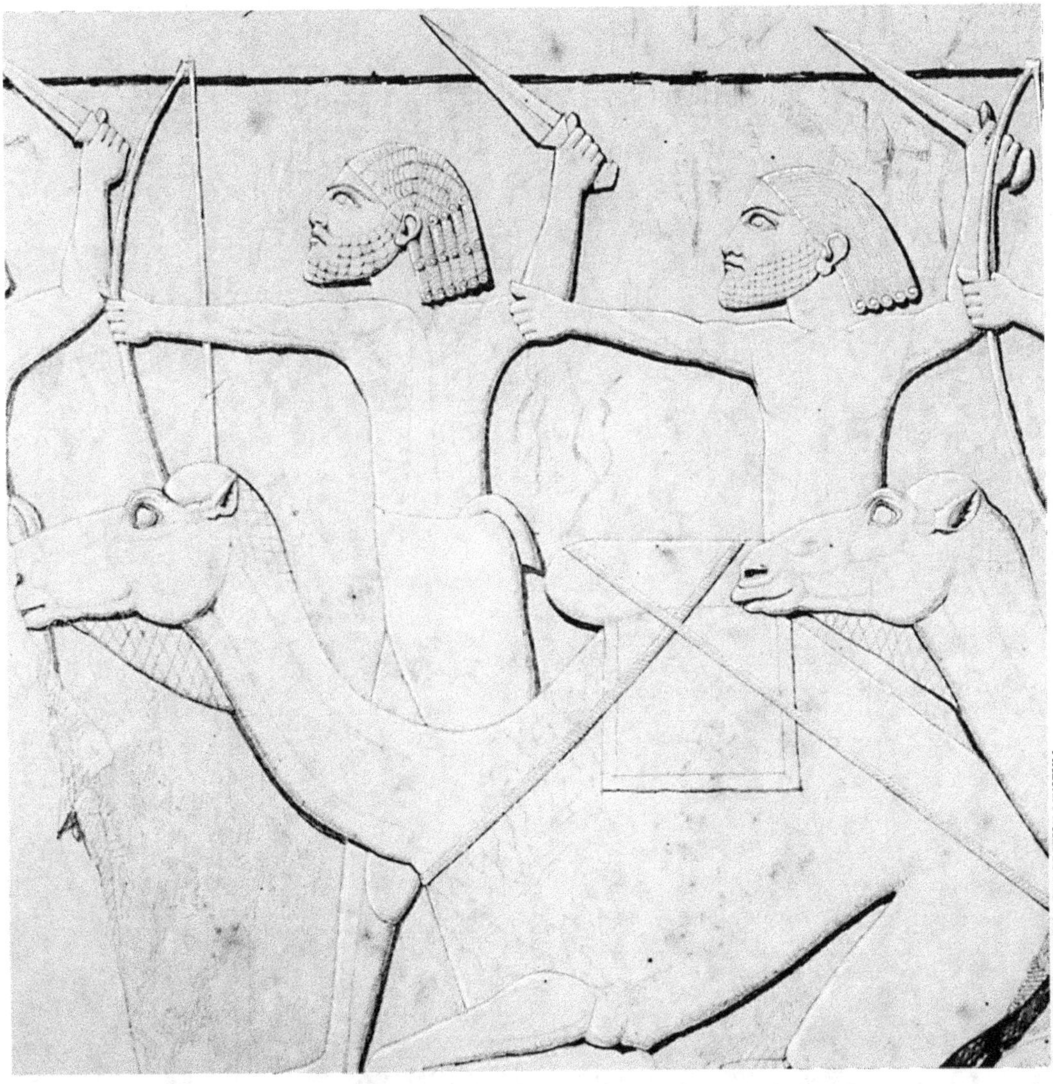

COURTESY TRUSTEES OF THE BRITISH MUSEUM

FIG. 22. *Arabs arrayed for battle (reign of Assurbanipal).* ORIGINAL DRAWING VII, 28.

Late Treaties (626-612)

COURTESY TRUSTEES OF THE BRITISH MUSEUM

FIG. 23. *A late Assyrian king, possibly Aššur-etelli-ilani or Sin-šarru-iškun.*
BM 124825.

11. Sin-šarru-iškun's Treaty with Babylonian Allies

MLC 1302

1 [*a-de*]-*e ša* ^{md}30—⸢MAN!—GAR!⸣-[*un* MAN KUR—*aš-šur*.KI]
2 [DU]MU ^{m}AN.ŠÁR—DÙ—A [MAN ŠÚ MAN KUR—*aš-šur*.KI]
3 [T]A* ^{md}AG—A—[S]UM-*na* [*x x x x x x x x x*]
4 [T]A* ^{m}ITI!.AB-⸢*a*!⸣-*a* [*x x x x x x x x*]
5 [T]A* ^{m}*aq-ri* [*x x x x x x x x*]
6 [*i-n*]*a ma-har* ^{d}S[AG!.ME.GAR ^{d}*dil-bat x x x*]
rest broken away

Rev. beginning broken away
1′ [*x x x x x*] ⸢*x x*⸣ [*x x x x x x x*]
2′ [MU AN.ŠÁR] EN *ṣi*!-⸢*i*!⸣-*r*[*i*? *x x x x*]
3′ [*ša*] ⸢*a-a*⸣-*bi ra-im-a-nu ša* [*ke-nu-ti*]
4′ [*ša* LUG]AL ⸢ÁG!⸣-*ú-ni za-ia-ra-an*-⸢*šú*!⸣ [*ú-hal-li-qu-ni*]
5′ [*man-nu š*]*a da*!-*bab ṭup-pi an-ni-e* ⸢*e*⸣-[*nu-u-ni*]
6′ [0! *a-de*]-*e* DINGIR.MEŠ GAL.MEŠ *i-haṭ-ṭ*[*u*!-*u-ni*]
7′ [*x x*] *šá* AN-*e u* KI.TIM *ar-rat la na*[*p-šu-ri*]
8′ [GIG-*t*]*ú li-ri-im-šú-nu e-liš i-na* T[I.LA.MEŠ]
9′ [*li-su-uh-š*]*ú-nu šap-liš i-na* KI.TIM ⸢*e*!⸣-[*ṭím-ma-šú-nu*]
10′ [A.ME]Š *lu-u-za-am-me* ^{d}30 ^{d}ŠEŠ.KI A[N-*e u* KI.TIM]
11′ [SAHAR].ŠUB-*pu ki-ma na-ah-lap-ti lu-u-hal-lip-šú-*[*nu*]
12′ *ma*!-*za-sa-šu*!!-*nu* TA* ŠÀ É.KUR É.GAL *lu-hal-liq* [0]

BRM 4 50

The treaty of Sin-šarru-išk[un, king of Assyria], son of Assurbanipal, [king of Assyria], with Nabû-apla-iddina [......], with *Ṭebetaya* [......], (and) with Aqri [......] in the presence of Ju[piter, Venus ...

(Break)

r.1 [*By Aššur*], *augu*[*st*] lord, [*defeater of*] enemies, lover of [the just], [who] loves the [kin]g and [destroys] his enemy:

5 [Whoever] a[lters] the wording of this tablet, or sins against the [trea]ty of the great gods,

7 May [......] of heaven and earth cover (sic) them with an evil, irremovable curse. Above, may [he uproot] them from amongst the living, (and) below, in the underworld, deprive [their] ghosts of water.

10 May Sin, light of heaven and earth, clothe them in leprosy as in a cloak (and) destroy their stands from temple and palace,

11 Previous edition: A.K. Grayson, JCS 39 (1987) 150ff. Collated for the present edition by B.Foster and Gary Beckman in February, 1988. Collations and comments cited below with no indication of source originate with Foster, those marked (GB) with Beckman. 1 See coll. Last sign "not GIŠ, copy is excellent. I would read SI" (BF). "Certainly not GIŠ" (GB). 4 See coll. "Signs ITI and AB are clear. There is only one sign in break, I believe E or A." 6 See coll. "I see R[I, Z[I, etc. There seems to be a second vertical, and the initial wedge is a horizontal, not a Winkelhaken" (GB). r.2 See coll. "There is a clear vertical after the alleged AD; I think you have to read ṢI. Then there are what appears to be two horizontals, hence *ṣi*-⸢*i*⸣-[ ]*x*. No sure reading possible for *x*. I would read *ṣi*-⸢*i*⸣-[*ru/i*]." 3 "[*ša*] okay with space. *a-a-bi* first A aligns with PA in last line. 4 See coll. "At end of line read -*an*-⸢*šú*⸣; [last] sign just like *šú* in line 8′. Room for 3-4 signs at end, or even 5, if one of the signs is a small one." 5 "First ŠA aligns with LUG]AL of preceding line. *man-nu* therefore just possible. Clay's copy is good for the [next] two signs (see copy). Last trace as copied, ⸢*e*⸣ is good, looks like sign next to it; ⸢*ú*⸣ is not good." 6 "No space for *ina* at beginning. Traces of last sign (see copy) seem fine for *ṭ*[*u*" (GB). "Trace of DI is in alignment with MEŠ of second to last line. Not really room for *ina a-*; Grayson probably correct." 8 "First trace (see copy) not too good for UD. *li-ri-im-šú-nu* is correct." 9 Last sign: "Definite E" (GB). "I would read E and exclude GIDIM." 12 "KIB excluded. First sign does indeed seem to be *ma*. Fourth sign Clay's copy good. The left vertical is clear. You cannot read ŠU without emending the tablet. The wedge to make it "KI" is low and cramped compared to the other two KI signs in the text. I would read *ku-nu* and ignore the little wedge as a slip or chip. I don't think the scribe wanted to write KI."

13′ NUMUN.MEŠ-*šú-nu ṣa-lam-*(*a*)*-ni-šú-nu i-na* IZI *i-kar-ru-r*[*u*]
14′ *di-pa-ra-šú-nu i-na* A.MEŠ *ú-bal-*⸢*lu*⸣-[*ú*]

13 (so that) their offspring and their statues be thrown into the fire, (and) their torches be extinguished with water.

12. Extract from a Treaty of Sin-šarru-iškun

Ass 13955z

1 *šum-ma at-tu-nu ina* ŠÀ *a-de-e*
2 *an-nu-te šá* ^{md}30—MAN—GAR-*un*
3 LUGAL KUR—*aš-šur*.KI EN-*ku-nu*
4 DUMU.MEŠ-*šú* DUMU—DUMU.MEŠ-*šú*
5 *ta-ha-ṭi-a-ni*
6 ^{d}U.GUR EN *gít-ma-lu*
7 [*d*]*a-me-ku-nu ina har-ri* [*n*]*a-da-*[*b*]*a-k*[*i*]
Rev. uninscribed

AfO 13 pl. 14

If you should sin against this treaty of Sin-šarru-iškun, king of Assyria, your lord, and his sons and grandsons,

6 may Nergal, the perfect lord, (pour out) your blood into ditches and ravines.

12 Previous editions: E. Weidner, AfO 13 (1939/41) 215 and pl.14; A.K. Grayson, JCS 39 (1987) 154. 7 There is no room for [*litbuk*] restored in JCS 39 at the end of the line.

Varia

13. A Vassal Treaty

K 4439

I entirely broken away
II beginning broken away
1′ *[x x x x x x x]* ⸢*x*⸣
2′ *[x x x x x x]-ka-šú*
3′ *[is-si]-šú* ⸢*la*⸣ *ta-*⸢*sa-lim*⸣
4′ *[pi-i i]s-si-šú* ⸢*la*⸣ *ta-šá-kan*
5′ *[ta]-pa-l[àh-an]-ni*
6′ [SI]G$_5$-*ia te-*⸢*pa*⸣*-áš-*⸢*ma*⸣
7′ *[šum-ma]* ⸢SIG$_5$-*ia*⸣ *te-ta-pa-áš*
8′ *[x x x* KUR$^?$.*a$^?$-r]u-bu gab-bu*
9′ *[x x x x x x]-bu*
10′ *[x x x x x x]-di-u*

11′ *[šum-ma a-na-ku ina* U]GU-*hi-ka*
12′ *[x x x x x a]l-lak*
13′ *[x x x x x x]*⸢*x*⸣*-bi pi-i-šú*
14′ *[x x x x x]* ⸢TA*⸣ IGI-*ka pa-ti-u-ni*
15′ *[x x x x t]u-še-ṣa*
16′ *[x x x š]ak-na-šu-u-ni*
17′ *[x x lu-š]am-ri-ṣu*
18′ *[x x]* 1-⸢*en ina*⸣ ŠÀ ARAD.MEŠ-*ka*
19′ *[x x x]* ⸢KUR⸣ *šá-ni-*⸢*tim*⸣*-ma*
20′ *[x x x x x x]* ⸢*at x*⸣

Reverse

III 1 *lu-u ina* ŠU.2 KU$_6$ *šá tam-*⸢*tim*⸣
2 *lu-u ina* ŠU.2 MUŠEN *šá* AN-*e*
3 *la ta-šap-par*
4 *šum-ma at-ta ta-qab-bu-u-ni*
5 *[ma]-*⸢*a*⸣ *a-lik a-na* LUGAL *am-mì-e qi-bi*
6 *[ma-a] an-nu-rig* LUGAL KUR—*aš-šur*
7 *[ina* UG]U-*hi-ka il-la-ka*
8 *[nik-l]u me-me-ni us-se*-IL$^?$
9 *[ina* UGU*]-hi-ka a-na e-pa-ši*
10 *[ù] a-bu-tú am-mar ta-šam-mu-ni*
11 *[lu-u* T]A *pi-i* 1-*en* LUGAL.MEŠ
12 *[lu-u* T]A *pa-an* 1-*et* KUR.MEŠ
13 *[ša ina* UG]U-*hi-ni ina* UGU KUR—*aš-šur*
14 *[qur]-bu-u-ni la ṭa-bu-u-ni*
15 [TA] IGI-*ia la tu-pa-zar*

JCS 39 188

(Beginning destroyed)

ii 2 [...] him.
3 You will not make peace [with] him
4 nor make [common cause] with him,
5 but will fe[ar] me
6 and do what is [good] to me.
7 [If] you do what is good to me,
8 all [*Ar*]*abia* [...
(Break)

---

11 [Should] I march
12 [...] against you
13 [...] his *mouth*
14 [...] keeping at a distance from you
15 [...] you will bring forth
16 [...] is set to him
17 [... let them] make *difficult*
18 [...] one of your servants
19 [...] another country
20 [...] ...
iii 3 You will send no [messages],
1 neither with a fish of the sea
2 nor with a bird of the sky.
4 You shall not say:
5 "Go and tell that king:
6 'Now, the king of Assyria
7 is marching against you,
8 he has ...ed a certain [strat]agem
9 to use against you.'"
15 [Nor] will you conceal from me
10 anything that you hear,
11 be it from the mouth of a king
12 or on account of a country,
14 (anything) that bears upon or is harmful
13 to us or Assyria,

13 Previous edition with commentary: S. Parpola, JCS 39 (1987) 175ff.
II 1f, 16, 19f See coll. The proposed restoration is tentative.
III 8 See coll.

16 [*a-na*] ⌈*a*⌉-*a-ši ta-šap-pa-ra*
17 [*tu-š*]*á-áš-man-ni*
18 [*dib-bi*] *am—mar šá a-na-ku*
19 [*is-si-ka a-d*]*a-bu-ub-u-ni*
20 [*x x x x x-p*]*i am—mar šá a-me-lu-ti*
21 [*x x x x x x x*]-*ṣa*
22 [*x x x x x x x*]-*su*
23 [*x x x x x x x-k*]*a*
rest (at least 15 lines) broken away
IV entirely broken away

16 but you will write to me
17 and bring it to my attention.
18 Whatever [matters]
19 I may discu[ss with you],
20 whatever [...] mankind
(Rest destroyed)

14. Esarhaddon's Treaty Inscription

BM 50666 + 50857 + 53678 + 53728 (+) 51098

JCS 39 158 (+) 160

I 1 [*x x*] ⌈^{d}⌉*be-lit*—DINGIR.ME ⌈*eš*$^{?}$⌉-*ra-ti mìn-si a-šá-lu šá a-x*[*x*]
2 [*x x*] *ra ú*$^{?}$ *tú* ⌈*x x x-nu*⌉-*ti dan-niš ma-har* [*x*]
3 [*ṭu*]-*ub-ti ina gi-mir* ⌈*x*⌉ [Á].KAL-*a-a šu x*[*x x*]
4 [*x x*]*x* 7 MUL.UDU.IDIM.MEŠ AN-*e šá a-na ma-mit* LUG[AL]
5 [*x x*]*x-tú*$^{!}$ *i-ra-ru-ma la i-tur-*[*ru*]
6 [*x*]*x-ši-ti* DINGIR-*ti be-lit*—DINGIR.ME *ina a-mat pi-i-šú el-lit* [*at-kal*]

i 1 [...] I asked ... Belet-ili, "Why?" ... [...]
2 [...]...... exceedingly before [......]
3 [... *goo*]*dness* with all my strength [......]
4 [...] the seven planets of the sky which [...] the oath of the king,
5 will curse [...] and not return [*to his side*].
6 [*I obeyed*] the divinity of Belet-ili, [*trusting*] in her holy command.

---

7 ⌈*i*⌉-*na* UD-*mi-šu-ma šá a-de-e šu-a-ti šu-uṣ*$^{!}$-[*bu-tu*]
8 [*um-m*]*a* LUGAL *be-lí ma-mit iš-ku-nu it-ti ka-l*[*i* KUR.KUR.MEŠ]
9 [*iš-me*]-*e-ma* NUN$^{!}$ ^{d}AMAR.UTU *a-na šu-pu-uš kiš-šu-t*[*ú*]
10 [*a-na*] KUR—*aš-šur*.⌈KI⌉ *it-ru-uṣ bu-*[*ni-šú*]
11 [*qa-at*] ^{m}AN.ŠÁR$^{!}$—*ba-an*—DUMU.UŠ DUMU—LUGAL É—*re-du-*[*ti*]
12 [*qa-at* ^{md}UT]U—⌈MU—GIN⌉ DUMU—LUGAL É—*re-du-*[*ti*]
13 [*šá* KÁ.DINGIR.RA.KI *x*]*x šá šu-lu-ku* [*a-na e-peš* LUGAL-*ti*]
14 [*iṣ-bat-ma x x x*]*x-a*$^{!}$ *u* ⌈^{d}*be-lit*—DINGIR.MEŠ⌉ [*x x x x x*]
short break
about 4 lines with traces at the ends of lines
19′ [*x x x x x x x x*]*x* [*x x x*]
20′ [*x x x x x x x x*]*x-bil-x*[*x*]

7 At that time, when that treaty was imp[osed] and it was said: "The king my lord has imposed an oath on all [the lands]," Prince Marduk heard it, and turned [his attention to] Assyria to help (it) establish world dominion.

11 [He took the hand] of Assurbanipal, the crown prince designa[te], [and that of] Šamaš-šumu-ukin, the crown prince designate of [Babylon], [*princes*] superbly suitable for [the exercise of kingship],

14 [......] Belet-ili [......]
(Break)

14 Previous edition: A.K. Grayson, JCS 39 (1987) 135ff and 155ff. Collation (both by Parpola and Watanabe) indicates that the fragments published by Grayson as separate texts belong together and are in fact parts of the same tablet.

I 1 See coll.; the sense of the line remains obscure. 2 The restoration and rendering [*mi-ša*]-*ra kit-tú* "law (and) justice" proposed by Grayson must be rejected since the word order required is *kittu (u) mīšaru*, not vice versa. 7 See coll.; Grayson's copy agrees with the reading -*uṣ*-. 14 See coll. After [*iṣ-bat-ma* one may plausibly restore

21′ [DUMU.MEŠ ^{m}AN.ŠÁR–ŠEŠ]–⸢SUM⸣-*na* LUGAL *kiš*$^{!}$-⸢*šá*$^{!}$⸣-*t*[*i*$^{!}$]
22′ [LÚGAL *kib-ra-a-t*]*i er-bet-ti šu-nu*
23′ [*x x x x*]-*du qer-bu-uš-un* [0$^{?}$]
24′ [*la ha*]-*la-qu* LUGAL-*ú-ti-šu-nu*
25′ [*ku-un u*]*š-še-e* GIŠ.GU.ZA-*šú-nu šu-a-ti*
26′ [KUR.KUR.ME]Š *nap-har-ši-na i-na ni-iš* DINGIR.MEŠ
27′ [GAL.MEŠ *m*]*a-mit ú-šá-aṣ-bit-su-nu-ti*

21 ... sons of Esarhad]don, king of the universe, [king of the] four [quarters, in order to ...] in their midst, [to *preserve*] their sovereignty, [and to *establish*] the foundations of their throne, made all the [lands] take an oath by the [great] gods.

28′ [*i-na ni-iš aš-šur*] *u* ⸢$^{d!}$⸣*ši*-EDIN$^{!}$-*ú*$^{!}$-*a* DINGIR.ME É.ŠÁR.RA
29′ [*ma-mit ú-šá-aṣ*]-*bit-su-nu-ti-ma*
30′ [*ár-rat la nap-šur i*]*š-ku-un i-na pi-i-šú-un*
31′ [*i-na ni-iš* ^{d}*a-nu-u*]*m ù an-tum*
32′ [*i-na ni-iš* ^{d}EN.LÍL] ⸢*ù* ^{d}NIN.LÍL⸣
rest broken away

28 [By Aššur and] Šerua, gods of Ešarra, [he made] them take [an oath] and put [a curse which cannot be dispelled] in their mouths.

31 [By Anu] and Antu, [and by Illil] and Mulliltu, [he made them take an oath and put a curse which cannot be dispelled in their mouths.]

(Break)

II beginning broken away
1′ [*i-n*]*a* [*ni*]-*iš* ^{d}⸢EN$^{?}$ *u*$^{?}$⸣ [^{d}GAŠAN-*ia*$^{?}$ *x x*]
2′ *i-na ni-iš* 7 MUL.[UDU.IDIM.MEŠ AN-*e*]
3′ *ma-mit ú-šá-aṣ-bit-s*[*u-nu-ti-ma*]
4′ *ár-rat la nap-šur* GAR-*un ina p*[*i-i-šú-un*]
5′ *ù i-na mim-mu ši-pir*$^{!}$ É.GAL [*x x x*]
6′ *šá a-na mu-ú-ti ha-x*[*x x x x*]
7′ *ú-na-si-su su-*[*um-mi-iš*$^{?}$ *x x*]

ii 1 By *Bel* and [*Beltija*], by the seven planets of the sky, he made [them] take an oath [and] put a curse which cannot be dispelled in [their mouths.]

5 And *through whatever skill* of the palace [......], which [......] to/for death, they moaned like d[oves ...].

8′ *man-nu ša-a-ša šá a-na* [*a-de-e šu-a-ti*]
9′ *i-ha-ṭu-ú x*[*x x x x*]
10′ DINGIR.MEŠ GAL.MEŠ EN.MEŠ *eš-*[*re-e-ti*$^{?}$ *li-ši-mu-šu*]
11′ *ši-ma-*[*ti ar-ra-ti*]
12′ *ma-la i-na* ŠÀ-*bi a-de-*[*e šu-a-ti*]
13′ *šur-šu-du na-*[*x x x*]
14′ NÍG.GIG *šá du-ur* UD-*me li-*[*x x x*]
15′ *za-mar la* ⸢*i*$^{?}$⸣-[*x x x*]

8 Whoever sins against [that treaty, may] the great gods, lords of the sh[rines *decree an evil*] fat[e for him]; may all [the *curses*] established in [that] treaty [*bring upon him*] eternal hardship so that he does not [*die*] quickly.

16′ AN.ŠÁR *a-gu-um* ^{d}*a-num an-*⸢*tum*⸣ [*x x x x*]
17′ *a-na* ŠU.2 LUGAL-*šu*$^{?}$ *lu* GAR-*niš-šu* ⸢*ú*⸣-[*x x x*]
18′ GÍR.AN.BAR-*šú lik-šu-*⸢*ud*⸣-[*su*]
19′ ^{d}*ši*-EDIN$^{!}$-*ú*$^{!}$-*a be-lit* DINGIR.ME GAL-⸢*ti*⸣ [*x x x*]
20′ *li-kar-ru x*[*x x x*]
21′ ^{d}*a-num ù an-tum an-n*[*a-šu x x*]
22′ *la i-*⸢DU$_{8}$⸣ [*x x x*]
23′ ⸢^{d}⸣EN.LÍL *ù* ^{d}NI[N.LÍL *x x x*]
24′ *a-na le-m*[*u-ut-ti x x x*]
25′ ⸢^{d}⸣AMAR.UTU *ù* [^{d}*zar-pa-ni-tu x x*]
26′ [*t*]*e*$^{?}$-*bi* [*x x x x x x*]

16 May Aššur, (Lord) Crown, Anu and Antu *deliver him* into the king's hands, may [...], may his own sword make an end of him.

19 May Šerua, the great lady of the gods, shorten [his life].

21 May Anu and Antu pun[ish him] (and) not absolve [his crime].

23 May Illil and Mu[lliltu ... *consign* him] to misfortune.

25 May Marduk and [Zarpanitu ...]...

[^{d}*ši*-EDIN]-*u-a (*Šerua) in view of II 19′. 21, 32 See coll. 26 The feminine suffix in *nap-har-ši-na* requires restoring "lands" rather than "people" in the break.

II 5, 17, 22 See coll. 5-7 The meaning of these lines escapes us. 8 Cf. I 7. The restoration suggested by Grayson is unacceptable as the text cannot be considered a treaty document proper. 17 *lu* GAR-*nu-niš-šu*: The proposed rendering involves various orthographic and grammatical difficulties and must be regarded as tentative only.

27′ [*x x x*]*x*[*x x x x x x x*]
rest broken away
Reverse
I entirely broken away
II beginning broken away
1′ [*x x x*] ⌜*x x x*⌝ [*x x x x*]
2′ [*x x x*]*x šá a*$^{!}$-[*x x x x*]
3′ [*x x a*]-*a-ši* LUGAL *šá* EN GAL-*ú* [^{d}AMAR.UTU]
4′ [*ki-niš ú*]-*ma-ʾi-ir-an-ni-ma* [*x x x x*]
5′ *x*[*x x*] ⌜*um*⌝-*ma áš-šú ru-qiš t*[*a*$^{!}$-*x x x*]
6′ *la ta-tur-ru áš-ru-uk-*[*ku-nu x x*]
7′ ^{d}⌜EN⌝ GAL-*ú* ^{d}AMAR.UTU *a-na* ⌜*ti*?⌝-[*x x x x*]
8′ [*x x*]*x-su-ku-nu-ši-ma iš-ku-un x*[*x x x x*]
9′ [*x x x*]*x-na i-na ku-un* ŠÀ-*bi ki*$^{!}$-*n*[*i-iš x x x*]
10′ [*x x*]*x*-⌜*x*⌝-*ku-nu-šim-ma mug-ra q*[*í-bi-ti x x*]
11′ [*x x*] *dam-qa-a-ti* MUL.NIN.MAH [*x x x x*]
12′ [*x x*]*x e hi ṣa ti kiš-šu-t*[*i x x x x*]
13′ [*x x*]-*ti* DINGIR-*ti* ^{d}*be-lit*—DINGIR.M[EŠ *x x x x*]
14′ [*x x ta-n*]*a-da-at a-me-lut-t*[*i x x x x*]
15′ [*x x*]*x* ⌜BALA⌝-*ú ta-nam-din-nu* ^{md}*x*[*x x x x*]

(Break)

r.3 [... m]e, the king whom the great lord [Marduk had truly] commissioned to [...,
5 [...]... Because you (pl.) [have *gone*] far away and not returned to y[our] place [......],
7 the great lord Marduk [...ed] you (pl.) to [......] and established [......].
9 In steadfast heart [I have] tru[ly ...] to you (pl.); please accept [my prayers]!
11 Beautiful [...] the constellation of Ninmah [......]
12 [...]... world power [......]
13 [...] divinity, Belet-ili [......]
14 [...] the praises of mankind [......]
15 [...] the reign you will give [......]

r.II 1f, 9 See coll. 3f, 9f The literary topoi and other stylistic features in these lines definitely establish the present text as a royal inscription. 12 Sic; see coll.

GLOSSARY AND INDICES

Logograms and Their Readings

A → *mar'u;* A.AN → *zunnu;* A.KAL → *mīlu;* A.MEŠ → *mê;* A.ŠÀ → *eqlu;* Á.2 → *ahu;* Á.KAL → *emūqu;* Á.MUŠEN → *arû;* AD → *abu;* ÁG → *ra'āmu;* AMA → *ummu;* AMBAR → *appāru;* AN → *šamê;* AN.BAR → *parzillu;* AN.NA → *annuku;* AN.ŠÁR → *Aššūr;* ANŠE; ANŠE.NITÁ → *imāru;* ANŠE.GÌR.NUN → *parû;* ANŠE.GÌR.NUN.NA → *parû;* ANŠE.KUR.RA → *sissû;* ARAD → *urdu;* ARHUŠ → *rēmu;*

BALA → *palû;* BÁR.SIPÁ.KI → *Barsipa;* BE → *šumma;* BURU$_{14}$ → *ebūru;* BURU$_{5}$; BURU$_{5}$.MUŠEN → *erbiu;*

DAM → *aššatu;* DI → *šulmu;* DI.KUD.GAL → *diqugallu;* DINGIR → *ilu;* DINGIR.MAH → *Bēlet ilī;* DU → *alāku;* DÙ → *kalu;* DU$_{6}$ → *tillu;* DÙG.GA → *ṭābtu; ṭiābu;* DUH.LÀL → *iškuru;* DUL → *tillu;* DUMU → *mar'u;* DUMU—DUMU → *mār mar'i;* DUMU—LUGAL; DUMU—MAN → *mār šarri;* DUMU.MÍ → *mar'utu;* DUMU—SIG$_{5}$ → *mār damqi;* DUMU—ŠEŠ—AD → *mār ah abi;* DUMU.UŠ → *aplu;* ^{d}7.BI → *Sebetti;* ^{d}A.A → *Nūr;* ^{d}AG → *Nabû;* ^{d}AMAR.UTU → *Marduk;* ^{d}BA.Ú → *Bābu;* ^{d}BE → *Illil;* ^{d}DI.KUD → *Madānu;* ^{d}É.A → *Ea;* ^{d}EN → *Bēl;* ^{d}EN.LÍL → *Illil;* ^{d}GA.GA → *Kakka;* ^{d}GAG.SI.SÁ → *Šukūdu;* ^{d}GAM—KUR → *Kippat māti;* ^{d}GAŠAN → *Bēltīa;* ^{d}GIŠ.BAR → *Girra;* ^{d}IB → *Uraš;* ^{d}IGI.DU → *Pālil;* ^{d}IM → *Adad;* ^{d}INNIN → *Issār;* ^{d}IŠ.TAR → *Issār;* ^{d}LÁL → *Tašmētu;* ^{d}MAŠ → *Inurta;* ^{d}ME → *Gula;* ^{d}NIN.É.GAL → *Ninegal;* ^{d}NIN.GAL → *Nikkal;* ^{d}NIN.GÍR.SU → *Ingirsu;* ^{d}NIN.KILIM → *šikkû;* ^{d}NIN.LÍL → *Mullissu;* ^{d}NIN.URTA → *Inurta;* ^{d}NUMUN.DÙ → *Zarpānītu;* ^{d}PA → *Nabû;* ^{d}PA.TÚG → *Nusku;* ^{d}SAG.ME.GAR → *Sagmegar;* ^{d}ŠEŠ.KI → *nannaru;* ^{d}U.GUR → *Nērigal;* ^{d}UDU.IDIM.GUD.UD → *Šihṭu;* ^{d}UDU.IDIM.SAG.UŠ → *Kaiamānu;* ^{d}UTU → *šamšu; Šamaš;*

É → *bētu;* É—AD → *bēt abi;* É—EN.MEŠ → *bēt bēli;* É.GAL → *ekallu;* É.KUR → *ekurru;* É.SAG.ÍL → *Esangil;* É.ŠÁR.RA → *Ešarra;* É—UŠ → *bēt rēdūti;* È → *uṣû;* EDIN → *ṣēru;* EGIR → *urki;* EN → *bēlu;* EN.LÍL.KI → *Nippur;* EN—MÚD.MEŠ → *bēl dāmi;* EN—URU → *bēl āli;* ERIM.MEŠ → *ṣābu;* EŠ.BAR → *purussû;*

GAL → *rabû; rabiu;* GÁL → *bašû;* GAR → *šakānu;* GAŠAN → *bēltu;* GAZ → *dēktu;* GEŠTIN → *karānu;* GI → *qanû;* GI.AMBAR → *appāru;* GIDIM → *eṭimmu;* GIG → *marāṣu; murṣu;* GIM → *kî;* GÍR; GÍR.AN.BAR → *patru;* GÌR.2 → *šēpu;* GÌR.BAL → *rihṣu;* GIŠ.ABXAD.TIM → *paššūru;* GIŠ.APIN → *epinnu;* GIŠ.BAL → *pilaqqu;* GIŠ.BAN → *qassu;* GIŠ.BANŠUR → *paššūru;* GIŠ.GIGIR → *mugirru;* GIŠ.GU.ZA → *kussiu;* GIŠ.IG → *dassu;* GIŠ.MÁ → *eleppu;* GIŠ.MI → *ṣillu;* GIŠ.NÁ → *eršu;* GIŠ.PA → *haṭṭu;* GIŠ.SAR → *kiriu;* GIŠ.TUKUL → *kakku;* GÚ.GAL → *gugallu;* GÚ.ZI → *kāsu;* GUD → *alpu;* GUR → *tuāru;*

HABRUD → *hurrutu;* HUL → *lemuttu;* HÚL → *hadû;*

Ì.GIŠ; Ì.MEŠ → *šamnu;* ÍD → *nāru;* IDIM → *nagbu;* IGI; IGI.MEŠ → *pānu;* IGI.2 → *ēnu;* IM → *ṭuppu;* ITI → *urhu;* ITI.GUD.SI.SÁ → *aiāru;* IZI → *išātu;*

KA → *pû;* KÁ → *bābu;* KÁ.DINGIR.KI; KÁ.DINGIR.RA.KI → *Bābili;* KAB → *šumēlu;* KAR → *kāru;* KASKAL; KASKAL.2 → *hūlu;* KÀŠ → *šīnāti;* KÉŠ → *riksu;* KI → *kaqquru;* KI.MIN → KI.MIN; KI.TA → *šapal;* KI.TIM → *kaqquru;* KÚ → *akālu;* KU$_{6}$ → *nūnu;* KUG.GI → *hurāṣu;* KUR → *mātu;* KUR.EME.KU → *māt Šumeri;* KÚR → *nakāru; nakru;* KUŠ → *mašku;* KUŠ.E.SÍR → *maš'ennu;*

LÀL → *dišpu;* LÚ → *amēlu;* LÚ.A—KIN → *mār šipri;* LÚ.ARAD → *urdu;* LÚ.EN—GIŠ.GIGIR → *bēl mugirri;* LÚ.EN—KÚR → *bēl nakāri;* LÚ.EN.NAM → *pāhutu;* LÚ.EN—URU → *bēl āli;* LÚ.ENGAR → *ikkāru;* LÚ.ERIM → *ṣābu;* LÚ.GAL—SAG → *rab ša-rēši;* LÚ.GAR.KUR → *šaknu;* LÚ.GUB—IGI → *mazzāz pāni;* LÚ.GURUŠ → *eṭlu;* LÚ.KÚR → *nakru;* LÚ.NAM → *pāhutu;* LÚ.NUN → *rubû;* LÚ.SAG → *ša-rēši;* LÚ.ŠÁM → *ša-šīmi;* LÚ.TU—KUR → *ērib ekalli;* LÚ.ÚŠ → *pagru;* LUGAL → *šarru;*

MAH → *ṣīru;* MAN → *šaniu; šarru;* MAŠ.DÀ → *ṣabītu;* MÈ → *tāhāzu;* MI → *mūšu;* MÍ → *issu;*

MÍ.DAM → *aššatu;* MÍ.HUL → *lemuttu;* MÍ.KUR → *ekallītu;* MÍ.NIM → *hurāptu;* MÍ.PEŠ$_4$ → *arītu ;* MÍ.UDU.NIM → *hurāptu;* MIN → MIN; MU → *šumu;* MU.AN.NA → *šattu;* MÚD → *dāmu;* MÚD—GIŠ.ERIN → *dām erēni ;* MUL → *kakkubu;* MUL.GAG.SI.SÁ → *Šukūdu;* MUL.NIN.MAH → *Ninmah;* MUL.SAG.ME.GAR → *Sagmegar;* MUL.UDU.IDIM → *Bibbu;* MUL.UDU.IDIM.GUD.UD → *Šihṭu;* MUL.UDU.IDIM.SAG.UŠ → *Kaiamānu;* MUN → *ṭābtu;* MUNU$_4$ → *buqlu;* MURUB$_4$ → *qablu;* MUŠ → *ṣerru;* MUŠEN → *iṣṣūru;*

NA$_4$.KIŠIB → *kunukku;* NA$_4$.UR$_5$ → *arû;* NAG → *šatû;* NAM → *šīmtu;* NAM.ÚŠ → *mūtānu;* NÍG.GIG → *ikkibu; maruštu;* NIM → *elû;* NIN → *bēltu;* NINA; NINA.KI → *Nīnua;* NINDA → *kusāpu;* NINDU → *tinūru;* NITA → *zikaru;* NU → *la;* NUM → *zumbu;* NUMUN → *zarʾu;* NUN → *rubû;* NUN.ME → *apkallu;*

PAB → *ahu; gimru;* PI.2 → *uznu;* PÚ → *būrtu;*

SAG → *rēštû;* SAG.DU → *kaqqudu;* SAG.KAL → *ašarēdu;* SAHAR → *epru;* SAHAR.ŠUB; SAHAR.ŠUB.BA → *saharšuppu;* SI → *qarnu;* SIG$_4$ → *libittu;* SIG$_5$ → *damāqu; dunqu;* SILA → *sūqu;* SU → *zumru;* SU.KÚ → *bubūtu;* SUM → *tadānu;*

ŠÀ → *libbu;* ŠÀ.ŠÀ → *liblibbu;* ŠAH → *huzīru;* ŠE.PAD → *uṭṭutu;* ŠEŠ → *ahu;* ŠEŠ.AD → *ah abi;* ŠÉŠ → *piššatu;* ŠU.2 → *qātu;* ŠU.SI → *ubānu;* ŠÚ → *kiššatu;* ŠUKU → *kurummatu;*

TA → *issi;* TI → *laqû;* TI.LA → *balāṭu;* TIM.KI → *kaqquru;* TIN.TIR.KI → *Bābili;* TU$_{15}$ → *šāru;* TÚG → *lubultu;* TUK → *rašû;* TUR → *ṣahāru;* TUR.DIŠ → *šerru;*

U$_8$ → *agurrutu;* UD → *ūmu;* UD.DA → *ṣētu;* UD.KA.BAR → *siparru;* UD.NÁ.ÀM → *ūm bubbuli;* UDU → *immeru;* UDU.NIM → *hurāpu;* UDU.SISKUR → *niqiu;* UGU → *muhhu;* UKKIN → *puhru;* UN → *nīši;* UR.KU → *kalbu;* UR.MAH → *nēšu;* UR.SAG → *qarrādu;* ÚR → *sūnu;* URI.KI → *māt Akkadî;* URU → *ālu;* URU.BÀD—LUGAL → *Dūr-Šarrukku;* URU.KASKAL → *Harrānu;* URU.NINA; URU.NINA.KI → *Nīnua;* URU.ŠÀ—URU → *Libbi-āli;* URU.ŠE → *kapru;* UZU → *šīru;* UZU.ZAG → *imittu;*

ZAG → *imittu;* ZÉ → *martu;* ZI → *napištu; napšutu;* ZU.AB → *apsû*

Glossary

abālu "to bring, (Gtn) to serve": *ab-lu* 9: 31, *ta-tan-nab-bal-a-šú-u-ni* 6: 98F, *ta-ta[n-nab-bal-a-šú-u-ni* 6: 98E, *ta-ta-nab-bal-a-šá-nu-u-ni* 6: 98frg, *ta-ta-nab-bal-a-šú-u-ni* 6: 236N, *ta-ta-nab-bal-a-[šú-u-ni]* 6: 236X, *ta-ta-nab-bal-šú-u-ni* 6: 98A, *ta-ta-na-bal-a-šú-nu-u-ni* 6: 98I, *ta-ta-na-bal-a-šú-u-ni* 6: 236J, *ta-ta-na-b[al-a-šú-u-ni* 6: 98frg, *ta-(ta)-nab-bal-šú-u-ni* 6: 236A, *t[a-ta-n]a-bal-[a-šú-u-ni]* 6: 236f,

abātu "to destroy, (N) to flee": *in-nab-tu-u-ni* 6: 217J, frg, *in-na[b-tu-u-ni* 6: 217u, *in-n]a-bi-tu-ni* 1: 14, *ta-bat-a-ni* 6: 413A, *ta-b[a-x* 6: 413B, *ta-[bat-a-ni]* 6: 413C,

abbūtu "intercession": *ab-bu-tu]-ku-un* 6: 418frg, *ab-bu-tú-k[u-un]* 6: 418C, *ab-bu-tu-ku-un* 6: 418A, *a-bu-us-[su]* 1 r. 6, *[ab-bu-su* 4 r. 25,

abu "father": *a-b]i* 1 r. 3, AD 2 v 5, 4 r. 16, 6: 25A, frg, 405A, 518V, iiiA, B, F, H, Y, frg, 9 r. 5, AD-*ka* 6: 203J, 351F, AD-*ku-nu* 6: 334B, 358frg, AD-*šu* 6: 317J, AD-*šú* 6: 90A, I, frg, d, 317A, C, 319J, 320A, 324B, C, N, c, 326B, C, N, 331B, 332B, AD-*šú-nu* 6: 273A, B, frg, 370frg, AD-*š[ú-nu* 6370R, AD-*u-ka* 6: 351B, AD-*[x* 6: 351A, AD]-*ka* 6: 203frg, A[D-*ku-nu* 6: 334frg, 358B, A[D.MEŠ-*ku-nu*] 10: 14, A[D-*šú* 6: 326c, 332frg,

abutu "word, matter": *a]-bu-tú* 6: 107y, *a]-bu-t[u* 6: 107frg, *a-bat-su* 4 r. 4, 6: 325B, C, N, c, *a-bu-tu* 6: 57frg, r, 108frg, 186F, I, 347R, *a-bu-tú* 3: 2, 6: 57A, 67A, S, W, 73A, H, 107E, frg, 108frg, y, 183frg, 186frg, 295C, 347F, frg, 363R, 8: 12, 13 iii 10, *a-bu-t[u* 6: 183I, *a-bu-t]u* 6: 347A, *a-bu-t]ú* 6: 73x, 295H, 347w, *a-bu-(tú)* 6: 295B, *a-b]u-tu* 6: 108frg, *[a]-bu-tú* 6: 295A, *[a-bu]-tu* 6: 363z, *[a-bu-tú* 8 r. 3,

abūbu "deluge": *a-bu-bu* 6: 488D, frg, *a-bu-bi]* 1 r. 15,

adê "treaty": *a]-de-e* 6: 153frg, 390H, *a-de]-e* 6: 291H, 555frg, 11 r. 6, *a-de-e* 1 e. 15, 2 i 13, 15, 24, r. iv 17, 29, v 8, 14, 16, 24, 6: 1A, F, G, H, T, frg, 10A, F, G, H, T, 12A, 41A, E, frg, 64A, W, 96A, F, I, frg, 104E, frg, 132A, E, frg, 153A, E, 175A, B, I, S, 283A, B, Y, frg, 289A, 291A, B, C, 351R, w, 358R, 382D, s, 387A, D, s, 390A, D, 398D, 400D, 513D, V, 517A, 573Q, 666Q, 8: 9, 9 r. 3, 12: 1, 14 i 7, *a-de-e]* 2 i 31, *a-de-e-ku-nu* 6: 292A, B, *a-de-[e* 6: 289C, 351B, F, 14 ii 12, *a-de-[e]* 6: 616frg, *a-d[e]-e* 5: 420E, 6: 526B, *a-d[e-e* 6: 573frg, 666frg, *a-d[e-e]* 6: 358frg, *a-d]e-e* 6: 612K, *a-[de-e* 6: 175M, *[a]-de-e* 6: 1a, 666frg, *[a-de]-e* 5 i 1, 6: 175frg, 11: 1, *[a-de-e* 14 ii 8, *[a-de-e-k]u-nu* 6: 292H, *[a-d]e-e* 8: 1,

adi "until, plus": *a-di* 2 i 9, 18, r. iv 2, 6: 6A, F, G, H, T, a, 207C, O, frg, 612A, G, K, M, 9: 17, 33, *a-d[i* 5 iii 1, 6: 207J, *a-d]i* 6: 382D, 612frg, *a-[d]i* 6: 382s, *[a-di* 9: 3,

aganutillû "dropsy": *a-ga-nu-til-la-a* 6: 522I, *a-ga-nu-ti-l[a-a* 6: 522A, *a-ga-nu-ti-l]a-a* 6: 522frg, *a-g[a-nu-ti-la-a* 6: 522B,

agāru "to hire": *in-na-ga-ru-u-ni* 5 iii 27,

aggiš "grimly": *ag-giš* 6: 475D,

agurrutu "ewe": U_8 6: 547A, frg,

agû A "crown": *a-gu-um* 14 ii 16,

agû B "tide": *a-gu-u* 5 iv 13,

ah abi "uncle": ŠEŠ.MEŠ—AD.MEŠ-*šú* 6: 76H, x, 114frg, 214J, e, 319N, ŠEŠ.MEŠ—AD-*šú* 6: 76A, ŠEŠ—AD.MEŠ-*šú* 6: 114E, 214C, 319A, B, C, 337frg, ŠEŠ—AD.M[EŠ-*šú* 6: 337F, ŠEŠ]—AD.MEŠ-[*šú* 6: 337frg, ŠE]Š—AD.MEŠ-*šú* 6: 214frg, Š[EŠ—A]D.MEŠ-*šú* 6: 214frg, [Š]EŠ—AD.MEŠ-*šú* 6: 114frg,

ahāiš "each other": *a-ha-iš* 2 v 23, *a-ha-meš* 6: 156E, H, *a-h]a-meš* 6: 212frg, *a-he]-iš* 6: 212e, 640frg, *a-he]-i[š* 6: 648frg, *a-he-iš* 6: 156A, P, 212C, J, frg, 327B, C, N, frg, 557A, D, 559A, 640frg, 648U, frg, *a-[he-iš* 6: 559D, frg, *a-na-he-iš* 6: 640A,

ahiu "strange": *a-hu-u* 5: 419E, 6: 430A, B, *a-[hu-u* 6: 430frg,

ahītu "outlying area": *a-hi-ta-te-šú-nu-u-ni* 5 iii 26,

ahāmiš see *ahāiš*,

ahu A "brother": PAB 8: 3, PAB.MEŠ-*ku-nu* 8 r. 22, PAB.MEŠ-*šú* 8: 5, r. 21, ŠEŠ 6: 86A, G, d, ŠEŠ-*ku-nu* 6: 335frg, ŠEŠ.ME 10: 14, ŠEŠ.ME-*ku-nu* 6: 624L, ŠEŠ.ME-*šú* 6: 55A, ŠEŠ.MEŠ 6: 171frg, 319J, 345w, 624K, ŠEŠ.MEŠ-*ku-nu* 6: 115E, 549A, 577D, v, 583D, b, v, 585Q, Z, frg, 589Q, b, 591Q, j, 597h, 606H, T, frg, 636F, 10: 14, ŠEŠ.MEŠ-*ku-n[u]* 6: 591h, ŠEŠ.MEŠ-*ku-(nu)* 6: 618K, ŠEŠ.MEŠ-*ku-[nu]* 6: 115frg, ŠEŠ.MEŠ-*k]u-nu* 6: 577Q, 589j, ŠEŠ.MEŠ-*šu* 6: 270i, 633L, ŠEŠ.MEŠ-*šú* 6: 4a, 69A, W, 76A, H, x, 94A, F, I, 103E, F, frg, 113E, 171A, P, S, 214J, u, 270A, frg, 285B, J, 318B, C, J, 330B, frg, 337F, frg, 341F, 343F, frg, p, 345F, 346F, R, w, 354R, 363R, 496D, frg, 504D, V, ŠEŠ.MEŠ-*š[ú* 6: 354A, ŠEŠ.MEŠ-[*ku*]-*nu* 6: 597T, ŠEŠ.MEŠ-[*ku-nu* 6: 618frg, ŠEŠ.MEŠ-[*ku-nu*] 6: 538frg, ŠEŠ.MEŠ-[*šú* 6: 103frg, 285frg, ŠEŠ.MEŠ]-*ku-nu* 6: 549frg, 606h, ŠEŠ.MEŠ]-*šú* 6: 345frg, 346frg, 504q, ŠEŠ.ME[Š-*šú* 6: 285A, ŠEŠ.M[EŠ-*šú* 6: 94frg, ŠEŠ-*šú-nu* 6364R, frg, z, ŠEŠ.[MEŠ-*ku-nu* 6: 543F, 577b, ŠEŠ.[MEŠ-*ku-nu*] 6: 585v, ŠEŠ.[MEŠ-*šú* 6: 341frg, 345B, 496frg, ŠEŠ-[*x* 6: 214u, ŠEŠ].MEŠ-*šú* 6: 337B, 341B, 343frg, 345p, 504A, ŠE[Š.MEŠ-*šú* 6: 346B, 363frg, z, ŠE[Š-*x* 6: 363frg, ŠE]Š-*ku-nu* 6: 335frg, ŠE]Š.MEŠ-*šu* 6: 171M, ŠE]Š.MEŠ-*šú* 6: 214e, ŠE]Š.MEŠ-*šú-nu* 6: 364frg, Š[EŠ 6: 114frg, Š[EŠ-*ku-nu* 6: 335B, Š[EŠ.MEŠ-*šú* 6: 404A, Š[EŠ.ME]Š-*š[ú* 6: 363frg, Š[EŠ].MEŠ-*šú* 6: 318N, Š]EŠ 6: 86I, Š]EŠ.MEŠ-*ku-nu* 6: 618A, Š]EŠ.MEŠ-*šú* 6: 55n, Š]EŠ-*šú-nu* 6368R, [ŠEŠ.ME]Š-*šú* 6: 496q, [ŠEŠ].MEŠ-*šú* 6: 515A, [ŠE]Š.MEŠ-*ku-nu* 6: 597j, [Š]EŠ.MEŠ-

šú 6: 94frg, 171I,

ahu B "arm": Á.2]-*ku-nu* 6: 271frg, Á.2-*ku-nu* 6: 271A, B, F, Á.2.MEŠ-*šú-nu* 6: 627F, K, L, frg, Á.2.MEŠ-*šú-un*] 14 i 5, [Á.2]-*ku-nu* 6: 271frg,

ahû see *ahiu,*

ahūla "woe": *a-hu-la* 2 i 18, r. v 14,

ai "may not": *a*]-*a* 6: 416A, 418A, 452frg, *a-a* 1 r. 9, 2 iv 6, 7, 19, 21, 4 r. 17, 25, 6: 418C, 420c, 423C, c, 430B, 432B, C, I, frg, 444A, 452A, frg, 481H, 484D, 651U, frg, *a-(a)* 6: 418B, *a-*[*a* 6: 452g, 460frg, *a-*[*a*] 6: 481D, [*a-a* 1 r. 7,

aiābu "enemy": *a-a-bi* 11 r. 3,

aiāru (Iyyar, name of the 2nd month): ITI.GUD.SI.SÁ 6: 664Q, ITI.GUD.[SI.SÁ 6: 664frg, [ITI.GU]D.SI.SÁ 6: 664frg,

aiāši "me": *a*]-*a-ši* 14 ii 3, *a-a-ši* 13 iii 16,

aiulu "stag": *a-a*]-*lu* 6: 576Q, *a-a-lu* 6: 576D, b, v,

akālu "to eat": *ak-la* 6: 324B, C, N, c, 342F, R, p, 449g, l, *a*[*k-la* 6: 449A, *ek-la* 6: 485D, KÚ 2 vi 1, KÚ-*šú-nu* 2 iv 14, *le*]-*ku-lu-šú* 6: 636K, *le-e-kul* 6: 450g, *le-e-ku-lu* 6: 451g, *le-kul* 6: 448A, g, 450A, 451A, *le-kul-a-šú* 6: 635L, frg, 636frg, *le-kul-š*[*ú*] 6: 636A, *le-ku*]-*lu* 6: 451frg, *le-ku-la-šú* 6: 635F, frg, 636F, frg, *le-ku-lu* 6: 451l, *le-ku-lu-ma* 2 iv 10, *le-k*[*u-la-šú*] 6: 636frg, *le-*[*k*]*ul-a-šu* 6: 636L, *li-šá-kil* 6: 427B, *lu-šá-kil* 6: 427N, *lu-šá-kil-ku-n*[*u*] 6: 550A, *lu-šá-kil-u-ku-nu* 6: 550frg, *lu-šá-ki-li-ku-n*[*u*] 6: 550frg, *lu-šá-ki-lu* 6: 600A, *lu-šá-*[*ki-lu*] 6: 600j, *l*]*e-ku-lu-šú* 6: 635K, *ta-kal-a-ni* 6: 270A, F, *ta-kal-a-n*[*i*] 6: 270frg, *ta-kul* 6: 572D, frg, *ta-kul-u*]-*ni* 6: 570frg, *ta-kul-u-ni* 6: 570D, Q, frg, *ta-k*]*al-a-ni* 6: 270frg, *ta-*[*kal-a-ni*] 6: 270i, *ta-*[*kul*] 6: 572Z, *tu*]-*šá-kal-a-šú-u-ni* 6: 262I, *tu-šá-kal-a-šú*]-*u-ni* 6: 262p, *tu-šá-kal-a-šú-u*]-*ni* 6: 262A, *tu-šá-kal-a-šú-u-ni* 6: 262B, *tu-šá-kal-a-šu-u-ni* 6: 262i, *t*[*a-kul*] 6: 572frg, *t*]*a-kal-ni* 6: 270frg, [*ak-l*]*a* 6: 342B, [*a*]*k-la* 6: 342frg, [*ek-k*]*al-u-ni* 6: 332B, [*li-šá-kil*] 6: 520A, [*lu-š*]*á-kil* 6: 427A,

aki "as": *a-ki-i* 9: 22,

akītu "festival chapel": É.*á-ki-it* 3: 11, r. 8, É.*á-ki-it*] 3 r. 5,

alala "harvest song": *a-la-la* 2 iv 19,

alāku "to go, come": *a*]*l-lak* 13 ii 12, *a-lik* 2 vi 19, 13 iii 5, *a-l*]*ik* 4 r. 3, *a-l*]*i-*[*ku* 1 r. 16, DU-*ak* 6: 532A, F, DU-*ku* 1 e. 16, DU-*k*[*u-ni*] 2 iv 1, 3, *i-lak* 6: 532M, *il-lak* 6: 206C, *il-lak-u-ni* 6: 209e, u, 635F, L, 636A, F, L, *il-lak-u-n*[*i* 6: 635A, *il-lak-*[*u-ni*] 6: 190frg, *il-la*]*k-u-ni* 6: 635frg, *il-la-ka* 13 iii 7, *il-la-ku-u-ni-ni* 5 iii 5, *il-li-ka*] 9: 8, *il-l*[*ak* 6: 532B, *il-l*[*ak-u-ni*] 6: 635frg, *il-*[*lak* 6: 206frg, *it-la-ka* 6: 424c, *it-tal-ka* 6: 203J, frg, *it-ta*]-*lak* 6: 238N, *it-ta-lak* 6: 46A, E, 84A, G, 238A, J, X, 361R, *it-ta-l*[*ak* 6: 361frg, *it-ta-*[*lak* 6: 84d, *it-*[*tal-ka* 9: 30, *i*[*l-lak-u-ni* 6: 209O, *i*]*l-lak* 6: 532G, *i*]*l-lak-ú-ni* 6: 190Y, *i*]*t-ta-lak* 6: 84I, *i*]-*tal-la-ka* 6: 424A, *i-lak-u-ni* 6: 209J, *i-tal-la-k*[*a*] 6: 424C, *lil-li-ka* 6: 204J, *lil-l*]*i-k*[*a*] 6: 204frg, *lu-šá-li-ku* 6: 567D, frg, *lu-šá-l*[*i-ku*] 6: 567Q, *ni-tal-la-ka*] 9 r. 10, *šu-lu-ku* 14 i 13, *tal-lak-a-ni* 6: 634F, K, frg, *tal-lak-a-ni-ni* 6: 151P, 158A, P, 179A, 349F, w, *tal-lak-a-n*[*i*] 6: 634frg, *tal-lak-a-*[*ni-ni*] 6: 179I, *tal-lak-ni-ni* 6179S, *tal-la-ka* 6: 211B, J, frg, e, *tal-la-ka-nin-ni* 8 r. 5, 15, *tal-la-k*[*a*] 6: 211frg, *tal-l*[*a-ka*] 6: 211u, *tal-l*]*ak-a-ni* 6: 634G, *tal-*[*lak-a-ni-ni* 6: 158S, *ta*]*l-lak-a-ni-ni* 6: 151frg, *ta*]*l-la-ka-nin-ni* 8 r. 10, *ta*]-*lak-a-ni* 6: 151A, *ta-lak*]-*a-ni-ni* 6: 349frg, *ta-lak-an-*[*ni* 5 iii 11, *ta-lak-a-ni-ni* 3: 4, 6: 81A, H, I, x, 120E, frg, 151E, 158E, 179B, M, *ta-lak-a-ni-*[*ni* 6: 120A, 349B, *ta-lak-a-ni-*[*ni*] 6: 81G, 179frg, *ta-lak-ni* 2 iii 17, *ta-la*]*k-a-ni-ni* 6: 120O, *t*]*al-la-ka* 6: 211C, *t*]*a-lak-a-ni-ni* 6: 349R, [*il-la-ku* 1 e. 16, [*il*]-*lak-u-ni* 6: 209frg, [*i*]*t-tal-ka* 9: 37, [*tal-la*]*k-a-ni* 6: 634L, [*tal-la*]-*ka* 6: 211frg, [*ta*]-*lak-a-ni-*[*ni*] 6: 151H,

ali "where?": *a-le-e*ʾ 6: 332B,

alluttu "crab": *al-lut-te* 6: 619frg, *al-lu*]-*ti* 6: 619L, *al-lu-ti* 6: 619A, G, *al-*[*lu-ti* 6: 619m, [*al-lu-t*]*i* 6: 619K,

alpu "ox": GUD 2 iv 7, GUD.MEŠ 6: 277A, B, Y, frg,

amatu "word, matter": *a-mat* 1: 8, 6: 117E, frg, 417A, 501D, V, q, 9: 13, 14 i 6, *a-mat*]-*su* 4 r. 25, *a-mat-su* 1 e. 16, *a-*[*mat* 6: 417C,

amatu see also *abutu,*

amāru "to see": *am-mar* 13 iii 10, *e-mar-u-ni* 6: 210J, frg, u, *e-mar-u-ni*] 2 i 17, [*em-mar*] 2 i 20, [*e-mar*]-*u-ni* 6: 210e,

amēlu "man": LÚ 2 vi 5, 6: 450A, g, l, L[Ú 6: 450A,

amēlūtu "mankind": *a-me-lut-t*[*i* 14 ii 14, *a-me-lu-te* 6: 296H, 604T, frg, h, *a-me-lu-ti* 13 iii 20, *a-m*]*e-lu-ti* 6: 604K, LÚ-*ti* 6: 296A, C, 604A, LÚ-*u-te* 6: 604H, [L]Ú-*ti* 6: 604j,

ammar see *mar,*

ammiu "that": *am-mì-e* 13 iii 5,

ana "to": *ana* 2 iv 15, v 5, 6, 7, 11, 6: 235frg, 471D, 567D, *a*]-*na* 4 r. 3, 5 ii 10, 6: 105frg, 294B, 387A, 640frg, *a-na* 1: 7, 2 i 6, 10, 11, 12, 13, 17, 20, iii 23, r. iv 1, 3, 4, 13, 14, 15, vi 3, 4, 5, 3: 3, 4, 4 r. 2, 3, 7, 5 iii 18, 19, 25, iv 14, 15, 6: 10F, H, T, a, 44A, E, 46frg, 62A, W, 66A, 72A, W, 81A, G, H, a, x, 84A, G, H, d, 120frg, 127E, frg, 128A, E, frg, 129A, E, frg, 130A, E, frg, 134frg, 150A, E, H, P, 156A, E, H, P, 165A, I, P, S, 170A, S, frg, 190frg, 212frg, 213J, O, frg, u, 238X, 239A, X, 243A, X, 260A, I, i, 266A, F, frg, i, 278B, Y, 288A, B, J, frg, 289A, 294A, C, H, 295H, 298A, B, C, H, 300B, H, 304B, frg, 307A, frg, 327B, C, frg, c, 349F, R, frg, w, 361frg, 383D, s, 387s, 393D, H, 396D, 410C, 434I, 444g, l, 486D, 506D, V, 524G, 550A, 566D, 575D, Q, b, 577D, b, v, 580b, 583D, Q, Z, frg, v, 606A, frg, 618G, frg, m, 619A, G, K, L, frg, 626G, K, L, frg, 632A, 634F, K, L, frg, 635A, F, L, frg, 636A, F, 640frg, 645A, U, frg, 7: 2, 3, 9: 9, 13, 14, 16, 24, 27, 30, 31, 34, 35, 37, 38, r. 3, 10: 5, 13, 13 iii 5, 9, 14 i 4, 9, ii 6, 8, 17, 24, r. ii 7, *a-n*[*a* 1 r. 15, 2 i 12, 6: 62frg, 260B, 295B, 304A, 444A, 524A, 564D, 634A, 9: 36, *a-n*[*a*] 6: 199frg, *a-n*]*a* 6: 46E, 120frg, o, 199Y, 300C, *a-(na)* 6: 266B, 278A, *a-*[*na* 6: 278frg, 524B, 575v, 640frg, *a-*[*na*] 6: 304C, 581b, *a-*[*n*]*a* 6: 361R, (*a-na)* 6: 636L, [*a*]-*na* 6: 361z, [*a-na* 1 r. 5, 6: 523G, 14 i 13, [*a-na*] 13 iii 16, 14 i 10, [*a-n*]*a* 6: 46A, 239J, 278frg, 327N, 618frg,

anāku "I": *a-na-ku* 4 r. 10, 13 ii 11, r. iii 18, *a-na-ku-u-ni* 4 r. 8, *a-na-k*]*u* 4 r. 4,

anīnu "we": *a*]-*ni-nu* 6: 494V, *a-ni-ni* 9: 15, r. 3, *a-ni-nu* 6: 494D, 507D, V, *a-*[*ni*]-*nu* 6: 507A,

anniu "this": *an*]-*ni-e* 6: 382s, *an*]-*ni-tú* 6: 623frg, *an*]-*nu-ti* 6: 494frg, *an-ni*]-*tu* 6: 623frg, *an-ni-e* 6: 473D, 616frg, 8 r. 2, 11 r. 5, *an-ni-i* 6: 397D, 400D, 573Q, 618G, 9: 3, 17, 33, *an-ni-tu* 6: 296H, 347A, R, 385D, 612K, *an-ni-tú* 2 i 29, 6: 296B, 347F, w, 380A, 561A, 612A, 623A, *an-ni-t*[*u* 6: 623L, *an-ni-*

u 2 i 16, 21, 25, 6: 603H, frg, *an-ni-u*] 2 i 32, *an-ni-ú* 2 i 10, *an-ni-x*[*x* 6: 397H, *an-ni-*[*x*] 6: 296C, *an-nu-te* 5 iii 4, 18, 6: 291A, 494D, 513D, V, 637frg, 8: 10, 12: 2, *an-nu-ti* 2 i 32, r. iv 29, v 8, 6: 283B, J, 291H, 555frg, 612K, *an-nu-ti*] 1 e. 15, *an-nu-t*[*i* 2 i 24, *an-nu-t*]*i* 2 v 16, *an-nu-u-ti* 6: 291B, *an-nu-*[*x*] 6: 291C, *an-n*[*i-e* 6: 382D, *an-n*]*u-te* 5 iii 4, *an-n*[*u-x* 6: 283frg, *an-*[*ni-e* 6: 526B, *an-*[*ni-tu* 6: 380D, frg, s, 561D, *an-*[*ni-tú*] 6: 347frg, *an-*[*nu-ti* 2 i 15, 6: 283A, *a*[*n-ni*]*-tu* 6: 623K, *a*[*n-ni-ti*] 6: 385A, *a*[*n-ni-tu* 6: 623m, *a*[*n-ni-tú* 6: 612m, *a*[*n-nu-ti* 9 r. 3, *a*[*n-nu-t*]*i* 6: 283Y, *a*]*n-nu-te* 2 iii 18, *a*]*n-nu-ti* 2 iii 4, *ha*]*-an-nu-um-ma* 6: 60W, *ha-an-ni*]*-i* 6: 561A, 580Q, *ha-an-ni-e* 6: 531A, B, 548A, 580b, 604A, 610H, 613A, G, K, 623K, 629K, L, 638frg, *ha-an-ni-i* 6: 580v, 604H, 629F, *ha-an-nu-ma* 6: 60A, *ha-an-nu-um-ma* 6: 60n, r, *ha-an-*[*ni-i* 6: 580frg, *ha-a*]*n-nu-um-ma* 6: 60frg, *ha-ni-e* 6: 638A, *ha-ni-i* 6: 604L, *ha-ni-*[*i* 6: 580frg, *h*]*a-an-ni-e* 6: 610A, 629frg, *h*]*a-an-ni-i* 6: 580Z, [*an-ni*]*-tu* 6: 623G, [*an-ni*]*-tú* 6: 547A, [*ha-an*]*-ni-e* 6: 629G,

annu "crime": *an-n*[*a-šu* 14 ii 21,

annuku "lead": AN.NA 6: 534F, AN.N]A 6: 534A,

annurig "now": *an-nu-rig* 13 iii 6,

apkallu "sage": NUN.ME 1 r. 7,

aplu "heir": DUMU.UŠ 1 r. 1, 6: 433I, 9 r. 17, DUMU.U]Š 6: 433B,

appāru "reed": *a-pa-*[*ri* 6: 630frg, AMBA[R 6: 630L, GI.AMBAR 6: 630F,

apsû "Abyss": ZU.AB 6: 521A, I, 9 r. 13,

arāku "to be long": *a-rak* 6: 415A,

arāmu "to cover": *li-ri-im-šú-nu* 11 r. 8,

arāru "to curse": *i-ra-ru-ma* 14 i 5, *li-ru-ru-ku-nu* 5 iv 9, 6: 475D, *li-*[*ru-ru-ku-nu*] 3 r. 6, [*li-ru-ru-ku-nu* 3: 12,

ardatu "young woman": *ar-da-te-ku-nu* 6: 481D,

ardu see *urdu,*

arhu "month": ITI.MEŠ 1 r. 12,

arītu "pregnant": MÍ.*a-ri-ti* 6: 249A, MÍ.*a-r*[*i-ti*] 6: 249frg, MÍ.PEŠ$_4$ 6: 249I, frg,

arki see *urki,*

arû "millstone": NA$_4$.UR$_5$ 6: 443g, NA$_4$.[UR$_5$ 6: 443l,

arratu "curse": *ar*]*-rat* 3: 11, *ár-rat* 14 ii 4, *ár-ra-tu* 6: 475D, *ar-rat* 3 r. 6, 5 iv 9, 11 r. 7, *ar-ra-ti*] 14 ii 11, [*ár-rat* 14 i 30,

arrāru "curser": *a-ra-ri* 6: 626frg, *a-ra-ru* 6: 626K, L, *a-ra-r*]*i* 6: 626G, *a-r*]*a-ru* 6: 626frg,

arû "eagle": Á.MUŠEN 6: 426A, B, frg, 520A, I,

aṣû see *uṣû,*

aṣūdu (a bowl): *a-ṣu-da-ti-ku-nu* 6: 447g,

ašarēdu "leader, vanguard": *a-šá-rid* 6: 425B, C, *a-šá-ri*]*d* 6: 425frg, *a-šá-ri-x*[*x* 6: 425frg, *a-*[*šá-ri-du* 6: 519I, SAG.KAL 6: 519frg, [*a*]*-šá-*[*ri-du* 6: 519A,

ašābu "to sit, live": *li-še-šib-ku-nu* 6: 454frg, *li-še-ši-ib-ku-nu* 5: 419E, *li-š*]*e-šib-ku-nu* 6: 454frg, *l*]*i-še-ši-ib-šú* 4 r. 21, see also *ušābu,*

ašru "site": *a-šar* 1 r. 6, *áš-ru-uk-*[*ku-nu* 14 ii 6,

aššatu "wife": *áš-šá-tu-šú* 2 v 12, DAM 6: 250A, B, I, MÍ.DAM 6: 250frg,

aššu "because": *áš-šú* 14 ii 5,

atta "you": *at-ta* 4 r. 12, 13, 13 iii 4, *a*]*t-ta* 2 iii 26, *a*]*t-t*[*a* 4 r. 14,

attunu "you": *at*]*-tu-nu* 6: 318N, 377s, 383D, s, 10 r. 1, *at-tu*]*-nu* 6: 200frg, *at-tú-nu* 6: 123E, 167P, 180frg, 205frg, 212frg, 229f, 242X, 513V, 558frg, *at-tu-nu* 6: 55A, frg, r, 62A, W, frg, 73A, 135A, 167A, I, S, 176A, B, I, S, 178G, I, 205C, 212J, O, 214J, O, u, 229X, frg, 242A, 249A, I, frg, 259A, B, I, i, 266F, i, 269A, B, F, i, 318A, C, J, 344F, R, 355B, 360R, frg, 377frg, 385s, 389D, 410C, 535F, M, frg, 555frg, 558D, 580Q, b, 606T, 612K, 632F, frg, 638A, frg, 8 r. 2, 12, 18, 10: 12, 12: 1, *at-tu-n*[*u* 6: 62frg, 123frg, 178frg, 229J, *at-tu-n*]*u* 6: 242C, *at-tu-*[*nu* 6: 123A, *at-t*[*ú-nu* 6: 135t, *at-t*[*u-nu* 6: 135E, 344B, 7 r. 4, *at-t*[*u-nu*] 6: 266A, 647U, *at-t*[*u-n*]*u* 6: 73H, 212u, 266B, *at-t*]*u-nu* 6: 385A, D, 589b, 632A, *at-t*]*u-n*[*u*] 6: 355A, *at-*[*tu-nu* 6: 249B, *at-*[*tu-nu*] 6: 647frg, *a*[*t-tu-nu* 6: 180I, 269frg, 410A, 589D, *a*[*t-tu-nu*] 6: 200J, *a*]*t-tú-nu* 6: 123o, [*at*]*-tu-nu* 6: 647frg, [*at-tu*]*-nu* 8 r. 8, [*at-t*]*u-nu* 6: 266frg, 344frg, 535A, K, [*a*]*t-tu-nu* 6: 135frg, 167E, 344p, 558A,

azugallatu "chief woman physician": *a-zu-gal-la-tú* 6: 461frg, *a-zu-gal-la-t*[*ú* 5 iv 3, *a-*[*zu-gal-la*]*-tú* 6: 461frg,

ākilu A "man-eating": *a-ki-li* 5 iv 7, 6: 468D,

ākilu B (a field pest): *a-ki-lu* 6: 599A, j,

ālu "city, town": URU 2 vi 5, 6: 49A, E, frg, n, 99A, F, frg, 166A, E, P, S, URU-*ku-*[*nu* 6: 545A, URU.MEŠ 5 iii 4, 20, 21, 22, 24, URU.MEŠ-*ka* 2 v 6, URU.MEŠ-*ku-nu* 6: 600A, URU.MEŠ-*šú* 5 iii 25, URU-*šú* 1 r. 15, 4 r. 23, URU-*šú-n*[*u* 2 v 10, UR[U.MEŠ-*ku-nu* 6: 600j, UR]U 6: 166M, [URU 2 vi 3,

ba'āšu "to stink": *bi*]*-ʾi-šu-u-n*[*i*] 6: 603K, *bi-ʾi-šú-u-ni* 6: 603A, *bi-ʾi-šu-ú-ni* 6: 603T, j, *bi-ʾi-šu-u-ni* 6: 603H, L, frg, *lib-ʾi-iš* 6: 605H, *lib-ʾi-ši* 6: 605h, *lib-iš* 6: 605L, *li-ib*]*-ʾi-ši* 6: 605K, *li-ib-ʾi-iš* 6: 605T, *li-ib-*(*ʾi*)*-ši* 6: 605A, [*bi-ʾ*]*i-šu-u-ni* 6: 603h, [*l*]*u-ba-i-šu* 6: 605frg,

ba''û "to seek": *lu-ba-ʾi-ú* 6: 512D, *lu-ba-ʾi-*[*u*] 6: 512V, *lu-ba-ʾ*]*i-ú* 6: 512frg, *lu-*[*ba-ʾi-u*] 6: 512frg, *nu-ub-te-ʾu-ú* 9: 35, *tú-*[*b*]*a-ʾu-u-ni* 2 v 4, *tu-ba-a-ni* 6: 232J, *tu-ba-ʾa-a-ni* 6: 197frg, 232A, X, frg, *tu-ba-*[*ʾa-a-ni*] 6: 197J, *tu-b*[*a-ʾa-a-ni*] 6: 197frg, *tu-b*]*a-ʾa-a-ni* 6: 197F, *t*[*u-b*]*a-a-ni* 6: 232N, *t*]*ú-ba-ʾa-a-ni* 6: 232f, *t*]*u-ba-a-ni* 6: 197Y, [*tu-b*]*a-ʾu-ú-*[*n*]*i* 2 iii 27,

balāt "without": *ba-lat* 6: 334B, *ba-la-at* 5 iii 12, 13, *b*]*a-lat* 6: 334frg,

balāṭu "to live; life": *bal-lu-ṭí* 6: 193Y, *bal-ṭa-a-ni* 9: 3, 33, *bal-ṭa-a-ni-ni* 6: 508D, V, *bal-ṭu-te-ku-nu* 6: 571D, Q, 598T, h, *bal-ṭu-te-ku-nu*] 6: 598L, *bal-ṭu-ti-ku-nu* 6: 598j, *bal-ṭ*]*u-ti-ku-nu* 6: 571frg, *ba*[*l-ṭa-a-ni* 9: 17, *ba-laṭ-ka-ni* 2 v 2, *ba-*[*la-ṭi*]*n-ni* 2 v 1, TI 2 v 11, 6: 334B, TI.LA 2 v 2, 4, 6: 521G, TI.LA.MEŠ 6: 476D, TI.LA.MEŠ] 9 r. 13, T[I.LA.MEŠ] 11 r. 8, *ú-bal*]*-laṭ-u-ni* 6: 194F, frg, *ú-bal-laṭ-u-ni* 6: 194J, *ú-bal-*[*laṭ-u-ni* 6: 194frg, *ú-ba-la-ṭ*[*a* 6: 194frg,

baltu "shame": *bal-tu-šú-nu* 2 v 13,

banû A "to create": *ba-ni-tu* 6: 73x, 501D, q, *ba-ni-tú* 6: 73A, 109E, frg, 501V,

banû B "to be good, nice": *nu-ban-nu-ú* 9: 26,

barmu (a pest): *bar-mu* 6: 599A,

bašû "to exist": *ba-šu*]*-u* 6: 223f, *ba-šú-u* 6: 5A, H, 80H, 118frg, 164B, P, S, *ba-šú-ú* 6: 5T, *ba-šu-u* 6: 5F, 80A, x, 118E, frg, 164A, 223H, 340F, *ba-šu-ú* 6: 5G, 80G, I, 223C, *ba-š*]*ú-u* 6: 340B, *b*[*a-šu-u*] 6: 223J, GÁL 6: 164E, 340frg, GÁL-*ši* 6: 444A, *ib*]*-ba-áš-šu-u-ni* 6: 384s, *ib-ba-áš-ši-u-*[*ni* 6: 383D, *ib-ba-áš-šú-u-ni* 6: 10F, H, 384D, 388D, *ib-ba-áš-š*[*u-*

u-n]i 6: 290A, ib-ba-šú-u-ni 6: 10A, 290B, ib-ba-šu-ú-[ni] 6: 10T, ib-ši 2 iv 7, ib-[ba-áš-šú-u-ni 6: 388s, it-tab-ši 6: 252A, B, I, i[b-ba]-šu-u-ni 6: 10G,

batāqu "to trim, cut off": ú-bat-ti-qu-ni 6: 627L, ú-bat-ti-qu-u-ni 6: 627frg, ú-bat-tú-qu-u-ni 6: 627F, ú-b[at-ti-qu-u-ni] 6: 627frg, ú-pa-ti-qu-u-ni 6: 627G, ú-pa-t[i-q]u-u-ni 6: 627K,

bābu "gate, doorway": KÁ 2 v 26, KÁ-šú 2 v 25, [KÁ-šá 6: 448A,

bārtu "rebellion": bar]-tu 6: 107frg, 169S, bar-te 6: 136E, t, 145E, 147H, 159E, S, 166S, 8: 20, r. 3, bar-ti 6: 147P, 159A, P, 169A, P, 254A, B, I, bar-tu 6: 67A, 133A, 166A, 169I, 186I, 198J, 303A, C, 498D, q, bar-tú 6: 67W, 107E, frg, 133E, 166E, P, 169E, 186frg, 198frg, 498V, bar-t[u 6: 166I, bar-t]e 6: 169M, bar-t]i 6: 136O, bar-[tu 6: 198frg, bar-[tu] 6: 303B, b[ar-te 6: 147E, b[ar-tu 6: 67frg,

bēl āli "city ruler": EN—URU 6: 3A, F, T, d, LÚ.EN—URU 6: 3G, H, a,

bēl dāmi "avenger": EN—MÚD.MEŠ-ku-nu 6: 583Q, frg, EN—MÚD.M]EŠ-ku-nu 6: 577Z, EN—[MÚD.MEŠ-ku]-nu 6: 577Q, EN—[MÚD.MEŠ-ku-nu] 6: 577D, E[N—MÚD.MEŠ-ku-nu] 6: 583v, E]N—MÚD.MEŠ-ku-nu 6: 583b, [E]N—MÚD.MEŠ-ku-nu 6: 583Z,

bēl hiṭṭi "criminal": EN—hi-ṭi 6: 159A, B, P, EN—hi-[ṭ]i 6: 159E,

bēl mugirri "chariot fighter": LÚ.EN—GIŠ.GIGIR 2 iii 21,

bēl nakāri "enemy": LÚ.EN—KÚR 9: 8, LÚ.EN—na-kar 9: 20,

bēl piqitti "official": LÚ.EN—pi-qit-ti 9: 11, 14,

bēl salāmi "ally": LÚ.EN—sa-lam-i-ni 9: 21,

bēltu "lady, mistress": be-let 4 r. 20, be-lit 6: 453g, l, 9 r. 22, 14 ii 19, be-l]it 2 v 12, GAŠAN 2 v 12, NIN 2 vi 15, 16,

bēlu "lord": be-lí 14 i 8, be-lí-ku-nu 8 r. 4, 11, 14, 17, be-lí-ni 6: 506D, be-lum 1 r. 3, EN 1 e. 16, r. 9, 10, 2 iv 4, 6: 25A, frg, 71A, S, W, 72A, 129E, frg, 159S, 196J, 204J, 301B, C, H, 431B, C, I, frg, 453A, 466frg, 519A, I, frg, 521I, 659frg, ii A, F, G, H, T, a, d, 8 r. 22, 9: 34, r. 6, 19, 11 r. 2, 12: 6, 14 ii 3, EN-a-ni 9: 4, EN-a-ni] 9: 33, EN-iá 4 r. 7, EN-i-ni 6: 497frg, q, 505q, 9: 8, 10, 11, 13, 14, 16, 20, 26, 30, 31, 32, 35, EN-i-ni] 9: 21, 23, r. 3, EN-i-[ni 9: 27, 28, EN-ku-nu 3: 4, 6: 44A, 59A, 110E, frg, 131frg, 157A, E, H, P, S, 174A, I, M, 189frg, 190J, 211C, J, frg, 230J, X, frg, f, 237X, 261B, i, 267A, B, frg, i, 360frg, 381D, s, 394A, H, 517V, 632L, 8: 14, 21, 24, r. 9, 10: 8, 12: 3, EN-ku-nu] 3: 1, 3, EN-ku-n[u 6: 211frg, EN-ku-n[u] 6: 59frg, EN-ku-n]u 6: 261p, EN-ku-(nu) 6: 230A, EN-ku-[nu 6: 131A, EN-k[a-nu-ni] 6: 191frg, EN-k[u-nu 6: 110y, 174frg, EN-k[u-nu] 6: 267frg, EN-k]u-nu 6: 174frg, 261A, EN.MEŠ 14 ii 10, EN.MEŠ-ia 6: 401D, EN-ni 6: 495frg, 506A, V, EN-ni-ni 6: 509D, EN-ni-n[i 6: 509V, EN-šu 6: 207J, O, 209J, O, EN-šú 6: 207frg, u, 209frg, u, EN-[i-ni 9: 5, EN-[ku-nu 6: 110frg, 131E, EN-[ku-nu] 6: 360B, 513D, EN]-ka-nu-u-ni 6: 191Y, EN]-ku-nu 6: 131O, 174S, 230N, 237N, E[N 6: 129A, 204O, frg, 328c, E[N-iá] 4 r. 9, E[N-ku-nu] 6: 360R, E]N-ku-nu 6: 189frg, 8 r. 7, [be-lí-ku-nu 8: r. ii 7E, [EN 6: 400D, [EN-ku-nu 8: 18, [EN-k]u-nu 6: 394D, [EN]-ku-nu 6: 44E, [E]N-ku-[nu] 6: 59W,

bēlūtu "lordship, dominion": be-lut 6: 298A, be-lu-te 6: 298H, be-lu-ti 6: 298C, be-lu-tu 6: 7A, EN-tu 6: 7F, G, 61r, EN-tú 6: 7T, 48E, 61W, 228X, f, EN-ut 6: 298B, EN-u]-tú 6: 48n, EN-ú-[tú] 6: 225H, EN-u-tu 6: 7H, EN-u-tú 6: 48A, 61A, n, EN-u-t[u 6: 228J, EN-[u-tu 6: 225J, EN]-tú 6: 228frg,

bēt abi "father's house, dynastic line": É—AD-šu 6: 115frg, 320J, c, É—AD-šú 6: 4a, 77A, H, x, 115E, 215J, frg, e, u, 320B, C, N, 338F,

bēt bēli "government, ruling family": É—EN.MEŠ-šu 6: 208J, É—EN.MEŠ-šú 6: 208C, É—EN.MEŠ]-šú 6: 208frg,

bēt redûti "Palace of Succession": É—re-du]-u-ti 6: 286frg, É—re-du-[ti] 14 i 11, 12, É—re-d]u-ú-ti 6: 165B, É—re-(du)-u-ti 6: 284A, É—re-[du-ti 6: 173frg, É—UŠ-te 6: 45E, frg, 75H, 82H, x, 85d, 86frg, 92frg, 95F, frg, 104E, 109frg, 124E, frg, 130E, 137O, 157E, P, 165P, 167E, 171P, 179frg, 184frg, 226X, 229J, frg, f, 240J, X, 258i, 260i, 266frg, i, 269F, frg, i, 284frg, 286J, 324c, 350w, 353A, 367frg, 392H, 503V, 505V, 506V, 508V, 515V, 633F, frg, É—UŠ-ti 3: 5, 6: 11A, 43A, E, 45A, 47A, 59A, n, 62A, 75A, 82A, G, I, 85A, G, 86A, G, 92A, I, 95A, I, 101A, 104frg, 109E, 121A, 124A, 137A, E, 144t, 150frg, 157A, 165A, E, 167A, S, 171A, I, M, S, 173A, I, M, S, 179I, M, 184I, 226C, f, 240N, 247A, 251A, B, 258A, I, 260A, p, 266A, B, 269A, B, 280A, Y, 284B, 286B, 298B, 316C, 324B, C, N, 350B, R, 362R, 367z, 381D, 394D, H, 403D, 495D, 496D, 503A, D, q, 505A, D, 506A, D, 508A, D, 633L, 667Q, frg, 669Q, É—UŠ-t[e] 6: 101frg, 514V, É—UŠ-t[i 6: 165M, 371z, É—UŠ-t[i] 6: 167M, 247frg, 269frg, 284Y, É—UŠ-t]e 6: 121O, 179frg, 362frg, É—UŠ-t]i 6: 85I, 86I, 179B, S, 633frg, É—UŠ-u-te 6: 316J, É—UŠ-[ti 6: 350A, 669Z, frg, É—UŠ-[ti] 6: 229C, 495q, É—UŠ-[x] 6: 101E, 260frg, É—UŠ]-te 6: 47E, 240frg, 495frg, É—UŠ]-ti 6: 403A, 506frg, É—U[Š-te 6: 350F, É—U[Š-te] 6: 229X, É—U[Š-ti 6: 75S, 95frg, 144E, P, 367R, É—U[Š-ti] 6: 150P, 157H, 226J, 353B, 508frg, É—U[Š-t]i 6: 258B, 286A, É—U[Š-x 6: 104y, É—U[Š-x] 6: 137t, 167P, É—U[Š]-ti 6: 298C, É—U]Š-te 6: 75x, 86d, 121E, 157B, 226H, 667frg, É—U]Š-ti 6: 92frg, 130O, 171frg, 179A, 506q, 555frg, 633frg, É—U]Š-t[i 6: 280frg, É—⌜UŠ⌝-ti 6: 251I, É—[UŠ-ti 6: 82a, É—[UŠ-ti] 6: 59r, 92frg, 101F, 109frg, 188frg, É—[UŠ-x 6: 251frg, 362z, É—[U]Š-ti 6: 165S, É]—UŠ-te 6: 367frg, 496q, É]—UŠ-ti 6: 124O, 260B, 280B, 353R, 392D, É]—UŠ-[x] 6: 266I, É—U]Š-ti 6: 316B, [É—re-du]-ú-[ti 6: 669frg, [É—UŠ]-ti 6: 150H, [É]—UŠ-[x] 6: 316A,

bētu "house, family": É 2 i 28, r. vi 3, 6: 115o, 171frg, 406A, 558A, D, frg, É-ka 2 v 6, É-ku-un 6: 430B, frg, É.MEŠ 2 vi 3, 6: 275A, frg, É.MEŠ-ku-nu 6: 418C, 444A, 493D, frg, 581Q, Z, b, v, É.MEŠ-ku-n[u 6: 581D, É.MEŠ-k[u-nu 6: 444g, É.MEŠ-šú-nu 6: 272A, B, É.MEŠ-šu-nu 6: 272frg, É.[MEŠ 6: 275frg, É.[MEŠ-šú-nu 6: 272F, É—[x 6: 165I, 179frg, 188frg, 269M, 286Y, É].MEŠ-ku-nu 6: 493V, 581frg,

biālu "to rule, govern": i-bé-lu 6: 430B,

bibbu "planet": MUL.UDU.IDIM.MEŠ 14 i 4, MUL.[UDU.IDIM.MEŠ 14 ii 2,

bibil libbi "ardent desire": bi-bil ŠÀ-bi-ni 9: 25,

bikītu "weeping": bi-k[it-su-nu 2 v 14,

birti "between": bir]-tu-šú-nu 6: 342w, bir-ti 6: 49A, frg, 99A, F, 166A, S, 326B, C, N, bir-tuk-ku-nu 8 r. 20, bir-tu-šú 6: 326B, C, N, c, bir-tu-šú-nu 6: 342F, bir-tu-š]ú-nu 6: 342A, bir-t]i 6: 99frg, bir-[ti] 6: 326c, bi[r-tu-šú-nu] 6: 342frg, bi[r-t]u-šú-nu 6:

342p, *b]ir-te* 6: 49E,

biškānu "cocoon": *bé-eš-ka-n[i-šá* 6: 580frg, *biš-ka-ni-šá* 6: 580Z, b, *bi-iš-ka-ni-šá* 6: 580D, Q, v,

bīrtu "fort": URU.*bi-ra-a-ti* 1: 7,

bītu see *bētu,*

bu''û see *ba''û,*

bubbulu "flood": *bu-bu-lu* 6: 488D, [UD.N]Á.À[M 6: 488frg,

bubūtu "hunger": *bu-bu-tu* 6: 480D, *bu-bu-t]i* 1 e. 19, *bu-b[u-ti]* 6: 449g, SU.KÚ 2 iv 9,

bullû "to extinguish": *li-bal-li* 6: 456g, *ú-bal-lu-[ú]* 11 r. 14, *[li-ba]l-li* 6: 456l, *[l]i-bal-l[i]* 6: 456A,

buqlu "malt": M[UNU$_4$ 6: 540F, frg, k,

burdišahhe "caterpillar": *bur-di-šá-hi* 6: 579D, b, v, *bu[r-di-šá-hi* 6: 579frg,

būnu "countenance; attention": *bu-[ni-šú]* 14 i 10,

būru "hunger": *bu-ri-ku-nu* 6: 449A, 550A, *bu-ri-ku-n]u* 6: 550frg,

da'ānu "to be strong, violent": *da]-ʾa-a-ni* 6: 177S, *da-a-ni* 6: 177I, *da-ʾa-ni* 6: 177A, *da-[ʾa-a-ni* 6: 177frg, *d[a-ʾa-a-ni* 6: 177G, *d]a-a-ni* 6: 177B, *d]a-ʾa-a-ni* 6: 177M, *tu]-da-a-n[a]* 6: 206e, *tu-da-a-na* 6: 206J, O, *t]u-da-a-na* 6: 206frg,

dababtu "talk": *da-bab-ti* 6: 386A, D, *d[a-bab-ti* 6: 386s,

dabābu "to talk, conspire": *a-d]a-bu-ub-u-ni* 13 iii 19, *da-bab* 6: 502D, V, q, 11 r. 5, *da-ba-a-bu* 8: 16, *du-ub]-ba* 6: 559D, *du-ub-ba* 6: 559A, *i-da-ba-bu-u-ni* 6: 557A, D, *ta-dáb-bu-ba-a-ni* 8: 22, *ta-dáb-bu-ba-a-[ni]* 8: 24, *ta-da-bu-ba-a-ni* 6: 52A, n, *ta-da-bu-ba-ni* 6: 99A, *ta-da-bu-ub-a-ni* 6: 99I, *ta-da-bu-[ba-ni]* 6: 99F, *ta-[da-bu-ba-a-ni* 6: 52E, *[i-dáb-bu]-bu-u-ni* 8 r. 5, *[ta-dáb-bu-b]a-a-ni* 8: 19,

dagālu "to look": *a-dag-gal-u-ni* 4 r. 9, *i-da-gal-u-ni* 2 iv 30, *lid-gu-lu* 6: 494D, *lid-g]u-lu* 6: 494frg, *l[id-gu-lu* 6: 494frg, *ta-da]-gal-ni* 6: 579Q, *ta-da-gal* 5 iii 14, *ta-da-gal-a-ni* 6: 60frg, 251A, B, I, *ta-da-gal-a-n[i]* 6: 60frg, *ta-da-gal-a-[ni]* 6: 251frg, *ta-da-gal-[u-ni]* 6: 579v, *ta-da-ga[l-a-ni]* 6: 60W, *ta-d[a-ga-la-ni* 6: 353B, *ta-[da-gal-u-ni]* 6: 579D, *tú-šad-ga-[la* 6: 89frg, *tu-šad-ga-la* 6: 89A, I, d, *tu-šad-ga-l]a* 6: 89frg, *tu-šad-g[a-la* 6: 89G, *t[a-da-gal-u-ni]* 6: 579b, *t[a-d]a-gal-a-ni* 6: 60A, *t]a-da-gal-u-ni* 6: 579Z, frg, *t]a-da-ga-la-n[i* 6: 353R,

dahû "to push": *lid-hu-šú-nu* 2 v 11,

daiānu "judge": *da-a-a-nu* 1 r. 8,

dalīlu "praise": *di-li-li* 2 vi 5,

daltu see *dassu,*

damāqu "to be good, nice": *dam-qa-a-ti* 14 ii 11, *dam-qu* 6: 234frg, *da-an-qu* 8: 16, r. 13, *de-iq-tú* 3: 2, 6: 108E, 8: 12, r. 3, *de-iq-[tú]* 6: 125E, *de-i[q-t]ú* 4 r. 4, *de-i]q-tú* 6: 621frg, 8: 20, SIG$_5$ 6: 52A, W, r, 54A, r, 234A, J, N, 621G, SIG$_5$.MEŠ 6: 368frg, z, 10: 10, SIG$_5$-*tu* 6: 148frg, 325C, N, 621L, SIG$_5$-*tú* 6: 68A, W, 73A, 125o, 148P, 325B, c, 621K, SIG$_5$-*t[ú* 6: 621A, SIG$_5$-*t[ú]* 6: 73H, SI[G$_5$ 6: 368frg, 621frg, SI]G$_5$ 6: 52n, 54frg, 234f, SI]G$_5$-*tu* 6: 148frg, SI]G$_5$-*tú* 6: 183A, S[IG$_5$-*tú]* 6: 148P, S]IG$_5$ 6: 234X, S]IG$_5$-*tú* 6: 108frg, S]IG$_5$-*t[ú]* 6: 148A,

damiqtu see *deʾiqtu, damāqu,*

danānu "to be strong, big": *dan-ni* 4 r. 20, 5: 418E, 6: 442A, g, 453frg, *dan-nu* 5 iv 12, 6: 192J, 470D, *da[n-ni* 6: 453A, LÚ.*dan-nu* 8: 9, *ú-dan-nin-u-ni* 6: 65A, W, 286A, B, *ú-dan-nin-[u-ni]* 6: 23A, *ú-dan-ni]n-u-ni* 6: 286frg, *ú-dan-ni-[x* 6: 23frg, *ú-dan-[nin-u-ni* 6: 286J, *ú-d[an-nin-u-ni* 6: 286C, *ú-[dan]-nin-[u-ni]* 6: 23U, *ú-[dan-nin-u-ni]* 6: 23G,

danānu see also *daʾānu,*

dandannu "strongest": *dan-dan-nu* 4 r. 26, *dan-nu-dan-nu* 9 r. 18,

danniš "greatly": *dan-niš* 14 i 2,

dassu "door": GIŠ.IG 6: 662frg, GIŠ.IG.MEŠ-*ku-n[u* 6: 663frg, GIŠ.I[G-*x* 6: 663frg, G[IŠ.IG 6: 662frg,

dāgil pāni "vassal": *da]-gíl*—IGI 6: 162B, *da-gíl—pa-ni* 6: 162A, E, P, S, *da-gíl—pa-[ni* 6: 162M,

dâku see *duāku,*

dâlu see *duālu,*

dām erēni "cedar balsam": MÚD—GIŠ.ERIN 6: 644A,

dāmu "blood": *da-a-me* 6: 256B, *da-a-mu* 5 iv 4, *da-me* 6: 256A, I, i, *da-mu* 6: 462frg, MÚD.MEŠ 6: 568Q, frg, 613G, H, K, frg, 615G, K, frg, MÚD.MEŠ-*ku-nu* 6: 426B, C, frg, MÚD.MEŠ-*k[u-nu* 6: 426frg, MÚD.M]EŠ 6: 615L, MÚD].MEŠ 6: 568D, *[d]a-me-ku-nu* 12: 7,

dātu "after": *[i—d]a-tu-uš-[šu* 10 r. 3,

de'iqtu "goodness": *de-iq-ta-šú-nu* 6: 279A, B, *de-iq-t[a-šú-nu* 6: 279frg, *de-iq-[ta-š]ú-nu* 6: 279Y, *[de-i]q-tú-šú* 4 r. 8,

dekû "to mobilize": *ni-de-ek-ku-ú-ma* 9: 23,

dēktu "defeat": *de-ek-tu-šú* 6: 314A, C, J, GAZ-*šú* 2 iii 16,

dēnu "judgment": *di-in* 6: 422A, B, C, c, *di-i-ni* 9 r. 9, *di-in-šu* 1 r. 9,

dibbi "words": *di-ib-bi-šú-nu* 6: 368frg, *di-ib-[bi-šú-nu* 6: 368B, *[dib-bi]* 13 iii 18, *[di-i]b-bi-šú-nu* 6: 368z,

diliptu "sleeplessness": *di]-lip-ti* 6: 487frg, *di-lip-tu* 6: 418C, *di-lip-tú* 6: 418frg, *d]i-lip-tu* 6: 487D,

dimmatu "moaning": *[dim-ma-ti* 1 r. 12,

dipāru "torch": *di-pa-ra-šú-nu* 11 r. 14,

diqugallu "supreme judge": DI.KUD.GAL 9 r. 8,

dišpu "honey": LÀL 6: 568D, Q, 594T, h, 644A, frg, LÀL.MEŠ 6: 644U, frg, LÀ[L 6: 568frg,

dī'u "malaria": *di-ʾu* 6: 418C,

duāku *da-a-ki* 8 r. 8, *de-ku-ú-[ni]* 6: 576Q, *de-ku-u-ni* 6: 576D, *du-a]-ki-šú-nu* 6: 142P, *du-a-ki* 6: 193J, frg, 8: 23, *du-a-ki-šu* 6: 307C, *du-a-ki-šú* 6: 307A, 10 r. 6, *du-a-ki-šú-nu* 6: 139E, 142E, *du-a-k[i-šú* 6: 307B, *du-a-k]i-šú-nu* 6: 142frg, t, *du-a-x[x* 6: 307frg, *du-u-a-ki-šú-nu* 6: 139A, *du-ú-ku* 1: 9, *d[u-a-ki]-šu* 6: 133A, *d[u-a-ki-šu* 6: 133E, *d]e-ku-u-ni* 6: 576Z, *i-du-ak* 6: 240A, C, frg, *i-du-ku-u-ni* 6: 193J, *i-du-ku-[u-ni* 6: 193frg, *i-[du-ak]* 6: 240N, X, *li-du-ku-ku-[nu]* 6: 578D, *li-d[u-ku-ku-nu]* 6: 578b, v, *l]i-du-ku-ku-nu* 6: 578Z, *ta]-du-ka-a-ni* 6: 160B, 170frg, *ta]-du-ka-šá-nu-u-ni* 6: 140t, *ta-du-ka-a-ni* 6: 160A, E, 170M, P, S, 255A, B, I, 314C, *ta-du-ka-a-n[i* 6: 170I, *ta-du-ka-a-šá-nu-ni* 6: 140E, *ta-du-ka-a-šú-u-ni* 6: 306A, C, *ta-du-ka-a-šú-u-n[i* 6: 306B, *ta-du-ka-a-[ni]* 6: 160S, *ta-du-ka-ni* 6: 314J, 8 r. 25, *ta-du-ka-šá-nu-u-n[i* 6: 140A, *ta-du-ka-šú-u-ni* 6: 127A, 246A, frg, *ta-du-ka-[a-ni]* 6: 146t, *ta-du-k[a-a-ni* 6: 255M, *ta-du-k[a-a-ni]* 6: 146P, *ta-du-k[a-šú-u-ni]* 6: 246frg, *ta-du-k]a-šú-u-ni* 6: 246frg, *ta-du-(ka)-a-ni* 6: 160P, *ta-du-[ka]-a-ni* 6: 170A, *ta-d[u-ka-a-šú-u-ni]* 6: 306frg, *ta-d[u-k]a-šú-u-ni* 6: 127E, *ta-d[u-x* 6: 146frg, *ta-[du-ka]-a-ni* 6: 314A, *t]a-du-ka-a-[ni]* 6: 146E, *[du-a-k]i-šú-nu* 6: 139t, *[ta-du]-ka-šú-u-n[i* 6: 127o, *[ta-du-k]a-šu-u-ni* 6: 127frg,

duālu "to run": *lu]-šá-di-lu* 6: 575Z, *lu-šá-di-lu* 6: 575D, *lu-šá-di-lu-ku-nu* 6: 620G, K, L, *l]u-šá-di-il-*

lu 6: 575Q, [*lu-š*]*á-di-lu-ku-nu* 6: 620frg, [[*lu-šá*]-*di-lu-ku-nu* 6: 620A,

dunqu "fortune, advantage": *du-un-qu* 6: 148E, H, *du-un-*[*qu*] 6: 148E, SIG$_5$-*ia* 13 ii 7, [SI]G$_5$-*ia* 13 ii 6,

dūru "eternity": *du-ur* 14 ii 14,

ebūru "harvest": BURU$_{14}$-*ku-nu* 6: 443A, g,

edēlu "to bar, close": *li-di-il*] 6: 448A,

edû "wave": *e-du-u* 5 iv 12,

egirtu "letter": *e-gír-tú* 5 iii 13,

egû "to disregard": *e-gu-u* 6: 397D, [*e*]-*gu-ma* 6: 399D,

ekallītu (reading uncert.) "queen": MÍ.KUR 8: 1, 10,

ekallu "palace": É.GAL 6: 198J, frg, 202J, frg, 209C, J, e, 211J, O, frg, u, 217C, J, e, 218H, J, 9 r. 12, 11 r. 12, 14 ii 5, É.[GAL 6: 218u, É].GAL 6: 202C,

ekēmu "to deprive": *li-kim* 2 v 13,

ekletu "darkness": *ek-let-te* 6: 424c, *ek-le-ti* 6: 424C, 9 r. 10, *ek-le-tú* 6: 485D, *ek-*[*le-ti* 6: 424B, *e*]*k-le-tu* 6: 485frg, *e*]*k-le-*[*tu*] 6: 485frg, *e*]*k-l*[*e-ti* 6: 424A,

elapû "duckweed": *e-la-pu-u* 6: 492frg, *e-la-pu-u-a* 6: 492D,

eleppu "ship": GIŠ.MÁ 5 iii 15, 17, GIŠ.MÁ.MEŠ 5 iii 9, GIŠ.MÁ.MEŠ-*ku-nu* 5 iv 11, GIŠ.MÁ.MEŠ-*šú-nu* 5 iii 24, 28, GIŠ.MÁ-*ni* 5 iii 16,

eliš "above": *e-liš* 6: 476D, 9 r. 13, 11 r. 8,

ellu "pure, holy": *el-lit* 14 i 6,

eli "upon": *e-li-ku-nu* 5 iv 13,

elû "to rise": *il-la-a* 9 r. 16, *li-la-a-ma* 6: 489D, *li-*[*la-a-ma* 6: 489frg, *li-l*[*i-a*] 5 iv 13, NIM 6: 551A, frg, *še-lu-a* 2 i 11, 12, *še-lu-a*] 2 i 12, *še-lu-*[*a*] 2 i 10, *še-lu-*[*u-ni*] 2 i 16, *še-*[*lu-a*] 2 i 11, 14,

emādu "to lean, impose": *li-mid-su*] 4 r. 16, *ta-nim-me-da* 6: 479D, [*li-mid-su-ma*] 1 r. 11,

emūqu "force; (pl.) troops": Á.KAL.MEŠ-*šú* 2 iv 2, *e-mu-qí* 1: 4, [Á].KAL-*a-a* 14 i 3,

enāšu "to be weak": *lu-ni-šú-ku-nu* 6: 630L, frg, *lu-ni-šú-u-ku-nu* 6: 630K, *lu-ni-šu-ku-nu* 6: 630G, *lu-n*[*i-šú-ku-nu*] 6: 630F, *l*[*u-ni-šú-ku-nu*] 6: 630frg,

enû "to alter": *e-nu-u* 6: 397D, *e-*[*nu-u-ni*] 11 r. 5, *te-na-a-ni* 6: 58A, frg, *te-*[*na-a-ni* 6: 58W, *t*[*e-na-a-ni* 6: 58r,

epāšu "to do": *e-pa*]*-šu-u-ni* 4 r. 12, *e-pa-áš-šu-ni-šu-u-ni* 6: 169S, *e-pa-ši* 13 iii 9, *e-pa-šú-ni-šú-un-ni* 6: 169E, *e-pa-šú-ni-šú-u-ni* 6: 169A, *e-pa-šu-niš-šu-un-ni* 6: 169M, *e-pa-šu-*[*u-ni*] 4 r. 11, *e-peš* 6: 74A, H, x, 14 i 13, *e-pu-šu-niš-*[*x* 6: 169I, *e-pu-šú-niš-šú-*[*x* 6: 169P, *e-p*[*u-šu-u-ni*] 10 r. 5, *e-tap-áš* 6: 303B, C, *e-tap-pa-šu* 6: 166M, *e-tap-pa-*[*áš* 6: 200frg, *e-tap-šu* 6: 166E, S, *e-tap-šú* 6: 166P, *e-ta-pa-áš* 6: 200J, 303A, *in-n*]*é-piš* 2 iii 7, *i-pu-šu* 9: 7, *le-e-pu-šú* 6: 528B, *le-pa-šú-ku-nu* 6: 601A, h, 617A, *le-pa-šú-ku-n*]*u* 6: 617H, *le-pa-šu-ku-nu* 6: 601T, frg, j, 617G, L, *le-pa-šu-*[*ku-nu*] 6: 601K, *le-pu-šu* 6: 528G, *le-pu-šú* 6: 528F, *le-pu-š*[*u* 6: 528A, *l*[*e-p*]*a-šú-(ku)-nu* 6: 617K, *né-ep-pa-áš-u-ni* 6: 498D, q, *te*]*-pa-šá-ni-šu-*[*u-ni*] 6: 187frg, *te*]*-pa-šu-u-ni* 4 r. 13, *te-ep-pa-áš-a-ni* 6: 232A, *te-ep-pa-šá-a-ni* 6: 232X, 8: 15, *te-ep-pa-šá-niš-šú-un-ni* 6: 233X, *te-ep-pa-šá-niš-un-ni* 6: 264F, *te-ep-pa-šá-ni-šú-u-ni* 6: 68A, 233A, *te-ep-pa-šá-ni-šú-x*[*x* 6: 126A, *te-ep-pa-š*]*á-a-ni* 6: 376frg, *te-ep-pa-*[*šá-a-ni* 6: 196frg, *te-ep-p*]*a-šá-a-ni* 6: 376s, *te-e*[*p-pa-šá-a-ni*] 6: 376frg, *te-pa*]*-šá-a-ni* 6: 196F, *te-pa-áš-a-ni* 6: 232N, *te-pa-áš-ma* 13 ii 6, *te-pa-šá-a-ni* 6: 196Y, 232f, *te-pa-šá-a-ni-niš-šu-un-ni* 6: 233f, *te-pa-šá-ni* 6: 232J, *te-pa-šá-niš-šú-ni* 6: 68W, 264frg, *te-pa-šá-niš-šu-un-ni* 6: 233N, *te-pa-šá-niš-*[*x* 6: 187frg, *te-pa-šá-ni-šú-nu-ni* 6: 107E, *te-pa-šá-ni-šu-un-ni* 6: 233J, 264i, *te-pa-šá-*[*ni-šu*]*-nu-u-ni* 6: 107frg, *te-pa-šu-u-ni* 4 r. 14, *te-pa-*[*x* 6: 187I, *te-p*[*a-šá-a-ni* 6: 196frg, *te-p*[*a-x* 6: 233frg, *te-p*]*a-a-šá-a-ni* 6: 196frg, *te-ta-pa-áš* 13 ii 7, *te-*[*pa-šá-a-ni*] 6: 196J, *tu-pa-áš-a-ni* 6: 311C, *tu-pa-šá-ni* 6: 311J, *t*[*e-e*]*p-pa-šá-ni-šú-u-ni* 6: 264A, *t*]*e-ep-pa-šá-a-ni* 6: 376B, *up-pa*]*-áš* 6: 49n, *up-pa-áš* 6: 49A, W, *up-pa-áš-ú-ni* 6: 8T, *up-pa-áš-u-ni* 6: 8F, G, *up-pa-áš-u-n*[*i*] 6: 228C, *up-pa-šú-u-ni* 6: 8H, *up-*[*pa-áš-u-ni*] 6: 228J, *ú-ba-šu-u-ni* 6: 8A, *ú-pa-áš-ú-ni* 6: 228f, *ú-(pa)-áš-u-ni* 6: 61A, *ú-*[*pa*]*-áš-*[*u-ni*] 6: 61frg, [*né-ep-pa*]*-áš-u-ni* 6: 498V, [*te-e*]*p-pa-šá-ni-šu-un-ni* 6: 126frg, [*t*]*e-ep-pa-šá-niš-šú-u-ni* 6: 264B, [*t*]*e-pa-šá-a-ni* 6: 380s, [*t*]*e-pa-šá-ni-šú-un-ni* 6: 126E, [*up*]*-pa-*[*áš-u-ni*] 6: 8a,

epēšu "to do": *ni-ip-pu-šu* 9: 22, 24, *ni-te-ep-šu* 9: 19, *nu-ul-te-pi-šu* 9: 19, *šu-pu-uš* 14 i 9,

epinnu "plough": GIŠ.APIN 6: 545frg, [GI]Š.APIN 6: 545A,

epru "dust": *ep-ri* 6: 412A, SAHAR.MEŠ 2 iv 14,

epšu "venture": *ep-šu* 6: 67frg, 186I, *ep-šú* 6: 67A, W, 107E, frg, 186frg, *ep-*[*šú* 6: 107A,

eqlu "field": A.ŠÀ 6: 49A, frg, 99A, F, 165P, S, A.ŠÀ.MEŠ 6: 275A, B, frg, A.ŠÀ.MEŠ-*ku-nu* 6: 531A, F, M, A.ŠÀ.MEŠ-*ku-*[*n*]*u* 6: 531G, A.ŠÀ-*šú* 6: 165A, A.Š]À.MEŠ 6: 275frg, A].ŠÀ 6: 165E,

erābu "to enter; to set": *er-rab-u-ni* 6: 556D, frg, 560D, 622L, frg, *e-rab* 6: 431A, B, *e-rab-ku-nu* 6: 420C, c, *e-rab-u-ni* 5 iii 24, 6: 556A, 560A, 622G, K, *e-rab-u-*[*ni* 6: 210O, *e-rab-u-*[*ni*] 6: 622frg, *e-ra*[*b*]*-u-ni* 6: 622A, *e-r*]*ab* 6: 431C, *e-(re)-eb-ku-*[*nu* 6: 420B, *e-*[*rab* 6: 431I, *e-*[*reb-šú* 4 r. 17, *lu-še-ri-bu* 6: 562D, 625G, *lu-še-ri-b*[*u*] 6: 625K, *lu-še-r*[*i-bu*] 6: 562A, *lu-š*[*e-ri-bu*] 6: 625frg, *te*]*-rab-a-ni* 6: 392D, *te-rab*]*-a-ni* 6: 392A, *te-rab-a-ni* 6: 392H, *te-rab-a-ni-ni* 6: 183I, *te-rab-a-n*[*i-ni*] 6: 183frg, *te-rab-ba* 6: 558A, *te-ra-ba* 6: 558D, [*lu-še*]*-ri-bu* 6: 625A, [*lu-še-r*]*i-bu* 6: 625L, [*lu-š*]*e-ri-bu* 6: 625frg,

erbettu "four": *er-bet-ti* 14 i 22,

erbiu "locust": BURU$_5$ 6: 442g, 599j, BU]RU$_5$ 6: 442l, 599A, [BURU$_5$.MUŠEN 2 vi 1,

erēbu "to enter": *e-re-ba-nu* 9 r. 12, *e-reb* 6: 6A, G,

erimtu (mng. uncert.): *e-rim-tú* 5 iii 29,

eršu "bed": GIŠ.NÁ 6: 559frg, G[IŠ.N]Á 6: 559D,

esāru "to besiege": *e-ta-as-ru-šu* 6: 166E, M, *e-ta-as-ru-šú* 6: 166A, P, S, *e-ta-as-ru-uš* 6: 166I, *e-ta-a*]*s-ru-šú* 6: 166B,

eṣintu "bone": *eṣ-ma-a-te-ku-nu* 6: 640frg, *eṣ-ma-ti-ku-nu* 6: 445g, *eṣ-ma-*[*x* 6: 445l, *eṣ-*[*ma-te-ku-nu* 6: 640frg, *eṣ-*[*ma-ti-ku-nu*] 6: 445A, [*e*]*ṣ-ma-te-ku-nu* 6: 640A, frg,

eširtu "sanctuary": *eš-*[*re-e-ti* 14 ii 10,

ešrati (mng. uncert.): *eš-ra-ti* 14 i 1,

eṭēru "to remove": [*li-ṭir-šu*] 1 r. 13,

eṭimmu "ghost, spirit": *e-ṭím-ma-a-nu* 9 r. 14, *e-ṭím-ma-ku-nu* 6: 452frg, 477D, *e-*[*ṭím-ma-šú-nu*] 11 r. 9, GIDIM-*ku-nu* 6: 452I, G[IDI]M-*ku-nu* 6: 452A,

eṭlu "young man": LÚ.GURUŠ.MEŠ-*ku-nu* 6: 482D, frg,

eṭû "to be dark": *e-ṭu-u* 6: 485D, *e-ṭu-ú* 6: 485frg,

ezābu "to save": *li-ni-zib* 2 vi 5, *li-z[i-b]u-ku-nu* 6: 479D, *tu-še-za-ba-a-ni-ni* 6172S, *tu-še-za-ba-ni-ni* 6: 172A, *tu-še-za-b[a-ni]-ni* 6: 172M, *t]u-še-za-ba-a-ni-ni* 6: 172frg,

ezziš "angrily": *ez-zi-iš* 1 r. 15,

ezzu "angry": *ez-zu-ti* 6: 465frg, *ez-zu-u-ti* 6: 518frg, [*ez-zu-ti* 5 iv 5,

ēnu "eye": *e-ni-šú* 4 r. 9, IGI.2 1: 11, IGI.2-*ku-nu* 6: 423B, c, 428B, 482D, IGI.2-*k]u-nu* 6: 423A, IGI.2.MEŠ-*ku-nu* 6: 423C, 565frg, IGI.2.MEŠ-*š[ú-nu]* 6: 628F, IGI.2.ME[Š]-*ku-nu* 6: 428A, IGI.2-*ni* 9 r. 10, IGI.2-*šú-nu* 2 vi 2, IGI.2.[MEŠ-*šú-nu* 6: 628A, [IGI.2.MEŠ-*k]u-nu* 6: 565D, [IGI.2.MEŠ-*šú-n]u* 6: 628frg, [IG]I.2.MEŠ-*šú-nu* 6: 628K,

ēpišānu "maker": *e-piš-a-nu-te* 6: 136E, t, *e-piš-a-nu-ti* 6: 159E, P, 254B, *e-piš-a-n[u-ti* 6: 145P, *e-pi-š-šá-nu-te* 6: 159S, *e-pi]š-a-nu-ti* 6: 147P, *e-pi-šá-nu-te* 6: 145t, 147H, *e-pi-šá-nu-ti* 6: 136A, 145frg, 147A, 159A, 254A, I, *e-p]iš-a-nu-te* 6: 145E, [*e-pi]-šá-nu-t[i* 6: 136frg,

ērib ekallu "palace personnel": LÚ.TU—KUR 8: 8,

ēṣu "scarce": *e-ṣu-ti* 6: 147P, *e-ṣ]u-ti* 6: 147frg, *e-[ṣ]u-te* 6: 147H, *i-ṣu-ti* 1 r. 4,

gabbu "all": *gab[-b[u* 5 iii 21, *gab-bu* 5 iii 16, 6: 5A, F, G, H, T, a, d, 245frg, 8: 8, 11, r. 23, 10: 6, 13 ii 8, *gab-b]i-šú* 5 i 3, *gab-[bu* 5 iii 19, 20, *ga[b-bu* 6: 245frg,

gadiu "male kid": *ga-de-e* 6: 636frg, *ga-[de-e]* 6: 636F,

galālu "to blind": *ú]-gal-lil-u-ni* 6: 628L, *ú]-ga-lil-u-ni* 6: 628G, *ú-gal-lil-u-ni* 6: 628F, *ú-ga-lil-u-[ni]* 6: 628frg, *ú-ga-li-lu-u-ni* 6: 628K, *ú-g]a-lil-u-ni* 6: 628frg,

gallû "demon": *gal-le-e* 1 r. 2,

galû "to go into exile": *ta-ga-lu-ni* 2 iv 33, *ul-te-eg-lu-ma* 1: 6,

gamālu "to spare": *ga-me-li* 6: 455A, frg, k, *g[a-me-li* 6: 455frg, *i-gam-mi-la* 1 r. 2,

gamāru "to finish": *gam-mur-u-ni* 6: 152P, frg, *ga-ma-ru-[ni]* 6: 152A, *ga-mur-u-ni* 6: 152E, *ga-mur-[u-ni* 3: 4, *gu-um-mu-ru* 9: 5, *lig-ma-ru-ku-nu* 6: 629G, *lig-ma-ru-ku-[nu]* 6: 629frg, *lig-ma-r[u-ku-nu]* 6: 629frg, *li-ga-am-ru* 6: 593h, *li-gi-(ma)-ru-ku-nu* 6: 629frg, *li-ig-mur-u-ku-nu* 6: 629K,

gammurtu "totality": *gam-mur-te* 6: 53E, *gam-mur-ti* 6: 53A, n, r, 169A, S, *gam-mur-t[i* 6: 310A, *ga]m-mur-te* 6: 169P, *ga-mur-ti* 2 iv 3, *gu-mur-ti* 6: 310C, *gu-mur-(ti)* 6: 387D, *gu-m[ur-ti* 7 r. 5, *gu-[mur-t]i* 6: 387s,

garû "to contest": *ta-ga-ri-šú-nu-ni* 6: 356frg, *ta-g[a-x* 6: 356B, *tu-ga-ri-a-šá-nu-u-[ni]* 6: 356R,

gaṣṣu "gypsum": *gaṣ-ṣi* 2 i 9,

gimlu "compassion": *gim-lu* 5 iv 2, 6: 459A, k, *gi-im-li* 6: 257B, *gi-im-lu* 6: 257A, I, i, *g[i-im-lu]* 6: 459frg,

gimru "total": *gi-mir* 14 i 3,

girru "fire (god)": ᵈGIŠ.BAR 6: 155A, E, H, P, 410A, C, 610G, K, M, ᵈGIŠ.BA]R 6: 610L, ᵈGIŠ.BAR 6: 610A,

gišparru "trap": *giš-par-ri* 6: 650U, frg,

gitmālu "perfect": *gít-ma-lu* 12: 6,

gugallu "canal inspector": GÚ.GAL 1 r. 13, 2 iv 8, 6: 440g, GÚ.GAL-*la* 9 r. 15,

habātu "to plunder": *ta-hab-bat-a-ni-ni* 6: 313C, J, *ta-hab-bat-[a-ni-ni]* 6: 313A,

habbātu "robber": *hab-ba-ti* 2 v 26,

habû "to draw water": *ih-ba-a* 2 iv 21,

hadû "to be glad": HÚL 8: 11, *ta-ha-du-a-ni* 6: 305B, *ta-ha-[du-a]-ni* 6: 305A, *ta-ha-[du-a-ni]* 6: 305frg, *tah-du-a-ni* 6: 305C,

haerušhu (a beast): *ha-e]-ru-uš-hi* 6: 588b, *ha-e-ru-u]š-hi* 6: 588Q, *ha-e-[ru-uš-hi* 6: 588D,

halālu "to sound": *i-ha-lul-u-ni* 6: 637A,

halāpu "to clothe": *li-hal-lip-ku-nu* 6: 420c, *lu-u-hal-lip-šú-[nu]* 11 r. 11, *l[i-hal-lip]* 2 iv 5, [*li-h]al-lip-ku-nu* 6: 420A,

halāqu "to disappear, (D) to destroy": *ha-lu-[qi* 10: 5, *ha]-la-qu* 14 i 24, *hul-lu-qí* 8 r. 8, *hul-lu-qi-šú* 6: 134A, *hul-lu-qi-šú-nu* 6: 134O, *hu[l-x* 6: 134frg, *h[ul-x* 6: 134E, *li]-ih-liq* 6: 539F, *li-hal-li-qa* 6: 432A, B, I, *li-hal-l]i-qa* 6: 432C, *li-hal-[liq* 1 r. 14, *li-hal-[liq]* 6: 661frg, *li-ih-liq* 2 i 7, 6: 645A, *li-ih-[liq]* 6: 544frg, *li-tah-li-qa-ku-nu* 6: 445A, *li-[ih-liq]* 2 i 19, 6: 539k, 544k, *lu-hal]-liq* 6: 436B, *lu-hal-liq* 6: 436I, 661Q, 11 r. 12, *lu-hal-li-qu* 5: 417E, *lu-h]al-liq* 6: 436A, *l[i-ih-liq]* 6: 539A, *l]i-ih-liq* 6: 544F, *tah-[li-qa-ku-nu]* 6: 445g, *ta-hal-laq-a-[x* 6: 178frg, *ta-hal-liq-a-ni* 6: 178A, S, *ta-hal-liq-a-ni-ni* 6: 178I, *ta-hal-li-qa-a-ni-ni* 6: 178M, *ta-hal-l]i-qa-a-ni-ni* 6: 178B, *tu]-hal-laq-qa-ni* 6: 141t, *tu]-hal-la-qa-a-ni* 6: 161B, *tu-hal-laq-a-ni* 6: 161P, 315J, *tu-hal-laq-qa-a-ni* 6: 141E, 161A, 256A, B, *tu-hal-laq-q[a-ni]* 6: 141A, *tu-hal-la-qa* 6: 293A, *tu-hal-la-ka-a-[ni]* 6: 161S, *tu-hal-la-qa-a-ni* 6: 256I, 315C, *tu-hal-la-q[a-a-ni* 6: 413C, *tu-hal-la-[qa]* 6: 293B, *tu-hal-l]a-qa* 6: 293H, *tu-h[al-laq]-a-ni* 6: 315A, *tu-h[al-laq-qa-ni]* 6: 141P, *tu-[hal-la-qa-a-ni]* 6: 413A, *t[ú]-hal-laq-qa-a-ni* 6: 161E, [*h]ul-lu-q[i-šu* 6: 134t, [*li-hal-liq* 1 e. 19, [*t]u-[ha]l-la-qa-a-[ni* 6: 256M, [*ú-hal-li-qu-ni*] 11 r. 4,

hamāṭu "to glow": *ha-am-ṭ[u* 6: 458frg, *ha-an-ṭu* 5 iv 1, 6: 458k, *ha-a]n-ṭu* 6: 458B, [*ha-an-ṭ]u* 6: 458A,

hanāqu "to strangle": *li-ih]-nu-qu-ku-nu* 6: 607L, *li-ih-na-qu-ku]-nu* 6: 607h, *li-ih-na-qu-ku-nu* 6: 607A, frg, *li-ih-nu-qu-ku-nu* 6: 607M, *li-ih-n[a]-qu-ku-nu* 6: 607K, *li-ih-n]u-qu-ku-nu* 6: 607T, *li-i]h-nu-qu-ku-nu* 6: 607H,

hapû "to break, destroy": *ah-pu-n[i* 5 iii 4, *ha-bé-e* 6: 294C, *ha-pe-e* 6: 294A, H, *ha-p[e]-e* 5 iv 14, *h[a-p]e-e* 6: 294B, *ta-hi-bi* 6: 654U,

harammāma "later": *ha-ra-ma-a-ma* 6: 210e, *ha-ra-me-ma* 6: 210J, frg, *ha-ra-me-[ma* 6: 210u,

harbatu "wasteland, ruins": *har-ba-ti* 2 v 7, *har-ba-t[i* 2 i 4,

harimtu "whore": MÍ.*ha-rim-tú* 2 v 9, 10,

harrānu see *hūlu,*

harru "ditch": *har-ri* 12: 7,

hasāsu "to think": *ta-ha-sa-sa-[a-ni]* 6: 379A, *ta-ha-sa-[sa-a-ni]* 6: 379frg, *ta-ha-s[a-sa-a-ni]* 6: 379D,

haṣānu "to protect": *ta-ha-ṣi-nu-[u]-ni* 2 iii 22,

haṭṭu "sceptre": GIŠ.PA-*šú* 1 r. 3,

haṭû "to sin": *ih-ti-ṭi* 2 v 9, *ih-ṭu-u-ni* 6: 626K, *ih-ṭ[u]-u-ni* 6: 626L, *ih-ṭ[u-u-ni]* 6: 626frg, *i[h]-ṭu-u-ni* 6: 626G, *i-haṭ-ṭu-ú* 1 e. 15, *i-haṭ-ṭ[u-u-ni]* 11 r. 6, *i-ha-ṭi* 5 iii 28, *i-ha-ṭi]* 2 i 15, *i-ha-ṭi-u* 5 iii 17, *i-ha-ṭu-ni]* 2 i 24, *i-ha-ṭu-u* 6: 398H, *i-ha-ṭu-ú* 14 ii 9, *i-ha-ṭu-u-ni* 2 iv 18, *i-ha-ṭu-[ni* 2 i 32, *ni-ih-ti-ṭi* 2 v 15, *ni-ih-ṭu-ú]* 9: 27, *ni-i]h-ti-ṭi* 2 iv 28, *ta-ha-ṭa-a-ni* 6: 66A, 105E, 272frg, 555frg, *ta-ha-ṭa-a-n]i* 6: 517V, *ta-ha-ṭa-a-[ni]* 6: 66W, *ta-ha-ṭa-ni* 6: 105frg, 272A, *ta-ha-ṭa-[a-ni]* 6: 517frg, *ta-ha-ṭi-a* 6: 292H, *ta-ha-ṭi-a-ni* 12: 5, *ta-ha-ṭu-[ni]* 2 iii 15, *ta-ha-ṭ[i-a]* 6: 292A, *t[a]-ha-[ṭ]a-a-ni* 6: 272B, *t[a-ha-ṭa-a-ni]* 6: 272frg, *t]a-ha-ṭu-ni* 2 iii 14, *[ih-ti-ṭi* 2 v 17, *[ih-ṭu-u-n]i* 6: 626frg, *[i-ha-ṭu-ni* 2 iv 30, *[i-ha-ṭ]u-u* 6: 398D, *[ta-ha]-ṭa-a-ni* 6: 612K, *[t]a-ha-ṭa-[ni]* 6: 272F,

hābītu "woman drawing water": [M]Í.*ha-bi-t[i* 2 iv 21,

hā'iru "spouse": *[ha-ʾi-ri-šá]* 4 r. 24,

hiāru "to select": *li-hi-ru* 6: 493D, V, frg,

hiṭṭu "crime; punishment": *hi-i-ṭu* 6: 433B, *hi-ṭu* 6: 433A, I, *hi-ṭu-ú-ni* 9: 26,

hīrtu "spouse": *hi]-ir-tu* 4 r. 18, *hi-ir-tu* 6: 417C, *hi-ir-t]u* 6: 417A, *hi-ra-a-te-[k]u-nu* 6: 428B, *hi-ra-ti-ku-nu* 6: 428A,

hubtu "plunder; captives": *hu-ub-ta-a-ni* 1: 12, *hu-ub-tu-šú* 6: 313A, J, *hu-ub-t[u]-šú* 6: 313C,

huhāru "bird trap": *hu-ha-ru* 6: 649U, frg,

huppu "hole": *hu-up-pi* 6: 641frg, *hu-up-pu* 6: 641A, *hu-up-p]i* 6: 641frg,

hurādu "guard duty(?)": *hu-ra-a-[di* 6:180I, hu-ra-di 6: 180A, *hu-ra-di]* 6: 180frg,

hurāptu "female spring lamb": MÍ.NIM 2 iv 11, MÍ.NIM-*tú* 6: 551A, D, MÍ.[NIM-*tú* 6: 551frg, MÍ.UDU.NIM-*tú* 6: 551frg,

hurāpu "male spring lamb": UDU.NIM 2 i 10, 16, 21, 25, 32, r. iv 11, 6: 551D, frg, 636F, frg, UDU.NI]M 6: 636frg, UDU.[NIM 2 i 29,

hurāṣu "gold": KUG.GI 6: 567D, Q, frg,

hurbabillu "chameleon": *hur-ba-bíl-li* 6: 593h, *hur-ba-bi-li* 6: 593j, *hur-ba-bi-l[i* 6: 593L, *h]ur-ba-bíl-li* 6: 593Q,

hurrutu "hole": HABRUD 6: 598T, j, HABRUD.MEŠ 6: 595h, j, 598h, HABRUD.M[EŠ 6: 595T, HABRUD.[MEŠ 6: 598L, *hu-ri-te* 6: 555A, *hu-ri-ti* 6: 555D, frg,

hušahhu "famine": *hu-šah-hi* 1 e. 19, 2 iv 9, *hu-šah-hi]* 1 r. 14, *hu-šah-hu* 6: 450A, 480D, *hu-[šah-hi]* 1 r. 4,

huzīru "pig": ŠAH 6: 451g, ŠAH.MEŠ 6: 451A, 482D, 484D,

hūlu "road": *hu-li* 4 r. 3, KASKAL 6: 54A, r, 199J, 235A, J, X, KASKAL.MEŠ 5 iii 18, KASKAL.2 9: 37, KAS]KAL 6: 199frg,

ia'nu "is not": *ia-aʾ-nu* 9: 28,

idu "side": *i-di-ku-nu* 6: 454A, g, l, *[i-di-ku-n]u* 6: 454frg,

idû see *udû,*

ikkāru "farmer": LÚ.ENGAR-*šú* 2 iv 19,

ikkibu "taboo": *ik-kib-ku-nu* 6: 489D, *ik-kib-ku-[nu]* 6: 489frg, *ik-ki-bi-šú-nu* 2 iv 13, NÍG.GIG]-*ku-nu* 6: 523G,

ikkillu "noise": *ik-kil* 2 iv 12, 6: 438I, 443g, *i[k-kil* 6: 438F, *i]k-kil* 6: 443l, *kil-lu* 6: 637A, frg,

ilku "duty": *il-ka-šu* 1 e. 15,

iltu "goddess": *i-lat* 9 r. 24,

ilu "god": DINGIR 4 r. 17, 6: 117frg, 264frg, 296A, 420B, 431B, 455g, l, 604A, H, frg, DINGIR-*ku-nu* 6: 393D, H, DINGIR-*ku-n[u* 6: 409A, DINGIR.ME 6: 373frg, 14 i 28, ii 19, DINGIR.MEŠ 1 r. 3, 7, 10, 2 v 5, 22, 3 r. 5, 4 r. 16, 26, 5 iv 5, 8, 9, 6: 21G, U, frg, 22A, G, U, frg, 23A, G, frg, 25A, frg, 31A, G, frg, 32A, G, frg, 33A, G, frg, 34A, frg, 35A, fr 36A, frg, 37A, frg, 38A, frg, 39A, E, frg, 40A, frg, 41A, E, 117E, 153E, 264B, F, i, 296C, H, 373frg, 401D, 405A, D, 414C, 418B, C, 420C, c, 425B, 431I, 494D, 511D, 518V, 523A, B, 526A, B, 573Q, b, 604h, 616m, 618G, frg, 660Q, i A, F, G, H, T, a, d, iiiA, B, F, Y, 9: 2, r. 5, 6, 18, 10: 2, 11 r. 6, 14 i 26, ii 10, DINGIR.MEŠ-*ni* 6: 153E, P, frg, 407A, DINGIR.ME[Š 6: 425frg, 464frg, DINGIR.ME[Š] 6: iiifrg, DINGIR.M[EŠ 6: 34G, DINGIR.M]EŠ 6: 431A, DINGIR-*[ku-nu]* 6: 393A, DINGIR.[MEŠ 6: 23U, 431frg, 494frg, DINGIR.[MEŠ] 6: 153A, DINGIR.[ME]Š 6: iiiH, DIN[GIR 6: 296B, DIN[GIR.MEŠ 6: 153A, 472D, DIN[GIR.MEŠ] 6: 660frg, DI]NGIR.MEŠ 6: 414A, [DINGIR.MEŠ 3: 11, 9 r. 2, [DINGIR.M]EŠ 6: 38E, [DINGIR].MEŠ 6: 21A, 31E, 32E, 33E, 37E, 40E, [DING]IR.MEŠ 6: 34E, 40frg, 616frg, [DIN]GIR.MEŠ 6: 35E, 36E, [DI]NGIR.MEŠ 6: 511V,

ilūtu "divinity": DINGIR-*ti* 14 i 6, r. ii 13,

imāru "donkey": ANŠE 2 iv 7, 15, ANŠE.MEŠ 6: 277A, B, Y, frg, ANŠE.NITÁ 6: 491D, AN]ŠE.NITÁ 6: 491frg,

imittu A "shoulder": UZU.ZAG 2 i 29, 30, UZU.Z[AG 2 i 32, UZ[U.ZAG 2 i 34,

imittu B "right side; south": ZAG 4 r. 3, 6: 634F, K, L, frg, 635A, F, L, frg, Z[AG 6: 634frg, Z]AG 6: 634frg, 8 r. 1,

immeru "sheep": UDU.MEŠ 2 iv 7, 6: 277A, B, Y, frg,

ina "in": *ina* 1: 5, e. 15, 16, 19, r. 10, 11, 13, 14, 2 i 5, 15, 24, 26, 28, 31, 33, 35, iii 15, 21, r. iv 1, 7, 8, 16, 17, 19, 27, 29, v 8, 10, 14, 16, 21, 24, vi 5, 3 r. 1, 7, 4 r. 17, 20, 23, 24, 5 ii 13, r. iii 3, 6, 7, 11, 14, 15, 16, 17, 19, 20, 21, 24, 26, 28, 29, iv 3, 4, 5, 7, 11, 12, 16, 417E, 418E, 421E, 6: 8A, F, G, H, T, a, 10A, G, 11A, 12A, 13A, K, frg, 16A, K, frg, 41A, E, 43A, 47A, E, 49A, E, frg, r, 50A, r, 51A, r, 54A, frg, r, 56A, frg, r, 61A, W, frg, r, 64A, W, 66A, W, 67A, W, 68A, W, frg, 70A, S, 71A, S, W, 74A, H, x, 76A, H, x, 77A, H, a, x, 78A, 79A, G, H, I, a, x, 83A, G, H, I, 87A, d, 89A, I, frg, d, 95A, F, frg, 97A, F, I, frg, 98A, F, I, frg, 99A, F, 104E, frg, 105E, frg, 106A, E, frg, y, 109frg 111A, E, frg, y, 112frg, 113A, frg, 115E, frg, 116E, frg, 118A, frg, 131frg, 135A, frg, 137A, E, 141A, E, 153A, E, frg, 154A, E, H, P, 161A, E, P, S, 164E, M, P, S, 165A, P, S, 166A, E, P, 169A, S, 174A, G, I, M, S, frg, 178A, B, I, M, frg, 182I, frg, 185F, I, frg, 189frg, 197J, frg, 198J, frg, 199J, frg, 201J, frg, 203O, frg, 207C, 208C, J, 209C, J, e, 211J, O, frg, u, 213J, O, frg, u, 216C, J, O, e, 217J, 218C, H, J, e, 219H, J, 220C, H, J, 221H, J, f, 222C, H, J, 223J, 224H, J, 228J, X, f, 229X, f, 231A, J, X, f, 235A, N, X, 236A, C, J, X, 237A, B, J, N, X, 245frg, 249A, I, frg, 256A, B, I, 269A, B, i, 272A, B, F, frg, 278A, B, Y, frg, 279A, B, Y, frg, 281A, B, 284A, B, C, Y, frg, 292A, H, 296A, B, C, H, 297A, B, C, 301B, C, frg, 302A, B, C, frg, 303A, B, C, frg, 309A, C, frg, 310A, C, 315A, C, J, 317A, 324B, C, N, c, 326B, C, N, c, 327B, C, N, frg, 331B, 332B, frg, 333B, 334B, 339F, R, 341F, R, frg, p, 342F, frg, p, 345F, R, frg, p, 351R, 353R, 357B, R, frg, 358R, frg, 362R, frg, 364B, R, frg, z, 365B, R, frg, z, 368frg, z, 370frg, 373B, 375B, frg, 380s, 385D, 387D, s, 389A, D, 391H, 407A, 408A, 410A, 411B, C, 412A, C, 419c, 420B, C, c, 421c, 424B, C, c, 425B, 428B, 429B, frg, 431A, B, C, I, 436I, 437C, F, I, 439F, I, 440F, 442A, C, g, 444A, g, 447A, g, 449A, g, 453A, g, 454A, g, 455A, g, 456A, 462frg, 464frg, 468D, 470D, 473D, 476D, 478D, 482D, 483D, 484frg, 487D, 494D, V, 495D, frg, 503D, V, 510D,

V, 511D, V, 513D, V, 517frg, 518A, V, 526A, 529A, B, F, 531A, G, M, 533A, M, 534A, F, 535F, frg, 536M, 541A, F, k, 544k, 545A, frg, 548A, frg, 555A, D, frg, 557A, frg, 558A, D, frg, 559D, frg, 560A, D, 561A, 563D, 567D, Q, frg, 569Q, frg, 571D, Q, 573D, Q, frg, b, 574D, b, 577Q, 580D, Q, Z, frg, v, 581D, Z, b, v, 582D, b, v, 583Z, v, 588Q, Z, b, 590D, b, 594K, L, h, j, 596K, L, T, h, j, 598L, T, h, j, 601A, T, frg, h, j, 604A, H, frg, 607A, frg, 608A, M, frg, 609A, G, M, 610A, G, K, M, 611G, M, 612K, 613G, frg, 614G, K, L, frg, m, 615G, K, frg, 616frg, m, 617G, K, L, frg, m, 618G, 622K, frg, 623A, G, frg, 630F, G, K, 631frg, 648U, frg, 649U, frg, 650U, frg, 653U, 657frg, 658frg, 661Q, frg, 662frg, 666Q, frg, 668frg, 7 r. 5, 8: 9, 10, 17, 18, 21, 23, r. 4, 13, 16, 20, 21, 22, 23, 26E, 9: 11, 15, 25, 27, 28, r. 13, 14, 16, 18, 10: 10, r. 4, 5, 6, 12: 1, 7, 13 ii 11, 18, r. iii 1, 2, 13, 14 i 3, 6, ii 4, *ina*] 4 r. 26, 5 iii 6, 6: 78x, 567frg, 630frg, 666frg, 8 r. 25, *in*[*a* 6: 180frg, 181I, 292B, 455I, 483H, *in*]*a* 3 r. 8, 6: 105y, 341frg, 408C, 462k, 494frg, *i*[*na* 6: 249frg, 567Q, *i*]*na* 3: 12, *i-na* 1 r. 6, 12, 9 r. 20, 11 r. 8, 9, 13, 14, 14 i 7, 26, 30, ii 2, 5, 12, r. ii 9, *i-n*[*a* 1 r. 5, 9 r. 10, (*ina*) 6: 112E, 526B, [*ina* 1 r. 8, 4 r. 21, 6: 16G, 50n, 185frg, 202J, frg, 379frg, 461A, 614A, 655U, 8: 14, 21, 9 r. 25, 10: 7, 13 iii 7, 9, [*ina*] 6: 514V, 623K, [*in*]*a* 6: 390H, 407C, 483frg, 613K, [*i*]*na* 6: 13G, 573Q, [*i-na* 14 i 28, 31, 32, [*i-n*]*a* 11: 6, 14 ii 1,

irru "entrails, intestines": *ir-ri* 6: 553A, frg, 560A, 562D, *ir-ri-ku-nu* 6: 553D, *ir-ri-šú-nu* 6: 552A, frg, *ir-ri-*[*ku-nu*] 6: 560D, 561A, *ir-r*[*i-ku-nu*] 6: 561D, [*ir*]*-ri* 6: 553D, [*ir-ri*]*-šu-nu* 6: 552D,

isītu "tower": *i-si-ta-*[*te* 4 r. 2,

issēn "one": I-*en* 4 r. 5, 6, 6: 91A, I, d, 207C, O, 213J, O, frg, u, 224J, 558A, D, frg, 13 ii 18, r. iii 11, I-*e*[*n* 6: 91frg, 207frg, 224H,

issēt "one": I-*et* 6: 555A, D, frg, 559D, frg, 13 iii 12, I-*e*[*t* 6: 555frg,

issi "with": *is*]*-si-šu* 6: 176M, *is*]*-si-šú* 6: 242frg, *is-si*]*-ku-nu* 6: 175frg, *is-si*]*-šu* 6: 176frg, *is-si*]*-šú* 6: 152P, *is-si-ku-nu* 6: 9A, F, G, H, a, 12A, 42A, 64A, 96A, F, G, I, frg, 104E, y, 132A, E, frg, 175A, B, I, S, 281A, B, Y, frg, 286A, B, frg, 517A, V, *is-si-ku-n*[*u*] 6: 104frg, 281frg, *is-si-ku-*[*nu*] 6: 64W, 104frg, *is-si-k*[*u-nu* 6: 42frg, *is-si-k*[*u-nu*] 6: 286frg, *is-si-k*]*u-nu* 6: 64frg, *is-si-ni* 6: 351R, *is-si-šu* 6: 152E, 242C, 265M, *is-si-šú* 6: 52A, E, n, r, 91A, frg, d, 99A, 144E, 152A, frg, 171S, 176A, B, I, 242A, J, 245A, frg, 265A, B, F, i, 311A, C, 312A, C, *is-si-šú-nu* 5 iii 8, 6: 99E, F, frg, 148A, H, 176S, *is-si-*[*ku-nu* 6: 96frg, 175frg, *is-si-*[*šu* 6: 176frg, *is-si-*[*šú* 6: 152H, *is-s*[*i-ku-nu*] 6: 9T, *is-s*]*i-ku-nu* 6: 96frg, *is-s*]*i-šú* 6: 245frg, 311J, *is-*[*si-šú*] 6: 144frg, *i*[*s-si-ku-n*]*u* 6: 132O, *i*]*s-si-šú* 6: 245X, 13 ii 4, TA 2 i 10, 16, 19, 4 r. 5, 6, 5 i 2, 7, r. iv 15, 6: 3A, F, G, H, T, a, 4A, F, G, H, T, a, 6A, F, G, H, T, a, 9T, 55A, r, 69A, W, frg, 167A, B, E, I, P, S, 173A, G, I, M, P, S, frg, 202J, 210J, frg, 214J, u, 273A, frg, 318A, C, J, N, 320B, C, J, 321B, C, N, c, 322B, C, N, c, 337frg, 343F, 346B, F, R, w, 366R, frg, z, 481D, 498D, V, q, 530A, B, F, G, frg, 539A, k, 552A, D, frg, 553A, D, frg, 8: 3, 4, 5, 7, 8, 11, r. 2, 10: 12, 11 r. 12, TA 13 ii 14, TA] 10: 14, TA] 6: 498q, T[A 4 r. 5, 6: 214O, 273B, 337A, 343frg, 366frg, T[A] 6: 320N, 343frg, T]A 4 r. 6, 5 iii 1, 6: 210C, frg, 343w, 552frg, 13 iii 11, 12, [*is*]*-si-šu* 6: 91G, [*is-si*]*-šú* 13 ii 3, [*is-si*]*-šú-nu* 6: 99I, [*is-si-ka* 13 iii 19, [*is-si-šú*]*-nu* 6: 148P, [*is-si-š*]*u* 6: 91frg, [*is-si-š*]*ú* 6: 91frg, [TA 4 r. 4, 6, 5 i 2, 3, 8: 23, 10: 1, [TA] 2 iii 25, 6: 544A, 13 iii 15, [T]A 2 i 14, iii 24, 6: 4G, 320A, 11: 3, 4, 5,

issu "woman; wife": MÍ 6: 617G, K, L, frg, m, MÍ.MEŠ 2 v 9, 12, MÍ.MEŠ-*ku-nu* 6: 558A, D, frg, 564D, 568D, Q, frg, 571D, frg, 581D, Z, b, v, 585b, v, 591h, 596T, h, 606A, frg, 624G, 636F, frg, 638A, frg, 647A, U, frg, MÍ.MEŠ-*ku-*[*nu* 6: 638frg, MÍ.MEŠ]*-ku-nu* 6: 585Q, 589Q, 591Q, MÍ.M[EŠ-*ku-nu*] 6: 571Q, 596j, MÍ.M[EŠ-*ku-n*]*u* 6: 585Z, MÍ.[MEŠ-*ku-nu* 6: 638frg, M[Í.MEŠ-*ku-nu* 6: 591K, M]Í.MEŠ-*ku-nu* 6: 585frg, 636frg, 638frg,

iṣ qāti "handcuffs": *iṣ—qa-ti*] 9: 15,

iṣṣūru "bird": MUŠEN 6: 582D, b, v, 13 iii 2,

išātu "fire": IZI 6: 534A, F, M, 608A, L, M, frg, 621G, K, 11 r. 13, IZ]I 6: 608K, I[ZI 6: 621m,

išdu "foundation": *i*]*š-di-šu* 4 r. 28,

iškuru "wax": DUH.LÀL 6: 608A, M, frg,

itti "with": *it-ti* 9: 5, 14 i 8, *it-ti-ku-nu* 5 iv 1, 6: 458A, B, *it-ti-ku-n*]*u* 6: 458frg, *it-t*[*i* 9: 23,

kabātu "to be weighty; (D) to honour": *kab-tu* 6: 433B, *kab-tú* 4 r. 16, *ka*[*b-tu*] 6: 433I, *ka*[*b-t*]*ú* 6: 433A, *k*]*ab-bi-da* 6: 335B, [*kab-ta-at*] 1 r. 6,

kabsu "young sheep": *kab-su* 6: 551A, frg, *k*]*ab-su* 6: 551D,

kabsutu "young ewe": *kab-su-tú* 6: 551A, D, frg, *kab-s*]*u-tú* 6: 551frg,

kabūtu "dung": *ka-bu-ut* 2 iv 7,

kakku "weapon": GIŠ.TUKUL.MEŠ-*šú-nu* 5 iv 5, GIŠ.TUKUL.MEŠ-*šú-nu*] 6: 464frg, GIŠ.TUKUL.MEŠ-[*šú* 6: 518A, GIŠ.TUKUL.ME[Š-*šú* 6: 518V,

kakkubu "star": MUL.MEŠ 6: 428B, frg,

kal mūši "nighttime": *kal* MI 6: 199frg, 201 *kal* M[I 6:199J, 201. *kal m*[*u-ši* 6:201J *kal*] *mu-ši* 6:201C

kal ūmi "daytime": *kal* UD-*me* 6: 198frg, 201J, frg, *k*[*al* UD-*me*] 6: 198J, *k*]*al* UD-*me* 6: 198Y,

kalbu "dog": UR.KU 6: 482D, 484D, UR.KU.MEŠ 6: 451A, g, UR.[KU 6: 484frg,

kallumu "to show, present": *ú-kal-lim*]*-ú-ka-nu-ni* 3: 6, *ú-kal-lim-ku-nu* 6: 432B, *ú-kal-lim-ku-*[*nu* 6: 432frg, *ú-kal-lim-ú-ka-nu-*[*ni*] 6: 63W, 93frg, *ú-kal-lim-ú-*[*ka-nu-ni*] 6: 93frg, *ú-kal-lim-u-ka*]*-nu-ni* 6: 93frg, *ú-kal-lim-u-ka-nu*]*-u-ni* 6: 93frg, *ú-kal-lim-u-ka-nu-ni* 6: 63A, 93A, *ú-kal-lim-u-ka-*[*nu-ni*] 6: 93F, *ú-kal-lim-u-šú-nu-*[*ni* 6: 370z, *ú-kal-lim-*[*ku-nu*] 6: 432I, *ú-kal-lim-*[*u-ka-nu-ni*] 6: 93G, [*ú*]*-kal-lim-k*[*a*]*-nu-*[*ni* 6: 60W, [*ú-kal*]*-lim-u-ka-nu-ni* 6: 60n, [*ú-kal-l*]*im-u-ka-nu-u-ni* 6: 93I,

kalmutu "louse": *kal-mu-tú* 6: 599A,

kalu "all": DÙ.A.BI 6: 89A, G, I, DÙ.A.B[I] 6: 89d, [DÙ].A.BI 6: 89frg, DÙ-*šú-nu* 6: 23A, G, frg, 31A, E, frg, 32A, E, G, frg, 33A, E, frg, 34A, E, frg, 35E, frg, 36A, E, frg, 37frg, 38A, 39A, frg, 40A, E, frg, DÙ-*šú-nu*] 10: 2, DÙ-*šú-n*[*u* 6: 40frg, DÙ-*šú-*[*nu* 6: 35A, DÙ]*-šú-nu* 6: 23U, D[Ù]*-šú-nu* 6: 31G, D[Ù]*-šú-*[*nu* 6: 33G, *ka-l*[*i* 14 i 8, [DÙ]*-šú-nu* 9: 2,

kalû "to hold back": *tak-la-a* 6: 91I, *ta-kal-la-a* 6: 91A, *ta-kal-*[*la-a*] 6: 91frg, *ta-*[*ka*]*l-la-a* 6: 91d,

kalzu "group of people": *kal*]*-zi* 6: 218u, *kal-za-a-ni* 6: 218C, H, e, *kal-za-ni* 6: 218J, *kal-zi* 6: 217J, 218H, J, *ka*]*l-zi* 6: 217frg,

kamānu "honeycomb": *ka-ma-a-ni* 6: 594T, h, j, *ka-m*[*a-a-ni* 6: 594L,

kamāsu "to kneel": *li-šak-mì-is-an-n[a-ši* 9 r. 25,
kamiš "like a captive": *ka-mì-iš* 4 r. 21,
kanāku "to seal": *ka-nik-u-ni* 6: 408A,
kanāšunu "you": *ka-na-šú-nu* 6: 606A, frg,
kapādu "to plan, contrive": *ta-kap-pu-d[a-a-ni]* 10 r. 6, *ú-šak-pa-ad-u-ka-nu-ni* 6: 322c, *ú-šak-pa-du-ka-nu-u-ni* 6: 322N, 336frg, *ú-šak-pa-du-u-ka-(nu)-u-ni* 6: 322C, *ú-šak-pa-d]u-k[a-nu-u-ni* 6: 336frg, *ú-[šak-pa-du-ka]-nu-u-ni* 6: 336F, *[ú]-šá-ak-pa-du-ka-nu-ni* 6: 322B,
kappu "wing": *kap-pi* 6: 627F, K, frg,
kapru "village": URU.ŠE.MEŠ-*šú* 5 iii 25, 29,
kaqqudu "head": SAG.DU 2 i 21, 22, 23, 25, S[AG.D]U 2 i 27,
kaqquru "earth, ground, area": *kaq]-qar* 6: 527M, *kaq]-qa-ri* 6: 422A, *kaq-qar* 6: 385A, D, s, 422C, 471D, 653U, 657frg, *kaq-qar-ku-nu* 6: 528A, F, *kaq-qa-ri* 6: 422c, 544A, *kaq-qa-ru* 2 i 5, *kaq-qu-ru* 6: 527A, B, KI 2 vi 6, KI.TIM 1 r. 8, 13, 2 iv 8, 4 r. 16, 5 iv 8, 6: 21G, U, 40A, frg, 42A, 419B, C, c, 440g, 472D, 476D, 483D, 488D, frg, 523G, 9: 2, r. 7, 8, 11, 14, 15, 11 r. 7, 9, KI.TIM] 11 r. 10, K[I 6: 541k, K[I.TIM 6: 523B, TIM.KI 6: 40E, TIM.[KI 6: 42E, *[kaq]-qar* 6: 527F, *[ka]q-qu-ru* 6: 527G, [K]I.TIM 6: 523A,
karāku "to roll": *kar-ku-u-ni* 6: 552A, D, frg, *kar-[ku-u-ni]* 6: 552frg, *li-kar-ku* 6: 554A, D, frg, *li-kar-[ku]* 6: 554frg,
karānu "wine": GEŠTIN 6: 560A, GEŠTIN.MEŠ 6: 560D,
karāru "to throw": *i-kar-ru-r[u]* 11 r. 13, *ka-[ar-ru]* 2 i 28, *ta-[kar-ra-ra-a-ni* 6: 412A,
karṣu "calumny": *kar-ṣi* 6: 232B, 323C, N, c, 341F, frg, *kar-ṣi-šú* 6: 332B, frg, *kar-ṣi-šú-nu* 6: 270A, frg, i, *kar-ṣi-[šú* 6: 332frg, *kar-ṣ]i-šú-nu* 6: 270F, *k[ar-ṣi* 6: 341p,
karšu "belly": *kar-ši* 6: 484D, frg,
karû "to be short": *li-kar-ru* 14 ii 20,
kasû "to bind": *lik-si* 6: 454A, frg, l, *li-ik-si* 6: 454g,
kašādu "to reach, chase": *ka-šu-du-ni* 6: 576Q, *ka-šu-du-u-ni* 6: 576D, *ka-šu-d[u-ni* 6: 576v, *k[a-šu-du-ni* 6: 576b, *lik-šu-ud-[su]* 14 ii 18, *li-ik-ta-ši-du-ku-nu* 6: 478D, *lu-ka-ši-du* 6: 578D, b, v,
kāru "port of trade": KAR.MEŠ 5 iii 18, KAR.MEŠ-*šú* 5 iii 25,
kāsu "cup": GÚ.ZI 6: 154P, G[Ú.ZI] 6: 154frg, *ka-si* 6: 154E,
kāšunu "you": *ka-a-šú-nu* 6: 636F, *ka-a-š]ú-nu* 6: 636frg, *ka-a-[šú-nu* 6: 636frg, *ka-šú-nu* 6: 577D, v, 583D, Q, Z, frg, v, 618G, frg, *ka-šú-[nu* 6: 618m, *ka-šu-nu* 6: 134frg, *ka-šu-n[u* 6: 618frg, *ka-šu-[n]u* 6: 577b, *ka-š]ú-nu* 6: 134A, *ka-[šú-nu* 6: 618frg, *k]a-šú-nu* 6: 564D, 618K, *k]a-šu-nu* 6: 583b, 618L,
kânu see *kuānu,*
kettu "truth": *ket-te* 6: 98F, 422c, *ket-ti* 6: 51A, W, r, 98A, I, frg, 422C, *ket-tu* 6: 96A, frg, *ket-t]u* 6: 96frg, *ket-[tu* 6: 96F, *kit-ti* 4 r. 22, *k[et-ti]* 6: 422B, *k[et-tu* 6: 96frg, *k[et-t]i* 6: 422A,
KI.MIN (reading uncert.) "ditto": KI.MIN 2 iv 31, vi 7, 8, 9, 10, 11, 12, 13, 14, 15, 16, 17, 18, 19, 20, 21, 22, 23, 6: 526A, B, 527F, 537k, 547frg, 560D, 563D, 567D, 568D, frg, 570D, 573D, b, 576D, Q, b, 579D, 582D, 585D, 588D, 591D, 594D, 599j, 601K, T, h, j, 606frg, 612M, m, 637frg, 649U, frg, KI.M[IN 6: 594D, KI.[MIN 6: 563D, K[I.MIN 6: 599A, K[I.M]IN 6: 591D, [KI.M]IN 6: 555D, [KI].MIN 6: 606frg, [K]I.MIN 6: 568frg,
kibirtu "horizon; quarter": *kib-ra-a-ti* 6: 472D, *kib-ra-a-t]i* 14 i 22,
kiniš "truthfully": *ki-n[i-iš* 14 ii 9, *[ki-niš* 14 ii 4,
kippu "snare": *kip-pi* 6: 588Q, b, *kip-p[i]* 6: 588Z,
kiriu "orchard": GIŠ.SAR.MEŠ 6: 275A, B, frg,
kiṣru "joint": *ki-ṣir* 6: 446A, g, *ki-[ṣir* 6: 446l,
kišdu "attainment": *[k]i-šid* 6: 416A,
kišpi "sorcery": *kiš-pi* 6: 264A, B, F, frg, i,
kiššatu "totality, universe": *kiš-šat* 9 r. 7, *kiš-šá-t[i]* 14 i 21, *k]iš-šat* 4 r. 16, ŠÚ 6: 1A, F, H, T, a, 2A, F, H, a, 11: 2,
kiššūtu "world dominion, hegemony": *kiš-šu-t[i* 14 ii 12, *kiš-šu-t[ú]* 14 i 9,
kittu see *kettu,*
kīma "when, after, if": *ki-ma* 5 iv 4, 6: 46A, frg, 252A, B, I, 421B, 463frg, 471D, 11 r. 11, *ki-[ma* 6: 360R, *k[i-ma* 6: 360frg, *k]i-ma* 6: 360frg, *[ki]-ma* 6: 421A, *[k]i-ma* 6: 83H,
kî "as": GIM 1 e. 18, 2 i 8, 9, r. iv 5, 11, v 10, 6: 421C, *ki* 6: 580v, *ki]-i* 6: 537frg, 579frg, *ki-i* 1: 3, 2 i 16, 25, r. v 2, 5 iii 26, 30, 6: 177A, G, I, frg, 181A, I, frg, 182I, frg, 195J, 268A, frg, i, 356R, 385A, D, s, 409A, 421c, 528A, B, F, 530A, B, F, G, frg, 531A, B, 534A, F, 537F, frg, k, 540F, k, 547A, frg, 548A, 551A, frg, 555A, D, frg, 560D, 568D, frg, 570D, Q, 576D, b, v, 579D, b, v, 580frg, b, 582D, frg, v, 588D, 593h, j, 594K, L, j, 601A, K, T, frg, h, j, 603A, H, K, T, frg, h, j, 604A, H, L, 608A, M, 612G, K, M, m, 613G, 616G, m, 617G, K, frg, m, 619A, G, K, m, 621G, K, m, 622G, K, m, 623K, 626K, 629A, F, G, L, 630A, F, G, L, 631A, 636F, 637A, frg, 638A, 641U, 643A, U, frg, 646U, frg, 652U, 9 r. 3, *ki-[i* 6: 356A, 636frg, *k[i]-i* 6: 613A, *k[i-i* 6: 409C, 540A, 593K, *k]i-i* 2 i 32, 6: 528G, M, 563D, 582b, 616frg, 619frg, 637frg, *[ki]-i* 6: 540frg, 586v, 616L, 617L, 629K, 641frg, *[ki-i* 6: 561A, 610A, 8 r. 13, *[ki-i]* 9: 3, *[k]i-i* 6: 268B, 608G, 610H, 613K, 616K, 617frg, 638frg, 641A, frg, 646frg, 656frg,
kuānu "to be firm, true": *ke]-na-a-te* 6: 236N, *ke-na-a-te* 6: 97A, F, 236A, J, X, 502V, *ke-na-a-ti* 6: 236C, 502D, q, *ke-na-a-[te* 6: 97I, *ke-na-te* 6: 97frg, *ke-nu-ni* 2 iii 24, *ke-n]a-a-ti* 6: 236frg, *kun-nu* 5: 420E, *ku-un* 14 ii 9, *ku-u]n* 1: 5, *ku-[nu]-ni* 2 v 3, *k]e-na-[a-t]i* 6: 502A, *ta-kun* 6: 333B, *ta-[kun]* 6: 333frg, *[ke-nu-ti]* 11 r. 3, *[ku-un* 14 i 25,
kullu "to hold": *tu-kal-la-a-ni* 6: 97A, F, I, *tu-kal-la-ni* 6: 97frg, *tu-kal-[la-a-ni* 6: 97frg,
kullumu see *kallumu,*
kunukku "seal": NA_4.KIŠIB 6: 405A, 407C, i A, F, G, H, T, frg, iiiA, F, H, I, NA_4.KI[ŠIB 6: 407A, [NA_4.K]IŠIB 6: i a,
kupru "pitch": *ku-up-ri* 6: 587D, frg, v, *ku-up-ru* 6: 490D, *ku-[up-ru* 6: 490frg, *k]u-up-ru* 6: 490frg, *[ku-up-r]i* 6: 587Q, *[ku-u]p-ri* 6: 587b,
kursinnu "knuckle": *[ku]r-sin-nu-šu* 2 i 26,
kurummatu "food": ŠUKU.MEŠ 5 iv 16,
kusāpu "bread": NINDA.MEŠ 6: 479D, 560D, 567D,
kussiu "throne": GIŠ.GU.ZA 6: 47A, 56A, frg, r, 70A, S, W, 85A, G, I, d, 87A, G, I, d, 224J, f, 227H, J, X, f, 248A, frg, 253A, B, I, 303A, B, C, frg, 317A, C, J, 362R, frg, 659frg, GIŠ.GU.ZA-*e* 6:

47E, GIŠ.GU.ZA-*šú-nu* 14 i 25, GIŠ.GU].ZA 6: 362z, GIŠ.G[U.ZA 6: 70frg, GIŠ.G[U.ZA] 6: 47frg, GIŠ.G]U.ZA 6: 87frg, 224X, GIŠ].GU.ZA 6: 56n, GI]Š.GU.ZA 6: 362frg, [GIŠ.GU.Z]A 6: 253frg, [GIŠ.G]U.ZA-*ku-n*[*u* 6: 659frg, [G]IŠ.GU.ZA 6: 248frg,

kuzippu "garment": *ku-zip-pi* 5 iv 16,

kūdunu "mule": ANŠE.GÌR.NUN 2 v 11, ANŠE.GÌR. NUN.NA 6: 276B, frg, ANŠE.GÌR.NUN.N[A 6: 537A, ANŠE.*k*[*u-di-ni* 6: 537frg, k,

kūmu "instead": *ku-mu-šu* 6: 56frg, *ku-mu-šú* 6: 56A, r, 70A, S, *ku-um* 6: 256A, B, I, i, 445A, g, l, 532A, G, *ku-u*]*m* 6: 532K,

la "not": *la* 1: 5, e. 15, 17, r. 2, 4, 11, 2 i 10, 11, 12, 17, 20, 21, 29, iii 9, 10, 24, 25, r. iv 3, 20, v 1, 02, 4, 3: 2, 4, 6, 11, r. 6, 4 r. 4, 7, 8, 22, 5 i 8, 9, r. iii 3, 5, 11, 12, 13, 14, 17, 28, iv 2, 9, 6: 50A, E, frg, n, 51A, E, 52A, E, n, r, 53A, E, W, n, r, 54W, n, r, 60A, W, frg, r, 61A, frg, 65A, W, frg, 67A, S, W, 68A, W, 73A, H, S, x, 74A, H, 75A, H, x, 81A, G, H, I, x, 82A, G, H, I, x, 85G, 91A, I, frg, d, 97A, F, I, frg, 98A, E, F, frg, 99A, E, F, I, frg, 100E, F, frg, 107E, frg, y, 108E, frg, y, 109E, frg, 110E, 111frg, 120A, E, frg, 122A, frg, o, 125E, frg, o, 136A, E, O, t, 138A, E, O, 139E, frg, t, 140A, E, 141A, E, P, 143P, frg, t, 144frg, t, 145E, 146E, P, frg, t, 148E, H, P, frg, 151E, H, P, 152E, P, frg, 158A, E, P, S, 160A, E, P, S, 161A, E, P, S, 168A, E, I, M, P, S, 170A, G, I, M, P, S, frg, 172A, G, M, S, frg, 178I, S, 179A, B, I, M, S, frg, 183frg, 187I, frg, 191J, frg, 192J, Y, 193J, frg, 194J, frg, 195J, frg, 196J, frg, 201frg, 202J, 205J, frg, 20 frg, 227H, f, 228C, J, X, f, 230A, C, J, X, frg, f, 231J, X, frg, f, 232J, N, X, frg, f, 233A, C, J, X, frg, f, 234A, 235A, J, X, 236A, N, X, f, 244A, X, frg, 245A, X, frg, 246A, X, frg, 248A, frg, 251A, B, I, 252A, B, I, 253A, B, I, 254A, B, I, 255A, I, M, 256A, I, M, 257A, I, M, i, 259A, B, i, 268A, B, M, frg, i, 271A, B, F, 278A, B, Y, frg, 280A, frg, 281A, Y, 282A, B, Y, 290A, 291A, 292A, C, H, 293A, B, C, 295A, C, H, 301H, 305B, C, frg, 306A, B, C, frg, 307A, C, 310A, C, 311A, C, J, 312A, C, 313A, C, J, 314A, C, J, 315A, C, J, 317A, C, J, 325B, C, N, c, 333B, 344A, F, R, frg, w, 349A, B, F, w, 350R, 356B, frg, 358R, frg, 363B, R, frg, z, 368frg, z, 387D, 388A, 389A, D, 392H, 409C, 415A, C, 418C, 433A, B, I, 447A, g, 455A, frg, k, 479D, 486D, frg, 488D, 501D, V, q, 502D, V, q, 507D, 509D, V, frg, 521G, 529A, F, 530A, F, G, frg, 532A, F, M, 534M, 535F, 541F, frg, k, 542F, frg, 556A, D, frg, 558A, D, 559D, frg, 579D, b, v, 580D, b, v, 581Z, frg, b, v, 621A, G, K, L, frg, 639A, frg, 640A, frg, 650U, ii A, F, G, H, I, frg, a, d, iv A, F, H, Y, 7: 7, 10, r. 2, 8: 12, 16, 20, r. 5, 7, 13, 15, 17, 27E, 9: 13, 18, 21, 30, r. 5, 16, 10: 4, r. 6, 7, 11 r. 7, 13 ii 3, 4, r. iii 3, 14, 15, 14 i 5, 30, ii 4, 15, 22, r. ii 6, *la*] 4 r. 9, 6: 280frg, 281B, 8 r. 3, *la-a* 6: 143E, *l*[*a* 6: 50W, 51n, 54frg, 61frg, 81a, 108frg, 125frg, 149A, 168I, 178G, 179frg, 187F, 206O, 234X, 246frg, 259M, 292B, 344frg, 358A, 455g, 502A, 521frg, 530B, 534A, 558frg, 621K, 650frg, iv B, *l*[*a*] 6: 234frg, *l*]*a* 2 iv 30, 33, 6: 54E, 158B, 161M, 178A, M, frg, 193frg, 202frg, 234J, 236J, 248X, 251frg, 301C, 350F, 356R, 363frg, 387s, 388s, 460B, 529G, M, 650frg, 8 r. 24, NU 6: 418B, (*la*) 6: 54A, 232A, 532B, [*la* 2 i 17, 3: 3, 4, 6: 100I, 111y, 120O, 122E, O, frg, 140t, 145P, 194F, 280Y, 536M, 8: 13, 17, 20, r. 10, 12, 25, 14 i 24, [*la*] 6: 152A, [*l*]*a* 1: 14, 6: 98I, 100A, 107frg, 168E, 195frg, 231A, 246frg, 255B, 256B, 257B, 278B, 280B, 305A, 556D,

labāšu "to dress": *li-la-biš* 6: 451A, l, *l*[*i-la-biš*] 6: 451g, [*li-la-bi*]*š* 6: 451frg,

labīru "old": *la-bi-ri* 5 iii 30, *la-bi-*[*ri* 5 iii 26,

labû "to surround": *lu-šal-bu-ku*]*-nu* 6: 621frg, *lu-šal-bu-ku-nu* 6: 621G, K, L, *lu-šal-*[*bu-ku-nu*] 6: 621frg, *l*]*u-šal-bu-ku-nu* 6: 621A,

lakû "baby": *la-ke-e* 6: 438F, I,

lamādu "to learn": *tu-šal-mad-a-ni* 6: 388A, *tu-šal-mad-a-*[*ni*] 6: 388s, *t*]*u-šal-ma-da-ni* 6: 388D,

lamānu "to be bad, evil": *lem-nu* 5 iv 11, 6: 493D, *lem-nu-ti* 1 r. 2, *li-lam-mín-ma* 6: 418C, *li-lam-mìn* 4 r. 25, [*li-la*]*m-mín-ma* 6: 418B,

laplaptu "parching thirst": *lap-lap-tu* 6: 653U,

laššu "is not": *la-á*]*š-šu-u-ni* 6: 537F,

lazāzu "to persist": *la-zu* 5 iv 4, 6: 462frg,

lānu "figure": *la-an-ku*]*-nu* 6: 610T, *la-an-ku-nu* 6: 610A, G, M, *la-an-ku-n*]*u* 6: 610K, *la-an-k*[*u-nu* 6: 610frg, *la-ni-ku-nu* 5 iv 16,

lemēnu see *lamānu,*

lemuttu "evil (intentions), misfortune": HUL-*ti* 6: 66A, HUL-*tim* 6: 66W, 105E, frg, y, 365frg, 501q, HUL-*t*[*im*] 6: 105frg, HUL-[*t*]*i* 6: 365R, H[UL-*x* 6: 365B, H]UL-*ti* 6: 414A, H]UL-*tim* 6: 105frg, *le-m*[*u-ut-ti* 14 ii 24, MÍ.HUL 1: 8, 6: 414C, 501D, V, MÍ. HUL-*ti* 9 r. 5,

lēšu "dough": *le-e-še* 6: 447g, *le-ši* 6: 447A, *l*[*e-šu*] 6: 447A,

libbu "heart": *lib-ba-ku-nu* 6: 152A, *lib-bu* 6: 641frg, *li*[*b-bu* 6: 641frg, ŠÀ 1 e. 15, 2 i 10, 19, 31, r. vi 5, 4 r. 5, 6, 5 iii 16, 17, 24, 28, 6: 55A, 69W, frg, 166E, P, 202J, frg, 273frg, 318C, 320B, C, J, 321B, C, c, 322B, C, c, 358R, 488frg, 513D, V, 530A, B, F, G, 531A, 541A, F, 555frg, 558D, frg, 560D, 561D, 563D, 594L, h, j, 596L, T, h, j, 612K, 615K, 622frg, 623K, frg, 8: 9, r. 2, 11 r. 12, 12: 1, 13 ii 18, ŠÀ-*ba-*[*ku-nu* 6: 642U, ŠÀ-*bi* 6: 69A, 214J, u, 273A, 292A, H, 318J, N, 320A, N, 321N, 322N, 337frg, 358frg, 407A, 529A, B, F, 530frg, 541k, 555A, D, 558A, 560A, 561A, 596K, 623A, G, 9 r. 16, 14 ii 12, r. ii 9, ŠÀ-*bi*]*-ku-nu* 6: 51E, 98E, 224H, ŠÀ-*bi-ku*]*-nu* 8: 21, ŠÀ-*bi-ku-nu* 6: 51A, n, r, 53A, E, n, r, 98A, 169A, I, 207C, J, 213J, u, 224J, 310C, 456A, 8: 18, ŠÀ-*bi-ku-nu*] 6: 461A, ŠÀ-*bi-ku-n*]*u* 6: 224f, ŠÀ-*bi-k*]*u-nu* 5 iv 3, 6: 98frg, ŠÀ-*bi-ni* 9: 25, ŠÀ-*bi-ni*] 9: 4, ŠÀ-*bi-šú* 2 iv 3, 3 r. 1, 6: 66A, W, 67A, W, ŠÀ-*bi-šú-nu* 1: 5, 6: 106E, frg, 272F, frg, 357R, frg, 365R, ŠÀ-*bi-šú-n*[*u* 6: 106frg, ŠÀ-*bi-šú-(nu)* 6: 272A, ŠÀ-*bu* 6: 641A, frg, ŠÀ-*b*[*i* 6: 390H, 594K, ŠÀ-*b*[*i-ku-nu*] 6: 185I, ŠÀ-*b*]*i* 6: 320A, ŠÀ-*b*]*i-ku-nu* 6: 169M, 185frg, 456frg, ŠÀ-*b*]*i-šú-*[*nu*] 6: 357A, ŠÀ-*ku-nu* 6: 152E, 169S, 185frg, 213frg, 387D, 470D, ŠÀ-*k*[*u-nu* 6: 213O, ŠÀ-*šú* 2 iii 15, ŠÀ-*šú-nu* 5 iii 17, 6: 272B, 357B, 365frg, ŠÀ-*šú-*[*nu* 6: 106y, ŠÀ-[*ba-k*]*a* 2 iii 24, ŠÀ-[*bi* 9: 24, ŠÀ-[*bi*] 6: 321A, ŠÀ-[*b*]*i* 6: 321N, ŠÀ]-*bi* 6: 320N, Š[À 6: 358A, Š[À-*bi-ku-nu*] 6: 51W, Š[À-*x* 6: 106A, 169P, Š]À 6: 292B, 318B, 555frg, 594T, 622frg, 8: 18, Š]À-*ba-ku-nu* 3: 4, Š]À-*bi* 6: 622G, Š]À-*bi-šú-nu* 6: 272frg, Š]À-*ku-nu* 6: 456B, [*li*]*b-bi-ku-nu* 6: 642A, [ŠÀ-*bi*]*-ku-nu* 6: 642frg,

libittu "brick": SIG_4 2 i 5, 6: 527A, B, F, G,

liblibbu "grandson": ŠÀ—ŠÀ-*bi-šá* 8: 11,

lihšu "whisper": *li-ih-šu* 6: 500D, *li-ih-šú* 6: 500V, *li-ih-*[*šu*] 6: 500q, [*li-ih*]*-šu* 6: 500q,

limmu "eponym year": *lim-mu* 6: 665Q, frg, [*lim-m*]*u* 6: 665frg,
littūtu "extreme old age": *lit-tu-*[*ti* 6: 416A, *li-tu-tu* 2 v 12,
lu "let, may, be it": *lu* 2 i 27, 28, 35, iii 21, r. iv 16, 20, 22, 23, v 9, 11, 5 iii 15, iv 2, 6: 76A, H, 77A, a, 78A, a, 79A, G, a, 111A, E, frg, y, 112E, 113A, frg, 115E, frg, 116E, frg, 147P, frg, 162A, E, P, S, 163A, B, E, I, P, S, 164A, E, I, P, S, 165P, 166P, 180frg, 181I, 182frg, 198J, frg, 199J, frg, 201frg, 216C, J, O, 218C, J, 219H, 220C, 221J, f, 222C, J, f, 238A, B, C, J, N, X, 297A, B, C, H, 299B, C, 300C, frg, 330B, frg, 338F, R, 339F, R, 374B, frg, 375frg, 403A, 404A, 445g, 447A, g, 484D, 485D, 489D, frg, 490D, frg, 491D, frg, 492D, V, 532A, B, F, 572frg, 598L, T, 615L, 640A, frg, 648A, U, frg, 654U, 662frg, 7: 1, 14 ii 17, *lu*] 6: 485D, *lu-u* 5 i 5, 6, 7, 6: 76x, 77H, 78H, 79H, I, x, 111frg, 112frg, 113frg, 115frg, 118A, frg, 147H, 163A, M, 164A, I, 182I, 201J, 216J, u, 217J, O, 218H, J, O, 219J, 220H, J, 221H, J, 222H, J, 223J, 363frg, 402D, 8 r. 20, 21, 22, 13 iii 1, 2, *lu-ú* 9: 5, 6, 7, 12, 14, 29, 36, *lu-ú*] 9: 7, 28, *l*[*u* 6: 147P, 164S, 572Q, *l*[*u*] 6: 529A, *l*]*u* 6: 162P, 198frg, 201frg, 300B, 339F, 572Z, frg, *l*]*u-u* 6: 164M, 199J, 201J, 375B, [*lu* 6: 238A, J, X, 460B, [*lu*] 2 iii 21, 6: 572D, [*lu*]-*u* 6: 118o, 199J, [*lu*]-*ú* 9: 36, [*lu-u* 13 iii 11, 12, [*lu-u*] 8 r. 23, [*l*]*u* 2 i 35, 6: 79H, 181frg, 339frg, 529F,
lubultu "clothing": *lu-bul-*[*ta-ku-nu*] 6: 374frg, *lu-bu-uš-ti-šú-nu* 2 iv 15, TÚG.*lu-bul-ta-ku-n*[*u*] 6: 374B,
ma "thus": *ma* 6: 323c, 325c, *ma*]-*a* 6: 342frg, *ma-a* 2 v 14, 5 i 11, 6: 203J, 204J, O, frg, 232B, 291A, B, C, 292A, B, C, H, 294C, H, 295C, 323C, N, 325C, 326B, 330B, frg, 333B, 334B, 335A, B, frg, 341F, R, p, 342F, frg, 343B, F, p, 351A, B, F, 358B, frg, 365R, frg, z, 8 r. 19, *m*[*a-a* 6: 342B, R, p, *m*]*a-a* 2 iv 27, v 14, [*ma*]-*a* 6: 330frg, 343frg, 13 iii 5, [*ma-a*] 13 iii 6, [*m*]*a-a* 6: 341frg,
ma'ādu "to be much": *ma-a'-du-te* 6: 147H, *ma-a'-d*[*u-ti*] 6: 147frg,
magāru "to agree": *mug-ra* 14 ii 10, *ta-ma-gúr-a-ni* 6: 308A, *ta-*[*ma-gúr-a-ni* 6: 308B, *t*[*a-ma-gúr-a-ni* 6: 308frg, [*ta*]-*ma-g*[*úr-a*]-*ni* 6: 308C,
mahar "before": *ma-har* 1 r. 6, 4 r. 17, 24, 11: 6, 14 i 2,
mahāhu "to dissolve": *i-mah-ha-hu*]-*u-ni* 6: 609frg, *i-mah-ha-hu-u-ni* 6: 609A, frg, *i-mah-h*]*a-hu-u-ni* 6: 609K, L, *i-ma-ha-hu-u-ni* 6: 609M,
mahāru "to accept; to oppose": *im-hur* 6: 484D, *lim-hu-ru* 2 v 10, *mah*]-*rat* 6: 297A, *mah-rat* 6: 297C, H, *mah-rat-u-ni* 6: 296A, C, *mah-ru* 6: 488D, *ma*]*h-rat-u-ni* 6: 296B, [*mah-rat-u-n*]*i* 6: 296H,
mahāṣu "to strike, fight": *lim-ha-ṣu-ku-nu* 6: 474D, *šam-hi-ṣa* 6: 342frg, *šá-an-hi-ṣa* 6: 342F, *šá-an-hi-*[*ṣa* 6: 342frg, *ta-mah-ha-ṣu-u-ni* 5 iii 16, *tu-šam-ha-ṣa-a-ni* 6: 326C, *tu-šam-ha-ṣa-ni* 6: 326B, *tu-šam-h*]*a-ṣa-a-ni* 6: 326c, (*tu*)-*šam-*[*ha-ṣa-a-ni*] 6: 326N,
mahhû "ecstatic": LÚ.*mah-he-e* 6: 117frg, LÚ.*mah-*[*he-e* 6: 117A, [LÚ.*ma*]*h-he-e* 6: 117o,
mahru "front": *mah-ri* 1 e. 16, 2 vi 19,
maiālu "sleeping place": *ma-a-a-al-šú-nu* 2 iv 16,
mala "as much/many as": *ma-la* 6: 5F, G, H, 80G, I, 164B, E, P, 340F, frg, 473D, 511D, V, 526A, B, 573Q, 616frg, m, 618G, 9: 3, 17, 21, 33, 14 ii 12, *ma-l*[*a* 6: 5a, 618frg, *ma-l*]*a* 6: 573frg, *m*[*a-la* 9: 29, [*m*]*a-la* 6: 80H, *mal* 6: 5A, T, 80A, a, x, 118E, frg, 164A, S, 223H, J, *ma*[*l* 6: 164M, 223f, *ma*]*l* 6: 223C,
malāku "to advise, counsel": *ta-mal-lik-a-šú-u-ni* 6: 234J, *ta-mal-lik-a-š*[*ú-u-ni*] 6: 234X, *ta-mal-li-ka-šú-u-n*[*i*] 6: 234f, *ta-mal-l*[*ik-a-šú-u-ni*] 6: 53W, *ta-mal-*[*lik-a-šú-u-ni*] 6: 234frg, *ta-ma-lik-a-šú-u-ni* 6: 53n, 234A, C, N, *ta-*[*mal*]-*li-ka-šú-u-ni* 6: 53A, [*ta-mal-l*]*ik-a-ni* 8: 22,
malû "to be full": *li-mal-la* 6: 426B, *li-mal-li-ku-nu* 6: 522G, *li-*[*mal-li* 6: 426C, frg,
mamma "anyone": *mam-ma* 9: 12, 38,
mannu "who(ever)": *man-nu* 8: 9, 12, 14 ii 8, [*man-nu* 11 r. 5,
manû "to assign, hand over": *lim-nu-ku-nu* 6: 468frg, [*lim-nu-u-k*]*u-nu* 5 iv 7,
maqātu "to fall": *li-šam*]-*qit-*[*ku-nu*] 6: 518V, *li-šam-qit* 1 e. 19, *li-šam-qit-ku-nu* 6: 425A, *li-šam-qit-k*]*u-nu* 6: 425frg, *li-*[*šam-qit-ku-nu*] 6: 518frg, *lu-šam-qit-*[*ku-nu*] 6: 425c, *l*[*i-šam-qit-ku-nu*] 6: 425B, *l*]*i-ša*[*m-qit-ku-nu*] 6: 425C, *ta-m*[*a-qut-a-ni*] 6: 230frg, *ta-ma-qut*]-*a-ni* 6: 230c, *ta-ma-qut-a-ni* 6: 50A, n, 230A, C, J, f, *ta-ma-qut-a-n*]*i* 6: 230frg, *ta-ma-qut-a-*[*ni*] 6: 230X, *ta-ma-*[*qut-a-ni*] 6: 50frg, *t*]*a-ma-qut-a-ni* 6: 50E,
mar "as much/many as": *am—mar* 2 i 3, 4, 5, 5 iii 16, 17, 22, 24, 26, 6: 7A, F, G, T, a, 90A, G, frg, d, 138E, t, 142E, t, 194J, frg, 306A, C, frg, 507A, D, V, 527A, B, F, 13 iii 18, 20, *am—ma*]*r* 6: 194Y, *am—m*]*ar* 6: 527G, *a*[*m—mar* 6: 142frg, [*am—m*]*ar* 6: 7d,
marāru "to be bitter": *lim-ru-ur* 2 v 14, *mar-rat-u-ni* 6: 646U, frg, *mar-ra-ku*]-*nu* 6: 648frg, *mar-ra-ku-nu* 6: 648A, *mar-ra-ku-*[*nu*] 6: 648frg, *mar-ra-tú-u-ni* 6: 646A, *mar-*[*rat-u-ni*] 6: 646frg, *ma-ra-ku-*[*nu*] 6: 648U,
marāsu "to squash": *lim-ri-is-ku-nu* 6: 602frg, *li-im-ri-is-ku-nu* 6: 602A, T, *li-*[*i*]*m-ri-is-ku-nu* 6: 602h, [*li-im-r*]*i-is-ku-nu* 6: 602L,
marāṣu "to be sick, painful, troublesome": *lu-š*]*am-ri-ṣu* 13 ii 17, *ma-ru-uš-tu* 6: 475D, *ma-ru-u*]*š-tu* 3 r. 6, *ma-r*[*u-uš-tu*] 3: 11, *mar-ṣa-áš-šú-un-ni* 6: 208frg, *mar-ṣa-šú-u-ni* 6: 208O, *mar-ṣa-šu-un-ni* 6: 208J, *mar-ṣa-šu-u-ni* 6: 208u, *mar-ṣi* 2 i 12, *tu-šam-ri-iṣ-an-na-ši* 9 r. 23, [GIG-*t*]*ú* 11 r. 8,
mar'u "son": A 6: 157H, 174S, 10: 1, DUMU 5 i 1, 6: 2A, F, G, H, T, 11A, 44A, 94A, F, I, frg, 103E, F, frg, 110frg, 117o, 121E, O, 131A, frg, 151A, 157A, B, E, P, 163A, B, E, M, P, S, 164I, P, S, 171A, I, M, S, frg, 174A, G, I, frg, 189I, J, 220C, H, J, e, f, 222H, J, 230X, frg, f, 247A, X, frg, 261A, B, i, 267A, B, F, M, i, 270A, frg, 285B, C, J, frg, 321B, C, N, c, 322B, C, N, c, 338F, 339F, frg, 341F, p, w, 343F, frg, 363z, 381D, 496D, frg, q, 497D, frg, 504D, V, q, 515A, 633frg, 8: 11, DUMU-*ka* 2 iii 26, DUMU.MEŠ 3: 5, 6: 164A, 171frg, 497q, 504A, 505q, 516V, 633L, frg, 8: 8, 9: 7, DUMU.MEŠ-*ka* 2 v 3, DUMU.MEŠ-*ku-nu* 6: 9A, F, G, H, T, 116frg, 383D, s, 387A, D, 395D, H, 429A, B, 446A, g, 449A, g, l, 535M, frg, 538F, k, 549A, frg, 553A, D, frg, 564D, 569D, Q, frg, 572D, Q, 577D, 581frg, b, 583b, v, 586D, Q, Z, b, 589Q, 592L, h, j, 597K, T, h, j, 606A, h, 618A, G, K, L, 624G, K, frg, 636F, L, frg, 638A, frg, 647A, U, frg, DUMU.MEŠ-*ku-(nu)* 6: 577Q, 606H, DUMU.MEŠ-*ku-*[*nu* 6: 116A, 549frg, DUMU.MEŠ-*ku-*[*nu*] 6: 649frg, DUMU.

MEŠ-*k*[*u-nu* 6: 624L, DUMU.MEŠ-*k*]*u-nu* 6: 583Z, 606M, DUMU.MEŠ-*ni* 6: 507A, D, 508D, 510D, V, DUMU.MEŠ-*šu* 6: 237C, DUMU.MEŠ-*šú* 2 i 2, 6, 18, 23, r. iv 17, v 4, 6: 4A, F, G, H, T, a, 83H, I, 237A, J, N, 278A, B, Y, frg, 12: 4, DUMU.MEŠ-*šú-nu* 2 iv 10, DUMU.MEŠ-[*ku-nu* 6: 581v, 647frg, DUMU.MEŠ-[*šú* 2 i 34, DUMU.ME[Š-*šú*] 6: 83A, DUMU.M[EŠ-*ku-nu* 6: 9a, 572frg, DUMU.M[EŠ-*k*]*u-nu* 6: 288J, DUMU.M]EŠ-*ku-n*[*u* 6: 577Z, DUMU-*šá* 6: 547frg, DUMU.[MEŠ-*šú* 2 i 27, DUMU.[MEŠ]-*ni* 6: 507V, DUMU-[*šá*] 6: 547frg, DUMU] 6: 94G, 285A, DUMU].MEŠ 6: 624A, DUMU].MEŠ-*ku-nu* 6: 383A, DUMU].MEŠ-*šú* 6: 83G, 612K, DUM[U 6: 285Y, 363R, DUM[U.MEŠ-*ku-nu* 6: 387s, DUM[U—MEŠ-*šú*] 2 iv 4, DUM[U—X 6: 319A, DUM]U.MEŠ-*ku-nu* 6: 606K, 624frg, DUM]U.MEŠ-*k*[*u-nu* 6: 549frg, DUM]U—DUMU.MEŠ-*šu* 6: 4d, DU[MU 6: 131frg, DU[MU.MEŠ-*ku-nu* 6: 562D, DU[MU.MEŠ-*ku-nu*] 6: 538A, DU[MU.MEŠ-*šú* 2 i 30, DU[MU.MEŠ-*šú*] 6: 237X, DU]MU 6: 220frg, D[UMU 6: 110A, 230J, 270i, D[UMU.MEŠ-*ku-nu* 6: 543A, 572b, D[UMU.MEŠ-*ku-nu*] 6: 589j, D]UMU.MEŠ-*ku-nu* 6: 535F, [DUMU 6: 633L, [DUMU.MEŠ 14 i 21, [DUMU.MEŠ-*šú*] 2 i 7, [DUM]U 6: 261I, [DUM]U.MEŠ-*ku-nu* 6: 606frg, [DU]MU 6: 2a, 44E, 174frg, 230A, 11: 2, [D]UMU 6: 131E, 151H, [D]UMU.MEŠ-*ku-nu* 6: 569frg,

marʾutu "daughter": DUMU.MÍ-*ku-nu* 6: 592h, 619K, DUMU.MÍ-*ku-n*[*u*] 6: 592D, DUMU.MÍ.MEŠ-*ku-nu* 6: 116frg, 446A, 536F, M, 539F, 549A, 553A, D, 564D, frg, 569frg, 572D, Q, 581b, 586b, 590D, 592K, 597h, 607A, H, L, 619G, L, 624A, frg, 636F, 639A, frg, DUMU.MÍ.MEŠ-*ku-*[*nu* 6: 581frg, DUMU.MÍ.MEŠ-*ku-*[*nu*] 6: 647U, DUMU.MÍ.MEŠ-*k*[*u-nu* 6: 553frg, 569D, 636L, DUMU.MÍ.MEŠ-*k*[*u-nu*] 6: 624m, 647frg, DUMU.MÍ.MEŠ-*k*]*u-nu* 6: 572frg, 581Z, 647frg, DUMU.MÍ.MEŠ-*šú* 2 i 2, DUMU.MÍ.MEŠ-*šú-nu* 2 iv 10, DUMU.MÍ.MEŠ-[*ku*]-*nu* 6: 647A, DUMU.MÍ.MEŠ-[*ku-nu*] 6: 597K, DUMU.MÍ.ME[Š-*ku-nu* 6: 539frg, 586D, DUMU.MÍ.ME[Š-*šú* 2 i 6, DUMU.MÍ.ME]Š-*ku-nu* 6: 636frg, DUMU.MÍ.M[EŠ-*ku-nu* 6: 569frg, DUMU.MÍ-*šá* 6: 448A, DUMU.MÍ-[*ku-nu*] 6: 597j, DUMU.MÍ.[MEŠ-*ku-nu*] 6: 539k, 543frg, 624K, DUMU.M[Í-*ku-nu* 6: 116o, DUMU.M[Í-*šá* 6: 448g, DUMU.M]Í.MEŠ-*ku-nu* 6: 553frg, 562D, 571frg, DU[MU.MÍ.MEŠ-*ku-nu*] 6: 592L, DU[MU.MÍ-*šá* 6: 448l, DU[MU].MÍ.[MEŠ-*ku-nu* 6: 590h, D]UMU.MÍ.MEŠ-*ku-nu* 6: 562A, [DUMU.MÍ.MEŠ-*ku-n*]*u* 6: 619A, [DUMU.MÍ.MEŠ-*k*]*u-nu* 6: 536K, 590b, [DUMU.MÍ.MEŠ]-*ku-nu* 6: 539A, [DUMU.MÍ].MEŠ-*ku-nu* 6: 624G, [DUMU.M]Í.MEŠ-*ku-nu* 6: 650frg, [DUMU].MÍ.MEŠ-*šú* 2 i 8, [D]UMU.MÍ.MEŠ-*ku-nu* 6: 639frg,

markāsu "moorings": GIŠ.*mar-kas-ši-na* 5 iv 11,

martu "gall": *mar-tu* 6: 646A, U, frg, *mar-tú* 6: 646frg, ZÉ-*tú* 6: 646frg,

maruštu "trouble, hardship": NÍG.GIG 14 ii 14,

massītu "drink": *m*]*aš-ti-su-nu* 2 iv 23,

maṣṣartu "watch, guard": *ma-aṣ-ṣar-tú* 9: 10, *ma-aṣ-*[*ṣar-tú* 9: 11, *ma-ṣar-t*[*u* 6: 355A, *ma-ṣar-t*]*u-šú* 6: 206J, *ma-ṣar-*[*tu* 6355R,

maṣû "to be able to": *ma-ṣa-ku-nu* 6: 139E, t, 143t, 307A, C, *ma-ṣa-ku-n*[*u* 6: 139A, *ma-ṣa-*[*ku-nu* 6: 143frg, (*ma-ṣa-ku-nu)* 6: 143E,

mašāru "to drag": *li-in-da-šá-ru* 6: 483D,

mašʾennu "shoe": KUŠ.E.SÍR 6: 656U, KUŠ.E.SÍR.ME]Š-*ku-nu* 6: 657U, KUŠ.E.[SÍR 6: 656frg,

mašku "skin": KUŠ 6: 450g, l,

maškunu "tent": TÚG.*maš-ki-ni* 2 vi 4, TÚG.*maš-ku-nu* 2 vi 4,

mašqītu "potion, drink": *maš-qit-ku-nu* 6: 491D, frg, *maš-qit-ku-*[*nu* 6: 491frg,

matāhu "to lift": *i-ma-táh-u-ni* 6: 192Y,

matāqu "to be sweet": *li-*AH-*ti-iq* 6: 569D, *li-im-ti-iq* 6: 569frg, *li-in-ti-iq* 6: 569Q, *ma*]-*ti-qu-u-ni* 6: 568frg, *ma-ti-qu-u-ni* 6: 568Q, *ma-*[*t*]*e-qu-u-n*[*i* 6: 568D,

matnu "tendon, penis": *mat-nat* 6: 482D,

mazzassu "post, position": *ma-za-a-su* 6: 369z, *ma-za-sa-šu-nu* 11 r. 12, *m*]*a-za-s*[*u* 6: 369frg,

mazzāz pāni "entourage": LÚ.GUB—IGI 8: 7,

mākalu "food, meal": *ma*]-*ka-al-šu-nu* 2 iv 22,

mākalû "food": *ma-ka-la-ku-nu* 6: 490D, *ma-ka-le-e* 6: 524G, *ma-ka-li* 6: 524A, B, *ma-ka-*[*x* 6: 490frg,

māmītu "oath": *ma*]-*mit* 6: 397D, *ma-mit* 4 r. 10, 6: 72A, S, 376frg, 378frg, 379s, 397H, 433A, B, C, I, 14 i 4, 8, ii 3, *ma-mit-su-un* 6: 399D, *ma-m*[*it* 6: 129frg, *m*]*a-mit* 14 i 27, [*ma-mit* 4 r. 11, 14 i 29,

mār ah abi "cousin": DUMU—ŠEŠ.MEŠ—AD.MEŠ-*šú* 6: 76A, 215J, 319N, DUMU—ŠEŠ.MEŠ—[AD.MEŠ-*šú*] 6: 114frg, DUMU—ŠEŠ.ME[Š—AD].M[EŠ]-*šú* 6: 319J, DUMU—ŠEŠ—AD-*šú* 6: 319C, DUMU—ŠEŠ—AD.MEŠ-*šú* 6: 114E, 215C, DUMU—ŠEŠ—AD.MEŠ-[*šú* 6: 215O, [DUMU—ŠEŠ].MEŠ—AD.MEŠ-*šú* 6: 337frg, [DUMU—ŠE]Š.MEŠ—AD.MEŠ-*šú* 6: 76x,

mār damqi "rich, nobleman": DUMU—SIG$_5$.MEŠ 6: 220J, D]UMU—SIG$_5$.MEŠ 6: 220H,

mār marʾi "grandson": DUMU—DUMU.MEŠ-*ku-nu* 6: 9A, F, G, H, 288A, 395D, H, DUMU—DUMU.MEŠ--*ku-*[*nu*] 6: 9T, DUMU—DUMU.MEŠ-*ni* 6: 510D, DUMU—DUMU.MEŠ-*šú* 6: 4A, F, G, H, T, 612K, 12: 4, DUMU—DUMU].MEŠ-*k*[*u-nu*] 6: 395A, DUMU—DUMU].MEŠ-*ni* 6: 510frg, DUMU—DUM]U.MEŠ-*ni* 6: 510frg, DUMU—DU[MU.MEŠ-*ku-nu* 6: 288C, DUMU—[DUMU.MEŠ-*ku-nu* 6: 288J, D[UMU—DUMU—MEŠ-*ni* 6: 510V, [DUMU—DUMU].MEŠ-*ni* 6: 508V, [DUMU—DUM]U. MEŠ-*ni* 6: 508frg, [DUM]U—DUMU.[MEŠ-*ni* 6: 508frg,

mār šarri "crown prince": DUMU—LUGAL 6: 509D, V, 14 i 11, 12, DUMU—LU]GAL 6: 203J, 509frg, DUMU—MAN 3: 5, 6: 11A, 43A, 47A, frg, n, 58A, frg, r, 62A, 72W, 75A, H, 81A, G, H, a, 84A, G, d, 86A, G, d, 92A, G, frg, 94A, I, frg, 101E, F, frg, 103E, frg, y, 109E, frg, y, 120frg, o, 123frg, 137A, E, t, 143E, frg, 150A, E, H, P, frg, 156A, E, H, P, 165A, E, P, S, 167A, E, M, P, 170A, G, M, S, frg, 173I, M, S, frg, 179I, 184I, 188I, frg, 210C, frg, 226H, 229C, J, X, frg, f, 239A, J, X, 247A, frg, 250A, B, I, 258A, B, i, 260i, 266A, B, F, frg, i, 269A, B, M, frg, 279A, B, frg, 284A, B, Y, 285A, B, frg, 298C, H, 316A, C, J, 324B, C, N, c, 349A, B, F, 353R, 362R, frg, z, 366frg, 380D, s, 391A, D, H, 394D, H, 495D, q, 496D, q, 503D, q, 504A, D, V, q, 506A, D, V, 508D, 514D, V, 515V, 555frg, 633F, K, L, 667Q, frg, 669q, frg, DUMU—MA[N 6: 173A, 250frg, DUMU—MA]N 6: 94frg, 239frg, DUMU—M[AN 6: 43E, 58W, 167I, 173frg, 239B, 371frg, DUMU—M]AN 6: 285Y, DUMU—[MAN 6: 130frg, 203O, 366B, 633A, DUMU—[MA]N 6: 633frg, DUMU—[M]AN 6: 165I, DUMU]—MAN 6: 92I, 260A, frg, 495frg, 496frg, DUM[U—MAN 6: 92frg, 362frg, 508V, DUM]U—MAN 6: 508A, DU[MU—MAN 6: 101y, 123o, 284J, DU[MU—MAN] 6: 210J, DU[MU—M]AN 6: 503A, DU]MU—MAN 6: 81I, 203frg, 260B, 403D,

D[UMU—MAN 6: 170P, 633frg, D]UMU—MAN 6: 143P, 226f, 250frg, [DUMU—MAN 6: 130E, [DUMU—M]AN 6: 669frg, [DUMU]—MAN 6075S, [DUM]U—MAN 6: 179frg, 258I, [D]UMU—MAN 6: 503V,

mār šarrūtu "crown-princeship": DUMU—MAN-*ti* 6: 44A, DUMU—MAN-*u-te* 6: 44E,

mār šipri "messenger": LÚ.A—KIN 5 iii 14, 9: 6, 36, LÚ.A—*šip-ri* 6: 202J, frg,

māru see *mar'u,*

mātu "land, country": KUR 2 iii 23, r. v 11, 6: 141A, E, 161A, E, P, S, 164A, I, P, S, 181A, I, frg, 199frg, 216C, J, frg, e, u, 222H, J, f, 256A, B, I, 299B, C, H, 315A, C, J, 322B, C, N, c, 339F, frg, 436I, 443A, g, 539A, k, 544k, 661Q, frg, 8: 11, 9: 29, 36, 10: 15, 13 ii 19, KUR-*ka* 2 iii 26, r. v 5, 5 iii 7, KUR-*ku*]-*nu* 6: 533G, KUR-*ku-nu* 5 iv 14, 15, 6: 294C, H, 437C, I, 442g, 533A, M, 600A, KUR-*ku*-[*nu* 6: 442A, KUR-*k*[*u-nu* 6: 440F, KUR-*k*[*u-nu*] 6: 567D, KUR-*k*]*u-nu* 6: 437A, KUR.MEŠ 13 iii 12, KUR-*su* 2 i 4, r. iv 9, vi 1, KUR-*s*[*u*] 1 e. 18, KUR-*šu* 1: 12, 6: 40E, KUR-*šú* 2 i 7, 8, 9, 19, 20, 31, r. iv 5, 7, 9, 32, 9: 18, KUR-*šú*] 2 i 2, 34, KUR-*šú-nu* 5 iii 17, KUR-*š*]*u* 6: 40frg, KUR.KUR 6: 23A, G, frg, 25A, frg, 40A, E, frg, 245A, frg, 312A, ii A, F, G, T, a, d, 9 r. 6, KUR.KUR.MEŠ] 14 i 8, KUR.K[UR] 6: ii H, KUR]-*ku-nu* 6: 567Q, KUR]-*su* 1 r. 15, KUR].KUR 6: ii I, frg, KU]R-*ku-nu* 6: 294A, K[UR-*šú* 2 i 23, K[UR.KUR 3 r. 7, K]UR 6: 222frg, 8 r. 23, K]UR-*ku-n*[*u* 6: 533B, [KUR-*k*]*u-nu* 6: 437F, [KUR-*su* 1 r. 14, [KUR.KUR.ME]Š 14 i 26, [KU]R.KUR 6: 312C, [KU]R.KUR.MEŠ 6: 245frg,

memmēni "anybody, anything": *me*]-*me-ni* 6: 336frg, *me-me-ni* 5 iii 6, 27, 6: 130A, E, frg, 135O, 198J, 302C, 336F, frg, 528B, F, G, 10 r. 4, 13 iii 8, *me-me-(ni)* 6: 302frg, *m*]*e-me-ni* 6: 302A,

mēšāru "justice": *me-šá-ri* 6: 422A,

mê "water": A.MEŠ 1 e. 18, 2 iv 21, 6: 155A, E, H, P, 411C, 452A, g, 463frg, 477D, 479D, 521G, I, frg, 523A, G, 563D, 609A, M, 611G, M, frg, 630F, G, K, frg, 655U, 9 r. 13, 14, 11 r. 14, A.MEŠ-*šá* 6: 652U, A.MEŠ] 5 iv 4, A.M[EŠ 6: 411B, A].ME 2 iv 21, A].MEŠ 6: 411A, 452frg, 609frg, 611A, H, 630L, frg, [A.ME]Š 11 r. 10,

mêsu "to crush": *ni-mi-is-su* 9 r. 4,

milku "advice, counsel": *mil-ki* 5 iii 7, *mil-ku* 6: 52A, r, 234A, X, 8: 20, *mi*]*l-ku* 6: 52W,

mimma "anything": *mim*]-*ma* 6: 412A, *mim-ma* 1 r. 7, 6: 412C, 489D, 490D, 9: 21, r. 16, *mim-m*[*a* 1: 4, *mim-mu* 14 ii 5,

mimmû "property, belongings": *mim-mu-ku-un* 6: 430A, B, *mim*-[*mu-ku-nu*] 5 iv 19E,

MIN (reading uncert.) "ditto": MIN 6: 26G, 27G, 28A, G, 29A, 30A, frg, 31A, frg, 32A, frg, 33A, frg, 34A, frg, 35A, 36A, E, frg, 37E, frg, 38A, 39A, E, frg, 40A, E, frg, MIN] 6: 37A, M[IN] 6: 31E, 32E, 33E, 34E, 35E,

minsi "why?": *mìn-si* 14 i 1,

mīlu "flood": A.KAL 1 r. 13, A.[KAL 6: 440g,

muātu "to die; death": *mu-at-ka* 2 v 1, *mu-a-tin-ni* 2 v 1, *mu-a-ti-šú* 6: 262B, frg, i, *mu-u-ta* 6: 655U, *m*[*u-a-ti-šú* 6: 262A, *ša*]-*mut-ti-šú-nu* 6: 133O, *ša-mut-ti-šu* 6: 133frg, *ša-mut-t*]*i-šu* 6: 133frg, *ša-m*]*ut-te-šu* 6: 133E, *ta-mut-ta*]-*a-ni* 6: 231c, *ta-mut-ta-a-ni* 6: 51A, 231A, X, f, *ta-mu-ta-a-n*[*i*] 6: 231J, *ta-mu-t*[*a-a-n*]*i* 6: 51E, *ta*-[*m*]*u-ta-a*-[*ni* 6: 231frg, *t*]*a-mut-ta-a-ni* 6: 51n, 231N,

mu''uru "to send, commission": *ú*]-*ma-'i-ir-an-ni-ma* 14 ii 4,

mugirru "chariot": GIŠ.GIGIR 6: 612K, M, m, GIŠ.GIGIR-*ku-nu* 6: 614m, GIŠ.GIGIR.MEŠ 6: 612G, GIŠ.GIGIR.MEŠ-*ku-nu* 6: 575D, b, 614A, G, H, K, frg, GIŠ.GIGIR.M[EŠ-*ku-nu*] 6: 575Q, GIŠ.GI[GIR.MEŠ-*šú*] 2 iv 2, GI]Š.GIGIR 6: 612A, [GIŠ.GIGIR.MEŠ-*ku*]-*nu* 6: 575v, [GIŠ.GIGIR.MEŠ-*ku-n*]*u* 6: 614L, [GIŠ.GIGIR]-*ku*-[*nu* 6: 575frg, [GI]Š.GIGIR-*ku-nu* 6: 575Z,

muhhu "top; on": UGU 5 iii 1, 6: 11A, 43A, 74A, x, 109frg, 137A, E, 178A, B, I, M, frg, 203O, 208C, J, 229X, frg, f, 284A, B, Y, frg, 302A, B, C, frg, 331B, 373frg, 389A, D, 391D, H, 418B, C, 448A, g, l, 494D, V, frg, 495D, 503D, V, 514V, 544A, 555frg, 557A, frg, 559D, frg, 581D, Z, b, v, 648U, 666Q, frg, 668frg, 8: 10, 17, 21, 23, r. 4, 13, 25, 26E, 9: 27, 13 iii 13, UGU-*hi* 5 iii 3, 6: 74H, 648frg, 9: 13, 14, UGU-*hi*]-*šú* 6: 245X, frg, UGU-*hi-ka* 5 iii 6, UGU-*hi-ku*]-*nu* 6: 228C, UGU-*hi-ku-nu* 6: 49A, 61A, frg, 71A, S, W, 228X, f, 297A, B, C, 301B, 649U, 10: 10, UGU-*hi-ku*-[*nu* 6: 61W, UGU-*hi-k*[*u-nu* 6: 61r, UGU-*hi-k*]*u-nu* 6: 228J, UGU-*hi-ni* 6: 510D, UGU-*hi-ni*] 9: 11, UGU-*hi-šu* 6: 174G, 309C, UGU-*hi-šú* 6: 12A, 50W, 64A, W, 166A, E, P, 174A, I, M, S, 185F, I, frg, 197J, frg, 231A, J, X, frg, f, 301frg, UGU-*hi-šú-nu* 6: 8F, G, H, T, a, 95A, 104E, frg, UGU-*hi-šú*-[*nu*] 6: 95frg, UGU-*hi-š*[*ú* 6: 197frg, UGU-*hi-š*[*ú*] 6: 174frg, UGU-*hi-š*]*u* 6: 231C, UGU-*hi-š*]*u-nu* 6: 517A, UGU-*hi*-[*šu*] 6: 309A, UGU-*hi*-[*š*]*u* 6: 50A, UGU-*h*[*i-šú-nu* 6: 517frg, UGU-*h*]*i-ku-nu* 6: 649frg, UGU-*ku-nu* 6: 49E, UGU-*ku-un* 6: 460A, UGU-*ni* 6: 510V, UGU-*šú-nu* 2 iv 11, 6: 8A, UGU-[*hi-ku-nu* 6: 649frg, UGU-[*hi-šú* 6: 50r, 245frg, UGU-[*x* 6: 174frg, 309frg, UGU] 6: 380s, UGU]-*hi-ka* 13 iii 9, UGU]-*hi-šú* 6: 50n, 197frg, UG[U 6: 495frg, 658frg, UG[U-*hi-šú* 6: 245frg, UG[U-*hi-šú-nu*] 6: 95frg, UG[U-*ku-un*] 6: 460B, UG]U 5 ii 13, 6: 373frg, 666frg, 8: 14, UG]U-*hi-ka* 13 iii 7, UG]U-*hi-ni* 13 iii 13, UG]U-*hi-šu* 6: 166M, UG]U-*hi-šú* 6: 50frg, 166S, UG]U-*ku-un* 6: 460k, U[GU 2 iii 21, 6: 203frg, 284C, 373B, U[GU-*hi-ni* 9: 34, U[GU-*hi-šú-nu*] 6: 95F, U]GU 6: 43E, 109y, 284J, 503q, 514D, 559A, U]GU-*hi-ka* 13 ii 11, U]GU-*hi-šú* 6: 131E, U]GU-*hi*-[*šú*] 6: 185frg, U]GU-*ku-un* 5 iv 2, U]GU-[*hi-šu* 6: 301C, [UGU 1 r. 15, [U]GU 10 r. 6, [U]GU-*hi-šú* 6: 245frg, [U]GU-⌜*ka*⌝ 6: 351R,

munnabtu "fugitive": *mun-nab-t*[*u*] 1: 13,

mūnu "caterpillar": *mu-nu* 6: 599A, j,

murṣu "disease": GIG 5 iv 3, 6: 418B, C, 461k, 490D, GI]G 6: 461A, 490frg, G]IG 6: 389A, [GI]G 6: 389D,

mušadbibu "agitator of conspiracy": LÚ.*mu-šad-bi-bu* 9: 13, *mu-šad-bi-bu-u-te* 8 r. 20,

mušadbibūtu "agitation": *mu-šad-bi-bu-tu* 6: 500D, q, *mu-šad-bi-bu-tú* 6: 500V,

mušamhiṣu "instigator of armed rebellion": LÚ.*mu-šam-hi-ṣu*] 9: 12, *mu-šam-hi-iṣ-ṣu-u-te* 8 r. 19,

mušamhiṣūtu "instigation": *mu-šam-hi-ṣu-tu* 6: 500V, q, *mu-šam-hi-ṣu-u-tú* 6: 500D,

muškēnu "poor, beggar": *muš-ke-nu-te* 6: 220frg, e, *muš-ke-nu-ti* 6: 220C, J, *muš-ke-n*[*u-t*]*i* 6: 220H, *muš-k*]*e-n*[*u-ti*] 6: 220f,

muštēširu "just ruler": *m*[*uš-te-šir*] 1 r. 8,

mūdû "knowledgeable": *mu-de-e* 1 r. 7,

mūšu "night": MI 6: 199frg, *mu-ši* 6: 201C, M[I 6: 199J, M[I] 6: 201frg, *m*[*u-ši*] 6: 201J,

mūtānu "pestilence": *mu-t[a-a]-nu* 6: 456A, NAM.ÚŠ 6: 456k, NAM.ÚŠ.MEŠ 4 r. 26, NAM.[Ú]Š.MEŠ 6: 480D,

mūtu "death": *mu-ú-ti* 14 ii 6,

nabalkattu "revolt": *na-bal-kàt-tu* 8: 13,

nabalkutu "to revolt, reverse": *bal-kàt-a]-ni* 6: 244frg, *ib-bal-kàt-u-ni* 6: 175A, I, M, *ib-bal-kàt-u-n[i]* 6: 175G, *ib-bal-kàt-[u-ni]* 6: 175frg, *i]b-bal-kàt-u-ni* 6175S, *i]b-bal-k[àt-u-ni]* 6: 175frg, *lu-šá-bal-kit* 6: 574Q, *lu-šá-bal-kit]* 6: 659frg, *lu-šá-bal-ki-[tu]* 6: 574D, *lu-[šá-b]al-ki[t]* 6: 546A, *l[u-šá-bal-kit]* 6: 546frg, *ta-bal-kàt-a-ni* 6: 186frg, 244A, 310A, C, *ta-bal-k[àt-a-ni* 6: 186F, *ta-bal-k[àt-a-ni]* 6: 186I, *ta-bal-[kàt-a-ni* 6: 244frg, *ta-ba]l-kàt-a-ni* 6: 244X, *ta-b]al-kàt-ni* 6: 310J, *ta-[ba]l-kàt-a-ni* 6: 244frg, *[lu-šá-bal]-kit* 6: 546F, *[ta-ba]l-kàt-a-ni* 6: 186frg,

nabiu "bright": *na-bat* 6: 428B, frg,

nabnītu "creation": *nab-ni-ti* 6: 437I, *nab-n[i-t]ú* 6: 437F,

nabû "to call": *na-bi* 6: 300B, C, *n[a-bi* 6: 300frg,

nadānu "to give": *na-din* 2 v 5, 6: 524A, B, *na-di]-nat* 6: 435B, *na-di-na-at* 6: 435I, 9 r. 21, *na-d]in* 6: 524G, *ni-nam-du-ši-na* 9: 16, *ta-nam-din-nu* 14 ii 15,

nadānu see *tadānu,*

nadû "to throw, cast": *li-di-ku-nu* 6: 651U, *ta-na-da-a-ni* 6: 411A, *ta-na-da-a-[ni]* 6: 411C, *[li-d]i-ku-nu* 6: 651frg,

nagbu "spring": IDIM 6: 521G, I, frg, 9 r. 23, *nag-bi* 1 r. 8, 13, 2 iv 21, 9 r. 13,

nagiu "district": *na]-gi-k[u-nu]* 6: 545frg, *na-gi-e* 5 iii 19, *na-gi-ku]-nu* 6: 545F, *na-gi-ku-nu* 6: 545frg, 600A, j, *na-gi-šu* 6: 40E, frg, *na-gi-šú* 5 iii 29,

nahlaptu "cloak": *na-ah-lap-ti* 11 r. 11, *na-ha-lap-ti* 2 iv 5,

nakālu "to elaborate, devise a scheme": *i-nak-ki-l-an-ni* 8 r. 14, *ta-nak-kil-a-nin-ni* 8: 18,

nakāru "to be hostile; (D) to change, remove; (Š) to make hostile": KÚR-*ru* 1 r. 11, *ta-na-kír-a-ni* 6: 244frg, *ta-na-kir-[a-ni]* 6: 244X, *ta-na-ki-ir-ra-ni* 6: 244A, *ta-na-ki-ra-ni* 6: 244frg, *tu]-šam-kar-a-ni* 6: 312J, *tu-nak-kar]-a-šú-ni* 6: 128O, *tu-nak-kar-a-šu-ni* 6: 55r, *tu-nak-kar-šú-u-ni* 6: 55A, 69A, *tu-nak-ka-ra-š[ú-ni]* 6: 69W, *tu-nak-k[ar-šú-u-ni* 6: 55W, *tu-nak-[ka]r-a-šú-u-[n]i* 6: 128E, *tu-nak-[ka-ra-šú-ni* 6: 69S, *tu-na-kar-a]-ni* 6: 410A, *tu-na-kar-a-šá-n[u-u-ni]* 6: 367frg, *tu-na-kar-[a-ni]* 6: 410C, *tu-na-ka[r-a-šá-nu-u-ni]* 6: 367z, *tu-n[ak-kar-šú-u-ni* 6: 55frg, *tu-n[a-kar-a-šá-nu-u-ni]* 6: 367frg, *tu-šam-kar-a-ni* 6: 245A, frg, *tu-šam-kar-[a-ni]* 6: 245X, *tu-šam-[k]ar-a-ni* 6: 312C, *tu-š[am-k]a[r-a-ni]* 6: 312A, *t]u-na-kar-a-š[á-nu-u-ni]* 6: 367R, *ú-na-kar-šú-[nu-u-ni]* 6: 372frg, *ut-tak-k]a-ru* 1 r. 4,

nakāsu "to cut": *na-kas* 6: 557A, 559A, D, *na-kás* 6: 559frg,

nakru "enemy": KÚR-*ku-nu* 6: 573Q, 601T, KÚR-*šú* 2 iv 1, LÚ.KUR 6: 430frg, LÚ.KUR-*šú* 4 r. 21, LÚ.KÚR 5: 419E, 6: 430B, 9: 35, LÚ.KÚR-*ku-nu* 6: 429B, frg, 454B, frg, 590b, h, 601frg, h, 602A, K, L, T, frg, h, 614G, frg, 617G, K, L, 631K, L, frg, 643A, frg, LÚ.KÚR-*ku-nu]* 5: 418E, LÚ.KÚR-*ku-n[u* 6: 643frg, LÚ.KÚR-*ku-n[u]* 6: 573D, 614K, L, LÚ.KÚR-*ku-n]u* 6: 643frg, LÚ. KÚR-*ku-[nu* 6: 535F, LÚ.KÚR-*k[u-nu* 6: 454A, 631G, LÚ.KÚR-*šu* 6: 127frg, LÚ.KÚR-*šú* 6: 111E, 127E, 499D, q, 9: 24, 25, LÚ.KÚR-*[ku-nu* 6: 602j, LÚ.KÚR-*[šu]* 6: 111frg, LÚ.KÚ]R-*ku-nu* 6: 573Z, 590Q, 614A, frg, LÚ.KÚ]R-*šu* 6: 127O, LÚ.K[ÚR-*ku-nu* 6: 617frg, LÚ.K[ÚR-*ku-nu]* 6: 573b, LÚ.[KÚR-*šú* 9: 32, LÚ].KÚR-*ni* 9 r. 25, L[Ú.KÚR-*ku-nu* 6: 631F, 643U, L]Ú.KÚR 6: 430A, L]Ú.KÚR-*ku-nu* 6: 617A, L]Ú.KÚR-*[ku-nu* 6: 535A, ⌜KÚR⌝-*ku-nu* 6: 601A, [LÚ.KÚR.M]EŠ-*šú* 6: 499V,

nalšu "dew": *na]-al-šu* 6: 531M, *na]-al-šú* 6: 531A, *na-al]-šu* 6: 531G, *na-al-šú* 6: 531B, *n[a-al-šú* 6: 531frg, *n]a-al-[šú* 6: 531F, *[na-a]l-šú* 6: 532A,

namāru "to be bright": *na-ma-a-r[i* 6: 486frg, *na-[ma-a-ri]* 6: 486D,

nannaru "brigthness, luminary": dŠEŠ.KI 11 r. 10, *na-an-nar* 6: 419C, c, *na-an-na-ru* 9 r. 11, *na-nar* 6: 419B, *n]a-an-nar* 6: 419A,

naparšudu "to escape": *na-par-šú-di* 6: 650frg, *na-par-šu-di* 6: 650U,

napāhu A "to blow": *li-p[u-h]u-ku-nu* 6: 565D, *ta-nap-pa-ha-a-ni* 6: 563D,

napāhu B "to light up, rise": *na-pah* 6: 6A, *na-pa]-ah* 6: 6d, *na-pa-ah* 6: 6F, G, H, T, a,

napālu (D) "to blind": *lu-na-pi-il* 2 vi 2, *nu-up-pil* 1: 9,

napharu "totality, sum": *nap]-har* 6: 79I, *nap-har* 3 r. 7, 6: 79A, G, H, a, x, 118frg, o, 164S, 223J, 339F, 418C, *nap-har-ši-na* 14 i 26, *nap-ha[r* 6: 339R, *nap-[har* 6: 223H, *na[p-har* 6: 118A, *n[ap-har]* 6: 418B,

napištu "life": *na-piš-ta-ku-n[u* 6: 487frg, *n[a-piš]-ta-ku-nu* 6: 487D, ZI-*tim* 1 r. 9,

napšutu "life; throat": *nap]-šat-ku-nu* 6: 651frg, *nap-šat-kun* 6: 651U, *nap-šat-ku-nu* 6: 268A, 455B, *nap-šat-ku-un* 6: 432A, B, *nap-šat-ku-[nu]* 6: 455A, *nap-šat-ku-[un]* 6: 432I, *nap-šat-su* 1 r. 2, *nap-šá-te-ku-nu* 6: 268i, *nap-[šat-ku-nu]* 6: 651frg, *na[p-šat-ku-un]* 6: 432C, *na]p-šat-ku-nu* 6: 455frg, ZI.MEŠ 6: 557A, frg, 559A, D, frg, ZI.MEŠ-*ku-nu* 6: 268B, 293H, 335B, ZI-*šú* 1 e. 18, ZI.[MEŠ]-*ku-nu* 6: 293B, ZI.[ME]Š-*ku-nu* 6: 293C, Z[I.MEŠ]-*ka* 2 v 2, Z]I.MEŠ 6: 557D, *[nap-ša]t-ku-nu* 6: 293A,

napṭu "naphtha": *nap-ṭi* 6: 587D, Q, frg, b, v, *nap-ṭu* 6: 491D, *na]p-ṭu* 6: 587Z,

napultu "throat": *na-pul-ta-ku-nu* 6: 374frg,

naqbaru "burial place": *naq-bar-qa-ku-nu* 6: 484D, *n]a-aq-bar-ku-[nu]* 6: 484frg,

naqû "to libate, sacrifice": *iq-qu-u-ku[n-u-ni* 7: 8, *na-aq* 6: 452A, g,

narāmtu "beloved": *na-ram-ta-šú* 6: 417A, C, *na-ram-ta-[šu* 4 r. 18,

nasāhu "to uproot, tear out": *li-is-suh-an-na-a-šú* 9 r. 14, *li-is-su-hu* 5 iv 12, *li-sa-hu-ku-nu* 6: 476D, *na-as-ha-at* 2 i 35, *na-as-ha-tu-ni* 2 i 33, *[lis-su-h]u-ku-nu* 5 iv 15, *[li-su-uh-š]ú-nu* 11 r.9,

nasāsu "to moan": *ú-na-si-su* 14 ii 7,

naṣāru "to guard, protect": *na-ṣir* 6: 299B, *ni-na-aṣ-ṣa-ru* 9: 11, 12, *ta-na-ṣar-a-ni* 6: 65A, *ta-na-ṣar-a-šú-nu-u-ni* 6: 100A, *ta-na-ṣar-a-šú-n[u-u-ni]* 6: 100E, *ta-na-ṣar-a-šú-u-ni* 6: 168E, S, *ta-na-ṣar-a-šú-[u]-ni* 6: 168M, *ta-na-ṣar-a-[ni]* 6: 409C, *ta-na-ṣar-ra-ni* 6: 65W, *ta-na-ṣar-šá-n[u-ni* 3: 6, *ta-na-ṣar-šú-nu-u-[ni]* 6: 100frg, *ta-na-ṣar-šú-u-ni* 6: 50A, E, 168A, *ta-na-ṣar-[a-šú-nu-u-ni]* 6: 100F, *t[a-n]a-ṣar-a-šú-u-ni* 6: 168P, *t]a-na-ṣar-a-ni* 6: 409A, *t]a-na-ṣar-a-šú-nu-u-ni* 6: 100I, *uṣ-ra* 6: 292H, 335B, *u[ṣ]-ra-a* 6: 292C, *[na]-ṣir* 6: 299C, *[ta-na-ṣa]r-šú-u-ni* 6: 50n, *[u]ṣ-ra* 6: 292A,

našpantu "devastation": *na-áš-pan-ta-k]u-nu* 5 iv 5, *na-aš-pan-ta-ku-nu* 6: 489D, *na-aš-pan-ta-k]u-*

nu 6: 489frg, *na-aš-pan-*[*ta-ku-nu* 6: 465frg,

našû "to lift, take, bring": *it*]*-te-ši* 6: 204frg, *it-ti-ši* 6: 241A, J, X, *i*]*t-ti-ši* 6: 204J, 241frg, *i-ti-ši* 6: 204O, *li-ši-ma* 6: 423B, *li-ši-mu* 6: 423c, *li-ši-*[*ma*] 6: 423C, *liš-ši* 9 r. 10, *liš-ši-ma* 6: 423A, *na-še-e* 5 iii 25, *na-ši* 6: 660frg, *ta-na-áš-šá-a-ni* 6: 274A, B, *ta-na-šá-a-ni* 6: 274frg, [*na*]*-ṣa-ku-nu* 5 i 11,

natāku "to drop": *lit-ta-tuk* 6: 471D,

natbāku "ravine": [*n*]*a-da-*[*b*]*a-k*[*i*] 12: 7,

nazāru "to curse; (Š) to make hateful, detestable": *na-az-ru* 9: 12, *tu-šá-an*]*-zar-a-ni* 6: 364z, *tu-šá-an-za-ra-ni* 6: 364frg, *tu-šá-an-*[*za-ra-ni*] 6: 364R, *ú-šá-an*]*-za-ar-u-ni* 6: 331frg, *ú-šá-an-za-ar-u-ka-nu-ni* 6: 329frg, *ú-šá-an-za-ru-ka-nu-ni* 6: 329B, *ú-šá-an-za-ru-k*[*a-nu-ni* 6: 329frg, *ú-*[*šá-an-z*]*i-ru-u-ni* 6: 331B,

nādu "waterskin": KUŠ.*na-a-du* 6: 652U, KUŠ.*na-da-ku-nu* 6: 654U,

nāru "river": ÍD 6: 492D, frg, ÍD.MEŠ*-ku-nu* 6: 565D, ÍD.[MEŠ*-šú*] 1 r. 7,

nekelmû "to frown": *li-kil-mu-ku-nu* 6: 474D,

nēšu "lion": UR.MAH 5 iv 7, UR.M[AH 6: 468D,

niālu "to lie": *li-ni-la* 2 v 27, *li-šá*]*-ni-il* 6: 429A, *li-šá-ni-il* 6: 429B, *l*[*i-šá-ni-il* 6: 429frg, *ta-ta-la* 6: 559D, *ta-*[*ta-la*] 6: 559frg,

niāru "papyrus": *ni-a-ru* 2 iv 15,

nidnu "gift": *nid-n*]*u* 2 v 10,

nikiltu "cunning, scheme": *ni-kil-ti* 6: 412A, C,

niklu "trick, stratagem": *nik-l*]*u* 8 r. 13, [*nik-l*]*u* 8: 16, 13 iii 8,

niphu "kindling, conflagration": *ni-pi-ih* 6: 155A, E, P, [*ni*]*-pi-ih* 6: 155H,

nipšu "breath": *ni-piš-ku-nu* 6: 605A, H, T, frg, h, *ni-piš-ku-*[*n*]*u* 6: 605L,

niqiu "sacrifice": UDU.SISKUR 2 i 10,

nissatu "worry": *ni-is-sa-tu* 6: 418C, *ni-i*]*s-sa-tú* 6: 418B,

niṭlu "sight": *ni-iṭ-lu* 9 r. 10, *ni-ṭil* 6: 423C, c, 428A, B, 482D, *n*]*i-ṭil* 6: 423B,

nīš "by": *ni-iš* 14 i 26, 28, 31, 32, ii 2, [*ni*]*-iš* 14 ii 1,

nīši "people": UN.MEŠ 2 i 2, 8, 9, 19, 23, 31, iii 26, r. iv 5, 9, 32, 5 iii 15, 17, 6: 276A, B, frg, 299B, C, H, 8: 11, UN.MEŠ*-ka* 2 v 6, UN.MEŠ*-ku-nu* 5 iv 15, 6: 294A, B, UN.MEŠ*-šú* 1 e. 17, 19, 6: 77H, UN.MEŠ-[*šú* 2 v 26, 4 r. 27, UN.ME[Š*-ku-nu*] 6: 294C, UN.M[EŠ 8 r. 23, UN.[MEŠ 2 i 34, U[N.MEŠ*-šú* 7: 6, [UN.MEŠ-*k*]*u-nu* 6: 294H, [U]N.MEŠ 2 i 7,

nuāhu "to rest": *ta-nu*]*-ha* 6: 639frg, *ta-nu-ha* 6: 639A, frg, *ta-nu-h*[*a* 6: 639frg,

nūnu "fish": KU_6 13 iii 1,

nūru "light": *nu-úr* 6: 422B, C, c,

pagru "corpse": LÚ.ÚŠ.MEŠ*-ku-nu* 6: 483D, LÚ.ÚŠ.MEŠ*-ku-n*[*u* 6: 483frg,

pahû "to close": *li-pi-hi-ma* 2 v 25,

palāhu "to fear": *lip-lu-hu* 6: 396D, H, [*ta*]*-pa-l*[*àh-an*]*-ni* 13 ii 5,

palāšu "to pierce": *lu-p*[*al-x* 6: 598j, *lu-ú-pal-li-šu* 6: 598h, *pal-lu-šá* 6: 598T, *pal-lu-šá-a-ni* 6: 595L, *pal-lu-šá-a-*[*ni*] 6: 595j, *pa-*[*l*]*u-šá-a-ni* 6: 595h,

palû "reign, regnal year": BALA*-ú* 14 ii 15, *pa*]*-le-e-šú* 1 r. 12, *pa-le-e* 1 r. 4,

paqāru "to contest, dispute": *pa*]*-qa-a-ri* 6: iv frg, *pa-qa*]*-a-ri* 6: iv frg, *pa-qa-a*]*-ri* 6: iv c, *pa-qa-a-ri* 6: iv A, F, *pa-qa-*[*a-ri*] 6: iv Y, *pa-q*]*a-a-ri* 6: iv p, *pa-*[*qa*]*-a-ri* 6: iv H,

paqādu "to appoint, entrust, take care": *ip-qid-du-šú-u-ni* 6: 45E, *ip-qí-du* 9: 12, *ip-qi-*[*du-ni*] 5 iii 18, *pa-qid* 9 r. 7, *pa-qi-du* 6: 452A, g, *pa-*[*qi-du* 6: 452I, *ta-pa-qid-a-*[*ni*] 6: 411C, *ta-pa-q*[*i-x* 6: 411A, [*ip*]*-qi-du-šú-u-ni* 6: 45A,

paquttu "brier": *pa-qut-ti* 6: 657frg,

parā'u "to sprout": *i-par*]*-ru-ʾa* 6: 529frg, *i-par-ru-a* 6: 529G, M, *i-par-ru-ʾa* 6: 529F, *i-par-ru-ʾu-u-ni* 6: 541k, *i-par-ru-u-*[*ni*] 6: 541F, *i-p*[*ar-ru-u-ni*] 6: 541frg, *i-*[*par-ru-a*] 6: 529A,

parāmu "to tear": *li-par-ma* 6: 658frg,

parāru "to scatter": *lip-p*[*ar-ri-ir*] 2 i 9,

parāsu "to cut off, separate": *lip-ru-us* 6: 438F, I, *lip-ru-*[*us*] 6: 440C, *pur*]*-sa* 6: 343B, *pur-sa* 6: 343A, F, w, *pur-*[*sa*] 6: 343p, *ta-par-ra-sa-šú-ni* 6: 346R, *ta-par-ra-sa-šú-nu-u-ni* 6: 346F, *ta-par-r*]*a-sa-a-šú-u-ni* 6: 346A, *t*]*a-par-*[*x* 6: 346frg, [*ta-par-r*]*a-sa-šú-u-ni* 6: 346w,

parāṣu "to transgress": *i-par-ra-ṣu* 6: 399D,

pariktu "injustice": *pa-rik-ti* 9 r. 9,

paršumu "elder": LÚ.*par-šá-mu-te* 5 iii 7,

parzillu "iron": AN.BAR 6: 528A, B, F, G, M, 545A, AN.B[AR 6: 545frg,

pasāsu "to erase": *i-pa-sa-si* 6: 398D, *i-pa-sa-su* 6: 398H, *ni-pa-as-s*[*a-su* 9 r. 4,

paṣānu "to hide, conceal": *ni-ip-te-eṣ-nu* 9: 9,

pašāru "to undo, dissolve": *nap-šur* 3: 11, r. 6, 14 i 30, ii 4, *nap-šú-ri* 5 iv 9, *na*[*p-šu-ri*] 11 r. 7, *pa-šá-a*]*-ri* 6: 379A, *pa-šá-a-ri* 4 r. 15, 6: 379s, *pa-šá-ri* 6: 376frg, 433A, B, I, *p*]*a-šá-a-ru* 4 r. 11, *ta-pa-šar-a-*[*ni* 6: 378frg, *t*]*a-pa-šar-a-ni* 6: 378s,

pašāšu "to anoint": *pa-šá-ši-ku-nu* 5: 417E, *ta-pa*]*-šá-áš-a-šú-ni* 6: 263I, *ta-pa-šá-áš-a-ni* 6: 375frg, *ta-pa-šá-šá-a-šú-u-ni* 6: 263B, *ta-pa-šá-šá-šu-u-ni* 6: 263i, *ta-p*[*a-šá*]*-áš-a-*[*ni* 6: 375B,

pašāṭu "to erase": *lip-ši-ṭi* 6: 661frg, *lip-ši-*[*ṭi* 6: 661Q,

pašīru "secrecy": *pa-ši-ri* 9: 9,

paššūru "table": GIŠ.ABXAD.TIM 6: 154A, E, GIŠ.BANŠUR 6: 154H, P,

patāhu "to pierce": *ú-pa-ta-hu-ka-nu-ni* 6: 643A, *ú-pa-t*[*a-x* 6: 643frg, *ú-*[*pa-ta-hu-ka*]*-nu-n*[*i*] 6: 643frg,

patru "sword": GÍR.MEŠ 6: 635F, frg, GÍR.MEŠ*-ma* 6: 636A, F, frg, GÍR*-šú* 6: 455A, g, k, GÍR.AN.BAR 5 iv 1, 10: 7, GÍR.AN.BAR*-šú* 14 ii 18, GÍR.AN.B]AR*-ma* 6: 636frg, GÍR.AN].BAR.MEŠ 6: 635frg, GÍR]*-šú* 6: 455frg, GÍ]R*-šú* 6: 455frg, G]ÍR.MEŠ*-ma* 6: 636frg, G]ÍR.AN.BAR 10: 5, *pat-ri* 6: 458k, *pat-ru* 6: 458frg, [GÍR.ME]Š 6: 635L, [GÍR.ME]Š*-ma* 6: 636L, [GÍ]R.AN.BAR 6: 458A,

patû "to open": *ta-pat-ti* 5 iii 14, *ta-pat-t*[*i* 5 iii 13, *tú-pat-ta-a-ni* 6: 144E, *tu-pat-ta-a-ni* 6: 144frg, 8 r. 7, *tu-pat-t*[*a-a-ni* 6: 144t, *tu-pa*]*t-ta-a-ni* 8 r. 12,

patiu "remote": *pa-ti-ú-ti* 6: 218H, *pa-ti-u-ni* 13 ii 14, *pa-ti-u-te* 6: 218J, *pa-ti-u-t*]*i* 6: 218C,

paṭāru "to undo, release": *ip-pi-ṭir* 6: 481D, *i-*DU_8 14 ii 22, *lip-ṭu-ur* 5 iv 11, *pa-aṭ-ru* 6: 389D, [*pa*]*-aṭ-ru* 6: 389A,

pazzuru "to conceal": *nu-pa-zar-u-ni* 6: 505A, *nu-pa-za-ar-u-ni* 6: 505V, *nu-pa-za-ru-u-ni* 6: 505D, *tu-ba-za-ra-ni* 6: 80H, *tu-pa-zar* 13 iii 15, *tu-pa-zar-a-ni* 6: 80a, *tu-pa-za*[*r_4-a-ni*] 6: 80G, *tu-pa-za*]*r_4-a-ni* 6: 80G, *tu-pa-za-ra-a-ni* 6: 80A, I, 119frg, *tu-pa-za-ru-ni* 2 iii 22, *tu-pa-*[*za-ra-ni*] 6: 119o, *tu-p*[*a-x* 6: 311A, *t*]*u-pa-za-ra-a-ni* 6: 119frg, [*tu-pa-za*]*r_4-a-ni* 6: 80x,

pāhutu "governor": LÚ.EN.NAM 1: 3, LÚ.NAM 6: 321B, C, LÚ.NAM.MEŠ 6: 77A, a, x, 8: 6, LÚ.N[AM 6: 321N, L]Ú.NAM.MEŠ 6: 77H, [LÚ.NAM.MEŠ] 4 r. 5,

pānīu "former": *pa-ni-ú-ti* 6: 320B, *pa-ni-ú-ut-ti* 6: 320C, *pa-ni-u-ti* 6: 320N, *pa-ni-u-tú* 6: 320c,

pānu "face": IGI 2 iv 20, v 21, 6: 13A, G, K, frg, 16A, K, frg, 41A, 153A, E, frg, 249A, I, frg, 269A, B, i, 279A, B, Y, frg, 296A, B, C, H, 324B, C, N, c, 327B, C, N, frg, 332B, frg, 346B, F, R, w, 353R, 364B, R, frg, z, 366R, frg, z, 370frg, 420B, c, 534A, F, 535F, 604A, H, frg, 617G, K, L, frg, m, 8 r. 16, IGI-*ia* 13 iii 15, IGI-*ka* 5 iii 11, 13 ii 14, IGI-*ku-nu* 6: 408C, 481D, IGI.MEŠ-*ku-nu* 6: 662frg, IGI.MEŠ-*ku-n*[*u* 6: 297B, IGI.MEŠ-*šú* 6: 345frg, IGI-*ni-šú* 6: 89A, 281A, IGI-*ni*-[*šú* 6: 281B, IGI-*šú* 5 iii 14, 6: 89I, frg, d, 341F, R, frg, 343w, 345F, R, IGI-*šú-nu* 6: 278B, IGI-*š*[*u*] 6: 341frg, IGI-[*šú* 6: 343frg, IG[I 6: 368frg, z, IG]I 6: 41E, 153P, 534M, I[GI 6: 535frg, I]GI 6: 16G, I]GI-*ni* 6: 379frg, *pa*]-*ni-šú* 6: 343A, *pa-an* 9: 7, 25, 28, 13 iii 12, *pa-ni* 2 i 17, 20, 6: 544A, 9: 8, 38, *pa-ni-ku-nu* 6: 297C, 374frg, *pa-ni-ni* 9: 30, *pa-ni-ni*] 9: 36, *pa-ni-šú* 6: 89frg, 341p, 343F, 10: 10, *pa-ni-šú-nu* 6: 278A, *pa-ni-šú*-[*nu* 6: 278Y, *pa-n*]*i-ku-nu* 6: 297H, *pa*-[*ni* 9: 37, *pa*-[*ni-šú* 6: 345p, *p*[*a-ni-šú-nu* 6: 278frg, [*pa-ni*]-*ku-nu* 6: 374B, [*pa-n*]*i* 4 r. 9, [(IGI⌉ 10: 2,

pe'ettu "coal": *pe-e*ʾ-*na-a-ti* 6: 533B, G, *pe-eh-n*[*a-a-ti*] 6: 533A, [*pe-e*ʾ-*na*]-*a-ti* 6: 533M,

pilaqqu "spindle": GIŠ.BAL 6: 616G, GIŠ.*pi-laq-qi* 6: 616L, frg, GIŠ.*pi-laq*-[*qi* 6: 616m, *pi-laq-qi* 6: 616K,

pirku "injustice": *pi-ir-k*[*u* 5 iii 27,

pirru "(tax) collection": *pi-ir-ri* 6: 182A, I, frg,

pispisu "bug": *pi-is-pi-su* 6: 603A, H, T, h, *pi-is-pi-s*[*u* 6: 603j, *pi-is-p*]*i-su* 6: 603L, *pi-is-(pi)-su* 6: 603frg, *pi-is*-[*pi-su* 6: 603K,

piššatu "unguent, ointment": *pi-šat-ku-nu* 6: 491D, ŠÉŠ-*šú-nu* 2 iv 14,

pithu "wound": *pi-it-hi-ku-nu* 6: 645A, *pi-it-hi*-[*ku-nu* 6: 645frg, *pi-i*[*t-hi-ku-nu* 6: 645frg,

pitiltu "cord": *pi-til-te* 6: 607frg, *pi-til-ti* 6: 607A, *pi-ti-i*]*l-ti* 6: 607K,

pitqu "fold": *pit-qí-šú* 2 i 10, 16, 17,

pitti "according to": *pi-it* 6: 567frg, *pi*-[*it-ti* 6: 567frg, *pi-it*]-*ti* 6: 567Q, *pit-ti* 5 iii 23, *p*]*i-it-ti* 6: 567Q, *p*]*u-ut* 6: 567D, [*pit-ti* 10: 4,

puhru "assembly": *pu-uh-ri* 6: 373frg, *pu-uh-ru* 6: 212frg, *pu-uh-r*[*i*] 6: 373B, UKKIN 6: 212J, O, u,

purussû "decision": EŠ.BAR 1 r. 6,

puzru "shelter": *pu-uz-ri* 6: 478D,

pūlu "limestone": *pu-l*[*i* 2 i 8,

pūtu "in accordance with": *pu-ut* 10 r. 5,

pû "mouth, utterance, command": KA-*šú* 2 i 26, 6: 417A, *pi* 6:115E, *pi*]-*i* 4 r. 4, 6: 113E, 10: 7, *pi-i* 4 r. 5, 6, 5 ii 10, 6: 76A, H, x, 77A, H, a, x, 78A, x, 79A, G, H, I, a, 111E, frg, 112E, frg, 113A, frg, 115frg, 116E, frg, 118A, 135A, 13 iii 11, *pi-i*]-*ku-nu* 6: 569D, *pi-i-ku-nu* 5 iv 16, 6: 569Q, frg, *pi-i-ni* 6: 498D, V, *pi-i-šá* 6: 548A, *pi-i-šú* 5 iii 12, 6: 195J, frg, 13 ii 13, 14 i 6, *pi-i-šú-un* 14 i 30, *pi-i*-[*ni* 6: 498q, *pi*-[*i-šá* 6: 548frg, *pi*-[*i-šú* 9: 22, *p*[*i-i* 6: 111A, 113frg, 115frg, 135frg, *p*[*i-i-šú-un*] 14 ii 4, *p*]*i-i* 6: 112frg, 135O, [*pi*]-*i-ni* 6: 498q, [*pi-i* 10: 5, 13 ii 4,

qabassu "middle; within": *qab-si* 6: 199frg, *qab*-[*si* 6: 199J,

qablu "middle; within": MURUB₄ 4 r. 20, 6: 181A, I, 453A, g, l, 614A, G, K, L, frg, MUR[UB₄ 6: 614m, *qa-bal* 6: 181frg,

qabû "to say, tell": *a-qab-bi* 4 r. 3, *a-qab-b*[*u-u-ni*] 4 r. 7, *iq-ba*]-*ka-nu-ni* 6: 102A, *iq-ba-ka*]-*nu-u-ni* 6: 134t, *iq-ba-ka-nu-ni* 6: 64A, *iq-ba-ka-nu-u-ni* 6: 102E, *iq-ba-ka-nu-u-n*[*i*] 6: 348F, *iq-ba-ka-nu-u*-[*ni* 6: 348w, *iq-ba-ka-nu-u*-[*ni*] 6: 102frg, y, *iq-ba-ka-n*[*u-u-ni*] 6: 102frg, *iq-ba-ka*-[*nu-u-ni* 6: 125A, *iq-ba-k*[*a-nu-u-ni*] 6: 102F, *iq-ba-k*]*a-nu-u-ni* 6: 134frg, *iq-ba*-[*ka*]-*nu-ni* 6: 64W, *iq-bi* 6: 420c, *iq-bi*] 4 r. 17, *iq-bu-u-ni* 6: 333B, frg, *iq-b*[*a-ka-nu-u-ni* 6: 348A, *iq-qa-ba-kan-u-ni* 6: 323N, *iq-ta-bu-ú* 1: 9, *iq*-[*ba-k*]*a-nu-u-ni* 6: 125E, *i*[*q-ba-ka-nu-u-ni* 6: 125o, *i*]*q-ba-ka-nu-ni* 6: 134E, *i-qab*]-*bu-u-ni* 6: 194frg, *i-qab-ba-ak-ka-nu-u-ni* 6: 323c, *i-qab-ba-an-na-a-šú* 9: 22, *i-qab-ba-áš-šú* 1: 14, *i-qab-ba-kan-u-ni* 6: 340R, *i-qab-ba-ka-nu-ni* 6: 232B, 323C, *i-qab-ba-ka-nu-u-ni* 6: 340F, p, *i-qab-ba-ka*-[*nu-ni*] 6: 336F, *i-qab-bu-ú* 9: 14, 15, *i-qab-bu-u-ni* 6: 194Y, *i-qab-b*[*u-u-ni*] 6: 194J, *i-q*]*ab-ba-ka-nu-u-ni* 6: 134O, *li*]*q-bi* 1 e. 18, *ni-iq-ta*-[*bi* 9: 19, *ni-qa-bu*]-*u-ni* 6: 507A, q, *ni-qa-bu-u-ni* 6: 507D, *ni-qa-bu-u-n*]*i* 6: 507frg, *ni*]-*qa-bu-u-ni* 6: 507V, *qi-bi* 13 iii 5, *qi-bi-a* 6: 325B, C, N, c, *ta-qab-ba*]-*a-ni* 3: 3, 6: 122O, *ta-qab-ba-a*]-*ni* 6: 149A, 271frg, *ta-qab-ba-a-ni* 6: 82A, x, 152P, 158A, B, E, P, 271A, 280A, 290A, 345F, R, 350F, R, 371frg, 8 r. 17, *ta-qab-ba-a-ni-šú-ni* 6: 290B, *ta-qab-ba-a*-[*ni*] 6: 350frg, *ta-qab-ba-a*-[*n*]*i* 6: 364R, *ta-qab-ba-ni* 6: 122frg, *ta-qab-ba-niš-šú-un-ni* 6: 82H, *ta-qab-ba-niš*-[*x* 6: 290C, *ta-qab-ba*-[*a-ni* 6: 271i, *ta-qab-ba*-[*a-ni*] 6: 364frg, *ta-qab-bu-u-ni* 13 iii 4, *ta-qab-b*]*a-a-ni* 6: 122E, *ta-qab-b*]*a-a*-[*ni*] 6: 122frg, *ta-qab*-[*ba*]-*a*-[*ni*] 6: 82G, *ta-qa*[*b-ba-a-ni* 6: 364frg, *ta-qa*]*b-ba-a-ni* 6: 345w, *ta-qa-ba-a-ni* 6: 82I, 271frg, 280frg, *ta-q*[*ab-ba-a-ni* 6: 364frg, *ta-q*[*ab-ba-a-ni*] 6: 152E, 280frg, *ta*-[*qab-b*]*a-a-ni* 6: 280B, *t*[*a-qab-ba-a-ni* 6: 364z, *t*[*a-qa*]*b-ba*-[*a-ni* 6: 369frg, *t*]*a-qab-ba-a-ni* 6: 345A, *t*]*a-qab-ba-ni* 6: 280Y, [*ta-qab-ba-a*]-*ni* 6: 271B, [*iq-ba*]-*kan-u-n*[*i* 6: 64frg, [*iq-ba-ka-nu*]-*u-ni* 6: 348R, [*iq-ba-ka-nu-u*]-*ni* 6: 348frg, [*iq-b*]*a-ka-nu-u-ni* 6: 125frg, [*i*]*q-ba-ka-nu-u-n*[*i* 6: 348B, [*i-qab*]-*ba-kan-u-ni* 6: 336frg, [*ta-qab*]-*ba-a-ni* 6: 271F, 369z,

qallu "small; boy": LÚ.[*qà*]*l-lu* 8: 9,

qamû "to burn": *liq-mu* 6: 525G, *liq-mu-u* 6: 610A, K, L, *liq-mu-ú* 6: 610M, *liq-mu*-[*u*] 6: 610G, *liq-m*[*u-u*] 6: 610m, *l*]*iq-mu-u* 6: 610frg,

qanû A "reed": GI.MEŠ 6: 631frg, *qa-né*-[*e* 6: 631A,

qanû B "to acquire": *iq-nu-u-ni* 6: 274A, frg, *iq-qi-nu-u-n*[*i*] 6: 274B,

qaqqadu see *kaqqudu,*

qaqqaru see *kaqquru,*

qarābu A "battle": *qa-ra-a-bu* 6: 311C, *qa-ra-bu* 6: 311A,

qarābu B "to approach, arrive": *i-qar-ri-ba* 6: 640frg, *i-qa-ri-ba* 6: 640A, *qur*]-*bu-u-t*[*i*] 6: 217frg, *qur-bu* 5 iii 14, *qur-bu-ti* 6: 217C, J, frg, e, *ta-qar-rib-a-ni* 10: 13, [*qur*]-*bu-u-ni* 13 iii 14,

qardu "heroic": *qar-du-te* 5 iv 5, *qar-du-ti* 2 vi 20, *qa*]*r-d*[*u-te* 6: 464frg,

qarītu "banquet": *qa-ri-ti* 2 i 11,

qarnu "germinal shoot": *qar-nu* 6: 540k, SI 6: 540F, frg,

qarrādu "hero": *qar-ra-du* 1 r. 16, *qar-rad* 6: 455g, *qar-r*[*ad* 6: 455A, UR.SAG 6: 455l,

qassu "bow": GIŠ.BAN 6: 574D, Q, b, GIŠ.BAN-*ku-nu* 5: 418E, 6: 453frg, 573D, Q, GIŠ.BAN.MEŠ-*ni*

9: 23, GIŠ.BAN-*su-nu* 2 v 13, [GIŠ.BAN-*šú* 4 r. 20,

qatāpu "to pluck, cut off": *qa-ti-ip* 2 i 27, *qa-[ti-pu-u-ni]* 2 i 25,

qatû "to end": *liq-qat-ti-ma* 2 iv 10, *liq-ti* 6: 487D, *li-qa]t-ta-a* 4 r. 27, *li-šaq-ti]* 1 r. 12,

qābiānu "speaker": *qa-bi-a-nu* 6: 347F, *qa-bi-a-nu-ti* 6: 347R, *qa-bi-a-n[u* 6: 347B, w,

qātu "hand": *qa-at-ku-nu* 6: 105E, ŠU.[2 6: 590D, ŠU.2 5 iv 7, 6: 468D, 577Q, 583Z, frg, v, 590b, h, 601A, T, frg, h, 10 r. 4, 13 iii 1, 2, 14 ii 17, ŠU.2]-*ku-nu* 6: 374frg, 574Q, ŠU.2-*i-ni* 6: 511D, ŠU.2-*ka* 6: 365R, frg, z, ŠU.2-*ku-nu* 6: 66A, W, 105frg, 374frg, 536M, 574D, b, ŠU.2-*ku-n[u* 6: 66frg, ŠU.2-*k[a* 6: 365frg, ŠU.2-*šú* 6: 5F, G, H, T, a, d, ŠU.2-[*ni*] 6: 511V, Š]U.2-*ni* 6: 511frg, [*qa-at* 14 i 12, [*qa-at*] 14 i 11, [ŠU.2]-*ku-nu* 6: 374B,

qerbu "inside, between": *qer-bu-uš-un* 14 i 23,

qēpu "royal delegate": LÚ.*qe-e-bi* 5 iii 13, LÚ.*qe-e-pu* 5 iii 6, 8, 14, LÚ.[*qe*]-*e-bi* 5 iii 12,

qiāšu "to grant, bestow": *i-qiš-ku-nu* 6: 416A,

qi''u "envy": EN—*qi-ʾi* 6: 328B, frg,

qibītu "utterance, command": *qí-bi-sa* 1 r. 4, *qí-bit* 2 iv 1, *qí-bit-sa* 1 r. 5, *q[í-bi-ti* 14 ii 10,

qinītu "purchase, acquisition": *qí-ni-ti* 2 i 11, *qi-ni-tu* 6: 274A, *qi-ni-tú* 6: 274B, F, [*q*]*i-ni-tu* 6: 274frg,

qinniš "backwards": *qí-in-niš* 6: 566frg, 619A, *qí-niš-ši* 6: 619K, *qí-[i]n-niš* 6: 566D, *qí-[niš* 6: 575Q, *qi-in-niš* 6: 619G, L, *q[í]-niš* 6: 575D, *q[í-in-niš]* 6: 619frg,

qinnu "family, kin": *qin-ni-šu* 6: 115frg, 215J, 337frg, *qin-ni-šú* 6: 4a, 77A, x, 115A, 337F, *qin-n]i-šú* 6: 337B, *q]in-ni-šú* 6: 215u, 319c,

qīru "pitch": *qi-i-ru* 6: 490D, *qi-ru* 2 iv 14, 6: 586v, *q]i-i-ru* 6: 490frg,

qutāru "fumigant": *qu-ta-a-r[i* 7: 9,

ra'āmu "to love": ÁG-*ú-ni* 11 r. 4, *i-ra-a-mu-u-ni* 6: 207J, *i-ra-a-mu-u-n[i]* 6: 207u, *i-ra-ʾa-mu-u-ni* 6: 207e, *i-ra-ʾa-mu-u-[ni]* 6: 207frg, *i-ra-ʾa-mu-[u-ni]* 6: 207O, *ni-ra-ʾa-a-mu* 9: 32, *tar-a-ma-a-ni* 6: 268B, *tar-a-ma-a-[ni]* 6: 268frg, *tar-a-ma-ni* 6: 268M, *tar-ʾa-ma-a-ni* 6: 268A, *ta-ram-ma-ni* 6: 268i,

rab ša-rēši "chief eunuch": LÚ.GAL—SAG 11: 1,

rabāṣu "to lie down": *i-rab-bi-[ṣu-u-ni]* 6: 556frg, *i-rab-b[i-ṣu-u-ni]* 6: 556D, *i-ra-bi-ṣu-u-ni* 6: 556A,

rabiu "magnate": GAL.MEŠ-*ka* 2 v 3, GAL.MEŠ-*šu*] 2 i 27, GAL.MEŠ-*šú* 2 i 8, 23, r. iv 2, 5, 17, v 4, GAL.MEŠ-*šú*] 2 i 6, 30, 34, G[AL.MEŠ-*šú* 2 i 2, LÚ.GAL 6: 321C, LÚ.GAL.MEŠ 6: 77A, a, x, 8: 6, LÚ.GA[L 6: 321A, L]Ú.GAL.MEŠ 4 r. 5, [GAL.MEŠ-*šú*] 2 i 18,

rabû A "to be great, grow": GAL 3: 5, 5 i 3, 6: 5A, F, G, H, T, a, 11A, 43A, 47A, frg, 58A, 62A, W, 75A, S, 81A, G, I, a, 84A, 92A, I, frg, 94A, I, frg, 101E, F, 103y, 109E, frg, 130E, 137E, 143E, P, frg, 150E, P, 156A, E, P, 165A, E, I, P, S, 167A, E, M, P, 170A, M, S, frg, 173I, M, S, frg, 179frg, 188frg, 226f, 229C, X, frg, f, 239A, X, frg, 247A, frg, 250A, B, frg, 258A, B, I, 260B, frg, 266A, F, 269A, B, M, frg, 279A, 284A, B, Y, 285A, B, Y, frg, 298B, 316A, C, 324B, C, c, 349B, F, 353B, R, 362R, z, 371frg, 380s, 391D, 394H, 403D, 495D, q, 496D, q, 503A, D, q, 504A, D, q, 506A, D, 508A, D, 514D, 555frg, 633F, K, L, 667Q, frg, 669frg, GAL-*e* 6: iiiA, H, GAL.MEŠ 5 iv 8, 6: 41A, E, 56A, E, W, frg, n, r, 69A, W, 219C, H, J, frg, e, 401D, 523A, B, 524G, 11 r. 6, 14 ii 10, GAL.M[EŠ 9: 2, GAL-*ti* 14 ii 19, GAL-*tu* 1 r. 5, GAL-*tú* 4 r. 18, 5 iv 3, 6: 461frg, GAL-*u* 1 r. 16, 2 iv 4, 6: 58r, 75H, 81H, 84G, d, 94frg, 101frg, 103E, frg, 120frg, 123frg, 137t, 150H, 156H, 179I, 184I, 188I, 239J, 247frg, 250I, 258i, 260i, 266frg, i, 269frg, 285frg, 298H, 316J, 324N, 362frg, 366frg, 391H, 496frg, 503V, 504V, 506V, 514V, 515V, 633frg, GAL-*ú* 1 e. 16, r. 8, 6: 495frg, 14 ii 3, 7, GAL-[*e*] 6: iiiF, GAL-[*u*] 6: 120o, GAL]-*e* 6: iiiB, Y, frg, GAL]-*u* 6: 143t, 226J, 266p, GA[L 6: 101frg, 109y, 226H, 394D, GA[L.MEŠ 6: 219H, GA[L-*u*] 6: 103frg, 120frg, GA[L] 6: 58frg, 170G, 260A, 349A, GA]L 6: 123E, 137O, G[AL 6: 92G, frg, 137A, 150A, G[AL-*tú* 6: 461frg, G[AL] 6: 391A, G]AL 6: 173A, 366R, G]AL.MEŠ 6: 472D, G]AL-*u* 6: 58W, G]A[L] 6: 101A, *ra-bi-ta* 1 r. 11, *tu-rab-ba-a-ni* 6: 252A, B, *tu-ra-ba-a-ni* 6: 252I, [GAL-*e* 6: 405A, [GAL.MEŠ 14 i 27, [G]AL 6: 266B, 298C, [G]A[L 6: 77H,

rabû "to set": *ra-ba* 6: 6F, T, *ra-b[a* 6: 6a, *ra-bé-e* 6: 6H,

radû "to lead": *li-ir-di-šu* 1 r. 1,

raggimu "prophet": LÚ.*ra-gi-me* 6: 116frg, LÚ. *ra-g[i-me]* 6: 116frg, *ra-gi-me* 6: 116E,

rahāṣu "to spatter": *li*]-*ra-ah-ṣa* 6: 615H, *li-ra*]-*ah-[ṣa]* 6: 615frg, *li-ra-ah-ṣa* 6: 615G, *li-ra-ah-[ṣa]* 6: 615frg, *lu-šar-hi-ṣu* 6: 615A, *lu-ša[r-hi-ṣu]* 6: 615K, *ra*]-*ah-ṣa-at* 6: 615L, *ra-ah-ah-ṣa-tu-[u]-ni* 6: 613K, *ra-ah-ṣa-tu-u-ni* 6: 613frg, *ra-ah-ṣa-tu-u-[ni]* 6: 613G, *ra-ah-ṣa-[tu-u-ni* 6: 613frg, *r*]*a-ah-ṣa-tú-u-ni* 6: 613A, *r*]*a-ah-ṣa-tu-u-ni* 6: 613L,

rakāsu "to tie, bind": *li-ir-ku-su* 6: 458A, *li-ir-ku-su*] 5 iv 1, *li-ir-ku-[su]* 6: 458B, frg, *li-i*]*r-ku-su* 6: 458k, *ta-rak-kás-a-ni* 6: 376frg, *ta-rak-kas-a-[ni]* 6: 376B, *ta-rak-kas-ni* 6: 376frg,

ramanu "self": *ra-ma-ni-ku-nu* 6: 615G, frg, *ra-ma-ni-ku-[nu* 6: 615m, *ra-ma-ni-[ku-nu* 6: 615frg, *ra-ma-n[i-ku-nu* 6: 615L, *ra-ma-[ni-ku-nu* 6: 356R, *ra-me-ni-ku-nu* 6: 615K, *r[a-ma-ni-k]u-nu* 6: 390D, *r*]*a-me-ni-ku-nu* 6: 615A,

ramāku "to bathe": *ru-un-ka* 5 iv 4, *ru-[un-ka]* 6: 463frg,

rammû "to leave, let go": *tu-ram-ma-a-ni* 6: 634A, F, *tu-ra-ma*]-*šú-u-ni* 6: 348A, *tu-ra-ma-šá-nu-u-ni* 6: 348R, *tu-ra-ma-šu* 6: 205J, *tu-ra-ma-šú*]-*u-ni* 6: 348w, *tu-ra-ma-šú-nu* 6: 205frg, *tu-ra-ma-šú-u-ni* 6: 348F, *tu-ra-ma-š[ú-u-ni]* 6: 348frg, [*t*]*u-ram-ma-a-ni* 6: 634L, [*t*]*u-ra-ma-a-ni* 6: 634frg,

rapādu "to run, roam": *li-ir-pu-du* 2 iv 6, *ru-up-da* 6: 421c, *ru-up-d*]*a* 6: 421A, *ru-[u]p-da* 6: 421C,

rašû "to get": *ir-še* 6: 452frg, *ir-ši* 6: 452frg, *ir-[ši]* 6: 452A, TUK-*šú-nu* 2 iv 6,

rā'imānu "lover": *ra-im-a-nu* 11 r. 3,

rā'imu "lover": LÚ.*ra-ʾi-ma-ni-šú* 9: 18,

rābiṣu (an evil demon): *ra-bi-ṣu* 6: 493D,

redû see *radû*,

rēbītu "square, plaza": *re-bit* 2 v 10, 4 r. 23, 6: 439I, 483D, frg,

rēhtu "rest": *re-eh-te* 8: 5, *re-eh-ti* 3: 5, 6: 497D, frg, q, 633frg, *re-eh-t]i* 6: 505q, *re-e[h-ti* 6: 516V,

rēmu "mercy": ARHUŠ 6: 459frg, *re-e-mu* 2 iv 6, 5 iv 2, 6: 459A, k, 9 r. 22, *r*]*e-e-mu* 6: 459frg,

rēštû "foremost, eldest": *reš-tu-u* 6: 433B, I, *reš-t*]*u-u* 6: 433A, SAG-*tu-ú* 9 r. 17,

rēšu "head": *re-eš-k[a* 6: 204frg, [*re*]-*eš-ka* 6: 204C,

riāqu "to be empty, free": *li*]-*ri-qu* 6: 642frg, *li-ri-qu* 6: 642A, *ra-qi* 6: 181A, *ra-q*]*i* 6: 181I, *ra-qu-u-ni* 6: 641A, frg, *ra-qu-*[*u-ni*] 6: 641frg,

rihṣu "downpour, devastation": GÌR.BAL 2 v 6, *ri-ih-ṣi* 6: 442A, g, *r*[*i-ih-ṣi* 6: 442C,

riksu "setup, bond, bundle": KÉŠ 6: 154A, E, P, *rik-si* 6: 631F, frg, *rik-s*]*i* 6: 631K, *ri*]*k-si* 6: 631G, *ri-k*[*is*] 6: 154H,

rimṭu (a venereal disease): *ri-im-ṭu* 6: 470D,

rubû "ruler, prince": LÚ.NUN 6: 321N, NUN 9 r. 23, 14 i 9, NUN-*e* 6: 321B, c, 405A, iiiA, F, H, NUN-[*e* iiiI,

rūqiš "far": *ru-qiš* 14 ii 5,

sahāpu "to overwhelm": *li-is-hu-pu* 6: 650frg, *li-is-hu-up* 6: 650U,

sahāru "to return": *lu-sa-hi-r*[*u*] 6: 566frg, *lu-*[*sa-h*]*i-ru* 6: 566D, *ta-sa*]-*hu-ra* 6: 581Q, *ta-sa-ah-hu-ra* 6: 581Z, *ta-sa-har-u-ni* 6: 542k, *ta-sa-ha*[*r-u-ni*] 6: 580v, *ta-sa-hu-ra* 6: 581b, *ta-sa-hu-r*[*a*] 6: 581frg, *ta-sa-h*[*ar-u-ni* 6: 580D, *ta-sa-h*[*ar-u-ni*] 6: 542F, *ta-sa-h*[*u-ra*] 6: 581v, *ta-sa-*[*har-u-ni*] 6: 542frg, *ta-s*[*a-ha*]*r-u-*[*ni*] 6: 580b, *t*]*a-sa-har-u-ni* 6: 580frg, *ú-sa-hu-ru* 5 iii 17,

sakāpu "to reject": *li-is-kip* 1 r. 9, *ni-sek-ki-pu* 9: 25,

salāmu "to make peace": *ta-sa-lim* 13 ii 3,

salmu "ally": *sa-li-me-*[*šú*] 6: 112E *sa-l*]*i-me-šú* 6: 112frg, *sa-*[*x x x*] 6: 112frg, *sal-me-šú* 6: 112frg,

salû "to lie": *t*]*a-sa-li-a-ni* 8: 15,

samāhu "to unite": *ú-sa-ta-a-mah-u-ni* 6: 282B, *ú-sa-ta-mah-u-ni* 6: 282A,

samiktu "misdeed(?)": *sa-an-ka-a-te* 10 r. 5,

sapāhu "to disperse": *sa-pa-ah* 1 e. 17,

sapāku "to catch": *is-sa-pa-ku-u-ni* 6: 589D, [*is-s*]*a-pa-ku-u-ni* 6: 589Z,

sapānu "to level, deface": *ta-sa-pan-a-ni* 6: 413A,

sarbu (mng. uncert.): *sar-bu* 6: 373frg, [*sa*]*r-bu* 6: 373B,

sartu "fine, punishment": *sar-ti* 2 v 22,

sassu "base-board": *sa-se-e-*[*šá*] 6: 612A, *sa-se-šá* 6: 612G, M, frg, [*sa-s*]*e-e-šá* 6: 612K,

sasû "to shout": *li-is-si-ma* 1 r. 15,

sekēru "to dam": *lis*]-*kir* 1 r. 8,

semeru "manacles": *se-me-re-e* 9: 16,

siāqu "to be tight": *li-si-q*[*u-ni-ku-nu*] 6: 527B, *li-s*[*i-qu-ni-ku-nu*] 6: 527A, *lu-si-qu-ni-ku-nu* 6: 527F, G,

simmu "sore, wound": *si-im-mu* 5 iv 4, *si-mu* 6: 462frg, [*si*]-*mu* 6: 462frg,

simunu "time": *si*]-*me-ni-šú* 6: 202J, *si-la-ma-n*[*i-šú* 6: 202frg,

siparru "bronze": UD.KA.BAR 6: 530A, B, F, 649U, frg, UD.KA].BAR 6: 530M,

sirrimu "wild ass": *sír-ri-me* 6: 421A, B, C, c,

sissû "horse": ANŠE.KUR.RA.MEŠ 2 iv 7, 6: 276A, frg, ANŠE.KUR.RA.[MEŠ] 6: 276B, ANŠ]E.KUR.RA.ME[Š 1: 2,

sīhu "conspiracy, rebellion": *si-hi* 8: 20, r. 3, *si-hu* 6: 133A, E, 166A, I, P, S, 245frg, 303B, C, 498D, V, *si-h*[*u* 6: 498q, [*si*]-*hu* 6: 166E, [*si-h*]*u* 6: 303A, 498q,

sīqu "lap": *si-qi-ku-nu* 6: 375B, *si-qi-k*[*u-nu*] 6: 375frg, *si-qi-k*]*u-nu* 6: 375frg,

sīsu "teat(?)": *si-si* 6: 481D,

su''u "dove": *su-ʾi* 6: 637A, frg, *s*[*u-ʾi* 6: 637frg,

summiš "like a dove": *su-*[*um-mi-iš* 14 ii 7,

sunqu "want": *su-un-qi* 2 iv 8, *su-un-qu* 6: 480D, *s*[*u-un-qu* 6: 480H,

surrāti "lies, treason": *sur-ra-a-ti* 6: 502D, *su*]-*ra-a-ti* 6: 502q, *su-ra-a-ti* 6: 502V, *su-*[*ra-a-ti* 6: 502q, *s*]*u-ra-a-te* 6: 502A,

sūnu "bosom": ÚR 6: 429B, frg,

sūqu "street": SILA 6: 439I, SI[LA 6: 439F,

ṣabāru "to spin": *lu-šá-aṣ-bir-ku-nu* 6: 616G, *lu-šá-aṣ-bi-ru-ku-nu* 6: 616A, L, *lu-šá-ṣa-bir-ku-nu* 6: 616K, [*lu-šá*]-*ṣa-*[*bi-ru-ku-nu*] 6: 616frg,

ṣabātu "to seize, take hold of": *aṣ*]-*ṣab-bat-ni* 6: 582Q, *iṣ-bat* 4 r. 25, 6: 418C, *iṣ-bat*] 1 r. 7, *iṣ-ba-ta* 6: 418A, *iṣ-ba-tú* 6: 24A, *iṣ-b*[*a-ta* 6: 418B, *iṣ-ṣab-bat-u-ni* 6: 582Z, b, *iṣ-ṣab-bat-u-*[*ni*] 6: 582v, *iṣ-ṣab-tu-ku-nu* 6: 177A, B, M, *iṣ-ṣab-tu-ku-*[*nu*] 6: 177I, *iṣ-ṣi-bat-tu* 6: 24frg, *i*]*ṣ-ṣab-tu-ku-nu* 6: 177frg, *i*]*ṣ-ṣab-tu-ma* 1: 7, *i*]*ṣ-ṣa-bat-u-ni* 6: 582frg, *na*]-*aṣ-b*[*i-ta*] 6: 590j, *na-aṣ-b*[*i-ta*] 6: 590h, *na-aṣ-b*]*i-ta* 6: 590Z, *na-ṣa-bi-ta* 6: 590Q, *ni-ṣab-bat-ú-ma* 9: 31, *ṣa-ba-te-šú* 6: 306frg, *ṣa-ba-te-šú-nu* 6: 142E, *ṣa-ba-ti-šu* 6: 306C, *ṣa-ba-ti-šú* 6: 306A, *ṣa-ba-ti-šú-nu* 6: 138E, *ṣa-ba-*[*te-šú-nu* 6: 142t, *ṣa-ba-*[*ti-šú-nu*] 6: 138t, *ṣa-bat-ti-šú* 6: 306B, *ṣu-ub-*[*bit* 1: 9, *šu-uṣ-*[*bu-tu*] 14 i 7, *ta-ṣab-bat-a-ni* 6: 160P, 254A, *ta-ṣab-bat-a-ni-ni* 6: 136A, O, 160S, 254I, *ta-ṣab-bat-a-ni-šú-u-ni* 6: 246A, 305A, *ta-ṣab-bat-a-šá-nu-ni* 6: 139E, *ta-ṣab-bat-a-šú-u-ni* 6: 246frg, 305C, *ta-ṣab-bat-*[*x* 6: 246frg, *ta-ṣab-ba-ta-nin-ni* 8 r. 24, *ta-ṣab-*[*bat-a-ni-ni*] 6: 136t, *ta-ṣab-*[*x* 6: 139t, 246X, *ta-ṣa-bat-a-ni-ni* 6: 136E, 160E, 254B, *ta-ṣa-bat-a-šú-u-ni* 6: 305frg, *ta-ṣa-ba*]*t* 6: 536K, *ta-ṣa-ba*]-*t*[*a*] 6: 536M, *ta-ṣa-ba-ta-šu-u-ni* 6: 126E, *ta-ṣa-ba-ta-*[*šu-u-ni*] 6: 126frg, *ta-ṣa-ba-*(*ta*)*-a-ni-ni* 6: 160A, *ta-ṣ*]*ab-bat-a-ni* 6: 146P, *ta-*[*ṣab-bat-a*]-*niš-šú-u-ni* 6: 305B, *tú-šá-aṣ-bat-a-ni* 6: 224f, 227f, *tú-šá-aṣ-ba-ta* 6: 85I, *tú-šá-a*[*ṣ-bat-a-ni*] 6: 70W, *tu-šá*]-*aṣ-bat-a-ni* 6: 317B, *tu-šá-aṣ*]-*bat-a-ni* 6: 227C, *tu-šá-aṣ-bat-a-ni* 6: 70A, 85G, 224C, 253A, B, I, 317C, J, *tu-šá-aṣ-bat-a-*[*ni*] 6: 224J, *tu-šá-aṣ-bat-ta* 6: 85A, *tu-šá-aṣ-bat-u-ni* 6: 248A, *tu-šá-aṣ-bat-*[*a-ni*] 6: 248frg, *tu-šá-a*[*ṣ-bat-a-ni*] 6: 248X, *tu-*[*šá-aṣ*]-*bat-a-ni* 6: 227H, *tu-*[*šá-a*]*ṣ-bat-a-ni* 6: 224H, *t*[*u-šá-a*]*ṣ-bat-ta* 6: 85d, *t*]*a-ṣa-ba-ta* 6: 536F, *t*]*u-šá-aṣ-bat-a-*[*ni*] 6: 227J, *ú-šá-aṣ*]-*bit-su-nu-ti-ma* 14 i 29, *ú-šá-aṣ-bit-su-nu-ti* 14 i 27, *ú-šá-aṣ-bit-s*[*u-nu-ti-ma*] 14 ii 3, (*ta*)*-ṣab-ba-tú-ni* 2 iii 9, [*iṣ-bat-ma* 14 i 14, [*na-aṣ-bi*]-*ta* 6: 590b, [*tu-šá-a*]*ṣ-bat-t*[*a-a-ni*] 6: 317A,

ṣabītu "gazelle": MAŠ.DÀ 6: 421A, B, C, c,

ṣahāru "to be small, young": *mu-ṣa-hi-ir* 6: 443A, g, *ṣa-ha-ri* 6: 83A, H, I, 237A, J, N, *ṣa-ha-r*[*i* 6: 237B, *ṣa-ha-r*]*i* 6: 237C, *ṣa-ha-*[*ri* 6: 83G, *ṣa-ha-*[*ri*] 6: 237X, TUR 5 i 3, 6: 5A, F, G, H, T, a, TUR.MEŠ 6: 56A, W, frg, n, r, 69A, W, 219C, H, J, frg, e, 524G, TUR.MEŠ-*te* 6: 219J, TU]R.MEŠ 6: 219H, T]UR.MEŠ 6: 69S,

ṣalālu "to sleep": *ta-ṣa-la-la* 6: 639A, frg, *t*[*a-ṣa-la-la*] 6: 639frg,

ṣalāmu "to be black": *li-ṣal-li-mu* 6: 587Z, *lu-ṣal-li-mu* 6: 587Q, b, *lu-ṣa-li-m*[*u*] 6: 587frg, *l*[*u-ṣal-li-mu*] 6: 587v,

ṣalmāt qaqqadi "human being": *ṣal*]-*mat*—SAG.DU 6: 79G, *ṣal-mat—qaq-q*]*a-di* 6: 118E, *ṣal-mat*—SAG.DU 6: 79A, I, a, 118frg, 164S, 223J, f, 339F, *ṣal-mat*—SA[G.DU 6: 118o, *ṣal-mat*—SA]G.DU 6: 339frg, *ṣ*]*al-mat*—SAG.DU 6: 118frg, [*ṣal*]-*mat*—SAG.DU 6: 79H, [*ṣal-mat*—S]AG.DU 6: 79x,

ṣalmu "statue, image": *ṣal-mu* 6: 608A, *ṣa-lam* 6: 402D, 403A, 404A, 608M, frg, *ṣa-lam-(a)-ni-šú-nu* 11 r. 13,

ṣaltu "battle": *ṣal-ti* 9: 24,

ṣapāhu (D) "to scatter, spill": *ṣa-ap-pa-hu-u-ni* 6: 653U,

ṣarāmu "to think, plan": *ta-ṣa[r]-rim-a-ni* 10 r. 7,

ṣābu "men, troops": ERIM.MEŠ 6: 159E, S, 8 r. 19, LÚ.ERIM.MEŠ 6: 5F, H, T, a, d, 159A, P, 169A, I, LÚ.ERIM.[MEŠ-*šú*] 2 v 9, [LÚ.E]RIM.MEŠ 6: 169E, [L]Ú.ERIM.MEŠ 6: 5G,

ṣerru "snake": MUŠ 6: 555A, frg, MU[Š] 6: 555D,

ṣēru "open country, desert": EDIN 2 iv 6, 19, 20, 6: 421B, C, c, 426A, B, 9 r. 20,

ṣētu "heat": UD.DA 6: 477D,

ṣibtu "seizure": *ṣi-bit* 6: 155A, E, [*ṣ*]*i-bit* 6: 155P,

ṣillu "shadow": GIŠ.MI 6: 477D, H,

ṣīru "exalted, august": MAH 6: 431A, M[AH] 6: 431I, *ṣi-i-ru* 6: 431B, *ṣi-i-r*[*i* 11 r. 2, *ṣi-ru* 1 r. 1,

ṣīt libbi "offspring": *ṣi-it*—ŠÀ-*bi* 6: 497D, q, 505q, 516A, 633L,

ṣītu "exit": *ṣa-a-ti* 6: 10A, F, G, H, 289A, 393D, H, *ṣa-*[*a-ti*] 6: 10T, *ṣ*[*a-a-t*]*i* 6: 384D, *ṣ*]*a-a-ti* 6: 393A,

ṣumāmītu "thirst": *ṣu-ma-mit* 6: 653U,

ṣūmu "thirst": *ṣ*]*u-um* 6: 655U,

ša "that; what; of": *ša* 2 i 21, 27, 32, 34, iii 5, 13, r. v 11, 26, vi 25, 3: 1, 5, 9, r. 4, 4 r. 5, 5 iii 13, 16, 25, 6: 1A, H, a, 10A, F, G, H, a, 11A, 12A, 20A, G, U, frg, 30A, E, G, frg, 31A, E, 32A, E, G, 33E, 34E, 35E, 36A, E, 41E, 53n, 57frg, n, 59r, 74A, 92frg, 93frg, 94frg, 95frg, 101E, 103frg, 104E, 109E, frg, 124E, frg, 133A 137E, 144E, 153A, E, 157E, 167E, 171frg, 173A, 179frg, 207J, O, 209frg, 226f, 247frg, 248frg, 262i, 269frg, 270frg, 273A, 283frg, 296C, 308A, frg, 316J, 323c, 324c, 331B, 332frg, 345F, w, 363frg, 371frg, 373frg, 382D, 386D, 387D, 469D, 496frg, 501D, 515A, 537frg, 544A, 557D, 594h, 603h, 615m, 633frg, 635frg, 649frg, 667frg, 669Z, frg, ii A, F, G, H, I, frg, a, iv B, H, Y, 9: 2, 11: 1, r. 3, *šá* 1: 8, e. 16, r. 5, 8, 11, 2 i 6, 13, 16, 17, 20, 22, 23, 25, 29, 30, 32, r. iv 9, 17, 18, 29, v 2, 4, 08, 15, 16, vi 17, 18, 3: 11, r. 3, 4, 4 r. 9, 15, 5 i 1, r. iii 4, 6, 7, 9, 10, 11, 15, 16, 17, 18, 20, 21, 23, 24, 26, 30, iv 8, 420E, 6: 1F, G, T, 10T, 11A, 31frg, 32frg, 33frg, 34frg, 35frg, 36frg, 40A, E, frg, 42A, 43A, 44A, frg, 45A, 4 49A, 51A, W, r, 53A, r, 56frg, 57A, r, 59A, frg, n, r, 61W, n, r, 62A, W, 63A, W, frg, 70S, 74A, H, x, 75A, H, S, 82A, G, I, a, x, 83H, I, 85A, G, I, d, 86A, G, 87A, G, d, 92A, I, 93A, F, I, frg, 94A, F, frg, 95A, F, I, frg, 98A, F, 101A, F, frg, 102E, F, 103E, F, 104A, y, 109frg, 121A, 124A, E, frg, 131frg, 133E, 136A, E, t, 137O, t, 143E, frg, t, 144P, t, 145E, frg, 147A, E, H, P, 150H, P, frg, 153P, 157A, H, P, 159A, E, P, S, 162A, B, E, P, S, 165A, E, M, P, 167A, M, P, 169A, E, I, P, 171A, I, M, P, S, 173A, G, M, P, S, frg, 174A, G, I, M, S, frg, 179I, 184I, frg, 188frg, 189frg, 193J, frg, 209C, J, 216C, J, O, 224X, 225H, 226J, 227H, J, X, f, 228X, f, 229C, J, X, frg, f, 231A, J, X, f, 232B, 237A, C, J, N, X, 240J, X, frg, 241J, X, frg, 247A, frg, 248A, frg, 250A, I, frg, 251A, B, I, frg, 253A, B, I, frg, 254A, B, I, 258A, B, I, i, 260A, frg, i, 262A, B, frg, 266A, B, frg, i, 269A, B, M, i, 270A, i, 273B, F, 274A, B, F, frg, 277A, B, Y, frg, 280A, Y, 283B, Y, 284A, B, Y, frg, 285A, B, 286A, B, J, Y, 289A, C, 296A, B, H, 298B, C, 308C, 316A, C, 323C, N, 324B, C, N, 328B, frg, 333B, 335B, 341F, frg, 345B, 347F, R, frg, 350A, B, F, w, 353A, B, 362R, frg, z, 363R, frg, z, 367R, frg, 369z, 373B, frg, 376B, frg, 379frg, 381D, s, 382A, D, s, 383s, 386A, s, 387A, 391D, H, 392H, 394H, 397H, 403D, 406A, 407A, C, 446g, 472D, 481D, 482D, H, 492D, frg, 495D, q, 496D, q, 497D, 501q, 503A, D, V, q, 504A, D, V, q, 505A, D, V, 506A, D, V, 508A, D, 513D, V, 514V, 515V, 516A, 517frg, 523A, B, 530A, B, F, G, 534F, 537F, frg, k, 538A, frg, 540F, frg, k, 543A, F, 545A, frg, 547A, frg, 549A, frg, 551A, frg, 553A, D, frg, 555A, D, frg, 557A, 559A, D, frg, 560D, 562D, 563D, 568D, Q, frg, 570D, Q, frg, 571D, Q, frg, 576D, b, v, 579D, frg, b, v, 582D, frg, b, v, 585b, v, 588D, 591K, h, j, 593L, j, 594K, L, j, 596T, h, j, 603A, H, K, T, frg, j, 608A, M, frg, 609M, 612G, K, M, m, 615K, L, frg, 622G, K, 624G, K, L, 626K, 627F, K, frg, 633F, L, frg, 635A, F, L, 636A, F, 637A, frg, 641A, U, frg, 646A, U, frg, 649U, 650U, frg, 652U, 656frg, 666Q, frg, 667Q, frg, 669Q, frg, ii d, 7 r. 4, 8: 1, 9, 10, 12, 20, r. 3, 6, 8, 10, 11, 9: 6, 7, 8, 10, 11, 13, 14, 17, 20, 26, 29, 35, 36, 38, r. 1, 3, 19, 25, 10 r. 5, 11 r. 7, 12: 2, 13 iii 1, 2, 18, 20, 14 i 1, 4, 7, 13, ii 6, 8, 14, r. ii 2, 3, *š*[*a* 6: 87frg, 150E, 193J, 286frg, 345p, 622m, 636frg, *š*[*á* 6: 47frg, 171frg, 328frg, *š*[*á*] 6: 165I, *š*]*a* 6: 35A, 51n, 86frg, 87frg, 174frg, 179frg, 207frg, 333frg, 387s, 523G, 594h, 627frg, 11 r. 5, *š*]*á* 6: 130E, 167S, 394D, 633L, 9 r. 2, 10: 4, (*ša*) 6: 41A, 44E, [*š*]*a* 6: 31G, 33A, 34A, 42E, 102frg, 104frg, 609G, iv A, [*š*]*á* 6: 173I, 636L, [[*šá*]] 8 r. 20,

ša'ālu "to ask": *a-šá-lu* 14 i 1,

šabāru "to break": *liš*]*-bir* 6: 453I, *liš-bir* 1 r. 3, 6: 453frg, *liš-bir*] 4 r. 20, *liš-bi-ru* 6: 573Q, *liš-bi-*[*r*]*u* 6: 573D, *li-(iš)-bir* 5: 418E,

šadādu "to drag, tolerate": *i-šad-da-du* 9: 30,

šadû "mountain": KUR-*i* 5 iii 21,

šaggaštu "massacre": *šag-gaš-tú* 6: 456g, *šag-ga-aš-tu* 6: 456frg, *šá-ga-áš-tu* 6: 456k, *šá-ga-áš-t*[*ú*] 6: 456A,

šahātu "corner": *šá-h*[*a-ti*] 6: 478H,

šaharšuppu "leprosy": SAHAR.ŠUB-*pu* 6: 419c, SAHAR.ŠUB.BA-*a* 2 iv 5, SAHAR].ŠUB-*pu* 6: 419frg, [SAHAR].ŠUB-*pu* 11 r. 11,

šakānu "to place, set up": *áš-kun-u-ni* 5 iii 6, GAR-*niš-šu* 14 ii 17, GAR-*nu-n*[*i*] 6: 510frg, GAR-*un* 14 ii 4, *is-sa-kan* 6: 352R, 359frg, *is-sa-k*[*a-an* 6: 359R, *iš*]*-ku-na-k*[*a-nu-ni*] 3: 2, *iš-kun* 6: 460frg, *iš-kun-ak-ka-nu-u-ni* 10: 9, *iš-kun-u*]*-ni* 6: 517frg, *iš-kun-u-ka-nu-n*[*i*] 10: 7, *iš-kun-u-ni* 6: 65W, 96F, 10: 11, *iš-kun-*[*u*]*-ni* 6: 287B, *iš-kun-*[*u-ni* 6: 96frg, *iš-ku*]*-nu-u-ni* 6: 175frg, *iš-ku-nu* 14 i 8, *iš-ku-nu-ni* 6: 12A, 65A, 96A, frg, 175frg, *iš-ku-nu-n*[*i*] 6: 24A, *iš-ku-nu-u-ni* 6: 42A, 96I, 105E, 132O, frg, 175A, 287J, *iš-ku-nu-*[*ni*] 6: 24frg, *iš-ku-n*[*u-ni*] 6: 24frg, *iš-ku-un* 14 ii 8, *iš-ku-*[*nu-ni*] 6: 175I, *iš-k*[*un-u-ni* 6: 96G, *iš-k*[*u-nu-ni* 6: 175P, *iš-k*[*u-nu-u-ni* 6: 105y, 287A, *i*[*š-kun-u-ni* 6: 105A, *i*[*š-ku*]*n-*[*u-ni*] 6: 132A, *i*]*š-kun-u-ni* 6: 175M, *i*]*š-ku-nu-u-ni* 6: 42E, *i*]*š-ku-un* 14 i 30, *i-sa-kan* 6: 352A, B, *i-s*[*a-kan* 6: 359B, *i-šá*]*-kan* 6: 460A, *i-šá-kan* 5 iv 2, 6: 460B, *i-šá-kan-u-ka-*[*x* 6: 328frg, *i-šá-kan-u-ni* 6: 154P, *liš-ka-nu-ku-nu* 6: 584Q, Z, frg, b, *liš-ka-nu-ku-*[*nu*] 6: 584v, *liš-kun* 2 v 13, 5 iv 4, 5, 6: 456A, B, 470D, 489D, *liš-ku[n]* 6: 456frg, *liš-ku-nu* 6: 523G, *liš-ku-nu]* 6: 465frg, *liš-ku-[un* 6: 489frg, *liš-k[un* 6: 462frg, *liš-šá-kín* 2 iv 13, 16, *li]-iš-ku-nu* 6: 456k, *li-iš-ku-nu-ku-[nu]* 6: 584D, *l[i-iš-kun* 6: 462frg, *ni-il-ta-kan-ú* 9: 9, *ni-il-ta-kan-ú]* 9: 34, *ni-šak-kan-ú-ma* 9: 37, *ni-šá-kan-u-ni* 6: 499D, V, q, 510D, *ni-[šá-kan-u-ni]* 6: 510frg, *šak-na-tu-ni]* 2 i 33, *šak-na-tu-n[i* 2 i 26, *šak-nu-ni* 6: 541k, *šak-nu-u-n[i* 6: 541F, *šak-n[u-u-ni]* 6: 670frg, *šak-[nu-u-ni]* 6: 670frg, *šá]-kín-u-ni* 6: 408A, *šá-kan* 6: 645A, frg, *šá-ka-a-[ni* 6: 645U, *šá-ka-ni* 2 i 14, *šá-kín-u-ni* 6: 408C, 548A, *šá-ki-nu-ni* 2 iii 25, *š]ak-na-šu-u-ni* 13 ii 16, *taš-(ka)-na* 6: 301C, *ta]-šá-kan-a-ni* 6: 242X, *ta-šak-kan-[a-ni]* 6: 54W, *ta-šá]-kan-a-ni* 6: 242frg, *ta-šá-kan* 13 ii 4, *ta-šá-kan]-a-ni* 6: 212frg, *ta-šá-kan]-a-šu-n[u-ni]* 6: 327c, *ta-šá-kan-a-ni* 6: 54A, n, 71A, 148P, 154E, 176A, M, frg, 185I, frg, 212J, 235A, J, N, 242A, J, 245X, frg, 301B, 390D, H, *ta-šá-kan-a-n[i* 6: 212frg, *ta-šá-kan-a-n[i]* 6: 242frg, *ta-šá-kan-a-šá-nu-ni* 6: 327B, C, *ta-šá-kan-a-šú-nu-ni* 6: 327frg, *ta-šá-kan-a-[ni* 6: 148A, *ta-šá-kan-a-[ni]* 6: 235X, f, *ta-šá-kan-[a-ni* 6: 212u, *ta-šá-ka[n]-a-n[i]* 6: 71W, *ta-šá-ka[n]-šú-u-ni* 6: 291A, *ta-šá-ka]n-a-ni* 6: 212C, *ta-šá-ka-na* 6: 301H, *ta-šá-[kan]-a-ni* 6: 148H, *ta-šá-[kan-a-ni]* 6: 54r, *ta-ša-kan-a-[ni]* 6: 54E, *ta-š[á-kan-a-ni]* 6: 176I, *ta-š]á-kan-a-ni* 6: 176frg, *ta-[šá-kan]-a-ni* 6: 245frg, *ta-[šá-kan-a-ni* 6: 212O, *ta-[šá-kan-a-ni]* 6: 185frg, 235frg, *t]a-šá-kan-a-n[i]* 6: 242frg, *[iš]-kun-u-ni* 6: 105frg, *[iš-kun-u-ni* 6: 517V, *[iš-ku-nu]-u-ni* 6: 132E, *[i]š-kun-u-ni* 6: 105frg, *[i-sa-k]an* 6: 352F, *[liš-ka]-nu-ku-n[u]* 6: 578Q, *[šak-na-at]* 2 i 35, *[taš-k]un-u-ni* 8: 12,

šaknu "governor": LÚ.GAR.KUR 6: 665Q, LÚ.GAR].KUR 6: 665frg,

šalālu "to plunder": *šal-la-li* 6: 295H, *šal-l]a-li* 6: 295A, *šá-la-li* 5 iv 15,

šalāmu "to be safe, whole, well": *šal]-mu* 6: 235N, *šal-mu* 6: 235A, J, X, frg, *šá-lam-šu* 1 e. 17, *šá-lim-tu* 6: 96A, *šá-l[im-tu]* 6: 96frg, *šá-l[i-im-tu]* 6: 96frg, *š]á-lim-tu* 6: 96frg,

šalāpu "to pull out": *lu-šá-lip-ku-nu* 6: 631K, L, *lu-šá-li]p-ku-nu* 6: 631G, *[lu]-šal-lip-ku-nu* 6: 631frg,

šalāqu "to cut, slit open": *šal-qa-tu-u-ni* 6: 652U, 656U, *šal-qa-t]u-u-ni* 6: 547frg, *šal-qa-[tu-u-ni* 6: 547A, *šal-qu-u-ni* 6: 551D, *šal]-qu-u-[ni]* 6: 551frg, *šal-[q]u-u-ni* 6: 551A,

šamāmu "heaven": *šá-ma-me* 6: 422B, c, *šá-ma-mi* 6: 422C,

šamê "heaven": AN 2 vi 6, AN-*e* 1 r. 8, 10, 13, 2 iv 8, 3: 9, 4 r. 16, 5 iv 8, 6: 21U, frg, 40A, E, frg, 42A, E, 419B, c, 440g, 472D, 523A, B, G, 530B, G, frg, 9: 2, r. 7, 8, 11, 15, 11 r. 7, 13 iii 2, 14 i 4, AN-*e*] 3 r. 3, 14 ii 2, AN.MEŠ 6: 419C, AN-⌈*e* 6: 21G, AN-[*e* 6: 530A, A[N-*e* 11 r. 10, [AN]-*e* 6: 530F,

šammu "drug": *šam-mu* 6: 262A, B, frg, i, p,

šamnu "oil": Ì.MEŠ 5: 417E, 6: 155E, P, 523G, 622K, 644A, frg, Ì.ME[Š 6: 644U, Ì.[MEŠ 6: 523A, 622G, Ì.GIŠ 10: 9, Ì].MEŠ 6: 622frg,

šamru "fierce": *šam-ri* 6: 425A, B, c, *šam-ru* 5 iv 13,

šamšu "sun": ᵈ*šam-ši* 6: 6F, G, ᵈUTU-*ši* 6: 6A, F, H, T, a, ᵈUTU-*š]i* 6: 6d,

šamû "to hear": *a-šam-mu-[u-ni]* 4 r. 4, *ni-šam-mu-u-ni* 6: 505A, D, *ni-šá-mu-u-ni* 6: 505V, *taš-me-a-šú* 6: 201Y, *taš-me-a-[šú* 6: 201frg, *ta]-šam-ma-a-ni* 6: 195F, 344w, *ta-šam-ma]-a-ni* 6: 344frg, *ta-šam-ma-a-ni* 6: 80G, a, x, 119frg, 135O, 195J, frg, 344F, frg, 8 r. 9, 15, 18, 23, *ta-šam-ma-a-n[i]* 6: 344R, *ta-šam-ma-ni* 6: 80A, H, 135E, *ta-šam-ma-n[i* 6: 119A, *ta-šam-mu-ni* 13 iii 10, *ta-šam-m[a-a-ni]* 6: 135A, *ta-šam-m]e-a-šú* 6: 205J, *ta-šam-[m]a-a-ni* 6: 149A, *ta-šá-me* 5 iii 12, *ta-[šam-ma-a-ni* 6: 344p, *ta-[šam-me-a-šú* 6: 205frg, *t[a-šam-ma-a]-ni* 6: 149H, *t[a-šam-ma-a-ni* 6: 195frg, *(ta-šam-ma-a-ni)* 8 r. 5, *[a-šam-mu-u-ni]* 4 r. 7, *[iš-me]-e-ma* 14 i 9, *[ta-šam-ma-a-ni]* 3: 2, *[ta-šam-m]a-a-ni* 6: 149P, *[tu-š]á-áš-man-ni* 13 iii 17, *[t]a-šam-ma-ni* 6: 119o, *[t]a-šam-m[a-ni* 6: 119frg,

šaniu "other": MAN-*ma* 6: 71A, W, 72A, S, 129frg, 196J, 301B, H, 509D, V, frg, MA[N-*ma* 6: 339frg, MA[N-*m]a* 6: 301H, M]AN-[*m*]*a* 6: 301C, *šá-nam-ma* 9: 34, *šá-nim-ma* 6: 129A, E, *šá-nim-m[a* 6: 129E, *šá-nim-tim-ma* 6: 216C, 322C, *šá-ni-a-te* 6: 312A, *šá-ni-a-ti* 6: 245A, 312C, *šá-ni-ma* 6: 72W, *šá-ni-nim-ma* 6: 339R, *šá-ni-tim-ma* 6: 164P, S, 216J, e, u, 223C, J, frg, 322N, 13 ii 19, *šá-ni-ti-ma* 6: 164I, *šá-ni-tú* 9: 29, *šá-ni-tú-ma* 9: 36, *šá-nu]-um-ma* 6: 509A, *šá-nu-um-ma* 6: 71S, *šá-nu-u]m-ma* 6: 71S, *šá-n[im-ma* 6: 129o, *šá-(ni)-tim-(ma)* 6: 164A, *ša-ni-tim-ma* 6: 322c, [MAN-*ma* 6: 301C,

šanû (D) "to change": *li-šá-ni* 4 r. 19, *tu-šá-an-na-a-ni* 6: 58A, *tu-šá-an-na-ni* 6: 58frg, *t]u-šá-na-a-ni* 6: 58n,

šapal "under": KI.TA 6: 573D, Q, b, KI.[TA] 6: 454A, KI].TA 6: 454frg, K[I.TA 6: 454g, *šap-l[a* 5: 418E, *šá-pal* 4 r. 21, 9 r. 25,

šapālu "to be low": *šap-lu* 6: 192Y, *šap-[lu* 6: 192frg, *ú-šap]-pa-lu-u-ni* 6: 192frg, *ú-šap-pal-u-[ni* 6: 192J, *ú-ša]p-pal-u-ni* 6: 192frg,

šapāru "to send": *a-šap-par]* 4 r. 3, *a-šap-par-kan-ni* 5 iii 13, *il-tap-ru* 1: 4, *ni-šap-par-uš* 9: 10, *ni-šap-par-uš]* 9: 16, *ni-[šap-pa-ru* 9: 31, *ta-šap-par* 5 iii 5, 13 iii 3, *ta-šap-pa[r]-a-[ni-(šú-ni)]* 10 r. 4, *ta-šap-pa-ra* 13 iii 16, *[ni-šap-par]* 9: 38,

šapliš "below": *šap-liš* 6: 476D, 11 r. 9, *šap-l[iš* 9 r. 14,

šaptu "lip": *šap-ti* 6: 386A, D,

šaqû "to give to drink": *liš-qi-ku-nu* 6: 522A, G, *šá-qu-ú* 9 r. 19, *ta-šá-qi-a-šú-u-ni* 6: 263A, B, frg, i,

šarāpu "to burn": *iš-šar-rap-u-ni* 6: 608H, M, *i-šar-rap-u-ni* 6: 608L, frg, *i-šá-rap-u-ni* 6: 608A, K, *i-šá-r]a-pu-u-ni* 6: 608T,

šarku "pus": *šar-ku* 5 iv 4, *šar-ku]* 6: 462frg,

šarru "king": LUGAL 1: 4, 9, 10, 14, 3: 4, 5, 4 r. 16, 17, 6: 71A, W, 72A, W, 129A, E, frg, 196J, 209C, J, frg, 301B, H, 320B, 414C, 420B, C, c, 509D, 521A, 604A, H, frg, h, i A, F, G, H, T, a, d, 7: 3, 11, 8: 5, 9: 4, 5, 8, 10, 11, 13, 14, 18, 20, 21, 23, 25, 27, 28, 29, 31, 32, 33, 34, 35, 37, 38, r. 3, 6, 13, 20, 12: 3, 13 iii 5, 6, 14 i 8, 21, r. ii 3, LUGAL-*a-ni* 9: 4, 33, LUGAL-*ka-nu-[ni* 6: 191J, LUGAL.MEŠ 13 iii 11, LUGAL-*ni-ni* 6: 509D, V, LUGAL-*šu* 14 ii 17, LUGA]L 6: 604j, LUG[AL 14 i 4, LUG]AL 11 r. 4, LU[GAL 9: 6, LU]GAL 6: 604T, MAN 2 i 13, iii 25, r. iv 1, 18, 28, 29, v 8, 15, 16, vi 6, 3: 1, 3, 5 i 1, 2, r. iii 2, 16, 18, 22, 23, 6: 1A, F, G, H, T, *a, d,* 2A, F, G, H, T, a, d, 7A, F, G, T, a, 12A, 41A, 44A, E, 46A, E, frg, 57A, n, r, 59A, W, frg, n, r, 63A, frg, 83A, G, H, 90A, G, I, frg, d, 93A, F, I, frg, 95A, F, G, I, frg, 102E, F, 110E, frg, y, 121frg, o, 124E, frg, o, 131A, E, frg, 151A, E, H, P, 157A, E, H, P, 174A, G, I, M, P, S, frg, 189I, frg, 190J, frg, 200frg, 230A, X, frg, f, 237A, J, X, 250A, I, 261B, I, i, 267B, F, frg, i, 273B, F, frg, 277A, Y, 283A, B, Y, frg, 302A, B, 320C, N, 360R, 370frg, 381s, 391D, H, 401D, 402A, D, 407A, C, 418B, C, 495D, frg, q, 497D, q, 505q, 513D, 516A, 521I, 555frg, 612K, 632F, L, frg, 633frg, 666frg, 8: 2, 14, 17, 21, r. 4, 9, 11, 14, 17, 22, 10: 8, 11: 2, MAN.MEŠ-*ni* 2 v 21, MAN] 6: 63W, 277B, 8: 24, MA[N 6: 495V, MA]N 6: 200J, 267frg, 381D, 632K, M[AN 6: 174frg, 189J, M[AN] 5 i 1, [LUGAL 6: 301C, 9: 16, 14 i 22, [MAN 3: 6, 6: 121E, 8 r. 7, 26E, 11: 2, [MA]N 8: 2, [M]AN 6: 267A,

šarrūtu "kingship": LUGAL-*te* 6: 74x, 87frg, d, 128E, LUGAL-*ti* 2 v 5, 6: 48A, 68A, W, 74A, 87A, G, I, 88A, 303C, 362R, LUGAL-*ti*] 14 i 13, LUGAL-*ti-šú* 6: 303B, 304B, C, LUGAL-*tu* 6: 7A, F, G, 48frg, 61r, 88I, 362z, LUGAL-*tú* 6: 7T, 48E, 88frg, 213u, 228f, 241X, LUGAL-*ú-ti-šu-nu* 14 i 24, LUGAL-*ú-tú* 6: 225H, LUGAL-*ú*-[*ti* 6: 300B, LUGAL-*u-te* 6: 128frg, 300H, 303frg, 362frg, LUGAL-*u-te-šú* 6: 304frg, 307frg, LUGAL-*u-ti* 6: 128A, LUGAL-*u-ti-šú* 6: 307A, LUGAL-*u-tu* 6: 7H, 88d, 213J, 225J, 228J, LUGAL-*u-tú* 6: 48A, 61A, n, LUGAL-*u-t*[*i* 6: 68frg, LUGAL]-*ú-te* 6: 128o, LUGA]L-*tu* 6: 213C, LUGA]L-*tú* 6: 88frg, LUG[A]L-*tu* 6: 88G, LU[GAL-*tu* 6: 7a, LU[GAL-*u-t*]*i* 6: 300C, MAN-*ti* 6: 303A, MAN-*tim-ma* 6: 216frg, 322B, MAN-*u-te* 6: 74H, *šar-ru-su* 1 r. 9, [LUGAL]-*tú* 6: 61W, 213frg, [LUGA]L-[*x* 6: 61frg, [LUG]AL-*tú* 6: 228X, [LUG]AL-*u-tu* 6: 241J, [LU]GAL-*tú* 6: 241frg, [LU]GAL-*u-te* 6: 48n,

šaṣbutu (mng. uncert.): *šá*]-*aṣ*-[*bu-tu* 6: 570frg, *šá-aṣ-b*[*u-tu* 6: 570D, *šá-aṣ-bu*-[*t*]*ú* 6: 570Q, *šá*-[*aṣ-b*]*u-tu* 6: 570frg,

šasû "to shout": *il-sa-a* 2 iv 19,

šattu "year": MU.AN.NA.MEŠ-*ku*-[*nu* 6: 485frg,

šatû "to drink": NAG-*šú-nu* 2 iv 15, *šá-te-e* 6: 154E, *šá-ti-e* 6: 154frg, [*ša-t*]*e-e* 6: 154P,

ša-pēthalli "cavalryman": *šá—pet-hal-li* 2 iii 21,

ša-rēši "eunuch": LÚ.SAG 6: 78I, 163A, E, P, S, 221H, J, 238N, X, 321C, LÚ.SAG.ME 6: 78A, LÚ.SAG.MEŠ 6: 78a, x, 8 r. 21, LÚ.SAG.MEŠ] 4 r. 6, LÚ.SAG] 6: 238A, J, LÚ.SA]G 6: 221f, 321N, LÚ.S[AG 6: 163I, 238B, LÚ.S]AG 6: 163M, LÚ].SAG 6: 221e, 321c, L[Ú.SAG 6: 338F, [LÚ.S]AG 6: 321B, [L]Ú.SAG.MEŠ 8: 7,

ša-šīmi "bought (slave)": LÚ.ŠÁM.MEŠ 6: 222C, J,

ša-ziqni "bearded (courtier)": LÚ.*šá—ziq*]-*ni* 6: 221H, 338F, LÚ.*šá—ziq-ni* 4 r. 6, 6: 78A, I, 163A, I, P, 238N, 338R, 8: 6, r. 21, LÚ.*šá—ziq-ni*] 6: 238X, LÚ.*šá*—[*ziq*]-*ni* 6: 78H, LÚ].*šá—ziq-ni* 6: 163E, *šá*—LÚ.*ziq-ni* 6: 221J, 238J, *šá*—LÚ.*ziq-n*[*i* 6: 78x, *šá*—L]Ú.*ziq-ni* 6: 338B, *šá—ziq-ni* 6: 163S, 238A, C,

šā'ilu "inquirer": *šá-ʾi*]-*li* 6: 117E, *šá-ʾ*]*i-li* 6: 117frg, *šá*-[*ʾi-li* 6: 117o,

šāru "wind": TU$_{15}$ 5 iv 11,

šāša "him": *ša-a-ša* 14 ii 8,

šāšu "him": *šá*-[*a*]-*šú* 6: 396D,

šemû "to hear": *il-te-mu-šu-ma* 1: 10, *ni-il-te-mu-ú* 9: 15, see *šamû,*

šerru "child": TU]R.DIŠ 6: 438F, [TUR].DIŠ 6: 438I,

šēdu "genie": *še-e-d*[*u*] 6: 493D, [*še*]-*e-du* 6: 493frg,

šēpītu "toe": *še-pi-tu* 1: 11,

šēpu "foot": GÌR.2 9 r. 25, GÌR.2-*ku-nu* 6: 553D, GÌR.2.MEŠ-*ku-nu* 6: 553A, GÌR.2.MEŠ-*ku*-[*nu*] 6: 553frg, GÌR.2.MEŠ-*šu* 6: 54r, GÌR.2.MEŠ-*šú* 6: 54frg, GÌR.2.MEŠ-*šú-nu* 6: 552A, frg, 627G, K, frg, GÌR.2.MEŠ-*š*[*ú-nu*] 6: 627F, GÌR.2-*šú* 6: 54A, 235A, X, frg, f, 552D, 9: 37, 10 r. 2, GÌR.2-*šú-nu* 6: 552frg, 627L, GÌR].2-*šú* 6: 54n, G[ÌR.2]-*šú* 6: 235N,

šērtu "punishment": *še-ret-su* 1 r. 10, *še-ret-s*[*u* 4 r. 16, *šir-t*]*a* 1 r. 11,

šiāmu "to decree, destine": *li*]-*šim-šú* 1 r. 5, *li-šim* 6: 434A, B, *li-šim-an-na-a-ši*] 9 r. 5, *li-ši-i*-[*mu*] 6: 486frg, *li-ši-mu* 6: 486D, *li-ši-mu-šu*] 14 ii 10, *li-š*[*im*] 6: 434I, *li-š*[*im-ku-nu*] 6: 415C, *l*[*i-šim-k*]*u-nu* 6: 415A, *l*]*i-ši-m*[*u*] 6: 486frg, *mu-šim* 1 r. 3, 6: 414C, 9 r. 5, [*mu-š*]*im* 6: 414A,

šibṭu "plague": *šib-ṭi* 4 r. 26,

šiddi "along": *ši-di* 5 iii 20,

šikkû "mongoose": ^{d}NIN.KILIM 6: 555A, D, frg,

šiknat napišti "living being": *šik-nat*—ZI 6: 164A, M, *šik-nat*—ZI-*tim* 6: 164E, P, *šik-nat*—Z]I-*tim* 6: 164B, S, [*šik-nat*—ZI-*tim* 1 r. 9,

šiltāhu "arrow": *šil-ta-hi-šu* 6: 425B, *šil-t*]*a-hi-šú* 6: 425A,

šingāti (mng. obscure): *ši*]-*in-ga-te* 6: 378A, *ši*]-*i*[*n-ga-a-te* 6: 378frg, *ši-in-ga*-[*te* 6: 378s,

šipirtu "message, letter": *ši-pir-ti* 9: 35, 36, *ši-pir-ti*] 9: 5,

šipru "device, method": *ši-pir* 6: 412A, C, 14 ii 5,

šipṭu "judgment": *šip-ṭi* 1 r. 6,

šībūtu "old age": *še-bu-ti* 6: 415A,

šīmtu "fate, destiny": NAM.MEŠ 6: 660frg, NAM.M[EŠ] 1 r. 3, NA]M.MEŠ 6: 660Q, *ši-ma*-[*a-ti* 9 r. 5, *ši-ma*-[*ti* 14 ii 11, *šim-te* 6: 46E, 238X, *šim-ti* 1 r. 5, 6: 46A, 84A, G, H, d, 190frg, 361R, 486D, *šim-t*]*i-ku-nu* 6: 486frg, *šim*-[*ti* 6: 361frg, *ši*[*m-ti* 6: 46frg, 361z, *ši-im-ti-ku*]-*nu* 6: 434A, *ši-im-t*]*i-ku-nu* 6: 434B, *ši-im-(ti)-ku-nu* 6: 434I, *ši-mat* 6: 414C, 9 r. 5, *ši-mat-ku-nu* 6: 490D, *ši-mat-ku*-[*nu* 6: 490frg, [NAM.MEŠ] 6: 414C,

šīnāti "urine": KÀŠ 2 iv 15, 6: 491D, [KÀŠ].MEŠ-*ku-nu* 6: 470D,

šīru "flesh": UZU 2 iv 10, 11, 6: 418B, 449I, 450A, g, 547frg, 549A, frg, 571Q, 585b, 593j, 622frg, 624L, UZU.MEŠ 6: 449A, g, 585v, 591K, h, 593h, 596T, h, j, 622G, frg, 624G, K, UZU.MEŠ-*ka* 6: 426A, UZU.MEŠ-*ku-nu* 6: 451A, g, 571Q, 585D, v, 591h, j, 596L, T, h, j, 623A, G, K, frg, UZU.MEŠ-*ku-n*[*u* 6: 596K, UZU.MEŠ-*ku-n*]*u* 6: 622L, 623L, UZU.MEŠ-*ku*-[*nu* 6: 591L, UZU.MEŠ-*ku*-[*nu*] 6: 623frg, UZU.MEŠ-*k*[*u-nu* 6: 451frg, 571frg, UZU.MEŠ-*k*]*a* 6: 426C, UZU.MEŠ-*k*]*u-nu* 6: 585b, UZU.MEŠ-[*ku-nu* 6: 591D, UZU.M[EŠ-*ku-nu* 6: 571D, UZU.[MEŠ-*k*]*u-nu* 6: 622K, UZU].MEŠ-*ku-nu* 6: 622A, UZ[U 6: 585D, UZ[U-*ku-nu*] 6: 519frg, UZ[U].MEŠ 6: 591j, U[ZU-*k*]*u-nu* 6: 426B,

šīti "she, it": *ši-i-ti* 2 i 30, 31, *ši-i-ti*] 2 i 29,

šī "she, it": *ši-i* 6: 297B, C, H, *ši*-[*i* 6: 297A,

šuātu "that": *šu-a-ti* 14 i 7, 25, *šu-a-ti*] 14 ii 8, 12,

šulmu "health, well-being": DI-*mu* 6: 209C, J, frg,

šumēlu "left side, south": KAB 6: 634F, K, L, frg, 636A, F, L, [KAB 4 r. 3, 8 r. 1,

šumma "if; verily": BE-*ma* 2 iv 17, *šúm-ma* 4 r. 4, 12, 5 i 9, 10, r. iii 12, 14, 15, *šúm-ma*] 4 r. 5, *šúm-mu* 2 i 15, 31, iii 22, 24, r. v 1, 8, 16, 24, 6: 123E, 130E,

138E, 162E, 229f, *šúm-m[a* 4 r. 14, *šúm-m[u* 2 iii 23, *šúm-[ma]* 4 r. 13, *šum-ma* 1: 7, 8, 6: 55A, frg, r, 57A, frg, r, 58A, frg, n, r, 62A, frg, 73A, H, 83A, G, a, 92A, G, frg, 101F, y, 123A, frg, 130A, frg, 138t, 142t, 147A, H, 162A, S, 173A, G, I, S, frg, 177A, G, I, 180I, 188F, I, 198J, 212J, O, u, 214J, O, u, 226H, J, 229J, frg, 233A, C, X, 237X, 242X, 249A, B, frg, 259A, B, i, 266A, B, F, frg, i, 269A, B, frg, i, 275A, B, frg, 279A, B, Y, 281A, B, Y, 302C, frg, 304A, B, C, frg, 306A, C, frg, 318A, C, J, 336A, F, 347B, F, w, 349A, F, 353B, 360R, frg, 366R, frg, z, 373B, 377frg, 410A, B, C, 494D, 499D, q, 509D, 513D, 632F, 7: 4, 8 r. 12, 18, 10: 12, 12: 1, 13 iii 4, *šum-ma]* 8 r. 2, *šum-m[a* 6: 138A, 302B, 336B, 353A, 7 r. 3, *šum-[ma* 6: 360B, 10: 14, *šum-[ma]* 1: 10, 6: 347R, *šu[m-ma* 6: 494frg, *šu[m-ma]* 1: 6, *šu[m-m]a* 6: 389D, *šú]m-ma* 4 r. 10, *š[úm-m]u* 2 i 24, *š[um-ma* 6: 108A, 162P, *š[um-ma]* 6: 92d, *š[um-m]a* 6: 266M, *[šum]-ma* 6: 249I, 259I, 513V, *[šúm]-mu* 6: 188frg, *[šúm-ma* 4 r. 8, 9, *[šúm-mu* 2 iii 26, r. iv 29, *[šúm-m]u* 6: 226f, *[šum-ma* 1: 10, 3: 5, 6: 302A, 555frg, 612K, 13 ii 11, *[šum-ma]* 6: 62frg, 13 ii 7, *[šum-m]a* 6: 62W, 177frg, 180frg, 233J, 632frg, 10 r. 2, *[šú]m-mu* 6: 212frg, *[šu]m-ma* 6: 101frg, 108frg, 142frg, 229X, 249frg, 349B, 373frg, 385s, *[š]úm-mu* 2 iii 23, 6: 142E, *[š]um-ma* 6: 101frg, 233frg, 242A, 8 r. 7,

šumu "name": MU 6: 315C, 435B, I, MU-*ku-nu* 6: 435A, B, I, 525A, 538F, k, 661frg, MU-*ku-nu]* 6: 661Q, MU-*ku-n[u* 6: 538frg, MU.MEŠ 1 r. 4, 12, MU.MEŠ-*ku-nu* 6: 485D, MU-*ni* 9: 25, MU-*šu* 6: 300C, MU-*šú* 6: 45A, E, 300B, 315A, J, MU-*šú-nu* 6: 140E, t, 161A, E, P, S, 255A, B, I, 473D, 511D, V, 526B, 573Q, b, 618G, MU-*šú-[nu* 6: 140frg, MU-*šu-nu* 6: 616frg, MU]-*šu* 6: 300H, M[U 9 r. 21, M[U-*šú* 6: 45frg, M]U-*šú-nu* 6: 511frg, *šum-šu* 1 r. 7, [MU 11 r. 2, [MU-*ku-nu* 6: 538F, [MU-*k]u-nu* 6: 538K,

šulūtu "garrison": *šu-[lu-ti]* 1: 7,

šunnû "to alter": *šu-un-né-e* 6: ii A, F, H, d, *šu-un-né-[e]* 6: ii G, *šu-un-[né-e]* 6: ii I, *šu-[un-né-e]* 6: ii frg, a,

šunu "they": *šú-nu* 6: 274A, B, *šú-[nu* 6: 274F, *šu-nu* 6: 274frg, 14 i 22, *šu-nu-ni* 6: 216C, *šu-nu-u-ni* 6: 216J,

šūpû "pre-eminent": *šu-pa-a[t* 1 r. 10,

šuršudu "to establish, found": *šur-šu-du* 14 ii 13,

šūtu "he": *šu-tú* 2 i 9, *šu-tú]* 2 i 23, *šu-tú-u-ni* 6: 278A, *šu-tu-ú-ma* 9: 34, *šu-tu-u-ni* 6: 278B, *šu-t]u-ni* 6: 278frg, *[šu-tú]* 2 i 21, *[šu-u-tú]* 2 i 22,

šû "he": *šu-u* 6: 191J, *[šu]-u* 9: 4,

tabāku "to shed, pour": *lit-bu-uk* 1 e. 18, *ta-ta-bak-a-ni* 6: 257I, *ta-ta-ba-ka-a-ni* 6: 257A, B, i, *[ta-ta-ba]-ka-[a-ni* 6: 257M,

tabû "to rise, get up": *lit-ba]-am-ma* 2 vi 1, *lu-šat-ba* 5 iv 11, *[t]e-bi* 14 ii 26,

tadānu "to give": *id-din-áš-šá-nu-u-ni* 6: 273A, *id-din-na-šú-ni* 6: 90A, *id-din-u-ni* 6: 278A, *id-din-u-[ni* 10: 6, *id-di-na-áš-šú-[u-ni]* 6: 273frg, *it-tan-nu-ma* 1: 13, *i-din-na-šá-nu-ni* 6: 273frg, *i-din-[áš-šú-ni]* 5 iii 23, *i-din-u-ni* 6: 278B, *i-di-in-ku-nu* 6: 423C, c, *i-di-[na-šu-u]n-ni* 6: 90d, *i-[di-in]* 1 r. 9, *li-di-n[a-na-ši* 9: r 9, *li-di-nu* 5 iv 15, SUM-*šú-un-ni* 6: 90I, SUM-*šú-u[n-ni]* 6: 90frg, *ta-dan-a-ni* 6: 213J, e, *ta-dan-na-a-ni* 6: 213frg, *ta-da-na* 6: 295A, C, H, *ta-da-na-a-ni* 6: 213C, *ta-da-na-šu-u-ni* 6: 127E, *ta-da-n[a-x* 6: 225J, *ta-da-(na)-ni-šú-nu* 6: 225f, *ta-da-[na-š]u-[u]-n[i]* 6: 127frg, *ta-d]a-na-niš-šu-un-ni* 6: 225C, *t]a-dan-a-ni* 6: 213frg, *t]a-da-na-a-ni* 6: 213frg, *t]a-da-na-niš-šú-ni* 6: 225H, *[i]-din-u-ni* 6: 278frg, *[i-d]in-u-ni* 6: 278Y,

tahūmu "border, territory": *ta-hu-me* 5 iii 15, 20,

takālu "to trust": *it-ták-lu* 1: 5, *[at-kal-ma]* 14 i 6,

takkussu "tube": *ta[k-k]u-si* 6: 563D,

taktīmu "cover": *tak]-tim-[ku-nu]* 6: 492frg, *tak-tim-ku-nu* 6: 492D, V,

talittu "birth": *ta-lit-tu* 6: 437F, I,

talīmu "equal (brother)": *ta-li-me-šú* 6: 86A, G, I, 8: 3, *ta-li-mu* 6: 86d,

tamītu "oath": *ta]-me-tú* 6: 287A, *ta-me-ti* 6: 385A, *ta-me-tu* 6: 287C, 308C, 380D, s, 385D, 386D, s, 561D, 623G, L, *ta-me-tú* 6: 72W, 287B, 308A, 561A, 623K, m, *ta-me-[tú* 6: 287J, *ta-mit* 2 iv 27, *ta-mi-ti* 2 i 15, *ta-[me-tu* 6: 385s, *t]a-me-tu* 6: 380frg, *t]a-me-tú* 6: 386A,

tamû "to swear": *ta-ʾa-ku-nu* 6: 384D, *ta-ʾa-[ku-nu]* 6: 384s, *ta-ʾ]a-ku-[nu]* 6: 384A, *ta-tam]-ma-ni* 6: 129E, *ta-tam-ma]-a-ni* 6: 129O, *ta-tam-ma-a-ni* 6: 72A, x, 387D, s, *ta-tam-ma-ni* 6: 72S, *ta-ta-ma-a-ni* 6: 387s, *ti-t[am-ma-a]* 6: 25A, *tùm-ma-tú-nu* 2 vi 6, *tú-ta-[ma]-ni* 6: 213frg, *tu-ta-ma-a-ni* 6: 156E, *tu-tam-ma-a-ni* 6: 156A, E, P, 213C, J, frg, e, *tu-tam-[ma-a-ni]* 6: 156H, *t[a-tam-ma-a]-ni-šú-[u-ni]* 6: 309C, *ú-tam-ma-n[a-a-ši]* 6: 352F, *ú-tam-mu-ka-nu-ni* 6: 287B, *ú-tam-mu-ka-nu-u-ni* 6: 287frg, *ú-ta[m-ma-na-a-ši]* 6: 359frg, *ú-ta-mu-ka-nu-u-ni* 6: 287A, *[ta]-tam-ma-a-ni* 6: 387D, *[ta-tam]-ma-ni* 6: 72W, *[t]a-tam-ma-a-ni-šú-u-ni* 6: 309A, *[ú-t]a-ma-na-a-[ši]* 6: 352R,

tanattu "praise": *ta-n]a-da-at* 14 ii 14,

tarāṣu A "to extend, point": *it-ru-uṣ* 14 i 10, *ta-r[a-ṣu]* 1: 11,

tarāṣu B "to be correct, fitting": *tar]-ṣa-a-te* 6: 97E, *tar-ṣa-at-u-ni* 6: 110E, *tar-ṣa-a-te* 6: 236X, *tar-ṣa-a-ti* 6: 97A, 236A, *tar-ṣa-a-t]i* 6: 236f, *tar-ṣa-tú-u-ni* 6: 75H, *tar-ṣa-tu-u-ni* 6: 75A, x, *tar-ṣ[a-a-ti]* 6: 97F, *ta-ri-su* 6: 74A, *ta-r[i-s]u* 6: 74H, *[ta]r-ṣa-[a]-ti* 6: 236frg,

tebû see *tabû,*

tāhāzu "battle": MÈ 4 r. 20, 6: 453A, B, g, M[È 6: 453g, l, M]È 6: 453frg, *ta-ha-za-a-ti* 9 r. 24, *ta-ha-zi* 5: 418E, *t]a-ha-a-zi* 4 r. 20,

tāmirtu "meadow": *ta-me-rat-k[u]-nu* 6: 532A, *ta-me-ra-a-ti-ku-nu* 6: 441g, 532B, *ta-me-ra-a-ti-[ku-nu* 6: 441A, *ta-me-ra-ti-ku-nu* 6: 532G, *[ta-me-r]a-[ti-k]u-nu* 6: 532F,

tāmtu "sea": *tam-tim* 5 iii 20, 13 iii 1, *[tam-t]im* 5 iv 12,

tānēhu "sighing, weariness, exhaustion": *ta-né-hi* 1 r. 4, 12, *ta-né-hu* 5 iv 3, 6: 418C, 461A, k, *ta-n[é-hu* 6: 487D, *t[a-né-hu* 6: 418B,

tārītu "nurse": *ta]-rit-ku-un* 6: 439I, *ta-rit]-ku-un* 6: 439F,

tidintu "gift": *ti]-din-tú* 6: 273F, *ti-din-te* 6: 273frg, *ti-din-tu* 6: 273frg, 275B, frg, *ti-din-tú* 6: 89A, 273A, 275A, *ti-din-t[ú]* 6: 89frg, *ti-din-[tu]* 6: 89frg, *ti-[di]n-tu* 6: 89d,

tillu "mound": DUL.ME 2 v 6, DU_6 1 r. 15,

tinūru "oven": NINDU 6: 443g,

titābu "mash": *ti]-ta-bi* 6: 540F,

tīku "raindrop, mist": *ti-ki* 6: 471D,

tuāru "to turn": GUR-*ni* 2 i 17, GUR-*ra* 2 i 20, *i-tur-[ru* 14 i 5, *li-tur* 2 vi 3, 4, *lu-tir* 2 v 7, *ta-tur-ru*

14 ii 6, *ta-tu-ra*]*-a-ni* 6: 243frg, *ta-tu-ra-a-ni* 6: 243A, *ta-tu-r*]*a-a-ni* 6: 243J, *ta-tu-u*]*r-a-ni* 6: 243C, *ta-tu-*[*ra-a-ni*] 6: 243X, *tur-ri* 6: 379s, *tu-tar-ra-a-ni-ni* 6: 259B, i, *tu-tar-r*[*a-a-ni*] 6: 377A, *tu-tar-r*]*a-a-ni-ni* 6: 259I, M, *tu-tar-*[*ra-a-ni*] 6: 377s, *t*[*u-tar-r*]*a-a-ni-ni* 6: 259A, *t*]*a-tú-ra-a-ni* 6: 243frg, *t*]*u-tar-ra-*[*a-ni*] 6: 377frg, *u*]*t-tir-ru-ma* 1: 13, [*li-tir* 1 r. 16,

tubāqu (a kind of trap): *du-ba-qi* 6: 582v, *du-ba-q*[*i* 6: 582D, *du-ba-q*]*i* 6: 582Z, *tu-ba-qi* 6: 582b,

tubkinnu "dung heap": *tub-ki-ni* 2 iv 16,

tuissu "worm": *tu-is-su* 6: 572D, Q, *tu-is-si* 6: 572frg,

tukultu "confidence": *tuk*]*ul-ti* 1 r. 9,

tulû "breast": *tu-le-e* 6: 155A, E, H, P,

tušāru "battlefield": *tú-šá-ri* 2 v 5,

tūltu "worm": *tul-tú* 6: 570Q, tul-t[u 6: 570frg, tul]-tu 6: 570D, tul-t]u 6: 570frg,

tūrtu "backing out, revocation": *tur*]*-tu* 6: 379s, *tur-tu* 6: 377s, *tur-t*[*u* 6: 377frg, *tur-t*]*u* 6: 377A, [*tu*]*r-tú* 6: 379frg,

ṭabāhu "to slaughter": *ṭa-ba-hi* 2 i 12,

ṭabû "to sink": *i-ṭa-ab-b*[*u* 6: 447g, *i-ṭa-bu* 6: 447A, *li-ṭa-ab-bu-ú* 6: 611M, *li-ṭa-bi-ši-na* 5 iv 13, *li-ṭa-bu-u* 6: 611G, *lu*]*-ṭa-bu-u* 6: 611K, *lu-ṭa-bu*]*-u* 6: 611T, *lu-ṭa-bu-u* 6: 611H, *lu-ṭa-bu-ú* 6: 611A, *lu-ṭa-bu-*[*u*] 6: 611frg, *lu-ṭa-b*]*u-u* 6: 611L, frg,

ṭarkullu "mooring pole": GIŠ.*ṭar-kul-la-ši-na* 5 iv 12,

ṭābtānu "benefactor": MU[N-*a-nu*] 10: 4,

ṭābtu "goodness, favour": DÙG.GA-*ta-šú-nu* 6: 271F, MUN 10: 13, MUN-*šú-nu* 6: 271A, MUN-*šú-n*[*u* 6: 271B, *ṭa-ab-ti* 9: 13, *ṭa-ab-tú* 6: 125E, *ṭa-a*[*b-tu* 6: 107frg, *ṭa-ba-te-ku-nu* 8 r. 22, *ṭ*[*a-ab-ti* 9: 18, *ṭ*]*a-ab-tú* 8: 13,

ṭābu see *ṭiābu,*

ṭēmu "order; mind": *ṭè*]*-e-šú* 4 r. 19, *ṭè-e-mu* 6: 328B, frg, *ṭè-mu* 6: 290A, *ṭ*[*è-mu*] 6: 290B, *ṭ*]*è-e-m*[*u* 6: 328N,

ṭiābu "to be good": DÙG.GA 6: 67A, 418B, C, 489D, 621G, DÙG.GA-*ti* 6: 415A, 9 r. 5, DÙG.GA-*tu* 6: 73x, 108frg, 125frg, 187I, 233C, J, frg, 325B, C, N, 344A, w, 363R, frg, z, 415C, 501D, q, 621frg, DÙG.GA-*tú* 6: 67W, 73H, 107E, frg, 108E, frg, y, 183frg, 187frg, 233A, X, f, 325c, 344F, 363frg, 501V, 621A, frg, DÙG.GA-*t*[*ú*] 6: 67S, DÙG.GA-*u-ni* 6: 231f, DÙG.GA-[*tú* 6: 107y, DÙG.GA]-*tu* 6: 621K, L, DÙG.G]A 6: 489frg, DÙG.G]A-*tu* 6: 233N, DÙG.G]A-*tú* 6: 67E, DÙG.[GA-*tú*] 6: 344frg, *li-ṭib* 2 iv 11, *ṭa*]*-a-bu* 8: 17, *ṭa-a-bu* 8: 20, *ṭa-bat* 6: 297C, H, *ṭa-bat-u-ni* 6: 75A, 111frg, *ṭa-bat-*[*u*]*-ni* 6: 75H, *ṭa-ba*[*t*] 6: 297A, B, *ṭa-bu-u-ni* 6: 231A, C, J, X, frg, 13 iii 14, *ṭa-b*[*a-at-u-ni* 6: 111frg, *ṭa-b*]*at-u-ni* 6: 111y, *ṭa-b*]*u-u-ni* 6: 231N,

ṭiānu "to grind": *li-ṭi-nu* 6: 446A, l, *ṭi-ia-ni* 6: 444g, *ṭi-*[*ia-ni*] 6: 444l,

ṭiṭṭu "clay": IM 6: 609G, *ṭi-ṭi* 6: 609M, *ṭi-ṭ*]*i* 6: 609A,

ṭuppu "tablet": *ṭup*]*-pi* 6: 400D, *ṭup-pi* 5: 420E, 6: 397D, H, 473D, 526B, 573Q, frg, 616frg, 618G, 660frg, 11 r. 5, *ṭup-p*[*i* 6: 526A, 616m,

ṭūbtu "kindness": [*ṭu*]*-ub-ti* 14 i 3,

u "and": *u* 1: 6, 12, e. 17, 19, r. 6, 8, 13, 2 iv 31, 4 r. 16, 17, 20, 5 iv 4, 6: 5F, 22A, U, 39A, E, frg, 40A, E, frg, 42E, 88G, frg, d, 103F, 159A, E, S, 171I, S, 264B, F, frg, i, 296A, 299C, H, 401D, 419B, c, 420B, C, c, 422B, C, 435I, 438I, 443g, 453l, 462frg, 477D, 479D, 502V, 504V, 505q, 516V, 560A, D, 604A, H, frg, 633K, L, 634F, frg, 9: 2, 9, 11, 15, 18, 32, r. 2, 7, 8, 11, 12, 15, 21, 22, 23, 11 r. 7, 10, 14 i 14, 28, ii 1, *ù* 1 r. 12, 4 r. 3, 7, 8, 12, 13, 14, 26, 5 iii 13, 17, 20, 21, 24, iv 8, 6: 21G, 94A, F, I, frg, 103frg, 135A, E, frg, t, 159P, 171A, frg, 247A, X, frg, 250B, I, frg, 285frg, 333frg, 334B, 497D, 504D, 555D, 633A, F, frg, 668Q, Z, frg, 7: 6, 8: 4, 8, 13, r. 6, 7, 8, 11, 12, 16, 18, 26E, 14 i 31, 32, ii 5, 21, 23, 25,

ubālu "to bring": *tu*]*-bal-a-ni-ni* 6: 138t, *tú-bal-a-ni* 6: 67W, *tú-bal-a-ni-ni* 6: 138E, *tu-bal*]*-a-ni* 6: 272F, *tu-bal*]*-a-n*[*in-ni*] 8: r. ii 7E, *tu-bal-a-ni* 6: 67A, 106E, frg, 272A, frg, *tu-bal-a-ni-ni* 6: 138A, O, *tu-b*[*al-a-ni*] 6: 272B, *tu-še-bal-ni* 2 iii 23, *tu-š*[*e-ba-la-šú-nu*] 5 iii 5, *t*]*u-še-bal-an-n*[*i-n*]*i* 2 iii 10, *ub-bal* 6: 91G, frg, d, *ub-bíl* 6: 365frg, *ub-b*[*al* 6: 91frg, *ú-bal* 6: 91A, frg, *ú-bíl* 6: 365frg, *ú-bí*[]*l* 6: 365z,

ubānu "finger": ŠU.SI 1: 11, ŠU.SI-*ku-nu* 6: 446g,

udû "to know": *tu-da-a-ni* 8 r. 19, [*tu-da-a-ni* 8 r. 24,

ulâ "or, else": *ú-la-a* 4 r. 6, 5 iii 14, [*ú-la-a* 4 r. 5,

ultu "from": *ul-tu* 6: 488frg, 9: 3, 7, 8, 17, 32, 36, *ul-tú* 6: 382D, 488D, *u*[*l-tu* 6: 382A,

umāmu "beast": *ú-ma-mu* 6: 588Q, b,

umma "thus": *um-ma* 1: 9, 14 ii 5, [*um-m*]*a* 14 i 8,

ummānu "scholar": LÚ.*um-ma-ni* 6: 79A, G, H, I, x, LÚ.*um-ma-*[*ni*] 6: 79a,

ummu "mother": AMA 4 r. 18, 6: 448A, g, l, 8: 2, AMA-*šú* 6: 94A, F, G, I, 103E, F, frg, 171A, I, M, S, frg, 270A, frg, 285A, B, J, Y, frg, 341F, p, w, 343F, frg, 496D, q, 504A, D, q, 633L, 8 r. 6, 16, AMA-*šú*] 6: 270i, 363R, AMA-[*šú* 6: 496frg, AMA]-*šú* 6: 633frg, AM[A-*š*]*ú* 6: 504V, AM]A-*šú* 6: 363z, A]MA-*šú* 6: 94frg, *um-mu* 1 r. 5, [AMA-*šú* 6: 285C, 515A, 8: r. ii 6E, [AMA-*šú*] 8 r. 11,

unūtu "utensil, implement": *ú-nu-tu* 6: 276frg, *ú-nu-tú* 6: 276A, B,

urdānūtu "servitude": LÚ.ARAD-*nu-ti* 6: 308A, LÚ.ARAD-*nu-ti-šú* 6: 243A, LÚ.ARAD-[*x* 6: 308frg, LÚ].ARAD.MEŠ-*a-nu-*[*ti*] 6: 308B, LÚ].ARAD-*nu-*[*t*]*i* 6: 308J,

urdu "servant, subject": ARAD.MEŠ 6: 221H, ARAD.MEŠ-*ka* 13 ii 18, ARAD-*šú* 5 iii 18, ARAD-*šú*] 4 r. 8, LÚ.ARAD.MEŠ 6: 221J, LÚ.ARAD.MEŠ-*šú* 6: 243X, LÚ.ARAD.MEŠ-*ti* 6: 308C, LÚ.ARAD.[MEŠ-*ni*] 6: 330frg, LÚ.AR]AD.MEŠ-*ni* 6: 330B, L]Ú.ARAD.MEŠ 6: 221C, frg, L]Ú.ARAD.[MEŠ-*ni*] 6: 330N,

urki "after": EGIR 6: 10A, F, G, H, T, a, 289A, C, 300B, H, 382A, D, s, 387A, D, s, 393D, H, EG[IR 6: 300C,

urqītu "vegetation": *ur-qit* 2 iv 20,

ussuktu "suggestion": *us-su-uk-tú* 8: 19,

uṣû "to emerge": È-*a* 2 iv 20, È-*ni* 2 iv 3, *t*]*u-še-ṣa* 13 ii 15, *ú-še-ṣi* 6: 651U, frg,

ušābu "to sit, reside": *áš-ba-ka-*[*nu-ni*] 6: 182frg, *a-šib* 2 iv 4, *a-ši*]*-bat* 6: 459A, *a-ši-bat* 5 iv 1, 6: 457A, frg, 459frg, 9 r. 24, *a-ši-bu-ti* 6: 21G, frg, *a-ši-bu-tu* 6: 472D, *a-ši-*[*bu-ti* 6: 21A, *a-š*[*i-b*]*u-ti* 6: 21U, *a-*[*ši-bat* 5 iv 2, *it-tu-šib* 6: 304B, C, *it-t*[*u-šib*] 6: 304frg, 362frg, z, *lu-še-šib-šib-bu* 6: 574Q, *lu-še-šib-u-ku-nu* 6: 574frg, *lu-še-ši-bu-ku-nu* 6: 574D, *lu-še-ši-b*[*u-ku-nu* 6: 574Z, *tu-še-šab* 6: 88A, *tu-še-šab-a-ni* 6: 57A, frg, n, *tu-še-šab-ba* 6: 48A, *tu-še-šab-šu* 6: 88d, *tu-še-šab-šú* 6: 48frg, *tu-še-šá-b*[*a*] 6: 88G, *tu-še-š[ab-ba* 6: 48W, *tu-š[e-šá-ba* 6: 88frg, *ú]-ši-šá-bu-u-n[i* 6: 153H, *ú-še-šab-u-ni* 6: 153E, P, *ú-š]e-šá-bu-u-[ni]* 6: 153A, *[t]u-še-šá-ba* 6: 88I,

uššê "foundations": *u]š-še-e* 14 i 25,

utukku "ghost": *ú-tuk-ku* 6: 493D, frg,

uṭṭutu (reading uncert.) "barley": ŠE.PAD 6: 445l, ŠE.PAD.MEŠ 6: 444A, g, l, 445A, g,

uznu "ear": PI.2 6: 143t, *uz-ni* 8 r. 10, [P]I.2 6: 143E, *[uz-ni]* 8 r. 6,

uzuzzu "to stand": *iz-za-zu-u-n[i* 7: 5, *i-za-zu-u-ni* 6: 281A, B, 534M, *i-za-zu-[u-ni]* 6: 281Y, *i-za-z]u-u-ni* 6: 281frg, 534F, G, *ni-iz-zi-iz-zu-ú-ma* 9: 24, *ta-za-za-a-ni* 6: 168A, E, I, P, *ta-za-z]a* 6: 535G, *ta-za-(za)-a-ni* 6: 168S, *t]a-za-za* 6: 535M, *t]a-za-za-a-ni* 6: 145P, *t]a-za-za-ni* 6: 145t, *ú-zu-zi* 2 i 6, *ú-[zu-zi-šú]* 2 i 5, *[ta-za]-za-a-ni* 6: 386D, *[t]a-za-za-a-ni* 6: 386s,

ūmu "day": UD 6: 415A, UD-*me* 6: 10A, F, G, H, T, 39 H, 189frg, 198Y, frg, 201J, frg, 289A, 382D, 384D, 507V, 8 r. 2, 14 ii 14, UD.MEŠ 1 r. 4, 6: 507A, UD.MEŠ-*ku-n[u* 6: 485D, UD-*mi-šu-ma* 14 i 7, UD-*mu* 6: 507D, 9: 3, 17, 33, UD-*mu]* 9: 32, UD-*m[e* 5 iii 1, 6: 10a, 384s, UD.16.KÁM 6: 664Q, UD.18.KÁM 6: 664frg, ⌜UD⌝-*me* 6: 384D, [UD.MEŠ 1 r. 12, [UD].MEŠ-*ku-nu* 6: 485frg,

zaiārānu "foe": *za-ia-ra-an-šú* 11 r. 4,

zakāru "to pronounce, call": *a-zak-k[ar-u-ni]* 4 r. 8, *iz-kur-u-ni* 6: 45A, *iz-kur-[u-ni* 6: 45frg, *i[z-kur]-u-ni* 6: 45E, *zak-ru* 6: 511D, V, 573Q, 618G, *zak-ru]* 6: 526B, *zak-r[u* 6: 573b, *zak-r[u]* 6: 473D, *zak-[ru* 6: 616frg, *za[k-ru* 6: 511frg,

zakkû "exempt": LÚ.*zak-[ke-e]* 5 ii 13, LÚ.*zak-ke-e* 8: 7,

zamar "quickly": *za-mar* 14 ii 15,

zanānu "to rain": *i-za-nun-a-ni* 6: 530A, G, *i-za-nun-u-ni* 6: 530F, *i-za-nun-u-[ni]* 6: 530frg, *li-iz]-nu-na* 6: 533K, *li-iz-nun* 6: 533G, M, *li-iz-[nun]* 6: 533A, *li-šá-az-n[in]* 6: 418frg, *l[i-šá-a]z-nin* 6: 418C,

zanû "to be angry": *tu-šá-az-na-a-ni* 6: 265I, *tu-šá-za-a-na-a-ni* 6: 265B, *tu-šá-za-na]-a-ni* 6: 265p, *tu-šá-za-na-a-ni* 6: 265F, i, *t[u-šá-za-na-a-ni]* 6: 265M, *[tu]-šá-za-n[a-a-ni]* 6: 265A,

zar'u "seed, offspring": NUMUN 6: 4a, 77A, x, 115A, E, frg, 215J, frg, u, 320A, B, C, J, N, c, 338F, 418C, 435A, B, I, 537frg, k, 538A, frg, 543F, 599A, 8: 5, r. 22, 9 r. 21, NUMUN-*ku]-nu* 6: 538frg, NUMUN-*ku-nu* 6: 288A, B, frg, 435A, B, I, 525A, G, 538F, k, 661Q, frg, NUMUN-*ku-[nu]* 6: 435C, NUMUN.MEŠ 6: 543A, NUMUN.MEŠ-*ku-nu* 6: 525B, NUMUN.MEŠ-*šú-nu* 11 r. 13, NUMUN-*ni* 6: 512frg, NUMUN-*šú* 4 r. 4, 6: 315A, C, J, 7: 6, NUMUN-*šú-nu* 6: 140E, 161A, E, P, S, 255A, B, I, NUMUN-*[i-n]i* 6: 512D, NUMUN-*[šú-nu]* 6: 140t, NUMUN—NUMUN-*i-ni* 6: 512D, NUMUN—NUMUN-*ku-n[u* 6: 525B, NUMUN—NUMUN-*[ku-nu* 6: 289J, NUMUN]-*ku-nu* 6: 538F, NUM[UN] 6: 537F, NU[MUN 6: 537frg, 538k, 599j, NU]MUN 6: 115o, 215e, 320B, NU]MUN—[NUMUN-*ku-nu* 6: 289B, N]UMUN-*ku-nu* 6: 538A, [NUMU]N-*ku-nu* 6: 543A, [NU]MUN 6: 77H,

ziāru "to hate": *ni-ze-ʾi-i-ru* 9: 32, *zi-a-ri* 6: 327B, C, N, frg, *z[i-a-ri* 6: 327c,

zibānītu "scales": GI]Š.*zi-ba-ni-tum* 4 r. 22,

zikaru "male": NITA.MEŠ 2 v 12,

zinzaru'u "ginger(?)": *zi-in-za-ru-ʾu* 6: 644A, *zi-in-za-r[u-ʾu* 6: 644frg, *zi-i[n-za-ru-ʾu* 6: 644frg,

zību "vulture": *zi-i-bu* 6: 426A, 520A, *zi-i-b[u]* 6: 426frg, *z[i]-i-bu* 6: 426B, *z[i-i-bu* 6: 520I, *z[i-i-bu]* 6: 426C,

zuāzu "to divide": *li-za-i-za* 5: 419E, 6: 430B, *li-x-x-za* 6: 430A,

zumbu "fly": NUM 6: 601A, T, *zu-um-bi* 6: 601frg, h, j, *zu-u[m-bi* 6: 601K,

zummû "to deprive; thirst for": *li-za-a[m-mi* 6: 439I, *li-za-a[m-mi]* 6: 441g, *li-za-me-ú-ma* 2 iv 12, *li-za-me]* 9 r. 14, *li-za-mu-u* 6: 477D, *lu-u-za-am-me* 11 r. 10,

zumru "body": SU-*ku-nu* 6: 462frg, SU-*šú* 1 r. 11, *zu-mur-ku-n[u* 5 iv 4, *zu-um-ri-[ku-nu* 6: 462k, *zu-um-(ri)-ku-nu* 6: 462frg,

zunnu "rain": A.AN 6: 530A, B, F, G, M, 532G, A.AN.MEŠ 2 iv 13, A.A[N 6: 531A, A.A]N 1 r. 13, 6: 530frg, *zu-un-nu* 6: 531B, frg, 532K

Index of Names

Personal Names

Aqru: maq-ri 11: 5,

Aššūr-ahu-iddina (Esarhaddon, king of Assyria): [m]aš-š[ur—PAB—AŠ 6: 267M, [maš]-šur—PAB—AŠ 6: 200frg, [maš-šur—PA]B—AŠ 6: 494V, m]aš-šur—PAB—AŠ 6: 59W, 273frg, mAN.ŠÁR—ŠEŠ]—SUM-na 14 i 21, maš]-šur—PAB—AŠ 6: 63frg, 124o, 189frg, 632G, maš-šur]—PAB—AŠ 6: 90frg, 110y, 151P, 174M, maš-šur]—PAB—[AŠ 6: 381A, maš-šur—PAB—AŠ 3: 5, 5 i 1, r. iii 2, 16, 18, 23, 6: 1A, F, G, H, T, 7A, F, G, T, a, 11A, 41A, 44A, E, frg, 46A, frg, 57A, n, r, 59frg, n, r, 63A, frg, 83A, G, H, 90A, G, I, d, 93A, F, I, frg, 95A, F, I, frg, 102E, F, frg, 110frg, 121E, O, frg, o, 124E, frg, 131A, E, frg, 151A, H, 157A, B, E, H, P, 174A, B, G, I, P, S, frg, 189I, J, frg, 200Y, 230A, X, frg, f, 237X, 250A, I, frg, 261A, B, I, i, 267A, B, F, i, 273F, 277A, Y, 283A, B, Y, 302A, B, C, frg, 381s, 391H, 402A, D, 494D, 497D, q, 505q, 513D, 555frg, 612K, 632F, frg, 633L, 666frg, 8: 2, maš-šur—PAB—A]Š 6: 237A, maš-šur—PAB—SUM-na 4 r. 9, maš-šur—PAB—[AŠ 6: 277B, frg, maš-šur—PAB—[AŠ] 6: 189frg, 273B, maš-šur—PAB—[SUM]-na 4 r. 7, maš-šur—PAB]—AŠ 6: 237J, 283frg, 494q, maš-šur—PA]B—AŠ 6: 632L, maš-šur—P[AB—AŠ 6: 57frg, 90frg, 121frg, 7: 3, maš-šur—P[AB—A]Š 6: 59A, maš-šur—P]AB—AŠ 6: 1d, maš-šur—ŠEŠ—SUM-na 6: 1a, maš-šur—[PAB—AŠ 6: 63W, 516A, maš-šu]r—PAB—AŠ 6: 360R, 633frg, maš-š[ur—PAB—AŠ 6: 41E, 93frg, 110frg, 391D, maš-š[ur—PAB—AŠ] 6: 189frg, maš-š]ur—PAB—AŠ 5 iii 22, maš-[šur—PAB—AŠ 6: 360frg, m[aš-šur]—PAB—AŠ 6: 95G, m[aš-šur—PAB—AŠ] 6: 369z,

Aššūr-bāni-apli (Assurbanipal, king of Assyria): [m]aš-šur—[DÙ]—A 6: 81G, [mAN.ŠÁR—DÙ—DUMU.UŠ 9: 21, [maš-šur]—DÙ—A 10: 8, [maš-šur—DÙ]—A 6: 47n, [maš-šur—D]Ù—A 8: 11, m]aš-šur—DÙ—A 6: 109E, 165E, 279frg, 391A, 503q, 633L, 8 r. 4, m]aš-šur—D[Ù—A 6: 514A, mAN.ŠÁR—ba-an—DUMU.UŠ 14 i 11, mAN.ŠÁR—DÙ—A 11: 2, mAN.ŠÁR—DÙ—DUMU.UŠ 9: 4, 5, 8, 16, 20, 25, 27, 28, 29, 37, 38, r. 3, mAN.ŠÁR—DÙ—DUMU.UŠ] 9: 9, 10, 17, 31, mAN.ŠÁR—DÙ—[DUMU.UŠ 9: 33, 35, maš]-šur—DÙ—A 6: 269frg, maš]-šur—DÙ—[A 6: 92I, maš-šur]—DÙ—A 6: 167M, 496frg, 506A, 8 r. 9, maš-šur—DÙ—A 6: 11A, 43A, E, 47A, frg, 58A, n, r, 62A, 74A, H, x, 81A, H, a, x, 84A, I, 92A, G, frg, 94A, F, frg, 101F, frg, y, 103E, frg, 109y, o, 123E, o, 130E, frg, 137A, E, t, 143E, frg, 150A, E, H, P, 156A, H, P, 165A, I, P, S, 167A, B, E, I, P, S, 170A, S, frg, 173A, I, P, S, frg, 178A, B, M, 184I, frg, 188I, frg, 226H, 229X, frg, f, 232B, 239A, J, X, 247A, X, frg, 250A, B, I, frg, 258B, I, i, 260I, i, 266A, B, F, i, 269A, B, i, 279A, B, Y, 284B, J, frg, 285A, B, 298C, H, 316A, C, J, 323C, N, c, 349F, R, 353R, 361frg, 366frg, 370frg, 380s, 391D, H, 394D, H, 495D, 496D, q, 503D, V, 504A, D, V, q, 506D, V, 508D, V, 514D, 515A, 555frg, 633A, F, G, K, frg, 666Q, frg, 8: 14, 17, 21, 24, r. 6, 11, 13, 16, maš-šur—DÙ—DUMU.UŠ 9: 23, maš-šur—DÙ—⌈A⌉ 6: 156E, maš-šur—DÙ—[A 6: 62W, 173M, 226J, 250frg, 366R, 380A, maš-šur—DÙ—[A] 6: 84G, 361R, maš-šur—DÙ]—A 6: 58W, 84G, 170P, 229J, 361z, 8: r. ii 6E, maš-šur—D[Ù—A 6: 120frg, 260A, maš-šur—D[Ù—A] 6: 178frg, maš-šur—D]Ù—A 6: 94I, 170M, 285frg, 361frg, maš-šur—[DÙ—A 6: 103F, 130A, 173G, 279frg, 349frg, 366z, maš-šur—[DÙ—A] 6: 178I, 666frg, maš-šur—[DÙ]—A 6: 109frg, maš-šur—[D]Ù—A 6: 58frg, maš-šu]r—DÙ—A 6: 103frg, maš-š[ur—DÙ—A 6: 109frg, 143t, 226f, 247frg, 508A, maš-š[ur—DÙ—A] 6: 361B, maš-š[ur—DÙ]—A 6: 284A, maš-š]ur—DÙ—A 6: 84d, 101E, 109frg, 123frg, 173frg, 247frg, 258A, 380D, maš-š]ur—D[Ù—A] 6: 515V, maš-[šur—DÙ—A 6: 173frg, mA[N.ŠÁR—DÙ—DUMU.UŠ 9: 13, m[AN.ŠÁR—DÙ—DUMU.UŠ 9: 14, m[aš]-šur—DÙ—A 6: 514V, m[aš-šur—DÙ—A 6: 403A, m[aš-š]ur—DÙ—A 6: 92d, 503A,

Aššūr-nērāri (king of Assyria): [maš-šur—ER]IM.GABA 2 v 16, m]aš-šur—ERIM.GABA 2 iv 29, maš-šur—ERIM.GABA 2 i 13, iii 24, 25, r. iv 1, 18, 28, v 4, 15, maš-šur—ERIM.[GABA] 2 v 8,

Ba'lu (Baal, king of Tyre): mba-a-lu 5 iii 15, 18, 22, 420E, mba-a-l]u 5 i 2,

Bur-Dādi (ruler of Karzitalli): mbur—da-di 6: 3G,

Hatarna (ruler of Sikris): mha-tar-na 6: 3T,

Humbarēš (ruler of Nahšimarti): mhum-ba-re-eš 6: 3H,

Iauta' (king of Qedar): mia-ú-ta-a' 10: 4, 12, mia-ú-[ta-a' 10: 1,

Larkutla (ruler of Mazamua): mla-ar-ku-ut-la 6: 3a,

Marduk-rīmanni: mdAMAR.UTU—ri-man-ni 1: 8,

Marduk-zākir-šumi (king of Babylonia): mdAMA]R.UTU—MU—MU 1: 10,

Mati'-il (king of Arpad): mma-ti-i'—DINGIR 2 i 7, 14, 15, 18, 22, r. iv 2, 4, 9, 17, mma-ti-i['—DINGIR 2 i 31, mKI.MIN 2 i 24, 27, 30, r. iv 29, v 8, 9, 24, mKI.M]IN 2 iii 23, mKI.[MIN 2 v 11, mK[I.MIN 2 v 16, mK]I.MIN 2 i 34,

Nabû-aplu-iddina mdAG—A—[S]UM-na 11: 3,

Nabû-bēlu-uṣur (governor of Dur-Šarrukku,

eponym 672): ^{md}PA—EN—PAB 6: 665Q, ^{md}PA—E[N—PAB 6: 665frg, ^{md}PA—E]N—PAB 6: 665frg, ^{md}AG—E[N—PAB 6: 665frg,

Ramataia (ruler of Urakazabanu): ^{m}*ra-ma-ta-a-a* 6: 3A,

Sīn-ahhē-rība (Sennacherib, king of Assyria): ^{md}[30—PAB.MEŠ—SU 5 i 1, ^{md}30—PAB.MEŠ—SU 3: 3, 5, 6: 2A, F, G, H, T, a, ^{md}30—PAB.ME]Š—SU 6: 2d, ^{md}30—PAB.M]EŠ—SU 3: 1, ^{m}30—P[AB.MEŠ—SU] 8: 1,

Sīn-šarru-iškun (king of Assyria): ^{md}30—MAN—GAR-*un* 12: 2, ^{md}30—MAN—GAR-[*un* 11: 1,

Šamaš-mētu-uballiṭ (Assyrian prince, son of Esarhaddon): ^{md}GIŠ.ŠIR—UG$_5$.GA—TI.LA 8: 4,

Šamaš-šumu-ukīn (Assyrian prince, king of Babylonia): [^{md}GIŠ.ŠIR—MU—GI].NA 6: 86G, ^{md}GIŠ.ŠIR—MU—GI.NA 6: 86A, d, 668frg, 9: 6, 27, 29, ^{md}GIŠ.ŠIR—MU—GI.N]A 6: 668frg, ^{md}GIŠ.ŠIR—MU—GI.[NA] 6: 86G, ^{md}GIŠ.ŠIR—MU—GI].NA 6: 668A, ^{md}GIŠ.ŠIR—MU—G[I].NA 8: 3, ^{md}GIŠ.ŠIR—M[U—GI.NA] 6: 668Q, ^{md}UT]U—MU—GIN 14 i 12, ^{md}[GIŠ.ŠIR—MU—GI.NA 9: 7, ^{md}[GIŠ.ŠIR—MU—GI.NA] 6: 668Z, ^{m}GIŠ.ŠIR—MU—GI.NA 6: 668frg,

Šamšī-Adad (V, Assyrian king): ^{m}*šam-ši*—^{d}IM 1: 8,

Tunî (ruler of Ellipi): ^{m}*tu-ni-i* 6: 3F,

Ṭebētāiu (or Kanūnāiu): ^{m}ITI.AB-[*a*]-*a* 11: 4,

Zakūtu (Assyrian queen, mother of Esarhaddon): MÍ.*za-ku-te* 8 r. 10, 16, MÍ.*za-ku-t*[*e*] 8 r. 25, MÍ.*za-ku-u-te* 8: 1, 10, r. 6,

broken: ^{md}*x*[*x* 14 ii 15, ^{m}*x* 10: 1, ^{m}*x*[*x* 5 i 2, ^{m}[*x* 5 iii 24, 6: 174frg, 188F, 266frg, 284frg, 503q, 513V

Place Names

Akkû (Acre, class. Akko, city in Philistia): URU.*a-ku-u* 5 iii 19,

Arbail (class. Arbela, mod. Erbil): *arba*]-*il*.[K]I 3 r. 4, *arba-il* 6: 30frg, 34frg, 10 r. 10, *arba-il*.KI 9 r. 24, ^{d}*arba-il* 6: 30A, URU.*arba*]-*il* 6: 459k, URU.*arba-il* 2 vi 16, 5 iv 2, 6: 20G, U, 30E, 34A, E, 459frg, URU.*ar*[*ba-i*]*l* 6: 459A, URU.*ar*]*ba-il* 6: 20A, URU.[*arba-il*.KI] 3: 9, UR[U].*a*[*rba-il* 6: 30G,

Arubu (Arabia): KUR.*a-r*]*u-bu* 13 ii 8, [KUR.*a-ru-b*]*u* 10: 6,

Aššūr (ancient capital of Assyria, now Qalʿat Širqat): URU—^{d}*aš-šur* 3: 12, URU—*aš-š*[*ur* 6: 483frg,

Aššūrāiu "Assyrian": *aš-šur-a-a* 6: 162A, *aš-šur-i-tú* 3: 10, *aš-šur*-[*i-tú* 3 r. 4, LÚ.*aš-šur-a-a* 6: 162E, P, S,

Barsipa (class. Borsippa, mod. Birs Nimrud): BÁR.SIPÁ.KI 6: 37A, E, frg,

Bābili (Babylon): KÁ.DINGIR.RA.KI 6: 37A, E, frg, 87A, d, 669frg, 14 i 13, KÁ.DINGIR.RA].KI 6: 669frg, KÁ.DINGIR.R]A.KI 6: 87G, 669A, KÁ.DINGIR.KI 6: 87G, I, frg, KÁ.DINGIR.[KI] 6: 87G, KÁ.DING[IR.RA].KI 6: 87d, KÁ.DING]IR.RA.KI 6: 669frg, K[Á.DINGIR.RA.KI] 6: 87frg, TIN.TIR.KI 9: 6,

Dimašqa (Damascus): UR[U.*di-maš-qa* 2 vi 25,

Dū'ru (Bibl. Dor, city in Phoenicia): URU.*du-u*ʾ-*ri* 5 iii 19,

Dūr-Šarrukku (city in Babylonia, now Tell ed-Der): URU.BÀD—LUGAL-*uk-ku* 6: 665Q, URU.BÀD—LUGAL-*uk*-[*ku*] 6: 665frg, URU.BÀD—LUGAL-*u*]*k-k*[*a*] 6: 665frg,

Ebir nāri ("Across-the-River", upper Syria): *e-bir*—ÍD 5 iv 9,

Ellipi (kingdom in northern Luristan): KUR.*el-pa-a-a* 6: 3F, 4F,

Gargamis (Carchemish, mod. Kargamis/Jarablus) URU.*gar-g*]*a-mis* 6: 469frg, URU].*gar-ga-mis* 6: 469D,

Gubla (class. Byblos, mod. Jubayil): URU.*gu-ub-lu* 5 iii 21,

Hallab (Aleppo): URU.*hal-la-ba* 2 vi 18,

Harrānu (Bibl. Haran, class. Carrhae): URU.KASKAL 2 iv 4, 6: 36A, E, frg,

Hatti (Hittite land, North Syria): KUR.*hat-ti* 2 iii 5,

Izaia (Median city-state): URU.*i-za-a-a* 6: 3d,

Kalhu (capital of Assyria, Bibl. Calah, mod. Nimrud): URU.*kal-ha* 6: 33A, E, frg,

Karduniaš (Cassite name of Babylonia): KUR.*kar*—^{d}*dun-iá* 6: 88A, d, KUR.*kar*—^{d}*dun-iá*-[*áš*] 6: 88G, KUR.*kar*—[^{d}*dun-iá-aš*] 6: 88frg, KUR.*ka*[*r*—^{d}*dun-iá-aš*] 6: 88frg, KUR.*ka*]*r*—^{d}*dun-iá-àš* 6: 88I, K]UR.*kar*—^{d}*d*[*un-iá-aš*] 6: 88frg,

Karzitali (Median city-state): *ƙar-zi-ta-li* 6: 3G, URU.*kar-zi-ta-li-a-a* 6: 4G,

Kilizi (city in central Assyria, now Qasr Šamamok): URU.*kàl-zi* 6: 35A, E, frg,

Kurbail (city in Assyria): URU.*kur-ba-il* 2 vi 17,

Labnāna (Lebanon): KUR.*lab-na*-[*na*] 5 iii 21,

Libbi-āli (Inner City, appellative of Aššur): URU.ŠÀ—URU 6: 31A, E, frg,

māt Akkadî (Babylonia): KUR—URI.KI 1: 6, 5 iv 8, KUR—UR[I.KI 9 r. 2, URI.KI 6: 39A, E, frg, 88A, G, UR[I.KI 6: 88frg, UR[I].KI 6: 88frg, U[RI.KI] 6: 22A, [UR]I.KI 6: 88d, [UR]I.[KI] 6: 22U,

māt Aššūr (Assyria): KUR—*aš* 8: 2, 17, 21, 24, r. 4, 7, 9, 11, 14, 17, 9: 25, KUR—*aš*] 8: r. ii 6E, KUR—*aš*]-*šur* 6: 121E, KUR—*aš-šur* 2 iii 25, r. iv 1, 18, 28, 29, v 8, 16, 5 i 1, iii 18, 22, 6: 1A, G, H, T, a, 2G, H, a, 7A, F, G, T, a, 12A, 22G, frg, 38A, E, 41A, 44A, E, 46A, 49A, 56n, 57A, r, 59W, n, r, 61W, r, 63A, 68A, S, W, 70A, W, 83A, G, H, 85A, I, d, 90A, G, I, frg, d, 93A, F, G, I, frg, 95A, F, G, I, frg, 102E, F, 110frg, y, 121frg, o, 124E, o, 128E, frg, 131A, E, frg, 151A, E, H, P, 157A, E, H, P, 162P, S, 163E, P, S, 174A, I, M, 190J, 200J, frg, 216J, 222J, 224f, 225f, 227H, 228X, f, 230A, X, frg, f, 237A, J, X, 241J, X, 250A, 261I, i, 267A, B, F, frg, i, 273B, frg, 277A, 283A, frg, 302B, 321B, C, 338F, 360R, 370frg, 381A, D, s, 391H, 402A, D, 495D, frg, 497D, q, 513D, 516frg, 555frg, 612K, 632F, G, K, L, frg, 633frg, 667Q, 7: 3, 11, 8:

2, 8, 14, 10: 8, 13 iii 6, 13, KUR—*aš-šur-ma* 6: 2A, F, KUR—*aš-šur*.KI 1: 6, 3: 6, 5 i 1, r. iii 16, 20, iv 8, 6: 1F, d, 2T, d, 38frg, 56A, 57n, 59frg, 61n, 63W, 110E, 162A, B, E, 163A, B, 227f, 241A, 248A, frg, 250I, 253A, B, I, 277B, 283B, 321N, c, 666frg, 667frg, 9: 5, 10, 11, 13, 14, 16, 18, 21, 23, 27, 28, 32, 33, 35, r. 2, 3, 12: 3, 14 i 10, KUR—*aš-šur*.KI] 9: 29, 37, 11: 2, KUR—*aš-šur*.K[I] 5 iii 16, KUR—*aš-šur*.K]I 6: 667A, KUR—*aš-šur*.[KI 3: 3, 9: 4, KUR—*aš-šur*.[KI] 5 iii 23, KUR—*aš-šur*.[K]I 6: 22U, KUR—*aš-šu[r* 6: 227J, 241frg, 267frg, KUR—*aš-šu[r*.KI 3: 1, KUR—*aš-šu]r* 6: 216C, 224C, 370R, 497frg, KUR—*aš-šu]r*.KI 6: 85G, KUR—*aš-š[ur* 5 i 10, 6: 46E, 128A, 174P, 222H, 225H, 273F, KUR—*aš-š[ur]* 6: 85G, 95frg, 302A, KUR—*aš-š[ur*.KI 6: 253frg, 9: 20, KUR—*aš-š[ur*.KI] 6: 56r, KUR—*aš-š]ur* 6: 95frg, 225J, 267frg, 505q, KUR—*aš-š]ur*.KI 6: 222e, 391D, KUR—*aš-[šur* 6: 63frg, 174frg, 189frg, 227X, KUR—*aš-[šur]* 6: 163M, KUR—*aš-[šur*.KI 5 iii 2, 6: 248frg, KUR—*aš-[šur]* 6: 121frg, KUR—⌜*aš-šur*⌝ 6: 59A, KUR—[*aš-šur* 6: 59frg, 63frg, 174G, KUR—[*aš-šur]* 2 i 13, 6: 110frg, 667frg, KUR—[*aš-šur*.KI 9: 8, KUR—[*aš-š]ur* 6: 216O, KUR]—*aš-šur* 6: 7H, 93frg, 174frg, 189frg, 225X, 10: 2, KUR]—*aš-šur*.KI 6: 57W, KU[R—*aš-šur* 6: 174S, KU[R—*aš-šur]* 6: 261B, KU]R—*aš-šur* 6: 102frg, KU]R—*aš-šur*.KI 6: 61frg, K[UR—*aš-šur* 6: 46frg, 70S, 189I, 495q, K[UR—*aš-šur]* 6: 56frg, 667frg, K[UR—*aš-šur*.KI 6: 248frg, K]UR—*aš-šur* 6: 516V, [KUR—*aš-šur*] 2 v 15, [KUR—*aš-šur*.KI 9: 38,

māt Šumeri (Sumer): KUR—EME.KU 6: 22A, 39frg, 88A, d, KUR—EME.[KU 6: 22frg, KUR—*šu-me-ri* 6: 22U, 39A, E, 88G, I, frg,

Māzamua (province of Assyria, mod. Sulaimaniya): KUR—*za-mu-u-a* 6: 3a,

Nahšimarti (Median city-state): URU.*na-ah-ši-mar-ta-a-a* 6: 4H, URU.*na-ah-ši-mar-ti* 6: 3H,

Nippur (Babylonian city, mod. Nuffar): EN.LÍL.KI 6: 37E, frg, EN.L[ÍL 6: 37A,

Nīnua (Nineveh, capital of Assyria): NINA 6: 32frg, NINA.KI 3 r. 4, 6: 457frg, NINA.[KI 10 r. 9, NI]NA 6: 457k, NI]NA.KI 6: 457frg, URU.NINA 2 iv 31, 6: 20frg, 30frg, URU.NINA.KI 5 iv 1, 6: 20A, G, 30A, G, 32A, E, 457A, URU.NINA.KI] 3: 9, URU.*ni-na-a* 2 vi 15, URU.[NINA.K]I 6: 30E, U]RU.NINA 6: 20U,

Pilistu (Philistia): KUR.*pi-lis-te* 5 iii 19, KUR.*pi-lis-ti* 5 iii 15,

Qidru (Qedar, Arab kingdom): KUR.*qi-id-[ri* 10: 2,

Sikris (Median city-state): URU.*sik-ri-sa-a-a* 6: 4T, URU.*sik-ri-si* 6: 3T,

Ṣidūnu (Sidon, now Ṣaida): KUR.*ṣi-du-[na-a-a* 5 iii 30,

Ṣurru (Tyre, now Ṣur): KUR.*ṣur-ra-a-a* 5 iii 23, KUR.*ṣur-ri* 5 i 2, 3, r. iii 15, KUR.*ṣu[r-ra-a-a]* 5: 420E, URU.*ṣu]r-[r]i* 5 iii 3,

Urarṭu (Bibl. Ararat, Armenia): K]UR.*ú-ra-ar-ṭa-a-a* 2 iii 8,

Urākazabannu (Median city-state): URU.*ú-ra-ka-za-ba-nu-a-a* 6: 4A, *ú-ra-ka-za-ba-nu* 6: 3A,

broken: KUR—[*x* 6: 22G, 283Y, K[UR—*x* 6: 88frg, K[UR.*x* 5 iii 28, UR[U.*x* 2 vi 25, 7: 2

God, Star, and Temple Names

Adad (weather god): ^{d}IM 2 iv 8, 12, vi 9, 17, 18, 24, 3: 8, r. 3, 6: 17U, f, 27A, G, frg, 440F, g, 9 r. 15, ^{d}[IM 6: 440C, ^{d}[IM] 6: 17G, [^{d}IM 1 r. 13,

Anat Baiti-ili (Anath-Bethel; Canaanite god): ^{d}*a-na-ti—ba-a-[a-ti*—DINGI]R.MEŠ 5 iv 6, ^{d}*a-na-t]i—ba-a-a-ti*—DINGIR.[MEŠ] 6: 467frg,

Antu (consort of Anu) *an-tum* 2 vi 7, 3: 8, r. 3, 14 i 31, ii 16, 21,

Anu (sky god): ^{d}*a]-num* 6: 418B, ^{d}*a-num* 6: 16A, G, K, 26A, frg, 418C, 14 ii 16, 21, ^{d}*a-nu-um* 2 vi 7, ^{d}*a-nu-u]m* 14 i 31, ^{d}*a-n[um* 6: 26G, [^{d}*a-num* 1 r. 3, 3: 8, r. 3,

Aramiš (Syrian god): [^{d}]*a-ra-miš* 6: 466frg,

Astartu (Astarte; Canaanite god): ^{d}*as-tar-tú* 5: 418E,

Aššūr (national god of Assyria): AN.ŠÁR 6: 414C, 9 r. 5, 14 ii 16, AN.ŠÁR] 11 r. 2, AN.Š[ÁR 6: 414A, AN.[ŠÁR 6: 414B, *aš-šur* 2 v 5, 6: 16A, 333frg, 334frg, 393A, H, 483D, *aš-šur]* 14 i 28, *aš-š[ur]* 6: 334B, ^{d}*aš-šur* 2 vi 6, 6: 16G, K, frg, 25A, frg, 333B, 407C, 518V, i G, ^{d}*aš-šur]* 6: 407A, ^{d}*aš-š[ur* 6: 25G, ^{d}*a-šur*$_4$ 6: i A, F, H, T, a, ^{d}*a-š]ur*$_4$ 6: i d, ^{d}*a-[šur*$_4$ 6: i frg, [AN.ŠÁR 4 r. 16, [*aš-šur* 3: 7, r. 2, 8: 25, [*aš-šur*] 10: 3, [*aš-š]ur* 6: 393D, [^{d}*aš-šur* 10 r. 8, [^{d}*aš-šur*] 6: 401D,

Ba'al malagê (Phoenician god): ^{d}*ba-al—ma-la-ge-e* 5 iv 10,

Ba'al samême (Baal Shamaim, Phoenician god): ^{d}*ba-al—sa-me-me* 5 iv 10,

Ba'al Ṣapūnu (Baal Saphon, Phoenician god): ^{d}*ba-al—ṣa-pu-nu* 5 iv 10,

Baiti-ili (Bethel, Baitylos; Canaanite god): ^{d}*ba-a-a-ti*—DINGIR.MEŠ 5 iv 6, [^{d}*ba-a-a-ti*—DINGIR.MEŠ 6: 467frg,

Bābu (consort of Zababa): ^{d}BA.Ú 2 vi 12, ^{d}BA.Ú] 3 r. 4, ^{d}BA].Ú 3: 10,

Bēl (appellative of Marduk): ^{d}EN 6: 626G, K, L, frg, 14 ii 1, r. ii 7, ^{d}[E]N 6: 431A, [^{d}EN 10 r. 9,

Bēlet ilī (creation goddess): *be-lit*—DINGIR.ME 14 i 6, DINGIR.MAH 3 r. 5, 6: 19U, 29A, DINGIR.MA[H 6: 29frg, DING[IR].MAH 6: 19A, ^{d}*be-lit*—DINGIR.ME 14 i 1, ^{d}*be-lit*—DINGIR.MEŠ 6: 19G, 437F, I, 14 i 14, ^{d}*be-lit*—DINGIR.M[EŠ 6: 29G, 14 ii 13, ^{d}*be-lit*—[DINGIR.MEŠ 6: 437C, ^{d}*be-lit*—[*x* 9: 1,

Bēltīa (appellative of Zarpanitu): [^{d}GAŠAN-*ia* 14 ii 1,

Dagān (Canaanite god): ^{d}[*d*]*a-gan* 2 vi 21,

Damkina (consort of Ea): ^{d}*dam-ki-na* 2 vi 8, 3 r. 5,

Dilipat (Venus): ^{d}*dil-bat* 6: 13A, 428B, frg, 8: 25, 11: 6, ^{d}*d[il-bat]* 6: 13frg, MUL.*dil-bat* 6: 13G, MUL.

dil-[bat] 6: 13K,
Ekur (main shrine of Illil): É.KUR 9 r. 12, 11 r. 12, É.KUR] 1 r. 5,
Enlil see *Illil,*
Esangil (main shrine of Marduk): É.SAG.ÍL 6: 431B, É.*sag-gíl* 6: 431A, C, I,
Ešarra (main shrine of Aššur): É.ŠÁR.RA 14 i 28,
Ea (creation god, father of Marduk): dI 2 vi 8, dÉ.A 1 r. 7, 3 r. 5, 6: 16A, G, 26A, 521A, I, 9 r. 13, dÉ.[A 6: 26frg, dÉ.[A] 6: 26G,
Girra (fire god; cf. Glossary): dGIŠ.BAR 2 vi 15, 6: 524A, B,
Gula (goddess of healing) d*gu-la* 5 iv 3, 6: 461frg, dME 2 vi 11,
Humhum (city god of Dur-Šarrukku): d*hum-hum-mu* 2 vi 14,
Iasumūnu (Eshmun, Phoenician god): d*ia-s]u-mu-na* 2 vi 22, d*ia-su-mu-nu* 5 iv 14,
Illil (Enlil, head of the Sumerian pantheon): d+EN.LÍL 1 r. 3, 6, dBE 2 vi 7, 6: 16A, dEN.LÍL 3: 8, 6: 26A, frg, 659frg, 14 ii 23, dEN.LÍL] 14 i 32, dEN.LÍ[L 6: 26frg, dEN.LÍ]L 6: 26G, dEN.L[ÍL] 6: 16G, dE]N.LÍL 3 r. 3,
Ingirsu (Ningirsu, Sumerian god equated with Ninurta): dNIN.GÍR.SU 2 vi 13,
Inurta (Ninurta, Assyrian war god): dMAŠ 2 vi 11, 3: 10, 6: 425B, C, frg, dNIN.URTA 9 r. 17,
Issār (Ištar, Assyrian war goddess): dI[5 6: 20frg, 469D, dI]5 10 r. 9, d15 2 vi 15, 3: 9, r. 3, 4, 6: 20A, G, U, frg, 30A, E, G, frg, 264F, 10 r. 9, [d15 2 v 12, 3: 9, 10, r. 4, 4 r. 20, d+INNIN 9 r. 24, dINNIN 2 vi 16, dIŠ.TAR 5 iv 2, 6: 264B, i, 453A, g, l, 459frg,
Ištar see *Issār,*
Išum (god of war and fire): d*i-šum* 2 vi 14,
Kaiamānu (Saturn): [dUDU.IDIM.SAG].UŠ 8 e. 26, MUL.UDU.IDIM.SAG.UŠ 6: 14A, K, MUL.UDU.IDIM.SAG.U[Š 6: 14frg, [M]UL.UDU.IDIM.SAG.UŠ 6: 14G,
Kakka (messenger god incorporated into the Assyrian pantheon by Sennacherib): dGA.G]A 3 r. 5,
Karhuha (Hittite god): d*kar]-hu-ha* 2 vi 23,
Kippat māti (deified Orbis Terrarum; Assyrian god): d*kip-pat*—KUR 3: 8, [dGAM—KUR 3 r. 3,
Kubāba (Cybele, goddess of Carchemish): d*kù-b[a-ba* 2 vi 23, d*kù*-KÁ 6: 469D,
Lāṣ (consort of Nergal): d*la-aṣ* 2 vi 12,
Madānu (Assyrian god): dDI.KUD 2 vi 13,
Marduk (supreme god of Babylon): dAMAR.UTU 1 e. 16, 2 vi 10, 6: 17G, f, 27A, G, 433I, frg, 9 r. 6, 14 i 9, ii 25, r. ii 7, dAMAR.[UTU 6: 433C, dA[MAR.UTU 6: 27frg, d[AMAR.UTU 6: 433B, [dAMAR.UTU] 14 ii 3,
Milqartu (Melqarth, Tyrian god): d*mi-il-qar-tu* 5 iv 14, d*m[i-il-qar-tu* 2 vi 22,
Mulliltu see *Mullissu,*
Mullissu (consort of Aššur): dNIN.LÍL 1 r. 5, 2 vi 7, 3: 7, r. 2, 6: 19A, G, frg, 29A, G, frg, 417C, 457A, frg, 14 i 32, dNIN.[LÍL] 6: 19U, dNI[N.LÍL 14 ii 23, dNI[N].LÍL 10: 3, dNI]N.LÍL 10 r. 8, d[NIN.LÍL 5 iv 1, [dNIN.LÍL 4 r. 18,
Muṣurūna (Phoenician god, reading uncert.): d*[m]u-ṣur-u-na* 2 vi 21,
Nabû (Nebo, son of Marduk): dAG 1 r. 1, 2 vi 10, 6: 18G, frg, 28A, G, 9 r. 7, dPA 6: 18A, U, 660frg, dP]A 10 r. 9, d[A]G 6: 28frg,
Nanai (goddess of love): d*na-na-a* 9 r. 22,
Nergal see *Nērigal,*
Nērigal (Nergal, god of war and pestilence): d]U.GUR 10 r. 10, dU.GUR 2 vi 12, 3 r. 5, 6: 18A, G, U, 28A, G, 455A, g, 9 r. 18, 12: 6, [dU.GUR 4 r. 26, [dU.G]UR 6: 455I,
Nikkal (consort of Sin): dNIN.GAL 2 vi 8, 3: 7, r. 2, [dNIN.GAL 4 r. 24,
Ninegal (consort of Uraš): dNIN.É.GAL 2 vi 11,
Ningirsu see *Ingirsu,*
Ninurta see *Inurta,*
Ninmah (constellation Puppis + Carina): MUL.NIN.MAH 14 ii 11,
Nusku (son of Sin): dPA.TÚG 2 vi 15, 3: 10, 6: 18A, G, U, 28A, frg, [dPA.TÚ]G 6: 28G,
Nūr (consort of Šamaš; reading uncert.) dA.A 2 vi 9, dA.[A 3: 7, [dA.A 3 r. 2,
Pālil (Mesopotamian war god): dIGI.DU 2 vi 19, 6: 519I, 9 r. 20, [d]IGI.DU 6: 519A,
Rammānu (Aramean deity worshipped in Damascus): d*ra-ma-nu* 2 vi 24,
Sagmegar (Jupiter; reading uncert.): dSAG.ME.GAR 6: 13A, 431B, frg, 8: 25, dS[AG.ME.GAR 11: 6, [d]SAG.ME.GAR 6: 431I, MUL.SAG.ME.GAR 6: 13G, K, frg, 431C,
Sebetti (the Pleiades): d*si-bit-te* 5 iv 5, d*si-bit-ti* 6: 464frg, d7.BI 2 vi 20,
Sīn (moon god): d3[0 6: 17frg, d30 2 iv 4, vi 8, 3: 7, r. 2, 4 r. 24, 6: 17G, K, U, f, 27A, G, frg, 419B, C, c, 8: 25, 9 r. 11, 10 r. 8, 11 r. 10, [d30 1 r. 10,
Ṣalbatānu (Mars): [d*ṣal-bat]-a-[nu* 8 e. 27, MUL.*ṣal-bat-a-nu* 6: 15A, K, MUL.*ṣal-bat-a-[nu* 6: 15frg, [MU]L.*ṣal-bat-a-nu* 6: 15G,
Šala (consort of Adad): d*ša-la* 2 vi 9, 3 r. 3, d*š]a-la* 3: 8,
Šamaš (sun god): d*šá-maš* 6: 17G, 27G, dUTU 1 r. 8, 2 iv 20, vi 9, 3: 7, r. 2, 6: 17K, f, 27A, frg, 333frg, 334B, frg, 422B, C, c, 545A, frg, 649U, frg, 9 r. 8, 10 r. 8, dUTU] 8: 25, d[UT]U 6: 17U, [dUTU 4 r. 22,
Šērū'a (morning star, daughter of Aššur): d*še-ru-u-a* 6: 19A, G, U, 29A, G, frg, d*še-ru-u-a]* 3: 7, r. 2, d*ši*-EDIN-*ú-a* 14 i 28, ii 19, d*š[e-ru-u-a* 6: 19frg, d*š[e-ru-u-a]* 10: 3,
Šihṭu (Mercury): dUDU.[IDI]M.GUD.[UD] 8 e. 26, MUL.UDU.IDIM.GUD.UD 6: 14A, MUL.UDU.IDIM.[GUD.UD] 6: 14G, MUL.UD[U.IDIM.GUD.UD] 6: 14K,
Šukūdu (Sirius): dGAG.SI.SÁ 8 e. 27, MUL.GAG.SI.SÁ 6: 15A, G,
Tašmētu (consort of Nabû): dLÁL 2 vi 10,
Uraš (city god of Dilbat, equated with Ninurta): dIB 2 vi 11, 6: 18A, G, U, 28A, G,
Zabāba (city god of Kiš): d*za-ba$_4$-ba$_4$* 1 r. 16, 2 vi 12, 3: 10, r. 4, 9 r. 19,
Zarpānītu (consort of Marduk): dNUMUN.DÙ-*tú* 6: 435I, dNUMUN.[DÙ-*tú* 6: 435C, d*zar-pa-ni-tum* 2 vi 10, 9 r. 21, [d*zar-pa-ni-tu* 14 ii 25,
broken: d*za-[x* 2 vi 26, d*[x* 6: 16K, 17K, 18frg, 28frg, 467D, d*[x]* 2 vi 24, 6: 28frg, MUL.*[x* 6: 14U, 15K, U

Subject Index

abandon **6** 476
abase **6** 188
able **6** 138
abomination **9** r22
absent **5** iii
absolve **14** ii
Abyss **6** 521 **9** r13
acceptable **6** 292
accountable **6** 507
accursed **6** 328 360
acquisitions **6** 269
adjure **6** 212
advice **6** 46 **8** 19
age **6** 414
agitation **6** 500
agitator **9** 12
Akko **5** iii
alienate **6** 237 360
alive **6** 328 507 570 594 649
alas **2** i
Aleppo **2** vi
ally **6** 108 **9** 20
alter **4** 18 **6** 1 57 **11** r5
Anath-Bethel **5** iv **6** 467
anger **6** 472
angry **6** 259
annihilate **6** 292 410 626
anoint **6** 259
appointed **5** iii **6** 41 **9** 10
Arabia **10** 4 **13** ii
area **2** i
armed **6** 500 **8** r18
arms **4** 20 **6** 453
army **2** iv
arrow **6** 425
ascend **6** 83 360
ascertain **6** 201
ass **6** 488
assassinating **6** 130
assembly **6** 212 373
asses **2** iv
assigned **6** 360
assist **6** 138
Assur **6** 481
Assurbanipal **6** 11 41 46 57 62 73 83 92 101 108 123 130 138 147 153 162 167 180 188 226 229 237 249 259 266 269 279 283 292 302 318 336 353 360 377 385 397 500 507 513 555 632 664 **8** 9 12 16 19 23 r2 r7 r12 r18 **9** 3 6 10 12 17 20 21 26 32 38 r3 **10** 1 8 **11** 1 **14** i
Assyria **1** 6 13 **2** i iv v **3** 1 2 5 **5** i iii iv **6** 1 11 16 38 41 46 55 57 62 69 83 92 101 108 123 130 147 153 162 173 198 214 226 237 249 259 266 275 283 302 318 360 385 494 513 555 612 632 664 **7** 11 **8** 1 12 16 19 23 r2 r7 r12 r18 **9** 3 6 10 12 17 20 21 26 32 38 r2 r3 **10** 1 8 **11** 1 **12** 1 **13** iii **14** i
Assyrian **2** iv **3** 7 r2 **5** iii **6** 162 336
Assyrians **8** 3
Astarte **5** iv
attainment **6** 414
attention **13** iii **14** i
august **1** r1 **11** r1
available **6** 643
avenge **6** 249
avenger **6** 576 582
Baal **5** i iii iv
Baal Malage **5** iv
Baal Shamaim **5** iv
Baal Saphon **5** iv
Babylon **6** 37 83 664 **14** i
Babylonia **1** 6 13 **9** 6 r2
backwards **6** 563 573 618
banquet **2** i
bar **6** 440
barefooted **6** 656
base-board **6** 612
bathe **5** iv
battle **4** 20 **5** iv **6** 302 453 **9** 21 r24
battlefield **2** v
bearded **4** 4 **6** 73 162 214 237 336 **8** 3 r18
bearer **6** 660
bears **13** iii
beast **6** 588
bed **6** 555
behold **2** i
belly **6** 481
belongings **5** iv
beloved **4** 18 **6** 417
besiege **6** 162
Bethel **5** iv **6** 467
bind **4** 20 **6** 453
binding **6** 153
bird **6** 582 649 **13** iii
birth **6** 249 437
bitter **6** 646
bitterly **2** v
bitumen **6** 585
black **6** 585
blind **1** 8 **2** vi
blinded **6** 626
blood **5** iv **6** 249 425 461 568 612 **12** 6
blow **6** 563
body **1** r10 **5** iv **6** 461
bones **6** 440 637
born **6** 1 249 283 377 385
Borsippa **6** 37

bought **6** 214
bow **2** v **4** 20 **5** iv **6** 453 573 **9** r24
bowls **6** 440
bowmen **9** 21
brazen **6** 530
bread **6** 560 567
break **1** 22 **4** 20 **5** iv **6** 237 573 652 **9** r24
breasts **6** 153
breath **6** 603
brick **2** i **6** 526
brier **6** 656
brighten **6** 485
brightest **6** 428
brightness **6** 419
bronze **6** 649
brother **6** 83 328 360 397 **8** 3
brothers **6** 55 69 73 92 101 108 167 214 269 283 318 328 336 353 494 500 513 547 576 582 585 588 591 594 622 632 636 **8** 3 r18 **10** 14
bug **6** 603
bundle **6** 626
burial **6** 481
burn **6** 524
burning **6** 530
burnt **6** 608
bury **6** 410
Byblos **5** iii
Calah **6** 33
called **6** 573 616
calumniate **6** 269
campaign **2** iv **6** 198
canal **1** r13 **2** iv **6** 440 **9** r15
captives **1** 12
captivity **1** 16
Carchemish **6** 469
case **1** r8 **4** 24
cast **6** 649
caterpillar **6** 579
caterpillars **6** 599
cattle **6** 275
cavalryman **2** 19
cedar-resin **6** 643
chameleon **6** 591
change **6** 57 397
chapel **3** 7 r2
chariot **6** 612
chariotry **2** iv
chariots **6** 573 612
chariot-fighter **2** 19
chase **6** 476 576
chief eunuch **11** 1
children **6** 437
cities **2** v **5** iii **6** 545
citizen **6** 162 214
citizens **6** 318
city **1** r13 **2** vi **3** 7 **4** 22 **7** 2
city-ruler **6** 1
clay **6** 608
cloak **2** iv **11** r10
closed **2** v
clothe **2** iv **6** 419 440 **11** r10
clothes **5** iv
clothing **2** iv
coals **6** 530
cocoon **6** 579
collecting **5** iii
command **1** 16 22 **6** 195 328 **9** 21 **14** i
commissioned **14** r3
commit **6** 269
committed **9** 26
compassion **6** 459
conceal **2** 19 **6** 73 108 500 **9** 6 **13** iii
conceive **8** 16
conclude **2** i **6** 153
concluded **6** 11 13 41 62 92 101 130 173 283 513 664 **8** 9
confidence **1** r8
confirmed **6** 13 62 283
consent **6** 328
conspiracy **8** r18
conspirator **9** 12
consume **6** 632
contact **6** 147
continually **6** 233
convene **5** iii
cord **6** 606
corner **6** 476
corpses **6** 481
counsel **5** iii **6** 233
country **1** 11 16 **2** i iv v **5** iii **6** 46 92 162 214 **13** ii iii
courtier **6** 162 237 336
cousins **6** 73 108 214 318
cover **11** r7
covering **6** 488
crab **6** 618
creation **6** 437
cries **6** 437
crime **6** 269 **14** ii
crimes **9** 26
crouch **4** 20 **5** iv **6** 453 **9** r24
crown prince **3** 5 **6** 11 57 62 73 83 101 108 123 130 138 147 153 162 167 173 180 188 226 229 237 249 259 266 269 279 283 292 302 318 336 353 360 377 385 397 494 500 507 513 555 632 664 **14** i
crown-princeship **6** 41
crushed **2** i
cunning **6** 410
cup **6** 153
curse **3** 7 r2 **5** iv **6** 433 472 523 **11** r7 **14** i ii
Cursers **6** 626
curses **14** ii8
cut **2** i **6** 437 440 547 555 626
dam **1** r7
dark **6** 485
darkness **6** 422 485 **9** r8
daughter **6** 440
daughters **2** i iv **6** 108 440 534 537 540 547 551 560 568 570 579 585 588 591 594 606 618 622 636 637 646 649
day **6** 180 188 198 201 377 664 **8** r2 **9** 3 17 32
daylight **6** 476
days **1** 22 r10 **6** 1 485
deadly **6** 259 521
death **2** v **6** 123 138 153 188 237 302 **14** ii
decay **1** 16
decision **1** r5
decrease **2** vi
decree **1** 22 **6** 414 433 **9** r8 **14** ii
decreer **1** 22
deed **6** 360
deface **6** 410

defeat **6** 167 302
defeater **11** r1
deliberate **8** 19
deliver **5** iv **6** 582 **14** ii
demon **6** 488
demons **1** r1
deport **1** 6
deportation **5** iv **6** 292
deported **2** iv
depose **6** 55
deprive **1** r13 **6** 437 440 **11** r7
deprived **2** iv
deputy **5** iii
descendant **6** 318
desert **6** 419 **9** r20
deserves **6** 188
desire **9** 21
despatch **5** iii
destroy **1** 16 r13 **4** 26 **5** iv **6** 138 153 249 302 410 431 435 660 **11** r1 r10
destruction **5** iv **6** 292 **10** 4
detestable **9** 12
devastate **6** 488
devastation **2** v
device **6** 410
devil **6** 488
devoted **2** 19 **9** 3
devoting **3** 2
devour **2** vi **6** 440 599
dew **6** 530
die **6** 46 229 652 **14** ii
dim **6** 485
diminish **6** 440
dip **6** 440
direct **6** 233
disappear **6** 537 540
discuss **13** iii
disease **6** 418 469
disloyal **2** 19 **6** 500
dispell **14** i ii
dispersion **1** 16
dispute **6** 1
disregard **6** 397 **9** r3
dissolved **6** 608
distance **13** ii
district **5** iii **6** 40 599
districts **6** 545
ditches **12** 6
ditto **2** iv **6** 26 40 27 28 29 30 31 32 33 34 35 36 37 39 40 526 547 555 560 563 567 568 570 573 576 582 585 588 591 594 599 601 606 612 637 649
divide **5** iv **6** 336 428
divination **2** i
divine **2** v
divinity **14** i r13
dogs **6** 440 481
dominion **6** 57 **14** i
donkey **2** iv
donkeys **6** 275
door **2** v **6** 440 662
Dor **5** iii
dough **6** 440
doves **6** 637 **14** ii
downfall **5** iv
drag **6** 481
draw **2** iv
drink **2** iv **6** 259 488 521
drinking **6** 153
drip **6** 469
drive **9** r21
dropsy **6** 521
drug **6** 259
duckweed **6** 488
dung **2** iv
dust **2** iv
duty **1** 15 **6** 180
dwelling **6** 16
dwells **2** iv **6** 457 459
dynastic **6** 318
eagle **6** 425
eagles **6** 519
earth **1** r8 r13 **2** iv vi **4** 16 **5** iv **6** 16 40 41 410 419 422 440 472 481 488 523 **9** 1 r8 r11 r15 **11** r7 r10
eat **2** iv **6** 259 440 519 547 570
ecstatic **6** 108
effort **10** r5
elaborated **8** r12
elder **6** 55 69
elders **5** iii
eldest **6** 433
eliminate **8** r7
eliminating **6** 130
empty **6** 641
end **1** r10 **6** 485 **14** ii
enemies **11** r1
enemy **4** 20 **5** iv **6** 108 123 428 453 494 534 573 588 612 616 626 643 **9** 6 20 21 32 r24 **11** r1
entourage **8** 3
entrails **6** 551
entrance **6** 431
entrusted **5** iii
envious **6** 328
eponymy **6** 664
equal **6** 83 **8** 3
erase **6** 397 660 **9** r3
Esarhaddon **3** 5 **4** 4 8 **5** i iii **6** 1 11 41 46 57 62 83 92 101 108 123 130 147 153 173 188 198 229 237 249 259 266 275 283 302 360 377 385 397 494 513 555 612 664 **7** 3 **8** 1 **10** 1 **14** i
escape **6** 649
Eshmun **2** vi **5** iv
eunuch **6** 162 214 237 336 **11** 1
eunuchs **4** 4 **6** 318 73 **8** 3 r18
evil **1** 8 r1 **5** iv **6** 62 73 101 108 123 180 269 318 336 360 414 417 500 621 **8** 12 16 19 **9** 12 17 r5 **11** r7 **14** ii
ewe **6** 547
exalted **6** 431 **9** r19
exempts **8** 3
exhaustion **1** 22 **6** 418 485
extinguish **6** 455 **9** r18 **11** r13
eye **1** 11
eyes **2** vi **6** 428 481 626 662 **9** 21
eyesight **6** 422 **9** r8
fabricate **8** 12
face **4** 8 **6** 373 540 **10** 8
fall **6** 530
family **6** 108 214 318 73 **7** 6
famine **1** 16 22 r13 **2** iv **6** 440 476
farmers **2** iv
fate **6** 414 433 485 **9** r5 **14** ii
fates **1** 22 **6** 414 660 **9** r5

father **1** 22 **2** v **4** 16 **6** 1 25 73 83 108 201 214 269 302 318 328 336 353 397 518 **9** r5
favourite **8** 9
favourable **6** 147
fear **6** 353 385 **13** ii
feed **6** 425
feet **5** iv **6** 551 626 **9** r24 **10** r2
feign **6** 385
female **6** 551
few **6** 147
field **6** 599
fields **2** iv **6** 440 530
fierce **5** iv **6** 425 464 518
fiercely **1** r13
fight **6** 229 318 336 46
figure **6** 608
finger **1** 11
finger-joint **6** 440
fire **6** 153 410 534 608 621 **11** r13
first-born **1** r16
fish **13** iii
flaming **6** 457
flee **1** 13 **6** 173 214
flesh **2** iv **6** 425 440 519 547 570 585 591 594 622
flocks **6** 275
flood **1** r13 **6** 440 488
flow **6** 563
fly **6** 601
foes **9** 21
fold **2** i
fomenting **8** r18
food **2** iv **5** iv **6** 476 488 524
forbid **4** 16 **6** 419
forbidden **2** iv **6** 488
force **6** 173
forces **2** iv
foreign **5** iv
foreigner **6** 214 318 336
foremost **6** 425 519 **9** r17
forever **6** 385
forgiven **9** 26
forgiveness **5** iv
former **6** 318
formulate **8** 19
forsake **6** 632
forts **1** 7
foundations **14** i
free **6** 336
friendly **10** 8
friends **8** r18
front **2** vi
fugitives **1** 13
fumigants **7** 9
future **6** 283 377 385
gained **6** 269
gall **6** 646
garrisons **1** 7
gazelle **6** 419
ghost **6** 440 476
ghosts **9** r13 **11** r7
gift **2** v **6** 269 275
gifts **6** 83
ginger **6** 643
glory **2** vi
god **4** 16 **6** 1 292 385 397 603
goddess **2** v **6** 469 **9** r24 **14** r11
goddesses **6** 259
gods **1** 22 r10 r7 **2** i v **3** 7 r2 **4** 16 26 **5** iv **6** 1 153 16 25 259 31 32 33 34 35 36 37 38 39 397 40 41 414 418 419 425 431 455 472 494 507 518 523 526 560 573 599 616 660 **9** 1 r18 r2 r5 r6 **10** 1 **11** r5 **14** i ii
gold **6** 567
goodness **14** i
goods **6** 428
governor **1** 3 86 664
governors **4** 4 **6** 73 318 **8** 3
grain **6** 440
grandson **8** 9
grandsons **5** i **6** 1 283 385 507 612 **12** 1
grant **2** v **5** iv **6** 414 435
grievous **3** 7 r2
grimly **6** 472
grind **6** 440
ground **6** 469 526 540
groups **6** 214
guard **6** 180 201 292 397
guardians **6** 397
gypsum **2** i
Hadad **2** vi
handcuffs **9** 12
harm **5** iii
harmful **13** iii
harvest **2** iv **6** 440
hate **9** 32
hatred **6** 318
health **6** 418
heap **2** iv
hear **3** 2 **4** 4 **6** 73 108 130 147 500 **8** r2 r7 r12 r18 **13** iii **14** i7
hearken **6** 195
heaven **1** r8 r10 r13 **2** iv vi **3** 7 r2 **4** 16 **5** v **6** 16 40 41 419 422 440 472 523 530 **9** 1 r7 r8 r11 r15 **11** r7 r10
heavy **4** 16 **6** 433
heir **1** r1 **9** r17
help **6** 83 214 226 237 302 **14** i
helping **6** 69
hero **6** 455
heroic **2** vi **5** iv **6** 464
hide **9** 6
hired **5** iii
hole **6** 555 641
holes **6** 594
honey **6** 568 643
honeycomb **6** 594
honoured **6** 328
horses **1** 2 **2** iv **6** 275
hostile **6** 237
house **2** v vi **6** 201 428
houses **2** vi **6** 269 275 418 440 488 579
human being **6** 73 108 214 336
hunger **1** 16 **2** iv **6** 440 476 547
husband **4** 24
ill **6** 418 488
illness **5** iv **6** 385 **14** ii
image **6** 608
implements **6** 275
impose **4** 16 **6** 336 **14** i
improper **3** 2 **6** 73 108 123 233 318
incurable **6** 385
indissoluble **3** 7 r2 **5** iv **6** 433

inflict **1** r10
inform **6** 138 **8** r2 r7
inimical **6** 302
injustice **5** iii
Inner City **6** 31
inquirer **6** 108
inspector **1** r13 **2** iv **6** 440 **9** r15
install **9** 32
instigate **6** 237
instigating **8** r18
instigation **6** 500
insurrection **6** 101 130 147 153 162 198 302 494 **8** 19 r2
intent **6** 62
intercede **1** r5 **4** 24 **6** 417
intestines **6** 560
iron **6** 526 545 632 **10** 4
irremovable **11** r7
irresistible **6** 488
judge **1** r8 **6** 422 **9** r8
judgment **1** r5 **9** r8
Jupiter **6** 13 431 **8** 25 **11** 1
justice **1** r8 **6** 92
justly **6** 422
kid **6** 636
kids **6** 551
kill **1** 8 **2** iii **6** 130 576 **8** r7 r18 **10** r5
kin **2** iv v
kindle **6** 153
king **1** 3 8 13 **2** i iv v **3** 1 2 5 **4** 16 **5** i iii **6** 1 11 41 46 57 62 69 83 92 101 108 123 130 147 153 173 188 195 198 201 237 249 259 266 275 283 292 302 360 385 397 414 418 419 494 507 521 555 603 612 632 664 **7** 11 **8** 1 12 16 19 23 r12 r18 r2 r7 **9** 3 6 10 12 17 20 21 26 32 38 r6 r13 r20 **10** 1 8 **11** 1 r1 **12** 1 **13** iii **14** i ii r3
kings **2** v
kingship **1** r8 **2** v **6** 1 57 69 73 83 123 212 214 226 237 292 302 **14** i
knuckle **2** i
lady **2** v vi **4** 20 **6** 437 453 **14** ii
lamb **2** i **6** 636
lambs **2** iv **6** 551
land **1** r13 **2** 19 i iv v vi **5** iii iv **6** 40 138 153 180 198 249 292 302 437 440 530 537 567 599 660 **9** 17 26 32 r21
lands **3** r2 **6** 1 16 40 237 25 275 302 **9** r6 **14** i
lap **6** 373 428
Lebanon **5** iii
leprosy **2** iv **6** 419 **11** r10
letter **5** iii
libations **6** 440
lice **6** 599
life **1** 16 r1 **2** v **6** 431 455 476 485 555 **11** r1 **14** i ii
light **6** 422 **9** r11 **11** r10
limestone **2** i
line **6** 73 108 214 318 336 **8** r18
lingering **14** ii
lion **5** iv **6** 467
lips **6** 385
listen **1** 8 **5** iii **6** 201 **9** 12
live **6** 555 **9** 3 17 32 r18
locust **6** 440
locusts **2** vi **6** 599
lordship **6** 1 214 226 292 46
love **6** 201 266 **9** 17 32 r22 **11** r1
lover **11** r1
lowly **6** 188
loyal **4** 8 **6** 147
loyally **6** 46 167
loyalty **2** iv
magnates **2** i iv v **4** 4 **6** 73 318 **8** 3
malaria **6** 418
male **6** 551
malefactor **10** 4
malicious **6** 500
malign **6** 318
malt **6** 540
man **2** i vi **6** 440
mankind **6** 292 603 **13** iii **14** r14
man-eating **5** iv **6** 467
march **2** vi **13** ii iii
marsh **6** 626
Mars **6** 13 **8** 25
mash **6** 540
massacre **6** 464
meadows **6** 530
Melqarth **2** vi **5** iv
member **6** 336
members **6** 73 108 214
men **2** v **6** 1 167 481 **8** r18
merciless **6** 455 **9** r18
Mercury **6** 13 **8** 25
mercy **2** iv **5** iv **6** 459
message **9** 6
messages **13** iii
messenger **5** iii **6** 201 **9** 6 32
messengers **4** 1
mighty **6** 188
mill **6** 440
mind **4** 18
minority **6** 237
minors **6** 83
misfortune **14** ii
mistress **9** r22
moan **14** ii
moaning **1** r10
mongoose **6** 555
moorings **5** iv
mother **1** r5 **4** 18 **6** 92 101 167 269 283 336 360 440 494 513 632 **8** 1 r2 r7 r12 r18
mounds **2** v
mountains **5** iii
mouth **2** i **4** 4 **5** iv **6** 73 108 130 417 547 568 **13** ii iii
mouths **14** i ii
mule **2** v **6** 537
mules **6** 175
murder **8** 23
muscles **6** 481
muster **9** 21
mutually **6** 153
name **6** 138 153 249 292 302 435 472 507 524 526 573 616 618 660 **9** 21 r21
named **6** 41
naphtha **6** 488 585
nation **8** 9 r18
netherworld **6** 476
night **6** 198 201
Nineveh **2** iv vi **3** 7 r2 **5** iv **6** 16 30 32 457 **10** r8
nobleman **9** r22
noise **6** 637

north **4** 1 **6** 632 **8** 25
nurses **6** 437
oath **2** i iv **4** 10 **6** 69 123 153 283 302 336 373 377 385 397 560 **14** i ii
oaths **6** 397
obey **2** iv **6** 198 336 **14** i
official **9** 10 12
officials **2** v
offspring **6** 513 537 632 **11** r13
oil **5** iv **6** 153 523 622 643 **10** 8
ointment **2** iv **6** 488
old **2** v **5** i **6** 1 214 414
oppose **6** 353
oracles **6** 108
orchards **6** 275
ordain **9** r5
order **1** 16 **6** 62 101 123 153 **14** i
orders **2** iv **6** 283
our **2** v **6** 494 500 507 **9** 3 6 10 12 20 21 26 32 38 r3 r8 r11 r13 r18 r24
ourselves **9** 32
oust **6** 69 123
ousted **2** i
outskirts **5** iii
oven **6** 440
overthrow **6** 659
overturn **6** 545
overwhelm **9** 21
oxen **2** iv
painful **6** 472
palace **6** 198 201 214 **8** 3 **9** r11 **11** r10 **14** ii
papyrus **2** iv
pardon **6** 188
pass away **6** 46 83 188 237 360
paws **5** iv **6** 467
pay **5** iii
peace **9** r22 **10** 12 **13** ii
people **1** 16 **2** i iv v **4** 26 **5** iii iv **6** 73 292
peoples **6** 275
perfect **6** 92 **12** 6
perform **4** 10 **6** 377
permit **5** iii
perpetrators **6** 130 138 147 153 249
persistent **6** 637
person **5** iii **6** 328 **9** 12
pestilence **4** 26 **6** 455
pests **6** 599
Philistines **5** iii
physician **5** iv **6** 461
pierce **6** 594 643
pig **6** 481
pitch **2** iv **6** 488 585
plague **4** 26 **6** 476
plain **6** 425
plan **8** r7
planets **14** i ii
plaza **4** 22
Pleiades **2** vi **5** iv **6** 464
plot **6** 318 336 **8** 16 23
plough **6** 545
plunder **6** 302
point **1** 11 **6** 180
pole **5** iv
poor **6** 214
ports **5** iii
positions **6** 360
possession **6** 428 476
pour **1** 16 **6** 440 **12** 6
power **14** r12
practice **6** 259
praises **14** r14
prayers **14** r9
pregnant **6** 249
preserve **14** i
prince **3** 5 **6** 11 46 57 62 73 92 101 108 123 130 138 147 153 162 167 173 180 188 201 226 229 237 249 259 266 269 279 283 292 302 318 336 353 360 377 385 397 494 500 507 513 555 632 664 **9** r22 **14** i
princes **3** 5 **14** i
proclaim **2** vi **6** 292
progeny **4** 4 **9** r21
prohibit **9** r11
prophet **6** 108
prostitute **2** v8
protect **2** 19 v **3** 5 **6** 46 62 92 167 292 **9** 10
punish **14** ii
punishment **1** r10 **2** v **4** 16 **6** 433
purchase **2** i
pus **5** iv **6** 461
push **2** v
Qedar **10** 1
quarters **14** i
queen **8** 1 9
rain **1** r13 **2** iv **6** 418 530
raindrops **6** 469
Ramman **2** vi
ravines **12** 6
rebellion **6** 130 138 162 180 237 249 302 494 500 **8** 19 r2 r18
reed **6** 626
refuge **6** 476
region **6** 656
reign **1** 22 r10 **14** r15
reject **1** r8
rejoice **6** 302
relations **6** 336
remove **1** r10 **6** 360 410 422 476 **9** r8
report **6** 73 108 147 153 336 500 **9** 32
rescue **6** 167
revoke **6** 377
revolt **6** 62 167 173 180 302 **8** 12
rich **6** 214
rite **4** 10
ritual **6** 377
rivers **1** r7
road **9** 32
roam **2** iv
roar **1** r13
robbers **2** v
roll **6** 551
room **6** 555
routes **5** iii
royal **5** iii **6** 46 302 360 **8** 3 r18
royalty **6** 318
ruins **1** r13 **2** v
ruler **6** 1 397
sacrifice **2** i
sacrificed **7** 8
sage **1** r7
same **6** 92 101 167 283 494 500 513 555 632
Saturn **6** 13 **8** 25

say **1** 8 **6** 195 201 318 328 336 353 360 **13** iii **14** i
scales **4** 22
sceptre **1** 22
scheme **8** 16 r12
scholars **6** 73
sea **5** iv **13** iii
seacoast **5** iii
seal **6** 1 397
seasonal **1** r13 **6** 440
seat **6** 46 55 302
see **2** iv **6** 579
seed **6** 138 153 249 283 302 435 507 524 537 540 **7** 6 **8** 3
seek **2** 19 v **6** 195 229 **9** 32
seize **1** 6 8 **2** iii **6** 123 130 138 153 173 214 226 237 249 302 582 588 **8** r18 **9** 26
select **6** 488
send **1** 3 **2** i iii **4** 1 **5** iii **6** 455 **9** 6 12 32 **10** r2 **13** iii
Sennacherib **3** 1 2 5 **5** i **6** 1 **8** 1
serious **6** 469
servant **4** 8 **5** iii **6** 237
servants **6** 214 328 **13** ii
serve **6** 57 92 233
servitude **6** 302
severe **1** r10 **6** 652
sex life **2** v
shade **6** 476
shame **2** v
shedding **6** 249
sheep **2** iv
ships **5** iii iv
shipwrecked **5** iii
shoes **6** 656
shoulder **2** i
shrines **14** ii
sick **2** i
sickness **6** 461
Sidon **5** iii
sighing **1** r10
sin **1** 15 **2** i iii iv v **4** 12 **6** 62 101 292 513 555 612 626 **11** r5 **12** 1 **14** ii
sing **2** iv
sink **5** iv
Sirius **6** 13 **8** 25
skin **6** 440
sky **13** iii **14** i ii
slander **6** 328 336
slaughter **6** 455 636
slaughtered **2** i
slaves **6** 214
slay **6** 249
sleep **2** iv v **6** 637
sleeplessness **6** 418 485
slit **6** 551
smash **6** 453
smear **6** 373
snake **6** 555
snare **6** 588
soaked **6** 540
soldiers **2** v
son **5** i **6** 1 11 41 108 130 147 153 173 188 229 237 249 259 266 377 433 **10** 1 **11** 1
song **2** iv
sons **2** i iv v **5** i **6** 1 101 108 167 237 269 275 283 336 360 377 385 428 440 494 507 513 534 537 540 547 551 560 563 568 570 576 579 582 585 588 591 594 606 612 618 622 632 636 637 646 649 **9** 6 **12** 1 **14** i
sore **5** iv
sources **1** r7
south **4** 1 **6** 632 **8** 25
sovereignty **14** i
spare **1** r1 **2** vi
spattered **6** 612
speak **3** 2 **4** 8 **6** 46 92 130 269 279 283 318 336 360 **8** r12 **9** 12 17
spin **6** 616
spindle-whorl **6** 616
spirit **6** 488
split **6** 652 656
spoken **8** r2
spring **2** i iv **6** 551 636
springs **2** iv **6** 521 563
sprout **6** 526 540
square **2** v
squares **6** 437 481
squash **6** 601
stag **6** 576
stand **2** i **6** 167 279 385 534 **9** 21
standing **7** 5
stands **11** r10
stars **6** 428
statue **6** 397
statues **6** 153 **11** r13
steadfast **1** 5 **14** r9
stink **6** 603
strangle **6** 606
stratagem **13** iii
streams **6** 563
streets **6** 437
strength **14** i
strike **1** 16 **6** 472 518
strive **10** 12
subject **6** 573 **9** 26
subjects **9** 3
submerge **6** 440
submit **6** 302
suggestion **8** 19
suitable **14** i
summon **6** 201
sunlight **2** iv
sunrise **6** 1
sunset **6** 1
surround **6** 621
sway **6** 626
swear **6** 25 69 123 302 336 353 385 **9** 1 **10** 3
sweet **6** 568
swine **6** 440 481
sword **5** iv **6** 455 457 **9** r18 **10** 4 **14** ii
swords **6** 632
sworn **2** vi **6** 377
table **6** 153
tablet **4** 10 12 **5** iv **6** 397 472 526 573 616 618 660 **11** r5
talk **6** 500
tar **6** 488
taste **2** iv
tax-collection **6** 180
teach **6** 385
teats **6** 481
tell **4** 1 4 **9** 21 **13** iii
temple **9** r11 **11** r10

tent **2** vi
terrible **10** r5
territory **5** iii
think **6** 377 555
thirst **6** 476 652 **9** r13
thousand **2** vi
throat **6** 373
throne **6** 46 55 69 83 214 226 237 249 302 360 659 **14** i
thunder **2** iv
tide **5** iv
time **6** 201 **14** i7
toe **1** 11
tolerate **9** 26
toll **5** iii
torches **11** r13
totally **3** 2 **6** 147 **9** 3
towers **4** 1
town **6** 46 92 162
towns **5** iii **6** 599
trade **5** iii
traitorous **6** 153
transgress **9** r3 **6** 397
trap **6** 582 649
travellers **4** 1
treacherous **6** 500
treaty **1** 15 **2** i iv v **4** 10 12 **5** i iv **6** 1 11 41 62 92 101 130 153 173 283 292 336 353 377 397 507 513 526 555 573 612 616 618 **8** 1 9 **9** r3 **10** 1 **11** 1 r5 **12** 1 **14** i ii
troops **1** 3 **6** 153
true **6** 92 233 328
truly **14** r3 r9
trust **1** 5 **14** i
trustee **9** r7
truth **6** 46 92
tube **6** 563
Tyre **5** i iii iv
Tyrians **5** i
ugly **4** 4 **6** 108 **8** 12 16 19 r2 r12
unable **6** 138 302
unalterable **1** 16 22
uncles **6** 73 108 214 318 336 **10** 14
unction **5** iv
underground **1** r13
underworld **9** r7 **11** r7
undo **4** 10 12 **5** iv **6** 373 377
unexpected **6** 201
unfavourable **6** 147
unhealing **5** iv **6** 461
united **6** 279
universe **6** 472 **14** i
unpleasant **6** 414
unreservedly **6** 302
unseemly **6** 73 500
unsuitable **6** 73
untoward **9** r5
untruthful **4** 22
unwholesome **6** 233
uproot **5** iv **6** 472 **9** r13 **11** r7
urine **2** iv **6** 469 488
utterance **1** r5 **6** 417
vassal **6** 162
vegetation **2** iv
venereal **6** 469
Venus **6** 13 428 **8** 25 **11** 1
villages **5** iii
violent **5** iv **9** r8
vow **6** 507
vulture **6** 425
vultures **6** 519
war **2** iv **6** 453
warfare **4** 20
warrior **6** 464
wasteland **2** i
water **1** 16 r13 **2** iv **5** iv **6** 153 410 461 476 521 523 563 608 652 **9** r13 **11** r7 r13
waters **6** 563
waterskin **6** 652
wave **5** iv
wax **6** 608
weapons **5** iv **6** 464 518
weariness **5** iv **6** 461
weep **2** v
weight **1** r5
well-being **6** 201
whispers **6** 500
wholeheartedly **6** 385 **7** r5
wicked **6** 621
wife **4** 18 **6** 249 417
wild ass **6** 419
wine **6** 560
witchcraft **6** 259
witnesses **6** 494
wives **2** v **6** 428 570
woe **2** iv v
woman **6** 249 616
women **2** iv v **6** 481 555 563 568 579 585 588 591 606 636 637 646
word **1** 16 **4** 4 **6** 57 73 108 180 360 **8** r2
wording **11** r5
words **1** 8 **8** 16 **9** 12
world **6** 1 **10** 1 **14** i r12
worm **6** 570
worries **6** 418
wound **6** 461 643
write **13** iii
years **1** 22 r10 **6** 485
young **5** i **6** 1 214 481 547
younger **6** 55 69

Index of Texts

By Publication Number

ABL 1105	9	BRM 4 50	11	JCS 39 187	4
ABL 1239+	8	Iraq 32 pl.36	2	JCS 39 188	13
AfO 13 pl.14	12	JCS 39 158	14	JCS 39 189	8
AfO 8 17+	2	JCS 39 159	10	PKTA 31	3
AfO 8 28	1	JCS 39 160	14	VTE	6
Borger, Esarh. pl.3+	5	JCS 39 174	7		

By Museum Number

K 3500+	5	79-7-8,195	2	BM 50666+	14
K 4439	13	82-5-22,130	9	(BM 50857+)	14
(K 4444+)	5	83-1-18,45+	8	BM 51098	14
(K 10235+)	5	(83-1-18,266+)	8	(BM 53678+)	14
K 15272+	2	83-1-18,420	4	(BM 53728+)	14
Sm 964	5	83-1-18,493+	4	BM 134596	2
(Rm 120+)	2	Bu 91-5-9,22	7	Ass 13955z	12
(Rm 274+)	2	Bu 91-5-9,131	4	MLC 1302	11
Rm 2,427	1	Bu 91-5-9,178	10	VAT 11449	3

ND numbers (text 6) are listed under manuscript sigla.

List of Illustrations

AO 20185	20	Or. Dr. IV, 7	9
BM 90864	19	Or. Dr. IV, 8	8
BM 118892	1	Or. Dr. IV, 15	12
BM 124801	14 and 18	Or. Dr. IV, 25	3
BM 124825	23	Or. Dr. IV, 53	11
BM 124927	13	Or. Dr. IV, 54	10
BM 124941	15	Or. Dr. IV, 70	17
BM 124945-6	21	Or. Dr. VI, 19	16
Börker-Klähn, *Bildstelen* II, 219	7	Or. Dr. VI, 46	6
Hittite Museum, Ankara 94 and 116	4a-b	Or. Dr. VII, 28	22
Or. Dr. II, 25	5	VA 2817	2

Cover photograph and frontispiece (IM 65574) courtesy of the British School of Archaeology in Iraq

COLLATIONS AND COPIES

2	i	1	[x x 〈cuneiform〉 x x x x x x x x]
		3	〈cuneiform〉]
	iii	12	〈cuneiform〉
		13	〈cuneiform〉
		14	〈cuneiform〉-ha-ṭu-ni
		21	〈cuneiform〉
		26	(end) 〈cuneiform〉
		27	[〈cuneiform〉
	iv	22	〈cuneiform〉
		31	] 〈cuneiform〉 (KW)
	vi	22	〈cuneiform〉 (KW)
		23	〈cuneiform〉 (KW)
		24	〈cuneiform〉
5	i	1	[〈cuneiform〉
		3	[TA* KUR.ṣur-ri gab- 〈cuneiform〉
	iii	1	]〈cuneiform〉
		14	(end) ú-la-a 〈cuneiform〉
		17	(end) 〈cuneiform〉
		24	am-mar 〈cuneiform〉
	iv	21	〈cuneiform〉
6:		180I	〈cuneiform〉
		181I	〈cuneiform〉
		408A	ka- 〈cuneiform〉
		570Q	〈cuneiform〉
		D	〈cuneiform〉
		frg (50F)	〈cuneiform〉
		frg (50T)	〈cuneiform〉
		598h	〈cuneiform〉
		599A	〈cuneiform〉
7	r.	5	ina gu- 〈cuneiform〉
8	r.	1	[x x x x 〈cuneiform〉
		2	〈cuneiform〉
		27	〈cuneiform〉 ← obverse
9:		2	〈cuneiform〉

		10	(end) 〈cuneiform〉
		38	[ni-šap-par] 〈cuneiform〉
	r.	1	[x x x x x x x 〈cuneiform〉
10:		3	(end) 〈cuneiform〉
		6	〈cuneiform〉
	r.	3	〈cuneiform〉
11:		1	[a-d]e-e ša ^{md}30- 〈cuneiform〉 (BF)
		4	〈cuneiform〉 (BF)
		6	(end) 〈cuneiform〉 (GB), 〈cuneiform〉 (BF)
	r.	2	EN 〈cuneiform〉 (BF)
		4	first trace: 〈cuneiform〉 end: 〈cuneiform〉 (BF)
13	ii	1	(end) 〈cuneiform〉
		2	(end) 〈cuneiform〉
		16	〈cuneiform〉
		19	〈cuneiform〉
		20	(end) 〈cuneiform〉
	iii	8	us-se- 〈cuneiform〉
14	i	1	be-lit-DINGIR 〈cuneiform〉
		2	[x x] 〈cuneiform〉
		7	(end) šu- 〈cuneiform〉
		14	[iṣ-bat-ma x x x 〈cuneiform〉
		21	AN.ŠÁR-ŠEŠ- 〈cuneiform〉
		32	(end) 〈cuneiform〉
	ii	5	ù i-na 〈cuneiform〉
		17	LUGAL- 〈cuneiform〉 (different from 〈cuneiform〉)
		22	la 〈cuneiform〉
	r.ii	1	
		2	〈cuneiform〉
		9	ku-un ŠÀ-bi 〈cuneiform〉
		12	〈cuneiform〉

BF = Benjamin R. Foster
GB = Gary Beckman
KW = Kazuko Watanabe
Unmarked collations by Simo Parpola

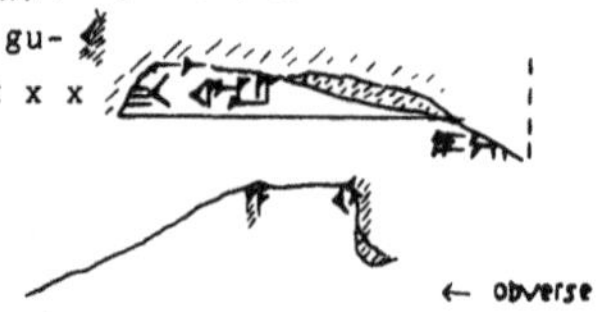

K 3500+ (no. 5), col. II

Sm 964 (no. 5, col. I)

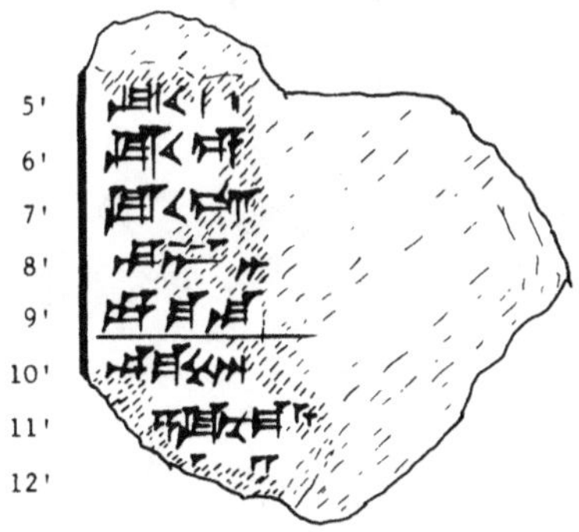

79-7-8,195 (no. 2, col. V)

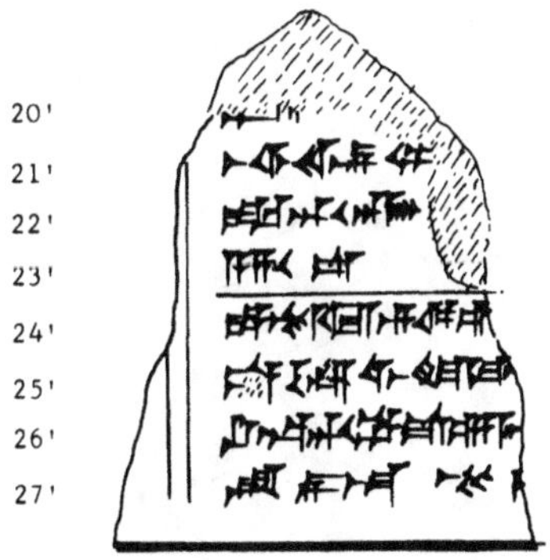

Obverse

Edge

Reverse

PLATE I. Rm 2, 427 (= No. 1)

COURTESY TRUSTEES OF THE BRITISH MUSEUM

Col. III

Col. I

COURTESY TRUSTEES OF THE BRITISH MUSEUM

PLATE II. K 15272+ (= No. 2), Obverse

Col. IV

Col. V

Col. VI

Plate III. K 15272+ (= No. 2), Reverse

COURTESY TRUSTEES OF THE BRITISH MUSEUM

Obverse (Col. III)

Reverse (Col. IV)

Plate IV. BM 134596 (= No. 2)

COURTESY TRUSTEES OF THE BRITISH MUSEUM

Plate V. 83-1-18,420+(= No. 4), Reverse

COURTESY TRUSTEES OF THE BRITISH MUSEUM

PLATE VI. K 3500+ (= No. 5)

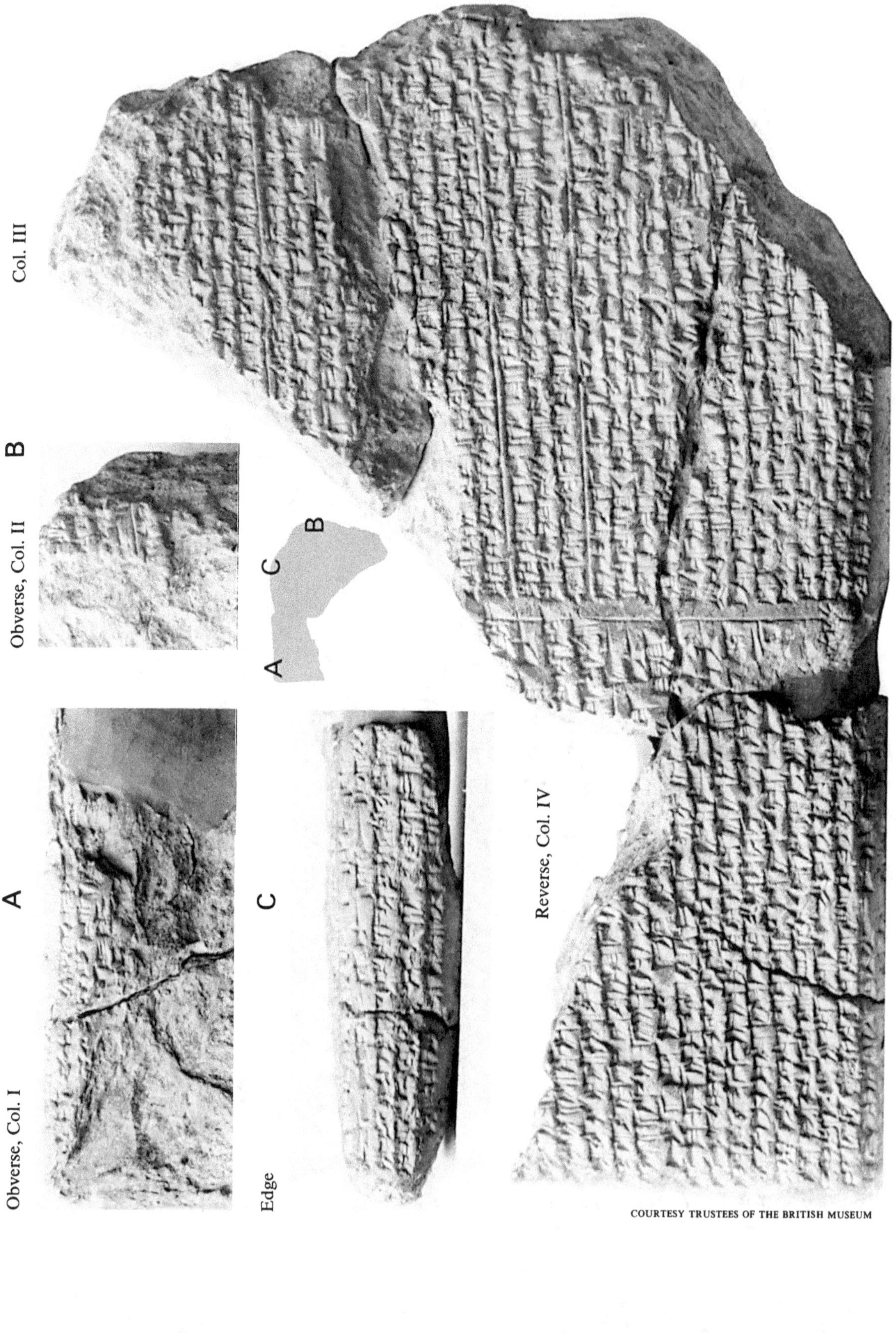

COURTESY TRUSTEES OF THE BRITISH MUSEUM

Plate VII. 82-5-22,130 (= No. 9), Obverse

COURTESY TRUSTEES OF THE BRITISH MUSEUM

PLATE VIII. 82-5-22,130 (= No. 9), Reverse

COURTESY TRUSTEES OF THE BRITISH MUSEUM

Reverse

Obverse

PLATE IX. Bu 91-5-9,178 (=No. 10)

COURTESY TRUSTEES OF THE BRITISH MUSEUM

Score of Text 6

10. Esarhaddon's Succession Treaty

ND 4336 etc. (for manuscript sigla see pp. lix–lxii)

i A NA$_4$.KIŠIB ^{d}*a-šur*$_4$ LUGAL DINGIR.MEŠ
G NA$_4$.KIŠIB ^{d}*aš-šur* LUGAL DINGIR.MEŠ
F NA$_4$.KIŠIB ^{d}*a-šur*$_4$ LUGAL DINGIR.MEŠ
T NA$_4$.KIŠIB ^{d}*a-šur*$_4$ LUGAL DINGIR.MEŠ
H NA$_4$.KIŠIB ^{d}*a-šur*$_4$ LUGAL DINGIR.MEŠ
a [NA$_4$.K]IŠIB ^{d}*a-šur*$_4$ LUGAL DINGIR.MEŠ
d [x x ^{d}*a-š*]*ur*$_4$ LUGAL DINGIR.MEŠ
_ NA$_4$.KIŠIB ^{d}⸢*a*⸣-[*šur*$_4$ x x x]
ii A EN KUR.KUR *ša la šu-un-né-*⸢*e*⸣
G EN KUR.KUR *ša la šu-un-né-*[*e*]
F EN KUR.KUR *ša la šu-un-*⸢*né*⸣*-e*
T EN KUR.KUR [x x x x x x]
H EN KUR.K[UR] *ša la šu-un-né-*⸢*e*⸣
I [x KUR].KUR *ša la šu-un-*[*né-e*]
a EN KUR.KUR *ša la šu-*[*un-né-e*]
d EN ⸢KUR⸣.KUR *šá la šu-un-né-*⸢*e*⸣
_ [x KUR].KUR *ša la šu-*[*un-né-e*]
iii A NA$_4$.KIŠIB NUN-*e* GAL-*e* AD DINGIR.MEŠ
F NA$_4$.KIŠIB NUN-*e* GAL-[*e*] AD DINGIR.MEŠ
B [x x x x GAL]-⸢*e*⸣ AD DINGIR.MEŠ
H NA$_4$.KIŠIB NUN-*e* GAL-*e* AD DINGIR-[ME]Š
I NA$_4$.KIŠIB LÚ.⸢NUN⸣ [x x x x x]
_ [x x x x GAL]-⸢*e*⸣ AD DINGIR.ME[Š]
Y [x x x x GAL]-⸢*e*⸣ AD DINGIR-⸢MEŠ⸣
iv A [*š*]*a la pa-qa-a-ri*
F *ša la pa-qa-a-ri*
B *ša l*[*a* x x x x]
H *ša la pa-*[*qa*]-⸢*a*⸣*-ri*
_ [x x *pa*]-⸢*qa-a-ri*⸣
p [x x *pa-q*]*a-a-ri*
_ [x x *pa-qa*]*-a-ri*
c [x x *pa-qa-a*]*-ri*
Y *ša la pa-qa-*[*a-ri*]
001 A *a-de-e ša* ^{m}*aš-šur*–PAB–AŠ MAN ŠÚ MAN KUR–*aš-šur*
G *a-de-e šá* ^{m}*aš-šur*–PAB–AŠ MAN KUR–*aš-šur*
F *a-de-e šá* ^{m}*aš-šur*–PAB–AŠ MAN ŠÚ MAN KUR–*aš-šur*.KI
T *a-de-e šá* ^{m}*aš-šur*–PAB–AŠ MAN ŠÚ MAN KUR–*aš-šur*
H *a-de-e ša* ^{m}*aš-šur*–PAB–AŠ MAN ŠÚ MAN KUR–*aš-šur*
a [*a*]*-de-e ša* ^{m}*aš-šur*–ŠEŠ–SUM-*na* MAN ŠÚ MAN KUR–*aš-šur*
d [x x x x ^{m}*aš-šur*–P]AB–AŠ MAN KUR–*aš-šur*.KI
_ *a-de-e* [x x x x x x x x x x x x x]

002 A DUMU ^{md}30–PAB.MEŠ–SU MAN ŠÚ MAN KUR–_aš-šur-ma_
G DUMU ^{md}30–PAB.MEŠ–SU MAN KUR–_aš-šur_
F DUMU ^{md}30–PAB.MEŠ–SU MAN ŠÚ MAN KUR–_aš-šur-ma_
T DUMU ^{md}30–PAB.MEŠ–SU MAN KUR–_aš-šur_.KI
H DUMU ^{md}30–PAB.MEŠ–SU MAN ŠÚ MAN KUR–_aš-šur_
a [DU]MU ^{md}30–PAB.MEŠ–SU MAN ŠÚ MAN KUR–_aš-šur_
d [x ^{md}30–PAB.ME]Š–SU MAN KUR–_aš-šur_.KI
003 A TA* ^{m}_ra-ma-ta-a-a_ EN–URU _ú-ra-ka-za-ba-nu_
G ⸢TA⸣ ^{m}_bur–da-di_ LÚ.EN–URU _kar-zi-ta-li_
F TA* ^{m}_tu-ni-i_ EN–URU KUR._el-pa-a-a_
T TA* ^{m}_ha-tar-na_ EN–URU URU._sik-ri-si_
H TA* ^{m}_hum-ba-re-eš_ LÚ.EN–URU URU._na-ah-ši-mar-ti_
a TA ^{m}_la-ar-ku-ut-la_ LÚ.EN–URU KUR–_za-mu-u-a_
d [x x x x x x x] EN–URU URU._i-za-a-a_
004 A TA* DUMU.MEŠ-_šú_ DUMU–DUMU.MEŠ-_šú_ TA* URU.⸢_ú-ra-ka_⸣-_za-ba-nu-a-a_
G [T]A DUMU.MEŠ-_šú_ DUMU–DUMU.MEŠ-_šú_ TA URU._kar-zi-ta-li-a-a_
F DUMU.MEŠ-_šú_ DUMU–DUMU.MEŠ-_šú_ TA* KUR._el-pa-a-a_
T DUMU.MEŠ-_šú_ DUMU–DUMU.MEŠ-_šú_ TA* URU._sik-ri-sa-a-a_
H DUMU.MEŠ-_šú_ DUMU–DUMU.MEŠ-_šú_ TA* URU._na-ah-ši-mar-ta-a-a_
a TA DUMU.MEŠ-_šú_ ŠEŠ.MEŠ-_šú qin-ni-šú_ NUMUN É–AD-_šú_
d [x x x x DUM]U–DUMU.MEŠ-_šu_ [x x x x x x]
005 A _gab-bu_ TUR GAL _mal ba-šú-u_
G [L]Ú.ERIM.MEŠ ŠU.2-_šú gab-bu_ TUR GAL _ma-la ba-šu-ú_
F LÚ.ERIM.MEŠ ŠU.2-_šú gab-bu_ TUR _u_ GAL _ma-la ba-šu-u_
T LÚ.ERIM.MEŠ ŠU.2-_šú gab-bu_ TUR GAL _mal ba-šú-ú_
H LÚ.ERIM.MEŠ ŠU.2-_šú gab-bu_ TUR GAL _ma-la ba-šú-u_
a ⸢LÚ.ERIM.MEŠ⸣ ŠU.2-_šú gab-bu_ TUR GAL _ma-l_[_a_ x x x]
d ⸢LÚ.ERIM.MEŠ⸣ ŠU.2-_šú gab-bu_ [x x x x x x x]
006 A TA* _na-pah_ ^{d}UTU-_ši a-di e-reb_ ^{d}UTU-_ši_
G TA _na-pa-ah_ ^{d}_šam-ši a-_⸢_di e_⸣-_reb_ ^{d}_šam-ši_
F TA _na-pa-ah_ ^{d}UTU-_ši a-di ra-ba_ ^{d}_šam-ši_
T TA* _na-pa-ah_ ^{d}UTU-_ši a-di ra!-ba_ ^{d}UTU-_ši_
H ⸢TA* _na-pa-ah_ ^{d}UTU-_ši a_⸣-_di ra-bé-e_ ^{d}UTU-_ši_
a TA* _na-pa-ah_ ^{d}UTU-_ši a-di ra-b_[_a_ x x x]
d [x _na-pa_]-_ah_ [x x x x x x x ^{d}UTU-_š_]_i_
007 A _am–mar_ ^{m}_aš-šur_–PAB–AŠ MAN KUR–_aš-šur_ LUGAL-_tu be-lu-tu_
G _am–mar_ ^{m}_aš-šur_–PAB–AŠ MAN KUR–_aš-šur_ LUGAL-_tu_ EN-_tu_
F _am–mar_ ^{m}_aš-šur_–PAB–AŠ MAN KUR–_aš-šur_ LUGAL-_tu_ EN-_tu_
T _am–mar_ ^{m}_aš-šur_–PAB–AŠ MAN KUR–_aš-šur_ LUGAL-_tú_ EN-_tú_
H [x x x x x x x x KUR]–⸢_aš-šur_⸣ LUGAL-_u-tu_ EN-_u-tu_
a _am–mar_ ^{m}_aš-šur_–PAB–AŠ MAN KUR–_aš-šur_ LU[GAL-_tu_ x x]
d [_am–m_]_ar_ [x x x x x x x x x x x x x x]
008 A _ina_ UGU-_šú-nu ú-ba-šu-u-ni_
G _ina_ UGU-_hi-šú-nu up-pa-áš-u-ni_
F _ina_ UGU-_hi-šú-nu up-pa-áš-u-ni_
T _ina_ UGU-_hi-šú-_⸢_nu_⸣ _up-pa-áš-ú-ni_
H ⸢_ina_ UGU-_hi-šú_⸣-_nu up-pa-šú-u-ni_
a _ina_ UGU-_hi-šú-nu_ [_up_]-⸢_pa_⸣-[_áš-u-ni_]

009 A *is-si-ku-nu* DUMU.MEŠ-*ku-nu* DUMU–DUMU.MEŠ-*ku-nu*
G *is-si-ku-nu* DUMU.MEŠ-*ku-nu* DUMU–DUMU.MEŠ-*ku-nu*
F *is-si-ku-nu* DUMU.MEŠ-*ku-nu* DUMU–DUMU.MEŠ-*ku-nu*
T *is-s*[*i-ku-nu*] TA* DUMU.MEŠ-*ku-nu* DUMU–DUMU.MEŠ-*ku-*[*nu*]
H ˹*is-si*˺*-ku-nu* DUMU.MEŠ-*ku-nu* DUMU–DUMU.MEŠ-*ku-nu*
a *is-si-ku-nu* DUMU.M[EŠ-*ku-nu* x x x x x]
010 A *ša* EGIR *a-de-e ina* UD-*me ṣa-a-ti ib-ba-šú-u-ni*
G *ša* EGIR *a-de-e ina* UD-*me* ˹*ṣa-a*˺*-ti i*[*b-ba*]*-šu-u-ni*
F *ša* EGIR *a-de-e a-na* UD-*me ṣa-a-ti ib-ba-áš-šú-u-ni*
T *šá* EGIR *a-de-e a-na* UD-*me ṣa-*[*a-ti*] *ib-ba-šu-ú-*[*ni*]
H *ša* EGIR *a-de-e a-na* UD-*me ṣa-a-ti ib-ba-áš-šú-u-ni*
a *ša* EGIR [x x x] *a-na* ˹UD?˺-*m*[*e* x x x x x x x x]
011 A *šá ina* UGU ^{m}*aš-šur*–DÙ–A DUMU–MAN GAL *ša* É–UŠ-*ti* DUMU ^{m}*aš-šur*–PAB–AŠ
012 A MAN KUR–*aš-šur ša ina* UGU-*hi-šú a-de-e is-si-ku-nu iš-ku-nu-ni*

---

013 A *ina* IGI ^{d}SAG.ME.GAR ^{d}*dil-bat*
G [*i*]*na* IGI MUL.SAG.ME.GAR ˹MUL˺.*dil-bat*
K *ina* IGI MUL.SAG.ME.GAR MUL.*dil-*[*bat*]
_ *ina* IGI MUL.SAG.ME.GAR ^{d}*d*[*il-bat*]
014 A MUL.UDU.IDIM.SAG.UŠ MUL.UDU.IDIM.GUD.UD
G [M]UL.˹UDU˺.IDIM.SAG.UŠ MUL.UDU.IDIM.[GUD.UD]
K MUL.UDU.IDIM.SAG.UŠ MUL.UD[U.IDIM.GUD.UD]
U MUL.[x x x x x x x x x] MUL.UDU.IDIM.SAG.U[Š x x x x x]
015 A MUL.*ṣal-bat-a-nu* MUL.GAG.SI.SÁ
G [MU]L.*ṣal-bat-a-nu* MUL.GAG.˹SI.SÁ˺
K MUL.*ṣal-bat-a-nu* MUL.[x x x]
U MUL.[x x x x x x x x]
_ MUL.*ṣal-bat-a-*[*nu* x x x x]
016 A *ina* IGI *aš-šur* ^{d}*a-num* ^{d}BE ^{d}É.A
G [*ina* I]GI ^{d}*aš-šur* ^{d}*a-*˹*num*˺ ^{d}EN.L[ÍL] ^{d}É.A
K *ina* IGI ^{d}*aš-šur* ^{d}*a-num* ˹^{d}˺.[x x x x]
_ *ina* IGI ^{d}˹*aš-šur*˺ [x x x x x x x x]
017 f ^{d}30 ^{d}UTU ^{d}IM ^{d}AMAR.UTU
G ^{d}30 ^{d}*šá-maš* ˹^{d}˺.[IM] ˹^{d}AMAR˺.UTU
K ^{d}30 ^{d}˹UTU˺ ^{d}[x x x x]
U ^{d}30 ˹^{d}˺.[UT]U ^{d}IM [x x x]
_ ^{d}3[0 x x x x x x x]
018 A ^{d}PA ^{d}PA.TÚG ^{d}IB ^{d}U.GUR
G ^{d}AG ^{d}PA.TÚG ^{d}IB ^{d}U.GUR
U ^{d}PA ^{d}PA.TÚG ^{d}IB ^{d}˹U.GUR˺
_ ^{d}AG ˹^{d}˺.[x x x x x x x]
019 A ^{d}NIN.LÍL ^{d}*še-ru-u-a* DING[IR].MAH
G ^{d}NIN.LÍL! ^{d}*še-ru-u-a*! ^{d}*be-lit*–DINGIR.MEŠ
U ^{d}NIN.[LÍL] ^{d}*še-ru-u-a* DINGIR.˹MAH˺
_ ^{d}NIN.LÍL ^{d}*š*[*e-ru-u-a* x x]
020 A ˹^{d}˺15 ˹*ša* URU.NINA.KI˺ [x x x URU.*ar*]*ba-ìl*
G ^{d}15 *ša* URU.NINA.KI ^{d}15 *ša* URU.*arba-ìl*
U ^{d}15 [*ša* U]RU.NINA ^{d}15 *ša* URU.*arba-ìl*
_ ^{d}15 *ša* URU.NINA ^{d}1[5 x x x x]

021 A [DINGIR].MEŠ *a-ši-[bu-ti* x x x x x]
G DINGIR.MEŠ *a-ši-bu-ti* AN-*(e)* ˹*ù* KI˺.TIM
U DINGIR.MEŠ *a-š[i-b]u-ti* AN-*e* KI.TIM
_ DINGIR.MEŠ *a-ši-bu-ti* AN-*e* [x x]
022 A DINGIR.MEŠ [x x x] DINGIR.MEŠ KUR–˹EME.GI$_7$˺ *u* U[RI.KI]
G DINGIR.MEŠ KUR–*aš-šur* DINGIR.MEŠ KUR–[x x x x x.K]I
U DINGIR.MEŠ KUR–*aš-šur*.[K]I DINGIR.MEŠ KUR–*šu-me-ri u* [UR]I.[KI]
_ DINGIR.MEŠ KUR–*aš-šur* DINGIR.MEŠ KUR–EME.[GI$_7$ x x x]
023 A DINGIR.MEŠ KUR.KUR DÙ-*šú-nu ú-dan-nin-[u-ni]*
G DINGIR.MEŠ KUR.KUR DÙ-*šú-nu* ˹*ú*˺-*[dan-nin-u-ni]*
U DINGIR.[MEŠ x x DÙ]-*šú-nu* ˹*ú*˺-*[dan]*-˹*nin*˺-*[u-ni]*
_ DINGIR.MEŠ KUR.KUR DÙ-*šú-nu ú-dan-ni-*[x x x x x x]
024 A *iṣ*-˹*ba-tú*˺ *iš-ku-nu-n[i]*
_ *iṣ-ṣi-bat-tu iš-ku-nu-[ni]* ˹x x x *iš-ku*˺-*n[u-ni]*

---

025 A ^{d}*aš-šur* AD DINGIR.MEŠ EN KUR.KUR *ti-t[am-ma-a]*
G ^{d}*aš-š[ur* x x x x x x x x x x]
_ ^{d}*aš-šur* AD DINGIR.MEŠ EN KUR.KUR [x x x x]
^{d}*aš-šur* AD DINGIR.MEŠ [x x x x x x x]
026 A ^{d}*a-num* ^{d}EN.LÍL ^{d}É.A [x]
G ^{d}*a-n[um* ^{d}EN.LÍ]L ^{d}˹É˺.[A] ˹MIN˺
_ ^{d}*a-num* ^{d}EN.LÍL ^{d}˹É˺.[A x] ^{d}*a-num* ^{d}EN.LÍ[L x x x x]
027 A ^{d}30 ^{d}UTU ^{d}IM ^{d}AMAR.UTU [x]
G ^{d}30 ˹^{d}*šá-maš*˺ ^{d}IM ^{d}AMAR.UTU MIN
_ ^{d}30 ^{d}UTU ^{d}IM ^{d}A[MAR.UTU x]
^{d}30 ^{d}UTU ^{d}IM [x x x x]
028 A ^{d}AG ^{d}PA.TÚG ^{d}IB ^{d}U.GUR MIN
G ^{d}AG [^{d}PA.TÚ]G ^{d}IB ^{d}U.GUR MIN
_ ^{d}[A]G ^{d}[x] ^{d}˹PA.TÚG˺ ^{d}[x x x x x]
029 A ^{d}NIN.LÍL ^{d}*še-ru-u-a* DINGIR.MAH MIN
G ^{d}NIN.LÍL ˹^{d}*še-ru*˺-*u-a* ^{d}*be-lit*–DINGIR.M[EŠ x]
_ ^{d}NIN.LÍL ^{d}*še-ru-u-a* DINGIR.MA[H x]
030 A ^{d}15 *ša* URU.NINA.KI ^{d}15 *ša* ^{d}˹*arba*˺-*ìl* MIN
G ^{d}15 *ša* ˹URU.NINA.KI˺ ^{d}15 *ša* UR[U].*a[rba-ìl* x]
_ ^{d}15 *ša* URU.NINA ^{d}15 *ša arba-ìl* MIN
E [x x] *ša* URU.[NINA.K]I ^{d}15 *ša* URU.*arba-ìl* [x]
031 A DINGIR.MEŠ DÙ-*šú-nu ša* URU.ŠÀ–URU MIN
G DINGIR.MEŠ D[Ù]-*šú-nu [š]a* [x x x x]
_ DINGIR.MEŠ DÙ-*šú-nu šá* URU.ŠÀ–URU MIN
E [DINGIR].MEŠ DÙ-*šú-nu ša* URU.ŠÀ–URU M[IN]
032 A DINGIR.MEŠ DÙ-*šú-nu ša* URU.NINA.KI MIN
G DINGIR.MEŠ DÙ-*šú-nu* ˹*ša*˺ [x x x x]
_ DINGIR.MEŠ DÙ-*šú-nu šá* NINA MIN
E [DINGIR].MEŠ DÙ-*šú-nu ša* URU.NINA.KI M[IN]
033 A DINGIR.MEŠ DÙ-*šú-nu [š]a* URU.*kal-ha* MIN
G DINGIR.MEŠ D[Ù]-*šú-[nu* x x x x x]
_ DINGIR.MEŠ DÙ-*šú-nu šá* URU.*kal-ha* MIN
E [DINGIR].MEŠ DÙ-*šú-nu ša* URU.*kal-ha* M[IN]

034 A DINGIR.MEŠ DÙ-*šú-nu* [*š*]*a* URU.*arba-ìl* MIN
G DINGIR.M[EŠ x x x x x x x x]
_ DINGIR.MEŠ DÙ-*šú-nu šá arba-ìl* MIN
E [DING]IR.MEŠ DÙ-*šú-nu ša* URU.*arba-ìl* M[IN]
035 A DINGIR.MEŠ DÙ-*šú-*[*nu š*]*a* URU.*kàl-zi* MIN
_ DINGIR.MEŠ DÙ-*šú-nu šá* URU.*kàl-zi* (MIN)
E [DIN]GIR.MEŠ DÙ-*šú-nu ša* URU.*kàl-zi* M[IN]
036 A DINGIR.MEŠ DÙ-*šú-nu ša* URU.KASKAL MIN
_ DINGIR.MEŠ DÙ-*šú-nu šá* URU.KASKAL MIN
E [DIN]GIR.MEŠ DÙ-*šú-nu ša* URU.KASKAL MIN
037 A DINGIR.MEŠ KÁ.DINGIR.RA.KI BÁR.SÍPA.KI EN.L[ÍL MIN]
_ DINGIR.MEŠ KÁ.DINGIR.RA.KI BÁR.SÍPA.KI EN.LÍL.KI DÙ-*šú-nu* MIN
E [DINGIR].MEŠ KÁ.DINGIR.RA.KI BÁR.SÍPA.KI EN.LÍL.KI MIN
038 A DINGIR.MEŠ KUR–*aš-šur* DÙ-*šú-nu* MIN
_ DINGIR.MEŠ KUR–*aš-šur*.KI
E [DINGIR.M]EŠ KUR–*aš-šur*
039 A DINGIR.MEŠ KUR–*šu-me-ri u* URI.KI DÙ-*šú-nu* MIN
_ DINGIR.MEŠ KUR–EME.GI$_{7}$! *u* URI.KI DÙ-*šú-nu* MIN
E DINGIR.MEŠ KUR–*šu-me-ri u* URI.KI MIN
040 A DINGIR.MEŠ KUR.KUR DÙ-*šú-nu* MIN DINGIR.MEŠ *šá* AN-*e u* KI.TIM MIN
_ DINGIR-⸢MEŠ⸣ KUR.KUR ⸢DÙ-*šú*⸣-*nu* MIN DINGIR.MEŠ *šá* AN-*e u* KI.TIM DÙ-*šú-n*[*u*
x DINGIR.MEŠ KUR-*š*]*u na-gi-šu* DÙ-*šú-nu* [x
[DING]IR.MEŠ [x x x x x x] DINGIR.MEŠ *šá* [x x x x x x x x x x]
E [DINGIR].MEŠ KUR.KUR DÙ-*šú-nu* MIN [DINGIR].MEŠ *šá* AN-*e u* TIM.KI! DÙ-*šú-nu* MIN
[DINGIR].MEŠ KUR-*šu*! *na-gi-šu* DÙ-*šú-nu* MIN

---

041 A *a-de-e* (*ša*) ^{m}*aš-šur*–PAB–AŠ MAN KUR–*aš-šur ina* IGI DINGIR.MEŠ GAL.MEŠ
_ *a-de-*⸢*e*⸣ [x x x x x x x x x x x x x x x x x x]
E ⸢*a*⸣*-de-e ša* ^{m}*aš-š*[*ur*–PAB–AŠ x x x x *ina* IG]I DINGIR.MEŠ GAL.MEŠ
042 A *šá* AN-*e* KI.TIM *is-si-ku-nu iš-ku-nu-u-ni*
_ [x x x x x] *is-si-k*[*u-nu* x x x x x]
E [*š*]*a* AN-*e u* TIM.[KI x x x x *i*]*š-ku-nu-u-ni*
043 A *ina* UGU ^{m}*aš-šur*–DÙ–A DUMU–MAN GAL *šá* É–UŠ-*ti*
E [x U]GU ^{m}*aš-šur*–DÙ–A DUMU–M[AN x x] É–UŠ-*ti*
044 A DUMU ^{m}*aš-šur*–PAB–AŠ MAN KUR–*aš-šur* EN-*ku-nu šá a-*⸢*na* DUMU–MAN-*ti*⸣
_ [x] *šá* ^{m}*aš-šur*–PAB–AŠ [x x x x x x x x x x x x x x]
E [DU]MU ^{m}*aš-šur*–PAB–AŠ MAN KUR–*aš-šur* [EN]-*ku-nu* (*ša*) *a-na* DUMU–MAN-*u-te*
045 A *šá* É–UŠ-*ti* MU-*šú iz-kur-u-ni* [*ip*]-*qi-du-šú-u-ni*
_ [x x x x x x] *iz-kur-*[*u-ni* x x x x x x x]
E [*ša*] É–UŠ-*te* MU-*šú i*[*z-kur*]-*u-ni ip-qid-du-šú-u-ni*
_ [*ša*] É–UŠ-*te* M[U-*šú* x x x x x x x x x x x]
046 A *ki-ma* ^{m}*aš-šur*–PAB–AŠ MAN KUR–*aš-šur* [*a-n*]*a šim-ti it-ta-lak*
_ [x x x x x x x x x x x x] *a-na ši*[*m-ti* x x x]
E [x x x x x x x x] MAN KUR–*aš-š*[*ur a-n*]*a šim-te it-ta-lak*
_ *ki-ma* ^{m}*aš-šur*–PAB–AŠ MAN K[UR–*aš-šur* x x x x x x x]

047 A ^{m}*aš-šur*–DÙ–A DUMU–MAN GAL *šá* É–UŠ-*ti ina* GIŠ.GU.ZA
_ [x x x x x x x x x x x x x x] ˹GIŠ˺.G[U.ZA]
E [x x x x x x x x x x É–UŠ]-*te ina* GIŠ.GU.ZA-*e*
_ ^{m}*aš-šur*–DÙ–A DUMU–MAN GAL *š*[*á* x x x x x x x x]
n [^{m}*aš-šur*–DÙ]–˹ DUMU–MAN˺ [x x x x x x x x x x]
048 A LUGAL-*ti tu-še-šab-ba* LUGAL-*u-tú* EN-*u-tú*
W [x x] *tu-še-š*[*ab-ba* x x x x]
E [x x x x x x] LUGAL-*tú* EN-*tú*
_ [x x] *tu-še-šab-šú* LUGAL-*tu* [x x]
n [LU]GAL-*u-te* [x x x x x x x EN-*u*]-*tú*
049 A *šá* KUR–*aš-šur ina* UGU-*hi-ku-nu up-pa-áš ina* A.ŠÀ *ina bir-ti* URU
W [x x x x x x x x x x] *up-pa-áš*
E *ina* UGU-*ku-nu* [x x x x x x x x x x x x x *b*]*ir-te* URU
n [x x x x x x x x x x *up-pa*]-*áš* [x x x x x x x x x x]-˹*ti* URU˺
r *ina* [x x x x x x x]
_ [x x x x x] *ina* A.ŠÀ *bir-ti* URU
050 A *la ta-na-ṣar-šú-u-ni ina* UGU-*hi*-[*š*]*u la ta-ma-haṣ-a-ni*
W [x x x x x x x x x] UGU-*hi-šú l*[*a* x x x x x x]
r [x x x x x x x x] *ina* UGU-[*hi-šú* x x x x x x]
E *la ta-na-ṣar-šú-u-ni* [x x x x x *t*]*a-ma-haṣ-a-ni*
_ [x x x x x x x x x UG]U-*hi-šú la ta-ma*-[*haṣ-a-ni*]
n ˹*la*˺ [*ta-na-ṣa*]*r-šú-u-ni* [*ina* UGU]-*hi-šú la ta-ma-haṣ-a-ni*
051 A *la ta-mut-ta-a-ni ina ket-ti šá* ŠÀ-*bi-ku-nu*
W [x x x x x x x x] *ket-ti šá* Š[À-*bi-ku-nu*]
r [x x x x x x x] *ina ket-ti šá* ˹ŠÀ-*bi-ku-nu*˺
E *la ta-mu-t*[*a?-a-n*]*i* [x x x x ŠÀ-*bi*]-*ku-nu*
n *l*[*a t*]*a-mut-ta-a-ni* [x x x *š*]*a* ŠÀ-*bi-ku-nu*
052 A *is-si-šú la ta-da-bu-ba-a-ni mil-ku* SIG$_5$
W [x x x x x x x x x x x *mi*]*l-ku* SIG$_5$
r ˹*is-si-šú la*˺ [x x x x x x x] *mil-ku* SIG$_5$
E *is-si-šú la ta*-[*da-bu-ba-a-ni* x x x]
n *is-si-šú* ˹*la*˺ *ta-da-bu-ba*-˹*a-ni*˺ [x x SI]G$_5$
053 A *šá gam-mur-ti* ŠÀ-*bi-ku-nu la ta*-[*mal*]-*li-ka-šú-u-ni*
W [x x x x x x x x x] *la ta-mal-l*[*ik-a-šú-u-ni*]
r *šá gam-mur-ti* ŠÀ-*bi-ku-nu la t*[*a*-x x x x x x x]
E [*ša*] *gam-mur-te* ŠÀ-*bi-ku-nu la* [x x x x x x x x]
n *ša gam-mur-ti* ŠÀ-*bi-ku-nu la ta-ma-lik-a-šú*-˹*u-ni*˺
054 A KASKAL SIG$_5$ *ina* GÌR.2-*šú* (*la*) *ta-šá-kan-a-ni*
W [x x x x x x x] *la ta-šak-kan*-[*a-ni*]
r KASKAL SIG$_5$ *ina* GÌR.2.MEŠ-*šu la ta-šá*-[*kan-a-ni*]
E [x x x x x x x *l*]*a ta-ša-kan-a*-[*ni*]
n [x x x GÌR].2-*šú la ta-šá-kan-a-ni*
_ [x SI]G$_5$ ˹*ina* GÌR.2.MEŠ-*šú*˺ *l*[*a* x x x x x x]
055 A *šum-ma at-tu-nu tu-nak-kar-šú-u-ni* TA* ŠÀ ŠEŠ.ME-*šú*
W [x x x x x x] *tu-nak-k*[*ar-šú-u-ni* x x x x x x]
r *šum-ma at-tu-nu tu-nak-kar-a-šu-ni* TA* [x x x x]
E [x x x x x x x x x x x x x x x x x]-*šú*
n [x x x x x x x x x x x x x x x Š]EŠ.MEŠ-*šú*
_ ˹*šum-ma*˺ *at-tu-nu tu-n*[*ak-kar-šú-u-ni* x x x x x x]

056 A GAL.MEŠ TUR.MEŠ *ina ku-mu*!-*šú ina* GIŠ.GU.ZA KUR–*aš-šur*.KI
W ⸢GAL.MEŠ TUR⸣.MEŠ [x x x x x x x x x x x x]
r GAL.MEŠ TUR.MEŠ *ina ku-mu-šú ina* GIŠ.GU.ZA KUR–*aš-š*[*ur*.KI]
E GAL.⸢MEŠ⸣ [x x x x x x x x x x x x x x]
n GAL.MEŠ TUR.MEŠ [x x x x x GIŠ].GU.ZA KUR–*aš-šur*
_ GAL.MEŠ TUR.MEŠ *ina ku-mu-šu ina* GIŠ.GU.ZA ⸢*šá*?⸣ K[UR?–*aš-šur*]
057 A *tu-še-šab-a-ni šum-ma a-bu-tú šá* ^{m}*aš-šur*–PAB–AŠ MAN KUR–*aš-šur*
W [x x x x x x x x x x x x x x x x x KUR]–⸢*aš-šur*.KI⸣
r [x x x x x] *šum-ma a-bu-tu šá* ^{m}*aš-šur*–PAB–AŠ MAN KUR–*aš-šur*
E ⸢*tu*⸣-[x x x x x x x x x x x x x x x x x x x x]
n *tu-še-šab-a-ni* [x x x x x] *ša* ^{m}*aš-šur*–PAB–AŠ MAN KUR–*aš-šur*.KI
_ *tu-še-šab-a-ni šum-ma a-bu-tu ša* ^{m}*aš-šur*–P[AB–AŠ x x x x x]
058 A *te-na-a-ni tu-šá-an-na-a-ni šum-ma* ^{m}*aš-šur*–DÙ–A DUMU–MAN GAL
W *te*-[*na-a-ni* x x x x x x x x ^{m}*aš-šur*–DÙ]–A DUMU–M[AN G]AL-*u*
r *t*[*e-na-a-ni* x x x x x x] *šum-ma* ^{m}*aš-šur*–DÙ–A DUMU–MAN GAL-*u*
n [x x x x *t*]*u-šá-na-a-ni šum-ma* ^{m}*aš-šur*–DÙ–A [x x x x]
_ *te-na-a-ni tu-šá-an-na-ni* ⸢*šum-ma* ^{m}*aš-šur*⸣–[D]Ù–A DUMU–MAN GA[L]
059 A *šá* É–UŠ-*ti šá* ^{m}*aš-šur*–P[AB–A]Š MAN KUR–(*aš-šur*) EN-*ku-nu*
W [x x x x x ^{m}]⸢*aš-šur*–PAB–AŠ⸣ MAN KUR–⸢*aš-šur*⸣ [E]N-*ku*-[*nu*]
r *ša* É–[UŠ-*ti*] *šá* ^{m}*aš-šur*–PAB–AŠ MAN KUR–*aš-šur*
_ [x x x x] *šá* ^{m}*aš-šur*–PAB–AŠ MAN KUR–[*aš-šur* x x x]
n [*ša*] É–UŠ-*ti šá* ^{m}*aš-šur*–PAB–AŠ MAN KUR–*aš-šur* [0?]
_ [x x x x] *šá* ^{m}*aš-šur*–PAB–AŠ MAN KUR–*aš-šur*.KI EN-*ku-n*[*u*]
060 A *ha-an-nu-ma la t*[*a-d*]*a-gal-a-ni*
W [*ú*]-⸢*kal-lim*⸣-*k*[*a*]-*nu*-[*ni ha*]-*an-nu-um*-⸢*ma*⸣ *la* ⸢*ta*⸣-*da-ga*[*l-a-ni*]
r ha-an-nu-um-ma la [x x x x x]
_ [x x x x x] *la ta-da-gal-a-n*[*i*]
n [*ú-kal*]-*lim-u-ka-nu-ni ha-an-nu-um-ma* [x x x x x-*n*]*i*
_ [x x x x x x x *ha-a*]*n-nu-um-ma la ta-da-gal*-⸢*a-ni*⸣
061 A LUGAL-*u-tú* EN-*u-tú ina* UGU-*hi-ku-nu la ú*-(*pa*)-*áš-u-ni*
W [LUGAL]-*tú* EN-*tú šá* KUR–*aš-šur ina* UGU-*hi-ku*-[*nu* x x x x x x]
r LUGAL-*tu* EN-*tu šá* KUR–*aš-šur ina* UGU-*hi-k*[*u-nu* x x x x x x]
_ [x x x x x x x x] *ina* UGU-*hi-ku-nu l*[*a* x x x x x]
n LUGAL-⸢*u-tú* EN⸣-*u-tú šá* KUR–*aš-šur*.KI [x x x x x x x x x x x]
_ [LUGA]L-[x x x KU]R–*aš-šur*.KI *ina* UGU-*hi-ku-nu la* ⸢*ú*⸣-[*pa*]-⸢*áš*?⸣-[*u-ni*]

---

062 A *šum-ma at-tu-nu a-na* ^{m}*aš-šur*–DÙ–A DUMU–MAN GAL *šá* É–UŠ-*ti*
W [*šum-m*]*a* ⸢*at-tu*⸣-*nu a-na* ^{m}*aš-šur*–DÙ–[A x x] GAL *šá* [x x x]
E [x x x x x x x x x x x x x x x x x x x]-*ti*
_ *šum-ma at-tu-n*[*u* x x x x x x x x x x x x x x x]
[*šum-ma*] *at-tu-nu a-n*[*a* x x x x x x x x x x x x x]
063 A *šá* ^{m}*aš-šur*–PAB–AŠ MAN KUR–*aš-šur ú-kal-lim-u-ka-nu-ni*
W *šá* ^{m}*aš-šur*–[PAB–AŠ MAN] KUR–*aš-šur*.KI *ú-kal-lim-ú-ka-nu*-[*ni*]
E [x x x x x x x x x x x x x x x x-*n*]*u-ni*
_ ⸢*šá* ^{m}*aš-šur*–PAB–AŠ⸣ MAN KUR–*aš*-[*šur* x x x x x x x]
[x ^{m}*aš*]-*šur*–PAB–AŠ MAN KUR–[*aš-šur* x x x x x x x]

064 A *iq-ba-ka-nu-ni a-de-e ina* UGU-*hi-šú is-si-ku-nu*
W *iq-ba-[ka]-nu-ni a-de-e ina* UGU-*hi-šú is-si-ku-[nu]*
E [x x x x x x x x x x x x]-*šú* [x x x x]
_ *[iq-ba]-kan-u-n[i* x x x x x x x x *is-si-k]u-⸢nu⸣*
065 A *ú-dan-nin-u-ni iš-ku-nu-ni la ta-na-ṣar-a-ni*
W *ú-dan-nin-u-ni iš-kun-u-ni la ta-na-⸢ṣar-ra⸣-ni*
E [x x x x x x x x x]-*ni* [x x x x x x]
_ ⸢*ú*⸣-[x x x x x x x x x x x x x x x] [x x x x x x x x x x] *la t[a-*x x x x]
066 A *ina* ŠÀ-*bi-šú ta-ha-ṭa-a-ni* ŠU.2-*ku-nu a-na* HUL?-⸢*ti*⸣
W *ina* ŠÀ-*bi-šú ta-ha-ṭa-a-[ni]* ŠU.2-*ku-nu ina* HUL-*tim*
E [x x x x x x x x]-*a-ni* [x x x x x x x x x]
_ [x x x x x x x x x x] ŠU.2-*ku-n[u* x x x x]
067 A *ina* ŠÀ-*bi-šú tu-bal-a-ni ep-šú bar-tu a-bu-tú la* DÙG.GA
W *ina* ŠÀ-*bi-šú tú-bal-⸢a-ni⸣ ep-šú bar-tú a-bu-tú la* DÙG.GA-*tú*
E [x x x]-*šú* [x x x x x x x x x x x x x DÙG.G]A-*tú*
S [x x x x x x x x x x x x x] ⸢*a-bu*⸣-*tú la* DÙG.GA-*t[ú]*
_ [x x x x x x x x x] *ep-šu b[ar-tu* x x x x x x x x]
068 A *la* SIG$_5$-*tú te-ep-pa-šá-ni-šú-u-ni ina* LUGAL-*ti* KUR–*aš-šur*
W *la* SIG$_5$-*tú te-pa-šá-niš-šú-ni ina* LUGAL-*ti* KUR–*aš-šur*
E [x x x x x x x x x x x x x x-*t]i*? [x x x]
S [x x x x x x x x x x x x x x]-*ti* KUR–*aš-šur*
_ [x x x x x x x x x x x x] *ina* LUGAL-*u-t[i* x x x]
069 A *tu-nak-kar-šú-u-ni* TA* ŠÀ-*bi* ŠEŠ.MEŠ-*šú* GAL.MEŠ TUR.MEŠ
W *tu-nak-ka-ra-š[ú-ni]* TA* ŠÀ ŠEŠ.MEŠ-*šú* GAL.MEŠ TUR.MEŠ
E [x x x x x]-*ni* [x x x x x x x x x x x]
S *tu!-nak!-[ka-ra-šú-ni* x x x x x x x x x T]UR.MEŠ
_ [x x x x x x] TA ŠÀ [x x x x x x x x]
070 A *ina ku-mu-šú* GIŠ.GU.ZA KUR–*aš-šur tu-šá-aṣ-bat-a-ni*
W GIŠ.GU.ZA KUR–*aš-šur tú-šá-a[ṣ-bat-a-ni]*
E [x x x]-*šu* [x x x x x x x x x x x x x]
S *ina ku-⸢mu⸣-šú* GIŠ.GU.ZA ⸢*šá*⸣ K[UR–*aš-šur* x x x x x x]
_ [x x x x] GIŠ.G[U.ZA x x x x x x x x x x]
071 A LUGAL MAN-*ma*! EN MAN-*ma*! *ina* UGU-*hi-ku-nu ta-šá-kan-a-ni*
W LUGAL MAN-*ma* EN MAN-*ma ina* UGU-*hi-ku-nu ta-šá-ka[n]-a-n[i]*
S [x *šá-nu-u]m-ma* EN *šá-nu-um-ma ina* UGU-*hi-ku-nu* [x x x x x]
072 A *a-na* LUGAL MAN-*ma*! EN MAN-*ma*! *ma-mit ta-tam-ma-a-ni*
W *a-na* LUGAL *šá-ni-ma* ⸢DUMU⸣–MAN *šá-ni-ma ta-me-tú [ta-tam]-ma-⸢ni⸣*
S [x x x x x] MAN-*ma ma-mit ta-tam-ma-ni*
x [x x x x x x x x x x] ⸢*ta-tam-ma-a-ni*⸣

---

073 A *šum-ma at-tu-nu a-bu-tú la* SIG$_5$-*tú la ba-ni-tú*
H *šum-ma at-t[u-n]u a-bu-tú la* DÙG.GA-⸢*tú*⸣ *la* SIG$_5$-*t[ú]*
S [x x x x x x x x x] *la* x x-*tú la* x[x x]
x [x x x x x *a-bu-t]ú la* DÙG.GA-*tu la ba-ni-tu*
074 A *la ta-ri-su ša e-peš* LUGAL-*ti šá ina* UGU ^{m}*aš-šur*–DÙ–A
H *la ta-r[i-s]u šá e-peš* MAN-*u-te šá ina* UGU-*hi* ^{m}*aš-šur*–DÙ–A
x [x x x x x] ⸢*e*⸣-*peš* LUGAL-*te šá ina* UGU ^{m}*aš-šur*–DÙ–A

075 A DUMU–MAN GAL *šá* É–UŠ-*ti la tar-ṣa-tu-u-ni la ṭa-bat-u-ni*

H DUMU–MAN GAL-*u šá* É–UŠ-*te la tar-ṣa-tú-u-ni la ṭa-bat*-[*u*]-*ni*

S [DUMU]–MAN GAL *šá* É–U[Š-*ti* x x x x x x x x x x x x]

x [x x x x É–U]Š-*te la tar-ṣa-tu-u-ni* [x x x x x]

076 A *lu ina pi-*˹*i*˺ ŠEŠ.MEŠ-*šú* ŠEŠ.MEŠ–AD-*šú* DUMU–ŠEŠ.MEŠ–AD.MEŠ-*šú*

H *lu ina pi-i* ˹ŠEŠ˺.MEŠ-*šú* ŠEŠ.MEŠ–AD.MEŠ-*šú*

x *lu-u ina pi-i* ŠEŠ.MEŠ-*šú* ŠEŠ.MEŠ–AD.MEŠ-*šú* [DUMU–ŠE]Š.MEŠ–AD.MEŠ-*šú*

077 A *qin-ni-šú* NUMUN ˹É˺–AD-*šú lu ina pi-i* LÚ.GAL.MEŠ LÚ.NAM.MEŠ

H *lu-u* UN.MEŠ-*šú* [NU]MUN É–AD-*šú lu-u ina pi-*˹*i*˺ [G]A[L L]Ú.NAM.MEŠ

a [x x x x x x x x x] *lu ina pi-i* LÚ.GAL.MEŠ LÚ.NAM.MEŠ

x *qin-ni-šú* NUMUN É–AD-*šú* [x x] *ina pi-i* LÚ.GAL.MEŠ LÚ.NAM.MEŠ

078 A *lu ina pi-i* LÚ.*šá–ziq-ni* LÚ.SAG.ME

H *lu-u* LÚ.*šá*–[*ziq*]-˹*ni*˺ LÚ.[x x]

I [x x x x x] LÚ.*šá–ziq-ni* LÚ.SAG

a *lu* [x x x x x x x] LÚ.SAG.MEŠ

x *šá*–LÚ.*ziq-n*[*i ina*] *pi-i* LÚ.SAG.MEŠ

079 A *lu ina pi-i* LÚ.*um-ma-ni lu ina pi-i nap-har ṣal-mat*–SAG.DU

G *lu ina pi-i* LÚ.*um-ma-ni lu ina pi-i nap-har* [x x x x]

H [*l*]*u ina pi-i* LÚ.*um-ma-ni lu-*˹*u*˺ *nap-har* [*ṣal*]-˹*mat*˺–SAG.DU

I *lu-u ina* ˹*pi-i*˺ LÚ.*um-ma-ni* [x x x x] *nap*]-*har ṣal-mat*–SAG.DU

a *lu ina pi-i* LÚ.*um-ma*-[*ni*] *lu ina pi-i nap-har ṣal-mat*–SAG.DU

G [x x x x x x x x x x x x x x *ṣal*]-*mat*–SAG.DU

x LÚ.*um-ma-ni lu-u ina nap-har* [*ṣal-mat*–S]AG.DU

080 A *mal ba-šu-u ta-šam-ma-ni tu-pa-za-ra-a-ni*

G *ma-la ba-šu-ú ta-šam-ma-a-ni tu-pa-za*[*r*$_4$*-a-ni*]

H [*m*]*a-la ba-šú-u ta-šam-ma-ni tu-ba-za-ra-ni*

I *ma-*˹*la*˺ *ba-šu-ú* [x x x]-*ni tu-pa-za-ra-a-ni*

a *mal* [x x x] *ta-šam-ma-a-ni tu-pa-zar-a-ni*

G [x x x x x x x x x x *tu-pa-za*]*r*$_4$*-a-ni*

x *mal ba-šu-u ta-šam-ma-a-ni* [*tu-pa-za*]*r*$_4$*-a-ni*

081 A *la ta-lak-a-ni-ni a-na* ᵐ*aš-šur*–DÙ–A DUMU–MAN GAL

G *la ta-*˹*lak-a-ni*˺-[*ni*] ˹*a-na*˺ [ᵐ]˹*aš-šur*˺–[DÙ]–˹A˺ DUMU–MAN ˹GAL˺

H ˹*la*˺ *ta-lak-a-ni-ni a-na* ᵐ*aš-šur*–DÙ–A DUMU–MAN GAL-*u*

I ˹*la*˺ *ta-lak-a-ni-ni* [x x x x x x x DU]MU–MAN GAL

a *l*[*a* x x x x x] *a-na* ᵐ*aš-šur*–DÙ–A DUMU–MAN GAL

x ˹*la*˺ *ta-lak-a-ni-ni a-na* ᵐ*aš-šur*–DÙ–A [x x x]

082 A *šá* É–UŠ-*ti la ta-qab-ba-a-ni*

G *šá* [x x x] *la ta-qab*-[*ba*]-*a*-[*ni*]

H [x] É–UŠ-*te la ta-qab-ba-niš-šú-un-ni*

I *šá* É–UŠ-*ti la ta-qa-ba-a-ni*

a *šá* ˹É˺–[UŠ-*ti* x x x x x x]

G [x] É–UŠ-*ti* [x x x x x]-*ni*

x *šá* É–UŠ-*te la ta-qab-ba-a-ni*

083 A *šum-ma* ^{m}*aš-šur*–PAB–AŠ MAN KUR–*aš-šur ina ṣa-ha-ri* DUMU.ME[Š-*šú*]
G *šum-ma* ^{m}*aš-šur*–PAB–AŠ MAN KUR–*aš-šur ina* ⸢*ṣa-ha*⸣-[*ri* x x x x]
H [*k*]*i-ma* ^{m}*aš-šur*–PAB–AŠ MAN KUR–*aš-šur ina ṣa-ha-ri šá* DUMU.MEŠ-*šú*
I [x x x x x x x x x x x] *ina* ⸢*ṣa*⸣-*ha-ri šá* DUMU.MEŠ-*šú*
a ⸢*šum-ma*⸣ [x x x x x x x x x x x x x x x x x x]
G [x x x x x x x x x x x x x x x x x DUMU].MEŠ-*šú*
x [x x x x x x x x x x x]x x[x x] ⸢x⸣ [x] ⸢x⸣ [x x]
084 A *a-na šim-ti it-ta-lak* ^{m}*aš-šur*–DÙ–A DUMU–MAN GAL
G *a-na šim-ti it-ta-lak* ^{m}*aš-šur*–DÙ–[A] DUMU–MAN GAL-*u*
H *a-na šim-ti* [x x x x x x x x x x x]
I [x x x x *i*]*t-ta-lak* ^{m}*aš-šur*–DÙ–A [x x x]
d *a-na šim-ti it-ta-*[*lak* ^{m}*aš-š*]*ur*–DÙ–A DUMU–MAN GAL-*u*
G [x x x x x x x ^{m}*aš-šur*–DÙ]–A [x x x]
085 A *šá* É–UŠ-*ti* GIŠ.GU.ZA *šá* KUR–*aš-šur tu-šá-aṣ-bat-ta*
G *šá* É–UŠ-*ti* GIŠ.GU.ZA *šá* KUR–*aš-š*[*ur*] ⸢*la tu*⸣-*šá-aṣ-bat-a-ni*
I [x É–UŠ-*t*]*i* GIŠ.GU.ZA *šá* KUR–*aš-šur tú-šá-aṣ-ba-ta*
d *šá* É–UŠ-*te* GIŠ.GU.ZA *šá* KUR–*aš-šur t*[*u-šá-a*]*ṣ-bat-ta*
G [x x x x x x x x KUR–*aš-šu*]*r*.KI [x x x x x]
086 A ^{md}GIŠ.ŠIR–MU–GI.⸢NA⸣ ŠEŠ *ta-li-me-šú* DUMU–MAN *šá* É–UŠ-*ti*
G ^{md}GIŠ.ŠIR–⸢MU–GI⸣.[NA] ŠEŠ *ta-li-me-šú* DUMU–MAN *šá* É–UŠ-*ti*
I [x x x x x x x ŠEŠ ⸢*ta*⸣-*li-me-šú* [x x x É–UŠ-*t*]*i*
d ^{md}GIŠ.ŠIR–MU–GI.NA ŠEŠ *ta-li-mu* DUMU–MAN [x É–U]Š-*te*
G [^{md}GIŠ.ŠIR–MU–GI].NA [x x x x x x x x x x x x]
_ [x x x x x x x x x x x x x x x *š*]*a* É–UŠ-*te*
087 A *šá* KÁ.DINGIR.RA.KI *ina* GIŠ.GU.ZA LUGAL-*ti šá* KÁ.DINGIR.RA.KI
G *šá* KÁ.DINGIR.[KI] GIŠ.GU.ZA LUGAL-*ti šá* KÁ.DINGIR.KI
I KÁ.DINGIR.KI GIŠ.GU.ZA LUGAL-*ti* [x x x x]
d *šá* KÁ.DINGIR.RA.KI *ina* GIŠ.GU.ZA LUGAL-*te* KÁ.DING[IR.RA].⸢KI⸣
G [x KÁ.DINGIR.R]A.KI [x x x x x x x x x]
_ *š*[*a* x x x x x GIŠ.G]U.ZA LUGAL-*te* K[Á.DINGIR.RA.KI]
[x x x x x x x x x x x x *š*]*a* KÁ.DINGIR.KI
088 A *tu-še-šab* LUGAL-*ti* KUR–EME.GI$_7$ URI.KI KUR.*kar*–^{d}*dun-iá*
G *tu-še-šá-b*[*a*] LUG[A]L-*tu* KUR–*šu-me-ri u* URI.KI KUR.*kar*–^{d}*dun-iá*-[*áš*]
I [*t*]*u-še-šá-ba* LUGAL-*tu* KUR–*šu-me-ri* [x x x KUR.*ka*]*r*–^{d}*dun-iá-àš*!
d *tu-še-šab-šu* LUGAL-*u-tu* KUR–EME.GI$_7$ ⸢*u*⸣ [UR]I.KI KUR.*kar*–^{d}*dun-iá*
_ [x x x x] ⸢LUGAL⸣-*tú* K[UR–x x x x x x x x x x x x x]
[x x x x x x x x x x x x x x] KUR.*kar*–[^{d}*dun-iá-aš*]
[x x x x LUGA]L-*tú* KUR–*šu-me-ri u* UR[I.KI x x x x x x]
tu-š[*e-šá-ba* x x x x x x x x K]UR.*kar*–^{d}*d*[*un-iá-aš*]
t[*u*-x x x x x x x x x] ⸢*u*⸣ UR[I].KI KUR.*ka*[*r*–^{d}*dun-iá-aš*]
089 A DÙ.A.BI! *ina* IGI-*ni-šú tu-šad-ga-la ti-din-tú*
G DÙ.A.BI [x x]-*šú tu-šad-g*[*a-la* x x x]
I DÙ.A.BI *ina* IGI-*šú tu-šad-ga-la* [x x x]
d DÙ.A.B[I] *ina* IGI-*šú tu-šad-ga-la ti-*[*di*]*n-tu*
_ [x x x] *ina pa-ni-šú t*[*u*-x x x x x x]
[x x x x x x x x x x x x] *ti-din-t*[*ú*]
[DÙ].A.BI *ina* IGI-*šú tú-šad-ga-*[*la* x x x]
[x x x x x x *tu-šad-ga-l*]*a ti-din-*[*tu*]

090 A *am–mar* ^{m}*aš-šur–*PAB–AŠ MAN KUR–*aš-šur* AD-*šú id-din-na-šú-ni*
G ⸢*am*⸣*–mar* ^{m}*aš-šur–*PAB–AŠ MAN KUR–*aš-šur* [x x x x x x x]
I [x x] ^{m}*aš-šur–*PAB–AŠ MAN KUR–*aš-šur* AD-*šú* SUM-*šú-un-ni*
d *am–mar* ^{m}*aš-šur–*PAB–AŠ MAN KUR–*aš-šur* AD-*šú i-di-*[*na-šu-u*]*n-ni*
_ *am–mar* ^{m}*aš-šur–*P[AB–AŠ x x x x x x x x x x x x]
[x x ^{m}*aš-šur*]–PAB–AŠ MAN KUR–*aš-šur* AD-*šú* [x x x x x]
[x x x x x x x x x x x x x-*š*]*ú* SUM-*šú-u*[*n-ni*]
am–mar [x x x x x x x x x x x x x x x x x]
091 A *is*!-*si*!-*šú ú-bal* 1-*en la ta-kal-la-a*
G [*is*]-⸢*si*⸣-*šu ub-bal* [x x x x x x x]
I [x x x x x] 1-*en la tak-la-a*
d *is-si-šú ub-bal* 1-*en la ta-*[*ka*]*l-la-a*
_ *is-si-šú ub-b*[*al* x x x x x x x]
ub-b[*al* x x x x x x x]
[*is-si-š*]*ú ub-bal* 1-*e*[*n* x x x x x]
[x x x x x x x] *la ta-kal-*[*la-a*]
[*is-si-š*]*u* ⸢*ú*⸣-*bal* [x x x x x x x]
092 A *šum-ma* ^{m}*aš-šur–*DÙ–A DUMU–MAN GAL *šá* É–UŠ-*ti*
G ⸢*šum*⸣*-ma* ^{m}*aš-šur–*⸢DÙ⸣–A ⸢DUMU⸣–MAN G[AL x x x x]
I [x x ^{m}*aš*]-*šur–*DÙ–[A DUMU]–MAN GAL *šá* É–UŠ-*ti*
d *š*[*um-ma*] ^{m}[*aš-š*]*ur–*⸢DÙ–A⸣ [x x x x x x x]
_ *šum-ma* ^{m}*aš-šur–*DÙ–A DUM[U–MAN x x x x x]
[x x x x x x x x x x x É–U]Š-⸢*ti*⸣
šum-ma ^{m}*aš-šur–*DÙ–A DUMU–MAN G[AL x x x x]
[x x] ^{m}*aš-šur–*DÙ–A DUMU–MAN GAL *ša* ⸢É⸣–[UŠ-*ti*]
[x x x x x x x x x x x] *ša* É–UŠ-*te*
093 A *šá* ^{m}*aš-šur–*PAB–AŠ MAN KUR–*aš-šur ú-kal-lim-u-ka-nu-ni*
G [x x x x x x x] ⸢KUR⸣*–aš-šur ú-*⸢*kal-lim*⸣-[*u-ka-nu-ni*]
F *šá* ^{m}*aš-šur–*PAB–AŠ MAN KUR–*aš-šur ú-kal-lim-u-ka-*[*nu-ni*]
I *šá* ^{m}*aš-šur–*PAB–AŠ MAN KUR–*aš-šur* [*ú-kal-l*]*im-u-ka-nu-*⸢*u*⸣-*ni*
_ *ša* ^{m}*aš-šur–*PAB–AŠ MAN [x x x x x x x x x x x]
šá ^{m}*aš-š*[*ur–*PAB–AŠ x x x x *ú-kal-lim-u-ka-nu*]-⸢*u*⸣-*ni*
[x x x x x x] MAN KUR–*aš-šur ú-kal-lim-ú-*[*ka-nu-ni*]
[x x x x x x x KUR]–*aš-šur ú-kal-lim-ú-ka-nu-*[*ni*]
šá ^{m}*aš-š*[*ur–*PAB–AŠ x x x x *ú-kal-lim-u-ka*]-*nu-ni*
094 A *ù* ŠEŠ.MEŠ-*šú* DUMU AMA-*šú šá* ^{m}*aš-šur–*DÙ–A DUMU–MAN GAL
G [x x x x DUMU] ⸢AMA⸣-*šú* [x x x x x x x x x]
F *ù* ŠEŠ.MEŠ-*šú* DUMU AMA-*šú šá* ^{m}*aš-šur–*DÙ–A [x x x]
I *ù* ŠEŠ.MEŠ-*šú* DUMU AMA-*šú* [x ^{m}*aš-šur–*D]Ù–A DUMU–MAN GAL
_ [x x x x x x x x x x x x x x DUMU–MA]N GAL-*u*
[Š]EŠ.MEŠ-*šú* [x x x x x x x x x x x x x]
ŠEŠ.M[EŠ-*šú* x x x x x x x x x DUMU–MA]N GAL-*u*
[x x x x x x x] *šá* ^{m}*aš-šur–*DÙ–A DUMU–MAN GAL
[x x x x DUMU A]MA-*šú šá* ^{m}*aš-šur–*DÙ–A DUMU–MAN
[x] [x x x x x x x] *ša* ^{m}*aš-šur–*DÙ–A [x x x]
ù ŠEŠ.M[EŠ-*šú* x x x x x x x x x] DUMU–MAN GAL

095 A šá É–UŠ-ti šá ^{m}aš-šur–PAB–AŠ MAN KUR–aš-šur ina UGU-hi-šú-nu
G [x x x x x] ^{m}[aš-šur]–PAB–AŠ MAN KUR–aš-šur [x x x x x]
F šá É–UŠ-te šá ^{m}aš-šur–PAB–AŠ MAN KUR–aš-šur šá! ina U[GU-hi-šú-nu]
I [ša] É–UŠ-ti šá ^{m}aš-šur–PAB–AŠ MAN KUR–aš-šur [x x x x x]
_ šá É–U[Š-ti x x x x x x x x KUR–aš-š]ur ina UGU-hi-šú-[nu]
šá É–UŠ-te šá ^{m}aš-šur–PAB–AŠ MAN KUR–aš-š[ur]
[x x x x-n]u šá É–U[Š-ti x x x x x x x x x x x x x x x x]
[x x x x x] ^{m}aš-šur–PAB–AŠ MAN KUR–aš-šur ina UG[U-hi-šú-nu]
[x x x x] ša ^{m}aš-šur–PAB–AŠ MAN [x x x x x x x x x]
šá É–U[Š-ti x x x x x x x x x x x x x x x x]
096 A a-de-e is-si-ku-nu iš-ku-nu-ni ket-tu šá-lim-tu
G [x x x] ⸢is-si-ku-nu iš⸣-k[un-u-ni x x x x x]
F a-de-e is-si-ku-nu iš-kun-u-ni ket-[tu x x x]
I a-de-e is-si-ku-nu iš-ku-nu-u-ni [x x x x x]
_ [x x x x x x x-n]u iš-kun-[u-ni x x x x x]x
a-de-e is-si-ku-nu iš-ku-nu-ni [x x š]á-lim-tu
[x x x is-s]i-ku-nu iš-ku-nu-ni k[et-tu x x x]
a-de-e is-si-[ku-nu x x x x] ket-tu šá-l[i-im-tu]
a-de-⸢e⸣ [x x x x x x x x ket-t]u šá-l[im-tu]
097 A la tu-kal-la-a-ni ina ke-na-a-te tar-ṣa-a-ti
F la tu-kal-la-a-ni ina ke-na-a-te tar-ṣ[a-a-ti]
I la tu-kal-la-a-ni ina ke-na-a-[te x x x x]
_ la tu-kal-[la-a-ni x x x x x x x x-t]e
E [x x x x x x x x x x x tar]-⸢ṣa⸣-a-te
_ la tu-kal-la-ni ina ke-na-te [x x x t]i
[x x x x x] ina ke-na-te [x x x x]
098 A la ta-ta-nab-bal-šú-u-ni ina ket-ti šá ŠÀ-bi-ku-nu
F la ta-tan-nab-bal-a-šú-u-ni ina ket-te šá [x x x]
I [l]a ta-ta-na-bal-a-šú-nu-u-ni ina ket-ti [x x x x]
_ la ta-ta-na-b[al-a-šú-u-ni x x x x ŠÀ-bi-k]u-nu
E la ta-ta[n-nab-bal-a-šú-u-ni x x x x ŠÀ-bi]-ku-nu
_ la ta-ta-nab-bal-a-šá-nu-u-ni [x x x x x x x x]
[x x x x x x x x x] ⸢ina ket-ti⸣ [x x x x x]
099 A is-si-šú la ta-da-bu-ba-ni ina A.ŠÀ bir-ti URU
F is-si-šú-nu la ta-da-bu-[ba-ni] ina A.ŠÀ bir-ti URU
I [is-si]-šú-nu la ta-da-bu-ub-a-ni [x x x x x x]
_ ⸢is⸣-si-šú-nu la ta-[x x x x x x x bir-t]i URU
E is-si-šú-nu la [x x x x x x x x x x x]
100 A [l]a ta-na-ṣar-a-šú-nu-u-ni
F la ta-na-ṣar-[a-šú-nu-u-ni]
I [la t]a-na-ṣar-a-šú-nu-u-ni
_ la ta-na-ṣar-šú-nu-u-[ni]
E la ta-na-ṣar-a-šú-n[u-u-ni]

101 A [x x x x x x x x x G]A[L] *šá* ˹É˺–UŠ-*ti*
F *šum-ma* ^{m}*aš-šur*–DÙ–A DUMU–MAN GAL *šá* ˹É˺–[UŠ-*ti*]
I [x x x x x x x x x x x x x x]-*ti*
_ [*š*]*um-ma* ^{m}*aš-šur*–DÙ–A DUMU–MAN GAL-*u šá* É–UŠ-*t*[*e*]
E [x x ^{m}*aš-š*]*ur*–DÙ–A DUMU–MAN GAL *ša* É–UŠ-[x]
y ˹*šum-ma* ^{m}*aš-šur*–DÙ˺–A DU[MU–MAN x x x x x]
_ [*šu*]*m-ma* ^{m}*aš-šur*–DÙ–A DUMU–MAN GA[L x x x x]
102 A [x x x x x x x x x x *iq-ba*]-*ka-nu-ni*
F *šá* ^{m}*aš-šur*–PAB–AŠ MAN KUR–*aš-šur iq-ba-k*[*a-nu-u-ni*]
_ [*š*]*a* ^{m}*aš-šur*–PAB–AŠ *iq-ba-ka-nu-u*-[*ni*]
E ˹*šá*˺ ^{m}*aš-šur*–PAB–AŠ MAN KUR–*aš-šur iq-ba-ka-nu-u-ni*
y [x x x x x x x x x x] *iq-ba-ka-nu-u*-[*ni*]
_ [x x x x x x x KU]R–*aš-šur iq-ba-ka-n*[*u-u-ni*]
103 F *u* ŠEŠ.MEŠ-*šú* DUMU AMA-*šú šá* ^{m}*aš-šur*–[DÙ–A x x x x]
_ [x] ŠEŠ.MEŠ-*šú* DUMU AMA-*šú ša* ^{m}*aš-šur*–DÙ–A DUMU–MAN GA[L-*u*]
E ŠEŠ.MEŠ-*šú* DUMU AMA-*šú šá* ^{m}*aš-šur*–DÙ–A DUMU–MAN GAL-*u*
y [x x x x x x x x x x x x x x] DUMU–MAN GAL
_ ˹*ù*˺ ŠEŠ.MEŠ-[*šú* x x x x x x x x x x x x x]
[x x x x x x x x ^{m}*aš-šu*]*r*–DÙ–A DUMU–MAN GAL-*u*
104 A *šá* x[x x x x x x x x x x x x x x x x]
_ [*š*]*a* É–UŠ-*ti ina* UGU-*hi-šú-nu a-de-e is-si*-˹*ku*˺-[*nu*]
E *ša* É–UŠ-*te ina* UGU-*hi-šú-nu a-de-e is-si-ku-nu*
y *šá* É–U[Š-x x x x x x x x x] *is-si-ku-nu*
_ [x] ˹É˺–UŠ-*ti* [x x x x x x x x x x x x]
[x x x x x x x x x x x]-*e is-si-ku-n*[*u*]
105 A *i*[*š-kun-u-ni* x x x x x x x x x x x]
_ [*i*]*š-kun-u-ni ta-ha-ṭa-ni* ŠU.2-*ku-nu ina* HUL-*tim*
E *iš-ku-nu-u-ni ta-ha-ṭa-a-ni qa-at-ku-nu ina* HUL-*tim*
y *iš-k*[*u-nu-u-ni* x x x x x x x x x *in*]*a* HUL-*tim*
_ [*iš*]-*kun-u-ni ta*-[x x x x x x x x x H]UL-*tim*
[x x x x x x x x x x x x x *a*]-˹*na*?˺ HUL-*t*[*im*]
106 A *ina* Š[À-x x x x x x x]
_ [x] ŠÀ-*bi-šú-nu tu-bal-a-ni*
E *ina* ŠÀ-*bi-šú-nu tu-bal-a-ni*
y *ina* ŠÀ-*šú*-[*nu* x x x x]
_ *ina* ŠÀ-*bi-šú-n*[*u* x x x x]
107 A *ep*-[*šú* x x x x x x x x x x x x x x x x x]
_ *ep-šú bar-tú a-bu-tú* [*l*]*a* DÙG.GA-*tú te-pa-šá*-[*ni-šu*]-*nu-u-ni*
E *ep-šú bar-tú a-bu-tú la* DÙG.GA-*tú te-pa-šá-ni-šú-nu-ni*
y [x x x x *a*]-*bu-tú la* DÙG.GA-[*tú* x x x x x x x x]
_ [x x *bar*]-*tu a-bu-tú la ṭa-a*[*b-tu* x x x x x x x x]
[x x x x *a*]-*bu-t*[*u* x x x x x x x x x x x x]

108 A *š*[*um-ma* x x x x x x x x x x]
_ [*šu*]*m-ma a-bu-tú l*[*a* x x x x S]IG$_5$-*tú*
E [x x x x x]x *la* DÙG.GA-*tú la de-eq-tú*
y [x x] *a-bu-tú la* DÙG.GA-*tú la* [x x]
_ [x x *a-b*]*u-tu la* DÙG.GA-*tú la* [x x]
[x x] ˹*a-bu*˺-*tu la* ˹DÙG.GA-*tu la*˺ [x x]

109 _ [x x x x] ⌜ša?⌝ [x x x x x x x x x x x x x x x]
la ba-ni-tú [x x] UGU ^{m}aš-š[ur–DÙ–A x x x x] É–UŠ-te
E la ba-ni-tú [x x x ^{m}]aš-šur–DÙ–A DUMU–MAN GAL ša É–UŠ-ti
y [x x x x x x U]GU ^{m}aš-šur–DÙ–A DUMU–MAN GA[L x x x x]
_ [x x x x x x x ^{m}aš-š]ur–DÙ–A DUMU–MAN GAL šá É–[UŠ-ti]
[x x x x x] ina UGU ^{m}aš-šur–[DÙ]–⌜A DUMU–MAN GAL⌝ [x x x x]
110 A D[UMU? x x x x x x x x x x x x x x x x x x x]
_ DUMU ^{m}aš-š[ur–PAB–AŠ x x x x x x x x x x x x x x]
[x x x x x x x x x x x]-ku-nu [x x x x x x]
E [x x x x x x] MAN KUR–aš-šur.KI EN-ku-nu la tar-ṣa-at-u-ni
y [x ^{m}aš-šur]–PAB–AŠ MAN KUR–aš-šur EN-k[u-nu x x x x x x]
_ [x x x x x x] MAN KUR–aš-šur EN-[ku-nu x x x x x x]
[x] ^{m}aš-šur–PAB–AŠ MAN KUR–[aš-šur] ⌜EN-ku-nu⌝ [x x x x x x]
111 A [x x x x x] lu ina p[i-i x x x]
_ la ṭa-⌜bat-u-ni lu⌝-u ina pi-⌜i⌝ [x x x]
[x x x]-u-ni [x x x x x x x]
E [x x x]-u-ni lu ina pi-i LÚ.KÚR-šú
y [la ṭa-b]at-u-ni lu ina [x x x x x]
_ la ṭa-b[a-at-u-ni x x x x x x x]
[x x x x x] lu ina pi-i ⌜LÚ.KÚR⌝-[šu]
112 _ lu-u ina pi-i sal-me-šú [x x x x x sa-l]i-me-šú
E lu (ina) pi-i LÚ.x-me?
_ [x x x p]i-i sa-[li-me-šú]
A lu ina pi-i [x x x]
113 _ lu-u ina p[i-i x x x]
E [x x x pi]-i ŠEŠ.MEŠ-šú
_ lu ina pi-⌜i⌝ [x x x]
114 _ ŠEŠ.MEŠ–AD.MEŠ-šú DUMU–ŠEŠ.MEŠ–[AD.MEŠ-šú]
E ŠEŠ–AD.MEŠ-šú DUMU–ŠEŠ–AD.MEŠ-šú
_ [Š]EŠ–AD.MEŠ-šú Š[EŠ? x x x x]
[x x x x x x x x–A]D.M[EŠ]-šu
115 A qin-ni-šú NUMUN [x x x x x x x x x x x]
_ qin-ni-šu NUMUN É–AD-šu lu-u ina p[i-i x x x x]
E [x x x] NUMUN É–AD-šú lu ina pi-⌜i⌝ ŠEŠ.MEŠ-ku-nu
_ [x x x x x x x] lu ina pi-i ŠEŠ.MEŠ-ku-[nu]
o [x x x NU]MUN ⌜É⌝ [x x x x x x x x x x]
116 A DUMU.MEŠ-ku-[nu x x x x x x x x x x x x x]
_ DUMU.MEŠ-ku-nu DUMU.MÍ.MEŠ-ku-nu lu [x x x] LÚ.ra-gi-me
E [x x x x x x x-k]u-[n]u lu ina pi-i ra-gi-me
_ [x x x x x x].MEŠ-ku-nu lu ina pi-i LÚ.ra-g[i-me]
o [x x x]-nu DUMU.M[Í!-ku-nu x x x x x x x x]
117 A LÚ.mah-[he-e x x x x x x x]
_ LÚ.mah-he-⌜e⌝ [x x x x] a-mat DINGIR
E [x x x x x šá-'i]-li a-mat DINGIR.MEŠ
_ [x x x x x šá-']i-li a-mat DINGIR
o [LÚ.ma]h-he-e DUMU šá-['i-li x x x]

118 A *lu-u ina pi-i na*[*p-har* x x x x x x x x]
_ *lu-u ina nap-har ṣal-mat*–SAG.DU *mal ba-šú-u*
E [x x x x x x x *ṣal-mat–qaq-q*]*a-di mal ba-šu-u*
_ [x x x x x x x *ṣ*]*al-mat*–SAG.DU *mal ba-šu-u*
o [*lu*]-*u ina nap-har ṣal-mat*–SA[G.DU x x x x]
119 A *ta-šam-ma-n*[*i* x x x x x x]
_ *ta-šam-ma-a-ni tu-pa-za-ra-a-ni*
E [x x x x x x x x x x-*n*]*i*
_ [x x x x x *t*]*u-pa-za-ra-a-ni*
o [*t*]*a-šam-ma-ni tu-pa-*[*za-ra-ni*]
_ [*t*]*a-šam-m*[*a-ni* x x x x x]
120 A *la ta-lak-a-ni-*[*ni* x x x x x x x x x x x]
_ *la ta-*⸢*lak-a-ni*⸣*-ni a-na* ^{m}*aš-šur*–DÙ–A DUMU–MAN GAL-*u*
E *la ta-lak-a-ni-ni* [x x x x x x x x x x x]
_ [x x x x x x *a-n*]*a* ^{m}*aš-šur*–DÙ–A DUMU–MAN GA[L-*u*]
O [*la ta-la*]*k-a-ni-ni* [x x x x x x x x x x x]
o [x x x x x x *a-n*]*a* ^{m}*aš-šur*–DÙ–A DUMU–MAN GAL-[*u*]
_ [x x x x x x *a-n*]*a* ^{m}*aš-šur*–D[Ù–A x x x x]
121 A *šá* É–UŠ-⸢*ti*⸣ [x x x x x x x x x x]
_ [x x x x x] ^{m}*aš-šur*–PAB–AŠ MAN KUR–*aš-šur*
E [x É–U]Š-*te* DUMU ^{m}*aš-šur*–PAB–AŠ [MAN KUR–*aš*]-*šur*
_ [x x x x x] ^{m}*aš-šur*–PAB–AŠ MAN KUR–*a*[*š-šur*]
O [x É–UŠ-*t*]*e* DUMU ^{m}*aš-šur*–PAB–AŠ [x x x x]
o [x x x x x] ^{m}*aš-šur*–PAB–AŠ MAN KUR–*aš-šur*
_ [x x x x x] ^{m}*aš-šur*–P[AB–AŠ x x x x]
122 A *la ta-*[x x x x]
_ *la ta-qab-ba-ni*
E [*la ta-qab-b*]*a-a*!*-ni*
_ [*la ta-qab-b*]*a-a-*[*ni*]
O [*la ta-qab-ba*]*-a-ni*
o *la t*[*a-*x x x x]

---

123 A ⸢*šum*⸣*-ma at-tu-*[*nu* x x x x x x x x x x]
_ *šum-ma at-tu-n*[*u* ^{m}*aš-š*]*ur*–DÙ–A DUMU–MAN GAL-*u*
E *šúm-mu at-tú-nu* ^{m}*aš-šur*–DÙ–A [x x GA]L
o [x x *a*]*t-tú-nu* ^{m}*aš-šur*–DÙ–A DU[MU–MAN x x]
124 A *šá* É–UŠ-*ti* [x x x x x x x x x x]
_ *šá* É–UŠ-*te ša* ^{m}*aš-šur*–PAB–AŠ MAN [x x x]
E *šá* É–UŠ-*te ša* ^{m}*aš-šur*–PAB–AŠ MAN KUR–*aš-šur*
O [x É]–UŠ-*ti* [x x x x x x x x x x]
o [x x x x x ^{m}*aš*]-*šur*–PAB–AŠ MAN KUR–*aš-šur*
125 A *iq-ba-ka-*[*nu-u-ni* x x x x x x x x]
_ [*iq-b*]*a-ka-nu-u-ni la* DÙG.GA-*tu l*[*a* x x x]
E *iq-*[*ba-k*]*a-nu-u-ni la ṭa-ab-tú la de-eq-*[*tú*]
O [x x x x x]-*ni* [x x x x x x x x]
o *i*[*q-ba-ka-nu-u-ni* x x x]-*tú la* SIG$_{5}$-*tú*

126 A *te-ep-pa-šá-ni-šú-*x[x x x x x x x x x]
_ [*te-e*]*p-pa-šá-ni-šu-un-ni ta-ṣa-ba-ta-*[*šu-u-ni*]
E [*t*]*e-pa-šá-ni-šú-un-ni ta-ṣa-ba-ta-šu-u-ni*
O [x x x x x x x]*-ni* [x x x x x x x]
127 A *ta-du-ka-šú-u-*⸢*ni*⸣ [x x x x x x x x x x x x]
_ [*ta-du-k*]*a-šu-u-ni a-na* LÚ.⸢KÚR⸣*-šu ta-da*⸣*-*[*na-š*]*u-*[*u*]*-n*[*i*]
ta-d[*u-k*]*a-šú-u-ni a-na* LÚ.KÚR*-šú ta-da-na-šu-u-ni*
O [x x x x x x x x LÚ.KÚ]R*-šu* [x x x x x x]
o [*ta-du*]*-ka-šú-u-n*[*i* x x x x x x x x x x x x]
128 A *a-na* LUGAL*-u-ti* KUR*–aš-š*[*ur* x x x x x x x]
_ *a-na* LUGAL*-u-te* KUR*–aš-šur tu-*[x x x x x x]
E *a-na* LUGAL*-te* KUR*–aš-šur tu-nak-*[*ka*]*r-a-šú-u-*[*n*]*i*
O [x x x x x x x *tu-nak-kar*]*-a-šú-ni*
o [x x LUGAL]*-ú-te* [x x x x x x x x x x]
129 A *a-na* LUGAL *šá-nim-ma* E[N x x x x x x x x x x]
_ *a-na* LUGAL MAN*-ma* EN MAN*-ma ma-m*[*it* x x x x]
E *a-na* LUGAL *šá-nim-ma* EN *šá-nim-m*[*a* x x *ta-tam*]*-ma-ni*
O [x x x x x x x x x x x x *ta-tam-ma*]*-a-ni*
o [x x x x x x x] ⸢*šá*⸣*-n*[*im-ma* x x x x x x]

---

130 A *šum-ma me-me-ni a-na* ^{m}*aš-šur–*[DÙ–A x x x x x x x x]
_ *šum-ma me-me-ni a-na* ^{m}*aš-šur–*DÙ–A DUMU–[MAN x x x x x]
E *šúm-mu me-me-ni a-na* ^{m}*aš-šur–*DÙ–A [DUMU–MAN GAL *š*]*á* É–UŠ*-te*
O [x x x x x x x x x x x x x x x x É–U]Š*-ti*
131 A DUMU ^{m}*aš-šur–*PAB–AŠ MAN KUR*–aš-šur* EN*-ku-*[*nu* x x x x x]
_ DUMU ^{m}*aš-šur–*PAB–AŠ MAN KUR*–aš-šur* EN*-ku-nu šá ina* [x x x]
E [D]UMU ^{m}*aš-šur–*PAB–AŠ MAN KUR*–aš-šur* EN-[*ku-nu* x x U]GU*-hi-šú*
_ DU[MU x x x x x x x x x x x x x x x x x x]
O [x x x x x x x x x x x EN]*-ku-nu* [x x x x x]
132 A *a-de-e is-si-ku-nu i*[*š-ku*]*n-*[*u-ni*]
_ ⸢*a-de-e is*⸣*-si-ku-nu iš-ku-nu-u-ni*
E *a-de-e is-si-ku-nu* [*iš-ku-nu*]*-u-ni*
_ [x x x] *is-si-ku-nu* [x x x x x]
O [x x x] *i*[*s-si-ku-n*]*u* ⸢*iš*⸣*-ku-nu-u-ni*
133 A *si-hu bar-tu ša d*[*u-a-ki*]*-šu* [x x x x]
_ [x x x x x x x x x *ša-mut-t*]*i-šu*
E *si-*⸢*hu*⸣ *bar-tú šá d*[*u-a-ki-šu ša-m*]*ut-te-šu*
_ [x x x x x x x x x] *ša-mut-ti-*⸢*šu*⸣
O [x x x x x x x x x *ša*]*-mut-ti-šú-nu*
134 A *hul-lu-qi-šú* [x x *ka-š*]*ú-nu* [x x x x x]
_ *hu*[*l-*x x x x x x x x *iq-ba-k*]*a-nu-u-ni*
E *h*[*ul-*x x x x x x x x *i*]*q-ba-ka-nu-ni*
_ [x x x x] *a-na ka-šu-nu* [x x x x x]
t [*h*]*ul-lu-q*[*i-šu* x x x x x *iq-ba-ka*]*-nu-u-ni*
O *hul-lu-qi-šu-nu* [x x x x x *i-q*]*ab-ba-ka-nu-u-ni*

135 A *ù at-tu-nu ina pi-i* [x x x] *ta-šam-m*[*a-a-ni*]
E *ù* ⸢*at*⸣*-t*[*u-nu* x x x x x x] *ta-šam-ma-ni*
_ ⸢*ù*⸣ [*a*]*t-tu-nu ina p*[*i-i* x x x x x x x x]
t *ù at-t*[*ú-nu* x x x x x x x x x x]*-ni*
O [x x x x x *p*]*i-i me-me-ni ta-šam-ma-a-ni*
136 A *e-pi-šá-nu-ti šá* [x x] *la ta-ṣab-bat-*⸢*a-ni-ni*⸣
E *e-piš-a-nu-te šá bar-te la ta-ṣa-bat-a-ni-ni*
_ [*e-pi*]*-šá-nu-t*[*i* x x x x x x x x x x]
t *e-piš-a-nu-te šá bar-te la ta-ṣab-*[*bat-a-ni-ni*]
O [x x x x x x *bar-t*]*i la ta-ṣab-bat-a-ni-ni*
137 A *ina* UGU ^{m}*aš-šur*–DÙ–A DUMU–MAN G[AL x] É–UŠ*-ti*
E *ina* UGU ^{m}*aš-šur*–DÙ–A DUMU–MAN GAL *ša* É–UŠ*-ti*
t [x x] ^{m}*aš-šur*–DÙ–A DUMU–MAN GAL*-u šá* É–U[Š-x]
O [x x x x x x x x x GA]L *šá* É–UŠ*-te*
138 A *la tu-bal-a-ni-ni šum-m*[*a* x x x x x x x]
E *la tú-bal-a-ni-ni šúm-mu am–mar ṣa-ba-ti-šú-nu*
t [x *tu*]*-bal-a-ni-ni šum-ma am–mar ṣa-ba-*[*ti-šú-nu*]
O *la tu-bal-a-ni-ni* [x x x x x x x x x]
139 A *du-u-a-ki-šú-nu ma-ṣa-ku-n*[*u* x x x x x x x x]
E *du-a-ki-šú-nu ma-ṣa-ku-nu la ta-ṣab-bat-a-šá-nu-ni*
t [*du-a-k*]*i-šú-nu ma-ṣa-ku-nu la ta-ṣab-*[x x x x x]
O ⸢x x x x⸣ [x x x x x x x x x x x x x x]
_ [x x x x x x x x*-n*]*u la t*[*a-*x x x x x x]
140 A *la ta-du-ka-šá-nu-u-n*[*i* x x x x x x]
E *la ta-du-ka-a-šá-nu-ni* MU*-šú-nu* NUMUN*-šú-nu*
t [*la ta*]*-du-ka-šá-nu-u-ni* MU*-šú-nu* NUMUN-[*šú-nu*]
_ [x x x x x x x*-n*]*i* MU*-šú-*[*nu* x x x]
141 A *ina* KUR *la tu-hal-laq-q*[*a-ni*]
P [x x] *la tu-h*[*al-laq-qa-ni*]
E *ina* KUR *la tu-hal-laq-qa-a-ni*
t [x x x *tu*]*-hal-laq-qa-ni*
142 A [x x x x x x x x x] *d*[*u*!-x x x x]
P [x x x x x x x x x *du-a*]*-ki-šú-nu*
E [*š*]*úm-mu am–mar ṣa-ba-te-šú-nu du-a-ki-šú-nu*
_ [x x x x x x x x x *du-a-k*]*i-šú-nu*
t *šum-ma am–mar ṣa-ba-*[*te-šú-nu du-a-k*]*i-šú-nu*
_ [*šu*]*m-*⸢*ma*⸣ *a*[*m–mar* x x x x x x x x x x]
143 P *la* [x x x x x x x x x x x x D]UMU–MAN GAL
E *la-*⸢*a*⸣ (*ma-ṣa-ku-nu*) [P]I.2 *šá* ^{m}*aš-šur*–DÙ–A DUMU–MAN GAL
_ *la ma-ṣa-*[*ku-nu* x x] *šá* ^{m}*aš-šur*–DÙ–A DUMU–MAN GAL
t *la ma-ṣa-ku-nu* PI.2 *šá* ^{m}*aš-š*[*ur*–DÙ–A x x GAL]*-u*
144 P *šá* É–U[Š*-ti* x x x x x x x x x]
E *ša* É–U[Š*-ti* x] *tú-pat-ta-a-ni is-si-šú*
_ [x x x x] *la tu-pat-ta-a-ni is-*[*si-šú*]
t *šá* É–UŠ*-ti la tu-pat-t*[*a-a-ni* x x x]
145 P [*la t*]*a-za-za-a-ni e-piš-a-n*[*u-ti* x x x]
E *la* [x x x x x *e-p*]*iš-a-nu-te šá bar-te*
_ [x x x x x x] *e-pi-šá-nu-ti šá* [x x]
t [x *t*]*a-za-za-ni e-pi-šá-nu-te* [x x x]

146 P [x *ta-ṣ*]*ab-bat-a-ni la ta-du-k*[*a-a-ni*]
E *la ta-*[x x x x x *t*]*a-du-ka-a-*[*ni*]
_ [x x x x x x] *la ta-d*[*u-*x x x]
t [x x x x x x] *la ta-du-ka-*[*a-ni*]

---

147 A *šum-ma e-pi-šá-nu-ti* ˹*šá*˺ [x x x x x x x x x x x x x]
H *šum-ma e-pi-šá-nu-te šá bar-te lu-u e-*[*ṣ*]*u-te lu-u ma-a'-du-te*
P [x x *e-pi*]*š-a-nu-ti šá bar-ti lu e-ṣu-ti l*[*u* x x x x]
E [x x x x]*-a-nu-te šá b*[*ar-te* x x x x x x x x x x x]
_ [x x x x x x x x x x x x *e-ṣ*]*u-ti lu ma-a'-d*[*u-ti*]
148 A *is-si-šú-nu ta-šá-kan-a-*[*ni* x x x S]IG$_5$*-t*[*ú*]
H *is-si-šú-nu ta-šá-*[*kan*]*-a-ni du-un-qu la du-un-qu*
P [*is-si-šú*]*-nu ta-šá-kan-a-ni* SIG$_5$*-tú la* S[IG$_5$*-tú*]
E [x x x x x x x x x] *du-un-qu la* ˹*du-un*˺*-*[*qu*]
_ [x x x x x x x x x SI]G$_5$*-tu la* SIG$_5$*-tu*
149 A *ta-šam-*[*m*]*a-a-ni l*[*a ta-qab-ba-a*]*-ni*
H *t*[*a-šam-ma-a*]*-ni*
P [*ta-šam-m*]*a-a-ni*
150 A *a-na* ^{m}*aš-šur*–DÙ–A DUMU–MAN G[AL x x x]*-u-ti*
H *a-na* ^{m}*aš-šur*–DÙ–A DUMU–MAN GAL*-u šá* [É–UŠ]*-ti*
P *a-na* ^{m}*aš-šur*–DÙ–A DUMU–MAN GAL *šá* É–U[Š*-ti*]
E *a-na* ^{m}*aš-šur*–DÙ–A DUMU–MAN GAL *š*[*a* x x x]
_ [x x x x x x x] DUMU–MAN *šá* É–UŠ*-ti*
151 A DUMU ^{m}*aš-šur*–PAB–AŠ MAN KUR–*aš-šur* [x *ta*]*-lak-a-ni*
H [D]UMU ^{m}*aš-šur*–PAB–AŠ MAN KUR–*aš-šur la* [*ta*]*-lak-a-ni-*[*ni*]
P [x ^{m}*aš-šur*]–PAB–AŠ MAN KUR–*aš-šur la tal-lak-a-ni-ni*
E [x x x x x x] MAN KUR–*aš-šur la ta-lak-a-ni-ni*
_ [x x x x x x x x x x x *ta*]*l-lak-a-ni-ni*
152 A *lib-ba-ku-nu is-si-šú* [*la*] ˹*ga-ma?-ru*˺*-*[*ni*]
H [x x x x x x x x x]*-nu is-si-*[*šú* x x x x x]
P *la ta-qab-ba-a-ni* [x x x x *is-si*]*-šú la gam-mur-u-ni*
E *la ta-q*[*ab-ba-a-ni*] ŠÀ*-ku-nu is-si-šu la ga-mur-u-ni*
_ [x x x x x x x*-k*]*u-nu is-si-šú la gam-mur-u-*˹*ni*˺
153 A *ša* DIN[GIR.MEŠ *ú-š*]*e-šá-bu-u-*[*ni*] *a-de-e ina* IGI DINGIR.[MEŠ]
H [x x x *ú*]*-ši-šá-bu-u-n*[*i* x x x x x x x]
P *šá* DINGIR.MEŠ*-ni ú-še-šab-u-ni* [x x x x IG]I DINGIR.MEŠ*-ni*
E *ša* DINGIR.MEŠ *ú-še-šab-u-ni a-de-e ina* IGI DINGIR.MEŠ*-ni*
_ [x x x x x x x x x x *a*]*-de-e ina* IGI DINGIR.MEŠ*-ni*
154 A [x x x x*-n*]*i ina* KÉŠ ˹GIŠ.ABxAD˺.TIM [x x x x x]
H [x x*-ka*]*n-u-ni ina ri-k*[*is*] GIŠ.˹BANŠUR˺ [x x x x x]
P *i-šá-kan-u-ni ina* KÉŠ GIŠ.BANŠUR [*ša-t*]*e-e* GÚ.ZI
E *ta-šá-kan-a-ni ina* KÉŠ GIŠ.ABxAD.TIM *šá-te-e ka-si*
_ [x x x x x x x x x] *šá-ti-e* G[Ú.ZI]
155 A *ni-pi-ih* ^{d}GIŠ.BAR A.MEŠ *ṣi-bit tu-le-e*
H [*ni*]*-*˹*pi*˺*-ih* ^{d}GIŠ.BAR A.MEŠ [x x x x] *tu-le-e*
P *ni-pi-ih* ^{d}GIŠ.BAR A.MEŠ Ì.MEŠ [*ṣ*]*i-bit tu-le-e*
E *ni-pi-ih* ^{d}GIŠ.BAR A.MEŠ Ì.MEŠ *ṣi-bit tu-le-e*

156 A *a-he-iš tu-tam-ma-a-ni a-na* ^{m}*aš-šur*–DÙ–A DUMU–MAN GAL
H *a-ha-meš tu-tam-*[*ma-a-ni*] *a-na* ^{m}*aš-šur*–DÙ–A DUMU–MAN GAL-*u*
P *a-na a-he-iš tu-tam-ma-a-ni a-na* ^{m}*aš-šur*–DÙ–A DUMU–MAN GAL
E *a-ha-meš tu-tam-ma-a-ni a-na* ^{m}*aš-šur*–DÙ–(A) DUMU–MAN GAL
157 A *šá* É–UŠ-*ti* DUMU ^{m}*aš-šur*–PAB–AŠ MAN KUR–*aš-šur* EN-*ku-nu*
B [x É–U]Š-*te* DUMU ^{m}*aš-šur*–PAB–AŠ [x x x x x x x]
H *šá* É–U[Š-*ti*] A ^{m}*aš-šur*–PAB–AŠ MAN KUR–*aš-šur* EN-*ku-nu*
P *šá* É–UŠ-*te* DUMU ^{m}*aš-šur*–PAB–AŠ MAN KUR–*aš-šur* EN-*ku-nu*
E *ša* É–UŠ-*te* DUMU ^{m}*aš-šur*–PAB–AŠ MAN KUR–*aš-šur* EN-*ku-nu*
S [x x x x x x x x x x x x x x] EN-*ku-nu*
158 A *la tal-lak-a-ni-ni la ta-qab-ba-a-ni*
B [x x x x x x *l*]*a ta-qab-ba-a-ni*
P *la tal-lak-a-ni-ni la ta-qab-ba-a-ni*
E *la ta-lak-a-ni-ni la ta-qab-ba-a-ni*
S *la* ⸢*tal*⸣-[*lak-a-ni-ni* x x x x x x]
159 A *e-pi-šá-nu-ti šá bar-ti u* LÚ.ERIM.MEŠ EN–*hi-ṭi*
B [x x x x x x x x x x x].MEŠ EN–*hi-ṭi*
P *e-piš-a-nu-ti šá bar-ti ù* LÚ.ERIM.MEŠ EN–*hi-ṭi*
E *e-piš-a-nu-ti šá bar-te u* ERIM.MEŠ EN–*hi-*[*ṭ*]*i*
S *e-piš-šá-nu-te šá bar-te u* ERIM.MEŠ EN [x x]
160 A *la ta-ṣa-ba-*(*ta*)*-a-ni-ni la ta-du-ka-a-ni*
B [x x x x x x x x x *ta*]-*du-ka-a-ni*
P *la ta-ṣab-bat-a-ni la ta-du-*(*ka*)*-a-ni*
E *la ta-ṣa-bat-a-ni-ni la ta-*⸢*du-ka*⸣*-a-ni*
S *la ta-ṣab-bat-a-ni-ni la ta-du-ka-*⸢*a*⸣-[*ni*]
161 A MU-*šú-nu* NUMUN-*šú-nu ina* KUR *la tu-hal-laq-qa-a-ni*
B [x x x x x x x x x *tu*]-*hal-la-qa-a-ni*
M [x x x x x x x x *l*]*a t*[*u*-x x x x x]
P MU-*šú-nu* NUMUN-*šú-nu ina* KUR *la tu-hal-laq-a-ni*
E MU-*šú-nu* NUMUN-*šú-nu ina* KUR *la t*[*ú*]-*hal-laq-qa-a-ni*
S MU-*šú-nu* NUMUN-*šú-nu ina* KUR *la tu-hal-la-qà-a-*[*ni*]

---

162 A *šum-ma lu aš-šur-a-a da-gíl–pa-ni šá* KUR–*aš-šur*.KI
B [x x x x x x x *da*]-⸢*gíl*?⸣–IGI *šá* KUR–*aš-šur*.KI
M [x x x x x x x] *da-gíl–pa-*[*ni* x x x x x]
P *š*[*um-ma l*]*u* LÚ.*aš-šur-a-a lu da-gíl–pa-ni šá* KUR–*aš-šur*
E *šúm-mu lu* LÚ.*aš-šur-a-a da-gíl–pa-ni šá* KUR–*aš-šur*.KI
S *šum-ma lu* LÚ.*aš-šur-a-a lu da-gíl–pa-ni šá* KUR–*aš-šur*
163 A *lu-u* LÚ.*šá–ziq-ni lu-u* LÚ.SAG *lu* DUMU KUR–*aš-šur*.KI
B [x x x x x x x x] *lu* DUMU KUR–*aš-šur*.KI
M [x x x x x x x x LÚ.S]AG *lu-u* DUMU KUR–*aš-*[*šur*]
I *lu* LÚ.*šá–ziq-ni lu* LÚ.S[AG x x x x x]
P *lu* ⸢LÚ⸣.*šá–ziq-ni lu* LÚ.SAG *lu* DUMU KUR–*aš-šur*
E [x LÚ].*šá–ziq-ni lu* LÚ.SAG *lu* DUMU KUR–*aš-šur*
S *lu šá–*⸢*ziq-ni*⸣ *lu* LÚ.SAG *lu* DUMU KUR–*aš-šur*

164 A *lu-u* DUMU.MEŠ KUR *šá-(ni)-tim-(ma) lu šik-nat*–ZI *mal ba-šu-u*
B [x x x x x x x x x x *šik-nat*–Z]I-*tim*? *ma-la ba-šú-u*
M [x x x x x x x x x *l*]*u-u ina šik-nat*–ZI *ma*[*l* x x x]
I *lu* DUMU KUR *šá-ni-ti-ma lu-*˹*u*˺ [x x x x x x x x x]
P *lu* DUMU KUR *šá-ni-tim-ma lu ina šik-nat*–ZI-*tim ma-la ba-šú-u*
E [x x x x x x-*m*]*a lu ina šik-nat*–ZI-*tim ma-la* GÁL
S *lu* DUMU KUR *šá-ni-tim-ma lu ina nap-har ṣal-mat*–SAG.DU *mal ba-šú-u l*[*u* x *šik-nat*–Z]I-˹*tim*˺ *mal ba-šú-u*
165 A *a-na* ^{m}*aš-šur*–DÙ–A DUMU–MAN GAL *šá* É–UŠ-*ti ina* A.ŠÀ-*šú*
B [x x x x x x x x x x x É–*re-d*]*u*?-*ú-ti* [x x x x]
M [x x x x x x x x x x] *šá* É–UŠ-*t*[*i* x x x x]
I *a-na* ^{m}*aš-šur*–DÙ–A DUMU–[M]AN GAL *š*[*á*] É–[x x x x x x]
P *a-na* ^{m}*aš-šur*–DÙ–A DUMU–MAN GAL *šá* É–UŠ-*te lu ina* A.ŠÀ
E [x x ^{m}]*aš-šur*–DÙ–A DUMU–MAN GAL *šá* É–UŠ-*ti* [x A].ŠÀ
S *a-na* ^{m}*aš-šur*–DÙ–A DUMU–MAN GAL [x] ˹É˺–[U]Š-*ti ina* A.ŠÀ
166 A *bir-ti* URU *e-ta-as-ru-šú si-hu bar-tu ina* UGU-*hi-šú e-*[x x]
B [x x x *e-ta-a*]*s-ru-šú* [x x x x x x x x x x x]
M [x x UR]U *e-ta-as-*˹*ru*˺-*šu* [x x x x x UG]U-*hi-šu e-tap-pa-šu*
I [x x x] *e-ta-as-ru-uš si-hu bar-t*[*u* x x x x x x x x]
P *lu ina* ŠÀ URU *e-ta-as-ru-šú si-hu bar-tú ina* UGU-*hi-*˹*šú*˺ *e-tap-šú*
E *ina* ŠÀ URU *e-ta-as-ru-šu* [*si*]-*hu bar-tú ina* UGU-*hi-šú e-tap-šu*
S *bir-ti* URU *e-ta-as-ru-šú si-hu bar-te* [x UG]U-*hi-šú e-tap-*˹*šu*˺
167 A *at-tu-nu* TA* ^{m}*aš-šur*–DÙ–A DUMU–MAN GAL *šá* É–UŠ-*ti*
B [x x x] TA* ^{m}*aš-šur*–DÙ–A [x x x x x]-*ti*
M [x x x x ^{m}*aš-šur*]–DÙ–A DUMU–MAN GAL *šá* É–UŠ-*t*[*i*]
I *at-tu-nu* TA ^{m}*aš-šur*–DÙ–A DUMU–M[AN x x x x x]
P *at-tú-nu* TA* ^{m}*aš-šur*–DÙ–A DUMU–MAN GAL *šá* É–U[Š-x]
E [*a*]*t-tu-nu* TA ^{m}*aš-šur*–DÙ–A DUMU–MAN GAL *ša* É–UŠ-*te*
S *at-tu-nu* TA* ^{m}*aš-šur*–DÙ–A [x x x *š*]*á* É–UŠ-*ti*
168 A *la ta-za-za-a-ni la ta-na-ṣar-šú-u-ni*
M [x x x x x x] *la ta-na-ṣar-a-*˹*šú*˺-[*u*]-*ni*
I *la ta-za-za-a-ni l*[*a* x x x x x x x]
P *la ta-za-za-a-ni la t*[*a-n*]*a-ṣar-a-šú-u-ni*
E [*l*]*a ta-za-za-a-ni la ta-na-ṣar-a-šú-u-ni*
S *la ta-za-(za)-a-ni la ta-na-ṣar-a-šú-u-ni*
169 A LÚ.ERIM.MEŠ *šá bar-ti e-pa-šú-ni-šú-u-ni ina gam-mur-ti* ŠÀ-*bi-ku-nu*
M [x x x x *bar-t*]*e e-pa-šu-niš-šu-*˹*un-ni*˺ [x x x x ŠÀ-*b*]*i-ku-nu*
I LÚ.ERIM.MEŠ *šá bar-tu e-pu-šu-niš-*[x x x x x x x] ŠÀ-*bi-ku-nu*
P L[Ú.x x] *šá bar-ti e-pu-šú-niš-šú-*[x x x *ga*]*m-mur-te* Š[À-x x x]
E [LÚ.E]RIM.MEŠ *šá bar-tú e-pa-šú-ni-šú-un-ni* [x x x x x x x x]
S [x x x x *bar*]-*tu e-pa-áš-šu-ni-šu-u-ni ina gam-mur-ti* ŠÀ-*ku-nu*
G L[Ú.x x x x x x x x x x x x x x x x x x x x x]

170 A *la ta-du-*[*ka*]*-a-ni a-na* ^{m}*aš-šur*–DÙ–A DUMU–MAN GAL
M *la ta-du-ka-a-ni* [x x ^{m}*aš-šur*–D]Ù–A DUMU–MAN GAL
I *la ta-du-ka-a-n*[*i* x x x x x x x x x x]
P *la ta-du-ka-a-ni* [x x ^{m}*aš-šur*–DÙ]–A D[UMU–MAN x]
S ⌈*la ta*⌉*-du-ka-a-ni a-na* ^{m}*aš-šur*–DÙ–A DUMU–MAN GAL
G *la t*[*a*-x x x x x x x x x x x x] DUMU–MAN GA[L]
_ [x *ta*]*-du-ka-a-ni* [x x x x x x x x x x]
[x x x x x x] ⌈*a-na* 1⌉.*aš-šur*–DÙ–A DUMU–MAN GAL
⌈*la ta*⌉-[x x x x x x x x x x x x x x x]

171 A *šá* É–UŠ-⌈*ti*⌉ *ù* ŠEŠ.MEŠ-*šú* DUMU AMA-*šú*
M *šá* É–UŠ-⌈*ti*⌉ [x ŠE]Š.MEŠ-*šu* DUMU AMA-*šú*
I *šá* É–UŠ-*ti u* [Š]EŠ.MEŠ-*šú* DUMU AMA-*šú*
P *šá* É–UŠ-*te* ŠEŠ.MEŠ-*šú* [x x x]
S *šá* É–UŠ-*ti u* ŠEŠ.MEŠ-*šú* DUMU AMA-*šú is-si-šú*
_ [x É–U]Š-*ti* [x x x x x x x]
š[*á* x x x] *ù* ŠEŠ.MEŠ DUMU.MEŠ AMA-*šú*
ša É U[Š-x x x x-*š*]*ú* DUMU AMA-*šú*

172 A *la tu-še-za-ba-ni-ni*
B [x x x x x x]-*ni*
M *la tu-še-za-b*[*a-ni*]-⌈*ni*⌉
S *la tu-še-za-ba-a-ni-ni*
G *la* [x x x x x x]
_ [x *t*]*u-še-za-ba-a-ni-ni*
la t[*u*-x x x x x]

---

173 A *šum-ma ša* TA* ^{m}*aš-šur*–DÙ–A DUMU–MA[N G]AL *šá* É–UŠ-*ti*
M [x x x] TA* ^{m}*aš-šur*–DÙ–[A DUMU–MAN GAL *šá* É–UŠ-*ti*
I *šum-ma* [*š*]*á* TA ^{m}*aš-šur*–DÙ–A DUMU–MAN GAL [x] É–UŠ-*ti*
P [x-*m*]*a šá* TA* ^{m}*aš-šur*–DÙ–⌈A⌉ [x x x x x x x]
S *šum-ma šá* ⌈TA 1⌉.*aš-šur*–DÙ–A DUMU–MAN GAL *šá* É–UŠ-*ti*
G *šum-ma šá* TA ^{m}*aš-šur*–[DÙ–A x x x x x x x]
_ [x x x x x x x x x x x x x x]–*re*-[*du-ti*
šum-ma šá ⌈TA* ^{m}*aš-šur*–DÙ⌉–A DUMU–M[AN x x x x x]
[x x x x ^{m}*aš-š*]*ur*–DÙ–A DUMU–MAN GAL *šá* [x x x]
[x x] ⌈*šá* TA*? 1⌉.*aš*-[*šur*–DÙ–A x x x x x x x]

174 A DUMU ^{m}*aš-šur*–PAB–AŠ MAN KUR–*aš-šur* EN-*ku-nu šá ina* UGU-*hi-šú*
B [x] ^{m}*aš-šur*–PAB–AŠ [x x x x x x x x x x x x x]
M [x ^{m}*aš-šur*]–PAB–AŠ MAN KUR–*aš-šur* EN-*ku-nu šá ina* UGU-*hi*-⌈*šú*⌉
I DUMU ^{m}*aš-šur*–PAB–AŠ MAN KUR–*aš-šur* EN-*ku-nu šá ina* UGU-*hi-šú*
P [x] ^{m}*aš-šur*–PAB–AŠ MAN KUR–*aš-š*[*ur* x x x x x x x x]
S A ^{m}*aš-šur*–PAB–AŠ MAN KU[R–*aš-šur* EN]-*ku-nu šá ina* UGU-*hi-šú*
_ [x x x x x x x x x x x x x x] ⌈*šá ina* UGU⌉-[x x]
G DUMU ^{m}*aš-šur*–PAB–AŠ MAN KUR–[*aš-šur* x x x] *šá ina* UGU-*hi-šu*
_ [x x x x x x x x x x EN-*k*]*u-nu* [x x x x x]
DUMU ^{m}[x x x x] ⌈MAN KUR–*aš*⌉-[*šur* x x x] *šá* [x x x x]
[x x x x x x x KUR]–*aš-šur* EN-*k*[*u-nu* x x x x x]
[DU]MU ^{m}*aš-šur*–PAB–AŠ M[AN x x x x x x *š*]*a ina* UGU-*hi-š*[*ú*]

175 A *a-de-e is-si-ku-nu iš-ku-nu-u-ni ib-bal-kàt-u-ni*
B *a-de-e is-si-ku-nu* [x x x x x x x x x x]x
M *a-*[*de-e* x x x x *i*]*š-kun-u-ni ib-bal-kàt-u-ni*
I *a-de-e is-si-ku-nu iš-*˹*ku*˺*-*[*nu-ni*] *ib-bal-kàt-u-ni*
P [x x x x x x x] ˹*iš*˺*-k*[*u-nu-ni* x x x x x]
S *a-de-e is-si-ku-nu* [x x x x *i*]*b-*˹*bal*˺*-kàt-u-ni*
_ [x x x x x x x *iš-ku*]*-nu-u-ni ib-bal-kàt-*[*u-ni*]
G [x x x x x x x x x x x] *ib-bal-kàt-u-n*[*i*]
_ [x x x *is-si*]*-ku-nu iš-ku-nu-ni* [x x x x x]
[*a-de*]*-e is-si-*[*ku-nu* x x x x x x x x x]
[x x x x x x x x x x x x *i*]*b-bal-k*[*àt-u-ni*]
176 A *at-tu-nu is-si-šú ta-šá-kan-a-ni*
B *at-tu-nu is-si-šú* [x x x x x]
M [x x x *is*]*-si-šu ta-šá-kan-a-ni*
I *at-tu-nu is-si-šú ta-š*[*á-kan-a-ni*]
S *at-tu-nu is-si-šú-nu* [x x x x x]
_ [x x x x x x x *ta-š*]*á-kan-a-ni*
[x x x *is-si*]*-šu ta-šá-kan-a-ni*
[x x x] *is-si-*[*šu* x x x x x]
177 A *šum-ma ki-i da-'a-ni iṣ-ṣab-tu-ku-nu*
B [x x x x *d*]*a-a-ni iṣ-ṣab-tu-ku-nu*
M [x x x x *d*]*a-'a-a-ni iṣ-ṣab-tu-ku-nu*
I *šum-ma ki-i da-a-ni iṣ-ṣab-tu-ku-*[*nu*]
_ [x x x x x x x x x x x*-n*]*u*
S [x x x x *da*]*-'a-a-ni* [x x x x x]
_ [x x x x x x x x *i*]*ṣ-ṣab-tu-ku-nu*
G *šum-ma ki-i d*[*a-'a-a-ni* x x x x x]
_ [*šum-m*]*a* ˹*ki-i da*˺*-*[*'a-a-ni* x x x x x]
178 A [x x x *l*]*a ta-hal-liq-a-ni ina* UGU ^{m}*aš-šur*–DÙ–A
B [x x x x *ta-hal-l*]*i?-qa-a-ni-ni ina* UGU ^{m}*aš-šur*–DÙ–A
M [x x x *l*]*a ta-hal-li-qa-a-ni-ni ina* ˹UGU˺ ^{m}*aš-šur*–DÙ–A
I *at-tu-nu la ta-hal-liq-a-ni-ni ina* UGU ^{m}*aš-šur*–[DÙ–A]
_ *at-tu-n*[*u* x x x x x x x x x x x x x x]
S [x x x] *la ta-hal-liq-a-ni* [x x x x x x x]
_ [x x x x x x x]*-a-ni-ni ina* UGU ^{m}*aš-šur*–D[Ù–A]
G *at-tu-nu l*[*a* x x x x x x x x x x x x x]
_ [x x x *l*]*a ta-hal-laq-a-*[x x x x x x x x x]
179 A [x x x x É–U]Š*-ti la tal-lak-a-ni-ni*
B [x x x x É–UŠ*-t*]*i la ta-lak-a-ni-ni*
M [x x x x] É–UŠ*-ti la ta-*˹*lak*˺*-a-ni-ni*
I DUMU–MAN GAL*-u šá* É–UŠ*-ti la tal-lak-a-*[*ni-ni*]
_ [DUM]U–MAN GAL *ša* É–[x x x x x x x x]
S [x x x x É–UŠ*-t*]*i la tal-lak-ni-ni*
_ [x x x x É–UŠ*-t*]*e la ta-lak-a-ni-*[*ni*]
[x x x *š*]*a* É–UŠ*-te l*[*a* x x x x x]

---

180 A [x x x x x x x x] *hu-ra-di*
I *šum-ma a*[*t-tu-nu* x x]*-e*! *hu-ra-di*
_ [*šum-m*]*a at-tú-nu lu in*[*a* x x *hu-ra-di*]

181 A [x x x x x x x x x] *ra!-qi ki-i* $MURUB_4$ KUR
I [x x x x x x] *lu in[a* x x *ra-q]i ki-i* $MURUB_4$ KUR
_ *[l]u ki-i qa-bal* KUR [x x x x x x x x x] *qa-bal* x[x]
182 A [x x x x x x x x] ⸢*pi*⸣*-ir-ri*
I *áš-*[x x x x] *lu-u ki-i ina pi-ir-ri*
_ *áš-ba-ka-[nu-ni] lu ki-i ina pi-ir-ri*
183 A [x x x x x x x x x SI]G_5*-tú*
I *te-rab-a-ni-ni a-bu-t[u* x x x]
_ *te-rab-a-n[i-ni] a-bu-tú la* DÙG.GA*-tú*
[x x x x x x x x x x*-t]ú*
184 I *šá* ^{m}*aš-šur*–DÙ–A DUMU–MAN GAL*-u šá* É–UŠ*-ti*
_ *šá* ^{m}*aš-šur*–DÙ–A [x x x] *šá* É–UŠ*-te*
[x x x x x x x x x x x x]*-ti*
185 F [x x x x x x x x x x] *ina* UGU*-hi-šú*
I *ina* ŠÀ*-b[i-ku-nu] ta-šá-kan-a-ni ina* UGU*-hi-šú*
_ *[ina* ŠÀ*-b]i-ku-nu ta-šá-kan-a-ni* [x x x x]
ina ŠÀ*-ku-nu ta-[šá-kan-a-ni] ina* UGU*-hi-šú*
[x x x x x x x x x x x U]GU*-hi-[šú]*
186 F *ta-bal-k[àt-a-ni* x x x x] *a-bu-tu*
I *ta-bal-k[àt-a-ni] ep-šu bar-tu a-bu-tu*
_ *[ta-ba]l-kàt-a-ni ep-šú bar-tú* [x x x]
ta-bal-kàt-a-ni [x x x x] *a-bu-tú*
187 F *l[a* x x x x x x x x x x]
I *la* DÙG.GA*-tu te-pa-*[x x x x x]
_ [x x x x *te]-pa-šá-ni-šu-[u-ni]*
la DÙG.GA*-tú te-pa-šá-niš-*[x x]

---

188 F ⸢*šum*⸣*-ma* ^{m}[x x x x x x x x x x x]
I *šum-ma* ^{m}*aš-šur*–DÙ–A DUMU–MAN GAL*-u* [x x x x]
_ [x x] ^{m}*aš-šur*–DÙ–A DUMU–MAN GAL *šá* É–[UŠ*-ti*]
[x x x x x x x] DUMU–MAN GAL *šá* É–[x x]
[šúm]-mu ^{m}*aš-šur*–DÙ–A DUMU–MAN GAL [x x x x]
189 I DUMU ^{m}*aš-šur*–PAB–AŠ MAN K[UR*–aš-šur* x x x x x x x x x x x x]
J DUMU ^{m}*aš-šur*–PAB–AŠ M[AN x x x x x x x x x x x x x x x]
_ [x x x x x x x x x x E]N-⸢*ku-nu*
ina UD⸣*-me šá* ^{m}*aš-šur*–PAB–[AŠ]
[x x x x x x x KUR]*–aš-šur* EN*-ku-nu*
ina UD*-me šá* ^{m}*aš-š[ur*–PAB–AŠ]
[x] ^{m}*aš-*⸢*šur*–PAB–AŠ⸣ MAN KUR*–aš-[šur* x x
x x x x x ^{m}*aš]-šur*–PAB–AŠ
190 J MAN KUR*–aš-šur* EN*-ku-nu* [x x x x x x x x]
_ [x x x x x x x x x x x x x x]*-ni*
[x x x x x x x] *a-na šim-ti il-lak-[u-ni]*
⸢MAN⸣ [x x x x x x x x x x x x x x]
Y [x x x x x x x x x x x x *i]l-lak-ú-ni*
191 J *šu-u la* LUGAL*-ka-nu-[ni* x x x x x x]
_ *š[u-*x x x x x x x x x x x x x]
[x x x x x]*-nu-ni la* EN*-k[a-nu-ni]*
Y [x x x x x x x x EN]*-ka-nu-u-ni*

192 J *dan-nu la ú-šap-pal-u-*[*ni* x x x x x x x x]
_ [x x x *ú-šap*]*-pa-lu-u-ni šap-*[*lu* x x x x x x]
[x x x *ú-ša*]*p-pal-u-*˹*ni šap*˺-[*lu* x x x x x x]
Y [x x x x x x x x] *šap-lu la i-ma-táh-u-ni*
193 J *šá du-a-ki la i-du-ku-u-ni š*[*a* x x x]
_ *šá du-a-ki la* [x x x x x x x x x]
[x x x x *l*]*a i-du-ku-*[*u-ni* x x x x]
Y [x x x x x x x x x x *ša*] *bal-lu-ṭí*
194 F [*la ú-bal*]*-laṭ-u-ni* [x x x x x x x]
J *la ú-bal-laṭ-u-ni am–mar i-qab-b*[*u-u-ni*]
_ [x] ˹*ú*˺*-ba-la-ṭ*[*a* x x x x x x x x]
[x *ú-bal*]*-laṭ-u-ni am–mar i-*[x x x x]
la ú-bal-[*laṭ-u-ni* x x *i-qab*]*-bu-u-ni*
[x x x x x x *am–ma*]*r i-qab-bu-u-ni*
195 F [x *ta*]*-šam-ma-a-ni* [x x x x x]
J *la ta-šam-ma-a-ni ki-i pi-i-šú*
_ [*l*]*a ta-šam-ma-a-ni* [x x x x x]
[x x x x x x x x] *pi-i-šú*
la t[*a-šam-ma-a-ni* x x x x x]
196 F [x *te-pa*]*-šá-a-ni* [x x x x x x]
J *la* ˹*te*˺-[*pa-šá-a-ni*] LUGAL MAN-*ma* EN MAN-*ma*
_ [x *te-p*]*a-a-šá-a-ni* [x x x x x x]
la te-p[*a-šá-a-ni* x x x x x x]
la te-ep-pa-[*šá-a-ni* x x x x x x]
Y [x] *te-pa-*˹*šá-a*˺*-ni* [x x x x x x]
197 F [x x x x *tu-b*]*a-'a-a-ni*
J *ina* UGU-*hi-šú tu-ba-*['*a-a-ni*]
_ [x] UGU-*hi-šú tu-ba-'a-a-ni*
[x UGU]-*hi-šú tu-b*[*a-'a-a-ni*]
ina UGU-*hi-š*[*ú* x x x x x]
Y [x x x x *t*]*u-ba-a-ni*

---

198 J *šum-ma me-me-ni ina* É.GAL *bar-tu lu ina k*[*al* x x]
_ [x x x x x x x x x x *l*]*u ina kal* UD-*me*
[x x x x x] *ina* É.GAL *bar-*[*tu* x x x x x]
[x x x x x x x x] ˹*bar-tú lu*˺ [x x x x]
Y [x x x x x x x x x x x *k*]*al* UD-*me*
199 J [*lu*]-˹*u*˺ *ina kal* M[I *l*]*u-u ina* KASKAL *lu ina qab-*[*si* x x x]
_ *lu ina kal* MI [x x x x x x x x x x]
[x x x x x x KAS]KAL *lu ina qab-si* KUR *a-n*[*a*?]
Y [x x x x x x x x x x x x *a-n*]*a*!
200 J [x x x x x MA]N KUR–*aš-šur e-ta-pa-áš a*[*t-tu-nu*]
_ [ᵐ*aš*]*-šur*–PAB–AŠ MAN KUR–*aš-šur e-tap-pa-*[*áš* x x x]
[x x x x x x x x x x x x x x *at-tu*]*-nu*
Y ᵐ*aš-šur*–PAB–AŠ [x x x x x x x x x x x]

201 C [x x x x x x x x x x x x x] ⸢*mu-ši*⸣
J [x x x x x *l*]*u-u ina kal* UD-*me lu-u ina kal m*[*u-ši*]
_ [x x x x x *l*]*u ina kal* UD-*me lu ina kal* M[I]
la taš-me-a-[*šú* x x x x x x x x x x]
Y [x] *taš-me-a-šú* [x x x x x x x x x x]
202 C [x x x x x x x x x x x x x É].GAL!
J [*ina la si*]-*me-ni-šú* LÚ.A–*šip-ri* TA* ŠÀ É.GAL
_ [x x x x x x] LÚ.A–*šip-ri* [x x x x]
[*ina l*]*a si-la-ma-n*[*i-šú* x x x x x] ŠÀ É.GAL
203 J [x x DUMU–LU]GAL *it-tal-ka ma-a* AD-*ka*
_ [x x DU]MU–MAN *it-tal-ka* [x x x x]
O ⸢*ina* UGU DUMU⸣–[MAN x x x x x x x]
_ *ina* U[GU x x x x x x x AD]-*ka*
204 C [*re*]-*eš-ka* [x x x x x x x x x]
J [x x x *i*]*t-ti-ši ma-a* EN *lil-li-ka*
_ [x x x *it*]-⸢*te-ši ma*⸣-*a* E[N x x x]
O [x x x] *i-ti-ši ma-a* E[N x x x]
_ *re-eš-k*[*a* x x x x x x *lil-l*]*i-k*[*a*]
205 C *at-tu-nu* [x x x x x x x x x]-⸢*ma*⸣-*šu*!
J [x x x x *ta-šam-m*]*e-a-šú la tu-ra-ma-šu*
_ *at-tú-nu la ta-*[*šam-me-a-šú* x x x x x]
[x x x x x x x x x x] *la tu-ra-ma-šú-nu*
206 C *la il-lak* [x x x x x x x x]
J [x x x *ma-ṣar-t*]*u-šú tu-da-a-na*
e [x x x x x x x *tu*]-⸢*da-a*⸣-*n*[*a*]
_ *la il-*[*lak* x x x x *t*]*u-da-a-na*
u [x x x x x]x-*tú-šú* [x x x x]
O *l*[*a* x x x x x x] *tu-da-a-na*
207 C ⸢*a*⸣-*di* 1-*en ina* ŠÀ-*bi-ku-nu* [x x x x x x x x-*n*]*i*
J *a-d*[*i* x x x] ⸢ŠÀ-*bi-ku*⸣-*nu ša* EN-*šu i-ra-a-mu-u-ni*
e [x x x x x x x x x x x x x] *i-ra-'a-mu-u-ni*
_ *a-di* 1-*e*[*n* x x x x x *š*]*a* EN-*šú i-ra-'a-mu-u-*[*ni*]
u [x x x x x x x x x x x] EN-*šú i-ra-a-mu-u-n*[*i*]
O *a-di* 1-*en* [x x x x x] *ša* EN-*šu i-ra-*⸢*'a-mu*⸣-[*u-ni*]
208 C *ina* UGU É–EN.MEŠ-*šú* [x x x x x]
J *ina* UGU É–EN.MEŠ-*šu mar-ṣa-šu-un-ni*
e [x x x x x x x x x x]-*ni*
_ [x x É–EN.MEŠ]-*šú mar-ṣa-áš-šú-un-ni*
u [x x x x x x] *mar-ṣa-šu-u-ni*
O [x x x x x x] *mar-ṣa-šú-u-ni*
209 C [x x]-*u-ni ina* É.GAL DI-*mu šá* LUGAL! [x x]
J *i-lak-u-ni ina* É.GAL DI-*mu šá* LUGAL EN-⸢*šu*?⸣
e *il-lak-u-ni ina* É.GAL [x x x x x x]
_ [*il*]-*lak-u-ni* DI-*mu ša* LUGAL EN-*šú*
u *il-lak-u-ni* [x x x x x x x] EN-*šú*
O *i*[*l-lak-u-ni* x x x] 0 [x x] EN-*šu*

210 C [x x x x x x x x T]A* DUMU–MAN
J *e-mar-u-ni ha-ra-me-ma* TA* DU[MU–MAN]
e *[e-mar]-u-ni ha-ra-ma-a-ma* [x x x]
_ *e-mar-u-ni ha-ra-me-ma* TA* DUMU–MAN
[x x x x x x x x T]A DUMU–MAN
u *e-mar-u-ni ha-ra-me-[ma* x x x]
O *e-rab-u-[ni* x x x x x x x]
211 C EN-*ku-nu* [x x x *t]al-la-ka*
B [x x x x x x] *tal-la-ka*
J EN-*ku-nu ina* É.GAL *tal-la-⸢ka⸣*
e [x x x x x x] *tal-la-⸢ka⸣*
_ EN-*ku-n[u* x] É.GAL *tal-la-ka*
E[N?-x x x x x] *tal-la-k[a]*
u [x x x] *ina* É.GAL *tal-l[a-ka]*
O [x x x] *ina* É.GAL [x x x]
_ ⸢EN-*ku-nu ina* É.GAL⸣ *[tal-la]-ka*

---

212 C [x x x x x x *ta-šá-ka]n-a-ni a-he-iš*
J *šum-ma at-tu-nu* UKKIN *ta-šá-kan-a-ni a-he-iš*
e [x x x x x x x x x x x *a-he]-iš*
_ *[šú]m-mu at-tú-nu ⸢pu⸣-uh-ru ta-šá-kan-a-n[i a-h]a-meš*
u *šum-ma at-t[u-n]u* UKKIN *ta-šá-kan-[a-ni* x x x]
O *šum-ma at-tu-nu* UKKIN *ta-[šá-kan-a-ni* x x x]
_ [x x x x x x *ta-šá-kan]-a-ni a-na a-he-iš*
213 C *tu-tam-ma-a-ni* [x x x x x x x x x LUGA]L-*tu ta-da-na-a-ni*
J *tu-tam-ma-a-ni a-na* 1-*en ina* ŠÀ-*bi-ku-nu* LUGAL-*u-tu ta-dan-a-ni*
e *tu-tam-ma-a-ni* [x x x x x x x x x x x] *ta-dan-a-ni*
_ *tú-ta-[ma]-ni a-na* 1-*en ina* ŠÀ-*ku-nu* [LUGAL]-*tú ta-⸢dan⸣-na-a-ni*
tu-tam-ma-a-ni [x x x x x x x x x x x *t]a-dan-a-ni*
u [x x x x x] *a-na* 1-*en ina* ŠÀ-*bi-ku-nu* LUGAL-*tú* [x x x x]
O [x x x x x] *a-na* 1-*en ina* ŠÀ-*k[u-nu* x x x x x x]
_ *tu-tam-ma-a-ni* [x x x x x x x x x x x *t]a-da-na-a-ni*

---

214 C [x x x x x x x x x x x] ŠEŠ–AD.MEŠ-*šú*
J *šum-ma at-tu-nu* TA* ŠÀ-*bi* ŠEŠ.MEŠ-*šú* ŠEŠ.MEŠ–AD.MEŠ-*šú*
e [x x x x x x x x ŠE]Š.MEŠ-*šú* ŠEŠ.MEŠ–AD.MEŠ-*šú*
_ [x x x x x x x x x x x ŠE]Š–AD.MEŠ-*šú*
u *šum-ma at-⸢tu⸣-nu* TA* ŠÀ-*bi* ŠEŠ.MEŠ-*šú* ŠEŠ-[x x x x]
O *šum-ma at-tu-nu* T[A* x x x x x x x x x x]
_ [x x x x x x x x x x x] Š[EŠ–A]D.MEŠ-*šú*
215 C DUMU–ŠEŠ–AD.MEŠ-*⸢šú⸣* [x x x x x x x]
J DUMU–ŠEŠ.MEŠ–AD.MEŠ-*šú qin-ni-šu* NUMUN É–AD-*šú*
e [x x x x x x x x x NU]MUN É–AD-*šú*
u [x x x x x x *q]in-ni-šú* NUMUN É–AD-*šú*
O DUMU–ŠEŠ–⸢AD.MEŠ⸣-[*šú* x x x x x x x]
_ [x x x x x x x x x] NUMUN É–AD-*šú*

216 C [x x x KUR–*aš-šu*]*r šu-nu-ni lu šá ina* KUR *šá-nim*!*-tim-ma*
J *lu-u šá ina* KUR–*aš-šur šu-nu-u-ni lu šá ina* KUR *šá-ni-tim-ma*
e [x x x x x x x x x x x x] *ina* KUR *šá-ni-tim-ma*
u *lu-u* [x x x x x x x x x x x] KUR *šá-ni-tim-ma*
O *lu šá ina* KUR–[*aš-š*]*ur* [x x x x x x x x x x x x]
_ [x x x x x x x x x x x x x x] KUR MAN-*tim-ma*
217 C [x x x x x x x x x x] ⸢É⸣.GAL *qur-bu-ti*
J *in-nab-tu-u-ni lu-u ina kal-zi* É.GAL *qur-bu-ti*
_ [x x x x x x x x *ka*]*l-zi qur-bu-ti*
e [x x x x x x x x x x] É.GAL *qur-bu-ti*
u *in-na*[*b-tu-u-ni* x x x x x x x x x x]
O [x x x x x] *lu-u* [x x x x x x x x]
_ *in-nab-tu-u-ni* [x x x x x x x *qur*]*-bu-u-t*[*i*]
218 C [x x x x x x x *pa-ti-u-t*]*i lu ina kal-za-a-ni*
H *lu-u ina kal-zi* É.GAL *pa-ti-ú-ti* ⸢*lu-u ina*⸣ *kal-za-a-ni*
J *lu-u ina kal-zi* É.GAL *pa-ti-u-te lu ina kal-za-ni*
e [x x x x x x x x x x x x] *ina kal-za-a-ni*
u [x x x *kal*]-⸢*zi* É⸣.[GAL x x x x x x x x x x]
O [x x x x x x x x x x x] *lu-u* [x x x x x]
_ [x x x x x x x x x x]-*ti* [x x x x x x x x]
219 C GAL.MEŠ TUR.MEŠ [x x x x x x]
H GAL.MEŠ TUR.MEŠ *lu ina* GA[L.MEŠ TU]R.MEŠ
J GAL.MEŠ TUR.MEŠ *lu-u ina* GAL.MEŠ TUR.MEŠ-*te*
_ GAL.MEŠ TUR.MEŠ [x x x x x x]
e GAL.MEŠ TUR.MEŠ [x x x x x x]
220 C [x x x x x].MEŠ *lu ina* DUMU *muš-ke-nu-ti*
H [x x x D]UMU–SIG$_5$.MEŠ *lu-u ina* DUMU *muš-ke-n*[*u-t*]*i*
J *lu-u ina* DUMU–SIG$_5$.MEŠ *lu-u ina* DUMU *muš-ke-nu-ti*
_ [x x x x x x x x x DU]MU *muš-ke-nu-te*
e [x x x x x x x x x] DUMU *muš-ke-nu-te*
f [x x x x x x x x x DUMU *muš-k*]*e-n*[*u-ti*]
221 C [x x x x x x x x x x x x x L]Ú.ARAD.MEŠ
H [x x LÚ.*šá–ziq*]-*ni* LÚ.SAG *lu-u ina* ARAD.MEŠ
J *lu šá*–LÚ.*ziq-ni lu* LÚ.SAG *lu-u ina* LÚ.ARAD.MEŠ
_ [x x x x x x x x x x x x L]Ú.ARAD.MEŠ
e [x x x x x x x LÚ].SAG [x x x x x x]
f [x x x x x x x LÚ.SA]G *lu ina* [x x x]
222 C *lu ina* LÚ.ŠÁM.MEŠ [x x x x x x x x x x]
H [x x x x x] *lu-u ina* DUMU KUR–*aš-š*[*ur* x] *ina* DUMU–KUR!
J *lu-u ina* LÚ.ŠÁM.MEŠ *lu ina* DUMU KUR–*aš-šur lu ina* DUMU–KUR
_ [x x x x x x x x x x x x x x x K]UR
e [x x x x x x x x x KUR–*aš-š*]*ur*.KI [x x x x]
f [x x x x x x x x x x x x x] *lu*! (*text ib*) DUMU–KUR.KUR?
223 C *šá-ni-tim-ma* [x x x x x x x x x *ma*]*l ba-šu-ú*
H [x x x x x x x] ⸢*nap*⸣-[*har* x x x x] ⸢*mal ba*⸣-*šu-u*
J ⸢*šá-ni-tim*⸣-*ma lu-u ina nap-har ṣal-mat*–SAG.DU *mal b*[*a-šu-u*]
_ *šá-ni-tim-ma* [x x x x x x x x x x x x]x-*u*
f [x x x x x x x x x] *ṣal-mat*–SAG.DU *ma*[*l ba-šu*]-*u*

224 C [x x x x x x x x x x KUR–aš-šu]r? ˹tu˺-šá-aṣ-bat-a-ni
H 1-e[n ina ŠÀ-bi]-ku-nu [x x x] tu-[šá-a]ṣ-bat-a-ni
J 1-en ina ŠÀ-bi-˹ku-nu ina GIŠ.GU˺.ZA tu-šá-aṣ-bat-a-[ni]
x [x x x x x x x x GIŠ.G]U.ZA ˹šá˺ [x x x x x x x x x]
f [x x x ŠÀ-bi-ku-n]u! GIŠ.GU.ZA KUR–aš-šur tú-šá-aṣ-bat-a-ni @Ā
225 C [x x x x x x x x x x ta-d]a-na-niš-šu-un-ni
H LUGAL-ú-tú EN-ú-[tú] šá KUR–aš-š[ur t]a-da-na-niš-šú-ni
J LUGAL-u-tu EN-[u-tu x KUR–aš-š]ur ta-da-n[a-x x x]
x [x x x x x x x KUR]–aš-šur ta-da-[x x x x]
f [x x x x x x x] KUR–aš-šur ta-da-(na)-ni-šú-nu
226 C [x x x x x x x x x x x x x] É–UŠ-ti
H šum-ma ^{m}aš-šur–DÙ–A DUMU–MAN GA[L x É–U]Š-te
J šum-ma ^{m}aš-šur–DÙ–[A x x GAL]-u šá É–U[Š-ti]
x [x x x x x x x x x x x x x] É–UŠ-te
f [šúm-m]u ˹^{m}aš˺-š[ur–DÙ–A D]UMU–MAN GAL ša É–UŠ-ti
227 C [x x x x x x x x tu-šá-aṣ]-bat-a-ni
H GIŠ.GU.ZA šá KUR–aš-šur la tu-[šá-aṣ]-bat-˹a˺-ni
J GIŠ.GU.ZA šá KUR–aš-šu[r x t]u-šá-aṣ-bat-˹a˺-[ni]
x GIŠ.GU.ZA šá KUR–aš-[šur x x x x x x x]
f GIŠ.GU.ZA šá KUR–aš-šur.˹KI˺ la tú-šá-aṣ-bat-a-ni
228 C [x x x x x x x x UGU-hi-ku]-˹nu˺ la up-pa-áš-u-n[i]
J LUGAL-u-tu EN-u-t[u ina UGU-hi-k]u-nu la ˹up˺-[pa-áš-u-ni]
x [LUG]AL-tú EN-tú šá KUR–aš-šur ina UGU-hi-ku-˹nu la˺ [x x x x x]
f LUGAL-tú EN-tú šá KUR–aš-šur ina UGU-hi-ku-nu la ú-pa-áš-ú-ni
_ [x x EN]-tú [x x x x x x x x x x x x x]-šú-ni

---

229 C [x x x x x x x x x x x x x] DUMU–MAN GAL šá É–UŠ-[ti]
J šum-ma at-tu-n[u x x ^{m}aš-šur–DÙ]–A DUMU–MAN [x] šá É–UŠ-te
x [šu]m-ma at-tu-nu ina UGU ^{m}aš-šur–DÙ–A DUMU–MAN GAL šá ˹É˺–U[Š-te]
f šúm-mu at-tú-nu ina UGU ^{m}aš-šur–DÙ–A DUMU–MAN GAL šá É–UŠ-te
_ [x x x x x x x x x x x x x x x x] šá É–UŠ-te
šum-ma at-tu-nu 0! UGU ^{m}aš-šur–DÙ–A DUMU–MAN GAL [x x x x]
230 A [DU]MU ^{m}aš-šur–PAB–AŠ MAN KUR–aš-šur EN-ku-(nu) la ta-ma-haṣ-a-ni
N [x x x x x x x x x x EN]-ku-nu [x x x x x x]
C [x x x x x x x x x x x x x x] la ta-ma-haṣ-a-ni
J D[UMU x x x x x x x x x] ˹EN-ku-nu˺ la ta-ma-haṣ-a-ni
x DUMU ^{m}aš-šur–PAB–AŠ MAN KUR–aš-šur EN-ku-nu la ta-ma-haṣ-a-[ni]
f DUMU ^{m}aš-šur–PAB–AŠ MAN KUR–aš-šur EN-ku-nu la ta-ma-haṣ-a-ni
c [x x x x x x x x x x x x x x x ta-ma-haṣ]-a-ni
_ [x x x x x x x x x x x x x x x ta-ma-haṣ-a-n]i
DUMU ^{m}aš-šur–PAB–˹K˺AŠ MAN KUR–aš-šur EN-ku-nu la ta-ma[h!-haṣ-a-ni]

231 A *[l]a ta-mut-ta-a-ni šá ina* UGU-*hi-šú ṭa-bu-u-ni*
N [x *t]a-mut-ta-a-ni* [x x x x x *ṭa-b]u-u-ni*
C [x x x x x x x x UGU-*hi-š]u ṭa-bu-u-ni*
J *la ta-˹mu˺-ta-a-n[i] ˹šá˺ ina* UGU-*hi-šú ṭa-bu-u-ni*
x *la ta-mut-ta-a-ni šá ina* UGU-*hi-šú ṭa-bu-u-ni*
f *la ta-mut-ta-a-ni šá ina* UGU-*hi-šú* DÙG.GA-*u-ni*
c [x *ta-mut-ta]-˹a˺-ni* [x x x x x x x x x]
_ [x x x x x x x x x x x x x x x]-*ni*
˹la˺ ta-[m]u-ta-a-[ni x x] UGU-*hi-šú ṭa-˹bu-u˺-ni*

232 A *(la) tu-ba-ʾa-a-ni (la) te-ep-pa-áš-a-ni*
N *la t[u-b]a-a-ni la te-pa-áš-a-ni*
C [x x x x x x x x x x]-*˹a-ni˺*
J *la tu-ba-a-ni la te-pa-šá-˹ni˺*
x *la tu-ba-ʾa-a-ni la te-ep-pa-šá-a-ni*
f [x *t]ú-ba-ʾa-a-ni la te-pa-šá-a-ni*
_ [x x x x x x x x x x x]-*ni*
la ˹tu˺-ba-ʾa-a-ni ˹la!˺ [x x x x x]

233 A *šum-ma la* DÙG.GA-*tú te-ep-pa-šá-ni-šú-u-ni*
N [x x x DÙG.G]A-*tu te-pa-šá-niš-šu-un-ni*
C *šum-ma la* DÙG.GA-*tu* [x x x x x x x x]
J *[šum-m]a la* DÙG.GA-*tu te-pa-šá-ni-šu-un-ni*
x *šum-ma la* DÙG.GA-*tú te-ep-pa-šá-niš-šú-un-ni*
f [x x] ˹ *la* DÙG.GA˺-*tú te-pa-šá-a-ni-niš-šu-un-ni*
_ [x x x x x x x x x x x x x x]-*ni [š]um-ma ˹la˺* DÙG.GA-*tu te-p[a*-x x x x x]

234 A *mil-ku la* SIG$_5$ *la ta-ma-lik-a-šú-u-ni*
N [x x x] SIG$_5$ *ta-ma-lik-a-šú-u-ni*
C [x x x x] *ta-ma-lik-a-šú-u-ni*
J [x x *l]a* SIG$_5$ *ta-mal-lik-a-šú-u-ni*
x *mil-ku l[a* S]IG$_5$ *ta-mal-lik-a-š[ú-u-ni]*
f [x x x SI]G$_5$ *ta-mal-li-ka-šú-u-n[i]*
_ [x x] *l[a] dam-qu ta-mal-[lik-a-šú-u-ni]*

235 A KASKAL *la šal-mu ina* GÌR.2-*šú ta-šá-kan-a-ni*
N [x x *šal*]-*mu ina* G[ÌR.2]-*šú ta-šá-kan-a-ni*
J KASKAL *la šal-mu* [x x x x]x *ta-šá-kan-a-ni*
x KASKAL *la šal-mu ina* GÌR.2-*šú ta-šá-kan-a-[ni]*
f [x x x x x] GÌR.2-*šú ta-šá-kan-a-[ni]*
_ [x x]x *šal-mu ana* ˹GÌR!˺.2!-*šú ta-[šá-kan-a-ni]*

236 A *ina ke-na-a-te tar-ṣa-a-ti la ta-(ta)-nab-bal-šú-u-ni*
N [x *ke]-na-a-te la ta-ta-nab-bal-˹a˺-šú-u-ni*
C *ina ke-na-a-ti* [x x x x x x x x x x]-*u-ni*
J *ina ke-na-a-te* [x x x x *l]a? ta-ta-na-bal-a-šú-u-ni*
x *ina ke-na-a-te tar-ṣa-a-te la ta-ta-nab-bal-a-[šú-u-ni]*
f [x x x x x *tar-ṣa-a-t]i la t[a-ta-n]a-˹bal˺-[a-šú-u-ni]*
_ [x *ke-n]a-a-˹ti˺ [ta]r-ṣa-[a]-ti!* [x x x x x x x x x]

237 A [x x ^{m}*aš-šur*–PAB–A]Š MAN KUR–*aš-šur ina ṣa-ha-ri šá* DUMU.MEŠ-*šú*
N [x x x x x x x x x x x x EN]-*ku-nu ina ṣa-ha-ri šá* DUMU.MEŠ-*šú*
C [x x x x x x x x x x x x x x x x *ṣa-ha-r*]*i šá* DUMU.MEŠ-*šu*
B [x x x x x x x x x x x x x x x] *ina ṣa-ha-r*[*i* x x x x]
J [x x ^{m}*aš-šur*–PAB]–AŠ MAN KUR–*aš-šur ina ṣa-ha-ri šá* DUMU.MEŠ-*šú*
x *šum-ma* ^{m}*aš-šur*–PAB–AŠ MAN KUR–*aš-šur* EN-*ku-nu ina ṣa-ha-*[*ri*] *šá* DU[MU.MEŠ-*šú*]
238 A [x x x x] *it-ta- lak lu šá–ziq-ni* [*lu* LÚ.SAG]
N [x x x x *it-ta*]-*lak lu* LÚ.SAG *lu* LÚ.*šá–ziq-ni*
C [x x x x x x x x x x x] *lu šá–ziq-ni*
B [x x x x x x x x] *lu* ⸢LÚ⸣.S[AG? x x x x x]
J [x x x x] *it-ta-lak lu šá*–LÚ.*ziq-ni* [*lu* LÚ.SAG]
x *a-na šim-te it-ta-lak lu* LÚ.SAG [*lu* LÚ.*šá–ziq-ni*]
239 A *a-na* ^{m}*aš-šur*–DÙ–A DUMU–MAN GAL
B [x x x x x x x x] DUMU–M[AN x]
J [*a-n*]*a* ^{m}*aš-šur*–DÙ–A DUMU–MAN GAL-*u*
x *a-na* ^{m}*aš-šur*–DÙ–A DUMU–MAN GAL
_ [x x x x x x x DUMU–MA]N GAL
240 A [x x x x] *i-du-ak*
N [x] É–UŠ-*ti i*-[*du-ak*]
C [x x x x] ⸢*i*⸣-*du-ak*
J *šá* É–UŠ-*te* [x x x]
x *šá* É–UŠ-*te* ⸢*i*⸣-[*du-ak*]
_ ⸢*šá*⸣ [x x x x x x] [x É–UŠ]-⸢*te i-du-ak*⸣
241 A [x x x] KUR–*aš-šur*.KI *it-ti-ši*
J [LUG]AL-*u-tu šá* KUR–*aš-šur it-ti-ši*
x LUGAL-*tú šá* KUR–*aš-šur it-ti-ši*
_ [LU]GAL-*tú šá* KUR–*aš-šu*[*r* x x x]
[x x x x x x *i*]*t-ti-ši*
242 A [*š*]*um-ma at-tu-nu is-si-šú ta-šá-kan-a-ni*
C [x x *at-tu-n*]*u is-si-šu* [x x x x x]
J [x x x x x] *is-si-šú ta-šá-kan-a-ni*
x *šum-ma at-tú-nu* [x x x *ta*]-*šá-kan-a-ni*
_ [x x x x x *is*]-⸢*si-šú ta-šá*⸣-*kan-a-n*[*i*]
[x x x x x x x x *t*]*a-šá-kan-a-n*[*i*]
[x x x x x x x x *ta-šá*]-*kan-a-ni*
243 A *a-na* LÚ.ARAD-*nu-ti-šú ta-tu-ra-a-ni*
C [x x x x x x x *ta-tu-u*]*r*!-*a-ni*
J [x x x x x x x *ta-tu-r*]*a-a-ni*
x *a-na* LÚ.ARAD.MEŠ-*šú ta-tu*-[*ra-a-ni*]
_ [x x x x x x x *t*]*a-tú-ra-a-ni*
[x x x x x x x *ta-tu-ra*]-*a-ni*
244 A *la ta-bal-kàt-a-ni la ta-na-ki-ir-ra-ni*
C [x x x x x x x x x x x x x]-*ni*
_ *la ta*-[*ba*]*l*-⸢*kàt-a-ni*⸣ *la ta-na-ki-ra-ni*
x [x *ta-ba*]*l-kàt-a-ni la ta-na-kir*-[*a-ni*]
_ [x *ta bal-kàt-a*]-*ni la ta-na-kír-a-ni*
la ta-bal-[*kàt-a-ni* x x x x x x]

245 A KUR.KUR *šá-ni-a-ti is-si-šú la tu-šam-kar-a-ni*
_ KUR.KUR *gab-*⸢*bu*⸣ *is-si-šú la* ⸢*tu-šam*⸣*-kar-a-ni*
si-hu ina [U]GU-*hi-šú la ta-*[*šá-kan*]-⸢*a*⸣-*ni*
x [x x x x *i*]*s-si-šú la tu-šam-kar-*[*a-ni*]
[x x x UGU-*hi*]-*šú la ta-šá-kan-a-ni*
_ [x x x x *is-s*]*i-šú la tu-šam-kar-a-ni*
[x x x UGU-*hi*]-*šú la ta-šá-kan-a-ni*
[KU]R.KUR.MEŠ *ga*[*b-bu* x x x x x x x x x]
si-hu ina UG[U-*hi-šú* x x x x x x]
[x x x x x x x x x x x x x x x x x x]
⸢*ina* UGU⸣-[*hi-šú* x x x x x x]
246 A *la ta-ṣab-bat-a-ni-šú-u-ni la ta-du-ka-šú-u-ni*
_ *la ta-ṣab-bat-a-šú-u-ni l*[*a ta-du-k*]*a-šú-u-ni*
x *la ta-ṣab-*[x x x x x x x x x x x]-*ni*
_ [x x x x x x]-*u-ni la ta-du-ka-šú-u-*⸢*ni*⸣
[*l*]*a ta-ṣab-bat-*[x x x x x x x x x x x]
[x x x x x x x x x] *ta-du-k*[*a-šú-u-ni*]
247 A *ù* DUMU ^{m}*aš-šur*–DÙ–A DUMU–MAN GAL *šá* É–UŠ-*ti*
_ [x x] ^{m}*aš-šur*–DÙ–A DUMU–MAN GAL-*u ša* [x x x]
x ⸢*ù*⸣ DUMU ^{m}*aš-šur*–DÙ–A [x x x x x x x]
_ [x x ^{m}*aš-š*]*ur*–DÙ–A DUMU–MAN GAL *šá* É–UŠ-*t*[*i*]
ù DUMU ^{m}*aš-š*[*ur*–DÙ–A x x x x x x x]
248 A GIŠ.GU.ZA *šá* KUR–*aš-šur*.KI *la tu-šá-aṣ-bat-u-ni*
_ GIŠ.GU.ZA *ša* KUR–*aš-šur*.KI *la* [x x x x x x]
x [x x x x x x x x *l*]*a tu-šá-a*[*ṣ-bat-a-ni*]
_ [x x x] *šá* KUR–*aš-šur*.KI *la tu-šá-aṣ-bat-*[*a-ni*]
[G]IŠ.GU.ZA *šá* K[UR–*aš-šur*.KI x x x x x x x]
[G]IŠ.GU.ZA *šá* KUR–*aš-*[*šur*.KI x x x x x x x]

---

249 A *šum-ma at-tu-nu ina* IGI MÍ.*a-ri-ti*
B *šum-ma at-*[*tu-nu* x x x x x x]
I [*šum*]-*ma at-tu-nu ina* IGI MÍ.⸢PEŠ$_4$⸣
_ *šum-ma at-tu-nu ina* IGI MÍ.*a-r*[*i-ti*]
[x x x x x x x] MÍ.PEŠ$_4$
[*šu*]*m-ma at-tu-nu i*[*na* x x x x x]
250 A *šá* ^{m}*aš-šur*–PAB–AŠ MAN KUR–*aš-šur* DAM ^{m}*aš-šur*–DÙ–A DUMU–MAN GAL
B [x x x x x x x x x x x] *ù* DAM ^{m}*aš-šur*–DÙ–A DUMU–MAN GAL
I *šá* ^{m}*aš-šur*–PAB–AŠ MAN KUR–*aš-šur*.KI *ù* DAM ^{m}*aš-šur*–DÙ–A DUMU–MAN GAL-*u*
_ [x x x x x x x x x x x x x] MÍ.DAM ^{m}*aš-šur*–DÙ–A DUMU–MA[N x]
šá ^{m}*aš-šur*–PAB–AŠ [x x x x x x x x x x x x x D]UMU–MAN GAL
[x x x x x x x x x x x x] *ù* [x] ^{m}*aš-šur*–DÙ–[A x x x]
251 A *šá* É–UŠ-*ti la ta-da-gal-a-ni*
B *šá* É–UŠ-*ti la ta-da-gal-a-ni*
I *šá* EŠ–(UŠ)-*ti la ta-da-gal-a-ni*
_ [x x x x *l*]*a* ⸢*ta-da*⸣-*gal-a-*[*ni*] *šá* É–[UŠ-x x x x x x x]
[x x x x x] *ta-da-gal-a-*[*ni*]

252 A *ki-ma it-tab-ši la tu-rab-ba-a-ni*
B *ki-ma it-tab-ši la tu-rab-ba-a-ni*
I *ki-ma it-tab-ši la tu-ra-ba-a-ni*
253 A GIŠ.GU.ZA *šá* KUR–*aš-šur*.KI *la tu-šá-aṣ-bat-a-ni*
B GIŠ.GU.ZA *šá* KUR–*aš-šur*.KI *la tu-šá-aṣ-bat-a-ni*
I GIŠ.GU.ZA *šá* KUR–*aš-šur*.KI *la tu-šá-aṣ-bat-a-ni*
_ [GIŠ.GU.Z]A *šá* KUR–*aš-š*[*ur*.KI x x x x x x x]
254 A *e-pi-šá-nu-ti šá bar-ti la ta-ṣab-bat-a-ni*
e-piš-a-nu-ti šá bar-ti la ta-ṣa-bat-a-ni-ni
I *e-pi-šá-nu-ti šá bar-ti la ta-ṣab-bat-a-ni-ni*
255 A *la ta-du-ka-a-ni* MU-*šú-nu* NUMUN-*šú-nu*
B [*l*]*a ta-du-ka-a-ni* MU-*šú-nu* ⸢NUMUN⸣-*šú-nu*
M *la ta-du-k*[*a-a-ni* x x x x x x]
I *la ta-du-ka-a-ni* MU-*šú-nu* NUMUN-*šú-nu*
256 A *ina* KUR *la tu-hal-laq-qa-a-ni da-me ku-um da-me*
B *ina* KUR [*l*]*a tu-hal-laq-qa-a-ni da-a-me ku-um da-a-me*
i [x x x x x x x x x] *da-me ku-um da-me*
M [x x] *la* [*t*]*u*-[*ha*]*l*-⸢*la-qa*⸣-*a*-[*ni* x x x x x x]
I *ina* KUR *la tu-hal-la-qa-a-ni da-me ku-um da-me*
257 A *la ta-ta-ba-ka-a-ni gi-im-lu*
B [*l*]*a ta-ta-ba-ka-a-ni gi-im-li*
i *la ta-ta-ba-ka-a-ni gi-im-lu*
M *la* [*ta-ta-ba*]-*ka*-[*a-ni* x x x]
I *la ta-ta-bak-a-ni* ⸢*gi-im*⸣-*lu*
258 A [x ^{m}*aš-š*]*ur*–DÙ–A DUMU–MAN GAL *šá* É–UŠ-*ti*
B ⸢*šá*⸣ ^{m}*aš-šur*–DÙ–A DUMU–MAN GAL *šá* É–U[Š-*t*]*i*
i *šá* ^{m}*aš-šur*–DÙ–A DUMU–MAN GAL-*u šá* É–UŠ-*te*
I *šá* ^{m}*aš-šur*–DÙ–A [DUM]U–MAN GAL *šá* É–UŠ-*ti*
259 A *la t*[*u-tar-r*]*a-a-ni-ni šum-ma at-tu-nu*
B *la tu-tar-*⸢*ra*⸣*-a-ni-ni šum-ma at-tu-nu*
i *la tu-tar-ra-a-ni-ni šum-ma at-tu-nu*
M *l*[*a tu-tar-r*]*a-a-ni-ni* [x x x x x]
I [x *tu-tar-r*]*a*-⸢*a-ni-ni*⸣ [*šum*]-*ma at-tu-nu*
260 A *a-na* ^{m}*aš-šur*–D[Ù–A DUMU]–MAN GA[L] *šá* É–UŠ-*ti*
B *a-n*[*a* x x x x x DU]MU–MAN ⸢GAL⸣ [x É]–UŠ-*ti*
i *a-na* ^{m}*aš-šur*–DÙ–A DUMU–MAN GAL-*u šá* É–UŠ-*te*
I *a-na* ^{m}*aš-šur*–DÙ–A [x x x x x x x]
p [x x x x x x x x x x x] É–UŠ-*ti*
_ [x x x x x x x DUMU]–MAN GAL *šá* É–UŠ-[x]
261 A DUMU ^{m}*aš-šur*–PAB–AŠ [x x x x EN-*k*]*u-nu*
B DUMU ^{m}*aš-šur*–PAB–AŠ MAN KU[R–*aš-šur*] EN-*ku-nu*
i DUMU ^{m}*aš-šur*–PAB–AŠ MAN KUR–*aš-šur* EN-*ku-nu*
I [DUM]U ^{m}*aš-šur*–PAB–AŠ MAN KUR–*aš-šur* [x x x]
p [x x x x x x x x x x EN-*ku-n*]*u*

262 A *šam-mu šá m[u-a-ti-šú tu-šá-kal-a-šú-u]-ni*
B *šam-mu šá mu-a-ti-šú tu-šá-kal-a-šú-u-ni*
i *šam-mu ša mu-a-ti-šú tu-šá-kal-a-šu-u-ni*
I [x x x x x x x *tu*]*-šá-kal-a-šú-u-ni*
p *šam-mu* [x x x x x *tu-šá-kal-a-šú*]-⸢*u*⸣*-ni*
_ *šam-mu šá mu-a-ti-šú* [x x x x x x x]
263 A *ta-šá-qi-a-šú-u-ni ta-pa-*[x x x x x]
B *ta-šá-qi-a-šú-u-ni* ⸢*ta*⸣*-pa-šá-šá-*⸢*a*⸣*-šú-u-ni*
i *ta-šá-qi-a-šú-u-ni ta-pa-šá-šá-šu-u-ni*
I [x x x x x x x *ta-pa*]*-šá-áš-a-šú-ni*
p [x x x x x x x x x x x x x*-š*]*ú-ni*
_ *ta-šá-qi-a-šú-u-ni* [x x x x x x x]
264 A *kiš-pi t*[*e-e*]*p-pa-šá-ni-šú-u-ni* [x x x x x x]
F *kiš-pi te-ep-pa-šá-niš-un-ni* DINGIR.MEŠ *u* ^{d}15
B *kiš-pi* [*t*]*e-ep-pa-šá-niš-šú-u-ni* DINGIR.MEŠ ⸢*u*⸣ ^{d}IŠ.TAR
i *kiš-pi te-pa-šá-ni-šu-un-ni* DINGIR.MEŠ *u* ^{d}IŠ.TAR
p [x x x x x x x x]*-ni* [x x x x x x]
_ *kiš-pi te-pa-šá-niš-šú-ni* DINGIR *u* [x x x]
265 A *is-si-šú* [*tu*]*-šá-za-n*[*a-a-ni*]
F *is-si-šú tu-šá-za-na-a-ni*
B *is-si-šú tu-šá-za-a-na-*⸢*a*⸣*-ni*
i *is-si-šú tu-šá-za-na-a-ni*
M *is-si-šu t*[*u-šá-za-na-a-ni*]
I [x x x]x *tu-šá-az-na-a-ni*
p [x x x *tu-šá-za-na*]-⸢*a*⸣*-ni*

---

266 A *šum-ma at-t*[*u-nu*] *a-na* ^{m}*aš-šur*–DÙ–A DUMU–MAN GAL *šá* É–UŠ*-ti*
F *šum-ma at-tu-nu a-na* ^{m}*aš-šur*–DÙ–A DUMU–MAN GAL [x x x x]
B *šum-ma at-t*[*u-n*]*u a-*(*na*) ^{m}*aš-šur*–DÙ–A DUMU–MAN [G]AL *šá* É–UŠ*-ti*
i *šum-ma at-tu-nu a-na* ^{m}*aš-šur*–DÙ–A DUMU–MAN GAL*-u šá* É–UŠ*-te*
M *š*[*um-m*]*a* [x x x x x x x x x x x x x x x x x x x]
I [x x x x x x x x x x x x x x x x x É]–UŠ-[x]
p [x x x x x x x x x x x x x x x GAL]*-u* [x x x x]
_ *šum-ma* [*at-t*]*u-nu a-na* ^{m}[x x x x x x x x x x x x]
[x x x x x x x x x x x x x] DUMU–MAN GAL*-u šá* É–UŠ*-te*
267 A DUMU ^{m}*aš-šur*–PAB–AŠ [M]AN KUR–*aš-šur* EN*-ku-nu*
F DUMU ^{m}*aš-šur*–PAB–AŠ MAN KUR–*aš-šur* [x x x]
B DUMU ^{m}*aš-šur*–PAB–AŠ ⸢MAN⸣ KUR–*aš-šur* EN*-ku-nu*
i DUMU ^{m}*aš-šur*–PAB–AŠ MAN KUR–*aš-šur* EN*-ku-nu*
M DUMU [^{m}]*aš-š*[*ur*–PAB–AŠ x x x x x x x]
_ [x x x x x x MA]N KUR–*aš-šu*[*r* x x x]
[x x x x x x x KUR–*aš-š*]*ur* EN*-ku-nu*
[x x x x x x] MAN KUR–*aš-šur* EN*-k*[*u-nu*]

268 A ki-i nap-šat-ku-nu la tar-ʾa-ma-a-ni
F [x x x x x]-ku-nu [x x x x x x]
B [k]i-i ZI.MEŠ-ku-nu la tar-a-ma-a-ni
i ki-i nap-šá-te-ku-nu la ta-ram-ma-ni
M [x x x x x x x] la tar-a-ma-ni
_ [x x x x x x x x x x]-ma-a-ni
[x x x x x]-ku-nu la tar-a-ma-a-[ni]
⸢ki-i⸣ [x x x x x x x x x x]
269 A šum-ma at-tu-nu ina IGI ^{m}aš-šur–DÙ–A DUMU–MAN GAL šá É–UŠ-ti
F [x x] at-tu-nu [x x x x x x x x x x x] É–UŠ-te
B šum-ma at-tu-nu ina IGI ^{m}aš-šur–DÙ–A DUMU–MAN GAL šá É–UŠ-ti
i šum-ma at-tu-nu ina IGI ^{m}aš-šur–DÙ–A [x x x] šá É–UŠ-te
M [x x x x x x x x x x x x] ⸢DUMU⸣–MAN GAL šá É–[x x]
_ [x x x x x x x x x x x x x x] GAL-u ⸢ša É–UŠ⸣-te
[x x x x x x x ^{m}aš]-šur–DÙ–A DUMU–MAN GAL ša É–UŠ-t[i]
šum-ma a[t-tu-nu x x x x x x x x x x x x x x]
270 A šá ŠEŠ.MEŠ-šú DUMU AMA-šú kar-ṣi-šú-nu ta-kal-a-ni
F [x x x x x x x kar-ṣ]i-šú-nu ta-kal-a-ni
i šá ŠEŠ.MEŠ-šu D[UMU AMA-šú] kar-ṣi-šú-nu ta-[kal-a-ni]
[x x x x x x x x x x x ta-k]al-a-ni
[x x x x] DUMU AMA-šú kar-ṣi-šú-nu ta-kal-a-n[i]
⸢ša⸣ ŠEŠ.MEŠ-⸢šú⸣ [x x x x x x x t]a-kal-ni
271 A la MUN-šú-nu ta-qab-ba-a-ni Á.2-ku-nu
F la DÙG.GA-ta-šú-nu [ta-qab]-⸢ba⸣-a-ni Á.2-ku-nu
B la MUN-šú-n[u [ta-qab-ba-a-]-ni Á.2-ku-nu
i [x x x x x x] ta-qab-ba-[a-ni x x x x]
_ [x x x x x x ta-qab-ba-a]-ni [x x x x]
[x x x x]x-šú-nu ta-qa-ba-a-ni [Á.2]-ku-nu
[x x x x x x x x x x x x Á.2]-ku-nu
272 A ina É.MEŠ-šú-nu tu-bal-a-ni ina ŠÀ-bi-šú-(nu) ta-ha-ṭa-ni
F ina É.[MEŠ-šú-nu tu-bal]-a-ni ina ŠÀ-bi-šú-nu [t]a-ha-⸢ṭa⸣-[ni]
B ina É.MEŠ-šú-nu tu-b[al-a-ni] ina ŠÀ-šú-nu t[a]-ha-[t]a-a-ni
_ ina É.MEŠ-šu!-nu tu-bal-a-ni [x Š]À-bi-šú-nu ta-ha-ṭa-a-ni
[x x x x x x x x x] ina ŠÀ-bi-šú-nu t[a-ha-ṭa-a-ni]
273 A TA* ŠÀ-bi ti-din-tú ša AD-šú-nu id-din-áš-šá-nu-u-ni
F [x x x ti]-din-tú šá ^{m}aš-šur–PAB–AŠ MAN KUR–aš-š[ur x x x x x x x x x x]
B T[A x x x x x] šá ^{m}aš-šur–PAB–[AŠ] MAN KUR–aš-šur AD-šú-nu i[d-x x x x x]
_ TA ŠÀ ti-din-tu [x ^{m}]aš-šur–PAB–AŠ MAN KUR–aš-šur AD-šú-nu
i-din-na-šá-nu-ni
[x x x] ti-din-te [x x x x x x x x x x x x x] id-di-na-áš-šú-[u-ni]
274 A qi-ni-tu šá šú-nu iq-nu-u-ni ta-na-áš-šá-a-ni
F qi-ni-⸢tú šá šú⸣-[nu x x x x x x x x x x]
B qi-ni-tú ⸢šá⸣ šú-nu iq-qi-nu-u-n[i] ⸢ta-na⸣-áš-šá-a-ni
_ [q]i-ni-tu šá šu-nu iq-nu-u-ni ta-na-šá-a-ni
[x x x x x x] iq-nu-u-ni ta-[x x x x x]
275 A šum-ma ti-din-tú A.ŠÀ.MEŠ É.MEŠ GIŠ.SAR.MEŠ
B šum-ma ti-din-tu A.ŠÀ.MEŠ [x x] GIŠ.SAR.MEŠ
_ šum-ma ti-din-tu A.ŠÀ.MEŠ É.MEŠ GIŠ.SAR.MEŠ
[x x x x x A.Š]À-⸢MEŠ⸣ ⸢É⸣.[MEŠ x x x]

276 A UN.MEŠ *ú-nu-*⸢*tú*⸣ ANŠE.KUR.RA.MEŠ ANŠE⸣.[x x x]
B UN.MEŠ *ú-nu-tú* ANŠE.KUR.RA.[MEŠ] ANŠE.GÌR.NUN.NA
_ UN.MEŠ *ú-nu-tu* ANŠE.KUR.RA.MEŠ ANŠE.⸢GÌR.NUN.NA⸣
277 A ANŠE.MEŠ GUD.MEŠ UDU.MEŠ *šá* ^{m}*aš-šur*–PAB–AŠ MAN KUR–*aš-šur*
B ANŠE.MEŠ GUD.MEŠ UDU.MEŠ *šá* ^{m}*aš-šur*–PAB!–[AŠ MAN] KUR–*aš-šur*.KI
_ ANŠE.MEŠ GUD.MEŠ UDU.MEŠ *šá* ^{m}*aš-šur*–PAB–[AŠ x x x x]
Y ANŠE.MEŠ GUD.MEŠ UDU.MEŠ *šá* ^{m}*aš-šur*–PAB–AŠ MAN [x x x]
278 A *a-*(*na*) DUMU.MEŠ-*šú id-din-u-ni la ina pa-ni-šú-nu la šu-tú-u-ni*
B *a-na* DUMU.MEŠ-*šú i-din-u-ni la ina* IGI-*šú-nu* [*l*]*a šu-tu-u-ni*
_ *a-*[*na* x x x x x x x] *la ina p*[*a-ni-šú-nu* x x x x x]
[*a-n*]*a* DUMU.MEŠ-*šú* [*i*]-*din-u-ni la a-*[*na* x x x x x *šu-t*]*u*?-*ni*
Y *a-na* DUMU.MEŠ-*šú* [*i-d*]*in-u-ni la ina pa-ni-šú-*[*nu* x x x x x]
279 A *šum-ma de-iq-ta-šú-nu ina* IGI ^{m}*aš-šur*–DÙ–A DUMU–MAN GAL
B ⸢*šum*⸣*-ma de-iq-ta-šú-nu* ⸢*ina* IGI 1⸣.*aš-šur*–⸢DÙ–A DUMU⸣–MAN [x]
_ [x x x x x x x] *ina* IGI ^{m}*aš-šur*–[DÙ–A x x x]
[x x] *de-iq-t*[*a-šú-nu* x x ^{m}]*aš-šur*–DÙ–A DUMU–MAN [x]
Y *šum-ma de*!-*iq-*[*ta-š*]*ú-nu ina* IGI ^{m}*aš-šur*–DÙ–A [x x x]
280 A *šá* É–UŠ-*ti la ta-qab-ba-a-ni*
B [x É]–UŠ-*ti* [*l*]*a* ⸢*ta*⸣-[*qab-b*]*a-a-ni*
_ [x x x x] *la ta-q*[*ab-ba-a-ni*]
[x É–U]Š-*t*[*i la*] ⸢*ta*⸣*-qa-ba-a-ni*
Y *šá* É–UŠ-*ti* [*la t*]*a-qab-ba-ni*
281 A *šum-ma ina* IGI-*ni-šú la i-za-zu-u-ni is-*⸢*si-ku*⸣*-nu*
B *šum-ma ina* IGI-⸢*ni*⸣-[*šú la*] *i-za-zu-u-ni is-si-ku-nu*
_ [x x x x x x x x x x x x x] *is-si-ku-n*[*u*]
[x x x x x x x *i-za-z*]*u-u-ni is-si-ku-nu*
Y *šum-ma* [x x x x] *la i-za-zu-*[*u-ni*] *is-si-ku-nu*
282 A *la* ⸢*ú*⸣*-sa-ta-mah-*⸢*hu-ni*⸣
B *la ú-sa-ta-a-mah-u-ni*
_ [x x x x x x]-*u-ni*
Y *la ú-*[x x x x x x]

---

283 A *a-de-e an-*[*nu-ti* x] ^{m}*aš-šur*–PAB–AŠ MAN KUR–*aš-šur*
B *a-de-e an-nu-ti šá* ^{m}*aš-šur*–PAB–AŠ MAN KUR–*aš-šur*.KI
J [x x x] ⸢*an-nu*⸣*-ti* [x x x x x x x x x x x x]
_ *a-de-e an-n*[*u-*x x x x x x x x x x x x x]
ša [x x x x x x x ^{m}*aš-šur*–PAB]–AŠ MAN KUR–*aš-šur*
Y *a-de-e a*[*n-nu-t*]*i šá* ^{m}*aš-šur*–PAB–AŠ MAN KUR–[x x x]
284 A *ina* UGU ^{m}*aš-š*[*ur*–DÙ]–A DUMU–MAN GAL *šá* É–*re-*(*du*)-*u-ti*
C *ina* U[GU x x x x x x x x x x x x x]
B *ina* UGU ^{m}*aš-šur*–DÙ–A DUMU–MAN GAL *šá* ⸢É–UŠ-*ti*⸣
J [x U]GU ^{m}*aš-šur*–DÙ–A DU[MU–MAN x x x x x]
_ *ina* UGU ^{m}[x x x x x x x x x x x x]
[x x x x x x x x x x x] *šá* É–UŠ-*te*
[x]x UGU ^{m}*aš-šur*–DÙ–A [x x x x x x x]
Y *ina* UGU [x x x x x] DUMU–MAN GAL *šá* É–UŠ-*t*[*i*]

285 A ŠEŠ.ME[Š-*šú* DUMU] AMA-*šú šá* ^{m}*aš-šur*–DÙ–A DUMU–MAN GAL
C [x x x] DUMU [AMA-*šú* x x x x x x x x x]
B ŠEŠ.MEŠ-*šú* DUMU AMA-*šú šá* ^{m}*aš-šur*–DÙ–A DUMU–MAN GAL
J ŠEŠ.MEŠ-*šú* DUMU AMA-*šú* [x x x x x x x x x]
_ *ù* ŠEŠ.MEŠ-[*šú* x x x x x x x x x] DUMU–MAN GAL
[x x x x x x x ^{m}*aš-šur*–D]Ù–A DUMU–MAN GAL-*u*
[x x x] DUMU AMA-*šú* [x x x x x x x x x]
Y [x x x] DUM[U AMA-*šú* x x x x x x DUMU–M]AN GAL
286 A *šá* É–U[Š-*t*]*i ú-dan-nin-u-ni is-si-ku-nu*
C [x x x x] *ú-d*[*an*!*-nin-u-ni* x x x x]
B *šá* É–UŠ-*ti ú-dan-nin-u-ni is-si-ku-nu*
J *šá* É–UŠ-*te ú-dan-*[*nin-u-ni* x x x x]
_ *š*[*a* x x x x x x x x x] *is-si-k*[*u-nu*]
[x x x x *ú-dan-ni*]*n-u-ni is-si-ku-nu*
[x É–*re-du*]-*u*!-*ti* [x x x x x x x x x]
Y *šá* ⸢É⸣–[x x] ⸢*ú*⸣-[x x x x x x x x]
287 A *iš-k*[*u-nu-u-ni ta*]-*me-tú ú-ta-mu-ka-nu-u-ni*
C [x x x x x] *ta-me-tu* [x x x x x x x]
B *iš-kun-*[*u*]-*ni ta-me-tú ú-tam-mu-ka-nu-ni*
J *iš-ku-nu-u-ni ta-me-*[*tú* x x x x x x x]
_ [x x x x x x x x] *ú-tam-mu-ka-nu-u-ni*
[x x x]-⸢*u-ni*⸣ [x x x x x x x x x x]
288 A *a-na* [x x x x] DUMU–DUMU.MEŠ-*ku-nu a-na* NUMUN-*ku-nu*
C [x x x x x x] DUMU–DU[MU.MEŠ-*ku-nu* x x x x x]
B [x x x x x x x x x x x]-*nu a-na* NUMUN-*ku-nu*
J *a-na* DUMU.M[EŠ-*k*]*u-nu* DUMU–[DUMU.MEŠ-*ku-nu* x x x x x]
_ [x x x x x x x x x x x x] ⸢*a-na*⸣ NUMUN-*ku-nu*
289 A *a-na* [x x x-*n*]*u šá* EGIR *a-de-e a-na* UD-*me ṣa-a-ti*
C [x x x x x x] *šá* EGIR ⸢*a-de*⸣-[*e* x x x x x x x x]
B [x x NU]MUN–[NUMUN-*ku-nu* x x x x x x x x x x x x]
J [x x] NUMUN–NUMUN-[*ku-nu* x x x x x x x x x x x x]
290 A *ib-ba-áš-š*[*u-u-n*]*i la ta-qab-ba-a-ni ṭè-mu*
C [x x x x x x x] *ta-qab-ba-niš-*[x x x x]
B *ib-ba-šú-u-ni* [x] *ta-qab-ba-a-ni-šú-ni ṭ*[*è-mu*]
_ [x x x x x x x x x x x]-⸢*ni*⸣ [x x]
291 A *la ta-šá-ka*[*n*]-*šú-u-ni ma-a a-de-e an-nu-te*
C [x x x x x x x] *ma-a* ⸢*a*⸣-*de-e an-nu-*[x]
B [x x x x x x x] *ma-a a-de-e an-nu-u-ti*
H [x x x x x x x x x *a-de*]-*e an-*⸢*nu-ti*⸣
292 A [*u*]*ṣ-ra ma-a ina* ŠÀ-*bi a-de-e-ku-nu la ta-ha-ṭ*[*i-a*]
C *la u*[*ṣ*]-*ra-a ma-*⸢*a*⸣ [x x x x x x x x x x x x x x]
B [x x] *ma-a in*[*a* Š]À *a-de-e-ku-nu l*[*a* x x x x]
H *uṣ-ra ma-a ina* ŠÀ-*bi* [*a-de-e-k*]*u-nu la ta-ha-ṭi-a*
293 A [*nap-ša*]*t*?-*ku-nu la tu-hal-la-qa*
C ZI-[ME]Š-*ku-nu la t*[*u*-x x x]
B ⸢ZI⸣.[MEŠ]-*ku-nu la tu-hal-*⸢*la*⸣-[*qa*]
H ZI.MEŠ-*ku-nu* x *tu-hal-l*]*a-qa*

294 A [x x KU]R-*ku-nu a-na ha-pe-e* UN.MEŠ-*ku-nu*
C *ma*!-*a* KUR-*ku-nu a-na ha-bé-e* UN!.ME[Š-*ku-nu*]
B [x x x x x *a*]-*na h*[*a-p*]*e-e* UN.MEŠ-*ku-nu*
H *ma-a* KUR-*ku-nu a-na ha-pe-e* [UN.MEŠ-*k*]*u-nu*
295 A [x x *šal-l*]*a-li la ta-da-*(*na*) [*a*]-*bu-tú*
C [x x x x x] *la ta-da-na ma-a a-bu-tú*
B *a-n*[*a* x x x x x x x x x x] *a-bu-*(*tú*)
H *a-na šal-la-li la ta-da-na* [x x *a-bu-t*]*ú*
296 A [x x x] *šá ina* IGI DINGIR *u* LÚ-*ti mah-rat-u-ni*
C *an-ni-*[x] *ša ina* IGI DINGIR.MEŠ LÚ-*ti mah-rat-u-ni*
B *an-ni-tú šá ina* IGI DIN[GIR x x *ma*]*h-rat-*˹*u*˺*-ni*
H *an-ni-tu šá ina* IGI DINGIR.MEŠ *a-me-lu-te* [*mah-rat-u-n*]*i*
297 A *ši*!-[*i* x x x x x x *mah*]-˹*rat*˺ *ina* UGU-*hi-ku-nu lu ṭa-ba*[*t*]
C ˹*ši-i*˺ *ina pa-ni-ku-nu* ˹*lu mah*˺*-rat ina* UGU-*hi-ku-nu lu ṭa-bat*
B *ši-i ina* IGI.MEŠ-*ku-n*[*u* x x x x] UGU-*hi-ku-nu lu ṭa-ba*[*t*]
H *ši-i* [x *pa-n*]*i-ku-nu lu mah-rat* [x x x x x] *lu ṭa-bat*
298 A [x x x x x x x x x x x x] *a-na be-lut*
C ^{m}*aš-šur*–DÙ–A DUMU–˹MAN˺ [G]AL *šá* É–U[Š]-˹*ti*˺ *a*!-*na be-lu-ti*
B [x x x x x x x] GAL *šá* É–UŠ-*ti a-na* EN-*ut*
H ^{m}*aš-šur*–DÙ–A DUMU–MAN GAL-*u* [x x x x] ˹*a*˺*-na be-lu-te*
299 C ˹KUR˺ *u* UN.MEŠ *lu* [*na*]-*ṣir*
B KUR [x] ˹UN.MEŠ˺ *lu na-ṣir*
H KUR *u* UN.MEŠ [x x x]
300 C EG[IR *a-n*]*a* LU[GAL-*u-t*]*i lu na-bi* MU-*šu*
B EGIR *a-na* LUGAL-˹*ú*˺-[*ti l*]*u na-bi* MU-*šú*
H EGIR *a-na* LUGAL-*u-te* [x x x MU]-*šu*
_ [x x x x x x] *lu n*[*a-bi* x x]
301 C [LUGAL M]AN-[*m*]*a* EN [MAN-*ma ina* U]GU-[*hi-šu l*]*a* ˹*taš*˺-(*ka*)-˹*na*?˺
B LUGAL MAN-*ma* EN MAN-*ma ina* UGU-*hi-*˹*ku*˺*-nu ta-šá-kan-a-ni*
H LUGAL MAN-*ma* EN MA[N-*m*]*a* [x x x x x] *la ta-šá-ka-na*
_ [x x x x x x] *ina* UGU-*hi-šú*? [x x x x x]

---

302 A [*šum-ma m*]*e-me-ni ina* UGU ^{m}*aš-šur*–PAB–AŠ MAN KUR–*aš-š*[*ur*]
C *šum-ma me-me-ni ina* UGU ^{m}*aš-šur*–PAB–AŠ
B *šum-m*[*a* x x x] *ina* UGU ^{m}*aš-šur*–PAB–AŠ MAN KUR–*aš-šur*
_ *šum-ma me-me-*(*ni*) *ina* UGU ^{m}*aš-šur*–PAB–AŠ
303 A [*si-h*]*u bar-tu e-ta-*˹*pa*˺*-áš ina* GIŠ.GU.ZA MAN-*ti*
C *si-hu bar-tu e-tap-áš ina* GIŠ.GU.ZA LUGAL-*ti*
B *si-hu bar-*[*tu*] *e-tap-áš ina* GIŠ.GU.ZA LUGAL-*ti-šú*
_ [x x x x x x x] *ina* GIŠ.GU.ZA LUGAL-*u-te*
304 A [x x x] *šum-ma a-n*[*a* x x x]
C *it-tu-šib šum-ma* ˹*a*˺-[*na*] LUGAL-*ti-šú*
B *it-tu-šib šum-ma a-na* ˹LUGAL˺-*ti-šú*
_ *it-t*[*u-šib*] *šum-ma a-na* LUGAL-*u-te-šú*
305 A *ta-ha-*[*du-a*]-*ni* [*l*]*a ta-ṣab-bat-a-ni-šú-u-ni*
C *tah-du-a-ni la ta-ṣab-bat-a-šú-u-ni*
B *ta-ha-du-a-ni la ta-*[*ṣab-bat-a*]-*niš-šú-u-ni*
_ *ta-ha-*[*du-a-ni*] *la ta-ṣa-bat-a-šú-u-ni*

306 A la ta-du-ka-a-šú-u-ni šum-ma am–mar ṣa-ba-ti-šú
C la ta-du-ka-a-šú-u-ni šum-ma am–mar ṣa-ba-ti-šu
B la ta-du-ka-a-šú-u-n[i x x x x] ṣa-bat-ti-šú
_ la ta-d[u-ka-a-šú-u-ni] šum-ma am–mar ṣa-ba-te-⸢šú⸣
307 A du-a-ki-šú ⸢la⸣ ma-ṣa-ku-nu a-na LUGAL-u-ti-šú
C du-a-ki-šu la ma-ṣa-ku-nu [x x x x x x]
B du-⸢a⸣-k[i-šú x x x x x x x x x x]-ti
_ ⸢du-a⸣-x[x x x x x x x] a-na LUGAL-u-te-šú
308 A ta-ma-gúr-a-⸢ni⸣ ta-me-tú ša LÚ.ARAD-nu-ti
C [ta]-ma-g[úr-a]-ni ta-me-tu šá LÚ.ARAD.MEŠ-⸢ti⸣
B ta-[ma-gúr-a-ni x x x x LÚ].ARAD.MEŠ-a-nu-[ti]
J [x x x x x x x x x LÚ].⸢ARAD⸣-nu-[t]i
_ t[a-ma-gúr-a-ni x x x] ša LÚ.ARAD-[x x]
309 A [t]a-tam-ma-a-ni-⸢šú⸣-u-ni ina UGU-hi-[šu]
C t[a-tam-ma-a]-ni-šú-[u-ni] ina UGU-hi-šu
_ [x x x x x x x x] ina ⸢UGU⸣-[x x]
310 A ⸢la⸣ ta-bal-kàt-a-⸢ni⸣ ina gam-mur-t[i x x x x]
C la ta-bal-⸢kàt-a⸣-ni ina gu-mur-ti ⸢ŠÀ-bi⸣-ku-nu
J [x ta-b]al-kàt-ni [x x x x x x x x]
311 A qa-ra-bu is-si-šú ⸢la⸣ tu-p[a-x x x]
C qa-ra-a-bu is-⸢si⸣-šú la tu-pa-áš-⸢a-ni⸣
J [x x x is-s]i-šú la tu-pa-šá-ni
312 A KUR.KUR šá-ni-a-te is-si-šú la tu-š[am-k]a[r-a-ni]
C [KU]R.KUR šá-ni-a-ti is-si-šú la tu-šam-[k]ar-⸢a⸣-ni
J [x x x x x x x x x x tu]-šam-kar-a-ni
313 A hu-ub-tu-šú la ta-hab-bat-[a-ni-ni]
C hu-ub-t[u]-šú la ta-hab-bat-a-ni-⸢ni⸣
J hu-⸢ub-tu-šú⸣ la ta-hab-⸢bat⸣-a-ni-ni
314 A de-ek-tu-šú la ta-[du-ka]-a-ni
C ⸢de⸣-ek-tu-šú la ta-du-ka-a-⸢ni⸣
J de-ek-tu-šú la ta-du-ka-ni
315 A MU-šú NUMUN-šú ina KUR la tu-h[al-laq]-⸢a-ni⸣
C MU NUMUN-šú ina KUR la ⸢tu-hal-la-qa-a-ni⸣
J MU-šú NUMUN-šú ina KUR la tu-hal-laq-a-ni
316 A ᵐaš-šur–DÙ–A DUMU–MAN GAL šá [É]–⸢UŠ⸣-[x]
C ᵐaš-šur–DÙ–A DUMU–MAN ⸢GAL šá É–UŠ-ti⸣
B [x x x x x x x x x É]–U]Š-ti
J ᵐaš-šur–DÙ–A DUMU–MAN GAL-u ša É–UŠ-u-te
317 A ina GIŠ.GU.ZA AD-šú la [tu-ša-aṣ-bat-t[a-a-ni]
N [x x x x x x x x x x-t]a-a-ni
C GIŠ.GU.ZA ⸢AD-šú la tu-šá⸣-aṣ-bat-a-ni
B [x x x x x x tu-šá]-aṣ-bat-a-ni
J GIŠ.GU.ZA AD-šu la tu-šá-aṣ-bat-a-ni

---

318 A šum-ma at-tu-nu TA* [x x x x x]
N [x x at]-tu-nu TA ⸢ŠÀ⸣-bi Š[EŠ].MEŠ-šú
C šum-ma at-tu-nu TA* ŠÀ ŠEŠ.MEŠ-šú
B [x x x x x x Š]À ŠEŠ.MEŠ-šú
J šum-ma at-tu-nu TA* ŠÀ-bi ŠEŠ.MEŠ-šú

319 A ŠEŠ–AD.MEŠ-_šú_ DUM[U–x x x x x]
N ŠEŠ.MEŠ–AD.MEŠ-_šú_ DUMU–ŠEŠ.MEŠ–AD.MEŠ-_šú_
C ŠEŠ–AD.MEŠ-_šú_ DUMU–ŠEŠ–˹AD!-_šú_!˺
B ŠEŠ–AD.MEŠ-_šú_ [x x x]-_šú_
J ŠEŠ.MEŠ AD-_šú_ DUMU–ŠEŠ.ME[Š–AD].M[EŠ]-˹_šú_˺
c [x x x x x x x x x x _q_]_in-ni-šú_
320 A [T]A* ŠÀ-_bi_ NUMUN AD-_šú_ [x ŠÀ-_b_]_i_ [x x x x x x]
N T[A] ŠÀ-_bi_ NUMUN É–AD-_šú_ [x ŠÀ]-_bi_ NUMUN MAN _pa-ni-u-ti_
C TA* ŠÀ NUMUN É–AD-_šú_ TA* ŠÀ NUMUN MAN _pa-ni-ú-ut-ti_
B TA*! ŠÀ NUMUN É–AD-_šú_ [x x NU]MUN LUGAL _pa-ni-ú-ti_
J TA* ŠÀ NUMUN É–AD-_šu_ [x x x x x x x x]
c NUMUN É–AD-_šu_ [(x x) x x] _pa-ni-u-tú_
321 A [x] ˹ŠÀ˺-[_bi_] ˹LÚ˺.GA[L x x x x x x x x x x x x]
N TA ˹ŠÀ˺-_bi_ LÚ.˹NUN˺ LÚ.N[AM LÚ.SA]G TA! ŠÀ-[_b_]_i_ DUMU KUR–_aš-šur_.KI
C TA* ŠÀ LÚ.GAL LÚ.NAM LÚ.SAG TA* ŠÀ DUMU KUR–_aš-šur_
B TA* NUN-_e_ LÚ.NAM [LÚ.S]AG TA* ŠÀ ˹DUMU˺ KUR–_aš-šur_
c TA* ŠÀ NUN-_e_ [x x LÚ].˹SAG˺ TA* ŠÀ DUMU KUR–_aš-šur_.KI
322 A [x x x x x] _šá_-[x x x x x x x x x x x]
N TA ŠÀ-_bi_ DUMU KUR _šá-ni-tim-ma ú-šak-pa-du-ka-nu-u-ni_
C TA* ŠÀ DUMU KUR _šá-nim-tim-ma ú-šak-pa-du-u-ka-_(_nu_)_-u-ni_
B TA* ŠÀ DUMU KUR MAN-_tim-ma_ [_ú_]-_šá-ak-pa-du-ka-nu-ni_
c ˹TA* ŠÀ DUMU˺ KUR _ša-ni-tim-ma ú-šak-pa-ad-u-ka-nu-ni_
323 N _iq-qa-ba-(ka-nu) ma-a_ ˹_kar_˺-_ṣi_ ˹_šá_˺ ^{m}_aš-šur_–DÙ–A
C _i-qab-ba-ka-nu-ni ma-a kar_!-_ṣi šá_ ^{m}_aš-šur_–DÙ–A
B _i-qab-ba-ka-nu-ni_ ˹_ma-a_˺ _kar-ṣi šá_ ^{m}_aš-šur_–DÙ–A
_c_ _i-qab-ba-ak-ka-nu-u-ni ma kar-ṣi_! _ša_ ^{m}_aš-šur_–DÙ–A
324 N DUMU–MAN GAL-_u šá_ É–UŠ-_ti ina_ IGI AD-_šú ak-la_
C DUMU–MAN GAL _šá_ É–UŠ-_ti ina_ IGI AD-_šú ak-la_
B DUMU–MAN GAL _šá_ É–UŠ-_ti ina_ IGI AD-_šú ak-la_
c DUMU–MAN GAL _ša_ É–UŠ-_te ina_ IGI AD-_šú ak-la_
325 N _a-bat-su la_ DÙG.GA-_tu la_ SIG$_5$-_tu qi-bi-a_
C _ma-a a-bat-su la_ DÙG.GA-_tu la_ SIG$_5$-_tu qi-bi-a_
B _a_-˹_bat_˺-_su la_ DÙG.GA-_tu la_ SIG$_5$-_tú qi-bi-a_
c _ma a-bat_-˹_su_˺ _la_ DÙG.GA-˹_tú_˺ _la_ SIG$_5$-_tú qi-bi-a_
326 N _ina bir-tu-šú bir-ti_ AD-_šú (tu)-šam-_[_ha-ṣa-a-ni_]
C _ina bir-tu_-˹_šú_!˺ _bir-ti_ AD-_šú tu-šam-ha-ṣa-a-ni_
B _ma-a ina bir-tu-šú ina bir-ti_ AD-_šú tu-šam-ha-ṣa-ni_
c _ina bir-tu-šú ina bir_-[_ti_] A[D-_šú tu-šam-h_]_a-ṣa-a-ni_
327 N [_a-n_]_a zi-a-ri ina_ IGI _a-he-iš_ [x x x x x x x]
C _a-na zi-a-ri ina_ IGI _a-he-iš ta-šá-kan-a-šá-nu-ni_
B _a-na zi-a-ri ina_ IGI _a-he-iš ta-šá-kan-a-šá-nu-ni_
_ _a-na zi-a-ri ina_ IGI _a-he-iš ta-šá-kan-a-šú_-˹_nu-ni_˺
c _a-na z_[_i-a-ri_ x x x x x _ta-šá-kan_]-_a-šu-n_[_u-ni_]

---

328 N [x x x x *ṭ*]*è*-˹*e*˺-*m*[*u* x x x x x x x x]
C [x x x x x x x x x-*k*]*a-nu*-x[x]
B EN–*qi-'i šá ṭè-e-mu* ˹*i*˺-[x x x x]-*nu-u-ni*
_ EN–*qi-'i šá ṭè-e-mu i-šá-kan-u-ka*-[x x]
c E[N x x x x x x x x x x x x x x]
_ EN–*qi-'i š*[*á* x x x x x x x x x x x]
329 N [x x x x x-*k*]*a-nu*-[*ni* x x x]
B *ú-šá-an-za-ru-ka-nu-ni* [x x]x-*šú*
_ *ú-šá-an-za-ar-u-ka-nu*-˹*ni*˺ [x]x x (x)
c ˹*ú*˺-[x x x x x x x x x x]
_ *ú-šá-an-za-ru-k*[*a-nu-ni* x x x]
330 N [x x x x x x x x x L]Ú.ARAD.[MEŠ-*ni*]
B *ma-a lu* ŠEŠ.MEŠ-*šú ma-a* [x LÚ.AR]AD.MEŠ-*ni*
_ [*ma*]-*a lu* ŠEŠ.MEŠ-*šú lu* LÚ.˹ARAD˺.[MEŠ-*ni*]
ma-a lu ŠEŠ.MEŠ-*šú* ˹*lu*˺ [x x x x]
331 B *ša ina* UGU AD-*šú ú*-[*šá-an-z*]*i-ru-u-ni*
_ [x x x x x *ú-šá-an*]-*za-ar-u-ni*
332 B *kar-ṣi-šú ina* IGI AD-*šú* [*ek-k*]*al-u-ni a-le-e'*
_ *ša kar-ṣi*-[*šú* x x x x x x x x x x x]
kar-ṣi-šú ina IGI A[D-*šú* x x x x x x x]
333 B *ma-a la šá* ^{d}*aš-šur* x[x *ina* K]A?-*šú iq-bu-u-ni ta-kun*
_ [x x x *š*]*a aš-šur* ^{d}UTU *ù* [x x x x x x x x x x]
[x x x x x x x x x x x x x x x] *iq-bu-u-ni ta*-[*kun*]
334 B *ma-a ina ba-lat aš-š*[*ur*] ˹*ù*?˺ ^{d}UTU AD-*ku-nu* LU TI *ú* ŠID
_ [x x x *b*]*a-lat aš-šur* ^{d}UTU A[D-*ku-nu* x x x x]
335 A *ma-a* [x x x x x x x x x x x x x x]
B *ma-a šá* Š[EŠ-*ku-nu k*]*ab-bi-da* ZI.MEŠ-*ku-nu uṣ-ra*
_ [x x x ŠE]Š-*ku-nu k*[*a*-x x x x x x x x x]
ma-a ŠEŠ-*ku-nu* [x x x x x x x x x]

---

336 A *šum-ma* [x x x x x x x x x x x x x x x x x x]
F *šum-ma me-m*USD *e-ni* ˹*ú*˺-[*šak-pa-du-ka*]-*nu-u-ni i-qab-ba-ka*-[*nu-ni*]
B *šum-m*[*a* x x x x x x x x x x x x x x x x x x]
_ [x x] *me-me-ni* [x x x x x x x x x x x x x x]
[x x *me*]-*me-ni ú-šak-pa-du-ka-nu-u-ni* [*i-qab*]-*ba-kan-u-ni*
[x x x x x *ú-šak-pa-d*]*u-k*[*a-nu-u-ni* x x x x x x]
337 A T[A x x x x x x x x x x x x x x x x x x x x x]
F [x x x] ŠEŠ.MEŠ-*šú* ŠEŠ–AD.M[EŠ-*šú* x x x x.M]EŠ-*šú qin-ni-šú*
B [x x x ŠEŠ].MEŠ-*šú* [x x x x x x x x x x *qin-n*]*i-šú*
_ TA ŠÀ-*bi* ŠEŠ.MEŠ-*šú* ŠEŠ–AD-˹MEŠ-*šú*˺ [DUMU–ŠEŠ].MEŠ–AD.MEŠ-*šú qin-ni*-˹*šu*˺
[x x x x x x ŠEŠ]–AD.MEŠ-[*šú* x x x x x x x x x x]
338 F NUMUN É–AD-*šú lu* L[Ú.SAG *lu* LÚ.*šá–ziq*]-*ni lu* DUMU KUR–*aš-šur*
B [x x x x x x x x x *šá*–L]Ú*.*ziq-ni* [x x x x x]
R [x x x x x x x x] *lu* LÚ.*šá–ziq-ni* [x x x x x]
_ [x x x x x x x x x x x]–*ziq-n*[*i* x x x x x]

339 F *lu* DUMU KUR *š[á-*x x x x *l]u ina nap-har ṣal-mat–*SAG.DU
B [x x x x x x*-m]a* [x x x x x x x x x]
_ [*l*]*u* DUMU KUR MA[N*-ma* x x x x *ṣal-mat–*SA]G.DU
R [x x x] *šá-ni-nim-ma lu ina nap-ha[r* x x x x]
340 F *ma-la ba-šu-u i-qab-ba-ka-nu-u-ni*
B [x x *ba-š*]*ú-u* [x x x x x x x x]
p [x x x x x] *i-qab-ba-ka-nu-u-*˹*ni*˺
_ *ma-la* GÁL [x x x x x x x x]
R [x x x x x] *i-qab-ba-kan-u-ni*
341 F *ma-a kar-ṣi šá* ŠEŠ.MEŠ*-šú* DUMU AMA*-šú ina* IGI*-šú*
B [x x x x x ŠEŠ].MEŠ*-šú* [x x x x x x]
p ˹*ma-a*˺ *k*[*ar-ṣi* x x x x] DUMU AMA*-šú ina pa-ni-šú*
w [x x x x x x x x x] DUMU AMA*-šú* [x x x]
_ [x x x x x x x x x x x x *in*]*a* IGI*-š*[*u*?]
[*m*]*a-a kar-ṣi šá* ŠEŠ.[MEŠ*-šú* x x x] *ina* IGI*-šú*
R *ma-a* [x x x x x x x x x x] *ina* IGI*-šú*
342 A [x x x x x x x x x x *bir-tu-š*]*ú-nu*
F *ak-la ma-a šá-an-hi-ṣa ina bir-tu-šú-nu*
B [*ak-l*]*a m*[*a-a* x x x x x x x x x x]
p *ak-la m*[*a-a* x x x x x] *ina bi*[*r-t*]*u-šú-nu*
w [x x x x x x x x x x *bir*]*-tu-šú-nu*
_ [x x *ma*]-˹*a*˺ *šam-hi-ṣa ina bi*[*r-tu-šú-nu*]
[*a*]*k-la ma-a šá-an-hi-*[*ṣa* x x x x x]
R *ak-la m*[*a-a* x x x x x x x x x x]
343 A [x x x x x x x x x x *pa*]*-ni-šú pur-sa*
F *ma-a* ŠEŠ.MEŠ*-šú* DUMU AMA*-šú* TA* *pa-ni-šú pur-sa*
B *ma-a* [x x x x x x x x x x x *pur*]*-sa*
p *ma-a* ŠEŠ.MEŠ-˹*šú*˺ [x x x x x x x x] *pur-*[*sa*]
w [x x x x x x x x x T]A IGI*-šú pur-sa*
_ [*ma*]-˹*a*˺ ŠEŠ.MEŠ*-šú* DUMU AMA*-šú* T[A*] ˹IGI˺-[*šú* x x]
[x x ŠEŠ].MEŠ*-šú* DUMU AMA*-šú* T[A x x x x]
344 A [x x x x x x x x x] *la* DÙG.GA*-tu*
F *at-tu-nu ta-šam-ma-a-ni la* DÙG.GA*-tú*
B *at-t*[*u-nu* x x x x x x x x x x]
p [*a*]*t-tu-nu ta-*[*šam-ma-a-ni* x x x x]
w [x x x *ta*]*-šam-ma-a-ni la* DÙG.GA!*-tu*
_ [*at-t*]*u-nu ta-šam-ma-a-ni l*[*a* x x x]
[x x x *ta-šam-ma*]*-a-ni la* DÙG.[GA*-tú*]
R *at-*˹*tu*˺*-nu ta-šam-ma-a-n*[*i*] *la ṭa-*[x x]
345 A [x x x x x x x x *t*]*a-qab-ba-a-ni*
F *ša* ŠEŠ.MEŠ*-šú ina* IGI*-šú ta-qab-ba-a-ni*
B *šá* ŠEŠ.[MEŠ*-šú* x x x x x x x x x]
p *š*[*a* ŠEŠ].MEŠ*-šú ina pa-*[*ni-šú* x x x x x]
w *ša* ŠEŠ.MEŠ [x x x *ta-qa*]*b-ba-a-ni*
_ [x ŠEŠ.MEŠ]*-šú ina* IGI.MEŠ*-šú* [x x x x x]
R [x x x x] *ina* IGI*-šú ta-qab-ba-a-ni*

346 A [x x x x x *ta-par-r]a-sa-a-šú-u-ni*
F TA* IGI ŠEŠ.MEŠ-*šú ta-par-ra-sa-šú-nu-u-ni*
B TA* IGI ŠE[Š.MEŠ-*šú* x x x x x x x x x]
_ [x x x x x *t]a-par-*[x x x x x x]
w TA* IGI ŠEŠ.MEŠ-*šú [ta-par-r]a-sa-šú-u-ni*
_ [x x ŠEŠ.MEŠ]-*šú ta-*[x x x x x x x]
R TA IGI ŠEŠ.MEŠ-*šú ta-par-ra-sa-⸢šú-ni⸣*
347 A [x x x x x x x *a-bu-t]u an-ni-tu*
F *šum-ma qa-bi-a-nu šá a-bu-tú an-ni-tú*
B *šum-ma qa-bi-a-n[u* x x x x x x x]
_ [x x x x x x] *šá a-bu-tú an-[ni-tú]*
w *šum-ma qa-bi-a-n[u* x *a-bu-t]ú an-ni-tú*
R *šum-[ma] qa-bi-a-nu-ti šá a-bu-tu an-ni-tu*
348 A *⸢iq⸣-b[a-ka-nu-u-ni tu-ra-ma]-⸢šú⸣-u-ni*
F *iq-ba-ka-nu-u-n[i] tu-ra-ma-šú-u-ni*
B *[i]q-ba-ka-nu-u-n[i* x x x x x x]
_ *[iq-ba-ka-nu-u]-ni tu-ra-ma-š[ú-u-ni]*
w *iq-ba-ka-nu-u-[ni tu-ra-ma-šú]-u-ni*
R *[iq-ba-ka-nu]-u-ni tu-ra-ma-šá-nu-u-ni*
349 A *šum-ma la* [x x x x x x x x x x x x] DUMU–MAN GA[L]
F *šum-ma la tal-lak-a-ni-ni a-na* ^{m}*aš-šur*–DÙ–A DUMU–MAN GAL
B *[šu]m-ma la ta-lak-a-ni-[ni* x x x x x x x] ⸢DUMU⸣–MAN GAL
_ [x x x *ta-lak]-a-ni-ni a-na* ^{m}*aš-šur*–[DÙ–A x x x]
w *la tal-lak-a-ni-ni a-na* [x x x x x x x x]
R [x x x *t]a-lak-a-ni-ni a-⸢na⸣* ^{m}*aš-šur*–DÙ–A [x x x]
350 A *šá* É–UŠ-*[ti* x x x x x]-*ni*
F *šá* É–U[Š-*te l]a ta-qab-ba-a-ni*
B *šá* É–UŠ-*⸢ti⸣* [x x x x x x]
_ [x x x x x] *ta-qab-ba-a-[ni]*
w *šá* É–UŠ-*te* [x x x x x x]
R [x] É–UŠ-*⸢ti⸣ la ta-qab-ba-a-ni*
351 A *ma-a* AD-[x x x x x x x]-*ni*
F *ma-a* AD!-*ka a-de-[e* x x x x x x]
B *ma-a* AD-*u-ka a-de-[e* x x x x x x]
w [x x x x] *a-de-e* [x x x x x x]
R [x x x x] *a-de-e ina* [U]GU-(*ka*) *is-si-ni*
352 A *i-⸢sa-kan⸣* [x x x x x x]
F *[i-sa-k]an ú-tam-ma-n[a-a-ši]*
B *i-sa-kan ú-*[x x x x x]
w [x x x] *ú-*[x x x x x]
R *is-sa-kan [ú-t]a-ma-na-a-[ši]*

---

353 A *šum-m[a* x x x x x x x x x x x x x x x x] *šá* É–UŠ-*te*
B *šum-ma ta-d[a-ga-la-ni* x x x x x x x x x] ⸢GAL⸣ *šá* É–U[Š-*ti*]
R [x x *t]a-da-ga-la-n[i? ina?* IGI ^{m}*aš-šur*–DÙ–A DUMU–MAN GAL x É]–UŠ-*ti*
354 A ŠEŠ.MEŠ-*š[ú* x x x x x-*k]u-u[š* x]
B [x x x x] *kan šu* x[x x x x x]
R ŠEŠ.MEŠ-*šú* [x x x x x]x-*ku-uš*

355 A ma!-ṣar-t[u x x x x x x x x at-t]u-n[u?]
B [x x x x x] at-tu-nu
R ma?-ṣar?-[tu x x x x x]
356 A ki-[i x x x x x x x x x]-˹ri˺-[x x x x]
B [x x x x x x x] la ta?-g[a?-x x x x x]
_ [x x x x x x x] ˹la ta-ga-ri-šú-nu-ni˺
R ki-i ra-ma-[ni-ku-nu l]a tu!-ga-ri-a-šá-nu-u-[ni]
357 A pu-x[x x x x x x x ŠÀ-b]i-šú-[nu]
B [x x x] ina ŠÀ-šú-nu
_ [x x x] ina ŠÀ-bi-šú-nu
R [x x x] ina ŠÀ-bi-šú-nu
358 A l[a x x x x x x x x x x x x] Š[À x x x]
B [x x x x x x] ma-a A[D-ku-nu x x x x x]
_ la tu-še-[x x x] ma-a AD-ku-nu ina ŠÀ-bi a-d[e-e]
R la tu-še-x[x x x x x x x x x] ina ŠÀ a-de-e
359 B i-s[a-kan x x x x x x]
_ is-sa-kan ú-ta[m-ma-na-a-ši]
R is-sa-k[a?-an x x x x x x]

---

360 B šum-[ma x x x x x x x x x x x x x x] EN-[ku-nu]
_ šum-ma at-tu-nu k[i-ma x x x x x x x x x x] EN-ku-nu
[x x x x x k]i-ma ᵐaš-[šur–PAB–AŠ x x x x x x x]
[x x x x x x x x x x x x x x x x x x x-n]u
R šum-ma ˹at˺-tu-nu ki-[ma ᵐaš-šu]r–PAB–AŠ MAN KUR–aš-šur E[N-ku-nu]
361 B [x x x x x x x] ᵐaš-š[ur–DÙ–A]
_ a-na [x x x x x] ᵐaš-šur–DÙ–A
z [a]-na ši[m-ti x x x ᵐaš-šur–DÙ]–A
_ [x x x x] it-ta-l[ak x x x x x]
a-na šim-[ti x x x ᵐaš-šur–D]Ù–A
R a-[n]a šim-ti it-ta-˹lak˺ ᵐaš-šur–DÙ–[A]
362 _ DUM[U–MAN x x x x x] ina GIŠ.GU.ZA [x x x x x]
z DUMU–MAN GAL šá ˹É˺–[UŠ-x x GIŠ.GU].ZA LUGAL-tu it-t[u-šib]
_ [x x x x É–UŠ-t]e ina GIŠ.GU.ZA [x x x x x]
DUMU–MAN GAL-u šá [x x x x GI]Š.GU.ZA LUGAL-u-te ˹it˺-t[u-šib]
R ˹DUMU˺–MAN GAL šá É–UŠ-ti ina GIŠ.GU.ZA LUGAL-ti [x x x]
363 B [x x x] la [x x x x x x x x x x]
_ [x x x x x x x x x] lu-u ŠE[Š-x x x x x]
z [a-bu]-tu la DÙG.GA-tu šá ŠE[Š.MEŠ-šú DUMU AM]A-šú
_ [x x x l]a DÙG.GA-tú šá ŠE[Š.MEŠ-šú x x x]
[x x x] la DÙG.GA-tu ša Š[EŠ.ME]Š-š[ú? x x x]
R a-bu-tú la DÙG.GA-tu šá ŠEŠ.MEŠ-šú DUM[U AMA-šú]
364 B ina IGI [x x x x x x x x] tu-ša[m?-x x x]
_ [x x x x x x] ˹ta˺-q[ab-ba-a-ni x x x x x x]
z ina IGI ŠEŠ-šú-nu t[a!-qab-ba-a-ni tu-šá-an]-zar-a-ni
_ [x x ŠE]Š.MEŠ-šú-nu ta-qa[b-ba-a-ni x x x x]-a-ni
ina IGI ŠEŠ-šú-nu ta-˹qab˺-ba-[a-ni] tu-šá-an-za-ra-ni
R ina IGI ŠEŠ-šú-nu ta-qab-ba-˹a˺-[n]i tu-šá-an?-[za-ra-ni]

365 B [x x x x x] *ina* H[UL-x x x x x x x x]
z *ma-a* ŠU.2-*ka ina* [x x x x x x x *ú-bí*]*l*
_ *ma-a* ŠU.2-*k*[*a* x x x x x x x x x] ⸢*ú*⸣-*bíl*
ma-a ŠU.2-⸢*ka ina* HUL-*tim*⸣ *ina* ŠÀ-*šú-nu ub-bíl*
R *ma-a* ŠU.2-*ka ina* ⸢HUL⸣-[*t*]*i ina* ŠÀ-*bi-šú-nu* [x x]
366 B [x x x x x x x x x] DUMU–[MAN x]
z *šum-ma* TA* IGI ^{m}*aš-šur*–[DÙ–A x x x]
_ *šum-ma* T[A x x x x x x x x x x]
šum-ma TA* IGI ^{m}*aš-šur*–DÙ–A DUMU–MAN GAL-*u*
R *šum-ma* TA ⸢IGI ^{m}*aš-šur*–DÙ⸣–[A x x G]AL
367 z [x] É–UŠ-*ti tu-na-ka*[*r-a-šá-nu-u-ni*]
_ [x É]–UŠ-*te tu-n*[*a-kar-a-šá-nu-u-ni*]
šá É–UŠ-*te tu-na-kar-a-šá-n*[*u-u-ni*]
R *šá* É–U[Š-*ti t*]*u*-⸢*na*⸣-*kar*-⸢*a*?⸣-*š*[*á-nu-u-ni*]
368 B *di-ib*-[*bi-šú-nu* x x x x x x x x]
z [*di-i*]*b-bi-šú-nu la* SIG$_5$.MEŠ *ina* IG[I x x x]
_ [x x x x x x] SIG$_5$.MEŠ *ina* IG[I x x x]
di-ib-bi-šú-nu la SI[G$_5$ x x x x x]
R [x x x x x x x x x x Š]EŠ-*šú-nu*
369 z [*ta-qab*]-*ba-a-ni ma-za-a-su šá* ^{m}[*aš-šur*–PAB–AŠ]
_ [x x x x x *m*]*a-za-s*[*u* x x x x x x]
t[*a-qa*]*b*-⸢*ba*⸣-[*a-ni* x x x x x x x x x x]
R *ta*-[x x x x x x x x x x x x x x]
370 z [x x x x x x x] *ú-kal-lim-u-šú-nu*-[*ni* x x x x x x x]
_ ⸢MAN KUR–*aš-šur*! AD-*šú-nu* [x x x x x x x] *ina* IGI ^{m}*aš-šur*–DÙ–A
R [x KUR–*aš-šu*]*r* ⸢AD⸣-*š*[*ú-nu* x x x x x x x x x x x x x x]
371 z [x x x x] É–UŠ-*t*[*i* x x x x x]
_ DUMU–M[AN GAL *ša* x x x] *ta-qab-ba-a-ni*
372 _ x[x x x x x x] *ú-na-kar-šú*-[*nu-u-ni*]

---

373 B *šum-ma* [*sa*]*r-bu šá ina* U[GU x x x] *pu*-⸢*uh*⸣-*r*[*i*]
_ [x x x x x x UG]U DINGIR.ME *ša pu-uh-ri*
[*šu*]*m-ma sar-bu šá* UGU DINGIR-⸢MEŠ⸣ ⸢x x x x⸣
374 B *lu* [*pa-ni*]-*ku-nu lu* [ŠU.2]-*ku-nu* TÚG.*lu-bul-ta-ku-n*[*u*]
_ [x x x x x x ŠU.2]-*ku-nu lu na-pul-ta-ku-nu*
lu pa-ni-ku-nu lu ŠU.2-*ku-nu lu-bul*-[*ta-ku-nu*]
375 B *ta-p*[*a-šá*]-*áš-a*-[*ni l*]*u-u ina si-qi-ku-nu*
_ [x x x x x x x x x *si-qi-k*]*u-nu ta-pa-šá-áš-a-ni lu ina si-qi-k*[*u-nu*]
376 B *ta-rak-kas-a*-[*ni*] *šá* [x x x x x *t*]*e-ep-pa-šá-a-ni*
_ *ta-rak-kas-ni* [x x x x x x *te-ep-pa-š*]*á-a-ni*
s [x x x x x x x x x x x *te-ep-p*]*a-šá-a*-⸢*ni*⸣
_ *ta-rak-kás-a-ni šá ma-mit pa-šá-ri te-e*[*p-pa-šá-a-ni*]

---

377 A [x x x x x *tur-t*]*u* ⸢*tu*⸣-*tar-r*[*a-a-ni*]
s [x x *at*]-*tu-nu tur-tu tu*-⸢*tar*⸣-[*ra-a-ni*]
_ *šum-ma at-tu-nu tur-t*[*u t*]*u-tar*-⸢*ra*⸣-[*a-ni*]
378 A [x x x x x x x *ši*]-*in-ga-te* [x x x]
s [x x *t*]*a-pa-šar-a-ni ši-in-ga*-[*te* x x x]
_ *ma-mit* ⸢*ta*⸣-*pa-šar*-⸢*a*⸣-[*ni ši*]-*i*[*n-ga-a-te* x x x]

379 A [x x x x x x x x x x x *pa-šá-a*]*-ri ta-ha-sa-sa-*[*a-ni*]
D [x x x x x x x x x x x x x x x] *ta-ha-s*[*a-sa-a-ni*]
s [x x x x *tur*]*-tu tur-ri ma-mit pa-šá-a-ri* [x x x x x x]
_ [*ina* I]GI-*ni šá* [*tu*]*r-*⸢*tú*!⸣ [x x x x x x x x x] *ta-ha-sa-*[*sa-a-ni*]
380 A [x x x x x x x x x] ⸢*an*?*-ni*?⸣*-tú* ^{m}*aš-šur*–DÙ–[A x x x]
D [x x x x x] *ta-me-tu an-*[*ni-tu* x x ^{m}*aš-š*]*ur*–DÙ–A DUMU–MAN [x]
s [*t*]*e-pa-šá-a-ni ta-me-tu an-*[*ni-tu ina* UGU?] ^{m}*aš-šur*–DÙ–A DUMU–MAN GAL
_ [x x x x x *t*]*a-me-tu an-*[*ni-tu* x x x x x x x x x x x]
381 A [x x x x x ^{m}*aš-šur*]–PAB–[AŠ x] KUR–*aš-šur* [x x x]
D *šá* É–UŠ-*ti* DUMU [x x x x x MA]N KUR–*aš-šur* EN-*ku-nu*
s *šá* [x x x x] ^{m}*aš-šur*–PAB–AŠ MAN KUR–*aš-šur* EN-*ku-nu*
382 A *šá u*[*l-tu* x x x x x x x x x] ⸢EGIR?⸣ [x x x]
D *šá ul-tú* UD-*me an-n*[*i-e a-d*]*i ša* EGIR *a-de-e*
s [x x x x x *an*]*-ni-e a-*[*d*]*i šá* EGIR *a-de-e*
383 A [x x x x x x x x x x DUMU].MEŠ-*ku-nu* [x x x]
D ⸢*ib*⸣*-ba-áš-ši-u-*[*ni at*]*-tu-nu* DUMU.MEŠ-*ku-nu* [x] ⸢*a*!⸣*-na*
s x[x x x x x x *at*]*-tu-nu* DUMU.MEŠ-*ku-nu šá a-na*
384 A [x x x x x x x x x x x x *ta-'*]*a-*⸢*ku*⸣*-*[*nu*]
D (UD)-*me ṣ*[*a-a-t*]*i ib-ba-áš-šú-u-ni ta-'a-ku-nu*
s UD-*m*[*e* x x x *ib*]*-ba-áš-šu-u-ni ta-'a-*[*ku-nu*]

---

385 A [x x *at-t*]*u-nu ki-i* GAG *kaq-qar ta-me-ti a*[*n-ni-ti*]
D [x x *at-t*]*u-nu ki-i ina kaq-*⸢*qar*⸣ *ta-me-tu an-ni-tu*
s [*šu*]*m-ma at-tu-nu ki-i kaq-qar ta-*[*me-tu* x x x]
386 A [x x x x x *t*]*a-me-tú šá da-bab-ti šap-*⸢*ti*⸣
D [*ta-za*]*-*⸢*za-a*⸣*-ni ta-me-tu ša da-bab-ti šap-ti*
s [*t*]*a-za-za-a-ni ta-me-tu šá d*[*a-bab-ti* x x]
387 A [x x x x x *a*]*-na* DUMU.MEŠ-*ku-nu šá* ⸢EGIR⸣ *a-de-*⸢*e*⸣
D [*ta*]*-tam-ma-a-ni ina gu-mur-*(*ti*) ŠÀ-*ku-nu la ta-tam-ma-a-ni*
[x x] DUMU.MEŠ-*ku-nu ša* EGIR *a-de-e*
s *ta-tam-ma-a-ni ina* ⸢*gu*⸣*-*[*mur-t*]*i* [x x x *l*]*a ta-ta-ma-a-ni*
⸢*a-na*⸣ DUM[U.MEŠ-*ku-nu š*]*a* EGIR *a-de-e*
388 A [x x x x x x] *la tu-šal-mad-a-ni*
D *ib-ba-áš-šú-u-ni* [x *t*]*u-šal-ma*!*-da-*⸢*ni*⸣
s *ib-*[*ba-áš-šú-u-ni l*]*a tu-*⸢*šal-mad*⸣*-a-*[*ni*]
389 A [x x x x x G]IG ⸢*la*⸣ [*pa*]*-*⸢*aṭ*?⸣*-ru*? *ina* UGU
D *šu*[*m-m*]*a at-tu-nu* [GI]G *la pa*!*-aṭ*!*-ru*! *ina* UGU
390 A [x x x x x x x x x x x x x x] *a-de-e*
H [x x x x x] *ta-šá-kan-a-ni* [*in*]*a* ŠÀ-*b*[*i a*]*-de-e*
D *r*[*a-ma-ni-k*]*u-nu ta-šá-kan-a-ni* [x x x] *a-de-e*
391 A [x x x x x x x x x x x x x x ^{m}]*aš-šur*–DÙ–A DUMU–MAN G[AL]
H *šá* ^{m}*aš-šur*–PAB–AŠ MAN KUR–*aš-šur šá ina* UGU ^{m}*aš-šur*–DÙ–A
DUMU–MAN GAL-*u*
D *šá* ^{m}*aš-š*[*ur*–PAB–AŠ MAN KUR–*aš-š*]*ur*.⸢KI⸣ [x x] UGU ^{m}*aš-šur*–DÙ–A
⸢DUMU–MAN GAL⸣
392 A [x x x x x *te-rab*]*-a-ni*
H *šá* É–UŠ-*te la te-rab-a-ni*
D [x É]–UŠ-*ti* [x *te*]*-rab-a-ni*

393 A [x x x x x x x x x *ṣ*]*a-a-ti aš-šur* DINGIR-[*ku-nu*]
H *a-na* EGIR UD-*me a-na* UD-*me ṣa-a-ti aš-šur* DINGIR-*ku-nu*
D *a-na* EGIR UD-*me a-na ṣa-a-ti* [*aš-š*]*ur* DINGIR-*ku-nu*
394 A [x x x x x x x x x x x x] EN-*ku-nu*
H ^{m}*aš-šur*–DÙ–A DUMU–MAN GAL *šá* ˹É–UŠ˺-*ti* EN-*ku-nu*
D ^{m}*aš-šur*–DÙ–A DUMU–MAN GA[L *š*]*á* É–UŠ-*ti* [EN-*k*]*u-nu*
395 A [x x x x DUMU–DUMU].MEŠ-*k*[*u-nu*]
H DUMU.MEŠ-*ku-nu* DUMU–DUMU.MEŠ-*ku-nu*
D DUMU.MEŠ-*ku-nu* DUMU–DUMU.MEŠ-*ku-nu*
396 H *a*-[x x]x-*šú lip-lu-hu*
D *a*-˹*na šá*˺-[*a*]-*šú lip-lu-hu*

---

397 H *šá ma-mit ṭup-pi an-ni*-x[x x x x x x x]
D [x *ma*]-*mit ṭup-pi an-ni-i e-nu-u e*-˹*gu*˺-*u*
398 H *i-ha-ṭu-u i-pa-sa-su* x[x x x x x x x]
D [*i-ha-ṭ*]*u-u i-pa-sa-si* x *šú a-de*-˹*e* x x˺
399 D [*e*?]-*gu-ma i-par-ra-ṣu ma-mit-su-un*
400 D [EN? *ṭup*]-*pi a-de-e an-ni-i*
401 D [^{d}*aš-šur*] MAN DINGIR.MEŠ *u* DINGIR.MEŠ GAL.MEŠ EN.MEŠ-*ia*
402 A [x x x x x x x x] ^{m}*aš-šur*–PAB–AŠ MAN KUR–*aš-šur*
D [x x x-*š*]*ú*? *lu-u ṣa-lam* ^{m}*aš-šur*–PAB–AŠ MAN KUR–*aš-šur*
403 A *lu ṣa-lam* ^{m}[*aš-šur*–DÙ–A x x x x É–UŠ]-*ti*
D [x x x x x x x x DU]MU–MAN GAL *šá* É–UŠ-*ti*
404 A *lu ṣa-lam* Š[EŠ?.MEŠ?-*šú* x x x x x x x x]
405 A NA$_{4}$.KIŠIB NUN-˹*e*!˺ [GAL-*e* AD DINGIR.MEŠ x x x]
D [x x x x x x x x x x x] ˹DINGIR˺.MEŠ
406 A *šá* É ˹x˺ [x x x x x x x x (x)]
407 A *ina* ŠÀ-*bi* ˹NA$_{4}$!˺.KI[ŠIB! *šá* ^{d}*aš-šur*] ˹MAN˺ DINGIR.MEŠ-*ni*
C [*in*]*a* NA$_{4}$.KIŠIB *šá* ^{d}*aš-šur* MAN [x x x]
408 A *ka*-˹*ni*˺*k*!-*u-ni ina* [x x x *šá*]-*kín-u-ni*
C [x x x x *in*]*a* IGI-*ku-nu šá-kín-u-ni*
409 A *ki-i* ˹DINGIR˺-*ku-n*[*u* x *t*]*a-na-ṣar-a-ni*
C *k*[*i-i* x x x] *la ta-na-ṣar-a-*[*ni*]

---

410 A *šum-ma a*[*t-tu-nu tu-na-kar-a*]-*ni ina* ^{d}GIŠ.BAR
C *šum-ma at-tu-nu tu-na-kar-*[*a-ni*] *a-na* ^{d}GIŠ.BAR
B *šum-ma* [x x x x x x x x x x x x x]
411 A *ta-pa-q*[*i*-x x x x A].MEŠ *ta-na-da-a-ni*
C *ta-pa-qid-a-*[*ni*] *ina* A.MEŠ *ta-na-da-a-*[*ni*]
B [x x x x x] *ina* A.M[EŠ x x x x x]
412 A *ina ep-ri ta-*[*kar-ra-ra-a-ni mim*]-*ma ši-pir ni-kil-ti*
C [x x x x x x x x x] *ina mim-ma ši-pir ni-kil-ti*
413 A *ta-bat-a-ni tu-*[*hal-la-qa-a-ni*] *ta-sa-pan-a-ni*
C *ta-*[*bat-a-ni*] *tu-hal-la*!-*q*[*a-a-ni* x x x x x]
B *ta-b*[*a*-x x x x x x x x x x x x x x]

---

414 A AN.Š[ÁR x DI]NGIR.MEŠ [*mu-š*]*im* [x x x x H]UL-*ti*
C AN.ŠÁR LUGAL DINGIR.MEŠ *mu-šim* [NAM.MEŠ] *ši-mat* MÍ.HUL
B AN.[ŠÁR x x x x x x x x x x x]

415 A *la* DÙG.GA-*ti l*[*i-šim-k*]*u-nu a-*˹*rak*!˺ UD *še-bu-ti*
C *la* DÙG.GA-*tu li-š*[*im-ku-nu*]
416 A [*k*]*i-šid lit-tu-*[*ti a*]*-a i-qiš-ku-nu*
C 0

---

417 A [x x x *hi-ir-t*]*u na-ram-ta-šú a-mat* KA-˹*šú*˺
C ^{d}NIN.LÍL *hi-ir-tu na-ram-ta-šú a-*[*mat* x x]
B [x x x] ˹x x x˺ [x x x x x x x x]
_ [x x x x x x x x x x x x x x]x ˹x˺
418 A [x x x x *a*]*-a iṣ-ba-ta ab-bu-tu-ku-un*
C *li-lam-mín-ma a-a iṣ-bat ab-bu-tú-k*[*u-un*]
^{d}*a-num* MAN DINGIR.MEŠ GIG *ta-né-hu di-ʾu di-lip-tu*
ni-is-sa-tu la DÙG.GA NUMUN UGU *nap-har*
É.MEŠ-*ku-nu l*[*i-šá-a*]*z-nin*
B [*li-la*]*m-mín-ma a.*(*a*) *iṣ-b*[*a-ta* x x x x x
^{d}*a*]*-num* MAN DINGIR.MEŠ GIG *t*[*a-ni-hu* x x x x x
ni-i]*s-sa*!*-tú*! NU DÙG.GA UZU UGU *n*[*ap-har*]
_ [x x x x x x x x *ab-bu-tu*]*-ku-un*
[x x x x x x x x x x x x]x *di-lip-tú* [x x x x] *li-šá-az-n*[*in*!]

---

419 A [x x *n*]*a-an-nar* [x x x x x x x x]
C ^{d}30 *na-an-nar* AN.MEŠ ˹KI.TIM˺ [x x x]
B ^{d}30 *na-nar* AN-*e u* KI.TIM [x x x]
_ [x x x x x x x x x x SAHAR].˹ŠUB!˺-*bu*
c ^{d}30 *na-an-nar* AN-*e u* KI.TIM *ina* ˹SAHAR.ŠUB˺-*bu*
420 A [*li-h*]*al-lip-ku-nu* [x x x x x x x x x x x x x x x x]
C [x x x x x] *ina* [x] DINGIR.MEŠ *u* LUGAL *e-rab-ku-nu* [x x x x]
B [x x x x x] *ina* IGI DINGIR *u* LUGAL *e-*(*re*)*-eb-ku-*[*nu* x x x x]
c *li-hal-lip-ku-nu ina* IGI DINGIR.MEŠ *u* LUGAL *e-rab-ku-nu a-a iq-bi*
421 A [*ki*]*-ma sír-ri-me* MAŠ.DÀ [x *ru-up-d*]*a*
C GIM *sír-ri-me* MAŠ.DÀ EDIN *ru-*[*u*]*p-*˹*da*˺
B *ki-ma sír-ri-me* MAŠ.DÀ EDIN [x x x]
c *ki-i sír-ri-me* MAŠ.DÀ *ina* EDIN *ru-up-da*

---

422 A [x x x x x x x x *kaq*]*-qa-ri di-*˹*in*˺ *k*[*et-t*]*i me-šá-ri*
C ^{d}UTU *nu-úr šá-ma-mi u kaq-qar* ˹*di-in*˺ *ket-ti*
B ^{d}UTU *nu-úr* ˹*šá*˺*-ma-me u di-*˹*in*˺ *k*[*et-ti*]
c ^{d}UTU *nu-úr šá-ma-me kaq-qa-ri di-in ket-te*
423 A [x x x x x x x x x IGI.2-*k*]*u-nu liš-ši-ma*
C *a-a i-di-in-ku-nu ni-ṭil* IGI.2.MEŠ-*ku-nu li-ši-*[*ma*]
B [x x x x x x x *n*]*i-ṭil* IGI.2-*ku-nu li-ši-ma*
c *a-a i-di-in-ku-nu ni-ṭil* IGI.2-*ku-nu li-ši-mu*
424 A [x *e*]*k-l*[*e-ti i*]*-tal-*˹*la-ka*˺
C *ina ek-le-ti i-*˹*tal*˺*-la-k*[*a*]
B *ina ek-*[*le-ti* x x x x]
c *ina ek-let-te* ˹*it*˺*-la-ka*

---

425 A [x x x x x x x x *šil-t*]*a-hi-šú* ⸢*šam*⸣*-ri* ⸢*li*⸣*-šam-qit-ku-nu*
C ^{d}MAŠ *a-šá-rid* [x x x x x x x x x *l*]*i-ša*[*m-qit-ku-nu*]
B ^{d}MAŠ *a-šá-rid* DINGIR.MEŠ *ina šil-ta-hi-šu šam-ri l*[*i-šam-qit-ku-nu*]
_ ⸢^{d}MAŠ *a-šá-ri*⸣-x[x x x x x x x x x x x x x x]
c [x x x x x x x x x x x x] ⸢*šam-ri lu*⸣*-šam-qit-*[*ku-nu*]
_ [x x *a-šá-ri*]*d* DINGIR.ME[Š x x x x x x x *li-šam-qit-k*]*u-nu*
426 A [x x x x x x x] EDIN UZU!.MEŠ-*ka* Á.MUŠEN *zi-i-bu*
C MÚD.MEŠ-*ku-nu* ⸢*li*⸣-[*mal-li* x UZU.MEŠ-*k*]*a* [x x] *z*[*i-i-bu*]
B MÚD.MEŠ-*ku-nu li-mal-la* EDIN U[ZU-*k*]*u-nu* Á.MUŠEN *z*[*i*]*-i-bu*
_ MÚD.MEŠ-*ku-nu li-*[*mal-li* x x x x] Á.MUŠEN *zi-i-b*[*u*]
MÚD.MEŠ-*k*[*u-nu* x x x x x x x] Á.MUŠEN [x x x]
427 A [*lu-š*]*á-kil*
N *lu-šá-kil*
B *li-šá-kil*

---

428 A [x x x x x x x x] *ni-ṭil* IGI.2.ME[Š]-*ku-nu hi-ra-*⸢*ti*⸣*-ku-nu*
B ^{d}*dil-bat na-bat* MUL.MEŠ *ina ni-ṭil* IGI.2-*ku-nu hi-ra-a-te-*[*k*]*u-nu*
_ ^{d}*dil-bat na-bat* MUL.MEŠ [x x x x x x x x x x x x x]
429 A [x x x x x x *li-šá*]*-ni-il* DUMU.MEŠ-⸢*ku*⸣*-nu*
B *ina* ÚR LÚ.KÚR-*ku-nu li-šá-ni-il* DUMU.MEŠ-*ku-nu*
_ *ina* ÚR LÚ.KÚR-*ku-nu l*[*i-šá-ni-il* x x x x]
430 A [x x x x x x x x L]Ú.KÚR *a-hu-u li-*⸢x-x⸣*-za mim-mu-ku-un*
B *a-a i-bé-lu* É-*ku-un* LÚ.KÚR *a-hu-u li-za-i-za mim-mu-ku-un*
_ [x x x x x] É-*ku-un* LÚ.KUR *a-*[*hu-u* x x x x x x x x]

---

431 A [x x x x x DINGIR.M]EŠ MAH *e-rab* ⸢*d*⸣.[E]N *ina* É.*sag-gíl*
C MUL.SAG.ME.GAR [x x x *e-r*]*ab* EN *ina* É.*sag-gíl*
B ^{d}SAG.ME.GAR EN DINGIR *ṣi-i-ru e-rab* EN *ina* É.SAG.ÍL
I [^{d}]SAG.ME.GAR EN DINGIR.MEŠ M[AH] *e-*[*rab* x] *ina* É.*sag-gíl*
_ ^{d}SAG.ME.GAR EN DINGIR.[MEŠ x x x x x x x x]
432 A [x x x x x x x] *li-hal-li-qa nap-šat-ku-un*
C *a-a* [x x x x x *li-hal-l*]*i-qa na*[*p-šat-ku-un*]
B *a-a ú-kal-lim-ku-nu li-hal-li-qa nap-šat-ku-un*
I *a-a ú-*⸢*kal*⸣*-lim-*[*ku-nu*] *li-hal-li-qa nap-šat-ku-*[*un*]
_ *a-a ú-kal-lim-ku-*[*nu* x x x x x x x x]

---

433 A [x x x x *reš-t*]*u-u hi-ṭu ka*[*b-t*]*ú ma-mit la pa-šá-ri*
C ^{d}AMAR.[UTU x x x x x x x x x] ⸢*ma*⸣*-mit* [x x x x]
B ^{d}[AMAR.UTU DUMU.U]Š *reš-tu-u hi-i-*⸢*ṭu*⸣ *kab-tu ma-mit la pa-šá-ri*
I ^{d}AMAR.UTU DUMU.UŠ *reš-tu-u hi-ṭu ka*[*b-tu*] *ma-mit la pa-šá-ri*
_ ⸢^{d}AMAR.UTU⸣ [x x x x x x x x x x x x x x x]
434 A [x x *ši-im-ti-ku*]*-nu li-šim*
B [x x *ši-im-t*]*i-ku-nu li-šim*
I *a-na ši-im-*(*ti*)*-ku-nu li-š*[*im*]

---

435 A [x x x x x x x x x] NUMUN MU-*ku-nu* NUMUN-*ku-nu*
C ^{d}NUMUN-[DÙ-*tú* x x x x x x x x x x] NUMUN-*ku-*[*nu*]
B [x x x x *na-di*]*-nat* MU NUMUN MU-*ku-nu* NUMUN-*ku-nu*
I ^{d}NUMUN-DÙ-*tú na-di-na-at* MU *u* NUMUN MU-*ku-nu* NUMUN-*ku-nu*

436 A [x x *lu-h*]*al-liq*
B [x x *lu-hal*]*-liq*
I *ina* KUR ⸢*lu*⸣*-hal-liq*

---

437 A [x x x x x x x x x x x x x x x KUR-*k*]*u-nu*
C ^{d}*be-lit*–[DINGIR.MEŠ x x x x x x x x x x] *ina* ⸢KUR⸣*-ku-nu*
F ^{d}*be-lit*–DINGIR.MEŠ ^{d}*be-lit nab-n*[*i-t*]*ú* ⸢*ta*⸣*-lit-tu ina* [KUR-*k*]*u-nu*
I ^{d}*be-lit*–DINGIR.MEŠ ^{d}*be-lit nab-ni-ti ta-lit-tu ina* KUR-*ku-nu*
438 C [x x x x x x x x x x]
F *lip-ru-us i*[*k-kil* TU]R.DIŠ *la-ke-e*
I *lip-ru-us ik-*⸢*kil*⸣ [TUR].DIŠ! *u*! *la-ke-e*
439 C [x x] *ri-*[x x x x x x x x x x x]
F *ina* SI[LA x x x x x x x x *ta-rit*]*-ku-un*
I *ina* SILA *ri-bit li-ṣa-a*[*m-mi ta*]*-rit-ku-un*

---

440 C ^{d}[IM x x x x x x x x x x x x x] *lip-ru-*[*us*]
F ^{d}IM [x x x x x x x x x] *ina* KUR-*k*[*u-nu* x x x]
g ⸢^{d}⸣IM GÚ.GAL AN-*e* KI.TIM ⸢A⸣.[KAL? x x x x x x x]
441 A *ta-me-ra-a-ti-*[*ku-nu* x x x x x]
C [x x x x x x x x x x x x x]
F [x x x x x x x] *l*[*i-*x x x x]
g *ta-me-ra-a-ti-ku-nu li-za-a*[*m-mi*]
442 A *ina ri-ih-ṣi dan-ni* KUR-*ku-*[*nu* x x x]
C *ina r*[*i-ih-ṣi* x x x x x x x x]
1 [x x x x x x x x x x x x BU]RU$_5$
g *ina ri-ih-ṣi dan-ni* KUR-*ku-nu* [x x x] BURU$_5$
443 A *mu-ṣa-hi-ir* KUR BURU$_{14}$*-ku-nu* ⸢*li*?⸣-[x x x x x x x]
1 *mu-*[x x x x x x x x *i*]*k-kil* NA$_4$.[UR$_5$ x x]
g *mu-ṣa-hi-ir* KUR BURU$_{14}$*-ku-nu* [x x] *ik-kil* NA$_4$.UR$_5$ *u* NINDU
444 A *ina* É.MEŠ-*ku-nu a-a* GÁL-*ši* ŠE.PAD.MEŠ *a-n*[*a* x x x]
1 [x x x x x x x x x x] ŠE.PAD.MEŠ *a-na ṭe-*[*ia-ni*]
g *ina* É.MEŠ-*k*[*u-nu* x x x x] ŠE.PAD.MEŠ *a-na ṭe-ia-ni*
445 A *li-tah-li-qa-ku-nu ku-um* ŠE.PAD.MEŠ *eṣ-*[*ma-ti-ku-nu*]
1 [x x x x x x] *ku-um* ŠE.PAD *eṣ-ma-*[x x x]
g *lu tah*!-[*li-qa-ku-nu*] *ku-um* ŠE.PAD.MEŠ *eṣ-ma-ti-ku-nu*
446 A DUMU.MEŠ-*ku-nu* DUMU.MÍ.MEŠ-*ku-nu li-ṭe-nu ki-ṣir* [x x x x x]
1 [x x x x x x x x x x] *li-ṭe-nu ki-*[*ṣir* x x x x x]
g DUMU.MEŠ-*ku-nu* [x x x x x x x x x] *ki-ṣir šá* ŠU.SI-*ku-nu*
447 A *ina* ⸢*le-ši lu la i-ṭa-bu*⸣ 0? ⸢x⸣-[*k*]*u-nu l*[*e-šu*]
1 [x x x x x x x x x x x]x x x[x x x x x x x x x x x]
g *ina le-e-še lu la i-ṭa-ab-b*[*u* x x x] *a-ṣu-da-ti-ku-nu le-e-še*
448 A *le-kul* AMA UGU DUMU.MÍ-*šá* [KÁ-*šá li-di-il*]
1 [x x] ⸢AMA⸣ UGU DU[MU.MÍ-*šá* x x x x x]
g *le-kul* AMA UGU DUMU.M[Í-*šá* x x x x x]
449 A *ina bu-ri-ku-nu* UZU.MEŠ DUMU.MEŠ-*ku-nu a*[*k-la* x x x x]
1 [x x x x x] UZU DUMU.MEŠ-*ku-nu* ⸢*ak-la*⸣ [x x x x]
g UZU.MEŠ DUMU.MEŠ-*ku-nu ak-la ina bu-b*[*u-ti*]

450 A *hu-šah-hu* LÚ UZU LÚ *le-kul* L[Ú x x]
l [x x x x x x x x x] LÚ KUŠ LÚ
g [0?] LÚ UZU LÚ *le-e-kul* LÚ KUŠ LÚ
451 A *li-la-biš* UZU.MEŠ-*ku-nu* UR.KU.MEŠ ŠAH.MEŠ *le-kul*
_ [x x x x x x x x x x x x x *le-ku*]-*lu*
l *li-la-biš* [x x x x x x x x x x] *le-ku-lu*
g *l*[*i-la-biš*] UZU.MEŠ-*ku-nu* UR.KU.MEŠ ŠAH *le-e-ku-lu*
_ [*li-la-bi*]*š* UZU.MEŠ-*k*[*u-nu* x x x x x *le-ku*]-*lu*
452 A G[IDI]M?-*ku-nu pa-qi-du na-aq* A.MEŠ *a-a ir*-[*ši*]
_ [x x x x x x x x x x x *a*]-*a ir-ši*
l GIDIM-*ku-nu pa*-[*qi-du* x x x x x x x x x]
g [x x x] *pa-qi-du na-aq* A.MEŠ *a*.[*a* x x]
_ *e-ṭém*-˹*ma-ku*˺-*nu* [x x x x x A].MEŠ *a-a ir-še*

453 A ^{d}IŠ.TAR EN MURUB$_4$ MÈ *ina* MÈ *da*[*n-ni* x x x x x x]
B [x x x x x x x x x] ˹MÈ?˺ [x x x x x x x x]
_ [x x x x x x x x x x M]È *dan-ni* GIŠ.BAN-*ku-nu liš-bir*
l ^{d}IŠ.TAR *be-lit* MURUB$_4$ *u* M[È x x x x x x x x *liš*]-*bir*
g ^{d}IŠ.TAR *be-lit* MURUB$_4$ MÈ *ina* M[È x x x x x x x x]
_ [x x x x x x x x x x] *dan-ni* GIŠ.BAN-*ku-nu* [x x]
454 A *i-di-ku-nu lik-si ina* ˹KI!˺.[TA] LÚ.KÚR-*k*[*u-nu* x x x x x]
B [x x x x x x x x x] LÚ.KÚR-*ku-nu* [x x x x x]
_ [x x x x x x x KI].TA LÚ.KÚR-*ku-nu li-še-šib-ku-nu*
l *i-di-ku-nu lik-si* [x x x x x x x x x x x x]
g *i-di-ku-nu li-ik-si ina* K[I.TA x x x x x x x x x]
_ [*i-di-ku-n*]*u lik-si* [x x x x x x x *li-š*]*e-šib-ku-nu*

455 A ^{d}U.GUR *qar-r*[*ad* x] *ina* GÍR-˹*šú*˺ *la ga-me-li nap-šat-ku*-[*nu*]
B [x x x x x x x x x x x x x x] *nap-šat-ku-nu*
_ [x x x x x x x GÍR]-*šú la g*[*a-me-li na*]*p*-˹*šat*˺-*ku-nu*
l [^{d}U.G]UR UR.SAG DINGIR *in*[*a* x x x x x x x x x x x]
g ^{d}U.GUR *qar-rad* DINGIR *ina* GÍR-*šú l*[*a* x x x x x x x x]
k [x x x x x x x] GÍR-*šú la ga-me-li* [x x x x]
_ [x x x x x x x GÍ]R-*šú la ga-me-li* [x x x x]
456 A [*l*]*i-bal-l*[*i*] *šá-ga-áš-t*[*ú*] *mu-t*[*a-a*]-*nu ina* ŠÀ-*bi-ku-nu liš-kun*
B [x x x x x x x x x x x x x Š]À-*ku-nu liš-kun*
l [*li-ba*]*l*-˹*li*˺ [x x x x x x x x x x x x x x x x]
g ˹*li*˺-*bal-li šag-gaš-tú* [x x x x x x x x x x x x]
k [x x x] *šá-ga-áš-tu* NAM.ÚŠ [x x x x x *li*]-*iš-ku-nu*
_ [x x x] *šag-ga-aš-tu* [x x x x x ŠÀ-*b*]*i-ku-nu liš-ku*[*n*]

457 A ^{d}NIN.LÍL *a-ši-bat* URU.NINA.KI
_ ^{d}NIN.LÍL *a-ši-bat* NINA.KI
k [x x x x x x NI]NA
_ [x x x x x x NI]NA.KI

458 A [GÍ]R.AN.BAR [*ha-an-ṭ*]*u it-ti-ku-nu li-ir-ku-su*
B [x x *ha-a*]*n-ṭu it-ti-ku-nu li-ir-ku-*[*su*]
k *pat-ri ha-an-ṭu* [x x x x *li-i*]*r-ku-su*
_ *pat-ru ha-am-ṭ*[*u it-ti-ku-n*]*u li-ir-ku-*[*su*]

459 A [x x x *a-ši*]*-bat* URU.*ar*[*ba-ìl*] *re-e-mu gim-lu*
_ ^{d}IŠ.TAR *a-ši-bat* URU.*arba-ìl* AMA [x x]
k [x x x x x x URU.*arba*]*-ìl re-e-mu gim-lu*
_ [x x x x x x x x x *r*]*e-e-mu g*[*i-mi-lu*]
460 A [x x *i-šá*]*-kan* UGU*-ku-un*
B [*lu l*]*a*! *i-šá-kan* UG[U*-ku-un*]
k [x x x x x UG]U*-ku-un*
_ ˹*a*˺.[*a iš-kun*? x x x]

461 A [x x x x x x x x x x GI]G ˹*ta*˺*-né-*˹*hu*˺ [*ina* ŠÀ*-bi-ku-nu*?]
_ ^{d}*gu-la a-zu-gal-la-tú* GAL*-tú* [x x x x x x x x x]
k [x x x x x x x x x]x*-tu* GIG *ta-né-hu* [x x x x x]
_ ^{d}*gu-la a-*[*zu-gal-la*]*-tú* G[AL*-tú* x x x x x x x x x]
462 _ [*si*]*-*˹*mu la-zu ina* SU˺*-ku-*˹*nu*˺ *l*[*i-iš-kun da-mu u šar-ku*]
k [x x x x *in*]*a zu-um-ri-*[*ku-nu* x x x x x x x x x]
_ *si-*˹*mu*˺ *la-zu ina zu-um-*(*ri*)*-ku-nu liš-k*[*un* x x x x x]
463 _ *ki-ma* A.MEŠ *ru-*[*un-ka*]

464 _ ^{d}*si-bit-ti* DINGIR.ME[Š *qa*]*r-d*[*u-te ina* GIŠ.TUKUL.MEŠ*-šú-nu*]
465 _ *ez-zu-ti na-aš-pan-*[*ta-ku-nu liš-ku-nu*]

466 _ [*d*].*a-ra-miš* EN *im*? x[x x x x x x x x x x]
[x x x x x x x x x x x x x x]*-ku-n*[*u* x x x x x x x x x x x x x]*-tu*

467 D ˹^{d}˺[x x x x x x x x x x x x x x x x x x]
_ [^{d}*ba-a-a-ti*–DINGIR.MEŠ ^{d}*a-na-t*]*i–ba-a-a-ti*–DINGIR.[MEŠ]
468 D *ina* ŠU.2 UR.M[AH *a-ki-li* x x x x]
_ [x x x x x x x x x] *lim-nu-ku-nu*

469 D ^{d}*kù-*KÁ ^{d}1[5 *ša* URU].*gar-ga-mis*
_ [x x x x x x URU.*gar-g*]*a-mis*
470 D *ri-im-ṭu dan-nu ina* ˹ŠÀ*-ku-nu liš-kun*˺ [KÀŠ].MEŠ*-ku-nu*
471 D *ki-ma ti*!*-ki ana kaq-qar lit-ta-tuk*!

472 D DIN[GIR.MEŠ G]AL.MEŠ *šá* AN*-e* KI.TIM *a-ši-bu-tu kib-ra-*˹*a-ti*˺
473 D *ma-la ina ṭup-pi an-ni-e* MU*-šú-nu zak-r*[*u*]
474 D *lim-ha-ṣu-ku-nu li-kil-mu-ku-nu*
475 D *ár-ra-tu ma-ru-uš-tu ag-giš li-ru-ru-ku-nu*
476 D *e-liš* TI.LA.MEŠ *li-sa-hu-ku-nu šap-liš ina* KI.TIM
477 H [x x x x x x x x x] GIŠ.MI [x x x]
D *e-ṭém-ma-ku-nu* A.MEŠ *li-ṣa-mu-u* GIŠ.MI *u* UD.DA

478 H [x x x x x x x x x x x x] *šá-h[a-ti]*
D *li-ik-ta-ši-⸢du-ku⸣-nu ina ⸢pu-uz-ri⸣* [x x x]
479 D *la ta-nim-me-da* ⸢NINDA⸣.MEŠ *u* A.MEŠ *li-z[i-b]u-ku-nu*
480 H *s[u-un-qu* x x x x x x x x x x]
D *su-un-qu hu-⸢šah⸣-hu bu-bu-tu* NAM.[Ú]Š.MEŠ
481 H [x x x x] *a.⸢a⸣* [x x x x x x x x x x x x]
D TA IGI-*ku-nu a.[a] ip-pi-ṭir! si-si šá ar-da-te-ku-nu*
482 H [x x] *šá* [x x x x x x x x x x x x x x x x x x]
D *mat-nat šá* LÚ.KAL.MEŠ-*ku-nu ina ni-ṭil* IGI.2-*ku-nu* UR.GI$_7$ ŠAH.MEŠ
_ [x x x] LÚ.KAL.MEŠ-*ku-nu* [x x x x x x x x x x x x]
483 H *in[a* x x x x x x x x x x x x x x x x x x x]
D *ina re-bit aš-šur li-in-da-šá-ru* LÚ.ÚŠ.MEŠ-*ku-nu* KI.TIM
_ *[in]a re-bit* URU.*aš-š[ur* x x x x x] LÚ.ÚŠ.MEŠ-*ku-n[u* x x]
484 D *a-a im-hur* [x] *kar-ši* UR.KU ŠAH.MEŠ *lu naq-bar-qa-ku-nu*
_ [x x x x] *ina kar-ši* UR.[KU x x x x x x x x]
[x x x x x x x x x x x x x *n]a-⸢aq-bar⸣-ku-[nu]*
485 D UD.MEŠ-*ku-n[u lu] ⸢e⸣-ṭu-u* MU.MEŠ-*ku-nu lu ek-la ek-le-tú*
_ [UD].MEŠ-*ku-nu* [x x x x x x x x x x x x x *e]k-le-[tu]*
[x x x x x] *⸢e⸣-ṭu-ú* MU.AN.NA.MEŠ-*ku-[nu* x x x *e]k-le-tu*
486 D *la na-[ma-a-ri] a-na šim-⸢ti⸣ li-ši-mu*
_ [x x x x x x x x x x *l]i-ši-m[u]*
la na-ma-a-r[i x x *šim-t]i-ku-nu li-ši-i-[mu]*
487 D *ina ta-n[i-hu d]i-lip-tu n[a-piš]-ta-ku-nu liq-ti*
_ [x x x x *di]-lip-ti na-piš-ta-ku-n[u* x x]
488 D *bu-bu-lu a-bu-bu la mah-ru ul-tú* KI.TIM
_ [UD.N]Á.À[M x x x x x x x x x x x x] [x x x] *a-bu-bu ul-tu* ŠÀ KI.TIM
489 D *li-la-a-ma na-aš-pan-ta-ku-nu liš-kun mim-ma* DÙG.GA *lu ik-kib-ku-nu*
_ *li-[la-a-ma na-aš-pan-ta-k]u-nu liš-ku-[un* x x DÙG.G]A *lu ik-kib-ku-[nu]*
490 D *mim-ma* GIG *⸢lu⸣ ši-mat-ku-nu qi-i-ru ku-up-ru lu ma-ka-la-ku-nu*
_ [x x GI]G *lu ši-mat-ku-[nu* x x x *k]u-up-ru lu ma-ka-*[x x x]
[x x x x x x x x x *q]i-⸢i-ru ku⸣-[up-ru* x x x x x x]
491 D KÁŠ ANŠE.NITÁ *lu maš-qit-ku-nu nap-ṭu lu pi-šat-ku-nu*
_ [x x x x] *maš-qit-ku-[nu* x x x x x x x x]
[x AN]ŠE.NITÁ *lu maš-qit-ku-nu* [x x x x x x x]
492 D *e-la-pu-u-a šá* ÍD *lu tak-tim-ku-nu*
V [x x x x x x x] *lu tak-tim-ku-nu*
_ *e-la-pu-u šá* ÍD [x x x x x] [x x x x x x x *tak]-⸢tim⸣-[ku-nu]*
493 D *še-e-d[u] ú-tuk-ku ra-bi-ṣu lem!-nu* É.MEŠ-*ku-nu li-hi-ru*
V [x x x x x x x x x x x x É].MEŠ-*ku-nu li-hi-ru!*
_ *[še]-e-du ú-tuk-ku* [x x x x x] É.MEŠ-*ku-nu li-hi-ru*

---

494 D DINGIR.MEŠ *an-nu-te lid-gu-lu šum-ma a-ni-nu ina* UGU ^{m}*aš-šur*–PAB–AŠ
V [x x x x x x x x x x x *a]-ni-nu ina* UGU [^{m}*aš-šur*–PA]B–AŠ
_ [x x x x x *lid-g]u-lu šu[m-ma* x x x x x x x x x x x]
q [x x x x x x x x x x x x x x x x ^{m}*aš-šur*–PAB]–AŠ
_ [x x x x x x x x x x x x x x *in]a* UGU [x x x x x]
DINGIR.[MEŠ *an]-⸢nu-ti⸣ l[id-gu-lu* x x x x x x x x x x x x x]

495 D MAN KUR–*aš-⸢šur⸣ ina* UGU ^{m}*aš-šur*–DÙ–A DUMU–MAN GAL *šá* É–UŠ-*ti*
V MA[N x x x x x x x x x x x x x x x x x x x]
_ [x] KUR–*aš-šur ina* UG[U x x x x x x x x x É–UŠ]-*te*
q MAN K[UR–*aš-šur* x x x x x x x] DUMU–MAN GAL *šá* É–⸢UŠ⸣-[*ti*]
_ [x x x x x x x x x x x DUMU]–MAN GAL-*ú* [x x x x]
MAN KUR–*aš-šur* EN!-*ni* [x x x x x x x x x x x x x x x]
496 D ŠEŠ.MEŠ-*šú* DUMU AMA-*šú šá* ^{m}*aš-šur*–DÙ–A DUMU–MAN GAL *šá* É–UŠ-*ti*
V [x x]x-*šú*
_ ŠEŠ.[MEŠ-*šú* x x x x x x x x x DUMU]–MAN GAL-*u* ⸢*ša*⸣ [x x x]
q [ŠEŠ.ME]Š-*šú* DUMU AMA-*šú šá* ^{m}*aš-šur*–DÙ–A DUMU–MAN GAL [x É]–UŠ-⸢*te*?⸣
_ [x x x x x x x ^{m}*aš-šur*]–⸢DÙ⸣–A [x x x x x x x]
ŠEŠ.MEŠ-*šú* DUMU AMA-[*šú* x x x x x x x x x x x x x x]
497 D *ú re-eh-ti* DUMU *ṣi-it*–ŠÀ-*bi šá* ^{m}*aš-šur*–PAB–AŠ MAN KUR–*aš-šur*
V 0
_ [x x x x x x x x x x x x x x x x KUR–*aš-šu*]*r* EN-*i-ni*
q *re-eh-ti* DUMU.MEŠ *ṣi-it*–ŠÀ-*bi* [x] ^{m}*aš-šur*–PAB–AŠ MAN KUR–*aš–šur* EN-*i-ni*
_ ⸢*re*⸣-*eh-ti* DUMU [x x x x x x x x x x x x x x x x x]
498 D *si-hu bar-tu né-ep-pa-áš-u-ni pi-i-ni* TA
V *si-hu bar-tú* [*né-ep-pa*]-*áš-u-ni pi*-⸢*i*⸣-*ni* ⸢TA⸣
q [*si-h*]*u bar-tu né-ep-pa-áš-u-ni* [*pi*]-⸢*i*⸣-*ni* TA*
si-h[*u* x x x x x x x x x] *pi-i-*[*ni* TA*]
499 D LÚ.KÚR-*šú ni-šá-kan-u*-⸢*ni*⸣ *šum-ma*
V [LÚ.KÚR.M]EŠ-*šú ni-šá-kan-u-ni* [x x]
q LÚ.KÚR-*šú ni-šá-kan-u-ni* [x x]
[x x x x x x x x x] *šum-ma*
500 D *mu-šam-hi-ṣu-u-tú mu-šad-bi-bu-tu li-ih-šu*
V *mu-šam-hi-ṣu*!-*tu mu-šad-bi-bu-tú li-ih-šú*
q *mu-šam-hi-ṣu-tu mu-šad-bi-bu-tu* [*li-ih*]-*šu*
[x x x x x x x x x x x] *li-ih-*[*šu*]
501 D *ša a-mat* MÍ.HUL *la* DÙG.GA-*tu la ba-ni-tu*
V [x] *a-mat* MÍ.HUL *la* DÙG.GA-*tú la ba*-⸢*ni*⸣-*tú*
q *šá a-mat* HUL-*tim la* DÙG.GA-*tu la ba-ni-tu*
502 A [x x *s*]*u*?-*ra-a-te l*[*a k*]*e-na-*[*a-t*]*i*
D *da-bab sur-ra-a-ti la ke-na-a-ti*
V *da-bab su-ra-a-ti u la ke-na-a-te*
q [x x *su*]-*ra-a-ti la ke-na-a-ti da-bab su-*[*ra-a-ti* x x x x x]
503 A [x x x] ^{m}[*aš-š*]*ur*–DÙ–A DU[MU–M]AN GAL *šá* É–UŠ-*ti*
D *šá ina* UGU ^{m}*aš-šur*–DÙ–A DUMU–MAN GAL *šá* É–UŠ-*ti*
V *šá ina* UGU ^{m}*aš-šur*–DÙ–A [D]UMU–MAN GAL-*u šá* É–UŠ-*te*
q [x x x ^{m}]*aš-šur*–DÙ–A DUMU–MAN GAL *šá* É–UŠ-*ti*
[x x U]GU ^{m}[x x x x x x x x x x x x]
504 A [x ŠEŠ].MEŠ-*šú* DUMU.MEŠ AMA-*šú šá* ^{m}*aš-šur*–DÙ–A DUMU–MAN GAL
D *ù* ŠEŠ.MEŠ-*šú* DUMU AMA-*šú šá* ^{m}*aš-šur*–DÙ–A DUMU–MAN GAL
V *u* ŠEŠ.MEŠ-*šú* DUMU AM[A-*š*]*ú*? *šá* ^{m}*aš-šur*–DÙ–A DUMU–MAN GAL-*u*
q [x ŠEŠ.MEŠ]-*šú* DUMU AMA-*šú šá* ^{m}*aš-šur*–DÙ–A DUMU–MAN GAL

505 A *šá* É–UŠ-*ti ni-šam-mu-u-ni nu-pa-zar-u-ni*
D *šá* É–UŠ-*ti ni-šam-mu-u-ni nu-pa-za-ru-u-ni*
V *šá* É–UŠ-*te ni-šá-mu-u-ni nu-pa-za-ar-u-ni*
q [x x x x *u re-eh-t*]*i* DUMU.MEŠ *ṣi-it*–ŠÀ-*bi* [*ša* ^{m}*aš-šur*–PAB–AŠ
MAN KUR–*aš-š*]*ur* EN-*i-ni* [x x x x x x x x x]-*u-ni*
506 A [x x ^{m}*aš-šur*]–DÙ–A DUMU–MAN GAL *šá* É–UŠ-*ti* EN-*ni*
D *a-na* ^{m}*aš-šur*–DÙ–A DUMU–MAN GAL *šá* É–UŠ-*ti be-lí-ni*
V ⸢*a-na* ^{m}*aš*⸣-*šur*–DÙ–A DUMU–MAN GAL-*u šá* É–UŠ-*te* EN-*ni*
q [x x x x x x x x x x x É–U]Š-*ti* [x x]
_ [x x x x x x x x x x x É–UŠ]-*ti* [x x]
507 A [x *ni-qa-bu*]-*u-ni* UD.MEŠ *am–mar a*-[*ni*]-*nu* DUMU.MEŠ-*ni*
D *la ni-qa-bu-u-ni* UD-*mu am–mar a-ni-nu* DUMU.MEŠ-*ni*
V [x *ni*]-*qa-bu-u-ni* UD-*me am–mar a-ni-nu* DUMU.[MEŠ]-*ni*
q [x *ni-qa-bu*]-⸢*u-ni*?⸣ [x x x x x x x x x x]
_ [x *ni-qa-bu-u-n*]*i* [x x x x x x x x x x]
508 A [x x x x x x x x x] ^{m}*aš-š*[*ur*–DÙ–A DUM]U–MAN GAL *šá* É–UŠ-*ti*
D DUMU.MEŠ-*ni bal-ṭa-a-ni-ni* ^{m}*aš-šur*–DÙ–A DUMU–MAN GAL *šá* É–UŠ-*ti*
V [DUMU–DUMU].MEŠ-*ni bal-ṭa-a-ni-ni* ^{m}*aš-šur*–DÙ–A DUM[U–MAN x x] É–UŠ-*te*
_ [DUM]U.⸢DUMU⸣.[MEŠ-*ni* x x x x x x x x x x x x x x x x x x]
[DUMU–DUM]U.MEŠ-*ni* [x x x x x x x x x x x x x x] É–U[Š-*ti*]
509 A [x x x x x x x x x x x x x x x *šá-nu*]-*um-ma*
D *la* ⸢LUGAL⸣-*ni-ni la* EN-⸢*ni*⸣-*ni šum-ma* LUGAL MAN-*ma* DUMU–LUGAL MAN-*ma*
V *la* LUGAL-*ni-ni la* EN-*ni-n*[*i* x x x x x] DUMU–LUGAL MAN-*ma*
_ [x x x x] *la* EN-x[x x x x x x x x x x x]
[x x x x x x x x x x x x x x DUMU–LU]GAL MAN-*ma*
510 A [x x x x x x x x x x x x x x x x]-*ni*
D *ina* UGU-*hi-ni* DUMU.MEŠ-*ni* DUMU–DUMU.MEŠ-*ni ni-šá-kan-u-ni*
V *ina* UGU-*ni* DUMU.MEŠ-*ni* D[UMU–DUMU-.MEŠ-*ni* x x x x x]
_ [x x x x x x x DUMU–DUMU].MEŠ-*ni ni*-[*šá-kan-u-ni*]
[x x x x x x x DUMU–DUM]U.MEŠ-*ni* GAR-*nu-n*[*i*]
511 D ⸢DINGIR⸣.MEŠ *ma-la* MU-*šú-nu zak-ru ina* ŠU.2-*i-ni*
V [DI]NGIR.MEŠ *ma-la* MU-*šú-nu zak-ru ina* ŠU.2-[*ni*]
_ [x x x x M]U-*šú-nu za*[*k-ru* x x x x]
[x x x x x x x x x x Š]U.2-*ni*
512 D NUMUN-[*i-n*]*i* NUMUN–NUMUN-*i-ni lu-ba-'i-ú*
V [x x x x x x x] *lu-ba-'i*-[*u*]
_ [x x x x x x x] *lu*-[*ba-'i-u*] NUMUN-*ni* [x x x *lu-ba-'*]*i-ú*

---

513 D *šum-ma ina* ŠÀ *a-de-e an-nu-te šá* ^{m}*aš-šur*–PAB–AŠ MAN KUR–*aš-šur* EN-[*ku-nu*]
V [*šum*]-*ma at-tú-nu ina* ŠÀ *a-de-e an-nu-te šá* ^{m}[x x x x x x x x x x x]
514 A [x x ^{m}]*aš-šur*–D[Ù–A x x x x x x x]
D [x U]GU ^{m}*aš-šur*–DÙ–A DUMU–MAN ⸢GAL⸣ [x x x x]
V [*ina*] UGU ^{m}[*aš*]-*šur*–DÙ–A DUMU–MAN GAL-*u šá* É–UŠ-*t*[*e*]
515 A [ŠEŠ].MEŠ-*šú* DUMU [AMA-*šú ša* ^{m}*aš-šur*–DÙ–A x x x x x x x]
V [x x x x x x x ^{m}*aš-š*]*ur*–D[Ù–A] DUMU–MAN GAL-*u šá* É–UŠ-*te*
516 A [x x x x x x] *ṣi-it*–ŠÀ-*bi šá* ^{m}*aš-šur*–[PAB–AŠ MAN x x x]
V *u re-e*[*h-ti* DUMU.MEŠ x x x x x x x x x x x K]UR–*aš-šur*
_ [x x x x x x x x x x x x x x x x x x] ⸢KUR–*aš-šur*⸣

517 A [x x x x x UGU-*hi-š*]*u-nu a-de-e is-si-ku-nu* [x x x x x x x x x]
V EN-*ku-nu is-si-ku-nu* [*iš-kun-u-ni ta-ha-ṭa-a-n*]*i*
_ ⸢*šá*⸣ *ina* ⸢UGU⸣-*h*[*i-šú-nu* x x x x x x x *iš-kun-u*]*-ni ta-ha-ṭa-*[*a-ni*]
518 A [x x x x x x] *ina* GIŠ.TUKUL.MEŠ-[*šú* x x x x x x x x x]
V ^{d}*aš-šur* AD DINGIR.MEŠ *ina* GIŠ.TUKUL.ME[Š-*šú* x x x x *li-šam*]-*qit*-[*ku-nu*]
_ [x x x x x x x x x x x] *ez-zu-u-ti li-*[*šam-qit-ku-nu*]

---

519 A [^{d}]IGI.DU EN [*a*]-*šá*-[*ri-du* x x x]
I ^{d}⸢IGI.DU⸣ EN ⸢*a*⸣-[*šá-ri-du* x x x]
_ [x x x] EN SAG.KAL UZ[U-*ku-nu*]
520 A ⸢Á⸣.MUŠEN *zi-i-bu* [*li-šá-kil*]
I Á.MUŠEN *z*[*i-i-bu* x x x]

---

521 A ^{d}É.A LUGAL ZU.AB [x x x x x x]
G [x x x x x x] IDIM A.MEŠ *la* TI.LA
I ^{d}É.A MAN ZU.AB EN IDIM A.MEŠ [x x x]
_ [x x x x x x x] IDIM A.MEŠ *l*[*a* x x]
522 A *liš-qi-ku-nu a-ga-nu-ti-l*[*a-a* x x x x x]
G *liš-qi-ku-nu* [x x x x x x] *li-mal-li-ku-nu*
B [x x x x] *a-g*[*a-nu-ti-la-a* x x x x x]
I [x x x x] *a-ga-nu-til-la-a* [x x x x x]
_ [x x x x *a-ga-nu-ti-l*]*a-a* [x x x x x]

---

523 A DINGIR.MEŠ GAL.MEŠ *šá* AN-*e* [K]I.TIM A.MEŠ Ì.[MEŠ x x x x x x x]
G [x x x x *š*]*a* AN-*e* KI.TIM A.MEŠ Ì.MEŠ [*a-na* NÍG.GIG]-*ku-nu liš-ku-nu*
B DINGIR.MEŠ GAL.MEŠ *šá* AN-*e* K[I.TIM x x x x x x x x x x x]

---

524 A ^{d}GIŠ.BAR *na-din ma-ka-li a-n*[*a* x x x x]
G [x x x *na-d*]*in ma-ka-le-e a-na* TUR.MEŠ GAL.MEŠ
B ^{d}GIŠ.BAR *na-din ma-ka-li* ⸢*a*⸣-[*na* x x x x]
525 A ⸢MU⸣-*ku-nu* NUMUN-*ku-nu* [x x]
G [x x x] NUMUN-*ku-nu liq-mu*
B NUMUN.MEŠ-*ku-nu* NUMUN–NUMUN-*ku-n*[*u* x x]

---

526 A KI.MIN KI.MIN DINGIR.MEŠ *ma-la ina ṭup-p*[*i* x x x x x x x x x x x]
G 0
B KI.MIN DINGIR.MEŠ *ma-la* (*ina*) *ṭup-pi a-d*[*e*]-*e an*-[*ni-e* MU-*šú-nu zak-ru*]
527 A *am–mar* SIG$_4$ *kaq-qu-ru* ⸢*li*⸣-*s*[*i-qu-ni-ku-nu*]
G [x x x x *am–m*]*ar* SIG$_4$ [*ka*]*q-qu-ru lu-si-qu-ni-ku-nu*
F KI.MIN KI.MIN *am–mar* SIG$_4$ [*kaq*]-*qar lu-si-qu-ni-ku-nu*
B *am–mar* SIG$_4$ *kaq-qu-ru* ⸢*li*⸣-*si-q*[*u-ni-ku-nu*]
M [x x x *kaq*]-*qar* [x x x x x x]
528 A *kaq-qar-ku-nu ki-i* AN.BAR *le-pu-š*[*u* x x x]
G [x x x x *k*]*i-i* AN.⸢BAR⸣ *le-pu-šu me-me-ni*
F *kaq-qar-ku-nu ki-i* ⸢AN⸣.BAR *le-pu-šú me-me-ni*
B [x x x x] *ki-i* AN.BAR *le-e-pu-šú me-me-ni*
M [x x x x *k*]*i-i* AN.BAR [x x x x x x]

529 A *ina* ŠÀ-*bi l*[*u*] *la i*-[*par-ru-a*]
G [x x x x *l*]*a i-par-ru-a*
F *ina* ŠÀ-*bi* [*l*]*u la i-par-ru-'a*
B *ina* ŠÀ-*bi* [x x x x x x]
M [x x x x *l*]*a i-par-ru-a*
_ [x x x x x *i-par*]-*ru-'a*
530 A *ki-i šá* TA* ŠÀ ⸢AN⸣-[*e šá*] UD.KA.BAR A.AN ⸢*la*⸣ *i-za-nun-a-ni*
G *ki-i šá* TA ŠÀ AN-*e* [x x x x] A.AN *la i-za-nun-a-ni*!
F *ki-i šá* TA* ŠÀ [AN]-*e šá* UD.KA.BAR A.AN *la i-za-nun-u-ni*
B *ki-i šá* TA* ŠÀ AN-*e šá* UD.KA.BAR A.AN *l*[*a* x x x x x x]
M [x x x x x x x x UD.KA].BAR A.AN [x x x x x x]
_ *ki-i* TA* ŠÀ-*bi* AN-⸢*e*⸣ [x x x x A.A]N *la i-za-nun-u*-[*ni*]
531 A *ki-i ha-an*-⸢*ni-e*⸣ A⸣.A[N *na*]-*al-šú ina* ŠÀ A.ŠÀ.MEŠ-*ku-nu*
G [x x x x x x x x *na-al*]-*šu ina* A.ŠÀ.MEŠ-*ku*-[*n*]*u*
F [x x x x x x x x *n*]*a-al*-[*šú* x] A.ŠÀ.MEŠ-*ku-nu*
B *ki-i ha-an-ni-e zu-un-nu na-al-šú* [x x x x x x x]
M [x x x x x x x x *na*]-*al-šu ina* A.ŠÀ.MEŠ-*ku-nu*
_ [x x x x x x] *zu-un-nu n*[*a-al-šú* x x x x x x x]
532 A *ta-me-rat-k*[*u*]-*nu lu la* DU-*ak ku-um* [*na-a*]*l-šú*
G *ta-me-ra-ti-ku-nu* [x x *i*]*l-lak ku-um* A.AN
K [x x x x x x x x x x *ku-u*]*m zu-un*-⸢*nu*⸣
F [*ta-me-r*]*a*?-[*ti-k*]*u-nu lu la* DU-*ak*
B *ta-me-ra-a-ti-ku-nu lu* (*la*) ⸢*il*?⸣-*l*[*ak* x x x x x]
M [x x x x x x x] *la i-lak* [x x x x x]
533 A *pe-eh-n*[*a-a-ti*] *ina* KUR-*ku-nu li-iz*-[*nun*]
G *pe-e'-na-a-ti* [x KUR-*ku*]-*nu li-iz-nun*
K [x x x x x x x x x *li-iz*]-*nu-na*
F 0
B *pe-e'-na-a-ti* [x K]UR-*ku-n*[*u* x x x x]
M [*pe-e'-na*]-*a-ti ina* KUR-*ku-nu li-iz-nun*

---

534 A *ki*-⸢*i*⸣ [x AN.N]A *ina* IGI IZI *l*[*a* x x x x x]
G [x x x x x x x x x *i-za-z*]*u-u-ni*
F [x x x x x x x x x *i-za-z*]*u-u-ni*
M [x x x x x x IG]I IZI *la i-za-zu-u-ni*
F *ki-i šá* AN.NA *ina* IGI IZI [x x x x x x]
535 A [*at-t*]*u-nu* [x x L]Ú.KÚR-[*ku-nu* x x x x x x x x]
G [x x x x x x x x x x *ta-za-z*]*a* [x x x x]
K [*at-t*]*u-nu* [x x x x x x x x x x x x x x]
F *at-tu-nu* [x x x x x x x x x x D]UMU.MEŠ-*ku-nu*
M *at-tu-nu* [x x x x x x x *t*]*a-za-za* DUMU.MEŠ-*ku-nu*
_ *at-tu-nu ina* I[GI x x x x x x x x] DUMU.MEŠ-*ku-nu*
F [x x x] *ina* IGI ⸢LÚ⸣.KÚR-*ku*-[*nu la* x x x x x x x]
536 K [DUMU.MÍ.MEŠ-*k*]*u-nu* [x x x x x x *ta-ṣa-ba*]*t*
F [x x x x x x x x x x x *t*]*a-ṣa-ba-ta*
M DUMU.MÍ.MEŠ-*ku-nu ina* ŠU.2-*ku-nu* [*la ta-ṣa-ba*]-*t*[*a*]
F DUMU.MÍ.MEŠ-*ku-nu* [x x x x x x x x x x]

---

537 A [x x x x x] ANŠE.GÍR.NUN.N[A x x x x x x]
F [x x x x x x x x x x *la-á*]*š?-šu-u-ni*
_ *ki-i šá* NU[MUN x x x x x x x x x x x]
F *ki-i šá* NUM[UN] *šá* A[NŠE.x x x x x x x x x]
k KI.MIN *ki-i šá* NUMUN *šá* ANŠE.*k*[*u-di-ni* x x x x x]
_ [x x *ki*]-˹*i*˺ *šá* NUMUN *ša* ANŠE.*k*[*u-di-ni* x x x x x]
538 A [x x x N]UMUN-*ku-nu* NUMUN *šá* DU[MU.MEŠ-*ku-nu*]
K [MU-*k*]*u-nu* [x x x x x x x x x x]
F [MU-*ku-nu* NUMUN]-*ku-nu* DUMU.MEŠ-*ku-nu*
_ MU-*ku-n*[*u* x x x x x x x x x x]
F MU-*ku-nu* NUMUN-*ku-nu* [x x x x x x]
k MU-*ku-nu* NUMUN-*ku-nu* NU[MUN x] DUMU.MEŠ-*ku-nu*
_ [x x x NUMUN-*ku*]-*nu* NUMUN *šá* ŠEŠ.MEŠ-[*ku-nu*]
539 A [DUMU.MÍ.MEŠ]-*ku-nu* TA* KUR *l*[*i-ih-liq*]
F [x x x x x x x *li*]-*ih-liq*
_ DUMU.MÍ.ME[Š-*ku-nu* x x x x x]
F DUMU.MÍ.MEŠ-*ku-nu* [x x x x x]
k DUMU.MÍ.[MEŠ-*ku-nu*] TA* KUR *li*-[*ih-liq*]

---

540 A *k*[*i-i* x x x x x x x x x x x]
F [x x x x x x x *ki-i ti*]-*ta-bi ki-i šá* SI *šá* M[UNU$_4$ x x x x x]
k *ki-i šá qar-nu šá* M[UNU$_4$ x x x x x]
_ [*ki*]-˹*i*˺ *šá* ˹SI˺ *šá* M[UNU$_4$ x x x x x]
541 A *ina* ˹ŠÀ˺ [x x x x x x x x x x x x x x]
F [x x x x x x x x x] *la* [x x x x x]
_ [x x x x x x x x x]x ˹*la i*˺-*p*[*ar-ru-u-ni*]
F *ina* ŠÀ *šak-nu-u-n*[*i* x x] *la i-par-ru-u*-[*ni*]
k *ina* ŠÀ-*bi šak-nu-ni* K[I x] *la i-par-ru-ʾu-u-ni*
542 A [x x] *šú? ra* x[x x x x x x x x x x x x]
F [x x x x x x x]x-*ni-šá* [x x x x x x]
_ [x x x x x x x x x x] *la ta-sa*-[*har-u-ni*]
F [x x x x x x x x x x] *la ta-sa-h*[*ar-u-ni*]
k [x x x x x x x x x x x] *ta-sa-har-u-ni*
543 A [NUMU]N-*ku-nu* NUMUN.MEŠ *šá* D[UMU?.MEŠ-*ku-nu* x x x x x]
F [x x x x x x x x x x]-*nu* [x x x x x]
_ [x x x x x x x x x]-*ku-nu* DUMU.MÍ.[MEŠ-*ku-nu*]
F [x x x] NUMUN *šá* ŠEŠ.[MEŠ-*ku-nu* x x x x x]
k [x x x x x x x x x x x x x x x-*n*]*u*
544 A [TA?] UGU *pa-ni ša kaq-qa-ri* [x x x]
F [x x x x x x x x x *l*]*i-ih-liq*
_ [x x x x x x x x x] *li-ih*-[*liq*]
k *ina* KUR *li*-[*ih-liq*]

---

545 A ^{d}UTU *ina* [GI]Š.˹APIN˺ *šá* AN.BAR URU-*ku*-[*nu* x x x x]
F [x x x x x x x x x x x x *na-gi-ku*]-*nu*
_ [x x x x x x x x x x x x *na*]-˹*gi*˺-*k*[*u-nu*]
^{d}UTU *ina* GIŠ.APIN *šá* AN.B[AR x x x] *na-gi-ku-nu*

546 A *lu-*[*šá-b*]*al*!*-ki*[*t*]
F [*lu-šá-bal*]*-kit*
_ *l*[*u-šá-bal-kit*]

---

547 A *ki-i šá* ˹U$_8$˺ [*an-ni*]*-tú šal-qa-*[*tu-u-ni* x x x x]
_ [x x x x x x x x x x x x *šal-qa-t*]*u-u-ni* UZU *šá* DUMU-[*šá*] KI.MIN KI.MIN
ki-i šá ˹U$_8$˺ [x x x x x x x x x] UZU *šá* DUMU-*šá*
548 A *ina pi-i-šá šá-kín-u-ni ki-i ha-an-ni-*˹*e*˺ [x x]
_ [x x x x x x x x x x x x x x x x x x]x *ina pi-*[*i-šá* x x x x x x x x x x x x x]
549 A UZU *šá* ŠEŠ.MEŠ-*ku-nu* DUMU.MEŠ-*ku-nu* DUMU.MÍ.MEŠ-*ku-nu*
_ UZU *šá* DUMU.MEŠ-*ku-*[*nu* x x x x x x]
[x x ŠEŠ.MEŠ]-*ku-nu* DUMU.MEŠ-*ku-nu* [x x x x x]
[x x x x x x DUM]U.MEŠ-*k*[*u-nu* x x x x x]
550 A *a-na bu-ri-ku-nu lu-šá-kil-ku-n*[*u*]
_ [x x x x x x] *lu-šá-ki-li-ku-n*[*u*]
[x x *bu-ri-ku-n*]*u lu-šá-kil-u-ku-nu*

---

551 A *ki-i šá kab-su kab-su-tú* NIM MÍ.NIM-*tú šal-*[*q*]*u-u-ni*
D [x x x *k*]*ab-su kab-su-tú* UDU.NIM ˹*šá*?*-al*˺*-qu-u-ni*
_ [x x x x x x x x x x x x x x *šal*]*-qu-u-*[*ni*]
[x x x x x *kab-s*]*u-tú* UDU.NIM MÍ.UDU.NIM-*tú* [x x x x]
ki-i šá kab-su kab-su-tú NIM MÍ.[NIM-*tú* x x x x]
552 A *ir-ri-šú-nu* TA* GÌR.2.MEŠ-*šú-nu kar-ku-u-ni*
D [*ir-ri*]*-šu-nu* TA GÌR.2-*šú kar-ku-u-ni*
_ [x x x x T]A* GÌR.2.MEŠ-*šú-nu kar-ku-u-ni*
ir-ri-šú-nu TA* GÌR.2-*šú-nu kar-*[*ku-u-ni*]
553 A *ir-ri šá* DUMU.MEŠ-*ku-nu* DUMU.MÍ.MEŠ-*ku-nu* TA* GÌR.2.MEŠ-*ku-nu*
D *ir-ri-ku-nu* [*ir*]*-ri šá* DUMU.MEŠ-*ku-nu* DUMU.MÍ.MEŠ-*ku-nu* TA GÌR.2-*ku-nu*
_ [x x x x x x x x x x x x DUMU.M]Í.MEŠ-*ku-nu* TA* GÌR.2.MEŠ-˹*ku*˺-[*nu*]
ir-ri šá DUMU.MEŠ-*ku-nu* DUMU.MÍ.MEŠ-*k*[*u-nu* x x x x x x]
554 A *li-kar-ku*
D ˹*li*˺*-kar-ku*
_ ˹*li-kar*˺*-ku li-kar-*[*ku*]

---

555 _ [*šum-ma at-tu-nu ina* ŠÀ *a-de*]*-e an-nu-ti šá* ^{m}*aš-šur*–PAB–AŠ MAN KUR–*aš-šur*
[*šá ina* UGU ^{m}*aš-šur*–DÙ–A DUMU–MAN GAL *šá* É–U]Š-*ti ta-ha-ṭa-a-ni*
[x x x x x x x x x x x x Š]À 1-*et hu-ri-ti*
A *ki-i šá* MUŠ ^{d}NIN.PÉŠ *ina* ŠÀ-*bi* 1-˹*et hu-ri*˺*-te*
D [KI.M]IN *ki-i šá* MU[Š] *ù* ^{d}NIN.PÉŠ *ina* ŠÀ-*bi* 1-*et hu-ri-ti*
_ *ki-i šá* MUŠ ^{d}NIN.PÉŠ *ina* ŠÀ 1-*e*[*t* x x x]
556 A *la e-rab-u-ni la i-ra-bi-ṣu-u-ni*
D *la er-rab-u-*˹*ni*˺ [*l*]*a i-rab-b*[*i-ṣu-u-ni*]
_ [x x x x x x x x x x x x]*-ni la er-rab-u-ni la i-rab-bi-*[*ṣu-u-ni*]
557 A *ina* UGU *na-kas* ZI.MEŠ *šá a-he-iš i-da-ba-bu-u-ni*
D [x x x x Z]I.MEŠ *ša a-he-iš i-da-ba-bu-u-ni*
_ *ina* UGU ZI.MEŠ [x x x x x x x x x]
558 A [*a*]*t-tu-nu* MÍ.MEŠ-*ku-nu ina* ŠÀ-*bi* 1-*en* É *la te-rab-ba*
D *at-tu-nu* MÍ-˹MEŠ-*ku*˺*-nu ina* ŠÀ 1-*en* É *la te-ra-ba*
_ *at-tú-nu* MÍ.MEŠ-*ku-nu ina* ŠÀ 1-*en* É *l*[*a* x x x]

559 A [x U]GU *na-kas* ZI.MEŠ *šá a-he-iš du-ub-ba*
D *ina* UGU 1-*et* G[IŠ.N]Á *la ta-ta-la ina* UGU *na-kas* ZI.MEŠ *šá a-*[*he-iš du-ub*]-*ba*
_ *ina* UGU 1-*et* GIŠ.NÁ *la ta-*[*ta-la*] *ina* UGU *na-kás* ZI.MEŠ *šá a-*[*he-iš* x x x]

---

560 A [x x x x x x x x x x] *u* GEŠTIN *ina* ŠÀ-*bi ir-ri e-rab-u-ni*
D KI.MIN KI.MIN *ki-i šá* NINDA.MEŠ *u* GEŠTIN.MEŠ *ina* ŠÀ *ir-ri-*[*ku-nu*] *er-rab-u-ni*
561 A [*ki-i ha-an-ni*]-*i ta-me-tú an-ni-tú ina* ŠÀ-*bi ir-*˹*ri*˺-[*ku-nu*]
D *ta-me-*˹*tu an*˺-[*ni-tu* x] ˹ŠÀ? *ir*˺-*r*[*i-ku-nu*]
562 A [x x x x x x x D]UMU.MÍ.MEŠ-*ku-nu lu-še-r*[*i-bu*]
D *ir-ri šá* DU[MU.MEŠ-*ku-nu* DUMU.M]Í.MEŠ-*ku-nu lu-še-ri-bu*

---

563 D KI.[MIN KI.MIN *k*]*i-i šá* A.MEŠ *ina* ŠÀ *ta*[*k-k*]*u-si ta-nap-pa-ha-a-ni*
564 D *a-n*[*a k*]*a-šú-nu* MÍ.MEŠ-*ku-nu* DUMU.MEŠ-*ku-nu* DUMU.MÍ.MEŠ-*ku-nu*
_ [x x x x x x x x x x x x x x] DUMU.MÍ.MEŠ-*ku-nu*
565 D *li-p*[*u-h*]*u-ku-nu* ÍD.MEŠ-*ku-nu* [IGI.2.MEŠ-*k*]*u-nu* ˹PÚ˺.MEŠ-*ši-na*
_ [x x x x x x x x x x] IGI.2.MEŠ-*ku-nu* PÚ.M[EŠ-*ši-na*]
566 D *a-na qí-*[*i*]*n-niš lu-*[*sa-h*]*i-ru*
_ [x x] *qí-in-niš lu-sa-hi-r*[*u*]

---

567 Q [x x x x x *ina p*]*i?-*˹*it*˺-*ti* KUG.GI *i*[*na* KUR]-*ku-nu lu-šá-l*[*i-ku*]
D KI.MIN KI.MIN *ana* ˹GI!˺.NA KUG.GI *ina* KUR-*k*[*u-nu*] *lu-šá-li-ku*
_ [x x x x x *ina*] *pi-it* KUG.GI *ina* [x x x] *lu-šá-li-ku*
[x x x x x x] *pi-*[*it* x x x x x x x x x x]

---

568 Q [x x x x x x] *šá* LÀL *ma-ti-qu-u-ni* MÚD.MEŠ *šá* MÍ.MEŠ-*ku-nu*
D KI.MIN *ki-i šá* LÀL ˹*ma*˺-[*t*]*e-qu-u-n*[*i* MÚD].MEŠ *šá* MÍ.MEŠ-*ku-nu*
_ *ki-i šá* LÀ[L *ma*]-*ti-qu-u-ni* MÚD.MEŠ *šá* MÍ.MEŠ-*ku-nu* [K]I.MIN KI.MIN
ki-˹*i šá*˺ [x x x x x x x x x x x x x x]
569 Q DUMU.MEŠ-*ku-nu ina pi-i-ku-nu* ˹*li*˺-*in-ti-iq*
D DUMU.MEŠ-*ku-nu* DUMU.MÍ.MEŠ-*k*[*u-nu* x *pi-i*]-*ku-nu* ˹*li*˺-AH-*ti-iq*
_ DUMU.MEŠ-*ku-nu* DUMU.MÍ.MEŠ-*ku-nu ina pi-i-ku-nu li-im-ti-iq*
[D]UMU.MEŠ-*ku-nu* DUMU.MÍ.M[EŠ-*ku-nu* x x x x x x x x x]

---

570 Q *ki-i šá šá-as-s*[*u-ru m*]*a-dul?-tú ta-kul-u-ni*
D KI.MIN *ki-i šá šá-as-r*[*u ma-dul*]-*tu ta-kul-u-ni*
_ [x x x x] *šá šá-*˹*as*˺-[*su-ru ma-dul*]-*tu ta-kul-u-ni*
[x x x x x *šá*]-˹*as?-su?*˺-[*ru* x x x x x x x]
[x x x x x x x x x x x x x *ta-kul-u*]-˹*ni*˺
571 Q *ina bal-ṭu-te-ku-nu* UZU.MEŠ-*ku-nu* UZU *šá* MÍ.M[EŠ-*ku-nu*]
D *ina bal-ṭu-te-ku-nu* UZU.M[EŠ-*ku-nu* x] *šá* MÍ.MEŠ-*ku-nu*
_ [x *bal-ṭ*]*u-ti-ku-nu* UZU.MEŠ-*k*[*u-nu* x] *šá* MÍ.MEŠ-*ku-nu*
Z [x x x x-*k*]*u-nu* x[x x x x x x x x x x x]
_ [x x x x x x x x x x x x x DUMU.M]Í.MEŠ-*ku-nu*

572 Q DUMU.MEŠ-*ku-nu* DUMU.MÍ.MEŠ-*ku-nu tu-is-su l*[*u* x x]
D DUMU.MEŠ-*ku-nu* DUMU.MÍ.MEŠ-*ku-nu tu-is-*⸢*su*⸣ [*lu*] *ta-kul*
b D[UMU.MEŠ-*ku-nu* x x x x x x x x x x x x]
_ DUMU.M[EŠ-*ku-nu* DUMU.MÍ.MEŠ-*k*]*u-nu tu-is-si lu t*[*a-kul*]
Z [x x x x x x x x x x x x x *l*]*u ta-*[*kul*]
_ [x x x x x x x x x x x x x *l*]*u ta-kul*

---

573 Q DINGIR.MEŠ *ma-la ina ṭup-pi a-de-e an-ni-i* MU-*šú-nu zak-ru* GIŠ.BAN-*ku-nu liš-bi-ru* [*i*]*na* KI.TA KÚR-*ku-nu*
D KI.MIN KI.MIN GIŠ.BAN-*ku-nu liš-bi-*[*r*]*u ina* KI.TA LÚ.KÚR-⸢*ku*⸣-*n*[*u*]
b KI.MIN DINGIR.MEŠ [x x x x x x x x x x x x] MU-*šú-nu zak-r*[*u* x x x x x x x] *ina* KI.TA LÚ.K[ÚR-*ku-nu*]
_ [x x x x *ma-l*]*a ina ṭup-pi a-d*[*e-e* x x x x x x x x x]
Z [x x x x x x x x x x x LÚ.KÚ]R-*ku-nu*
574 Q *lu-še-šib-šib-bu* GIŠ.BAN [x ŠU.2]-*ku-nu lu-šá-bal-kit*
D *lu-še-ši-bu-ku-nu* GIŠ.BAN *ina* ŠU.2-*ku-nu lu-šá-bal-ki-*[*tu*]
b [x x x x x x] GIŠ.BAN *ina* ŠU.2-*ku-nu* [x x x x x]
Z *lu-še-ši-b*[*u-ku-nu* x x x x x x x x x x x x]
_ *lu-še-šib-u-ku-nu* [x x x x x x x x x x x x x]
575 Q GIŠ.GIGIR.M[EŠ-*ku-nu*] *a-na qí-*[*niš l*]*u-šá-di-il-lu*
D GIŠ.GIGIR.MEŠ-*ku-nu a-na q*[*í*]*-niš lu-šá-di-lu*
b GIŠ.GIGIR.MEŠ-*ku-nu a-na* [x x x x x x]
v [GIŠ.GIGIR.MEŠ-*ku*]-*nu* ⸢*a*⸣-[*na* x x x x x x]
Z [GI]Š.GIGIR-*ku-nu* [x x x x *lu*]-*šá-di-lu*
_ [GIŠ.GIGIR]-⸢*ku*⸣-[*nu* x x x x x x x x]

---

576 Q KI.MIN [x x x *a.a*]-*lu ka-šu-du-ni de-ku-*⸢*ú*⸣-[*ni*]
D KI.MIN *ki-i šá a-a-lu ka-šu-du-u-ni de-ku-u-ni*
b ⸢KI.MIN⸣ *ki-i šá a-a-lu k*[*a-šu-du-ni* x x x x]
v *ki-i šá a-a-lu ka-šu-d*[*u-ni* x x x x]
Z [x x x x x x x x x x x x x *d*]*e-ku-u-ni*
577 Q [x x x x x ŠEŠ.MEŠ-*k*]*u-nu* DUMU.MEŠ-*ku-*(*nu*) *ina* ŠU.2 EN–[MÚD.MEŠ-*ku*]-*nu*
D *a-na ka-šú-nu* ŠEŠ.MEŠ-*ku-nu* DUMU.MEŠ-*ku-nu* EN–[MÚD.MEŠ-*ku-nu*]
b *a-na ka-šu-*[*n*]*u* ŠEŠ.[MEŠ-*ku-nu* x x x x x x x x x x x x]
v *a-na ka-šú-nu* ŠEŠ.MEŠ-*ku-nu* [x x x x x x x x x x x x x]
Z [x x x x x x x x x DUMU.M]EŠ-*ku-n*[*u* x x x EN–MÚD.M]EŠ-*ku-nu*
578 Q [*liš-ka*]-*nu-ku-n*[*u*]
D *lu-ka-ši-du li-du-ku-ku-*[*nu*]
b *lu-ka-ši-du li-d*[*u-ku-ku-nu*]
v *lu-ka-ši-du li-d*[*u-ku-ku-nu*]
Z [x x x x *l*]*i-du-ku-ku-nu*

---

579 Q [x x x x x x x x x x x *ta-da*]-*gal-ni*
D KI.MIN *ki-i šá bur-di-šá-hi la ta-*[*da-gal-u-ni*]
b *ki-i šá bur-di-šá-hi la t*[*a-da-gal-u-ni*]
_ [x x x x x x x x x x x *t*]*a-da-gal-u-ni*
v *ki-i šá bur-di-šá-hi la ta-da-gal-*[*u-ni*]
_ [x x *ki*]-*i šá bu*[*r-di-šá-hi* x x x x x x]
Z [x x x x x x x x x x x *t*]*a-da-gal-u-ni*

580 Q *ina bi-iš-ka-ni-šá* [x x x x x x x x *ha-an-ni*]-*i at-tu-nu*
D *ina bi-iš-ka-ni-šá la ta-sa-h*[*ar-u-ni* x x x x x x x x x]
b *a-na biš-ka-ni-šá la ta-s*[*a-ha*]*r-u-*[*ni*] *ki-i ha-an-ni-e at-tu-nu*
_ [x x x x x x x *t*]*a-sa-har-u-ni ki-i ha-ni-*[*i* x x x]
v *ina bi-iš-ka-ni-šá la ta-sa-ha*[*r-u-ni*] *ki ha-an-ni-i*
_ *ina bé-eš-ka-n*[*i-šá* x x x x x x] *ki-i ha-an-*[*ni-i* x x x]
Z *ina biš-ka-ni-šá* [x x x x x x x x *h*]*a-an-ni-i*
581 Q [x x x x x x x x x x x x x x x x x] ˹É.MEŠ-*ku*˺-*nu* [x *ta-sa*]-*hu-ra*
D *ina* UGU MÍ.MEŠ-*ku-nu ina* É.MEŠ-*ku-n*[*u* x x x x x]
b *ina* UGU MÍ.MEŠ-*ku-nu* DUMU.MEŠ-*ku-nu* DUMU.MÍ.MEŠ-*ku-nu a-*[*na*]
É.MEŠ-*ku-nu la ta-sa-hu-ra*
_ [x x x x]x-*ku-nu* DUMU.MEŠ-*ku-nu* [x x x x x x x É].MEŠ-*ku-nu la ta-sa-hu-r*[*a*]
v *ina* UGU MÍ.MEŠ-*ku-nu* DUMU.MEŠ-[*ku-nu* x x x x x] *ina* É.MEŠ-*ku-nu*
la ta-sa-h[*u-ra*]
_ [x x x x x x x x x x] DUMU.MÍ.MEŠ-*ku-*[*nu* x x x x x x x x x x]
Z *ina* UGU MÍ.MEŠ-*ku-nu* [x x x x DUMU.MÍ.MEŠ-*k*]*u-nu ina* É.MEŠ-*ku-nu*
la ta-sa-ah-hu-ra

---

582 Q [x x x x x x x x x x x x *iṣ*]-*ṣab-bat-ni*
D KI.MIN KI.MIN *ki-i šá* MUŠEN *ina du-ba-q*[*i* x x x x x]
b [x x x x *k*]*i-i šá* MUŠEN *ina tu-ba-qi iṣ-ṣab-bat-u-ni*
_ [x x x x x x x x x x x x *i*]*ṣ-ṣa-bat-u-ni*
v *ki-i šá* MUŠEN *ina du-ba-qi iṣ-ṣab-bat-u-*[*ni*]
_ *ki-i* ˹*šá*˺ [x x x x x x x x x x]
Z [x x x x x x x x x *du-ba-q*]*i iṣ-ṣab-bat-u-ni*
583 Q *a-na ka-šú-nu* [x x x x x x x x x x x] EN–MÚD.MEŠ-*ku-nu*
D *a-na ka-šú-nu* ŠEŠ.MEŠ-*ku-nu* [x x x x x x x x x x x x]
b [x x *k*]*a-šu-nu* ŠEŠ.MEŠ-*ku-nu* DUMU.MEŠ-*ku-nu* [x x x E]N–MÚD.MEŠ-*ku-nu*
_ *a-na ka-šú-nu* [x x x x x x x x x] ŠU.2 EN–MÚD.MEŠ-*ku-nu*
v *a-na ka-šú-nu* ŠEŠ.MEŠ-*ku-nu* DUMU.MEŠ-*ku-nu ina* ŠU.2 E[N–MÚD.MEŠ-*ku-nu*]
Z *a-na ka-šú-nu* [x x x x DUMU.MEŠ-*k*]*u-nu ina* ŠU.2 [E]N–MÚD.MEŠ-*ku-nu*
584 Q *liš-ka-nu-ku-nu*
D *li-iš-ku-nu-ku-*[*nu*]
b *liš-ka-nu-ku-nu*
_ *liš-ka-nu-ku-nu*
v *liš-ka-nu-ku-*[*nu*]
Z *liš-ka-nu-ku-nu*

---

585 Q [x x x x x x x x x x x MÍ.MEŠ]-*ku-nu* ŠEŠ.MEŠ-*ku-nu*
D KI.MIN KI.MIN UZU.MEŠ-*ku-nu* UZ[U x x x x x x x x x x]
b [x x x x UZU.MEŠ-*k*]*u-nu* UZU *šá* MÍ.MEŠ-*ku-nu* [x x x x]
_ [x x x x x x x x x x M]Í.MEŠ-*ku-nu* ŠEŠ.MEŠ-*ku-nu*
v UZU.MEŠ-˹*ku*˺-*nu* UZU.MEŠ *šá* MÍ.MEŠ-*ku-nu* ŠEŠ.[MEŠ-*ku-nu*]
Z [x x x x x x x x x x x] ˹MÍ˺.M[EŠ-*ku-n*]*u* ŠEŠ.MEŠ-*ku-nu*
586 Q DUMU.MEŠ-*ku-nu* [x x x x x x x x x]
D DUMU.MEŠ-*ku-nu* DUMU.MÍ.ME[Š-*ku-nu* x x x x]
b ˹DUMU˺.MEŠ-*ku-nu* DUMU.MÍ.MEŠ-*ku-nu* [x x x x]
v [x x x x] [*ki*?]-˹*i*? *qi*?˺-*ru*
Z DUMU.MEŠ-*ku-nu* [x x x x x x x x x]

587 Q [*ku-up-r*]*i nap-ṭi lu-ṣal-li-mu*
D *ku-up-ri nap-ṭi* [x x x x]
b [*ku-u*]*p-ri* ˹*nap*˺*-ṭi lu-ṣal-li-mu*
_ *ku-up-ri nap-ṭi lu-ṣa-li-m*[*u*]
v *ku-up-ri nap-ṭi l*[*u-ṣal-li-mu*]
Z [x x x *na*]*p-ṭu li-ṣal-li-mu*

---

588 Q [x x x x x *ha-e-ru-u*]*š-hi* ˹*ú*˺*-ma-mu ina kip-pi*
D KI.MIN *ki-i šá ha-e-*[*ru-uš-hi* x x x x x x]
b [x x x x x *ha-e*]*-ru-uš-hi ú-ma-mu ina kip-pi*
Z [x x x x x x x x x x x x x x] *ina* ˹*kip*˺*-p*[*i*]
589 Q [x x x x x x x x x MÍ.MEŠ]*-ku-nu* ŠEŠ.MEŠ*-ku-nu* DUMU.MEŠ*-ku-nu*
D *is-sa-pa-ku-u-*˹*ni*˺ *a*[*t-tu-nu* x x x x x x x x x x x x]
b [x x x x x x *at-t*]*u-nu* ŠEŠ.MEŠ*-ku-nu* [x x x x]
j [x x x x x x x x x x x x x x ŠEŠ.MEŠ*-k*]*u-nu* D[UMU.MEŠ*-ku-nu*]
Z [*is-s*]*a-pa-ku-u-ni* [x x x x x x x x x x x x x x x]
590 h DU[MU!].MÍ.[MEŠ*-ku-nu* x] ŠU.2 LÚ.KÚR*-ku-nu na-*˹*aṣ*˺*-b*[*i-ta*]
Q [x x x x x x x x LÚ.KÚ]R*-ku-nu na-ṣa-bi-ta*
D DUMU.MÍ.MEŠ*-ku-nu ina* ŠU.[2 x x x x x x x x]
b [DUMU.MÍ.MEŠ*-k*]*u-nu ina* ŠU.2 LÚ.KÚR*-ku-nu* [*na-aṣ-bi*]*-ta*
j [x x x x x x x x x x x x x *na*]*-aṣ-b*[*i-ta*]
Z [x x x x x x x x x x x x *na-aṣ-b*]*i-ta*

---

591 h UZU.MEŠ-˹*ku-nu*˺ UZU-˹MEŠ˺ *šá* MÍ.MEŠ*-ku-nu* ŠEŠ.MEŠ*-ku-n*[*u*]
Q [x x x x x x x x x x x MÍ.MEŠ]-˹*ku*˺*-nu* ŠEŠ.MEŠ*-ku-nu*
D KI.MIN K[I.M]IN UZU.MEŠ-[*ku-nu* x x x x x x x x x x x]
K [x x x x x x x x] UZU.MEŠ *šá* M[Í.MEŠ*-ku-nu* x x x x]
j UZU.MEŠ*-ku-nu* UZ[U].MEŠ *šá* [x x x x] ŠEŠ.MEŠ*-ku-nu*
L ˹UZU.MEŠ*-ku*˺-[*nu* x x x x x x x x x x x]
592 h ˹DUMU.MEŠ*-ku-nu*˺ DUMU.MÍ*-ku-nu*
D [x x x x] DUMU.MÍ*-ku-n*[*u*]
K [x x x x] DUMU.MÍ.MEŠ*-ku-nu*
j DUMU.MEŠ*-ku-nu* [x x x x x]
L DUMU.MEŠ-˹*ku-nu*˺ DU[MU.MÍ.MEŠ*-ku-nu*]
593 h *ki-i* UZU.MEŠ [*šá*] *hur-ba-bíl-li li-ga-am-ru*
Q [x x x x x *h*]*ur-ba-bíl-li* [x x x]*-ru*
K *k*[*i-i* x x x x x x x x x x x]
j *ki-i* UZU *šá hur-ba-bi-li* [x x x x]
L [x x x x] *šá hur-ba-bi-l*[*i* x x x x]

---

594 h [x x *š*]*a ina* ŠÀ *ka-ma-a*!*-ni ša* LÀL
T [x x x x Š]À *ka*!*-ma-a-ni* LÀL
D KI.MIN KI.M[IN x x x x x x x x x x x x]
K ˹*ki*˺*-i šá ina* ŠÀ*-b*[*i* x x x x x x]
j *ki-i šá ina* ŠÀ *ka*!*-ma-a-ni* [x x]
L *ki-i šá ina* ŠÀ *ka-m*[*a-a-ni* x x]

595 h HABRUD.MEŠ *pa-*[*l*]*u-šá-a-ni*
T HABRUD.M[EŠ x x x x x]
j HABRUD.MEŠ *pal-lu-šá-a-*[*ni*]
L [x x] *pal-lu-šá-a-*˹*ni*˺
596 h *ina* ŠÀ UZU.MEŠ-˹*ku*˺*-nu* UZU.MEŠ *šá* MÍ.MEŠ-*ku-nu*
T *ina* ŠÀ UZU.MEŠ-*ku-nu* UZU.MEŠ *šá* MÍ.MEŠ-˹*ku-nu*˺
K *ina* ŠÀ-*bi* UZU-˹MEŠ-*ku*˺*-n*[*u* x x x x x x x x]
j *ina* ŠÀ UZU.MEŠ-*ku-nu* UZU.MEŠ *šá* MÍ.M[EŠ-*ku-nu*]
L *ina* ŠÀ UZU.MEŠ-*ku-nu* [x x x x x x x x]
597 h ŠEŠ.MEŠ-*ku-nu* DUMU.MEŠ-*ku-nu* DUMU.MÍ.MEŠ-*ku-nu*
T ˹ŠEŠ.MEŠ˺-[*ku*]-˹*nu*˺ DUMU.MEŠ-*ku-nu*
K [x x x x] DUMU.MEŠ-*ku-nu* DUMU.MÍ.MEŠ-[*ku-nu*]
j [ŠE]Š.MEŠ-*ku-nu* DUMU.MEŠ-*ku-nu* DUMU.MÍ-[*ku-nu*]
598 h *ina bal-ṭu-te-ku-nu* HABRUD.MEŠ *lu-*˹*ú*!˺*-pal-li-šu*
T *ina bal-ṭu*!*-te-ku-nu* HABRUD *lu pal-lu-šá*
j *ina bal-ṭu-ti-ku-nu* HABRUD *lu-p*[*al*-x x]
L HABRUD.[MEŠ *ina bal-ṭu-te-ku-nu*] *lu* [x x x]

---

599 A K[I.MIN BU]RU$_5$! NUMUN! *bar*!*-mu kal-mu-tú mu-nu a-ki-lu*
j KI.MIN KI.MIN BURU$_5$! NU[MUN! x x x] *mu-nu a-ki-lu*
600 A URU.MEŠ-*ku-nu* KUR-*ku-nu na-gi-ku-nu* ˹*lu*˺*-šá-ki-lu*
j UR[U.MEŠ-*ku-nu* x x x] *na-gi-ku-nu lu-šá-*[*ki-lu*]

---

601 A *ki-i* NUM *ina* ŠU.2 (KÚR)-*ku-nu le-pa-šú-ku-nu*
h KI.MIN *ki-*˹*i*˺ *zu-um-bi ina* ŠU.2 LÚ.KÚR-*ku-nu le-pa-šú-ku-nu*
T KI.MIN KI.MIN *ki-i* NUM *ina* ŠU.2 KÚR-*ku-nu le-pa*!*-šu-ku-nu*
K KI.MIN KI.MIN *ki-i zu-u*[*m-bi* x x x x x x x x] *le-pa-šu-*[*ku-nu*]
j KI.MIN KI.MIN *ki-i zu-um-bi ina* [x x x x x x x x] *le-pa-šu-ku-nu*
_ *ki-i zu-um-bi ina* ŠU.2 LÚ.KÚR-*ku-nu le-pa-šu-ku-nu*
L [x x x x x x x x x x x x x x x x x x x x x x-*n*]*u*
602 A LÚ.KÚR-*ku-nu li-im-ri-is-ku-nu*
h LÚ.˹KÚR˺-*ku-nu li-*[*i*]*m-ri-is-ku-nu*
T LÚ.KÚR-*ku-nu li-im-ri-is-ku-nu*
K LÚ.KÚR-*ku-nu* [x x x x x x]
j LÚ.KÚR-[*ku-nu* x x x x x x]
_ LÚ.KÚR-*ku-nu lim-ri-is-ku-nu*
L LÚ.KÚR-*ku-nu* [*li-im-r*]*i-is-ku-nu*

---

603 A *ki-i šá pi-is-pi-su bi-*'*i-šú-u-ni*
K [x x x x x x x x x x *bi*]-˹'*i-šu*˺*-u-n*[*i*]
h ˹*ki-i*˺ *ša pi-is-pi-su* [*bi-*']*i-šu-u-ni*
T *ki-i šá pi-is-pi-su bi-*'*i-šu-ú-ni*
H *ki-i šá pi-is-pi-su an-ni-u bi-*'*i-šu-u-ni*
K *ki-i šá pi-is-*[*pi-su* x x x x x x x x x]
j *ki-i šá pi-is-pi-s*[*u* x x x] *bi-*'*i-šu-ú-ni*
_ *ki-i šá pi-is-*(*pi*)*-su an-ni-u bi-*'*i-šu-u-ni*
L [x x x *pi-is-p*]*i-*˹*su bi-*'*i*˺*-šu-u-ni*

604 A *ki-i ha-an-ni-e ina* IGI DINGIR *u* LUGAL LÚ-*ti*
K [x x x x x x x x x x x x *a-m*]*e-lu-ti*
h [x x] DINGIR.MEŠ LUGAL *a-me-lu-te*
T [x x x x LU]GAL *a-me-lu-te*
H *ki-i ha-an-ni-i ina* IGI DINGIR *u* LUGAL LÚ-*u-te*
j [x x x x x x x x x x LUGA]L [L]Ú-*ti*
_ *ina* IGI DINGIR *u* LUGAL *a-me-lu-te*
L *ki-i ha-ni-i* [x x x x x x x x]-*te*?
605 A *ni-piš-ku-nu li-ib-(ʾi)-ši*
K [x x x x *li-ib*]-*ʾi-ši*
h ˹*ni*˺-*piš*-˹*ku*˺-*nu lib-ʾi-ši*
T *ni-piš-ku-nu li-ib-ʾi-iš*
H *ni-piš-ku-nu lib-ʾi-iš*
_ *ni-piš*-˹*ku*˺-*nu* [*l*]*u-ba-i-šu*
L *ni-piš*-˹*ku*˺-[*n*]*u lib-iš*

---

606 A *a-na ka-na-šú-nu* MÍ.MEŠ-*ku-nu* DUMU.MEŠ-*ku-nu*
K [x x x x x x x x x x x x x x x x x x DUM]U.MEŠ-*ku-nu*
h [x x x x x x x x x x x x x x x ŠEŠ.MEŠ]-˹*ku-nu*˺ DUMU.MEŠ-*ku-nu*
T [x x x x x x x x x x x x x]x-*ku-nu* ŠEŠ.MEŠ-*ku-nu at-tu-nu*
H [x x x x x x x x x x x]x ˹ŠEŠ˺.MEŠ-*ku-nu* DUMU.MEŠ-*ku-*(*nu*)
M [x x x x x x x x x x x x x x x x x x DUMU.MEŠ-*k*]*u-nu*
_ [KI].MIN KI.MIN *a-na ka-na-šú-nu* MÍ.MEŠ-*ku-nu* ŠEŠ.MEŠ-*ku-nu* [DUM]U.MEŠ-*ku-nu*
L [x x x x x x x x x x x x x x x x x x x x x x-*n*]*u*
607 A DUMU.MÍ.MEŠ-*ku-nu ina pi-til-ti li-ih-na-qu-ku-nu*
K [x x x x x x *pi-ti-i*]*l-ti li-ih-n*[*a*]*-qu-ku-nu*
h [x x x x x x x x x x *li-ih-na-qu-ku*]-*nu*
T [x x x x x x x x x x *li-ih-n*]*u*?-*qu-ku-nu*
H DUMU.MÍ.MEŠ-*ku-nu* [x x x x x *li-i*]*h-nu-qu-ku-nu*
M [x x x x x x x x x x] *li-ih-nu-qu-ku-nu*
_ *ina pi-til-te li-ih-na-qu-ku-nu*
L DUMU.MÍ.MEŠ-*ku-nu* [x x x x *li-ih*]-*nu-qu-ku-nu*

---

608 A *ki-i šá ṣal-mu šá* DUH.LÀL *ina* IZI *i-šá-rap-u-ni*
G [*k*]*i-i* [x x x x x x x x x x x x x]
K [x x x x x x x x x IZ]I *i-šá-rap-u-ni*
T [x x x x x x x x x x *i-šá-r*]*a-pu-u-ni*
H [x x x x x x x x x x] *iš-šar-rap-u-ni*
M *ki*-˹*i šá*˺ *ṣa-lam šá* DUH.LÀL *ina* IZI *iš-šar-rap-u-ni*
_ [x x] *šá ṣa-lam* DUH.LÀL *ina* IZI *i-šar-rap-u-ni*
L [x x x x x x x x x] ˹IZI˺ *i-šar-rap-u-ni*
609 A [x *ṭi-ṭ*]*i ina* A.MEŠ *i-mah-ha-hu-u-ni*
G [*š*]*a* IM *ina* [x x x x x x x x]
K [x x x x x *i-mah-h*]*a-hu-u-ni*
M *šá ṭi-ṭi ina* A.MEŠ *i-ma-ha-hu-u-ni*
_ [x x x x x *i-mah-ha-hu*]-˹*u-ni*˺ [x x x A].MEŠ *i-mah-ha-hu-u-ni*
L [x x x x x *i-mah-h*]*a-hu-u-ni*

610 A [*ki-i h*]*a-an-ni-e la-an-ku-nu ina* ^{d}GIŠ.BAR *liq-mu-u*
G *la-an-ku-nu ina* ^{d}GIŠ.BAR *liq-mu-*[*u*]
K [x x x x x x *la-an-ku-n*]*u ina* ^{d}GIŠ.BAR *liq-mu-u*
T [x x x x x x *la-an-ku*]*-nu* [x x x x x x x]
H [*k*]*i-i ha-an-ni-e* [x x x x x x x x x x x]
M *la-an-ku-nu ina* ^{d}GIŠ.BAR *liq-mu-ú*
m [x x x x x x x x x x x x x x x] *liq-m*[*u-u*]
_ *la-*⸢*an*⸣*-k*[*u-nu* x x x x x x x]
[x x x x x x x x x x x x x x x *l*]*iq-mu-u*
L [x x x x x x x x x x x ^{d}GIŠ.BA]R *liq-mu*!*-u*
611 A [x A].MEŠ *lu-ṭa-bu-ú*
G *ina* A.MEŠ *li-ṭa-bu-u*
K [x x x *lu*]*-ṭa-bu-u*
T [x x x *lu-ṭa-bu*]*-u*
H [x A]-⸢MEŠ⸣ *lu-ṭa-bu-u*
M *ina* A.MEŠ *li-ṭa-ab-bu-ú*
_ [x] ⸢A⸣.MEŠ *lu-ṭa-bu-*[*u*] [x x x *lu-ṭa-b*]*u-u*
L [x x x *lu-ṭa-b*]*u-u*

---

612 K [*šum-ma at-tu-nu ina* ŠÀ *a-d*]*e-e an-nu-ti šá* ^{m}*aš-šur*–PAB–AŠ MAN KUR–*aš-šur*
[*u* DUMU]-⸢MEŠ-*šú*⸣ DUMU–DUMU.MEŠ-⸢*šú*⸣ [*ta-ha*]-⸢*ṭa*⸣*-a-ni*
ki-i šá GIŠ.GIGIR *an-ni-tu a-di* [*sa-s*]*i-i-šá*
A [x x x x x GI]Š.GIGIR *an-ni-tú a-di sa-se-e-*[*šá*]
G *ki-i šá* GIŠ.GIGIR.MEŠ *a-di sa-se-šá*
M KI.MIN *ki-i šá* GIŠ.GIGIR *a-di sa-se-šá*
m KI.MIN *ki-i šá* GIŠ.GIGIR *a*[*n-ni-tú* x x x x x]
_ [x x x x x x x x x x x *a-d*]*i sa-se-šá*
613 A [x x x *r*]*a-ah-ṣa-tú-u-ni k*[*i*]*-i ha-an-ni-e*
G *ina* MÚD.MEŠ *ra-ah-ṣa-tu-u-*[*ni*] *ki-i ha-an-ni-e*
K [*in*]*a* MÚD.MEŠ *ra-ah-ah-ṣa-tu-*[*u*]*-ni* [*k*]*i-i ha-an-ni-e*
H [x] MÚD.MEŠ [x x x x x x x x x x x x x]
_ *ina* MÚD.MEŠ *ra-ah-ṣa-*[*tu-u-ni* x x x x x x]
ina MÚD.MEŠ *ra-ah-ṣa-tu-u-ni*
L [x x x *r*]*a-ah-ṣa-tu-u-ni* [x x x x x x]
614 A [*ina* MURUB$_4$ LÚ.KÚ]R-*ku-nu* GIŠ.GIGIR.MEŠ-*ku-nu*
G GIŠ.GIGIR.MEŠ-*ku-nu ina* MURUB$_4$ LÚ.KÚR-*ku-nu*
K *ina* MURUB$_4$ LÚ.KÚR-*ku-n*[*u*] GIŠ.GIGIR.MEŠ-*ku-nu*
H GIŠ.GIGIR.MEŠ-*ku-nu* [x x x x x x]
m GIŠ.GIGIR-*ku-nu ina* MUR[UB$_4$ x x x x]
_ [x x x x x x x LÚ.KÚ]R-*ku-nu* GIŠ.GIGIR.MEŠ-*ku-nu ina* MURUB$_4$ LÚ.KÚR-*ku-nu*
L [GIŠ.GIGIR.MEŠ-*ku-n*]*u ina* MURUB$_4$ LÚ.KÚR-*ku-n*[*u*]

615 A [x x x x x *r*]*a-me-ni-ku-nu lu-šar-hi-ṣu*
G *ina* MÚD.MEŠ *ra-ma-ni-ku-nu li-ra-ah-ṣa*
K *ina* ŠÀ MÚD.MEŠ *šá ra-me-ni-ku-nu lu-ša*[*r-hi-ṣu*]
H [x x x x x x x x x x *li*]*-ra-ah-ṣa*
m [x x x x] *ša ra-ma-ni-ku-*[*nu* x x x x]
_ *ina* MÚD.MEŠ *šá ra-ma-ni-*[*ku-nu li-ra*]*-ah-*[*ṣa*]
ina MÚD.MEŠ *šá ra-ma-ni-ku-nu li-ra-ah-*[*ṣa*]
L [x x MÚD.M]EŠ ˹*šá*˺ *ra-ma-n*[*i-ku-nu lu ra*]*-ah-ṣa-at*

---

616 m DINGIR.MEŠ *ma-la ina ṭup-p*[*i* x x x x x x x x x x x] *ki-i* GIŠ.*pi-laq-*[*qi* x x x x x x]
_ [DING]IR.MEŠ *ma-la ina ṭup-pi a-de-*[*e*] *an-ni-e* MU-*šu-nu zak-*[*ru k*]*i-i*
GIŠ.*pi-laq-qi* [*lu-šá*]*-ṣa-*[*bi-ru-ku-nu*]
A [x x x x x x] *lu-šá-aṣ-bi-ru-ku-nu*
G *ki-i* GIŠ.BAL *lu-šá-aṣ-bir-ku-nu*
K [*k*]*i-*˹*i*˺ *pi-laq-qi lu-šá-ṣa-bir-ku-nu*
H [x x x x x x x x x x]*-ku-nu*
L [*ki*]-˹*i*˺ GIŠ.*pi-laq-qi lu-šá-aṣ-bi-ru-ku-nu*
617 A [x x x x x L]Ú.KÚR-*ku-nu le-pa-šú-ku-nu*
G *ki-i* MÍ *ina* IGI LÚ.KÚR-*ku-nu le-pa-šu-ku-nu*
K *ki-i* MÍ *ina* IGI LÚ*!.KÚR-*ku-nu l*[*e-p*]*a-šú-*(*ku*)*-nu*
H [x x x x x x x x x *le-pa-šú-ku-n*]*u*
_ ˹*ki-i*˺ [x x x x x x x x x x x x]
m *ki-i* MÍ *ina* IGI [x x x x x x x x x]
_ [*k*]*i-i* MÍ *ina* IGI LÚ.K[ÚR-*ku-nu* x x x x x]
L [*ki*]-˹*i*˺ MÍ *ina* IGI LÚ.KÚR-*ku-nu le-pa-šu-ku-nu*

---

618 G DINGIR.MEŠ *ma-la ina ṭup-pi an-ni-i* MU-*šú-nu zak-ru*
a-na ka-šú-nu DUMU.MEŠ-*ku-nu*
_ DINGIR.MEŠ *ma-l*[*a* x x x x x x x x x x x]
a-na ka-šu-n[*u* x x x x x x x x]
A [x x x x x Š]EŠ.MEŠ-*ku-nu* DUMU.MEŠ-*ku-nu*
K [x x *k*]*a-šú-nu* ŠEŠ.MEŠ-*ku-*(*nu*) DUMU.MEŠ-*ku-nu*
m *a-na ka-šú-*[*nu* x x x x x x x x]
_ [*a-n*]*a ka-*[*šú-nu* x x x x x x x x]
[x x] ˹*ka*˺*-šú-nu* ŠEŠ.MEŠ-[*ku-nu* x x x x]
L [x x *k*]*a?-šu-nu* DUMU.MEŠ-*ku-nu*
619 A [DUMU.MÍ.MEŠ-*ku-n*]*u ki-i al-lu-ti a-na qí-in-niš*
G DUMU.MÍ.MEŠ-*ku-nu ki-i al-lu-ti a-na qi-in-niš*
K DUMU.MÍ-*ku-nu ki-*˹*i*˺ [*al-lu-t*]*i a-na qí-niš-ši*
m [x x x x x] *ki-i al-*[*lu-ti* x x x x x]
_ [x x x x x *k*]*i-i al-lut!-te a-na q*[*í-in-niš*]
L DUMU.MÍ.MEŠ-*ku-nu* [x x *al-lu*]*-ti a-na qi-in-niš*
620 A [[*lu-šá*]*-di-lu-ku-*˹*nu*˺
G *lu-šá-di-lu-ku-nu*
K *lu-šá-di-lu-ku-nu*
_ [*lu-š*]*á-*˹*di-lu-ku-nu*˺
L *lu-šá-di-*˹*lu-ku*˺*-nu*

---

621 A [x x x x] DÙG.˹GA-*tú*˺ *la* SIG$_5$-*t*[*ú l*]*u-šal-bu-ku-nu*
G *ki-i* IZI *la* DÙG.GA *la* SIG$_5$ *lu-šal-bu-ku-nu*
K *ki-i* IZI *l*[*a* DÙG.GA]-*tu la* SIG$_5$-*tú lu-šal-bu-ku-nu*
_ [x x x x *de-i*]*q-tú la* ˹DÙG.GA-*tú lu-šal*˺-[*bu-ku-nu*]
m *ki-i* I[ZI x x x x x x x x x x x x x]
_ [x x x] *la* DÙG.GA-*tu* [x x x *lu-šal-bu-ku*]-*nu* [x x x x x x] *la* SI[G$_5$ x x x x]
L [x x x x DÙG.GA]-*tu la* SIG$_5$-*tu lu-šal-bu-ku-nu*

---

622 A [x x x x x x x UZU].MEŠ-*ku-nu e-ra*[*b*]-*u-ni*
G ˹*ki-i šá* Ì˺.[MEŠ x Š]À-*bi* UZU.MEŠ *e-rab-u-ni*
K *ki-i šá* Ì.MEŠ *ina* UZU.[MEŠ-*k*]*u-nu e-rab-u-ni*
_ [x x x Ì].MEŠ *ina* ŠÀ UZU.MEŠ *e-rab-u-*[*ni*]
m *ki-i š*[*a* x x x x x x x x x x x x x]
_ [x x x x x x Š]À UZU *er-rab-u-ni*
L [x x x x x x x UZU.MEŠ-*ku-n*]*u er-rab-u-ni*
623 A [x x x x x x x x x] *an-ni-tú ina* ŠÀ-*bi* UZU.MEŠ-*ku-nu*
G ˹*ta-me-tu*˺ [*an-ni*]-*tu ina* ŠÀ-*bi* UZU.MEŠ-*ku-nu*
K *ki-i ha-an-ni-e ta-me-tú a*[*n-ni*]-˹*tu*˺ [*ina*] ˹ŠÀ UZU˺.MEŠ-*ku-nu*
_ [x x x *an*]-*ni-tú ina* ŠÀ UZU.MEŠ-*ku-*[*nu*]
m [x x x x x x] *ta-me-tú a*[*n-ni-tu* x x x x x x]
_ [x x x x x x x x x *an-ni*]-*tu ina* ŠÀ UZU.MEŠ-*ku-nu*
L *ta-*˹*me*˺-*tu an-ni-t*[*u* x x UZU.MEŠ-*ku-n*]*u*
624 A [x x x x x x x DUMU].MEŠ DUMU.MÍ.MEŠ-*ku-nu*
G ˹UZU.MEŠ *šá* MÍ.MEŠ-*ku-nu* DUMU˺.MEŠ-*ku-nu* [DUMU.MÍ]-˹MEŠ-*ku*˺-*nu*
K UZU.MEŠ *šá* ŠEŠ.MEŠ DUMU.MEŠ-*ku-nu* DUMU.MÍ.[MEŠ-*ku-nu*]
_ [x x x DUM]U.MEŠ-*ku-nu* DUMU.MÍ.MEŠ-*ku-nu*
m [x x x x x x x x x x x] DUMU.MÍ.MEŠ-*k*[*u-nu*]
_ [x x x x x-*ku*]-*nu* DUMU.MEŠ-*ku-nu*
L UZU *šá* ŠEŠ.ME-*ku-nu* DUMU.MEŠ-*k*[*u-nu* x x x x x]
625 A [*lu-še*]-*ri-bu*
G *lu-še-ri-bu*
K *lu-še-ri-b*[*u*!]
_ *lu-š*[*e-ri-bu*] [*lu-š*]*e-ri-bu*
L [*lu-še-r*]*i*?-˹*bu*˺

---

626 G [x x x *a-ra-r*]*i*? ˹*a-na*˺ ^{d}EN *i*[*h*]-*ṭu-u-ni*
K *ki-i šá a-ra-ru a-na* ^{d}EN *ih-ṭu-u-ni*
_ [x x x *a-r*]*a-ru a-na* ^{d}EN *ih-ṭ*[*u-u-ni*]
[x x x] *a-ra-ri a-na* ^{d}EN [*ih-ṭu-u-n*]*i*
L [x x x] *a-ra-ru a-na* ^{d}EN *ih-ṭ*[*u*?]-*u-ni*
627 G [x x x x x x] ˹x x GÌR.2˺.MEŠ-*šú-nu ú-*˹*pa*!˺-*ti-qu-u-ni*
K *kap-pi šá* Á.2.MEŠ-*šú-nu* GÌR.2.MEŠ-*šú-nu ú-pa-t*[*i-q*]*u-u-ni*
F *kap-pi šá* Á.2.MEŠ-*šú-nu* GÌR.2.MEŠ-*š*[*ú-nu*] *ú-bat-tú*!-*qu-u-ni*
_ [x x *š*]*a* Á.2.MEŠ-*šú-nu* GÌR.2.MEŠ-*šú-nu ú-b*[*at-ti-qu-u-ni*]
kap-pi šá Á.2.MEŠ-*šú-nu* [x x x x x] ˹*ú*˺-*bat-ti-qu-u-ni*
L [x x x] Á.2?.MEŠ-*šú-nu* GÌR.2-*šú-nu ú-bat-ti-qu-ni*

628 A IGI.2.[MEŠ-*šú-nu* x x x x x x]
G [x x x x x *ú*]-⸢*ga-lil-u-ni*⸣
K [IG]I.2.MEŠ-*šú-nu ú-ga-li-lu-u-ni*
F IGI.2.MEŠ-*š*[*ú-nu*] *ú-gal-lil-u-ni*
_ [IGI.2.MEŠ-*šú-n*]*u ú-ga-lil-u-*[*ni*]
[x x x x x *ú-g*]*a-lil-u-ni*
L [x x x x x *ú*]-*gal-lil-u-ni*
629 A *ki-*⸢*i*⸣ [x x x x x x x x x x]
G ⸢*ki-i*⸣ [*ha-an*]-*ni-e lig-ma-ru-ku-*⸢*nu*⸣
K [*ki*]-⸢*i*⸣ *ha-an-ni-e li-ig-mur-u-ku-nu*
F *ki-i ha-an-ni-i*? [x x x x x x]
_ [x x *h*]*a-an-ni-e lig-ma-r*[*u-ku-nu*]
[x x x x x x] *lig-ma-*⸢*ru-ku*⸣-[*nu*]
[x x x x x x] *li-gi-(ma)-ru-ku-nu*
L *ki-i ha-an-ni-e* [x x x]x-⸢*ku*⸣-*nu*
630 A *ki-*⸢*i*⸣ [x x x x x x x x x x]
G *ki-i* [x x]x *ina* A.MEŠ *lu-*⸢*ni-šu-ku-nu*⸣
K [x x x x]x *ina* A.MEŠ *lu-ni-šú-u-ku-nu*
F *ki-i* GI.AMBAR *ina* A.MEŠ *lu-n*[*i-šú-ku-nu*]
_ [x x x] ⸢*a*⸣-*pa-*[*ri ina*] A.MEŠ *l*[*u-ni-šú-ku-nu*]
[x x x x x A].MEŠ *lu-ni-šú-ku-nu*
L *ki-i* AMBA[R x A].MEŠ *lu-ni-šú-ku-nu*
631 A *ki-*⸢*i qa-né*⸣-[*e* x x x x x x x x x x x x]
G [x x x x x x *ri*]*k*?-*si* LÚ.KÚR-*k*[*u-nu lu-šá-li*]*p-ku-nu*
K [x x x x x x *rik-s*]*i* LÚ.KÚR-*ku-nu lu-šá-lip-ku-nu*
F [x x x x x x] *rik-si* L[Ú.KÚR-*ku-nu* x x x x x]
_ [x x] ⸢GI!⸣.MEŠ *ina rik-si* LÚ.KÚR-*ku-nu* [*lu*]-*šal-lip-ku-nu*
L [x x x x x x x x] LÚ.KÚR-*ku-nu lu-šá-lip-ku-nu*

---

632 A [x x *at-t*]*u-nu a-na* [x x x x x x x x x]? [x x x]?
G [x x x x x x x ^{m}*aš*]-*šur*–PAB–AŠ [x] KUR–*aš-šur*
K [x x x x x x x x x x x x MA]N KUR–*aš-šur*
F *šum-ma at-tu-nu* ^{m}*aš-šur*–PAB–AŠ MAN KUR–*aš-šur*
_ [*šum-m*]*a at-tu-nu* ^{m}*aš-šur*–PAB–AŠ MAN KUR–*aš-šur*
[x x x x x x x x x x x x x] KUR–*aš-šur* 0?
L [x x x x x x x ^{m}*aš-šur*–PA]B–AŠ MAN KUR–*aš-šur* EN-*ku-nu*
633 A *ù* ^{m}*aš-šur*–DÙ–A DUMU–[MAN x x x x x]
G [x] ^{m}*aš-šur*–DÙ–A [x x x x x x x]
K *u* ^{m}*aš-šur*–DÙ–A DUMU–MAN GAL [x x x x]
F *ù* ^{m}*aš-šur*–DÙ–A DUMU–MAN GAL *šá* É–UŠ-*te*
_ ⸢*ù*⸣ ^{m}*aš-šur*–DÙ–A DUMU–[MA]N GAL-*u ša* É–UŠ-*te*
[x x x x x x x x x x É–U]Š-*ti*
[x x x x DUMU AMA]-*šú šá* ^{m}*aš-šur*–DÙ–A [x x x x É–UŠ-*t*]*i*
re-eh-ti DUMU.MEŠ [x x x x x ^{m}*aš-šu*]*r*–PAB–AŠ MAN KUR–*aš-šur*
ù ^{m}*aš-šur*–DÙ–A D[UMU–MAN x x x x x x]
L [x x x x x x x x x *š*]*á* É–UŠ-*ti*
u ŠEŠ.MEŠ-*šu* [DUMU AMA-*šú šá* ^{m}]*aš-šur*–DÙ–A DUMU–MAN GAL *šá* É–UŠ-*ti*
[x x x] DUMU.MEŠ *ṣi-it*–ŠÀ-*bi šá* ^{m}*aš-šur*–PAB–AŠ [x x x x]

634 A *tu-ram-ma-a-ni a-n*[*a* x x x x x x x]
G [x x x x x x x x x x x *tal-l*]*ak-a-ni*
K [x x x x x]x *a-na* ZAG KAB *tal-lak-a-ni*
F *tu-ram-ma-a-ni a-na* ZAG *u* KAB *tal-lak-a-ni*
_ [*t*]*u-ra-ma-a-ni a-na* Z[AG x x] ˹*tal*˺*-lak-a-ni*
[x x x x x] *a-na* ZAG KAB *tal-lak-a-ni*
[x x x x x x x x Z]AG *u* KAB *tal-lak-a-n*[*i*]
L [*t*]*u-ram-ma-a-ni a-na* ZAG KAB [*tal-la*]*k-a-ni*
635 A *šá a-na* ZAG *il-lak-u-n*[*i* x x x x x x]
K [x x x x x x x x x x x *l*]*e-ku-lu-šú*
F *šá a-na* ZAG *il-lak-u-ni* GÍR.MEŠ *le-ku-la-šú*
_ *ša a-na* ZAG *il-l*[*ak-u-ni*] GÍR.MEŠ *le-ku-la-šú*
[x x x *il-la*]*k-u-ni* GÍR.MEŠ *le-kul-a-šú*
[x x x x x x x x GÍR.AN].BAR.MEŠ *le-ku-la-šú*
L *šá a-na* ZAG *il-lak-u-ni* [GÍR.ME]Š *le-kul-a-šú*
636 A *šá a-na* KAB *il-lak-u-ni* GÍR.MEŠ*-ma le-kul-š*[*ú*]
K [x x x x x x x x x x x x *le*]-˹*ku-lu-šú*˺
F *šá a-na* KAB *il-lak-u-ni* GÍR.MEŠ*-ma le-ku-la-šú*
a-na ka-a-šú-nu MÍ.MEŠ*-ku-nu* ŠEŠ.MEŠ*-ku-nu* DUMU.MEŠ*-ku-nu*
DUMU.MÍ.MEŠ*-ku-nu*
ki-i UDU.NIM *ga-*[*de-e*] ˹*lu*-x x x˺-[*ku-nu*]
_ *š*[*a* x x x x x x x x G]ÍR.MEŠ*-ma le-k*[*u-la-šú*]
[x x x x x x x x x] GÍR.MEŠ*-ma le-kul-a-šú*
[x x *ka-a-š*]*ú-nu* MÍ.MEŠ*-ku-nu* 0?
[x x UDU.NIM *ga-de-e* [x x x x]x-*k*[*u-nu*]
[x x x x x x x x x GÍR.AN.B]AR*-ma le-ku-la-šú* [x x x x x x
M]Í.MEŠ*-ku-nu* DUMU.MEŠ*-ku-nu* [x x x x x x x x UDU.NI]M *ga-de-e* [x x x x]*-ku-nu*
L [*š*]*á* (*a-na*) KAB *il-lak-u-ni* [GÍR.ME]Š*-ma le-*[*k*]*ul-a-*˹*šu*˺
DUMU.MEŠ*-ku-nu* DUMU.MÍ.MEŠ*-k*[*u-nu* x x x x x x x x x x x x]x*-ku-*[*nu*]
_ [x x] *ka-*˹*a*˺*-*[*šú-nu* x x x x x x x x x x x x x DUMU.MÍ.ME]Š*-ku-nu*
ki-[*i* x x x x x x x x x x x x]

---

637 A *ki-i šá kil-lu šá su-'i i-ha-lul-u-ni*
_ KI.MIN *ki-i šá kil-lu* [x x x x x x x x x x x x]
[x x *k*]*i-i šá kil-lu šá su-'i* [x x x x x x x x x]
ki-i šá kil-lu šá s[*u-'i* x x x x x x x x x]
[x x x x x x x] *šá su-'i an-nu-te* [x x x x x]
638 A *ki-i ha-ni-e at-tu-nu* MÍ.MEŠ*-ku-nu* DUMU.MEŠ*-ku-nu*
_ [x x x x x x] *at-tu-nu* MÍ.MEŠ*-ku-*[*nu* x x x x]
[*k*]*i-i ha-an-ni-e at-tu-nu* MÍ.[MEŠ*-ku-nu* x x x x]
[x x x x x x] *at-tu-nu* MÍ.MEŠ*-ku-nu* [x x x x]
[x x x x x x x x x x M]Í.MEŠ*-ku-nu* DUMU.MEŠ*-ku-nu*
639 A DUMU.MÍ.MEŠ*-ku-nu la ta-nu-ha la ta-ṣa-la-la*
_ [x x x x x] *la ta-nu-h*[*a* x x x x x x]
[D]UMU.MÍ.MEŠ*-ku-nu la ta-nu-ha*! *la t*[*a-ṣa-la-la*]
DUMU.MÍ.MEŠ*-ku-nu la* [x x x] *la ta-ṣa-la-la*
[x x x x x x *ta-nu*]*-ha la ta-ṣa-la-la*

640 A *[e]ṣ-ma-te-ku-nu a-na-he-iš hi lu la i-qa-ri-ba*
_ *[e]ṣ-ma-te-ku-nu a-[na* x x x x x x x x x x]
eṣ-ma-a-te-ku-nu a-na a-he-iš lu la [x x x x]
eṣ-[ma-te-ku-nu a]-na a-he-iš [x x x x x x]
[x x x x x x x *a-he*]*-iš*! *lu la i-qar-ri-ba*

---

641 A *[k]i-i šaš* ŠÀ*-bu šá hu-up-pu ra-qu-u-ni*
U *ki-i šá* [x x x x x x x x x x]
_ *[ki]-⸢i⸣ šá li[b-bu* x x x x x x x x]
[k]i-i šá lib-bu šá hu-up-pi ra-qu-[u-ni]
[ki]-⸢i⸣ šá ŠÀ*-bu šá* [x x x x x x x]
[x x x x x x *hu-up-p]i ra-qu-u-ni*
642 A *[li]b-bi-ku-nu li-ri-qu*
U ŠÀ*-ba-[ku-nu* x x x]
_ [ŠÀ*-bi*]*-ku-nu* [x x x]
[x x x x *li*]*-ri-qu*

---

643 A *ki-i* LÚ.KÚR*-ku-nu ú-pa-ta-hu-ka-⸢nu⸣-ni*
U *ki-i* L[Ú.KÚR*-ku-nu* x x x x x x x]
_ *ki-i* LÚ.KÚR*-ku-nu ú-pa-t[a-*x x x x]
[x x LÚ.KÚR*-ku-n]u ⸢ú⸣-[pa-ta-hu-ka]-⸢nu⸣-n[i]*
[x x] LÚ.KÚR*-ku-n[u* x x x x x x x]
644 A LÀL Ì.MEŠ *zi-in-za-ru-'u* MÚD–GIŠ.ERIN
U LÀL.MEŠ Ì.ME[Š x x x x x x x x x]
_ LÀL.MEŠ Ì.MEŠ *zi-in-za-r[u-'u* x x x]
LÀL *zi-i[n-za-ru-'u* x x x]
645 A *a-na šá-kan pi-it-hi-ku-nu li-ih-liq*
U *a-na šá-ka-a-[ni* x x x x x x x x]
_ *a-na šá-kan pi-i[t-hi-ku-nu* x x x]
a-⸢na⸣ [x x x x x x x x x x]
[x x] *šá-kan pi-it-hi-[ku-nu* x x x]

---

646 A [x x] *šá mar-tu mar-ra-tú-u-ni*
U *ki-i šá mar-tu ⸢mar-rat-u-ni⸣*
_ *[k]i-i šá mar-tu* [x x x x]
ki-i šá ZÉ*-tú mar-rat-⸢u-ni⸣*
[x x] *šá mar-tú mar-[rat-u-ni]*
647 A [x x x] MÍ.MEŠ*-ku-nu* DUMU.MEŠ*-ku-nu* DUMU.MÍ.MEŠ*-[ku]-nu*
U *at-t[u-nu]* MÍ.MEŠ*-ku-nu* DUMU.MEŠ*-ku-nu* DUMU.MÍ.MEŠ*-ku-[nu]*
_ [x x x] MÍ.MEŠ*-ku-nu* DUMU.MEŠ*-[ku-nu* x x x x x]
[at]-tu-nu [x x x x x x x x DUMU.MÍ.MEŠ*-k]u-nu*
at-[tu-nu] MÍ.MEŠ*-ku-nu* DUMU.MEŠ*-ku-nu* DUMU.MÍ.MEŠ*-k[u-nu]*
648 A [x x x x x x] *lu mar-ra-ku-⸢nu⸣*
U *ina* UGU *a-he-iš lu ma-ra-ku-[nu]*
_ *ina* UGU*-hi* [x x x x *mar-ra-ku*]*-nu*
[x x x] *a-he-iš lu mar-ra-ku-[nu]*
[x x x *a-he*]*-i[š* x x x x x]

---

649 U KI.MIN ^{d}UTU *hu-ha-ru šá* UD.KA.BAR *ina* UGU-*hi-ku-nu*
_ [x x x x x x x x x x x x x UGU-*h*]*i-ku-nu*
DUMU.MEŠ!-*ku*-[*nu*] KI.MIN ^{d}UTU *hu-ha-ru ša* UD.KA.BAR *ina*
UGU-[*hi-ku-nu* x x x]
650 U *li-is-hu-up ina giš-par-ri šá la na-par-šu-di*
_ [x x x x x x x x x x x x x x x *l*]*a na-par-šú-di*
[DUMU.M]Í.MEŠ-*ku-nu li-is-hu-pu ina giš-par-ri šá l*[*a* x x x x x]
651 U ⸢*li*⸣-*di-ku-nu a-a ú-še-ṣi nap-šat-kun*
_ [x x x x x x x x x *nap*]-*šat-ku-nu* [*li-d*]*i-ku-nu a-a ú-še-ṣi nap*-[*šat-ku-nu*]

---

652 U *ki-i šá* KUŠ.*na-a-du šal-qa-tu-u-ni* A.MEŠ-*šá*
653 U *ṣa-ap-pa-hu-u-ni*! *ina kaq-qar ṣu-ma-mit lap-lap-tu*
654 U KUŠ.*na-da-ku-nu lu ta-hi-bi*
655 U [*ina ṣ*]*u-um* A.MEŠ *mu-u-ta*

---

656 U [x x x] ⸢KUŠ.E.SÍR *šal*⸣-*qa-tu-u-ni*
_ [*k*]*i-i šá* KUŠ.E.[SÍR x x x x x]
657 U [x x x x x x KUŠ.E.SÍR.ME]Š-*ku-nu*
_ *ina kaq-qar pa-qut-ti* [x x]x x[x x x x]
658 _ *li-par-ma ina* UG[U x x-*k*]*u-nu* x[x x x]

---

659 _ ^{d}EN.LÍL EN GIŠ.GU.ZA [GIŠ.G]U.ZA-*ku-n*[*u lu-šá-bal-kit*]

---

660 Q [x x x x x x NA]M.MEŠ DINGIR.MEŠ
_ ^{d}PA *na-ši ṭup-pi* NAM.MEŠ DIN[GIR.MEŠ]
661 Q ⸢*lip-ši*⸣-[*ṭi* MU-*ku-nu*] NUMUN-*ku-nu ina* KUR *lu-hal-liq*
_ MU-*ku-nu lip-ši-ṭi* NUMUN-*ku-nu ina* KUR *li-hal*-[*liq*]

---

662 _ GIŠ.IG *ina* IGI.MEŠ-*ku-nu lu* x[x x x x x] G[IŠ.IG x x x x x x x x x x x x]
663 _ GIŠ.IG.MEŠ-*ku-n*[*u* x x x]x[x x x x x] GIŠ.I[G-x x x x x x x x x x x]
A ————————————————————————
B ————————————————————————
664 Q ITI.GUD.SI.SÁ UD-16-KÁM
_ ITI.GUD.[SI.SÁ x x x]
[ITI.GU]D.SI.SÁ UD-18-KÁM [x x x x] UD-18-KÁM
665 Q *lim-mu* ^{md}PA–EN–PAB LÚ.GAR.KUR URU.BÀD–LUGAL-*uk*-⸢*ku*⸣
_ *lim-mu* ^{md}AG–E[N–PAB x x x x x x x x x]
[x x ^{md}PA–E]N–PAB [x x x x x x x x x]
[*lim-m*]*u* ^{md}PA–E[N–PAB LÚ.GAR].KUR URU.BÀD–LUGAL-*uk*-[*ku*]
[x x x x x x x x x x x URU.BÀD–LUGAL-*u*]*k-k*[*a*]
666 Q *a-de-e* ⸢*šá*!⸣ *ina* UGU ^{m}*aš-šur*–DÙ–A
_ [*a*]-*de-e šá* ^{m}*aš-šur*–PAB–AŠ MAN KUR–*aš-šur*.KI [*šá ina* UG]U ^{m}*aš-šur*–DÙ–A
⸢*a*⸣-*d*[*e-e* x x x x x x x x] [x x x *šá ina*] UGU ^{m}*aš-šur*–[DÙ–A]
667 A [x x x x x x x x x KUR–*aš-šur*.K]I
Q DUMU–MAN GAL *šá* É–UŠ-*ti šá* KUR–*aš-šur*
_ DUMU–MAN GAL *šá* É–UŠ-*ti* [x] KUR–*aš-šur*.KI
DUMU–MAN *šá* É–UŠ-*ti ša* ⸢KUR⸣–[*aš-šur*]
[x x x x É–U]Š-*te ša* K[UR–*aš-šur*]

668 A [x ^{md}GIŠ.ŠIR–MU–GI].NA
Q *ù* ^{md}GIŠ.ŠIR–M[U–GI.NA]
_ [*u*] *ina* UGU ^{m}GIŠ.ŠIR–MU–GI.NA
Z *ù* ^{md}[GIŠ.ŠIR–MU–GI.NA]
_ ⸢*ù*⸣ ^{md}GIŠ.ŠIR–MU–GI.NA
[x ^{md}GIŠ.ŠIR–MU–GI.N]A
669 A [x x x x x x x KÁ.DINGIR.R]A.KI
Q DUMU-MAN *šá* É–UŠ-*ti* [x x x x x]
_ DUMU–MAN GAL *šá* É–UŠ-[*ti* x KÁ.DING]IR.RA.KI
Z [x x] *ša* É–UŠ-[*ti* x x x x x]
_ [DUMU–M]AN *ša* [É–*re-du*]-*ú*-[*ti šá*] KÁ.DINGIR.RA.KI
[x x x x x x x KÁ.DINGIR.RA].KI
670 _ *šak*-[*nu-u-ni*]
šak-n[*u-u-ni*]

www.ingramcontent.com/pod-product-compliance
Lightning Source LLC
Chambersburg PA
CBHW081441070526
44586CB00019B/2196
* 9 7 8 1 5 7 5 0 6 3 3 2 4 *